Piedmont
College Library

Demorest, Ga.

96195

Law, Behavior, and Mental Health: Policy and Practice

LAW,
BEHAVIOR,
and
MENTAL HEALTH:
Policy and Practice

STEVEN R. SMITH
and
ROBERT G. MEYER

NEW YORK UNIVERSITY PRESS
New York *and* London

Library of Congress Cataloging-in-Publication Data

Smith, Steven R., 1946–
  Law, behavior, and mental health.

  Bibliography: p.
  Includes index.
  1. Mental health personnel—Legal status, laws,
etc.—United States.   2. Mental health laws—United
States.   3. Insanity—Jurisprudence—United States.
4. Psychology, Forensic.   I. Meyer, Robert G.,
1940– . II. Title.
KF2910.P75S46 1987   344.73'041   87–1544
ISBN 0–8147–7857–7   347.30441

Book designed by Laiying Chong.

3/30/88   R + T   60.00

CONTENTS

PREFACE

A friend of ours argues that lawyers and mental health professionals are forever separated by language, methodology, and approach to problems. He, like some others, affectionately (we think) refers to our efforts as "law and bananas." While there are important differences between our professions, there are even more important common interests and common problems. We address (in a common language, we hope) a wide range of the topics which involve law and the mental health professions.[1]

The study of law and the mental health professions is interesting and important for three reasons. First, they significantly affect each other. Laws relating to mental health licensure, malpractice, and limitations on human experimentations are a few examples of the ways in which the law directly affects mental health practice. At the same time, the law is increasingly dependent on the mental health professions and behavioral sciences. Mental health professionals commonly participate in a wide range of judicial and administrative proceedings such as those concerning emotional injuries, involuntary civil commitment, and child custody. It is likely that social science research will continue to inform the development of the law.[2]

A second reason for the study of law and the mental health professions is that they seek to solve common problems. In practice we often serve the same clients and patients and our research interests are often closely related: dealing with child abuse, violent behavior, and detecting deception are examples. In seeking solutions to social problems our disciplines can inform each other both in practice and in research.

These common concerns of the two professions suggest a third reason for studying them together. They both raise and face some similar fundamental philosophical questions concerning the nature of human behavior.[3] For example, the free will/determinism debate is of great importance to the mental health professions and many aspects of the law. Interdisciplinary consideration of these problems often provides a special perspective that differs from that provided by a single discipline. It also produces an interesting (and even enjoyable) opportunity to challenge the commonly accepted principles (and sacred cows) of a single discipline.

In this book we raise issues of common interest to our professions. We hope the book will be of value to legal and mental health professionals by discussing those issues and by raising some fundamental questions of policy and philosophy. Toward those ends, we have endeavored to avoid jargon, and therefore be useful to both professions. We hope it will provide an introduction to the issues to those who have not considered them before and will suggest new questions (or even a few solutions) to our colleagues to whom some of the issues are familiar.

We have organized the book in four general parts: The Law and Mental Health Practice, Human Behavior and the Courtroom, Behavioral Science and Social-Legal Policy, and Conclusion. While these divisions are a convenient way to consider law and mental health issues, they are somewhat arbitrary. In reality there is considerable overlap among these topics.

The first section, "The Law and Mental Health Practice," is concerned with law and the regulation of professional practice and research. Some of this regulation is self-imposed by the profession (e.g., codes of ethics), but more commonly they are imposed from outside the professions (e.g., legal prohibitions of the use of certain drugs and limitations on the use of human research subjects). Social controls sometimes are direct regulation (e.g., licensure), but often they are more indirect (e.g., malpractice, reimbursement for services, funding for research). The indirect regulation may be more important than the direct in defining the quality of care that is expected and determining what care will be available or what research will be undertaken. This section is also about the way society resolves the tension between permitting professionals to freely treat patients and clients without outside interference and the desire to protect the public (and other professionals) from inadequate or unfair practice.

Mental health professionals play increasingly active roles in the courtroom and in the study of the trial process. These roles are examined in "Human Behavior and the Courtroom." The most apparent role has been as expert witnesses in a wide variety of cases. Less obvious has been the expanded use of mental health professionals in the preparation of cases and in the selection of juries. A particularly noteworthy contribution of the behavioral sciences is the study of the courtroom process and the foundations of the trial process. For example, eyewitness testimony has traditionally been assumed to be among the best evidence available to courts, although behavioral science has now thrown considerable doubt on its reliability. The very essence of the trial process is the ability to determine the truth. The detection of deception and truth-finding are also concerns of the mental health professions. The reliability of eyewitnesses, the truth-finding process, and juries and the courtroom process are reviewed in "Human Behavior and the Courtroom."

Law may be seen as a form of social engineering where the power of society is applied to individuals in order to regulate or influence behavior. Whenever defined social standards are transgressed, society must determine a way to deal with this nonconforming conduct. The law has traditionally presumed that an individual is "a free agent confronted with a choice between doing right and doing wrong and choosing freely" which to do.[4] Under this model, a person who has violated social rules is morally blameworthy because he has freely chosen to do wrong (unless he has lost his free will because of mental illness). An alternative model is a strong behavioral model that views human conduct as a product of internal (genetic) and external (environmental) factors. Under this model one changes behavior by changing the stimuli (environment) to produce the desired response.

Two broad ways of dealing with undesirable behavior, punishment and treatment, are described in "Behavioral Science and Social-Legal Policy." Punishment has most commonly been identified with a free will model and treatment with a behavior model, but they cannot really be classified this clearly.[5] Reducing antisocial behavior is only one goal of society. That goal sometimes conflicts with other social values, such as privacy, freedom of choice and expression, and economic efficiency. This conflict of goals requires a balancing of competing values, and it limits the means which society is willing to employ to reduce antisocial behavior. This tension of values is apparent in all of the public policy issues considered in Part III.

In Part IV we summarize and draw a few conclusions. We note that the authority to make decisions and to be held responsible for those decisions are central to many of the issues facing law and the mental health professions. We suggest there an outline of the factors that should be considered in determining decision-making ability and responsibility.

NOTES

1. Of course the topics discussed in this book do not exhaust all of the legal issues related to mental health practice, or all mental health research relevant to the law. For example, business structures (e.g., partnerships) and taxation issues are not considered. Professor Sales has suggested that a comprehensive review of legal issues related to psychology would be useful. See B. Sales, *Laws Affecting Mental Health: Arizona* (1985).

2. See Haney, Psychology and Legal Change: On the Limits of Factual Jurisprudence, 4 *L. & Hum. Behav.* 147 (1980).

3. Professor Moore argues that there is a need to study further the philosophical bases of the law and of social policy. M. Moore, *Law and Psychiatry: Rethinking the Relationship* 423 (1984).

4. Pound, Introduction to F. Sayre, *Cases on Criminal Law* (1927).

5. One reason given for punishment of criminals, as we shall see, is to rehabilitate them. Rehabilitation, however, may be seen as a form of treatment. Thus, a form of treatment is one of the reasons for punishment. See generally, A. Brooks, *Law, Psychiatry and the Mental Health System* 218 (1974).

A NOTE ON NOTES

The disciplines from which we draw have significantly different conventions regarding footnotes and references. We, of course, had to adopt one citation form. We selected the common legal format as described in *A Uniform System of Citations* (13th ed. 1981). In a few instances we have modified the usual abbreviations to avoid confusion.

We assume that legal citation format and abbreviations will be familiar to most of our mental health readers. For those who may not be familiar with them, we provide a very brief outline. A much more complete description can be found in any law library or in "Legal Research Techniques: What the Psychologist Needs to Know," by Knapp, Vandecreek and Zirkel. It is in Volume 16 of *Professional Psychology: Research and Practice*, p. 363 (1985).

The legal citation format is reasonably easy to follow. Books are cited with the first initial and last name of the author, title and date of publication (information about the publisher is not included), as R. Meyer & P. Salmon, *Abnormal Psychology* (1984). One form that is not common in other disciplines is that the volume number precedes the name of the publication. Thus, Smith, Constitutional Privacy in Psychotherapy, 49 *Geo. Wash. L. Rev.* 1 (1980) refers to volume 49 of the *George Washington Law Review*, at page one, carrying a publication date of 1980.

A similar format is used in citing cases: name of case, volume, reporter, first page and date, for example, O'Connor v. Donaldson, 422 U.S. 563 (1975). The United States Reporter (U.S.) contains U.S. Supreme Court cases, the Federal Reporter (F. or F.2d) contains U.S. Courts of Appeals cases, and the Federal Supplement (Fed. Supp.) contains Federal District Court cases. State appellate cases are contained in regional reporters, Atlantic (A.2d), Northeastern (N.E.2d), Northwestern (N.W.2d), Pacific (P.2d), Southeastern

(S.E.2d), Southwestern (S.W.2d) and Southern (So.2d) reporters. There are several other reporters. Several states have official state reporters, there are a couple of commercial reporters that contain Supreme Court decisions, and a number of "specialized" reporters that contain cases from a number of courts related to a single subject.

Federal Statutes are contained in the U.S. Code (U.S.C.) or U.S. Code Annotated (U.S.C.A.). Federal regulations are usually found in the Code of Federal Regulations (C.F.R.), although recently adopted regulations may be found in the Federal Register (Fed. Reg.). Statutes (and codified regulations) are generally cited with the "title" or general division, code name, code section and date of the publication of the code (not the date the statute was passed); 42 U.S.C. §1983 (1982) deals with section 1983 of title 42, as published in the 1982 U.S. Code. State statutes follow the same general format.

We have tried to cite some of the important relevant literature in the notes that appear at the end of each chapter. However, the references are the end of the chapters are not meant to provide a full literature bibliography for the subject under consideration.

A NOTE OF THANKS

Many people have contributed to the completion of this book. Had we taken more of their advice, any errors which may remain undoubtedly would have been eliminated.[1]

We especially thank those whose contributions extended over several years:

Our colleagues interested in law and mental health who have encouraged this project and made useful suggestions.

Our students, especially those in our Law and Psychology seminar and our research assistants, who help maintain a fresh perspective on the issues.

The staff of the law school, department of psychology and manuscript preparation office of the University of Louisville who have spared no effort in interpreting our scribbling in preparing the manuscript.

The fine group at NYU Press who generously worked with us (and whose efforts at reducing the manuscript have prevented this book from becoming a three-volume set).

Several local innkeepers who have put up with our sometimes heated conversations about subjects in the book (seldom leading to blows) which periodically cleared entire sections of their establishments.

And, especially, our families who put up with this project for several years with good spirit and encouragement.

NOTES

1. We salute David Wexler's acknowledgment that demonstrates the unusual candor of those interested in law and mental health. Professor Wexler

thanked Dean Henderson who "has also taken the step of explicitly tying merit salary increases to scholarly productivity. As much as anything, this book is a test of his good word." D. Wexler, *Mental Health Law: Major Issues* viii (1981).

PART I

THE LAW
AND
MENTAL HEALTH PRACTICE

CHAPTER 1
ETHICS, MALPRACTICE, AND THE MENTAL HEALTH PROFESSIONS

Much of this book is about values: of society, of professions and professionals, and of individuals. Values, even those which are widely accepted, are often in conflict. In mental health law, there are fundamental conflicts between autonomy and paternalism; between protecting individual interests, and those of society; between confidentiality and openness; between protecting the interests of patients and clients, and those of mental health professionals.

Systems of law and ethics offer ways of selecting values to be protected, narrowing differences between conflicting values, and when necessary choosing those to be promoted at the expense of others. We begin with a consideration of ethical and legal issues. Both professional ethics and the malpractice issues considered in this chapter have as their primary purpose the protection of clients and patients.[1]

PROFESSIONAL ETHICS

This section will serve as only an introduction to ethical principles. Each chapter offers some discussion of ethical considerations for specific areas. Ethical issues come alive in the context of specific, substantive problems that must be addressed by professionals and are best considered as part of those problems.

Development of Ethics and Codes of Ethics

Ethical principles grow out of commonly accepted practices that develop within a profession or out of a consensus about what it should be doing. From time to time the threat of outside regulation causes a profession to adopt tougher standards, or existing principles become unenforceable because of external forces.[2] In addition, of course, the development of standards occurs within the context of the society. Ethical principles will therefore necessarily reflect the values of the times.[3] Thus, within limits, it is the profession itself that defines ethical principles.

Most professions adopt formal ethical principles or codes of responsibility, among them attorneys,[4] counselors,[5] nurses,[6] psychiatrists and physicians,[7] psychologists,[8] school counselors,[9] and social workers.[10] There is pressure for organizations without such codes to establish clear principles.[11]

Purpose of Ethics

The purpose of codes of ethics is primarily to protect the public—and in particular clients and patients—and secondarily to promote the welfare of the profession. In the long run, this will also promote the interest of the public by maintaining a robust, effective, and reliable profession. It is possible, of course, for these two purposes to be inconsistent, as when the profession acts as a guild to protect its members' economic interests.[12] The code may also protect other special interests, as for example that of the American Psychological Association, which contains provisions concerning the welfare of animals,[13] and that of the National Association of Social Workers, which requires that the profession take credit only for research work actually done.[14]

Advantages and Disadvantages of Codes

Codes ideally should give a clear understanding of what is expected of the professional. This has led states to include adherence to codes of conduct as a condition of licensure. There are two problems with many professional codes in defining these minimum expectations. First, they are often quite vague. For example, the professional "shall be dedicated to providing competent medical service with compassion and respect for human dignity."[15] A second problem is that codes often combine both minimum standards and aspirational standards. For example, the AMA code requires professionals to "safeguard patient confidences within the constraints of the law."[16] It also provides that "a physician shall recognize a responsibility to participate in activities contributing to an improved community."[17] The first of these is a minimum standard, and the failure to meet it could result in discipline or legal action. The second could certainly be a goal of the profession but cannot be a minimum standard in any enforceable way. Like those of most other professions, the AMA principles do not clearly indicate which standards are minimum and which are aspirational. This lack of clarity has the effect of making it more difficult to enforce codes of ethics.

Common Provisions of Codes of Ethics

The specific provisions of the codes vary considerably among professions. While attorneys, for example, are admonished to represent their clients zealously, psychologists would find such a principle to be of little relevance.[18] However, there are several aspects of the codes which are similar, if not universal. Professionals must provide competent or quality services, they have a fiduciary obligation to act in the best interests of clients and to avoid taking unfair advantage of them financially, emotionally, or sexually (which particularly requires the avoidance of any conflict of interest with clients or patients), and they are required to maintain within legal limits the confidentiality of information revealed to them. Most codes require that the patient be given the opportunity to make critical decisions or to give consent to treatment, and also suggest that professionals endeavor to make their services available to all people regardless of their ability to pay, and that professionals be involved in improving their profession and society.[19]

Complaints about Unethical Conduct

Professionals commonly have organizations for receiving and investigating complaints against its members. Normally, however, they respond only to complaints, and do not seek out the unethical practitioner. They are not very effective in pursuing unethical practitioners.[20] This is particularly true if the practitioner has violated, not the law, but "merely" the ethical standards. Even when ethical codes are part of the licensing laws, they are seldom enforced by the state.[21]

Training in Ethics

In theory, professional schools should ensure that their students receive adequate training in ethics. The educational accrediting standards of some professions require such training.[22] Arguments rage over whether ethical issues should be discussed throughout the curriculum, in a separate course, in an academic setting, or in a clinical setting.[23] Ideally, education about ethics includes the appropriate code and extends well beyond that into other issues facing professionals.[24] At any rate, in many institutions this instruction has probably been too little and too narrow. We hope that this state of affairs is slowly changing.

Ethics, the Law, and Malpractice

The law and ethical principles are related. The participation of the professional in the legal system may raise special ethical problems.[25] For example, it may be a problem determining whether a patient has consented to forensic treatment or evaluation. Legal principles may limit the ability of professionals to implement fully ethical goals, so that, say, legally required disclosure of information about a dangerous patient will limit the ability to maintain confidentiality (see chapter 2). Ethical principles and the law are also related when they define conditions for the retention of a professional license (see chapter 4).

The remainder of this chapter deals with malpractice. Ethics and malpractice are also related: both are intended to describe the obligations of professionals and to protect their clients. Although ethical principles do not specifically define malpractice, their violation will usually also be malpractice. (Aspirational principles are the exception.) Examples of activities which could subject a professional to civil liability (and would also be violations of professional ethics) are carelessly or incompetently provided services, unauthorized breaches of confidentiality, failure to obtain consent to treatment, and engaging in sexual relations with a patient. In short, the practitioner who engages in unethical conduct is often also engaged in malpractice.

MALPRACTICE

Mental health professionals experience fewer malpractice suits than do most medical specialists.[26] In one recent study, malpractice actions against psychiatrists accounted for less than 1 percent of the claims filed against all physicians.[27] Yet it appears malpractice suits against therapists are on the rise. During the first ten years (1961–71) of the malpractice insurance program of the American Psychological Association, no malpractice claims were paid. During the period 1976–80, however, 122 claims were processed, with estimated payments totaling $435,642.[28]

Most malpractice claims are based on the tort of negligence. A few are also based on intentional torts (such as battery, intentional infliction of mental distress or false imprisonment) or breach of contract.[29] Some commentators have suggested that malpractice should be based on strict liability, but this has not been widely accepted.[30] Both tort and contract liability are based on the breach of a duty. In the case of contracts, it is the breach of a duty voluntarily assumed through an agreement; in torts, it is the breach of a duty imposed by society.

In its simplest form, malpractice may be seen as a way of providing compensation to those injured by unethical or careless conduct. Liability is generally intended to compensate the victim through money damages, and to help prevent future undesirable conduct by penalizing the wrongdoer. Liability insurance is commonly purchased to cover the cost of defending lawsuits and paying damages.

Broadly stated, negligence is the breach of a duty to act reasonably to avoid injury. When negligence causes injury to another, the negligent party may be subject to liability. Professionals are obligated to use their special training and experience to avoid harming patients and clients. The general duty of a therapist is therefore to act as a reasonable or prudent therapist of similar training would act under the circumstances. Stating that standard settles very little; determining what a reasonable professional would do may be a difficult matter. It frequently depends upon the general or accepted practice of similar professions.[31]

REASONS FOR LOW RATES OF MALPRACTICE

Mental health professionals generally have avoided high rates of malpractice claims because of the nature of mental health therapy and the sorts of injuries that occur in therapy.

Establishing the Standard of Care

The standard of practice for mental health professionals is not as clearly or precisely defined as it is in many areas of medicine. The standard practice for treatment of appendicitis is fairly uniform and clear; the standard practice for treatment of schizophrenia is not. Therapists therefore find themselves with considerable latitude in determining what constitutes reasonable care.[32]

Causation

If it is often difficult to determine whether a breach of reasonable care has occurred in mental health, it is often equally difficult to determine whether a breach has *caused* an injury to the patient. The causes of emotional or psychological injuries are often very difficult to identify and explain with certainty. Therefore, a patient claiming therapy-related injury may have a difficult time demonstrating that faulty therapy was the cause. Indeed, since patients often are suffering from some form of mental illness before seeking the assistance of a therapist, any psychological injury received may appear to be nothing more than part of the pre-existing mental illness.[33]

Nature of the Injuries

The nature of most injuries likely to result from malpractice also makes recovery difficult. Emotional injuries are very real and may be very painful but generally not so obvious or gruesome as physical injuries. Emotional injuries are often difficult to effectively demonstrate to a jury. A mangled limb or scarred body presents to a jury dramatic evidence of injury; a mangled psyche is much less evident. In addition, the law has traditionally been reluctant to recognize emotional or mental injuries except when related to physical injuries.

Therapist-Client Relationship

Beyond the technical difficulties of demonstrating the elements of a claim of negligence, there are other factors which undoubtedly limit the number of malpractice claims against mental health practitioners, among them the relationship between the patient and the therapist. One reason for the increased rate of malpractice claims is a breakdown in the relationship between physician and patient. Patients may see a surgeon only briefly before and after surgery and are not likely to develop the kind of close relationship that would make them hesitant about filing suit. The very nature of mental health therapy, however, usually requires that the patient develop some closeness with the therapist. This relationship undoubtedly makes many patients reluctant to file suit against therapists.

Release of Private Information

Patients who have been injured in psychotherapy may also be reluctant to file a claim because they may suffer substantial embarrassment by bringing their emotional problems and histories into a public forum. Any privilege covering confidentiality or privacy in mental health care would probably not apply in such a lawsuit.[34] The court proceedings are public, so clients or patients may find their mental health and illnesses becoming matters of public record, with friends and family exposed to information previously considered confidential. Understandably, patients who have undergone mental health therapy might be more reluctant to have their condition and treatment discussed in public than a patient with a physical ailment.[35]

AREAS OF POTENTIAL MALPRACTICE CLAIMS

The kinds of activities giving rise to mental health care malpractice liability vary from one mental health profession to another. Psychiatrists may face liability resulting from the use of electroconvulsive therapy and drugs, risks which psychologists and social workers do not encounter.[36] The types of injury or forms of liability reported below, therefore, are not listed in order of importance for any particular profession. Although most attention has been focused on the liability for physical intervention (e.g. ECT, drugs), it appears that a substantial portion of the small number of claims that are filed against mental health professionals arise out of errors in diagnosis, treatment, and evaluation; breach of confidentiality; and most common of all, having sexual contact with or otherwise taking unfair advantage of clients.[37]

Not every negative result, or every mistake, results in negligence liability. Only injuries which occur as a result of unreasonable errors—that is, errors a reasonably careful practitioner would not have made under the circumstances—are actionable.

Electroconvulsive Therapy

The use of electroconvulsive therapy (ECT) has been thought to be the origin of most psychiatric malpractice.[38] Some insurance companies have, in fact, required surcharges to cover ECT because of the supposed risks. The claims arising from ECT do not fully justify this fear either in terms of the number or the size of the claims.[39]

Malpractice claims arising from ECT may be based on several theories of negligence: failure to obtain proper informed consent (described below), improperly prescribing ECT, or negligently administering it. When ECT is administered to patients whose conditions do not warrant it, they are subject to unnecessary risks and the psychiatrists may be liable for any injuries that may occur. For example, prescribing ECT as a treatment for Alzheimer's disease would be negligent because it is not effective against that disease.[40] The use of ECT with patients for whom it is contraindicated (such as some forms of organic brain damage) may also be a negligent use.

A therapist who does not administer ECT in a reasonably careful way will be subject to liability for any injuries that occur as a result of the carelessness. For example, neglecting to give medication to avoid extreme convulsions may give rise to liability if the patient suffers a fracture during them.[41]

Medications

The use of prescription drugs is a surprisingly common source of malpractice litigation against psychiatrists.[42] The bases of malpractice liability are similar to ECT: failure of informed consent, inappropriate and unnecessary prescription of drugs, or negligent administration of drugs. By definition the use of prescription drugs carries risks. Their inappropriate or improper prescription, or the failure to give adequate instruction, poses an unnecessary risk to patients, and therefore the possibility of negligence liability.[43]

Psychosurgery

Psychosurgery is not a significant area of malpractice liability because little is currently done. It can probably be characterized as an experimental procedure at this point, and therefore subject to special regulation[44] (see chapter 3).

Failure to Obtain Informed Consent

Informed consent is designed to protect patient privacy. One of the most fundamental concepts of privacy is the right to determine what is done to one's own body. Treatment conducted without informed consent may subject the practitioner to liability for negligence or battery.[45] The legal doctrine of informed consent to psychotherapy has not yet been fully developed by courts and legislatures.

To be legally effective, sufficient information must be given for the patient to make a reasonably informed judgment on whether or not to accept the treatment. Full informed consent requires that a patient understand: (1) the nature of the treatment which is proposed; (2) the major risks and benefits associated with the treatment;

(3) reasonable alternative forms of treatment; and (4) the consequence of no treatment.[46]

Courts have recognized that in some instances it is not feasible to obtain consent from the patient. When a patient is incompetent, substituted consent is acceptable, and someone (such as a guardian or relative) may consent to the treatment for the patient. Determining when a patient is incompetent to make decisions is sometimes difficult. The issue is considered in chapters 3, 16, 18 and 19. In emergency situations, where the patient is in no condition to exercise judgment, consent to emergency treatment is presumed. Where disclosure of risks would substantially adversely affect treatment by harming the patient's mental and emotional condition, informed consent may also be unnecessary.[47]

Issues regarding informed consent most often arise in areas of medical practice when there are substantial physical risks involved, such as surgery. But the same general principles of consent apply to other forms of treatment, such as the use of prescription drugs and ECT. Ordinarily, a patient's failure to object to significant or invasive procedures should not be seen as adequate informed consent unless it is clear that the patient has adequate information on which to base a decision, and intends the silence as consent.[48] Although written consent is not required, proof that consent was given is of course easier when given in writing. If the patient is misled about treatment by false representation from the therapist about the harm that can result from treatment, there is not adequate consent and the therapist is subject to liability. In one case, in which a patient suffered a compression fracture of the spine as a result of ECT, recovery was permitted on the basis that the therapist had assured the patient that he would suffer no injury from the therapy.[49] Aside from misrepresentations of the safety of ECT, the general rules regarding informed consent impose liability for the failure of a psychiatrist to adequately inform a patient of the major dangers associated with ECT and of alternatives available.[50]

Informed consent is necessary in several other areas of therapy, among them any other form of treatment which involves substantial physical contact or manipulation. Certainly any form of psychosurgery would require informed consent. Aversive therapies, in which a patient may be placed in some substantial discomfort, ordinarily require informed consent. Physicians are to provide information to patients about prescription drugs, and drug companies have an obligation to provide the information to physicians.[51] For example, a patient should be informed about potential serious side effects (such as tardive dyskinesia in the case of some antipsychotic drugs), changes in mood and outlook to be expected, and dangers of addiction to the drug. Psychiatrists prescribing drugs should make reasonable efforts to inform patients of how to use the drugs and the consequences of using them.[52]

A patient who chooses to see a psychotherapist has given consent to ordinary therapy by attending therapy sessions. Since there are relatively few risks involved with this form of therapy when done properly, little attention has been given to the need for some kind of informed consent to ordinary counseling or psychotherapy. It has been suggested, however, that patients have a right to know of some risks that do exist, such as the limits of confidentiality in therapy.[53] Because most patients apparently presume that whatever they tell a therapist will remain confidential, it seems reasonable they should be made aware that some kinds of communications will not necessarily remain secret.[54] It is unlikely that significant liability exists for the failure of informed consent to most forms of "talk therapy."

Many forms of behavior modification should include informed consent. This is especially true if such therapy involves treatment that will expose clients or patients to situations that they will find uncomfortable or if treatments are likely to inflict significant emotional distress.[55] For example, the taking of an acrophobic patient to an open, tall building, should include some form of informed consent.

The practical application of the principles of informed consent may be extremely difficult. There is reason to believe that, in practice, informed consent is frequently ignored.[56] Many factors may interfere with the consent process, including the limited mental competency of some patients that may reduce their ability to understand or make judgments, the failure to provide sufficient information in an understandable form, a feeling of paternalism toward patients, and the age of some patients.

Obtaining informed consent from patients presupposes that they are capable of making a reasoned decision, understanding the alternatives available for treatment, and selecting the treatment they desire. It is not unusual for patients of psychotherapists to be in a mental or emotional state where their ability to understand alternatives and make reasoned decisions can be questioned.[57] Patients who have been formally adjudged incompetent will have guardians appointed who can legally provide consent. Other patients may have impairments that do not justify a judicial determination of incompetence. In such cases professionals should take special steps to obtain informed consent. Those steps might include special or detailed discussions (particularly if the patient has lucid moments) and in some circumstances obtaining special informed consent from the next of kin.

Children present special informed consent problems. Traditionally, informed consent for children has been provided by their parents until the child achieves the age of majority.[58] In recent years, however, children have been playing a greater role in determining what treatment they will receive. The Supreme Court has held that parents may constitutionally "voluntarily" admit their children to mental hospitals even over the objection of the children, subject to review by a disinterested third party at the hospital.[59] The Court has also upheld the right of minors to make important treatment decisions even over the objections of their parents.[60] The extent to which parents may consent to particularly invasive therapy (for example psychosurgery or some aversive therapies) over the objection of their children is not clear. Inasmuch as these therapies may substantially change the thinking or "mentation" of children, a strong argument can be made that the children have legal rights which need to be protected from parental invasion.

Too little attention has been paid in the past to informed consent to therapy and counseling. Providing informed consent for many patients is difficult, but it is likely that ethical and legal pressures will continue to move toward requiring better informed consent.

Unfair Advantage and Excessive Force

Liability may result from taking unfair advantage of a patient, or using excessive force. Unfair advantage almost inevitably is an ethical violation, and commonly involves sexual contact between patient and professional.[61] One of the most notable cases involved a patient, Mrs. Zipkin, who was active in community activities and the mother of three children. She was referred to Dr. Freeman when no physical cause could be discovered for her chronic diarrhea and headaches.[62] At the doctor's suggestion she went on overnight trips with him and attended "group therapy" in the form of nude swimming parties. The doctor also advised Mrs. Zipkin to leave her husband, to sue her husband and brother, and to rid herself of hostility by breaking into her husband's home. There was expert testimony that the nude swimming party was not group therapy, that the "social contacts" between doctor and patient were improper, and that a therapist ought not to advise a patient to act out aggressive impulses toward others. Dr. Freeman was found liable for malpractice.

The *Zipkin* case undoubtedly represents an extreme in the mishandling of the transference phenomenon. Courts have recognized that because of the nature of the therapist-patient relationship, and the patient's great dependence on the therapist, it is easy for the therapist to take advantage of the patient. The therapist who does so is likely to be subject to liability for any harm which the patient experiences.[63]

It has been suggested that in some instances sexual relations between patients and therapists are not only proper but desirable.[64] Although such a position has not gained widespread acceptance among mental health professionals, it does represent one school of thought. A troubling question is the extent to which liability should be imposed for therapists who adhere to this school of thought and are involved sexually with patients. Aside from this "school of thought" question considered later in this chapter, the question of consent is also raised. Is there any way for a patient to give consent freely to engaging in this form of "therapy" given the nature of the relationship between patient and the therapist?[65] Although these legal questions are not absolutely settled, there is a good probability of liability if sexual relations between therapist and patient results in injury to the patient.

Liability may also arise from the use of therapy that includes a substantial painful or violent physical contact. A notable case dealing with excessive force involved a dramatic technique for treating schizophrenia, which required that communication be established between physician and patient on the patient's level.[66] For some patients this required varying degrees of physical contact, including substantial slapping and hitting as a means of opening up communication. Although consent was generally obtained from next of kin or from a guardian, suit was ultimately brought for damages resulting from the slaps and abuses suffered during Dr. Rosen's beating of one patient. Despite the existence of consent, the doctor was subject to liability for injuries suffered as a result of this treatment. Since Dr. Rosen did not call expert witnesses to testify to the reasonableness of his methods, it is difficult to speculate concerning the outcome of the case had this effort been made to prove the propriety of the technique. This case does raise the issue, however, of the circumstances under which promising new, and perhaps bizarre, means of psychotherapy may be attempted without the imposition of liability.

When a treatment deviates very substantially from generally recognized methods, patients should be aware of that fact and informed consent becomes particularly important. The basis for trying significant new therapies should be clearly stated and should be reviewed by an ethics committee or institutional review board. Therapies that are very aggressive or intentionally inflict significant emotional distress also demand full consent. (Issues regarding experimental treatment are considered in chapter 6.)

Wrongful Involuntary Civil Commitment and Detention

The tort of false imprisonment imposes liability when someone intentionally and wrongfully confines another. Participation in the civil commitment process may subject mental health professionals to liability for false detention. However, most states provide protection from liability for professionals who participate in the commitment process, so long as they act in good faith.[67] In a few states it may be possible for a patient committed as a result of a negligent examination to successfully sue the therapist.[68] If the professional is not acting in good faith, efforts to involuntarily detain or commit a patient may result in liability for malicious prosecution or false imprisonment.[69] As a practical matter, to sustain a malicious prosecution suit the patient usually must demonstrate that the therapist acted in a truly outrageous fashion, either conspiring with others to commit the patient for ulterior motives or attempting to confine the patient for the personal gain of the physician or out of hatred for the patient. In such circumstances, of course, punitive damages are possible.

The possibility of a new dimension to liability in the involuntary civil commitment process was raised by the Supreme Court in *O'Con-*

nor v. Donaldson.[70] Donaldson claimed that although he was not dangerous he had been held without treatment in the Florida State Hospital. At trial he was awarded $38,500 in compensatory and punitive damages from the state officials and psychiatrists involved in his lengthy confinement. Although officials like those in *Donaldson* have "no duty to anticipate unforseeable constitutional developments,"[71] liability may be imposed after constitutional rights have been defined. The Supreme Court indicated in *Donaldson* that a state cannot confine nondangerous individuals capable of surviving safely in freedom without providing some form of treatment. (It did not decide whether a dangerous person can be detained without treatment or whether a nondangerous person could be detained if treatment is provided.) Persons held in violation of this constitutional rule will be subject to liability in the future. However, the Court has also made it clear that professionals cannot be held individually liable or responsible for the failure of the state to provide adequate funds and facilities for involuntary patients.[72]

Thus mental health professionals who act reasonably and in good faith in the commitment system do not run any significant risks. Of course, the mistreatment of patients (beatings, unreasonable restraint), or the unreasonable withholding of available treatment may subject the professional to liability.

Breach of Confidentiality

Mental health professionals have ethical and legal obligations to maintain the secrets of their clients and patients. Failure to meet them may result in liability for invasion of privacy (public disclosure of private facts) or for negligence (breach of the duty to maintain secrets), or conceivably for breach of contract.[73] The duty to protect confidentiality exists whether or not a state has a testimonial privilege that covers the communications.

The duty of confidentiality is not absolute, and information from therapy may safely be released in some limited circumstances. Patients, when competent, may waive their rights of confidentiality—most commonly to some third parties who are paying for treatment. Patients' limited waivers do not permit an unlimited disclosure of the information by the counselor or therapist. For example, permission to inform an insurance company of therapy does not include the right of the professional to write a book describing the patient and the therapy. Therapists may also release information when they are obligated to breach confidentiality, such as when they receive information concerning child abuse. A valid court order may also require release of information, and professionals may, of course, obey the order without incurring liability. (Confidentiality is discussed in detail in chapter 2.)

Defamation

False statements about a patient may result in liability if they harm the patient's reputation. Libel (written or permanent), slander (oral or less permanent), and false light (a privacy action similar to defamation) may result from the release of false statements about patients or clients. To give rise to liability the untruth must be made negligently or intentionally, harm to reputation or standing must result, and the untruth must be communicated to third parties.

There are many exceptions to defamation liability. These "privileges" (not to be confused with testimonial privileges), apply to many of the activities of mental health professionals. There are absolute privileges (complete protection against liability) associated with testimony in court and before legislative bodies, and qualified privileges (based on a belief in the truth of the statements) in a wide variety of other circumstances such as some communications with employers, family members, and certain other organizations.

The law of defamation and false light is a highly technical combination of common-law tradition, statutes, and constitutional limitations, and a thorough discussion is well beyond the scope of this chapter. The continuing debate about the conflicting values between protection of reputation and freedom of speech make it likely that the law in this area will continue to be somewhat unstable. Although a few mental health professionals have had claims filed against them for defamation or false light, it is unlikely that these will become major areas of mental health liability. Nevertheless, because statements about mental illness are likely to harm reputations, special care is called for in avoiding harmful falsehoods.[74]

Inadequate Diagnosis or Testing

Many of the forms of liability discussed above may arise from the failure to conduct an adequate diagnosis or testing of patients or clients. A surprisingly large proportion of malpractice claims appears to be based on negligent testing or diagnosis.[75] The actual diagnosis or testing does not result in liability, unless that negligence causes an injury. For example, a negligently conducted examination that results in prescribing unnecessary medications that in turn results in injury to the patient may be the basis of liability. Negligent testing that results in the wrongful dismissal from employment may also subject the professional to liability. Not every incorrect diagnosis is the basis for liability, only those that result from negligence.[76]

Negligent diagnosis may result from the failure to perform an adequate examination or test, or to understand reasonably the information presented by or about the patient. The failure to understand the nature, limitations, and proper uses of tests; drawing conclusions not warranted by the testing and examination; improper administration of the test; or any unethical use of tests may also be negligent.

Failure to Refer

Some clients will present problems with which a particular mental health professional is not prepared to deal. For example, the patient may require sophisticated testing that a psychiatrist does not feel fully competent to complete. Or a patient requiring medical intervention may be seen by a psychologist. In such circumstances it is the obligation of the professional to refer the client or patient to a qualified professional. The failure to refer may be negligent and give rise to liability if it causes harm to the patient. This liability is consistent with the ethical standards of all mental health professionals requiring that professionals not practice beyond their competence and that the interests of the patient be considered paramount.

Determining when referral is required is often difficult. The legal standard is again the reasonable practitioner standard: Would a reasonable practitioner with similar training and experience have made the referral? Reluctance to refer because of a desire to keep a client or for economic reasons are not, of course, legitimate reasons not to refer.

In some circumstances mental health professionals may feel the need to refer because of personal feelings or conflicts with patients. In such cases it is important that the professional make arrangements for the patient to transfer to another therapist. After treatment has begun, the failure to attend to the patient or to make reasonable provision for the patient to see another competent professional may be "abandonment," a form of negligence.

Contracts

Although most malpractice claims involve torts, it is possible for contract liability to arise from the provision of mental health services. Contract liability is based on breach of promise, not on the absence of reasonable care. If there has been a legally binding promise to do something, the breach of the promise gives rise to liability.[77] If, for example, a psychiatrist warrants to a patient that ECT is perfectly safe, the psychiatrist may be making a contractual guarantee to the patient. Any injuries arising out of the ECT may give rise to liability even in the absence of any negligence in administering it. Such contract/warranty cases are unusual, but they have been known to occur.[78]

Common reassurances that are part of a good professional manner ("bedside manner") are not contracts. The issue is whether a reasonable person would have understood the assurances as a contractual promise and an inducement to undertake a course of action or therapy the professional is proposing. Such assurances may be particularly subject to interpretation if there is an effort to persuade the client to agree to an unusual or experimental treatment.

Some therapists use a "treatment contract" as part of therapy in which the patient agrees to certain undertakings as a part of therapy. These "contracts" may not contain some of the elements of a legally enforceable contract (e.g., an agreement by the therapist to do something in return for the promise of the patient to do something). However, it is possible that some are constructed in a way that meets all the requirements for a contract. If so, the contract will be enforceable and the therapist will be bound by it.

Failure to Prevent Suicide

Mental health professionals have an obligation to take reasonable steps to diagnose and supervise patients who are at risk for suicide.[79] This duty arises out of the therapeutic relationship with the patient. The negligence may result from failure to adequately examine the patient to determine the possibility of suicide; to recognize common indicia of potential suicide; or to adequately supervise, restrain, or treat the patient.[80] Hospitals also have a duty to restrain and supervise patients who may be suicidal.[81]

Of course, not all patient suicides give rise to liability. Professionals are not required to prevent all suicides, only to take reasonable steps to prevent them.[82] In addition, courts are recognizing that the threat of suicide must be balanced against other risks and values, such as freedom from restraint or the risks of some medication. "Calculated risks of necessity must be taken if the modern and enlightened treatment of the mentally ill is to be pursued intelligently and rationally. Neither the hospital nor the doctor are insurers of the patient's health and safety."[83] The tradeoffs must be reasonable, and when appropriate, accompanied with informed consent.

The imposition of liability for failure to prevent suicide is, in effect, to require that therapists protect patients from the patients' own wrongdoing. This is a somewhat unusual form of liability, but now well established.

DANGEROUS PATIENTS AND THIRD PARTIES

Undoubtedly the most controversial and interesting area in mental health malpractice is the obligation of mental health professionals to protect "third parties" from dangerous patients and clients. This form of liability raises a number of important issues. Among the most fundamental is the relationship among the patient, the professional, and society. Ordinarily the obligation of the mental health professional is to the client, not to others. When is it appropriate to interfere with this relationship to protect an interest of society? We examine that question from the perspective of two potential forms of "third party" liability: "the duty to warn" and "the duty to report."

Tarasoff and "The Duty to Warn"

Tarasoff is commonly recognized as the case that began to establish that therapists have a duty to take steps to protect potential victims. There have been a number of other cases which have adopted or expanded the duty to warn, several of which are cited in the notes. For convenience we will refer to the duty imposed by these cases as *Tarasoff*. Although commonly called the "duty to warn," this phrase does not accurately describe the duty, which requires reasonable steps to protect potential victims from dangerous patients.

Psychologists at the U.C.-Berkeley mental health clinic determined that one of their patients, Mr. Poddar, was dangerous and might kill a woman, Ms. Tarasoff, who he thought was spurning him.[84] The clinic called the campus police, who talked to Poddar and released him. Poddar later did kill Tarasoff and the University health service was sued for failure to take appropriate action to protect Tarasoff from Poddar. The California court held that the Tarasoff estate could sue the clinic on the basis that it failed to take reasonable action to protect her, such as warning Tarasoff about Poddar's intention to kill her.[85] The obligation described by the court was to take reasonable steps to protect the intended victim, but the emphasis has been on the "duty to warn" the intended victim of the danger so the victim could take steps to protect herself.

The *Tarasoff* decision was unusual in that it imposed a duty to the public arising out of the treatment of individual patients. It was seen by some commentators as violating the principle that one is not required to rescue those for whom one has no responsibility.[86] The court based this duty to warn on the therapist–client relationship and a balancing of the costs and benefits of such warnings. By voluntarily entering the practice of therapy, the therapist assumed a responsibility to the public to avoid this public harm.[87]

The arguments against imposing Tarasoff-type liability include the following: the duty to warn is based on the ability of mental health professionals to predict dangerousness, and such predictions cannot be made with any degree of confidence; warning intended victims will require that the confidences of therapy be revealed, and this breach of confidence will interfere with therapy among the very people (the potentially dangerous) whom we would like to have in therapy; the breach of the confidences of therapy will interfere with the privacy of those in therapy; there are substantial overpredictions of dangerousness, so many people who are in fact not dangerous will have their therapy interrupted by unnecessary warnings to victims; it is unusual and unfair to require "rescue" of third parties; once patients who have aggressive feelings understand that there is a duty to warn, they will not reveal these feelings in therapy for fear of the disclosure and therefore over the long run the duty to warn will largely be self-defeating by discouraging disclosure of aggression; even if some good can be accomplished by a duty to warn, the costs to therapy exceed the potential benefits of such disclosures.

Among the arguments in favor of imposing a Tarasoff-type duty to warn are the following: the opportunity to avoid unnecessary death or serious injury should be taken; avoiding unnecessary death or injury is so important that interference with therapy or the right of privacy is comparatively trivial; the duty imposed is not without precedent because professionals are sometimes required to act in the interest of society rather than a client or patient (e.g., the duty to isolate or report some serious, infectious diseases); patients are not likely to refuse to disclose matters in therapy because of the threat that the therapist will warn potential victims; although the prediction of dangerousness is not perfect, it is sufficiently accurate to be the basis of a warning when a patient is apparently dangerous; if these predictions can be the basis for involuntary commitment, they surely are accurate enough to provide the basis for a warning; overpredictions of dangerousness resulting in some unnecessary warnings is a relatively small price to pay to avoid murders and serious injury.

It is impossible to determine precisely what effect *Tarasoff* and similar cases have had on therapy, but there is some indication from studies conducted thus far that the impact is not overwhelming. It may have made therapists more concerned about the issue of dangerous patients, and made some patients more reluctant to discuss violence. There has been some increase in the breach of confidentiality to warn potential victims (some warning of potential victims occurred before *Tarasoff*).[88]

The *Tarasoff* decision left many unanswered questions about the duty it imposed: What is the nature of the duty and how can the duty be fulfilled? What professionals have this duty? How much information may or must be revealed when a warning is given? When several people know of the dangerousness, who has the duty to act?

Does the duty exist only when there is a specified, known victim, or does it exist whenever dangerousness exists? What does dangerousness include (physical injury, property damage, emotional injury to others)? At what level of certainty concerning dangerousness does the duty to act exist? Most of these questions have not yet been fully answered by those states adopting the duty.

Among the most discussed issues has been the "identifiable victim" issue—whether the duty applies only when the specific victim is known. The tendency in subsequent cases has been toward requiring a known victim. Under this approach, the duty does not apply when a therapist fears that a patient is likely to hurt someone, but does not know who may be harmed. The *Tarasoff* decision suggested that it was necessary that the victim be identifiable.[89]

A more recent decision seems to have expanded the concept of the known victim by permitting recovery by the son of a woman who was the intended victim. The son suffered emotional trauma when his mother was shot while covering him, in an attempt to protect him from injury. The court held that the son could recover because it was foreseeable that the son might be present during the attack on the mother. Therefore the son was a known victim to the therapist.[90] Not all courts have embraced the "known victim" approach.[91]

The known victim issue is related to the question of how the duty may be discharged. The emphasis has been on "the duty to warn."[92] If the duty is to warn, there generally must be a known victim in order to issue the warning. If, on the other hand, the therapist's duty is more clearly focused on taking reasonable steps to avoid injury from the violent patient, then there is no need for a known victim. When a therapist perceives a real threat to unspecified people, it is still possible to take action (civil commitment, warning to authorities) to avoid the injury.

The emphasis on "warning" is unfortunate.[93] Focus on taking some appropriate action to protect victims might allow greater protection for the public and potential victims and avoid some interference with therapy that warnings cause. Warnings have the advantage of being easy to prove: either they were given or they were not, but they are not nearly flexible enough to provide the protection *Tarasoff* sought. Over the long run it is probable that the duty will be more clearly defined to include actions other than warnings. However, it appears that therapists view the obligation as one of warning, and that in practice warnings to victims are the most common form of "reasonable action."[94]

Interesting questions about *Tarasoff* yet to be resolved revolve around the conflict between values of protection and confidentiality. It would not be unusual for a potential victim who is warned of danger to want more information about the dangerous patient. How much information can the therapist give to victims following the warning? The probable answer is that sufficient information may be given to allow potential victims to protect themselves. Defining just what that information is, however, is extremely difficult.

The duty to take reasonable steps to protect others from dangerous clients could be expanded to include other professionals, perhaps even lawyers.[95] In part the reason for imposing liability was on the basis of the special ability of psychotherapists to predict dangerousness. However, it is unlikely that any such special ability exists, and there is no apparent reason for other professionals to be exempt from the duty when they should, in light of their training and expertise, know of a client's threat to others.[96]

Most state courts that have considered the question have adopted an approach similar to California,[97] although some have been reluctant to impose liability.[98] It is always risky to predict whether a new legal theory will become widely accepted. Our guess is, however, that the duty to protect society from violent patients will become a part of the law of most states, although we expect that the duty will be modified as described above. It appears that therapists around the country already act as though *Tarasoff* applies to them. Many therapists identify a "duty to warn" as an ethical or moral duty as well as a legal duty.[99]

Legislatures are now considering *Tarasoff* issues. In some states mental health professionals have pressed for this legislation to clarify the law, or to narrow the scope of liability. California, for example, has adopted a statute that provides for liability only if the patient has told the therapist of a "serious threat of violence against a reasonably identifiable victim or victims." The duty is discharged by "reasonable efforts to communicate that threat to the victim . . . *and* to a law enforcement agency."[100] This statute generally follows the *Tarasoff* decision. It unfortunately emphasizes the duty to warn. Ironically, it may actually have somewhat expanded the duties of therapists by requiring that both victim *and* law enforcement agencies are warned.

Some states where no cases have clearly established a *Tarasoff* duty are considering a statute. For example, in 1986 Kentucky adopted a statute that imposed duties on therapists that went beyond those required in California by establishing a duty even when there is not an identifiable victim. That duty may be discharged by warning the police and/or (it is not clear which) by seeking civil commitment.[101]

Reporting Obligations

Another approach to protecting "third parties" from injury is to require the reporting of any past abuse that has occurred. All states have child-abuse reporting statutes, and an increasing number have laws requiring the reporting of other forms of abuse (e.g., spouse or elder abuse).[102] By requiring reporting, the state can intervene to prevent further injury and may prosecute if it chooses to do so.

Abuse-reporting statutes, which are discussed more thoroughly in the next chapter, vary from state to state. Many require the reporting of known or suspected physical or mental abuse (broadly defined), regardless of the source of the information. Therefore, a mental health professional learning of abuse from a patient who wishes to stop the abuse or from an abused person must report that to the state.

The failure to file the required reports may result in civil liability if the abused child suffers additional injury. This liability is specifically provided by statute in some states. Even in states without statutory liability, it is likely that negligence or liability would be imposed for the failure to report known or suspected abuse.[103] There have been only a limited number of civil cases resulting from the failure to report, but this is an area where, if reporting statutes are interpreted as broadly as they are written, failure to report could one day become more important than *Tarasoff*-type cases.[104]

OTHER ISSUES OF LIABILITY

Several other issues of liability may affect mental health professionals. In this section we consider issues related to practice by students and others in training, agents and employees, and "pop" psychotherapy.

Students and Others in Training

The education of mental health professionals is characterized by substantial clinical or practicum training. Since those still in training
assess, counsel and treat patients, there is the potential for harm.
This raises questions about the level of care those being treated can
expect, and the responsibilities to patients of students and of institutions and the faculty members, supervisors and treatment facilities.
Liability regarding student practice may arise for failure to provide
adequate supervision and review, for failure to meet acceptable levels
of care, or for the failure of informed consent.[105] There are few reported legal cases detailing the liability for injuries suffered because
of inadequate treatment by students.[106] It may be that most instances
in which student malpractice has occurred are not recognized. It may
be that attorneys, many of whom received little formal clinical training in law school, fail to notice the possibility of training-related
injuries.

Students must work under supervision that is adequate to ensure
that reasonable services are provided and that students do not extend
themselves beyond their level of training or expertise. Even when the
clinical work does not take place in the institution providing the
training, there must be adequate supervision. This obligation goes
beyond informing students when they have made mistakes or signing
treatment or assessment reports. The effort should be to ensure that
clients or patients do not receive inferior service because they are
being seen by a student. This level of supervision is often difficult
and expensive, and some training programs may not be meeting obligations to adequately supervise the work of students.

To what standard of care should students be held? While it seems
unfair to hold students to the same level of care and practice expected
of a fully trained professional, it is nevertheless unfair for patients to
receive a lower standard of care because they are being seen by a
student. Many patients are probably unaware about the status of their
therapists, who are sometimes not clearly identified. Certainly whenever a client has reason to believe that the student is actually a fully
trained professional, the student should be held to the professional
level of care.[107] In addition, supervision should be strong enough to
ensure that the care given by students does not fall below that accepted as ordinary professional care. Therefore, it is fair to hold the

care provided by students to the level commonly accepted as professional.

Informed consent may include permission to be seen by a student.[108] Deciding whether or not to accept treatment by someone in training may be an important matter for some patients. It is possible that treatment from a student will affect important legal rights, including the confidentiality of information revealed in therapy.[109] Certainly a patient should be able to decide whether or not to accept treatment from a student. It is not reasonable to assume that everyone who goes to a teaching facility agrees to treatment by students. Consent to treatment by those in training should be explicit. As we note in chapter 6, experimentation on humans has included great protections for human research subjects. Many of the considerations that cause concern for research subjects are present with "teaching subjects." Such patients may be at increased risk, their privacy may be invaded more frequently, and there may be conflicts between their treatment needs and the interests of instruction. There is no mechanism for protecting teaching subjects similar to those for protecting research subjects. Mental health professionals and students should, however, be sensitive to the special interests of teaching subjects.

Liability for Agents and Employees

Employers and other principals may be responsible for the torts of their employees or other agents in at least two ways: by failing to provide adequate supervision, and through vicarious liability (responsibility for the acts of others). Employers thus have some obligation to exercise at least limited supervision over employees to ensure that their conduct does not threaten the safety of those for whom the employer is responsible, and increasingly institutions have obligations to supervise nonemployees (such as private physicians) who use the institutions. In a mental health center, for example, the center has an obligation to supervise its staff and professional employees. It may also have some obligation to ensure a minimal level of care by those who are not direct employees, but who see clients at the center.[110]

Even if they have exercised reasonable care and supervision themselves, employers are vicariously responsible for the torts of their employees in the course of their employment. (The employees are individually responsible for those torts, but the employer is also responsible.) Thus, the mental health center will be responsible if a psychologist in its employ negligently harms a patient. Mental health professionals in private practice will be liable for the employment related negligence of their assistants, nurses, and receptionists.

"Pop" Therapy

A number of new, nontraditional, and "pop" therapies have developed and grown more popular. In some cases these have claimed to solve serious emotional problems; others have attracted people with serious problems. The training available to, or taken by, the practitioners of these various forms of therapy varies widely. In some instances the counselors have substantial training, in others little or none. As a general matter there is no state license required to "practice" nontraditional therapies.

To what extent should the practitioners of "pop" therapies be held liable when the counseling results in injury? If a client commits suicide or is substantially worse after therapy, should liability be imposed? To what standard of care should practitioners of nontraditional therapies be held, to the standard of care of psychotherapists generally or to a special standard of care defined by their own nontraditional therapy?

These are unsettled questions.[111] It is argued on one hand that to fully protect patients from ineffective therapy and charlatans, practitioners of nontraditional therapies should be held to the same standard of care, and charged with the same knowledge, as more traditional psychotherapists. To do anything less would permit the absence of substantial formal training to be an advantage to avoid liability and would, in fact, encourage the development of potentially harmful pop therapies. On the other side it is claimed that applying the standard of care of ordinary psychotherapy to nontraditional forms of therapy will discourage the development of new and effective therapies as well as the training of practitioners in nontraditional therapy.[112]

The law has usually defined a standard of care in terms of the "school of thought" of the practitioner involved and the training of the practitioner. A general practitioner would be held to a lower standard in treating a heart patient than a specialist in cardiology, and in some respects a chiropractor will not be held to the same standards as a physician. These principles suggest that practitioners of nontraditional therapy should not be held to the standard of care or level of training and knowledge of psychotherapists.

People are held to a higher standard of care or training if they claim to have or "hold themselves out" as having special qualifications. If general practitioners claim to be cardiologists, they should be held to that higher standard of care. These principles should also apply to the practitioners of "pop" therapies who present themselves to the public as therapists or trained counselors.[113]

There is a strong argument for the imposing on those practicing nontraditional forms of therapy a duty to be able to recognize people with serious emotional problems who may not be helped, and may in fact be harmed, by the pop therapy and to refer those people to qualified therapists. Consider, for example, a "growth" group that uses highly emotional and aggressive techniques in its sessions and does not screen applicants to eliminate those likely to be harmed by the sessions. If a participant who cannot take the emotional pressure and aggression generated by the session commits suicide as a result, liability should be imposed. By undertaking this form of "therapy" or counseling, adequate training and care to prevent serious injury should be expected of the practitioners.

These and similar issues have yet to be clarified by courts and legislatures. If the popular appeal of many forms of nontraditional therapy continues, however, it is reasonable to expect that liability will be imposed for the failure of nontraditional practitioners to take reasonable steps to be informed and understand the risks associated with the counseling or "therapy" that they are doing and for failure to take reasonable steps to protect particularly vulnerable people from harm. To the extent the nontraditional practitioners hold themselves out as therapists, they will undoubtedly be held to the standard of care of the formally trained and licensed psychotherapists.

LIABILITY IN PERSPECTIVE

The extended discussion of the possible forms of mental health malpractice liability must be viewed against the background of the very small number of successful cases filed against mental health professionals. Malpractice liability cannot be seen as a looming threat to most practitioners. And yet the potential certainly exists. New forms of liability such as *Tarasoff* and a greater recognition of emotional injuries may tend to increase the incidence of liability.

There are several ways to minimize the risks of malpractice that do exist. Among the steps a professional might take are: (1) Be particularly sensitive to the need to keep the confidences of therapy, and be sure that a good reason exists for breaching any confidences. (2) Be concerned with obtaining *informed* consent that includes a description of the hazards of treatment and the existence of alternative treatments. (3) Maintain accurate records. Do not tamper with records to try to cover up mistakes. (4) Be cautious of incomplete or sloppy testing, histories, and diagnoses. (5) Refer to another professional when the patient could benefit. (6) Give particular attention to the suicidal or dangerous patient. If you decide not to take action about a patient who may be dangerous, have sound reasons for the decision. (7) Engage in ethical practice. Unethical conduct is likely to also be illegal or subject to liability. (8) Do not suggest or engage in sexual relationships with patients, or former patients, or close relatives of patients, no matter what others may advocate.[114]

COMPENSATION FOR INJURED PATIENTS

Given the current extremely low level of liability claims, one might wonder whether the legal system is operating properly in providing compensation for those injured through negligence or misconduct. For reasons described earlier in this chapter, many more people are injured through therapy than ever receive compensation, and it is unlikely that society will soon become concerned with providing compensation for those injured. There has been a proposal to impose liability without fault (strict liability) for injuries "connected to" therapy.[115] There are a number of problems with this proposal that would make it difficult to implement.

An alternative might come from the mental health professions themselves in the form of a voluntary program to provide some compensation for those harmed in therapy. Similar plans have been adopted on a very modest scale in some states to assist clients harmed by unethical attorneys. Although compensation plans for clients would, of necessity, be somewhat complex and would impose some economic burden on professionals, it would be consistent with the compassionate traditions of the mental health professions. The plan could permit patients to seek compensation from a professional fund by proving misconduct or inappropriate conduct which probably caused harm. The patient would not be required to seek compensation in a public forum. Such a plan might be funded in part by the malpractice carriers to the extent that it would substitute for regular malpractice liability in some instances.

SUMMARY

Systems of law and ethics offer ways of protecting and balancing important social, professional, and individual values. One characteristic of a profession is the adoption of a code of ethics which protects the public (the clients or patients) and promotes the welfare of the profession. Codes typically include both minimum and aspirational standards of conduct. Common provisions of these codes are the obligation to provide competent service, confidentiality, fiduciary duties toward clients, and respect for client autonomy.

Both ethical principles and malpractice describe the obligations of professionals and protect clients. Ethical principles help to define legal duties, and are therefore related.

Mental health professionals have experienced relatively low rates of professional malpractice claims. This may be attributable to the difficulty in establishing a clear standard of care and causation, the absence of physical injuries, close client-therapist relationships, and the desire of patients to avoid releasing very private information in court.

Although malpractice claims are infrequent, they may arise in a number of areas. They may arise from sexual contact with clients, unnecessary or negligently conducted ECT, medications given unnecessarily or improperly, the failure to obtain informed consent to invasive or risky procedures or treatments, the use of excessive force or violence, wrongful commitment, the breach of the duty of confidentiality, inadequate diagnosis or testing, failure to refer to another professional, and failure to prevent suicide or to warn intended victims. In unusual circumstances therapists may make contractual guarantees to patients that will define additional legal duties.

Undoubtedly the most controversial issue in professional liability has been the imposition of a *"Tarasoff* duty to warn." This imposes a duty on therapists to take appropriate action to protect third parties when third parties are endangered by patients. The limits and nature of the *Tarasoff* duty have not been defined. Most states have not yet decided whether to impose this form of liability, but it is likely that in the long-run most will decide to do so. All states do, however, require reporting of certain kinds of injuries, such as child abuse. If the failure to report results in additional injuries to a child, there may be liability for the failure to report.

Students and others in training may see patients. It is important that there be adequate supervision of this treatment to ensure that the treatment is of high quality. We believe that ordinarily patients should understand when they will be seen by students.

Nontraditional therapies pose interesting malpractice issues. At a minimum, if practitioners hold themselves out as trained therapists they should be held to a fairly high standard of care. In addition, nontraditional practitioners should be held to a standard that requires them reasonably to determine who may be harmed by their therapy.

Despite the long list of potential forms of liability for mental health professionals, malpractice claims against them are infrequent. They are, in fact, sufficiently infrequent to raise doubts about whether the malpractice system is adequate to deal with injuries from therapy. Some have proposed a form of strict liability for therapy-related injuries. One alternative is a compensation plan provided by mental health professionals themselves.

NOTES

1. Some claim that professionals are bound by professional ethics even when not working as a trained professional (e.g., a psychologist working as an administrator). Goodstein, Ethical Pitfalls for Managers, 15 *Prof. Psychology: Research & Prac.* 749 (1984). See M. Carrol, H. Schneider & G. Wesley, *Ethics in the Practice of Psychology* (1985).

2. Examples of ethical standards which have been struck down by courts are minimum fee schedules (violations of antitrust laws) (e.g., Goldfarb v.

34

Virginia State Bar, 421 U.S. 773 [1975]) and prohibition on advertising (violations of free speech and freedom of the press) (Bates v. State Bar of Arizona, 433 U.S. 350 [1977]).

3. Changes in social values and technology may complicate ethical considerations. Busse, Ethics and Psychiatry: Old and New Issues, 141 *Am. J. Psychiatry* 410 (1984); Lichtenberg, Means and Ends in Counseling, 63 *J. Counseling & Development* 596 (1985); Tancredi & Edlund, Are Conflicts of Interest Endemic to Psychiatric Consultation?, 6 *Int'l J. L. & Psychiatry* 293 (1983). See P. Keith-Spiegal & G. Koocher, *Ethics in Psychology: Professional Standards and Cases* (1985).

It is interesting that modern consumer protection concepts are sometimes applied by analogy to some therapy practices. Williams, The Bait-and-Switch Tactic in Psychotherapy, 22 *Psychotherapy* 110 (1985).

4. American Bar Association, *Annotated Code of Professional Responsibility* (1981). (A revision of the code, *The Model Rules of Professional Conduct*, has been adopted in a few states.)

5. American Association for Counseling and Development, *Ethical Standards* (1981) (this was formerly the American Personnel and Guidance Association).

6. American Nurses' Association, *Code for Nurses with Interpretive Statements* (1968). Regarding special ethical issues in psychiatric nursing, see Hoeffer, The Private Practice Model: An Ethical Perspective, 21 *J. Psychosocial Nursing & Mental Health Services* 31 (1983).

7. American Psychiatric Association, *The Principles of Medical Ethics With Annotations Especially Applicable to Psychiatry* (1981); American Psychiatric Association, *Opinions of the Ethics Committee on the Principles of Medical Ethics With Annotations Especially Applicable to Psychiatry* (1980). See S. Block & P. Chadoff eds., *Psychiatric Ethics* (1981).

8. American Psychological Association, *Ethical Principles of Psychologists* (1981) (officially published at 36 *Am. Psychologist* 633); American Psychological Association, *Specialty Guidelines for the Delivery of Services By Clinical Psychologists* (1981), printed at, 36 *Am. Psychologist* 640 (1981). See generally, Haas & Fennimore, Ethical and Legal Works in Professional Psychology: Selected Works, 14 *Prof. Psychology: Research & Prac.* 540 (1983); Tokunaga, Ethical Issues in Consultation: An Evaluative Review, 15 *Prof. Psychology: Research & Prac.* 811 (1984).

9. American School Counselor Association, Ethical Standards for School Counselors, 32 *Sch. Counselor* 84 (1984).

10. National Association of Social Workers, *Code of Ethics* (1979). See Lewis, Ethical Assessment, 65 *Soc. Casework* 203 (1984).

11. Stephens, Personal Behavior and Professional Ethics: Implications for Special Educators, 18 *J. Learning Disabilities* 187 (1985).

12. See D. Hogan, *The Regulation of Psychotherapists* (vol. 1) (1979).

13. American Psychological Association, *Ethical Principles of Psychologists*, Principle 10 (1981).

14. National Association of Social Workers, *Code of Ethics*, standard I.E.

6 (1979). Unfortunately, even the honesty of reported research has become a serious ethical issues. See Knight, Exploring the Compromise of Ethical Principles in Science, 27 *Perspective in Biology & Med.* 432 (1984).

15. American Medical Association, *American Medical Association,* Section 1 (1980).

16. *Id.,* Section 4.

17. *Id.,* Section 7.

18. American Bar Association, *Annotated Code of Professional Responsibility,* Cannon 7 (1981).

19. For another view of the common elements of profession codes of ethics see, Abbott, Professional Ethics, 88 *Am. J. Soc.* 855 (1983).

20. D. Hogan, *The Regulation of Psychotherapists* (vol. 1) (1979). For a review of the cases investigated by one profession, see Hall & Hare-Mustin, Sanctions and the Diversity of Ethical Complaints Against Psychologists, 38 *Am. Psychologist* 714 (1983); Mills, Ethics Education and Adjudication Within Psychology, 39 *Am. Psychologist* 669 (1984).

21. See chapter 4 regarding licensing concerning the enforcement of licensing statutes.

22. For example, the American Bar Association requires that accredited law schools provide instruction in professional responsibility to all students.

23. E.g., as part of the debate, Barish, A Response to "Training for Responsible Professional Behavior in Psychology and Social Work," 11 *Clinical Soc. Work J.* 184 (1983); Pharis & Hill, The Training for Responsible Professional Behavior in Psychology and Social Work, 11 *Clinical Soc. Work J.* 178 (1983). Also see note 24, *infra.*

24. Regarding ethical training issues in social work see F. Reamer & M. Abramson, *The Teaching of Social Work Ethics* (1982); in law see Weinstein, On the Teaching of Legal Ethics, 72 *Colum. L. Rev.* 452 (1972); in nursing see Aroskar, Ethics in the Nursing Curriculum, 25 *Nursing Outlook* 260 (1977); in medicine see Chapman, On the Definition and Teaching of the Medical Ethic, 301 *New Eng. J. Med.* 630 (1979); in forensic psychiatry see Ciccone & Clements, The Ethical Practice of Forensic Psychiatry: A View from the Trenches, 12 *Bull. Am. Acad. Psychiatry & L.* 263 (1984); in counseling see Welfel & Lipsitz, Ethical Orientation of Counselors: Its Relationship to Moral Reasoning and Level of Training, 23 *Counselor Educ. & Supervision* 35 (1983).

25. Ciccone & Clements, Forensic Psychiatry and Applied Clinical Ethics, Theory and Practice, 141 *Am. J. Psychiatry* 395 (1984); Sadoff, Practical Ethical Problems of the Forensic Psychiatrist in Dealing with Attorneys, 72 *Bull. Am. Acad. Psychiatry & L.* 243 (1984). The American Academy of Psychiatry and the Law adopted ethical guidelines for forensic psychiatrists, see Weinstein, How Should Forensic Psychiatry Police Itself? Guidelines and Grievances: The AAPL Committee on Ethics, 12 *Bull. Am. Acad. Psychiatry & L.* 289 (1984).

26. For a review of malpractice cases involving psychotherapists see D. Hogan, *The Regulation of Psychotherapists: A Review of Malpractice Suits in*

the United States (vol. 3) (1979). A thorough review of psychiatric malpractice is J. Smith, *Medical Malpractice: Psychiatric Care* (1986).

27. Slawson & Guggenheim, Psychiatric Malpractice: A Review of the National Loss Experience, 141 *Am. J. Psychiatry* 979 (1984). These figures were based on claims filed between 1974 and 1978. The malpractice claims filed against psychiatrists are probably understated because the data did not include claims brought against V.A. or public hospital patients. See generally Deardorff, Cross & Hupprich, Malpractice Liability in Psychotherapy: Client and Practitioner Perspectives, 15 *Prof. Psychology: Research & Prac.* 590 (1984); Watkins & Watkins, Malpractice in Clinical Social Work, 1 *Behav. Sci. & L.* 55 (1983).

28. Wright, What to Do Until the Malpractice Lawyer Comes: A Survivor's Manual, 36 *Am. Psychologist* 1535 (1981).

29. There are many sources of information about these theories of recovery and their applicability to psychotherapy. E.g., E. Beis, *Mental Health and the Law* (1984); B. Furrow, *Malpractice in Psychotherapy* (1980); T. Gutheil & P. Appelbaum, *Clinical Handbook of Psychiatry and the Law* (1982); B. Schultz, *Legal Liability in Psychotherapy* (1982); R. Schwitzgebel & R. K. Schwitzgebel, *Law and Psychological Practice* (1980).

30. Furrow, Defective Mental Treatment: A Proposal for the Application of Strict Liability to Psychiatric Services, 58 *B.U. L. Rev.* 391 (1979); Comment, Injuries Precipitated By Psychotherapy: Liability Without Fault as a Basis for Recovery, 20 *S.D. L. Rev.* 401 (1975).

31. See Curran, Professional Negligence—Some General Comments, 12 *Vand. L. Rev.* 535 (1959); Keeton, Medical Negligence—The Standard of Care, 10 *Texas Tech L. Rev.* 351 (1979). However, in rare circumstances the standard or usual practice of a profession may be negligent. E.g., Helling v. Carey, 83 Wash.2d 514, 519 P.2d 981 (1974) (involving opthalmologists). It is possible to see Tarasoff v. Regents of the University of California, 17 Cal.3d 425, 551 P.2d 334, 131 Cal. Rptr. 14 (1976) (discussed later in this chapter) as a decision that found negligence in the common practice of mental health professionals in not warning potential victims.

32. The absence of clear standards has been criticized, "As long as therapists restrict their practices to talk, interpretations, and advice, they will remain relatively immune from suit, no matter how poor their advice, how damaging their comments, or how incorrect their interpretations." D. Hogan, *supra* note 26 at 322. See Knapp & VandeCreek, Malpractice as a Regulator of Psychotherapy, 18 *Psychotherapy: Theory, Research & Prac.* 354 (1981); Note, Malpractice in Psychotherapy: Is There a Relevant Standard of Care?, 35 *Case W. Res. L. Rev.* 251 (1984).

33. Neiland, Malpractice Liability of Psychiatric Professionals, 1 *Am. J. Forensic Psychiatry* 22 (1979).

34. Testimonial privileges such as psychotherapist-patient privileges commonly provide for a patient-litigant exception which waives the privilege when the holder of the privilege brings his or her mental condition or state into question. In a therapy malpractice action, the defendant would lose any

therapy privileges. Not only would any privilege be lost concerning the therapy on which the malpractice claim was based, but it could be lost for any therapy conducted by anyone if the information from that therapy might be relevant to the malpractice case. In practical fact, there might be very little limitation on therapy-related information which the defendant could seek from the plaintiff. See Slovenko, Psychotherapist-Patient Testimonial Privilege: A Picture of Misguided Hope, 23 *Cath. U. L. Rev.* 649 (1974). The patient-litigant exception is considered more completely in chapter 2.

35. See generally Dawidoff, The Malpractice of Psychiatrists, 1966 *Duke L. J.* 696; Note, The Liability of Psychiatrists for Malpractice, 36 *U. Pitt. L. Rev.* 108 (1974); Note, Medical Malpractice: The Liability of Psychiatrists, 48 *Notre Dame Law.* 693, 696–703 (1973).

36. A few claims have been filed against psychologists based on prescription drug use or ECT. Wright, Psychologists and Professional Liability (Malpractice) Insurance, 36 *Am. Psychologist* 1485, 1488, 1492 (1981).

37. Slawson & Guggenheim, Psychiatric Malpractice: A Review of the National Loss Experience, 141 *Am. J. Psychiatry* 979 (1984); Wright, *supra,* note 36. Some care must be used in reviewing these data because they may be incomplete or outdated. See Taub, Psychiatric Malpractice in the 1980s: A Look at Some Areas of Concern, 11 *L. Med. & Health Care* 97 (1983).

38. D. Hogan, *The Regulation of Psychotherapists: A Review of Malpractice Suits in the United States* (vol. 3) 15–16, 381 (1979).

39. Slawson & Guggenheim, note 37, *supra,* at 981.

40. It is possible that ECT might be used on an experimental basis to treat these conditions (or others for which ECT is not commonly used), but such experimental use would have to include the conditions for experiments. See chapter 3.

41. See, e.g., Stone v. Proctor, 259 N.C. 633, 131 S.E.2d 297 (1963), and an annotation on malpractice in connection with electroshock at 94 ALR3d 317.

42. One study reported that medication claims accounted for more than a third of malpractice claims arising from the major procedures employed in psychiatry. Slawson & Guggenheim, note 37, *supra,* at 980.

43. Appleton, Legal Problems in Psychiatric Drug Prescription, 124 *Am. J. Psychiatry* 877 (1968); Wettstein, Tardive Dyskinesia and Malpractice, 1 *Behav. Sci. & L.* 85 (1983).

44. See chapter 6 for discussions of the regulation of experimental practices.

45. Liability for the absence of consent, and the doctrine of consent to experimental treatment can be traced to Slater v. Baker and Stapleton, 95 Eng. Rep. 860 (K.B. 1767). Liability for the absence of informed consent is now firmly established by common law and statute. Meisel & Kabnick, Informed Consent to Medical Treatment: An Analysis of Recent Legislation, 41 *U. Pitt. L. Rev.* 407 (1980). The doctrine applies to psychotherapy. Note, The Doctrine of Informed Consent Applied to Psychotherapy, 72 *Georgetown L. J.* 1637 (1984).

46. Canterbury v. Spence, 464 F.2d 772 (D.C. Cir.), *cert. denied,* 409 U.S. 1064 (1972).

47. Meisel, The "Exceptions" to the Informed Consent Doctrine: Striking a Balance Between Competing Values in Medical Decisionmaking, 1979 *Wis. L. Rev.* 413.

48. Under limited circumstances consent to invasive procedures such as ECT may be presumed. See Wilson v. Lehman, 379 S.W.2d 478 (Ky. 1964). However, it would be a mistake to conclude that every patient who does not object to ECT has given informed consent to the procedure.

49. Woods v. Brumlop, 71 N.M. 221, 377 P.2d 520 (1962).

50. See Mitchell v. Robinson, 334 S.W.2d 11 (Mo. 1960).

51. See, e.g., Sterling Drug v. Yarrow, 408 F.2d 978 (6th Cir. 1969).

52. See generally Appleton, Legal Problems in Psychiatric Drug Prescription, 124 *Am. J. Psychiatry* 877 (1968); Merrill, Compensation for Prescription Drug Injuries, 59 *Va. L. Rev.* 1 (1973); Wettstein, Tardive Dyskinesia and Malpractice, 1 *Behav. Sci. & L.* 85 (1983).

53. E.g., Hare-Mustin, Marecek, Kaplan & Liss-Levinson, Rights of Clients, Responsibilities of Therapists, 34 *Am. Psychologist* 3 (1979); Noll, The Psychotherapist and Informed Consent, 133 *Am. J. Psychiatry* 1451 (1976); Smith, Unfinished Business With Informed Consent Procedures, 36 *Am. Psychologist* 22 (1981).

54. See Meyer & Smith, A Crisis in Group Therapy, 32 *Am. Psychologist* 638 (1977).

55. Such treatment runs the risk of liability through the tort of intentional infliction of emotional distress (outrage) if there is not some reasonable consent to it. W. P. Keeton, D. Dobbs, R. Keeton & D. Owen, *Prosser and Keeton on the Law of Torts,* 54–66 (W. P. Keeton 5th ed. 1984).

56. For an excellent review of informed consent in an evaluation center, a research ward and an outpatient clinic, see C. Lidz, A. Meisel, E. Zerubavel, M. Carter, R. Sestak & L. Roth, *Informed Consent: A Study of Decisionmaking in Psychiatry* (1984).

57. See Roth, Appelbaum, Salee, Reynolds & Huber, The Dilemma of Denial in the Assessment of Competency to Refuse Treatment, 139 *Am. J. Psychiatry* 910 (1982).

58. See Ewald, Medical Decision-Making for Children: An Analysis of Competing Interests, 25 *St. Louis U. L. J.* 689 (1982).

59. See Parham v. J. R., 442 U.S. 584 (1979). This case is discussed more thoroughly in chapter 17 dealing with involuntary civil commitment.

60. Minors who are sufficiently mature to make the decision to have an abortion, for example, may do so even over the objection of their parents. Akron v. Akron Center for Reproductive Health, 462 U.S. 416 (1983); Planned Parenthood of Kansas City v. Ashcroft, 462 U.S. 476 (1983). Minors may also obtain some contraceptives without parental consent. Carey v. Population Services, 431 U.S. 678 (1977). These rights of minors are based on constitutional privacy.

61. See principles 6 and 7, American Psychological Association, *Ethical*

Principles of Psychologists (1981); Section II.F.5, National Association of Social Workers, *Code of Ethics* (1979). Sexual attraction between therapist and patient is common. Pope, Keith-Spiegel & Tabachnik, Sexual Attraction to Clients, 41 *Am. Psychologist* 147 (1986). Sexual contact is often harmful to the patient. Bouhoutsos, Holroyd, Lerman, Forer & Greenberg, Sexual Intimacy Between Psychotherapists and Patients, 14 *Prof. Psychology: Research & Prac.* 185 (1983); Feldman-Summers & Jones, Psychological Impacts of Sexual Contact Between Therapists or Other Health Care Practitioners and Their Clients, 52 *J. Consulting & Clinical Psychology* 1054 (1984).

 62. Zipkin v. Freeman, 436 S.W.2d 753 (Mo. 1968).

 63. Another interesting form of potential liability where a therapist has been sexually involved with a married patient is the possibility of alienation of affection. In states still recognizing this cause of action, it may be brought by a spouse of a patient who has been enticed out of a marital relationship by a therapist. Anclote Manor Foundation v. Wilkinson, 263 S.2d 256 (Fla. 1972). See generally J. Smith, *Medical Malpractice: Psychiatric Care* 286–338 (1986).

 64. M. Shepard, *The Love Treatment: Sexual Intimacy Between Patients and Psychotherapists* (1971). See Marmor, Sexual Acting-Out in Psychotherapy, 32 *Am. J. Psychoanalysis* 3 (1972).

 65. See generally Roy v. Hartogs, 81 Misc. 2d 350, 366 N.Y.S. 2d 297 (Civ. Ct. 1975), *modified,* 85 Misc. 2d 891, 381 N.Y.S. 2d 587 (1976); Cummings & Sobel, Malpractice Insurance: Update on Sex Claims, 22 *Psychotherapy* 186 (1985).

 For a general discussion of possible criminal liability for therapist-patient sexual activity see Wis. Stat. Ann. §940.22 (West Supp. 1985); Leroy, The Potential Criminal Liability of Human Sex Clinics and Their Patients, 16 *St. Louis U. L. J.* 586 (1972); Stone, The Legal Implications of Sexual Activities Between Psychiatrist and Patient, 133 *Am. J. Psychiatry* 1138 (1976).

 66. Hammer v. Rosen, 7 N.Y.2d 376, 165 N.E.2d 756, 198 N.Y.S.2d 54 (1960).

 67. When psychotherapists testify in involuntary civil commitment hearings they are also generally protected from the defamation torts (libel and slander). Their in-court statements are generally covered by a "privilege" (not to be confused with a testimonial psychotherapist-patient privilege) that protects them from successful defamation suits. Other work done for courts or as part of the civil commitment process will generally be exempt from defamation suits as long as therapists have acted in good faith.

 68. Lanier v. Sallas, 777 F.2d 321 (5th Cir. 1985) (upholding a $50,000 award to a person committed on the basis of false affidavits by doctors who never examined her); Kleber v. Stevens, 39 Misc. 2d 712; 241 N.Y.S.2d 497 (1963), *aff'd,* 20 App. Div. 2d 896, 249 N.Y.S.2d 668 (2d Dept. 1964), but see Rhiver v. Rietman, 148 Ind. App., 265 N.E.2d 245 (1970).

 69. See Maben v. Rankin, 55 Cal.2d 139, 10 Cal. Rptr. 353, 358 P.2d 681 (1961); Whitree v. State, 56 Misc. 2d 693, 290 N.Y.S.2d 486 (Ct. Cl.

1968); Note, Tort Liability of the Psychotherapist, 8 *U. San Fran. L. Rev.* 405, 415–16 (1973).

70. O'Connor v. Donaldson, 422 U.S. 563 (1975).

71. *Id.* at 577.

72. Youngberg v. Romeo, 457 U.S. 307 (1982).

73. For an excellent review of therapist liability for breach of confidentiality see Eger, Psychotherapists' Liability for Extrajudicial Breaches of Confidentiality, 18 *Ariz. L. Rev.* 1061 (1976). See also Note, Roe v. Doe: A Remedy for Disclosure of Psychiatric Confidences, 29 *Rutgers L. Rev.* 191 (1975). Cf. Cooper, The Physician's Dilemma: Protection of the Right to Privacy, 22 *St. Louis U. L. Rev.* 379 (1978) (involving medical information generally).

74. See R. Cohen & W. Mariano, *Legal Guidebook in Mental Health* 394–403 (1982).

75. Slawson & Guggenheim, Psychiatric Malpractice: A Review of the National Loss Experience, 141 *Am. J. Psychiatry* 979 (1984); Wright, Psychologists and Professional Liability (Malpractice) Insurance, 36 *Am. Psychologist* 1485 (1981). See Kahn & Taft, The Application of the Standard of Care Doctrine to Psychological Testing, 1 *Behav. Sci. & L.* 71 (1983).

76. Kahn & Taft, The Application of the Standard of Care Doctrine to Psychological Testing, 1 *Behav. Sci. & L.* 71 (1983).

In some circumstances even negligent diagnosis will not result in liability. For example, most states provide some immunity for negligent diagnosis that results in wrongful civil commitment, so long as the professional acts in good faith or is not reckless.

77. Contracts for illegal acts are generally unenforceable. Therefore contracts to do something illegal, such as to withhold information even if ordered by a court to release it, are not enforceable agreements.

78. Johnston v. Rodis, 251 F.2d 917 (D.C. Cir. 1958).

79. E.g., Abille v. United States, 482 F. Supp. 703 (N.D. Cal. 1980); Meier v. Ross General Hospital, 69 Cal.2d 420, 445 P.2d 519, 71 Cal. Rptr. 903 (1968); Pisel v. Stamford Hospital, 180 Conn. 314, 430 A.2d 1 (1980).

80. See Cooper, Medical Treatment Facility for Patent Suicide and Other Self-Destruction, 3 *J. Leg. Med.* 8 (1975); Kjervik, The Psychotherapist's Duty to Act Reasonably to Prevent Suicide: A Proposal to Allow Rational Suicide, 2 *Behav. Sci. & L.* 207 (1984); Klein & Glover, Psychiatric Malpractice, 6 *Int'l J. L. & Psychiatry* 131 (1983); Schwartz, Civil Liability for Causing Suicide: A Synthesis of Law and Psychiatry, 24 *Vand. L. Rev.* 217 (1971).

81. E.g., Vistica v. Presbyterian Hospital, 67 Cal.2d 465, 432 P.2d 193, 62 Cal. Rptr. 577 (1967); Pisel v. Stamford Hospital, 180 Conn. 314, 430 A.2d 1 (1980).

82. See Berman & Cohen, Suicide and Malpractice: Expert Testimony and the Standard of Care, 14 *Prof. Psychology: Research & Prac.* 6 (1983); Kapp & Vandercreek, Malpractice Risks with Suicidal Patients, 20 *Psychotherapy* 274 (1983).

83. Baker v. United States, 226 F.Supp. 129, 135 (S.D. Iowa 1964), aff'd, 343 F.2d 222 (8th Cir. 1966). See, e.g., Johnson v. United States, 409 F.Supp. 1283 (M.D. Fla. 1976), later proceedings, 631 F.2d 34 (5th Cir. 1980), cert. denied, 451 U.S. 1018 (1981); Fiederlein v. New York Health and Hospital Corp., 80 App. Div. 2d 821, 437 N.Y.S.2d 321 (1st Dept. 1981), aff'd, 56 N.Y.2d 573, 435 N.E.2d 398, 450 N.Y.S.2d 181 (1982).

84. Tarasoff v. Regents of the University of California, 17 Cal.3d 425, 551 P.2d 334, 131 Cal. Rptr. 14 (1976).

85. The case has been the basis of a number of excellent articles. E.g., Roth & Meisel, Dangerousness, Confidentiality, and the Duty to Warn, 134 Am. J. Psychiatry 508 (1977); Stone, The Tarasoff Decision: Suing Psychotherapists to Safeguard Society, 90 Harv. L. Rev. 358 (1976); Note, Imposing a Duty to Warn on Psychiatrists: A Judicial Threat to the Psychiatric Profession, 48 U. Colo. L. Rev. 283 (1977).

86. There is ordinarily no legal duty to rescue another, even though the rescue may be accomplished without risk. One walking along a beach, and seeing someone drowning, is generally not legally obligated to throw a nearby lifesaver. A duty does exist, however, if the rescuer is in some way responsible for the victim—e.g., if the rescuer has pushed the victim into the water or there is a parent-child relationship. The rule has been criticized as inefficient and rewarding immoral conduct, and praised as an important part of individual freedom. The rule is probably beginning to break down as some states pass statutes requiring some forms of rescue. See Vt. Stat Ann. tit. 12, §519 (1973) requiring people to render aid to others in grave danger when the aid may be rendered without peril.

87. Goodman, From Tarasoff to Hopper: The Evolution of the Therapist's Duty to Protect Third Parties, 3 Behav. Sci. & L. 195 (1985); Note, Professional Obligation and the Duty to Rescue: When Must a Psychiatrist Protect His Patient's Intended Victims?, 91 Yale L. J. 1430 (1982).

88. See Givelber, Bowers & Blitch, Tarasoff: Myth and Reality: An Empirical Study of Private Law in Action, 1984 Wis. L. Rev. 443; Special Project, Where the Public Peril Begins: A Survey of Psychotherapists to Determine the Effects of Tarasoff, 31 Stan. L. Rev. 165 (1978). See Comment, Psychotherapists' Duty to Warn: Ten Years After Tarasoff, 15 Golden Gate U. L. Rev. 271 (1985).

89. Thompson v. County of Alameda, 27 Cal.3d 741, 614 P.2d 728, 167 Cal. Rptr. 70 (1980).

90. Hedlund v. Superior Court, 34 Cal.3d 695, 669 P.2d 41, 194 Cal. Rptr. 805 (1983).

91. See Bradley Center, Inc. v. Wessner, 250 Ga. 199, 296 S.E.2d 693 (1982).

92. Jablonski v. United States, 712 F.2d 391 (9th Cir. 1983).

93. Although Tarasoff did not speak solely in terms of the duty to warn, that has been the emphasis of many commentators and the California courts.

94. Givalber, Bowers & Blitch, supra, note 88.

95. See generally Crocker, Judicial Expansion of the Tarasoff Doctrine:

Doctor's Dilemma, 13 *J. Psychiatry & L.* 83 (1985); Merton, Confidentiality and the "Dangerous" Patient: Implications of *Tarasoff* for Psychiatrists and Lawyers, 31 *Emory L. J.* 263 (1982).

96. See generally J. Monahan, *Predicting Violent Behavior* (1981).

97. E.g., Bradley Center, Inc. v. Wessner, 250 Ga. 199, 296 S.E.2d 693 (1982); McIntosh v. Milano, 168 N.J. Super. 466, 403 A.2d 500 (1979); Peck v. Counseling Service of Addison County, 499 A.2d 422 (Vt. 1985) (this case is particularly interesting because it involved property damage rather than injury to persons).

98. Furr v. Spring Grove Hospital, 53 Md. App. 474, 454 A.2d 414 (1983). For a discussion of the issues see Note, The Scope of a Psychiatrist's Duty to Third Persons: The Protective Privilege Ends Where the Public Peril Begins, 59 *Notre Dame L. Rev.* 770 (1984).

99. Givelber, Bowers & Blitch, *supra*, note 88.

100. Cal. Civil Code §34.92 (West 1986) (emphasis supplied).

101. Ky. Rev. Stat. §202A.400 (Supp. 1986), 1986 Ky. Acts SB310.

102. Besharov, Child Protection: Past Progress, Present Problems and Future Directions, 17 *Fam. L. Q.* 151 (1983); Fraser, A Glimpse at the Future: A Critical Analysis of the Development of Child Abuse Reporting Statutes, 54 *Chi.-Kent L. Rev.* 641 (1978).

103. Issacson, Child Abuse Reporting Statutes: The Case for Holding Physicians Liable for Failure to Report, 12 *San Diego L. Rev.* 743 (1972); Note, Physicians' Liability for Failure to Diagnose and Report Child Abuse, 23 *Wayne L. Rev.* 1187 (1977).

104. Landeros v. Flood, 17 Cal.3d 399, 551 P.2d 389, 131 Cal. Rptr. 69 (1976); Brown & Truitt, Civil Liability in Child Abuse Cases, 54 *Chi.-Kent L. Rev.* 753 (1978).

105. Kapp, Supervising Professional Trainees: Legal Implications for Mental Health Institutions and Practitioners, 35 *Hosp. & Community Psychiatry* 143 (1984).

106. McBride v. United States, 462 F.2d 72 (9th Cir. 1972); Rush v. Akron General Hospital, 171 N.E.2d 378 (Ohio App. 1957); Kapp, Legal Implications of Clinical Supervision of Medical Students and Residents, 58 *J. Med. Ed.* 293 (1983).

107. See Slovenko, Legal Issues in Psychotherapy Supervision, in *Psychotherapy Supervision: Theory, Research and Practice* (A. Hess ed. 1980).

108. Hirsh, Which Physicians are Students? The Patient Has a Right to Know, 7 *Hosp. Med. Staff* 11 (1978); Kapp, Legal Implications of Clinical Supervision of Medical Students and Residents, 58 *J. Med. Ed.* 293 (1983).

109. Students should be viewed as assistants to their supervising faculty member, and therefore confidences revealed to a student should be considered protected by any psychotherapist-patient privilege that covers the supervising faculty member. Some doubt has been cast on whether all states will adopt this concept. One intermediate appellate court has suggested that the privilege would not apply to therapy conducted by students. See Hall v. State, 255 Ga. 267, 336 S.E.2d 812 (1985) (the Georgia Supreme Court

did not decide this issue). Another court suggested that some family court interns would not be covered by a privilege (but those under direct practice supervision would). People v. Gomez, 134 Cal. App. 3d 874, 185 Cal. Rptr. 155 (2d Dist. 1982).

110. Darling v. Charleston Community Memorial Hospital, 33 Ill.2d 326, 211 N.E.2d 253 (1965), cert. denied, 383 U.S. 946 (1966).

111. See R. Rosen, Psychobabble (1977); Gross, The New Therapies, The New Messiahs, in M. Gross, The Psychological Society 277–317 (1978); Glass, Kirsh & Parris, Psychiatric Disturbances Associated with Erhard Seminars Training: A Report of Cases, 134 Am. J. Psychiatry 245 (1977); Keen, Deliver Us From Shyness Clinics, 11 Psychology Today, March, 1978, at 18; Shastrom, Group Therapy: Let the Buyer Beware, in Clinical Psychology Today 149 (B. Henker, ed. 1967); Yalom & Lieberman, A Study of Encounter Group Casualties, 25 Archives Gen. Psychiatry 16 (1971).

112. Note, Standard of Care in Administering Non-Traditional Psychotherapy, 7 U. Cal. Davis L. Rev. 56 (1974), but see Hogan, Encounter Groups and Human Relations Training: The Case Against Applying Traditional Forms of Statutory Regulation, 11 Harv. J. Legis. 659 (1974). Encounter group sessions that are not adequately supervised by professionals, and because of their intensity cause severe psychological harm, may be the basis of liability. Bingham v. Lifespring, No. 82–5128 (E.D. Pa. July 31, 1984) reported in 28 ATLA L. Rep. 139 (1985). See Suskind v. Lifespring, No. 83-4370 (E.D. Pa. Nov. 1984) (significant settlement prior to trial reported in 28 ATLA L. Rep. 139 [1985]).

113. B. Schultz, Legal Liability in Psychotherapy 3–4 (1982); Knapp, A Primer on Malpractice for Psychologists, 11 Prof. Psychologist: Research & Prac. 606 (1980).

114. See Rothblatt & Leroy, Avoiding Psychiatric Malpractice, 9 Cal. W. L. Rev. 260 (1973). Other interesting suggestions for avoiding malpractice are provided in T. Gutheil & P. Appelbaum, Clinical Handbook of Psychiatry and the Law 178–203 (1982).

Even though malpractice claims are infrequently made, they may seriously disrupt the lives of those against whom they are filed. See S. Charles & E. Kennedy, Defendant: A Psychiatrist on Trial for Medical Malpractice (1985).

115. Comment, Injuries Precipitated by Psychotherapy Liability Without Fault as a Basis for Recovery, 20 S.D. L. Rev. 401, 413 (1975).

CHAPTER 2
CONFIDENTIALITY, PRIVILEGES, AND PRIVACY

Psychotherapists and counselors have long emphasized the importance of ensuring the privacy of their patients and clients, considering confidentiality a sine qua non for successful therapy.[1] In this chapter, we review the legal protection given to confidentiality and the circumstances in which the law permits or requires it to be breached. Information concerning therapy includes both records kept and recollections of information revealed in therapy.[2]

At least three related reasons have been identified for the importance of confidentiality in therapy. First, without a guarantee of confidentiality, patients may not be completely open or may be reluctant to enter therapy. In many forms of therapy, patients are expected to reveal the most intimate and private aspects of their lives including fantasies and fears. Patients believing that such communications might be repeated to others would be understandably reluctant to talk freely. Second, a very important ingredient in the therapeutic relationship is trust. Without the confidence that therapists will not reveal their secrets, some patients may not develop a trusting relationship. Finally, confidentiality promotes the privacy of individuals by allowing them to control extremely personal information about themselves.

It is important to distinguish between two related concepts: confidentiality and privilege. Confidentiality refers to broad ethical and legal obligations to protect the secrets of a client's life from disclosure to others. Privilege (testimonial privilege) refers to the protection of the communications of therapy from disclosure in court. Thus, privileges are one means of ensuring confidentiality. More testimonial privileges now apply to mental health treatment than ever before. Paradoxically, we suggest in this chapter that the real level of protection of the confidentiality of therapy may be lower now than ever before. In the next sections we will consider the limits and exceptions to full protection of confidentiality.

CONFIDENTIALITY

Ethical Obligations

Protecting the confidentiality of patients has been an ethical obligation of helping and healing professions for centuries.[3] All major mental health and counseling professional organizations currently recognize this obligation in their codes of ethics. The reference section of this chapter cites sources for ethical principles for psychologists,[4] psychiatrists,[5] social workers,[6] and counselors.[7]

Several features are common to these ethical guidelines. First, each offers a broad statement of the obligation of confidentiality. Second, they all stipulate that the client or patient can provide for release of the confidential information. This right implies an important principle: confidentiality protects clients or patients and the decision to release information is theirs, not the therapist's. A third common feature is the recognition of exceptions to confidentiality. The exceptions are generally not well defined, but rather set in terms such as "compelling professional reasons"[8] or "clear danger to the person or others."[9]

The codes of ethics also increasingly recognize some responsibility for therapists and counselors to inform patients of the consequences of releasing certain information. For example, the American Psychiatric Association provides "The continuing duty of the psychiatrist to protect the patient includes *fully apprising* him/her of the connotations of waiving the privilege of privacy."[10] The American Psychological Association code requires that, "*Where appropriate,* psychologists inform their clients of the legal limits of confidentiality."[11] The codes may also require special consideration or consent when the patient or client is a teaching or research subject.

Most codes do not deal explicitly with the confidentiality of information revealed to assistants or associates.[12] Nonetheless, there is an implied obligation to reasonably ensure that assistants and associates also maintain the confidentiality of clients and patients, and such communications are generally privileged as though the information were given directly to a therapist. Presumably, this "assistant" rule includes students and protects patient information given to students in training programs.[13]

Legal Obligations

Maintaining confidentiality is a legal as well as an ethical obligation. Some states provide statutory protection for confidentiality. Federal law also mandates protection for the confidences of some limited kinds of therapy, notably drug and alcohol abuse treatment programs.[14] Even without such statutes, however, the confidences of therapy have legal protection. Breaching confidentiality without legal justification will subject the therapist or counselor to liability for negligence or invasion of privacy.[15] For example, if a therapist reveals information about a patient while at a cocktail party and the patient loses his job as a result, the therapist may be liable for damages.

Special Problems of Confidentiality: Institutions and Children

Confidentiality presents special problems when therapy or counseling is conducted "for" someone (or something) other than the client or patient. An example is the industrial psychologist whose job is to consult with employees of the corporation for which he or she works. Suppose during therapy an employee discloses personal information that strongly suggests to the therapist that the person should not be promoted to a higher management position. Is the obligation of the therapist to report the information to the corporation or to maintain the confidences of the employee? Similar questions may arise from examinations conducted for courts, or by school psychologists or state mental facility therapists.

Strong arguments can be made both for the importance of maintaining the confidentiality of the therapy session and for the obligation to provide the organization important information disclosed in therapy. The degree to which confidentiality should be maintained may depend on the purpose of the consultation and the expectations of the participants.[16] For example, if a corporation wishes to provide counseling to help promote the emotional welfare of employees, confidentiality should be ensured. If it wishes to assess the emotional stability of its employees to determine job suitability, confidentiality cannot be fully protected. In some circumstances maintaining confidentiality is clearly inappropriate. The purpose of a court-ordered examination, for example, is to provide information to the court, which requires at least some breach of confidentiality. Serious problems arise when the purpose is unclear or in cases in which there are a number of incompatible purposes. For example, where a company wants to provide both personal counseling and employment evaluation.

One solution to this dilemma is to ensure a clear understanding about confidentiality before any information is revealed in therapy. It is critical to make clear the purpose of the interview or therapy session. It is one thing to release information from therapy by mutual agreement. It is quite another thing when the breach of confidentiality comes as a surprise.

Therefore, in circumstances where there may be a conflict between the interests of the patient and an organization, the patient should be clearly and specifically informed before therapy begins what the status of confidentiality is. In addition, treatment protocols, job descriptions, or other formal understandings between mental health professionals and institutions should make clear what the obligations are.

Children present similar problems. Ordinarily parents have the right to have information concerning their children until the children reach the age of majority, although this right has been modified somewhat by some states. The release of information from therapy often may be harmful. The age of the child is undoubtedly a factor in determining whether information should be released to parents; a five-year-old presents different problems than an adolescent. When parents are involved, the mental health professional may establish a contract with the parents in which the parents agree that they will not receive, or be able to demand, information from the therapy. A more difficult question arises when therapy is undertaken without the consent of parents, and parents discover the therapy and demand information concerning it. If therapy proceeded without an understanding with the minor about the release of information, the therapist should be reluctant to release any information. If the parents persist in their demand for the information, however, they may be able to obtain a court order for it. A very strong argument can be made for the adoption of statutes that protect the confidentiality of minors' therapy. Without such statutes, therapists should ensure that there is a clear understanding about confidentiality before therapy begins.

Third-Party Payment and Confidentiality

The increasing use of insurance, government-funded programs, and other third-party payments for therapy may threaten confidentiality in several ways. Most payers require some information concerning the basis of, reasons for, and extent of therapy. This information may be shared with other institutions and insurance companies. In some instances it may also be available to an employer who is paying for the insurance. In addition, third-party payers are increasingly establishing auditing and review systems that require the release of information to review committees or commissions. This means even more individuals will have access to private information. Hospitalization is particularly likely to result in this extensive review. In yet another instance, if the therapist is accused of fraud for wrongful billing, the criminal investigation may result in the subpoena of patient records to establish proof of fraud.[17]

Because the release of information may be necessary to obtain payment for service, mental health professionals may have a conflict between obtaining payment and protecting confidentiality. This conflict, and the significant breach of confidentiality associated with many forms of third-party payment, have resulted in some objections by mental health professionals to peer review of therapy.[18] However, the problems extend beyond peer review. Long-term storage and transfer of information from therapy poses additional threats to confidentiality. Rules regarding medical information are not sufficient to protect the more sensitive information regarding therapy.[19] Information given to one third-party payer may be transferred to other persons or used for purposes other than payment for services. For example, information given to an insurance company may be transferred to other insurance companies, or might be given to the employer who is providing the insurance, and the employer might use the information to make decisions about employment status. At the end of this chapter we suggest ways of limiting this kind of abuse of information.

EXCEPTIONS TO CONFIDENTIALITY

Confidentiality is not absolute. Circumstances occur in which a breach is permitted or even required. In reality there are probably few circumstances in which this distinction is of great importance. Often if a breach of confidentiality is permitted, it is also required.

Dangerousness to Others

Therapists may be required to breach the confidentiality of patients when the patients pose serious threats to other people. *Tarasoff* and similar cases (chapter 1) require that therapists with dangerous patients inform intended victims or take other steps to protect them.[20] This protection of third parties ordinarily involves a breach of patient confidentiality. Therefore, in states following *Tarasoff*, therapists are required to breach confidentiality in order to protect third parties at risk. Even in states that have not adopted *Tarasoff*-type liability, therapists often choose to breach confidentiality to protect intended victims from serious harm.[21]

States often permit a breach of confidentiality when mental health professionals determine that a patient is subject to involuntary civil commitment. (Civil commitment is discussed more fully in chapter 17.) Even without specific statutory authorization, therapists would probably be justified in breaching confidentiality to commence civil commitment proceedings if that were necessary to protect the patient from harming himself/herself or others.

All states require the reporting of known or suspected child abuse or neglect. Under these statutes therapists may be required to breach confidentiality to protect the child from further abuse. These statutes are considered later in this chapter.

Patient Suicide

Therapists have an obligation to take reasonable steps to prevent suicide by their patients. These steps often require some breach of confidentiality, which is permitted if reasonably necessary. For example, it may be necessary to inform the family that a patient is suicidal so the family can help prevent it.

When Telling Is Not a Breach

Therapists may generally release information to assistants, associates, and consultants when it is necessary as a part of treatment. Such releases are not considered breaches of confidentiality, because those receiving the information are part of the treatment and also carry an obligation to keep the confidences.

Voluntary Release

A patient or client may voluntarily choose to release information from therapy and mental health practitioners may release information as the patient directs. Patients should, however, be informed of the consequences of releasing the information. The release of information is effective, of course, only if the patient is legally competent to make decisions. Questions of competency should be resolved before any information is released on the basis of consent.

Research and Teaching

Information about a patient may ordinarily not be released in any identifiable form without the express consent of the patient. In some instances chart reviews of many patients is permitted without consent as long as the confidentiality of the information is fully protected by the investigator.

The use of patients as teaching subjects is likely to result in the release of the secrets of therapy to students. This practice is common, but difficult to justify if done without the knowledge and consent of patients. The mental health professions have emphasized the need for confidentiality for successful therapy. It would be somewhat inconsistent to claim that confidentiality may be breached at will for the purpose of training without potentially harming therapy. In addition, the information from therapy is the patient's, and the patient should decide whether or not the information should be released to help train others.

The Concept of Limited Release

When confidentiality must, or may, be breached under one of the situations described above, not all rights of confidentiality are destroyed. The disclosure of information should be as narrow as possible. Both the kinds of information released and the persons to whom it is released should be limited. Therefore, information about the threats may be disclosed to the intended victim, but should not be disclosed to the newspapers, nor should the intimate details of the patient's therapy be released if they do not relate to the threat.

PRIVILEGES

A fundamental principle of justice is that every person, when called upon to do so, must provide courts relevant information. The proper resolution of cases is of such importance that people may be required to give evidence despite promises not to reveal the information or the embarrassing or private nature of the information. Testimonial privileges are exceptions to this general rule in that they permit the withholding of some kinds of information from courts, and from some legislative and administrative bodies.[22]

Privileges exist because society's interest in knowing all the facts in a judicial proceeding is less important than maintaining the confidentiality required for certain relationships to exist. For example, it is generally acknowledged that it is extremely important that a client inform an attorney of the whole truth without reservation. To encourage openness, the attorney-client privilege assures clients that virtually anything they tell their attorney cannot be required to be disclosed by any court.

Since the effect of privileges is to prevent courts from obtaining relevant evidence, privileges are not favored by the courts. Few privileges have been recognized by courts as common-law privileges; among them are the attorney-client and husband-wife privileges. Others have been legislatively adopted. These statutory privileges cover a wide variety of relationships and vary considerably from state to state. Perhaps the most common statutory privileges are the physician-patient and clergy-parishioner (sometimes referred to as priest-penitent) privileges. Many other privileges, including those involving psychotherapist-patient, social-worker–client, accountant-client, parent-child, researcher-subject, and reporter-news source have all been suggested, and increasingly recognized.[23]

Justification for a Therapy Privilege

A privilege can be justified only if the benefits that it will provide are greater than its costs. The "Wigmore criteria" are commonly accepted as a method of assessing the justification for a privilege:

1. The communication must originate in a confidence that they will not be disclosed.
2. This element of confidentiality must be essential to the full and satisfactory maintenance of the relation between the parties.
3. The relation must be one which, in the opinion of the community, ought to be sedulously fostered.
4. The injury that would inure to the relationship by the disclosure of the communications must be greater than the benefit thereby gained for the correct disposal of litigation.[24]

A therapy privilege appears justified under the Wigmore criteria. Communications between therapist and patient, without question, ordinarily "originate in a confidence that they will not be disclosed." The general professional duty of confidentiality, as well as assurances of confidentiality by therapists, would reasonably lead patients to assume that communications to a therapist will not be disclosed.

There are some survey data to suggest that therapists and patients alike assume confidentiality in therapy.[25]

It is generally assumed that confidentiality is essential to successful psychotherapy. Perhaps nothing is more intensely personal and private than the information revealed therein. Therapy deals not only with information about a person, the disclosure of which may be embarrassing or harmful, but also with the patient's most intimate fantasies, fears, and anxieties. Empirical data has led some to believe that the absence of confidentiality may cause many people to avoid therapy or be considerably less open.[26]

The therapist-patient relationship appears to be important to the community. If we assume that successful therapy may reduce antisocial activity, particularly violent activity, then society has a clear interest in reducing this harm. There are substantial economic costs associated with mental illness—treatment costs as well as lost productivity—that may be reduced by successful treatment. There is quite apparently a strong social interest in reducing these costs. If confidentiality is important to successful therapy, and society has a strong interest in successful therapy, then society also has a strong interest in protecting confidentiality in therapy.

The most difficult of the Wigmore criteria to apply is the fourth—that the injury to the relationship by the disclosure of information would be greater than the benefit gained by the disclosure. Given the importance of psychotherapy to society, and the apparent importance of confidentiality to therapy, the benefits from a privilege seem great. Confidentiality can contribute to a reduction of suffering from mental illness, may reduce antisocial activity, and may reduce the economic losses associated with mental illness. At the same time there are probably few instances in which information essential to the correct disposal of litigation could not be obtained from a source other than the communications of therapy. Although it is impossible to weigh the costs and benefits of a privilege precisely, it seems most likely that the benefits are considerably greater than the costs.

The Wigmore criteria consider only the *social* benefits of privileges. In some relationships other values must also be considered. A privilege protecting the confidences of therapy, for example, also serves to protect *individual* rights of privacy by preventing the release of very personal information from therapy. A strong case has been made by commentators and by drafters of model codes of evidence for the need for therapy privileges.[27] Legislatures have been receptive to these privileges and they have been widely adopted in the last few years.

Description of Privilege

Most states now have some privileges covering therapy. These privileges vary considerably from state to state, the protection of the information revealed in therapy generally depending on the kind of therapist conducting the therapy. Most states have physician-patient privileges that include psychiatrists, but not other therapists. Several also have a specific psychiatrist-patient privilege.[28] An increasing number of states provide psychologist-patient privileges, and some have social worker and counselor privileges.[29]

Although the formulation of privileges varies from state to state, there are certain common features to all.[30] (1) A statement of the professionals covered by the privilege. (2) Coverage of the records and conclusions of therapist as well as the communications of the patient. (3) A requirement that the information protected by the privilege be "confidential." (4) Coverage limited to information developed in the course of a professional relationship between patient and therapist. (5) Provision for waiver of the privilege by the patient. (6) The existence of a number of exceptions to the privilege. These provisions define the privilege and the limitations on it.

Scope of the Privilege

Privileges are effective only if a professional relationship exists between therapist and client. Curbstone advice, or information exchanged in casual conversation, is not within the privilege. Generally, the consultation must be for diagnosis or treatment and have some indication of a formal therapy relationship. Privileges apply only to the types of therapist specified in the statute. This is particularly necessary because of the range of people who do some kind of counseling. Even the corner bartender is sometimes seen as a counselor.[31] Privileges are usually tied to licensing statutes.

Necessity of Confidentiality

Information loses the protection of a privilege if it is disclosed to third parties. If a patient repeats to a friend discussions he has had with a therapist, the discussions are no longer privileged. One reason for this rule is the belief that if information is made available to third parties, then courts should also have access to it because it is not really confidential. The requirement of confidentiality may be important to therapy privileges when group therapy or family therapy is used, or when information is transferred to third parties to pay for the therapy. We will note later in this chapter that these transfers of information may adversely affect privileges.

Disclosure of information to the professional's assistants and associates does not destroy the privilege, and information given by a patient to assistants or associates is generally privileged. It is sometimes difficult to determine when someone is an assistant and when he or she is acting as an independent professional. This issue may be important when one professional is covered by a privilege but the other is not. For example, a social worker who talks to a patient and the patient's family, reporting back to a psychiatrist only infrequently, may be providing independent treatment even though it is generally under the direction of the psychiatrist. In a state without a social worker privilege, it is entirely possible that the social worker would be seen as independent. Therefore the psychiatrist's privilege would not apply and the communications would not be privileged.[32]

Sources of Privileges

Three sources of therapy-related privileges are the common law, state statutes, and the constitutional right of privacy. The major source of privileges is state statutes. As a result, political considerations play an important role. As one would expect, professionals with more political clout have more control over obtaining privileges.

Courts have been reluctant to expand the common-law privileges beyond the attorney-client and husband-wife privileges because privileges deprive courts of material evidence.[33] At the state level, this reluctance has been coupled with a willingness by legislative bodies to provide statutory privileges. In a few states, and in federal courts, the existence of common-law privileges has been considered. There is not now a broadly accepted common-law therapy privilege, although such privileges may be accepted in the near future, as two cases, one state and one federal, illustrate.

In *Allred v. State* the Supreme Court of Alaska recognized a common-law psychotherapist-patient privilege.[34] The case arose in a criminal trial when the trial court ordered a social worker (who was assisting a psychiatrist) to testify regarding her conversations with the defendant. The court found that there was no statutory provision that protected the confidentiality of the communications between a psychotherapist and patient.[35] After reviewing the history of common-law privileges, however, the Supreme Court of Alaska concluded that a common-law psychotherapist-patient privilege was justified on the basis of the Wigmore criteria.[36] The court held that the privilege applied only to psychiatrists and psychologists who do therapy, as opposed to other professionals who do counseling.

In another case, *In re Zuniga*, patients' records were subpoenaed by two grand juries as part of an investigation of insurance billing fraud.[37] Therapists holding the records refused to release them. The federal court noted that the protection of confidentiality is essential to successful psychotherapy, and that the "inability to obtain effective psychiatrist treatment may preclude the enjoyment and exercise of many fundamental freedoms."[38] The court also noted the wide acceptance of the importance of privileges covering psychotherapy. On these bases it recognized a limited common-law privilege covering psychotherapy.

Because the operation of a privilege primarily affects the work of the judiciary, courts are justified, even without specific statutory authority, in establishing a common-law privilege covering therapy. Despite the past reluctance to consider new common-law privileges, the federal courts may now be more willing to do so.

Federal Privileges

The existence of common-law privileges is particularly important in federal courts, where state statutory privileges do not apply in all cases. The Supreme Court proposed a reform of federal rules of evidence that included a psychotherapist-patient privilege, but did not include a physician-patient privilege.[39] Congress rejected this proposal (although it did not specifically object to the psychotherapist-patient privilege) and substituted a general rule that in federal-law cases in federal courts, common-law privileges, as interpreted by the courts in "light of reason and experience," were to apply.[40] In cases in which federal courts apply state law (generally diversity of citizenship cases), federal courts must apply state rules regarding privileges. However, there may be no psychotherapist-patient privilege in federal cases even in states which have strong privileges.

The existence of privileges in federal courts, then, depends upon the nature of the case (whether it is a true federal case or a diversity case). This inconsistency regarding the existence of privileges in federal courts is undesirable. Confusion regarding the existence of privileges will raise doubts in the minds of patients about the protection given the confidences of therapy and reduce the effectiveness of privileges that do exist.

EXCEPTIONS TO PRIVILEGES

All privileges related to therapy have a number of important exceptions. Even those without specifically stated exceptions will have some which are usually enforced by courts. Exceptions, like privileges themselves, are matters of state law and therefore vary from state to state.

Waiver of Privilege

A patient may wish to permit disclosure of the content of therapy. Because the privilege belongs to the patient, not to the therapist (assuming the patient is competent to make decisions) the patient may voluntarily waive the privilege. The waiver of a privilege essentially destroys it, at least for any information related to the waiver. The mental health professional providing treatment can appropriately inform the patient of the consequences of releasing information, but generally the professional may not refuse to release it.

A patient may formally or explicitly waive the privilege by informing the court that the privilege is no longer claimed. The patient may also *implicitly* waive the privilege. Generally when a patient voluntarily discloses information that is protected by a privilege, the information is no longer protected. This form of waiver may be particularly harmful because the patient may not understand that the privilege is being lost by release to third parties.

Two important examples of ways in which privileges might inadvertantly be lost by disclosure to third parties are the payment system and group therapy. Strong arguments can be made that the privilege should not be destroyed in these circumstances, and it is likely that some courts would not find these kinds of release of information to be waivers of the privilege. But it is also likely that other courts would disagree. In general courts do not favor privileges. As a result, they tend to narrowly construe privileges, and therefore expand exceptions to them.[41]

If the release of information to third-party payers, including government programs and private insurance, serves as a waiver of privileges, then the privilege is of little value to many patients. The argument for waiver, of course, is that the information has been released to "third parties" who were not necessary for the therapy and therefore can also be released to courts.[42] Yet, the release of information to a payer should not be a public release of information. If privileges are to have any meaning, they cannot be destroyed by the information transmitted to payers. Even if courts determine that the release of information to payers is a waiver, they probably would (and should) determine that it is a limited waiver involving only the information transmitted to the payer, and not a general waiver of all of the confidences of therapy.[43]

Group therapy always involves "third parties" in the form of other members of the group. Few statutes make it clear that group therapy is covered by the privilege. This threat to group therapy and the confidences of groups has been recognized.[44] The coverage of group therapy may depend upon whether members of the group are seen as "assistants" to the therapist in dealing with the member of the group claiming the privilege. In reality group members participate to further their own therapy. Participants in group therapy generally expect confidentiality, and disclose very private information as they would in individual therapy. It seems clear courts should extend privileges to group therapy.[45] Such privileges must cover communications between therapist and patients and between patients who are members of the group.

Therapists should be aware of these potential "hidden" waivers of privileges and inform patients of them in appropriate cases. The potential problem associated with the release of information to third-party payers poses potential ethical dilemmas for therapists who, to ensure payment for services, may be inclined to urge disclosure, but who may be obligated to help the patient maintain the privilege.[46] As with other forms of consent, questions about the patient's competence to make decisions should be resolved before information is released.

Patient-Litigant Exception

Patients who bring their own mental conditions into question in litigation waive any privileges concerning relevant information from therapy. If, for example, a patient were to sue a therapist for malpractice or to raise the insanity defense in a criminal trial, he would lose the privilege of confidentiality. The reason for this exception is that it is unfair for a person to raise questions about a mental condition and then use the privilege to prevent opposing parties from obtaining the same information. The patient-litigant exception, however, means that a patient may face the unhappy choice of abandoning a valid claim or defense, or the confidentiality of therapy.

Courts could do much to limit this choice by reducing the intrusion into the confidences of therapy. Courts may limit the implicit waiver of the privilege to the mental conditions or defects which are directly relevant to the lawsuit, and by examining questionable evidence to determine if the introduction of it will do more harm than good.[47] Unfortunately, courts have been slow to provide protections for the confidences of therapy when the patient-litigant exception is invoked. As a result the exception has too often been an excuse for an opposing party to conduct a thorough examination into the mental and emotional history of a patient.[48]

Court-Ordered Examinations and Civil Commitment

Court-ordered examinations are ordinarily not within the scope of a privilege because they are not conducted with the expectation of confidentiality. It should be made clear to the patient that the examination is to obtain information for the court.

Examinations which states commonly make for civil commitment hearings are essentially court-ordered examinations. In addition, the commitment process may be an exception to the privilege so that information relevant to commitment-related hearings or treatment is not covered by the privilege. The basis for this exception appears to be that the commitment hearing is so important and mental conditions are so central to it that the invasion of the confidences of therapy is warranted.

Child Custody Exception

Courts have demonstrated a strong desire to have any information necessary to make awards of custody that are in the best interests of children. The psychological fitness of parents is seen as a critical aspect of awarding custody. Even without express statutory custody exceptions, some courts have, in effect, provided a child custody exception to therapy privileges.[49]

Future Crimes and Dangerous Patients

Information concerning the commission of future crimes may not be protected by a privilege.[50] Thus, a discussion regarding a planned bank robbery is not included in the privilege. The future crime exception is particularly important when a patient might take a violent or dangerous action. The general rules regarding privileges would not prevent the release of information about the future dangerous crime. Some states have gone further, stating that the therapist has a duty to take responsible steps to protect potential victims from a patient when it is, or should be, apparent to the therapist that the patient is likely to be dangerous.[51] Child abuse is generally not covered by the privilege, as we shall see later in this chapter.

Criminal Defense Exception

To present an adequate defense to criminal charges a defendant in a criminal case may require information revealed by another in therapy. A defendant, for example, might wish to present evidence that an adverse witness made statements to a therapist which were inconsistent with his courtroom testimony. A privilege may interfere with the ability of a defendant to obtain or present this evidence. The Supreme Court in *Davis v. Alaska* suggested that a state ban on the use of juvenile records in court was unconstitutional when those records were crucial to the defense in a criminal case.[52] Although the actual holding in *Davis* was relatively narrow, it has prompted some courts to hold that the constitutional rights of criminal defendants compel the disclosure of evidence which is protected by privileges.[53] In any case, criminal defendants may have a right to request certain information regarding the confidences of therapy. At the present time, however, such rights are not well defined but seem to be rather limited.

Other Exceptions

The statutes creating therapy privileges may provide for a number of additional exceptions. For example, the privilege may be lost entirely when a therapist determines that a patient is in need of hospitalization. This exception was supposedly to permit therapists to testify in involuntary civil commitment hearings, but is stated too broadly in some state statutes. The privilege may also not apply if the patient's will is contested. Other states void the privilege when the patient dies.

Subpoenas

A mental health professional presented with a subpoena requesting testimony or files pursuant to a patient-litigant exception (or other exception) should proceed with caution. The therapist, on behalf of the patient, may wish to challenge the subpoena. In any case, the patient, or the patient's attorney, should be contacted and given every opportunity to challenge the demand for information before it is released.

CHILD ABUSE REPORTING LAWS

A phenomenon that has had a significant effect on the confidentiality of some therapy is the development of child abuse reporting statutes and similar laws that require reporting of spouse abuse, elder abuse, or "endangered adults." The purpose of these statutes is to reduce violence by permitting early intervention by state authorities. In practice, however, abuse reporting statutes may interfere with therapy and even be counterproductive.[54]

Mandatory child abuse reporting statutes are relatively new and have been the subject of many changes during their short history. In 1963, the United States Children's Bureau proposed "principles and suggested language for legislation on reporting of the physically abused child."[55] Reporting laws were enacted at a rapid rate; within four years all 50 states had adopted them.[56]

Statutes may require or permit individuals to report child abuse. The tendency has been to expand the groups of persons required to report. The early statutes required physicians to report, but it is now common to require reports from medical personnel, psychologists, social service workers, teachers, and law enforcement officers. Other states require "anyone" or "any person" suspecting or knowing of child abuse to report it. In one way or another most states impose a duty on all psychotherapists and counselors to report child abuse or neglect.[57]

Definition of Abuse

Although states vary in the definition of abuse, it generally includes most or all of the following: physical injury, sexual molestation, emotional injury, and neglect. There is ordinarily a requirement that the injury be "serious" or a "serious threat to welfare." These terms are generally either left undefined or are so broadly defined as to be of little value.[58] It is therefore nearly impossible for those required to report to know what events must be reported. Naturally, this uncertainty has led to great confusion about what constitutes child abuse and neglect.

There are positive aspects of the expansion of the concept of child abuse and neglect. Emotional injuries are real and should be recognized by the law. Yet, the breadth of these statutes, coupled with the absence of any meaningful definition of terms, leaves professionals at a loss to know what they are required to report. This uncertainty can adversely affect the ability of authorities to discover and successfully deal with abuse. The *National Study of Child Abuse* found that nearly 60 percent of the cases of children reported to child protection agencies as suspected victims of child abuse could not be substantiated.[59] The problem of over reporting is significant: The National Study estimated that 1.1 million child abuse and neglect reports are filed with child protective service agencies each year, and more than 600,000 of these probably cannot be substantiated even using the broad definitions often employed by the protective service agencies.[60] More recent estimates of the number of reports of child abuse are as high as 1.8 million per year.[61]

Paradoxically the uncertainty concerning the definition of child abuse and neglect may also contribute to significant failure to report. The National Study found that 68 percent of the children who were reported as being within the scope of abuse and neglect (using a definition probably somewhat narrower than many statutes) were *not* reported to the child protection agency or otherwise known to the child protection agency. Only 21 percent of the cases of child abuse noted by agencies outside the child protection agency were reported. If anything, the actual rate of reporting nationwide may be even lower than indicated by the study.[62]

The significant failure to report combined with the large number of unsubstantiated reported cases suggests that there is considerable confusion about what constitutes child abuse or neglect.[63] A significant price is paid for this confusion. Actual abuse that is not dealt with may result in serious harm to the child. But false reports, even if made in good faith, may disrupt families, invade privacy,[64] and make some relationships more difficult to maintain.[65] Particularly when the report comes from a psychotherapist, it may disrupt therapy and reduce the chance of dealing successfully with the problems of the patient.

Legal Consequence of Failure to Report

The failure to report known or suspected child abuse or neglect may result in criminal or civil liability or professional discipline. Most states make the failure to report known or suspected abuse or neglect a criminal offense. Ordinarily this is a misdemeanor which may result in a fine or short jail sentence. Given the large number of abuse cases which are not reported, there are surprisingly few instances of criminal prosecution for failure to report.

Some states specifically provide that a child who is injured after someone's failure to make a required report has a civil claim against that person. Even without express statutory provisions, civil liability might be imposed for failure to diagnose or report child abuse on the basis of negligence *per se*[66] or on the basis of ordinary malpractice negligence.[67] In fact such civil liability has resulted in the past from failure to diagnose abuse or neglect.[68]

The failure to meet obligations imposed by statute, including reporting abuse, may be the basis for professional discipline including suspension of a license. It is unlikely, however, that the failure to report would result in such discipline except in extraordinary cases.

Dilemmas for Therapists

Special problems for psychotherapists arise from the nature of the information they receive during therapy and from the sources of that information. For example, therapists are more likely than other professionals to receive highly personal information from patients and clients. Therapists are given sensitive personal information, the release of which patients or clients will find embarrassing. Therefore, breaching the confidences of therapy may be highly distressing to patients or clients.

Information received from children in psychotherapy may give rise to "suspicions" of abuse or neglect, particularly of emotional abuse or neglect, and often these suspicions cannot be confirmed. Indeed, therapists may suspect that many children with significant emotional problems are experiencing broadly defined forms of abuse including emotional neglect. This kind of information poses a dilemma for therapists as to whether or not to report the suspicions.

Therapists are more likely than other professionals to receive information concerning abuse or neglect directly from the abuser. They are also likely to receive information from patients and clients about abuse by a spouse or relative. Therefore psychotherapists are likely to be required to report information revealed to them by the abuser or by someone close to the abuser. The obligation to disclose this self-reported information may be destructive of the process of psychotherapy.

Privileges

Most states abrogate the physician-patient privilege, and other privileges that might include psychotherapists, as part of their child abuse reporting statutes. Therefore therapists may be called into court to testify concerning the abuse that is discussed in psychotherapy, and it is entirely possible that a therapist will have to reveal in court information disclosed in treatment.[69] The therapist may even have to testify about secrets (confessions) revealed in therapy after the problem of child abuse was reported to the child protective agency. The abrogation of privileges in most states is much broader than it needs to be to fulfill the goals of the child abuse reporting statutes.

Modifications

Current abuse statutes have many problems and may discourage abusers from seeking therapy. To reduce the difficulties, several changes could be made: The definition of abuse and neglect should be narrowed and sharpened through clearer and more precise definitions of the kinds of abuse and neglect which must be reported, and the statutes should be modified to eliminate the reporting requirements when therapists receive information about child abuse from the abuser or the abuser's spouse. Therapists would be obligated to report child abuse when there is a threat of serious, permanent physical harm to the child or where therapy is not continuing and the threat of child abuse continues, but the psychotherapist-patient privilege should not be abrogated when the abuser reveals information intended to help stop the abuse.

Abusers might be further encouraged to seek therapy if a qualified immunity from prosecution were provided for abusers who voluntarily seek that psychotherapy. The immunity would not automatically apply if entered into in contemplation of prosecution or if death or serious permanent physical harm resulted from the abuse.[70] Nor would the immunity apply if the abuser continued after therapy began.

CONSTITUTIONAL PRIVACY AND PSYCHOTHERAPY

The recognition of the constitutional right of privacy is an important modern development in individual rights. If the right endures it is likely to have an important impact on therapy. This constitutional right had its genesis in decisions during the past century in which the federal courts invoked several provisions of the Bill of Rights to protect personal privacy. These earlier decisions relied on specific rights of the Constitution—particularly the search and seizure provisions of the Fourth Amendment—to implement a general concept of privacy. Not until 1965 in *Griswold v. Connecticut*[71] did the Supreme Court recognize a specific constitutional right of privacy when it struck down a statute prohibiting married couples from using contraceptives. In *Roe v. Wade* the Court struck down criminal abortion statutes.[72] Many of the subsequent privacy decisions have involved contraception or abortion.

Two aspects of privacy can be identified: autonomy privacy (the right to make fundamental personal decisions without government interference) and information privacy (the right to protect very personal information). Autonomy privacy has been clearly recognized by the Court, information privacy has received less judicial attention.

The right of privacy is not absolute. The Court has made it clear that the right of privacy may be invaded to protect a "compelling state interest." That concept has not been clearly defined by the courts, although it includes the protection of human life, national security, and fundamental political processes.

The constitutional right of privacy may apply to therapy if the government takes actions which interfere with the ability to decide to engage in psychotherapy or releases very private information from therapy.[73] Several cases illustrate the relevance of privacy to therapy.

A few courts have found a constitutionally-based psychotherapist-patient privilege, although at least one court has come to a contrary conclusion.[74] Several other courts have noted the relationship between the right of privacy and the need to protect a patient's communications to his psychotherapist, but have not resolved the issue of a privilege on constitutional grounds.[75] A third group of courts suggests, without expressly holding, that the Constitution may protect the privacy of psychotherapy and of mental health information.[76]

Constitutional Psychotherapist-Patient Privilege

California was the first jurisdiction to recognize a constitutional psychotherapist-patient privilege. In *In re Lifschutz,* one of Dr. Lifschutz's psychiatric patients filed a damage suit against another party for assault, claiming severe mental and emotional distress.[77] When the defendant tried to take Dr. Lifschutz's deposition regarding his treatment of the patient, he refused to answer any questions regarding the patient and refused to produce any of the requested records.[78] The patient neither directly consented nor objected to the release of information about his treatment. Dr. Lifschutz appealed a citation for contempt of court that resulted from his refusal to produce the records. Acknowledging the sensitive nature of the confidences that patients reveal in psychotherapy, the California Supreme Court indicated that the constitutional right of privacy protects those communications. The *Lifschutz* decision, in effect, recognized a constitutional psychotherapist-patient privilege.

Dr. Lifschutz argued for an absolute psychotherapist-patient privilege. Rejecting this broad extension of the right of privacy, the court held that the constitutional right can be limited by the state when necessary to protect or to advance a compelling state interest. The court recognized a patient-litigant exception to the constitutional privilege, but took care to emphasize that it would not sanction all inquiries into a patient's confidences under the guise of a compelling state interest. Rather, the court held that even when the state demonstrates a compelling interest requiring disclosure of the confidences of therapy, it must limit its inquiry into the confidential information as narrowly as possible to avoid unnecessary invasions of privacy. In the context of the patient-litigant exception, for instance, the state may conduct only a "limited inquiry into the confidences of the psychotherapist-patient relationship."

The United States Court of Appeals for the Ninth Circuit has also held that the constitutional right of privacy protects the confidentiality of psychotherapist-patient communications. In *Caesar v. Mountanos*,[79] a case factually similar to *Lifschutz*, Dr. Caesar refused to answer questions about one of his patients and was held in contempt of a California state court. Dr. Caesar then took the federal privacy claim to federal court. (The patient had filed suit against third parties alleging that two separate automobile accidents had caused her "pain and suffering not limited to her physical ailments.") Although the Ninth Circuit agreed that confidentiality is essential to psychotherapy and that the very nature of the communications brings them within the constitutional right of privacy, it rejected the argument that the privilege was absolute. Instead, the court held that the privilege may be limited when necessary to advance a compelling state interest. The court next proceeded to evaluate the state interest in obtaining disclosure and found that an invasion of the confidences of Dr. Caesar's patient was justified. In reaching this conclusion, however, the court failed to identify precisely the state interest that would be furthered by the release of information. Apparently, the state's interest in obtaining all material evidence, coupled with the implicit waiver by the patient in bringing her mental condition into issue, provided the necessary basis for finding a compelling interest in requiring the disclosure.

In *In re B*, the Pennsylvania Supreme Court, without a majority opinion, also recognized a constitutionally based psychotherapist-patient privilege.[80] Unlike the patients in *Caesar* and *Lifschutz*, the patient in *In re B* was not a party to the lawsuit for which her records were sought. Rather, the case involved a juvenile delinquency proceeding concerning "B." During the course of the predisposition investigation, juvenile court personnel discovered that B's mother had received psychiatric treatment at the Western Psychiatric Institute and Clinic of the University of Pittsburgh. Dr. Roth, acting for the director of the clinic, was ordered by the juvenile court to turn over the mother's psychiatric records. Dr. Roth refused to do so without the consent of the mother and was cited for contempt of the juvenile court. Although it ruled that the state's statutory doctor-patient privilege did not apply to the disputed records, the Pennsylvania Supreme

Court reversed the contempt citation on the ground that the constitutional right of privacy protected the information from involuntary disclosure. Noting that psychotherapy requires patients to reveal the most intimate details of their lives, the court concluded that the constitutional right of privacy includes protection of the confidences revealed in therapy. The court conceded that recognition of constitutional protection for the confidences of therapy might hamper the efforts of juvenile courts to obtain necessary information, but emphasized that the right of privacy must prevail over the interest of the court in obtaining the privileged information. The court also noted that the state's interest in securing access to a patient's files in such cases was diminished because, as a practical matter, courts could obtain most of the desired information from sources other than the psychotherapist.

In *In re B* the state sought access to a patient's psychiatric files in the disposition phase of a juvenile delinquency proceeding. The importance of juvenile proceedings and the quasi-criminal nature of delinquency proceedings emphasize the state's interest in obtaining all relevant information. Furthermore, because the information concerning the mother's therapy would have been used only in a disposition report in a juvenile proceeding, the court could have assured the confidentiality of the material by sealing the patient's records and by not disclosing the information at a public hearing. Despite the state's significant interest and the means available to limit disclosure, the court rejected the state's request because of the possibility that even a limited breach of the confidentiality of psychotherapist-patient communications could involve a significant invasion of privacy. The decision thus represents a vigorous endorsement of the privacy of communications between patient and psychotherapist.

Cases Not Involving Privileges

Other courts have extended some protection to confidential psychological information without recognizing a psychotherapist-patient privilege. These courts have held that the constitutional right of privacy protects some information concerning an individual's mental and emotional states and attitudes, and have acknowledged the obligation of the state to avoid releasing such information to the public.

In *Hawaii Psychiatric Society v. Ariyoshi,* a federal district court enjoined the state of Hawaii from enforcing a statute that permitted the issuance of "administrative inspection warrants" to review the medical (mental health) records of Medicaid patients.[81] The court held that "an individual's decisions whether to seek the aid of a psychiatrist, and whether or not to communicate certain personal information to that psychiatrist, fall squarely within" the constitutional right of privacy. Characterizing the significance of the privacy interest threatened by the statute, the court stated, "[N]o area could be more deserving of protection than communications between a psychiatrist and his patient." In the court's opinion, Hawaii's scheme for inspecting psychiatric records would interfere with therapy by destroying a patient's willingness to disclose intimate personal matters. Although the statute provided that patient information gathered from a psychiatrist's files was to remain confidential, the court found that given the extremely sensitive nature of the information, its disclosure, even to state officials, would invade the patient's privacy. Balanced against the patient's interest in privacy was the state's interest in protecting the Medicaid program from fraud, which the court accepted as compelling. Nevertheless, the court held that the state had not shown that warrants to inspect the confidential medical records of a psychiatrist were necessary to advance this compelling interest.

Merriken v. Cressman involved a junior high school program designed to identify emotionally handicapped students and provide "early intervention" to prevent drug abuse.[82] As part of the program, students were expected to complete a questionnaire dealing with matters of a personal nature and soliciting information regarding their emotional states. The purpose of the questionnaire was apparently to identify those students with an emotional propensity toward drug abuse. The court held that the program was unconstitutional. It acknowledged the state's interest in correcting drug abuse, but doubted whether the program would serve this objective. The court also mentioned that despite claims to the contrary, the state's subpoena power presented a threat to the confidentiality of the information collected about the students. This threat, combined with the questionable efficacy of the program in combatting drug abuse, persuaded the court to issue an injunction prohibiting the state from further efforts to collect sensitive psychological and emotional data.

The court in *Lora v. Board of Education* also found that the constitutional right of privacy protects records containing psychological information.[83] In a suit against the New York City school board alleging the discriminatory evaluation and placement of handicapped children, plaintiffs moved to compel production of the diagnostic and referral files of fifty students. Because they contained sensitive psychological information, plaintiffs requested that the files be randomly selected and that all names and identifying data be removed. The court noted the importance of privacy in protecting information a patient reveals to a psychotherapist. In granting the plaintiffs' motion, however, the court relied primarily on this scheme to ensure anonymity, as well as its own ability to fashion protective orders covering the use of the diagnostic files. In effect, there was no real invasion of privacy because the information would not be released in a personally identifiable form. The court cautioned, however, that even the anonymous intrusion into the psychological files was justifiable only because the plaintiffs demonstrated a genuine need for the information and because the data were unavailable from any other source.[84]

Applicants for positions as firefighters in Jersey City, New Jersey, objected in *McKenna v. Fargo* to the city's insistence that they undergo psychological testing as a prerequisite to being hired, and to the city's maintenance of the psychological profiles after it had made its hiring decisions.[85] The court acknowledged that the constitutional right of privacy limits the ability of the state to collect and to maintain certain kinds of very personal information concerning emotional and mental conditions, including the kind of information elicited through psychological testing. Nevertheless, the court upheld the psychological testing of the applicants because of the state's overriding interest in ensuring the selection of firefighters who would be emotionally stable under stress. Firefighting is inherently dangerous and pressured, the court observed. Consequently, firefighters must possess certain psychological traits to ensure the safety not only of the community, but also of their colleagues. The court characterized the state interest in psychologically screening applicants as "of the highest order" and "of an importance that would be found in very few occupations." The constitutionality of the psychological testing, however, was conditioned on the city's development of formal plans and regulations to preserve the confidentiality of the information obtained during the testing. The court further suggested that the city limit access to the information to the psychologist reviewing the applicant and to city employees who had specific reason to use the data. As final precautions, the court recommended that the city retain the records only for a specified period of time and that it establish a system for destroying those records not necessary to serve the compelling state interest.

In *United States v. Westinghouse Electric Corp.*, a somewhat similar case, objection was raised to the release of sensitive medical records.[86] The court found the information protected by the right of privacy, but found that a strong government interest, and a safeguard to prevent release of the information, justified the intrusion.

The foregoing cases suggest that in a variety of circumstances courts have recognized that the constitutional right of privacy limits the state's public disclosure of sensitive information concerning the mental and emotional condition of individuals. The principle that the confidences of therapy and other sensitive mental health information are protected by the constitutional right of privacy, however, has only recently begun to win judicial acceptance. The viability of this principle therefore depends upon the continued development and application of the broader constitutional right of privacy.

ARE CONFIDENCES PROTECTED?

An impressive number of legal and ethical doctrines protect the confidences of therapy. Privilege statutes are now common; common-law and constitutional privileges have been recognized in some jurisdictions; constitutional privacy protects some forms of information from release by the government; ethical codes require protection of confidentiality; common-law and statutory negligence and privacy actions impose liability for the wrongful release of therapy secrets; and a number of other statutes provide protection for some forms of therapy. Nevertheless, a strong argument can be made that in fact the confidences of therapy are less secure now than in the past. The reasons for this paradox include the law of privileges, the expanded use of third-party payers for therapy, and the increased importance of mental health issues in legal proceedings.

On Giving With One Hand and Taking With the Other

The protections of confidentiality the law has given with one hand have often been removed with the other. Privileges are filled with exceptions that may leave little left of them. In addition, in some states privileges may be destroyed if information from therapy is transmitted to third parties, constitutional protections of therapy may be invaded in pursuit of compelling state interests (which sometimes are not hard to find), federal privileges are uncertain, and the law may require a breach of confidentiality to report abuse or to warn intended victims. Courts have not favored privileges and many courts have narrowed privileges further. All of this reduces substantially the legal protection of the confidences of therapy. Professor Ralph Slovenko, one of the leading authorities on therapy privileges, referred to them as a "misguided hope" for protecting the secrets of therapy; his characterization is probably accurate.[87]

Part of the reason for the reduction in the protection of confidentiality is the increased reliance on and use of mental health information in the legal system. The topics described in this book are testimony to the wide range of legal issues that require mental health information presented in court. The more courts feel the need to have such information, the less likely they are to allow it to be withheld by means of privileges. In addition, in recent years there has been a general trend toward limiting most privileges.

Confidentiality has been further eroded by the use of third-party payers. These institutions understandably demand information to determine if claims should be paid. They ordinarily store the information and may share it with other institutions. Efforts to reduce claims may include "peer review" of treatment and such reviews may further reduce the protection of information from therapy.

Reforming the Protection of Confidentiality

Law reforms that could substantially improve the protection of confidentiality include the concept of limited release of information and "transferred privacy," modified privileges, and narrow reporting statutes (as described above). Many of these changes must occur at the federal level if they are to be effective. Information supplied to third-party payers generally crosses state lines, federal rules affect privileges, and federal law guides the development of the abuse reporting laws of many states.

Most laws protecting therapy information are based on the old concept that information was released by the patient to the therapist and not legitimately disclosed to anyone else. The law should recognize the reality that information must be passed to a limited number of others, notably third-party payers and their auditors, in the normal course of therapy. To protect the confidences revealed in therapy while recognizing this new need for information the law should define and limit the information concerning therapy that third-party payers may demand,[88] adopt a concept of extended privacy obligations that transfers the duty of confidentiality with the transfer of the information (an institution receiving information from therapy would have the same duty as the therapist to protect the information, and not to disclose it to others), and provide that the disclosure of information with transferred privacy would not destroy the privilege.

Privilege statutes should be part of a confidentiality statute that establishes a coherent policy concerning confidentiality. A single privilege statute should apply to all mental health professionals the state wishes to cover, and it should be clear concerning the professionals covered. It should also have very narrow and limited exceptions, and cover group and other multiple-party therapy, but should not be destroyed by limited disclosures to third-party payers.[89] Federal law should adopt a clearly defined privilege covering therapy.

Is Confidentiality Necessary?

There has been a strong assumption that confidentiality is necessary for successful therapy. Several studies support these opinions. Patients seem somewhat confused about the level of legal protection of the confidences of therapy. Some studies indicate that there are some kinds of information patients would reveal without legal protections for confidentiality.[90] Other studies indicate that people believe that they would be generally less open in therapy without the assurance of confidentiality.[91] A study of inpatients indicates that they highly value confidentiality but have very limited understanding of the legal protections of their rights.[92] Some patients may be reluctant to discuss violent feelings if they know that the therapist has an obligation to protect intended victims.[93] People may be more open in answering personal questions if confidentiality is assured.[94] These studies may provide some indirect information about the importance of confidentiality or privileges to therapy. They suggest that confidentiality plays a role in, but is not critical to all, successful therapy. They do not measure what effects confidentiality actually has. One effort to provide such information was inconclusive.[95] Additional research could help identify the kinds and levels of confidentiality that promote successful therapy.

The second major reason for protecting confidentiality, patients' interests in personal privacy, provides another basis for ensuring reasonable levels of secrecy. Even if confidentiality did not promote successful therapy, privacy interests surrounding the extremely sensitive information that may be revealed in therapy would be sufficient to justify substantial protection of confidentiality.

SUMMARY

Mental health professionals have long described confidentiality as essential to successful therapy. Assurances of confidentiality may encourage people to enter, and to be more open in, therapy; and it may promote the development of trusting relationships between patients and therapists. In addition, protecting the confidences of therapy promotes individual privacy rights of patients.

Ethical standards and the law require that mental health professionals maintain the confidences of therapy. Unauthorized disclosure of patient information may result in civil liability for negligence, breach of privacy, or breach of contract.

Many states provide privileges. An increasing number of states have adopted privilege statutes covering some forms of mental health services that limit courts' access to information revealed in therapy. Almost all therapy privileges are adopted by statute, although a few courts have recognized common law or constitutional privileges covering therapy.

A variety of exceptions are recognized to privileges and to obligations of confidentiality. Patients may voluntarily release information from therapy, or authorize professionals to release it. It is common, for example, to authorize the release of information to insurance companies or other third-party payers. A professional may release information as directed by the patient, but the release of the information may destroy the privilege. Therapists may also be obligated to breach confidentiality when it is necessary to prevent a patient from committing suicide. Some states now require that therapists take reasonable steps to prevent harm to third parties at the hands of their patients, even if a breach of confidentiality occurs. Other common exceptions to privileges are patient-litigant and child-custody cases, as well as court-ordered examinations.

Child abuse reporting statutes may seriously affect therapy. These statutes require the reporting to state authorities known or suspected child abuse. In many states the abuse must be reported even if the information comes from an abuser who is seeking therapy to stop his own abusive activity. Abuse is generally very broadly defined to include physical, mental, or sexual abuse or neglect. Failure to report known or suspected abuse may result in criminal or civil liability. These statutes are overly broad and may be counterproductive in some cases by discouraging abusers from seeking treatment.

The constitutional right of privacy has been a major development in individual rights. The extent and nature of this right has not yet been defined, but a few cases suggest that the right of privacy may provide some protections for highly personal information revealed in therapy. Even if the confidences of therapy are protected by the right of privacy, the state may invade these confidences if it is necessary in order to promote a compelling state interest, such as the prevention of death or serious injury.

It may appear that the confidences of therapy are enjoying increasing levels of legal protection. Statutes, common-law principles, and constitutional rights all seem to provide protection to therapy. In truth, however, exceptions, limitations, and narrow judicial decisions have all limited the protection of confidentiality. What the law has given with one hand, it has often taken away with the other. Several reforms might help ensure the privacy of therapy. For example, the concept of extended privacy obligations might be adopted obligating third parties receiving information about therapy to maintain confidentiality. Exceptions to privileges should be very limited and as narrow as possible, and child abuse reporting laws should be restructured to encourage abusers to seek therapy.

Legal principles protecting confidentiality have not changed as rapidly as the demand for and use of information about therapy. The challenge is to modify traditional rules to provide a meaningful level of protection to the highly personal information revealed.

NOTES

1. Group for the Advancement of Psychiatry, *Confidentiality and Privileged Communications in the Practice of Psychiatry,* Report No. 45 (1960). See S. Freud, 2 Collected Papers 356 (1959 ed.); Dubey, Confidentiality as a Requirement of the Therapist: Technical Necessities for Absolute Privilege in Psychotherapy, 131 *Am. J. Psychiatry* 1093 (1974); Shah, Privileged Communications, Confidentiality and Privacy, 1 *Prof. Psychology: Research & Prac.* 59 (1969); Siegal, Privacy, Ethics and Confidentiality, 10 *Prof. Psychology: Research & Prac.* 249 (1979); Slovenko, Psychotherapy and Confidentiality, 24 *Clev. St. L. Rev.* 375 (1975).

2. The issue of the confidentiality of records maintained in therapy has presented special problems. See Sloan & Hall, Confidentiality of Psychotherapeutic Records, 5 *J. Legal Med.* 435 (1984). Many of the privilege cases discussed later in this chapter involve the records of psychotherapy.

3. Hippocrates stressed the obligation of healers to refrain from repeating any personal information they might uncover in the course of treatment. See Schuchman, Confidentiality: Practice Issues in New Legislation, 50 *Am. J. Orthopsychiatry* 641 (1980); Shuman, The Origins of the Physician-Patient Privilege and Professional Secret, 39 *Sw. L. J.* 661 (1985).

4. American Psychological Association, *Ethical Principles of Psychologists* (1981).

"Principle V.—Confidentiality"

Psychologists have a primary obligation to respect the confidentiality of information obtained from persons in the course of their work as psychologists. They reveal such information to others only with the consent of the person or the person's legal representative, except in those unusual circumstances in which not to do so would result in clear danger to the person or to others. Where appropriate, psychologists inform their clients of the legal limits of confidentiality.

a. Information obtained in clinical or consulting relationships, or evaluative data concerning children, students, employees, and others, are discussed only for professional purposes and only with persons clearly concerned with the case. Written and oral reports present only data germane to the purposes of the evaluation and every effort is made to avoid undue invasion of privacy.

b. Psychologists who present personal information obtained during the course of professional work in writings, lectures, or other public forums either obtain adequate prior consent to do so or adequately disguise all identifying information.

c. Psychologists make provisions for maintaining confidentiality in the storage and disposal of records.

d. When working with minors or other persons who are unable to give voluntary, informed consent, psychologists take special care to protect these persons' best interests.

5. American Psychiatric Association, *The Principles of Medical Ethics with Annotations Especially Applicable to Psychiatry* (1981).

Section 4.

A physician shall respect the rights of patients, of colleagues, and of other health professionals, and shall safeguard patient confidences within the constraints of the law.

1. Psychiatric records, including even the identification of a person as a patient, must be protected with extreme care. Confidentiality is essential to psychiatric treatment. This is based in part on the special nature of psychiatric therapy as well as on the traditional ethical relationship between physician and patient. Growing concern regarding the civil rights of patients and the possible adverse effects of computerization, duplication equipment, and data banks makes the dissemination of confidential information an increasing hazard. Because of the sensitive and private nature of the information with which the psychiatrist deals, he/she must be circumspect in the information that he/she chooses to disclose to others about a patient. The welfare of the patient must be a continuing consideration.

2. A psychiatrist may release confidential information only with the authorization of the patient or under proper legal compulsion. The continuing duty of the psychiatrist to protect the patient includes fully apprising him/her of the connotations of waiving the privilege of privacy. This may become an issue when the patient is being investigated by an outside agency, is applying for a position, or is involved in legal action. The same principles apply to the release of information concerning treatment to medical departments of government agencies; business organizations, labor unions, and insurance companies. Information gained in confidence about patients seen in student health services should not be released without the student's explicit permission.

3. Clinical and other materials used in teaching and writing must be adequately disguised in order to preserve the anonymity of the individuals involved.

4. The ethical responsibility of maintaining confidentiality holds equally for the consultations in which the patient may not have been present and in which the consultee was not a physician. In such instances, the physician consultant should alert the consultee to his/her duty of confidentiality.

5. Ethically the psychiatrist may disclose only that information which is relevant to a given situation. He/she should avoid offering speculation as fact. Sensitive information such as an individual's sexual orientation or fantasy material is usually unnecessary.

6. Psychiatrists are often asked to examine individuals for security purposes, to determine suitability for various jobs, and to determine legal competence. The psychiatrist must fully describe the nature and purpose and lack of confidentiality of the examination to the examinee at the beginning of the examination.

7. Careful judgement must be exercised by the psychiatrist in order to include, when appropriate, the parents or guardian in the treatment of a minor. At the same time the psychiatrist must assure the minor proper confidentiality.

8. Psychiatrists at times may find it necessary, in order to protect the patient or the community from imminent danger, to reveal confidential information disclosed by the patient.

9. When the psychiatrist is ordered by the court to reveal the confidences entrusted to him/her by patients he/she may comply or he/she may ethically hold the right to dissent within the framework of the law. When the psychiatrist is in doubt, the right of the patient to confidentiality and, by extension, to unimpaired treatment, should be given priority. The psychiatrist should reserve the right to raise the question of adequate need for disclosure. In the event that the necessity for legal disclosure is demonstrated by the court, the psychiatrist may request the right to disclosure of only that information which is relevant to the legal question at hand.

10. With regard for the person's dignity and privacy and with truly informed consent, it is ethical to present a patient to a scientific gathering, if the confidentiality of the presentation is understood and accepted by the audience.

11. It is ethical to present a patient or former patient to a public gathering or to the news media only if that patient is fully informed of enduring loss of confidentiality, is competent, and consents in writing without coercion.

12. When involved in funded research, the ethical psychiatrist will advise human subjects of the funding source, retain his/her freedom to reveal data and results, and follow all appropriate and current guidelines relative to human subject protection.

13. Ethical considerations in medical practice preclude the psychiatric evaluation of any adult charged with criminal acts prior to access to, or availability of, legal counsel. The only exception is the rendering of care to the person for the sole purpose of medical treatment.

6. National Association of Social Workers, *Code of Ethics* (1979).

II. H.

H. Confidentiality and Privacy—The social worker should respect the privacy of clients and hold in confidence all information obtained in the course of professional service.

1. The social worker should share with others confidences revealed by clients, without their consent, only for compelling professional reasons.

2. The social worker should inform clients fully about the limits of confidentiality in a given situation, the purposes for which information is obtained, and how it may be used.

3. The social worker should afford clients reasonable access to any official social work records concerning them.

4. When providing clients with access to records, the social worker should take due care to protect the confidences of others contained in those records.

5. The social worker should obtain informed consent of clients before taping, recording, or permitting third-party observation of their activities.

7. American Personnel and Guidance Association, *Ethical Standards* (1981).

2. The counseling relationship and information resulting therefrom are to be kept confidential, consistent with the obligations of the member as a professional person. In a group counseling setting, the counselor must set a norm of confidentiality regarding all group participants' disclosures.

5. Records of the counseling relationship, including interview notes, test data, correspondence, tape recordings, and other documents, are to be considered

professional information for use in counseling and they should not be considered a part of the records of the institution or agency in which the counselor is employed unless specified by state statute or regulation. Revelation to others of counseling material must occur only upon the expressed consent of the client.

6. Use of data derived from a counseling relationship for purposes of counselor training or research shall be confined to content that can be disguised to ensure full protection of the identity of the subject client.

7. The member must inform the client of the purposes, goals, techniques, rules of procedure and limitations that may affect the relationship at or before the time that the counseling relationship is entered.

8. National Association of Social Workers, *supra* note 6, at H-1. See American Personnel and Guidance Association, *supra* note 7, at B-2.

9. American Psychological Association, *supra* note 4, Principle 5. See American Psychiatric Association, *supra* note 5, Section 4-8.

10. American Psychiatric Association, *supra* note 5, Section 4-2. Emphasis added.

11. American Psychological Association, *supra* note 4, Principle 5. Emphasis added.

12. See United States v. Lindstrom, 698 F.2d 1154 (11th Cir. 1982); United States v. Meagher, 531 F.2d 752 (5th Cir.), *cert. denied*, 429 U.S. 853 (1976).

13. Students should be considered assistants of a therapist (faculty supervisor) under whose direction the evaluation or therapy is undertaken. However, recently some question has been raised about this principle. In Hall v. State, 255 Ga. 267, 336 S.E.2d 812 (1985) the Georgia Supreme Court noted that an appellate court had refused to apply the psychologist-patient privilege to a student in training (the Georgia Supreme Court did not decide the issue). In People v. Gomez, 134 Cal. App.3d 874, 185 Cal. Rptr. 155 (2d Dist. 1982) the court held that family court interns were not covered by the privilege unless they were working under the supervision of a therapist to whom the privilege attached.

14. See 42 U.S.C. §290 dd-3 (Supp. 1984); 42 C.F.R. §2.31 (1985); Human, Release of Medical Records of Alcohol and Drug Abuse Patients: The Regulatory Maze, *J. Mo. Bar A.* 96 (1982); Saltzman, Protection for the Child or Parent? The Conflict Between the Federal Drug and Alcohol Abuse Confidentiality Requirements and the State Child Abuse and Neglect Reporting Laws, 1985 *S. Ill. U. L.J.* 181.

15. For an excellent review of therapist liability for breach of confidentiality see Eger, Psychotherapists' Liability for Extrajudicial Breaches of Confidentiality, 18 *Ariz. L. Rev.* 1061 (1976). See also J. Smith, *Medical Malpractice: Psychiatric Care* (1986); Note, *Roe v. Doe:* A Remedy for Disclosure of Psychiatric Confidences, 29 *Rutgers L. Rev.* 191 (1975). For a general review of confidentiality see H. Schuchman, L. Foster & S. Nye, *Confidentiality of Health Records* (1982).

16. See Cooper, Minors Participation in Therapy Decisions: A Written Therapist-Child Agreement, 1 *J. Child & Adolescent Psychotherapy* 93 (1984); Kobocow, McGuire & Blau, The Influence of Confidentiality Conditions on

Self-Disclosure of Early Adolescents, 14 *Prof. Psychology: Research & Prac.* 435 (1983); Melton, Minors and Privacy: Are Legal and Psychological Concepts Compatible?, 62 *Neb. L. Rev.* 455 (1983); Melton, Toward "Personhood" for Adolescents: Autonomy and Privacy as Values in Public Policy, 38 *Am. Psychologist* 99 (1983) (adolescents are competent to make decisions); Messenger & McQuire, The Child's Conception of Confidentiality in the Therapeutic Relationship, 18 *Psychotherapy: Theory, Research & Prac.* 123 (1981). For a broader view of children's mental health rights see N. Reppucci, L. Weithorn, E. Mulveys & J. Monahan eds., *Children, Mental Health and the Law* (1984); Kaser-Boyd, Adelman & Taylor, Minors' Ability to Identify Risks and Benefits of Therapy, 16 *Prof. Psychology: Research & Prac.* 398 (1985).

17. E.g., *In re* Zungia, 714 F.2d 632 (6th Cir.), *cert. denied,* 464 U.S. 983 (1983).

18. See Theaman, The Impact of Peer Review on Professional Practice, 39 *Am. Psychologist* 406 (1984).

19. See Bent, Multidimensional Model for Control of Private Information, 13 *Prof. Psychology: Research & Prac.* 27 (1982).

20. Tarasoff v. Regents of the University of California, 17 Cal.3d 425, 551 P.2d 334, 131 Cal. Rptr. 14 (1976).

21. See Givelber, Bowers & Blitch, *Tarasoff*: Myth and Reality: An Empirical Study of Private Law in Action, 1984 *Wis. L. Rev.* 443.

22. For a general review of the law of privileges see Developments, Privileged Communications, 98 *Harv. L. Rev.* 1550 (1985).

23. It has been suggested that it would be proper to include social workers or some counselors within the privilege. See e.g., Reynolds, Threats to Confidentiality, 21 *J. Nat'l A. Soc. Workers* 108 (1976); Robinson, Testimonial Privilege and the School Guidance Counselor, 25 *Syracuse L. Rev.* 911 (1974); Note, Underprivileged Communications: Extension of the Psychotherapist-Patient Privilege to Patients of Psychiatric Social Workers, 61 *Cal. L. Rev.* 1050 (1973); Note, Testimonial Privileges and the Student-Counselor Relationship in Secondary Schools, 56 *Iowa L. Rev.* 323 (1971).

It has in fact been suggested that a privilege limited to psychologists and psychiatrists is unconstitutional in that it violates the right of privacy and equal protection. Comment, The Psychotherapist-Patient Privilege: Are Some Patients More Privileged Than Others?, 10 *Pac. L.J.* 801 (1979). It has been suggested that the definition of a psychotherapist includes anyone "who, in the course of his or her regular profession or employment may be expected to practice psychotherapy." One difficulty with this approach is determinant with certainty what "psychotherapy" is, and therefore determining who practices psychotherapy.

24. J. Wigmore, *Evidence* §2285 (McNaughton's rev. 1961).

25. Willage, Group Therapists' Understanding of Privileged Communication and Confidentiality, paper presented to the American Psychological Association, Toronto, 1978. See also, authorities cited in notes 82 to 87, *infra.*

26. E.g., Meyer & Smith, A Crisis in Group Therapy, 32 *Am. Psychologist* 638 (1977); Shuman & Weiner, The Privilege Study: An Empirical Examination of the Psychotherapist-Patient Privilege, 60 *N.C. L. Rev.* 893 (1982); Willage & Meyer, The Effects of Varying Levels of Confidentiality on Self-Disclosure, 2 *Group* 88 (1978).

27. "On account of the special therapeutic need for assurance to the patient of protection against disclosures it is cogently argued . . . that even in states not having the physician-patient privilege generally, a privilege should be recognized, by statute or decision, for confidential disclosures to psychiatrists, qualified psychologists trained in the treatment of mental disorders, and (in the court's discretion) general practitioners consulted for diagnosis or treatment of mental disease. . . .

"A privilege of those receiving psychotherapy is necessary if the psychiatric profession is to fulfill its medical responsibility to its patients." *McCormick's Handbook on the Law of Evidence* §9 at 213 (Cleary, 2d. ed. 1972). See R. Slovenko, *Psychotherapy, Confidentiality and Privileged Communication* (1966); Dekruai & Sales, Privileged Communications of Psychologists, 13 *Prof. Psychology: Research & Prac.* (1982); Fisher, Psychotherapeutic Professions and the Law of Privileged Communications, 10 *Wayne L. Rev.* 609 (1964); Goldstein & Katz, Psychotherapist-Patient Privilege: The GAP Proposal and the Connecticut Statute, 36 *Conn. B. J.* 175 (1962); Guttmacher & Weihofen, Privileged Communications Between Psychiatrist and Patient, 28 *Ind. L. J.* 32 (1952); Ladd, Privileges, 1969 *L. & Soc. Order* 555, 581; Rappeport, Psychiatrist-Patient Privilege, 23 *Md. L. Rev.* 39 (1963); Slovenko, Psychiatry and a Second Look at the Medical Privilege, 6 *Wayne L. Rev.* 175 (1960).

28. Group for the Advancement of Psychiatry, *Confidentiality and Privileged Communications in the Practice of Psychiatry*, Rep. No. 45 (1960); Goldstein & Katz, *supra*, note 27.

29. For a summary of confidentiality laws, see S. Brakel, J. Parry & B. Weiner, *The Mentally Disabled and the Law* 592–604 (3d ed. 1986) (this is a fine work, which provides an excellent summary of mental health law related to the disabled); Ferster, Statutory Summary of Physician-Patient Privileged Communication Laws, in *Readings in Law and Psychiatry* (R. Allen, E. Ferster & J. Rubin eds. 1975) 171–94; Comment, Psychotherapist-Patient Privilege Under Federal Rule 501, 75 *J. Crim. L. & Criminology* 388, 396 (1984).

30. Courts will apply certain formulations whether or not they are specifically written into privileges. Even though a statutory privilege does not specify any exceptions, for example, courts will imply certain exceptions.

31. One sign posted by a bartender/counselor reads, "Need help? Don't visit a psychiatrist—See your bartender instead. He's more available, he's cheaper and he'll never tell you to quit drinking." See generally Slovenko, Commentaries on Psychiatry and Law: Shielding Communications With a Pet, 10 *J. Psychiatry & L.* 405 (1982); Note, The Psychotherapist-Client Privilege: Defining the Professional Involved, 34 *Emory L.J.* 777 (1985).

32. Lipsey v. Georgia, 170 Ga. App. 770, 318 S.E.2d 184 (1984).

33. See United States v. Lindstrom, 698 F.2d 1154 (11th Cir. 1982); United States v. Meagher, 531 F.2d 752 (5th Cir.), cert. denied, 429 U.S. 853 (1976).

34. Allred v. State, 554 P.2d 411 (Alaska 1976). A lower court in Illinois some years earlier also recognized a psychotherapist-patient privilege. Binder v. Ruvell, Civil Docket 52C2535, Circuit Court of Cook County, Illinois, June 24, 1952, Judge Harry M. Fisher presiding, reported in Note, Confidential Communications to a Psychotherapist: A New Testimonial Privilege, 47 Nw.U. L. Rev. 384 (1952).

35. Allred v. State, 554 P.2d at 418. The court could not agree on whether the privilege was broad enough to cover the communications to a social worker, as opposed to a psychotherapist. Two justices felt that communications to social workers were not covered by the common-law privileges; two were of the opinion they were, since there was a therapeutic relationship and because the social worker was the psychiatrist's "alter ego" in this case. Id. at 426. One justice found the communication between Allred and the social worker to be protected by the statute. Id. at 422.

36. The court relied upon Mullen v. United States, 263 F.2d 275, 279 (D.C. Cir. 1958) (Fahy, J. concurring) and Cook v. Carrol (1945) Ir.R. 515 (High Ct.) as examples of judicially created common law priest-penitent privileges. It also noted McTaggart v. McTaggart, 2 (1948) All E.R. Reprint 754, 755 (Ct. App.) as an example of the English judicial doctrine of "conversation without prejudice" covering statements made to marriage counselors attempting to effectuate reconciliation, and In re Kryschuk and Zulynik, 14 D. L. Rev. 2d 676 (Sask. Magist. Ct. 1958) establishing a similar Canadian doctrine.

37. In re Zuniga, 714 F.2d 632 (6th Cir.), cert. denied, 464 U.S. 983 (1983). See Note, The Case for a Federal Psychotherapist-Patient Privilege That Protects Patient Identity, 1985 Duke L.J. 1217.

38. In re Zuniga, 714 F.2d at 639.

39. Rule 504 of the Rules of Evidence proposed by the Supreme Court, 56 F.R.D. 183 (1972).

40. Federal Rules of Evidence, Rule 501.

41. E.g., Herbert v. Lando, 441 U.S. 153 (1979); United States v. Nixon, 418 U.S. 683 (1974).

42. See In re Pebsworth, 705 F.2d 261 (7th Cir. 1983).

43. Id.

44. E.g., Cross, Privileged Communications Between Participants in Group Psychotherapy, 1970 L. & Soc. Order 191; Meyer & Smith, A Crisis in Group Therapy, 32 Am. Psychologist 638 (1977); Slovenko, Group Psychotherapy: Privileged Communication and Confidentiality, 5 J. Psychiatry & L. 405 (1977).

45. See Minnesota v. Andring, 342 N.W.2d 128 (Minn. 1984).

46. Smith, Unfinished Business with Informal Consent Procedure, 36 Am. Psychologist 22 (1981).

47. Judge Hufstedler has proposed that to avoid unnecessary invasion of the confidences of therapy, the patient-litigant exception should ordinarily be limited to ascertaining the time, length, cost, and ultimate diagnosis of treatment. An adverse party would be permitted to demand additional information concerning therapy only if the party demonstrated a compelling need for the information. Caesar v. Mountanos, 542 F.2d 1064, 1074–75 (9th Cir. 1976), cert. denied, 430 U.S. 954 (1977) (Hufstedler, J., concurring and dissenting).

48. Slovenko, Psychotherapist-Patient Privilege: A Picture of Misguided Hope, 23 Cath. U. L. Rev. 649 (1974).

49. See Atwood v. Atwood, 550 S.W.2d 465 (Ky. 1976), Guernsey, The Psychotherapist-Patient Privilege in Child Placement: A Relevancy Analysis, 26 Vill. L. Rev. 955 (1981).

50. See McKenna v. Fargo, 451 F. Supp. 1355, 1381 (D.N.J. 1978), aff'd, 601 F.2d 575 (3d Cir. 1979); Tarasoff v. Regents of the University of California 17 Cal.3d 425, 440–42, 551 P.2d 334, 346–47, 131 Cal. Rptr. 14, 26–27 (1976).

51. Tarasoff v. Regents of the University of California, 17 Cal.3d 425, 551 P.2d 334, 131 Cal. Rptr. 14 (1976). This case is described in chapter 1.

52. Davis v. Alaska, 415 U.S. 308 (1974).

53. Salazar v. State, 559 P.2d 66 (Alaska 1976); State v. Hembd, 305 Minn. 120, 232 N.W.2d 872 (1975); State v. Roma, 140 N.J. Super. 582, 357 A.2d 45, aff'd on reargument, 143 N.J. Super. 504, 363 A.2d 923 (1976).

54. See Newberger, The Helping Hand Strikes Again: Unintended Consequences of Child Abuse Reporting, 12 J. Clinical Child Psychology 307 (1983).

55. U.S. Children's Bureau, The Abused Child-Principles and Suggested Language for Legislation on Reporting on the Physically Abused Child (DHEW, 1963). The medical community countered with its own proposed model act. American Medical Association, Physical Abuse of Children—Suggested Legislation (1965).

56. Besharov, Child Protection: Past Progress, Present Problems, and Future Directions, 17 Fam. L.Q. 151, 153–54 (1983).

57. See Fraser, A Glimpse at the Future: A Critical Analysis of the Development of Child Abuse Reporting Statutes, 54 Chi.-Kent L. Rev. 641, 650–67 (1978).

58. See J. Giovannoni & R. Becerra, Defining Child Abuse 4–13, 257–59 (1979).

59. See U.S. Center on Child Abuse and Neglect, National Study of the Incidence and Severity of Child Abuse and Neglect (DHHS 1981) [hereinafter cited as National Study of Child Abuse].

60. Id. at 39.

61. A later report suggested that by 1983 the annual number of children reported as abused or neglected had risen to 1.5 million. D. Whitcomb,

E. Shapiro & L. Stellwagen, *When the Victim Is a Child* 2 (1985). It is not unreasonable to expect that by now the figure is closer to 1.8 million.

62. The definition used by the *National Study* has been criticized by some, particularly as it relates to the definition of sexual abuse and the requirement that the abuser be a parent or other caretaker. Finkelhor & Hotaling, Sexual Abuse in the National Incidence Study of Child Abuse and Neglect: An Appraisal, 8 *Child Abuse & Neglect* 23 (1984).

63. See Swoboda, Elwork, Sales & Levine, Knowledge of and Compliance With Privileged Communication and Child Abuse Reporting Laws, 9 *Prof. Psychology: Research & Prac.* 448 (1978).

64. Child rearing or family integrity are part of the constitutionally protected right of autonomy privacy. E.g., H. L. v. Matheson, 450 U.S. 398, 411 (1981); Prince v. Massachusetts, 321 U.S. 158, 166 (1944); Pierce v. Society of Sisters, 268 U.S. 510, 535 (1925). The constitutional issues raised by state intervention to protect children are discussed in Note, Constitutional Limitations on the Scope of State Child Neglect Statutes, 79 *Colum. L. Rev.* 719 (1979). Other recent commentary concerning privacy and therapy includes Everstine, Everstine, Heymann, True, Frey, Johnson & Seiden, Privacy and Confidentiality in Psychotherapy, 35 *Am. Psychologist* 828 (1980); Melton, Minors and Privacy: Are Legal and Psychological Concepts Compatible?, 62 *Neb. L. Rev.* 455 (1983); Note, Privacy in Personal Medical Information: A Diagnosis, 33 *U. Fla. L. Rev.* 394 (1981).

65. See J. Giovannoni & R. Becerra, *Defining Child Abuse* 3–4 (1979); Bourne & Newberger. "Family Autonomy" or "Coercive Intervention?" Ambiguity and Conflict in the Proposed Standards in Child Abuse and Neglect, 57 *B.U. L. Rev.* 670 (1977).

66. The failure to adhere to a duty described in a criminal, or similar, statute may result in negligence per se liability if the statute was designed to protect the class of persons of which the plaintiff is a member and against the risk of harm and injury which occurred. W. P. Keeton, D. Dobbs, R. Keeton, D. Owen, *Prosser and Keeton on the Law of Torts,* 229–31 (W. D. Keeton 5th ed. 1984).

67. For a discussion of the negligence liability of the failure to report child abuse see Besharov, Child Abuse and Neglect: Liability for Failing to Report, 22 *Trial* 67 (Aug. 1986); Issacson, Child Abuse Reporting Statutes: The Case for Holding Physicians Civilly Liable for Failure to Report, 12 *San Diego L. Rev.* 743 (1972); Paulsen, Child Abuse Reporting Laws: The Shape of the Legislation, 67 *Colum. L. Rev.* 1, 34–36 (1967); Note, Physicians' Liability for Failure to Diagnose and Report Child Abuse, 23 *Wayne L. Rev.* 1187 (1977). See also Note, Civil Liability for Teachers' Negligent Failure to Report Suspected Child Abuse, 28 *Wayne L. Rev.* 183 (1981).

68. Landeros v. Flood, 17 Cal.3d 399, 551 P.2d 389, 131 Cal. Rptr. 69 (1976); Brown & Truitt, Civil Liability in Child Abuse Cases, 54 *Chi.-Kent L. Rev.* 753 (1978).

69. Besharov, "Doing Something" About Child Abuse: The Need to Narrow the Grounds for State Intervention, 8 *Harv. J. L. & Pub. Policy* 539

(1985); Hurley, Duties in Conflict: Must Psychotherapists Report Child Abuse Inflicted by Clients and Confided in Therapy, 22 *San Diego L. Rev.* 645 (1985); Note, Vanishing Exception to the Psychotherapist-Patient Privilege: The Child Abuse Reporting Act, 16 *Pac. L. J.* 335 (1984). Some courts have begun to protect psychotherapist privileges in child abuse cases. Minnesota v. Andring, 342 N.W.2d 128 (Minn. 1984); D.M. v. Hoeston, No. 47744 (Mo. Ct. App. Dec. 20, 1983) reported in 8 *Mental & Physical Disability L. Reporter* 121–22 (1984). See generally Saltzman, Protection for the Child or Parent? The Conflict Between the Federal Drug and Alcohol Abuse Confidentiality Requirements and the State Child Abuse and Neglect Reporting Laws, 1985 *S. Ill U. L. J.* 181.

70. Smith & Meyer, Child Abuse Reporting Laws and Psychotherapy: A Time for Reconsideration, 7 *Int'l J. L. & Psychiatry* 351 (1985). See Coleman, Creating Therapist-Offender Exception to Mandatory Child Abuse Reporting Statutes—When Psychiatrist Knows Best, 54 *Cin. L. Rev.* 1113 (1986).

71. Griswold v. Connecticut, 381 U.S. 479 (1965). This decision was followed by a decision that upheld unmarried persons' decisions to use contraceptives.

72. Roe v. Wade, 410 U.S. 113 (1973).

73. The theoretical and legal aspects of privacy and therapy are fully reviewed in Smith, Constitutional Privacy in Psychotherapy, 49 *Geo. Wash. L. Rev.* 1 (1980).

74. See Bremer v. State, 18 Md. App. 291, 334, 307 A.2d 503, 529 (1973), *cert. denied*, 415 U.S. 930 (1974) (denying the existence of a constitutional psychiatrist-patient privilege); *cf.* Felber v. Foote, 321 F. Supp. 85, 89 (D. Conn. 1970) (the right of privacy does not extend protection to the physician-patient relationship, even when the physician is a psychiatrist).

75. See Taylor v. United States, 222 F.2d 398, 401 (D.C. Cir. 1955) (noting the extraordinary sensitivity of psychotherapist-patient communications); State v. Looney, 294 N.C. 1, 28, 240 S.E.2d 612, 627 (1978) (upholding the refusal of a trial court to grant a defense request to order a psychiatric examination of a primary prosecution witness in part because such exams are a "drastic invasion" of the right of privacy); *cf.* Rennie v. Klein, 462 F. Supp. 1131, 1144 (D.N.J. 1978) [subsequent history not described] (because the right of privacy includes the right to protect mental processes from governmental interference, a patient has the right to refuse mind-altering drugs). Some courts have failed to consider the existence of a constitutional right of privacy, but have limited discovery of medical and psychiatric files by broadly construing statutory privileges to favor a general public policy against disclosure of psychotherapist-patient confidences. See Flora v. Hamilton, 81 F.R.D. 576, 578 (M.D.N.C. 1978) (construing a North Carolina statute that recognized a psychiatrist-patient privilege as favoring a policy of nondisclosure).

76. Robinson v. Magovern, 83 F.R.D. 79, 91 (W.D. Pa. 1979) (acknowledging the possibility of a constitutional psychiatrist-patient privilege, the

court made an exception for highly generalized information released under a confidentiality order); Miller v. Colonial Refrigerated Transp., 81 F.R.D. 741, 747 (M.D. Pa. 1979) (conceding that there may be a psychotherapist-patient privilege, the court held that the interests of the state in the fairness of the adversary process required a patient-litigant exception to confidentiality); United States *ex rel.* Edney v. Smith, 425 F. Supp. 1038, 1044 (E.D.N.Y. 1976) (recognizing a patient-litigant exception to any constitutionally based psychiatrist-patient privilege), *aff'd mem.,* 556 F.2d 556 (2d Cir.), *cert. denied,* 431 U.S. 958 (1977).

77. *In re* Lifschutz, 2 Cal.3d 415, 467 P.2d 557, 85 Cal. Rptr. 829 (1970).

78. *Id.* at 420, 467 P.2d at 559, 85 Cal. Rptr. at 831.

79. Caesar v. Mountanos, 542 F.2d 1064 (9th Cir. 1976), *cert. denied,* 430 U.S. 954 (1977).

80. *In re* B, 482 Pa. 471, 394 A.2d 419 (1978).

81. Hawaii Psychiatric Society v. Ariyoshi, 481 F. Supp. 1028 (D. Hawaii 1979).

82. Merriken v. Cressman, 364 F. Supp. 913 (E.D. Pa. 1973).

83. Lora v. Board of Education, 74 F.R.D. 565 (E.D.N.Y. 1977).

84. But see J. P. v. DeSanti, 653 F.2d 1080 (6th Cir. 1981) where the court permitted "social histories" of juveniles to be compiled for the juvenile court to be distributed among a number of government agencies.

85. McKenna v. Fargo, 451 F. Supp. 1355 (D.N.J. 1978) *aff'd,* 601 F.2d 575 (3d Cir. 1979).

86. United States v. Westinghouse Electric Corp., 638 F.2d 570 (3rd Cir. 1980).

87. Slovenko, Psychotherapist-Patient Testimonial Privilege: A Picture of Misguided Hope, 23 *Cath. U. L. Rev.* 649 (1974).

88. A D.C. ordinance passed in 1978 that included a provision to limit disclosure of mental health patient information was challenged by the insurance industry, including Blue Cross and Blue Shield. The ordinance limited the release of information to a brief statement of the fact of treatment, length of treatment and diagnosis, and provided for independent professional review in the case of dispute between an insurance company and mental health professional. See note 89 *infra.*

89. Some confidentiality statutes have been drafted to avoid some of the worst problems with laws dealing with confidentiality and privileges. Two statutes that are particularly good (but not perfect) are the District of Columbia Mental Health Information law (D.C. Code Ann. §6–2001 [1981]) and the Illinois Mental Health and Developmental Disabilities Confidentiality Act (Ill. Ann. Stat. ch. 91 1/2, §801 and ch. 110, §8–802 [Smith-Hurd Supp. 1985]). More recently, Massachusetts has made a similar effort.

90. Rosen, Why Clients Relinquish Their Rights to Privacy Under Sign-Away Pressure, 8 *Prof. Psychology: Research & Prac.* 17 (1977); Shuman & Weiner, The Privilege Study: An Empirical Examination of the Psychotherapist-Patient Privilege, 60 *N.C. L. Rev.* 893 (1982) (a thorough examination

of the attitudes of lay persons, patients, therapists, and judges); Simmons, Client Attitudes Toward Release of Confidential Information Without Consent, 24 *J. Clinical Psychology* 364 (1968); Weiner & Shuman, Privilege—A Comparative Study, 12 *J. Psychiatry & L.* 373 (1984) (finding little difference between a state with a privilege and another without).

91. Meyer and Smith found that 81.8 percent of respondents to a questionnaire on confidentiality indicated that they would refuse to enter group therapy or would be substantially less inclined to be open in therapy without the assurance of confidentiality. (The respondents were third-year university students.) Meyer & Smith, A Crisis in Group Therapy, 32 *Am. Psychologist* 638, 639–40 (1977). Another survey revealed that a substantial number of people felt they would be less open in therapy if they knew a psychotherapist was legally obligated to release information from therapy. Note, Functional Overlap Between the Lawyer and Other Professionals: Its Implications for the Privileged Communications Doctrine, 71 *Yale L.J.* 1226, 1262 (1962). See generally Miller & Thelen, Knowledge and Beliefs About Confidentiality in Therapy, 17 *Prof. Psychology: Research & Prac.* 15 (1986) (general population does not understand limits of confidentiality, but patients would like to have this information when in therapy). But see R. Kahl, *The Effects of Awareness of the Importance of Confidentiality and Lack of Privileged Communication Statutes for Group Psychotherapy* (dissertation, 1978), and studies cited in note 90, *supra.*

92. Schmid, Appelbaum, Roth & Lidz, Confidentiality in Psychiatry: A Study of the Patient's View, 34 *Hosp. & Community Psychiatry* 353 (1983). See Appelbaum, Kapen, Walters, Lidz & Roth, Confidentiality: An Empirical Test of the Utilitarian Perspective, 12 *Bull. Am. Acad. Psychiatry & L.* 109 (1984).

93. A survey of therapists revealed that about a fourth of them had, within one year, observed patients' reluctance to discuss violent tendencies when informed of the possibility of a breach of the confidences of therapy. Note, Where the Public Peril Begins: A Survey of Psychotherapists to Determine the Effects of Tarasoff, 31 *Stan. L. Rev.* 165, 183 (1978). See Beck, When the Patient Threatens Violence: An Empirical Study of Clinical Practice After *Tarasoff*, 10 *Bull. Am. Acad. Psychiatry & L.* 189 (1982); Givelber, Bowers & Blitch, *Tarasoff,* Myth and Reality: An Empirical Study of Private Law in Action, 1984 *Wis. L. Rev.,* 443. For a case study of using the "duty to warn" to therapeutic advantage, see Wulsin, Bursztajn & Gutheil, Unexpected Clinical Features of the *Tarasoff* Decision: The Therapeutic Alliance and the "Duty to Warn," 140 *Am. J. Psychiatry* 601 (1983).

94. Willage and Meyer found that subjects were more open and candid in answering personality inventories when confidentiality was assured than if they thought the results of their survey might be released. Willage & Meyer, The Effects of Varying Levels of Confidentiality on Self-Disclosure, 2 *Group* 88 (1978).

95. D. Willage, *The Effects of Informing Patients on the Limits of Confidentiality on Group Therapy,* 4 *Dissertation Abstracts International* 3595 (1981).

CHAPTER 3
THE INTRUSIVE THERAPIES: ELECTROCONVULSIVE THERAPY, PSYCHOSURGERY, AND PSYCHOTROPIC MEDICATIONS

The most controversial mental illness treatments—electroconvulsive therapy (ECT), psychosurgery, and psychotropic drug therapy—are called "intrusive" because they involve an invasion of the body. They have significant adverse side effects and are perceived as having the potential for science-fiction-like mind control, as suggested in the popular fictional representation, *One Flew Over the Cuckoo's Nest*. Concern about these treatments has manifested itself in limitation on their use with involuntary and even with voluntary mental patients.[1] This public concern was the basis for the proposition approved by ballot in Berkeley, California in 1982, to prohibit the use of ECT.[2]

A number of substantial legal issues are raised by these treatments: the circumstance in which there can be truly informed consent to the procedures; the use of the therapies without the consent of the patient; the degree to which they actually "work"; their cost/benefit ratios; the right of patients to choose these or other forms of treatment; the kinds of information patients should be given before treatment; and the appropriate forms of governmental regulation.

In this chapter, we consider the nature and consequences of psychosurgery, ECT, and psychotropic drugs, and the legal issues raised by these treatments. The process, benefits, dangers, and side effects of psychosurgery, ECT, and the major psychotropic drugs will be described. We will also explore the debates over the use of these treatments and their regulation by the government. These issues are particularly significant because of the wide use of ECT and psycho-tropic drugs and the potential return of psychosurgery as a legitimate therapy.[3] Other therapy, including "token economies" and other forms of behavior modification, may raise legal issues especially when used in prisons or on involuntary patients, but the problems with the more invasive forms of therapy raise legal problems for a wide range of patients and therapists. The right to treatment and right to refuse treatment are considered in chapter 18.

ELECTROCONVULSIVE THERAPY

ECT is a widespread psychiatric therapeutic technique. Unfortu-nately, accurate national statistics on its use are very difficult to ob-tain, and estimates range from 10,000 daily to 150,000 ECTs annually.[4] There is evidence, however, that the number of patients receiving ECT and the number of treatments being delivered are declining. A survey of the New York State area showed a 38 percent decrease in the absolute number of ECTs given, and a 28 percent decrease in the number of patients receiving shock treatment from 1972 to 1977.[5] Whether this is a nationwide trend and is continuing is difficult to say, but the results of the study may indicate a growing concern over the widespread application of ECT.

Shock therapy is a catchall term used to describe a variety of treat-ments, including pharmacological modes of inducing convulsions—such as insulin or drugs like metrazol—or electrically induced con-vulsions.[6] Pharmacological induction is seldom used today because of the unnecessary dangers inherent in this method. We will simply use ECT to designate electroconvulsive treatment.[7]

An ECT machine is basically a transformer that uses alternating current to apply electric shocks. The charge may last anywhere from 0.1 to 1.0 seconds, though applications are typically in the 0.5 to 1.0 second range. ECTs are usually administered in a series of threes, for no apparent theoretical or empirical reason. Two to four separate sets of three ECTs each is usually standard for an initial treatment response to depression, while those who administer it for schizo-phrenia may initially prescribe twice that number.[8]

There have been important innovations in ECT therapy, including the use of anesthetics and muscle-relaxant drugs to reduce pain and physical injuries, the application of unilateral rather than bilateral electrode placement, and the new technique of multiple monitored electroconvulsive therapy (MMECT). MMECT involves monitoring a variety of vital functions throughout the ECT administration, and includes the use of oxygenation to avoid anoxia. However, because of the apparatus problems involved, the need for an anesthesiologist, and the fact that in MMECT the patient does not stop breathing or "regress," its acceptance has been slow.[9]

How ECT Works

The exact processes that ECT initiates or causes in the body remain undefined. It appears that electrical stimulation *per se,* even at fairly high voltages, is not the factor. Many assume that the production of a severe or grand mal seizure, accompanied by unconsciousness and a period of amnesia, must be experienced if treatment is to be successful. There is evidence for a variety of physiological accompaniments to this event.[10] There may be as many as 50 theories as to how ECT causes eventual psychological changes. There is little agreement regarding the process by which ECT produces change. The variety of explanatory concepts offered is enormous.

One possible explanation that has not been thoroughly investigated is the placebo phenomenon. There is substantial pressure, both direct and indirect, on patients to report positive changes following ECT. Such expectancies can affect the reporting of mood, anxiety level, and satisfaction with treatment.[11] In a British hospital an ECT machine had been "successfully" and consistently used for two years of treatments before someone realized that the machine had not been working at all for those two years.[12]

Side Effects and Risks of ECT

Clearly, there are some dangers associated with the use of ECT. The idea that depressives cannot remember why they should feel guilty is consistent with the assertion that ECT can cause brain damage. This would not be surprising, since the electrodes, whether in a bilateral or unilateral placement, tend to discharge through the temporal lobes which contain the least stable cortex by EEG criteria. Close by are the hippocampal formations which have the lowest seizure threshold and the highest kindling propensity (reaction threshold) of the brain and which are crucial to the formation and retention of memories.

It is difficult to assess the level of brain damage from ECT, as bleeding in the form of petechial perivascular hemorrhages would be a typical side effect, and the longer the period there is between ECT and death, the greater the evidence of repair. However, given the anatomical situation described above and remembering the significant level of shock used, damage should not be surprising. As Friedberg notes, neuronal dropout is tough to detect but there is some clear evidence that this may be the case.[13] Karl Pribram, a world-renowned neurophysiologist, in a 1975 interview commented "I'd rather have a small lobotomy than a series of electroconvulsive shocks . . . I just know what the brain looks like after a series of shocks, and it's not very pleasant to look at."[14] Virtually everyone who has been involved in ECT work, including those who most advocate its use, agree that it causes significant cognitive confusion and memory loss in regard to those events that occur immediately before and after the application of ECT.[15]

While several early studies indicated that there may be little long-term effect on memory or intelligence from ECT, those studies were usually poorly controlled, and often used rather gross measures of deficit. In a study of 38 patients, Squire and Chase document that memory deficit is still evident at six to nine months after the last treatment, and that the ability to acquire new memories is also negatively effected.[16] More recently, Squire, Slater, and Miller compared 43 depressed patients who had received eight or nine bilateral ECT treatments (electrodes placed on both sides of the head) with a group of 7 depressed patients treated in other ways. Detailed memories were tested before starting ECT, after the fifth treatment, one week after completion of treatments, and seven months after the last treatments. The results indicated that one week after ECT was finished, memory was still seriously disrupted even for events which had occurred years previously. After seven months following treatment, patients' memories had recovered, but memory of their admission to the hospital was still disrupted, as was their memory of past public events.[17] Goldman, Gomer, and Templer matched 20 chronic male schizophrenics who had a history of 50 or more ECT treatments with 20 chronic male schizophrenics who had received no ECT.[18] The time from administration of last ECT to the administration of the test was 10 to 15 years. Two standard measures of visual motor memory and coordination were administered. They concluded that ECT produces irreversible brain damage and that the damage effects of treatments are cumulative.[19]

Friedberg cites additional data indicating cognitive disruption (change in thinking) and memory loss from ECT,[20] and supports the idea of cumulative damage from each treatment, an aspect also supported by Squire and Chase.[21] While it is true that oxygenation during treatment can help diminish this disruption, Friedberg notes that this would not prevent the major causes of damage, i.e., insult to the brain via the electrical current.[22]

Some might harbor the hope that the memory drugs, such as pirocetam (Nootropyl), could remove some of this loss, but so far evidence is that they are ineffective for these types of deficits and have undesirable side effects.[23] In summary, ECT in some patients has been associated with a number of negative results, including: memory impairment,[24] other cognitive impairments and movement disorders,[25] and, infrequently, continued seizures.[26]

"Unilateral" vs. "Bilateral" ECT

There has been a movement over the last several years to substitute the administration of unilateral for bilateral ECT.[27] The traditional bilateral ECT involves placement of the electrodes over the temporal lobes (usually near each temple) on each side of the head. Unilateral ECT requires placement of one electrode over the temporal lobe of the nondominant side with another placed at the back of the head on the same side.

While the research carried out and reviewed by Miller,[28] Annett,[29] and Blachly[30] has a variety of methodological flaws, there is enough overall consistency to allow a consensus on several issues. First, unilateral ECT can be as effective as bilateral ECT in altering depressive affect. Secondly, although some have reported that twice as many unilateral ECTs as bilateral ECTs may be necessary to produce the desired effect, this has not been supported by the recent literature.[31] Thirdly, even though one may administer many more unilateral ECTs, the problems with memory and other cognitive impairment do not occur in as significant a fashion as they do with the lesser number of bilateral ECTs.

The use of bilateral ECT with female patients in particular appears to cause a number of cognitive problems. In a well-designed study comparing the effects of right hemisphere, left hemisphere, and bilateral ECT treatments on men and women it was found that "women's performance improved most on right ECT, less on left ECT, and least on bilateral ECT."[32] In other words, bilateral ECT caused the most confusion of cognitive functioning and, as Kendell notes, "memory disturbance and confusion are unrelated to the therapeutic effect, and therefore to be avoided."[33]

Since the dominant side, or left hemisphere in most persons, controls logical thought process, it is not surprising that unilateral ECT to the nondominant causes far less disruption of memory and logical thought. This is especially reasonable if one accepts a direct insult theory, and in fact data that proponents for unilateral ECT have garnered can be seen as strong support of this concept. However, we are becoming more and more aware of the crucial part the nondominant hemisphere plays in creativity, constructive use of imaginal processes, and the like.[34] These types of thought processes are much harder to measure, hence standard measures that give rather gross scores or those that tap only outcomes of logical abstracting processes would be quite inappropriate and also give a spurious result. Data collected by d'Elia, et al. found that as few as three ECTs to the dominant side had negative effects on verbal memory processes, whereas a similar number of ECTs to the nondominant side had negative effects in complex nonverbal visual tasks.[35]

ECT and Schizophrenia

Although ECT has not been a successful therapy for schizophrenia, several studies have suggested that approximately 20 percent of all ECT treatments are given to schizophrenics.[36]

One study supported the efficacy of ECT in reducing hospitalization for schizophrenia,[37] but these results have not been supported by other research. Others simply continue to assert the value of ECT for overall treatment of schizophrenia.[38] There is a research need for systematic data collection, matched control groups, replication, and long-term followup of results. The consensus of the field certainly appears to be that ECT is not the treatment of choice for schizophrenia.[39] As Salzman concluded, chronic schizophrenics rarely respond to ECT. "ECT does not alter the fundamental psychopathology of schizophrenia."[40] Moreover, a major symptom of schizophrenia is cognitive confusion and a major side effect of ECT is cognitive confusion.

ECT and Depression

Many mental health professionals agree that severe depression warrants intervention by ECT.[41] Weiner and Power report that 79 percent of all ECT treatment in V.A. hospitals were given to people suffering from depression.[42] Hospitals in New York State delivered 83 percent of the ECT treatments to people with depressive symptomatology.[43] Taken together, these studies indicate that approximately 80 percent of all ECT treatments are given to people with depression, indicating that approximately 30 percent of all hospitalized people suffering from depression may receive ECT.[44] The tricyclic antidepressant drugs have also been found to be effective but, along with side effects and the requirement for maintenance medication, they do not have a therapeutic effect until a substantial time period has passed, often a week or more. The economic pressure on hospitals to reduce the length of hospitalization may also encourage the use of rapid response methods of treatment. Since depressions may include a potential for suicide, some argue the need for therapy with an immediate response. Evidence has been gathered which indicates remission of depression with ECT.[45] The question is whether the gain is worth the cost, an issue to which we will return.

Several problems have been noted with the treatment of depression using ECT. First, many patients who are depressed fail to respond positively to the treatments.[46] ECT has been found to be most effective on people suffering from a severe depression.[47] After extensively reviewing the literature, Scovern and Kilman concluded, "ECT is not more effective than antidepressant medication in treating neurotic depression, and ECT is probably not effective at all in depressed patients who lack signs of an endogenous (internally generated) sub-type."[48]

A second issue of concern is the high relapse rate associated with depression treated with ECT.[49] People with severe depression often do recover immediately following ECT, but the benefits may not last. Several studies have shown that long-term control of depression was better maintained by using such medications as lithium rather than ECT.[50]

In many cases where ECT is administered to depressed patients, there is no consideration of the initial causes of depression. A prominent theory as to how environment causes depression is that of "learned helplessness."[51] This theory purports that if people learn that they cannot influence or control situations, they cease behaviors and manifest depression. This raises a particular problem for a decision to administer ECT to a depressed person because of the strong feeling of helplessness during the period when one emerges from ECT. It seems reasonable that any significant set of ECT administrations is similar to laboratory-induced experiences of learned helplessness.[52] One's self-image is likely to be negatively influenced by such experiences. Certainly more attention to this specific issue is warranted in both ECT and psychosurgery research.

ECT and Other Disorders

McCabe and others assert some efficacy for ECT in the treatment of mania.[53] Methodological errors, however, cast some doubt on this assertion. Since chemotherapy based on lithium has been shown to be effective with mania, it would appear that any ECT treatment for mania should be labeled "experimental," or "nonstandard" treatment.

ECT has also been shown to be effective in the treatment of Parkinson's disease, but there are other treatments at least as effective without the side effects of ECT.

Mandel has demonstrated some reduction in the deep, chronic pain associated with terminal illnesses, but here the risks seem to outweigh the benefits of this treatment.[54]

PSYCHOSURGERY

Psychosurgery can be generally defined as surgery on normal or diseased brain tissue with a primary objective to change, control, or affect any emotional disturbance and abnormal behavior. Methods include the removal of tissue, the use of laser or ultrasound beams, or the direct application of substances to brain tissue. An estimated 500 such operations are now performed each year in the United States. Clearly, ECT is a more pervasive form of therapy. The use of psychosurgery has declined since the early 1960s, probably because of continued pressure from public, legal, and professional sources.[55] Yet there is some feeling that there may be a comeback for psychosurgery.[56]

Modern psychosurgery began when Moniz initiated frontal lobe surgery.[57] The first frontal leucotomy (selective destruction of brain tissue) was performed on a 63-year-old woman with a diagnosis of involutional melancholia. Two months later Moniz considered her cured. The first leucotomy in the United States took place in 1936. Within the following ten-year period, an estimated 6000 patients were operated on in the United States. Overall success rates were generally poor. Between 1950 and 1960, classical leucotomies fell into justified disrepute. Selection of patients for this procedure was uncritical, with a large proportion being chronic schizophrenics whose symptoms were not alleviated by the surgery. By 1960, classical psychosurgery was virtually abandoned as a therapeutic technique. Several patients who have undergone such treatments still live on in some back wards of state hospitals.

The use of psychosurgery to decrease aggressive behavior was influenced by the work of researchers such as Rosvold and Pribram who, in the mid-1950s, showed that male rhesus monkeys subjected to certain specific brain lesions lost their aggressive patterns of social dominance. Narabayashi, in Tokyo, was the first to report systematically on the amygdalotomies in man.[58]

Two more recent developments may encourage renewed interest in psychosurgery. First, there has been a trend toward destruction of smaller amounts of tissue, with correspondingly fewer side effects. An example of this is the development of the "prefrontal sonic treatment"—often referred to as PST or "ultrasound."[59] In addition, official sources have given tentative approval for experimentation with the procedure. While the National Association of Mental Health was rather negative toward the use of psychosurgery in 1974, the 1976 report of the prestigious and scientifically thorough National Commission for Protection of Human Subjects of Biomedical and Behavioral Research recognized the "potential merit" of psychosurgery, while noting the lack of adequate information as to effects at that time.[60] The position was again supported by the National Commission in 1977. The Commission also suggested a number of safeguards to prevent future misuse of psychosurgery. It recommended that a national committee be established to oversee policy regarding psychosurgery.[61] Case histories collected by the National Commission, reflect a diversity of issues.[62]

Efficacy of Psychosurgery

Over the years, psychosurgery has been used for a variety of psychiatric syndromes, but until fairly recently without any marked success. However, there are now some situations which may warrant it, at least after other treatments have failed. The conclusions of the National Commission relied substantially on the research it commissioned. This consisted of a thorough literature search, as well as independent evaluations by two separate teams, each headed by a research psychologist. They examined the results of at least four different techniques used during the period 1965 to 1975.[63]

It is not clear exactly how psychosurgery effects changes in depressive disorders, or in persistent pain cases. Lesions are usually directed at those aspects of the brain thought to control particular emotional and behavioral responses. The earliest forms of psychosurgery were aimed directly at causing an "emotional blunting" or a reduction in mood strength. More modern techniques have sought to avoid this as a side effect, however.[64] Virtually all would agree there is widespread controversy on which behaviors are controlled by which part of the brain, and even more basic, whether or not circumscribed parts of the brain even control specific responses. Also, both national research teams note that the placebo effect cannot be ruled out, and in fact many patients described their recoveries in quasi-religious terminology and became very devoted to their surgeons.[65]

In the majority of the studies dealing with psychosurgery a patient's improvement is usually based on subjective assessments done by the examiner.[66] In this situation, the examiner may feel pressured to report positive results. Moreover, patients undergoing psychosurgery often receive extensive postoperative care, which could be the crucial variable in bringing change. Without adequately controlled and empirically based research in this area, psychosurgery's actual effectiveness is impossible to assess fully.

Side Effects and Dangers of Psychosurgery

Because psychosurgery requires brain destruction there are a number of side effects and dangers associated with it. In addition to the normal dangers associated with surgery which may include infrequent cerebral hemorrhage and death, the older lobotomy procedures resulted in patients with stupor, substantial pain, convulsive seizures, incontinence and even "vegetable-like" personalities.[67] More recent surgical techniques have been developed which are meant to destroy only small specific portions of the brain. The techniques have fewer adverse side effects although substantially impaired intellectual ability, emotional blunting, and some physical symptoms are still observed.[68]

PSYCHOTROPIC MEDICATION

Psychotropic drugs are a group of medications used for the treatment and control of disorders characterized primarily by emotional, behavioral, or psychological disturbance. These medications usually act directly on the brain and functionally alter thought patterns and behavior by affecting the neurotransmission process. Included in this class are three major types of drugs: antipsychotic medications, antidepressants, and antianxiety agents.

Antipsychotic Drugs

Antipsychotic drugs are medications used to treat psychoses, especially schizophrenia.[69] Since their introduction in the 1950s, psychotropic medications have played a major role in the treatment of schizophrenia and in the reduction of the number of patients chronically hospitalized with that disorder. Today they are widely prescribed. The precise method of controlling or reducing psychotic episodes is not entirely understood. It appears, however, that they may block or reduce the reaction of dopamine in the brain.[70] While the efficacy of the psychotropic drugs is generally recognized, one review of the large number of studies which have considered the efficacy of these drugs describes the studies as being "frustratingly inconclusive."[71] Antipsychotic drugs seem to be more effective in the treatment of acute schizophrenia than in long-term, chronic cases.[72]

Side Effects. Substantial side effects are associated with the use of the antipsychotic drugs, the most common of which are related to the very dopamine-blocking activities which make them effective in reducing the psychosis.[73] These include blurred vision, anxiety, muscular rigidity, uncontrollable restlessness, spasms of the neck or spine, and tremors which resemble Parkinson's disease. They may also produce changes in emotion, motivation, and cognition, disoriented thinking, and flattening of all emotions to the point of apathy and lethargy. Reading, talking, and social interactions may become difficult or impossible. Death is an infrequent side effect of the drugs.

A serious side effect is tardive dyskinesia, an affliction characterized by involuntary movements of the head (notably the mouth or tongue) or arms or legs. These symptoms appear with varying intensity. Although tardive dyskinesia can occur after relatively short use of antipsychotic drugs, it is more commonly associated with their long-term use. In some instances it is irreversible, even if drugs are discontinued. The incidence of tardive dyskinesia has not been clearly established although the average reported incidence is 20 percent.[74] Other studies indicate that from 52 percent to nearly 60 percent of chronically hospitalized schizophrenics may suffer from it.[75]

Antidepressant Medication

Two major classes of antidepressant drugs, the tricyclic antidepressants[76] and the MAO inhibitors,[77] are frequently prescribed for the control of depression, certain phobias, and similar atypical mood disorders. More than 30 million prescriptions for antidepressant medication are written yearly.[78] One problem in using these drugs has been the relative slowness of therapeutic activation. Antidepressant medication may take as long as three to four weeks to have an effect, whereas unpleasant side effects may appear quite rapidly. Some patients find the side effects disruptive enough to discontinue treatment before improvement can occur. The considerable time lapse may also be a problem if the person is severely distressed or suicidal.

Side Effects. The side effects associated with the MAO inhibitors are of particular concern. Patients who take MAO drugs and do not avoid foods high in pyramine (aged cheese, chianti, sherry, certain beers, bananas, etc.) have been known to have marked increases in blood pressure, severe headaches, convulsions, and death in a few cases. The common availability of these foods have led many physicians to avoid prescribing the MAO drugs in favor of the tricyclic antidepressants, which do not have these risks. However, many people find that both groups of drugs produce a variety of other unpleasant side effects. The complications of both types of antidepressant medication may include dry mouth, constipation, increased heart rate, blurred vision, confusion, and agitation. Side effects may be aversive enough for some people to avoid continued treatment.

Antianxiety Medication

This class of drugs represents the most widely prescribed and used psychotropic medication in the United States. It is not uncommon for physicians to prescribe routinely from this class for patients who complain of anxiety, general unhappiness, insomnia, tension, or other difficulties they are unable to directly address.[79] Valium (Diazepam), Librium (Chlordiazepoxide), and Dalmane (Flurazepam) are the most commonly prescribed drugs from the benzodiazepine family, also known as barbituates. The use of antianxiety medication will usually result in sedation, a reduction in insomnia, and a general calm.

Side Effects. These drugs are well known to be especially susceptible to abuse and prolonged use can result in physical addiction. Because of this, drugs such as Valium and Elavil are usually prescribed on a time-limited basis and at a low dosage level. If addiction does occur, however, abrupt cessation of use will result in severe withdrawal symptoms, indistinguishable from those seen with alcohol dependence. Also, barbituates are often associated with death by overdose, especially when combined with alcohol. Pregnant women should be particularly careful, as barbituates taken during pregnancy can increase the likelihood of birth defects.[80]

Lithium

Lithium (usually lithium carbonate) has been more widely prescribed in recent years as a psychoactive agent. It has proven effective in treating patients with manic-depressive disorders. It is particularly useful in reducing the intensity of the manic phase and of severe depression. It produces relatively rapid results. If properly administered, it is relatively safe.[81]

Many seriously manic-depressive patients have benefited from the use of psychotropic drugs during the last thirty years. We now know, however, that they have serious side effects which must be considered.[82]

The potential for benefit, as well as the substantial risks, poses serious legal issues in the use of these drugs with voluntary and nonvoluntary patients alike.

LEGAL AND ETHICAL ISSUES

The use of ECT, psychosurgery, and psychotropic medication raises a number of important legal and ethical issues. The majority of litigation dealing with psychotherapy has involved these three forms of treatment. Malpractice claims, although infrequent, may arise from one of the intrusive treatments.[83] Because these therapies are physically "invasive" they are more likely to produce physical injuries which are obvious and demonstrable. Beyond malpractice claims, these treatments also raise special legal problems of consent, involuntary treatment, and the public control of therapy. These issues arise in two groups of patients: voluntary patients (those who can appreciate the nature and effects of the treatment) and "nonvoluntary" patients (those not fully free to choose or refuse treatment).

Availability

When a patient voluntarily wishes to receive ECT, psychosurgery, or psychotropic medication, and a therapist wishes to use it, should it be available to the patient? A clear example of cases in which society restricts treatment is that of prescription drugs. Only those licensed by the Food and Drug Administration (FDA) are available to patients, even with a physician's prescription. Similar federal limitations apply to the use of certain medical "devices" under the jurisdiction of the FDA. The federal government may also indirectly regulate or control certain treatments through federal funding of health care. It may, for example, refuse to pay for certain kinds of treatment or even prohibit certain kinds of treatment in facilities receiving any federal funding.[84] In addition, states may regulate or prohibit the use of certain forms of treatment. Civil liability also is a form of social control of therapy since these suits may make therapists reluctant to use it.

Federal and state governments have, within limits, the authority to exercise considerable control over the availability of the invasive forms of psychotherapy. Among the limits on state regulation is the constitutional right of privacy, which may curb the government's ability to prevent patients from obtaining some forms of therapy.[85] Efforts to severely restrict or prohibit ECT have been held to violate individual rights.[86]

The argument for personal freedom of choice, even when that choice is foolish or wrong, is a strong one. The case for some state intervention in health decisions is that these decisions are complex and technically beyond the competence of most people, patients are particularly subject to fraud where their health is concerned, and governments are increasingly called upon to finance a portion of health care costs. The strongest case can be made for governmental intervention to prevent fraud, including action aimed at assuring that patients receive accurate information regarding medical treatment. Preventing the use of therapies likely to be harmful may be based on the theory that no rational person would select such therapy, and therefore it is not limiting rational choice. Nevertheless, the activity is, in a real sense, paternalistic and does interfere with free choice.

The most extensive federal control of psychotherapy involves drugs. Federal law prohibits the introduction into interstate commerce of drugs without the approval of the Food and Drug Administration. It also requires proper labeling of the drug. Those which are particularly dangerous, or contain narcotics, require a physician's prescription before they are dispensed to patients. The FDA will not license any drug unless it has been demonstrated to be safe and effective. "Effective" means that the drug produces the results claimed for it; "safe" means that the expected therapeutic gain justifies the risk entailed by its use.[87] Once a drug is licensed by the FDA, however, it is available and may be prescribed by physicians for conditions other than that for which it was licensed.

As a result, not all drugs a physician might wish to prescribe are available, and this represents an interference with medical practice and the freedom of patients. The purpose of the law is to protect patients from fraudulent or dangerous medications. The balance between personal autonomy and regulation in the United States has been found to be clearly on the side of regulation, as it relates to medication.

ECT is subject to only limited direct regulation.[88] ECT generally must be ordered by a physician, and the mechanism used to produce the convulsion is subject to safety regulation. The effort in one community to ban ECT renews the debate regarding the availability of this treatment. At the heart of the debate is the issue of autonomy and the risks and benefits of ECT.[89] Even those willing to substantially limit the right of therapists and patients to select ECT would not do so if the benefits of the treatment exceeded the risk.

Costs will vary from person to person, and it is undoubtedly beneficial to some patients. The risks and benefits of ECT suggest it should be available for voluntary use by some patients. Research also suggests that the use of the technique for many conditions should be considered nonstandard or experimental.[90] The risks and limited efficacy of the treatment for many conditions underscore the importance of full informed consent before ECT is used.

Psychosurgery is not subject to the same direct federal control as is psychotropic medication. Nevertheless, the rate of psychosurgery has decreased markedly in the last two decades. The federal commission reviewing the issue suggested that psychosurgery be studied as an experimental technique under carefully controlled conditions.[91] Reflecting this view, Ayub Ommaya, Chief of the Surgical Neurology Branch of the National Institute of Neurological and Communicative

Disorders and Strokes, emphasized that regardless of the diagnosis, psychosurgery must always be viewed as a clinical procedure of last resort, experimental in nature, and one where the practitioner has the duty to collect data to provide information about the technique.[92] Because psychosurgery is experimental and is essentially irreversible, a strong argument can be made that it should not be widely available as a treatment technique. It should be subject to the rigorous review which accompanies other serious forms of experimental treatment, including drugs. At a minimum the precautions should include full animal testing (to the extent that could provide relevant information), particular attention to extensive and voluntary informed consent, the reasonable expectation that the benefits will exceed the risks of the experiment, and every effort to reduce the risks of the procedure.

Removing the choice to use one form of treatment or another is an interference with rights that we believe can be justified only in unusual circumstances. However, state intervention is warranted to ensure adequate informed consent. This interference may promote, rather than restrict, patient autonomy.

Informed Consent

The use of ECT, psychosurgery, and psychotropic medication raises particular problems of informed consent. The primary purpose of informed consent is to permit patients to make important treatment decisions for themselves. It is a way of protecting individual autonomy. Among the most important decisions facing an individual may be those that affect, perhaps irreversibly, the way they think. All psychotherapy, in some way, is designed to change the way a patient feels or thinks.[93] The intrusive therapies differ because they can be administered without the cooperation or participation of the patient and because they involve physical intrusion. The case for informed consent is particularly compelling where the treatment will make substantial, permanent changes in thought processes. In this sense psychosurgery may be seen as somewhat different than ECT and psychotropic drugs, as it is more likely irreversible than the other treatments.

Patients' decisions may differ from the recommendations of therapists for a number of reasons. A patient may have beliefs or value systems different than the therapist—a patient may, for example, reject some forms of therapy for religious reasons. A therapist's decision to recommend a particular form of therapy may be based on a number of factors which are not important to the patient; for example ECT may be particularly attractive because of ease of administration, limited personnel time involved, or the possibility of direct payment through health insurance. The cost-effectiveness of the procedure may not be so important to the patient as it is to the therapist. In addition the patient may have certain fears or hopes which may not be as fully considered by a therapist as by the patient himself. For example, a patient with a particular fear of losing memory might be reluctant to undergo repeated ECT treatments.

The goal of permitting patients to determine what they want done to and with their own bodies and minds assumes, of course, that patients are mentally competent to make decisions and that they are given enough adequate information. Despite its importance, informed consent is often difficult to obtain because the patients for whom the treatment would be appropriate are disoriented.[94] This does not suggest that informed consent is futile and may therefore be ignored, but rather that special efforts (discussed below) should be made to ensure that it is effectively and voluntarily given before the treatment is begun.

The fundamental elements of informed consent are that the patient be told what treatment is proposed, the important benefits and risks of the treatment, alternative forms of treatment, and the consequences of no treatment.[95] Informed consent need not be obtained when a real emergency exists and there is no opportunity to obtain consent (the emergency exception),[96] or when the process of obtaining consent is likely to have a very serious, adverse effect on the patient (the "therapeutic privilege"—a misleading label at best).[97] When a patient is legally incompetent, substituted consent may be given by a guardian or next of kin. These narrow exceptions are justified only infrequently. Psychiatrists giving these therapies to competent patients without consent or withholding critical information about them (particularly ECT and psychosurgery) do so at some peril of civil liability. The therapist who uses an exception to informed consent should be prepared to demonstrate that the exception was fully legitimate and legally justified.

Liability risk for the failure of informed consent, while real, is probably small. Some injury must occur to the patient during the treatment and it generally has to appear that a reasonable person "in the patient's position" would have refused the treatment (casual relationship).[98]

The principles of informed consent suggest that a patient about to receive ECT for depression should be told about the general nature of the procedure, the potential advantages which can reasonably be expected (a rapid reduction of depression), and the risks (short-term confusion, possible damage to certain mental functions such as memory loss especially after a number of treatments, and a very small chance of serious physical injury or death).[99] Alternative treatments such as antidepressant drugs or psychotherapy should also be discussed, as should the risks of no treatment at all (the potential for worsening depression and suicide). If ECT is being used for conditions other than severe depression, a strong case can be made for the patient also being told that ECT is not generally accepted as a standard treatment (e.g., for schizophrenia) or is experimental (e.g., for mania).

The same general kinds of information should be supplied to patients receiving psychotropic medication or psychosurgery. In the case of psychosurgery patients should be told of the experimental nature of the procedure. Patients are supposed to receive information about prescription drugs from their physicians, and the failure to provide information about drugs may subject a physician to civil liability.[100]

In practice, determining what information should be given to a patient may be difficult. As a general rule the facts that are important in reaching a decision should be revealed. The more likely an event, or serious a consequence of a risk, the more it should be disclosed. It is important that the information be given in language the patient can understand and appreciate.

The ideal of informed consent is often difficult to achieve when ECT, psychosurgery, or psychotropic medication is recommended because patients' mental conditions may make it difficult for them to receive, understand, and consider the information required to make decisions.[101] The patient may be impaired but not so incompetent as to be completely unable to participate in the decision. One might conclude that these impaired patients should not participate in decisions and should be treated as though they were incompetent, or that they should be given the same information that any other patient would receive, even if they cannot understand the information or deal with it. (In general, the law has emphasized that the information be given by the physician rather than that information be understood by the patient.)[102] Neither approach is likely to permit the patient to participate in deciding what treatment should be accepted. The better approach is to tailor the information given and the consent processes to the condition of the patient. In that way autonomy can be as fully protected as possible. For example, special efforts might be made to discuss and obtain consent to the proposed treatment during the patient's lucid intervals. The information may also be carefully couched in language the patient is most likely to understand, or the information may be repeated several times over the course of several visits.

One way to protect autonomy even when a patient is incompetent is to recognize a "treatment will," somewhat like a "living will." Living wills are documents in which patients describe the kind of medical treatment which they wish to have (or not have) if ever unconscious or mentally incompetent. The "treatment will" document could profitably be used to describe the kinds of psychotherapy or treatment one is willing to consent to if mentally incompetent. The "treatment will" could thus reduce the uncertainty of how to treat an incompetent patient, by allowing the patient maximum control.[103]

Nonvoluntary Patients

Among the most difficult issues involving the invasive treatments is their use among those patients not able to give consent themselves (incompetents), those given treatment against their wishes, and those who cannot give consent with relative freedom from coercion. In these cases someone other than the patient makes the decisions. These situations raise the questions of what standards should be employed, by whom, and under what circumstances. (These issues are more fully discussed in chapters 18 and 19.)

When a person is unable to make decisions, a guardian or next of kin is legally empowered to do so. In practice, of course, it is sometimes difficult to determine who is incapable of making decisions.

Clearly, however, the mere refusal of proposed treatment, even if it would ordinarily be accepted by the overwhelming majority of people, does not make a patient incompetent.

It is the guardian's obligation to make decisions which are in the ward's "best interest." Best interest may be difficult to define, because it should be considered from the point of view of the patient. In the case of a patient with lifelong religious beliefs against all invasive medical treatment, for example, psychosurgery is probably not in the patient's best interest and the guardian should not agree to it. In decisions about ECT, psychosurgery, and psychotropic medication, a form of "substituted judgment" (making treatment decisions as the ward would probably have made them if competent) is likely to lead to protecting what the ward would see as his own best interests. When it is impossible to base a decision on what the ward would have decided (e.g., for infants) decisions should ordinarily tend toward what most competent patients do when faced with the same decisions.

Special care must be exercised, of course, in consenting to experimental treatment because of concern that the ward not become an involuntary human guinea pig. These principles suggest that, where there is no indication that an incompetent patient would have decided otherwise, it is appropriate for a guardian to consent to psychotropic medication when the chance that it will improve the ward's condition is greater than the risks of the treatment and where the treatment is standard medical practice. That is, where the treatment has been demonstrated to be effective for the patient's condition. Consent to psychosurgery, which may be experimental, should be considered only in the most extraordinary circumstances and only after meeting the standards proposed by the National Commission for the Protection of Human Subjects of Biomedical and Behavioral Research.

Minors are generally considered to be incompetent and their parents are authorized to make decisions for them. Consent to invasive treatments for minors, particularly late adolescents, is troubling because these patients often have developed an independent sense of values and beliefs which may be different from those of their parents.[104] Permitting parents to consent to invasive treatment for these minors is inconsistent with the goals of informed consent, and at present the law in many jurisdictions appears to be unrealistic in failing to recognize the competence and independent autonomy interests of older minors.[105] The possibility of permanent injury from side effects associated with invasive therapies should increase the concern regarding their use.

In some instances these therapies may be used without consent on adults who are technically legally competent. This involuntary treatment may be imposed to prevent dangerous patients from harming themselves or others, or because of the belief that the patient really is not competent to make the decision.[106] It may also be imposed because of a strong feeling of paternalism, which is not uncommon.[107] One study has indicated that psychiatrists may agree to override the patient's right to refuse treatment as often as 78 percent of the time, depending on the nature and severity of the illness.[108] In Chapters 18 and 19 we argue that this form of paternalism, or an approach which assumes that nearly all mental patients are incompetent, is an inappropriate invasion of privacy.

Informed consent should be free of undue coercion (realistically, some coercion is often involved in obtaining consent). The therapist who threatens to refuse to treat patients if they reject ECT, for example, may be applying pressure to the point of coercion. The threat of losing a therapist, and the difficulty for a depressed patient of finding another, may amount to duress for that patient. Even if such threats are legal (assuming there is no technical abandonment of the patient), such an approach does raise ethical questions. Professionals certainly have the right not to provide treatment they consider unethical or immoral, but therapists have a special obligation to avoid using their position of trust and dependence to coerce consent.

The case of the incarcerated patient presents special problems of consent and coercion.[109] When someone believes that his only hope of freedom depends upon consenting to psychosurgery, ECT, or other invasive form of therapy, his agreement may be less than voluntary. This situation and the case which raised it, *Kaimowitz v. Department of Mental Health*,[110] have received more attention than the amount of psychosurgery involving the incarcerated would seem to justify.[111] In *Kaimowitz*, Louis Smith, committed to an institution as a criminal sexual psychopath, consented to psychosurgery. He was accepted as a subject for this only after he met a number of screening criteria. A review committee of physicians approved the surgery and a second review committee, which included a law professor, clergyman, and layperson, ensured the validity of the informed consent which was signed by Smith. Before the surgery took place Smith was released from custody. He rescinded his consent to the surgery but the Michigan court agreed to decide whether his original consent had been proper. It ruled that consent had not been completely valid in part because the institution was an inherently coercive atmosphere. The surgery would have interfered with fundamental rights, such as the right of privacy and the right to think implied by the First Amendment. The National Commission for the Protection of Human Subjects disagreed with the *Kaimowitz* court, suggesting that psychosurgery is an experimental procedure, and could be used under carefully controlled conditions on prisoners who request it.

In reality, the *Kaimowitz* court seemed particularly concerned that the psychosurgery suggested was experimental and high-risk. Had the proposed surgery been accepted practice, an involuntary patient probably could have consented to it.[112] The experimental nature of the surgery was critical to the *Kaimowitz* decision. Because of the "inherently coercive nature" of prison life, special protections have been proposed by the federal government for the use of prisoners as human subjects.[113] It is significant, however, that Smith, although he had given consent to psychosurgery in a manner approved by a review committee, withdrew his consent upon release. Inevitably, institutionalized people who believe, perhaps incorrectly, that treatment such as psychosurgery is the only way to gain release from prison will be driven toward that therapy. Whether that drive is so strong as to make legitimate informed consent impossible is the issue. At least the consent process in such a situation should be unusually thorough and subject to careful review.

The alternative to permitting prisoners to consent to treatment (even experimental therapies) may be to make the treatment unavailable to them. At least for therapies to which competent patients outside institutions consent, this seems unreasonably restrictive of the rights of institutionalized people to select treatment. A major objection to consent to this experimental treatment would be reduced by removing the suggestion, which at any rate is seldom true, that only through the acceptance of one form of treatment will the person be fit to be released.

Stigma

There is, realistically, a substantial stigma associated with having undergone the invasive therapies, particularly ECT and psychosurgery. This stigma may seriously affect the employment, professional opportunities, social standing, and personal life of the patient. The stigma attached to these procedures seems to exceed that of mental illness or hospitalization. In 1972, the fact that Vice Presidential candidate Thomas Eagleton had received shock therapy was seen as an indication of serious instability.

This stigma should be taken into account when decisions regarding therapy are made. Certainly it should be a factor in any nonvoluntary treatment. A strong argument can also be made for including stigma as a disclosed risk of therapy. The only legitimate reason for not including it is that most patients are probably aware of it. Patients with impaired capacity may have to be reminded of it. For some patients the stigma of ECT or psychosurgery may not be of great significance, for others, however, it may be critical.

Professional Considerations

Unlike most other psychotherapy, ECT, psychosurgery, and psychotropic medication may be administered by only one kind of therapist: psychiatrists (physicians). This may play at least a minor role in the way these therapies are viewed by professionals. Psychiatrists may tend to approve or promote these forms of therapy; other therapists may tend to disapprove of them. The debate over these forms of therapy, which should continue, might profitably include a recognition of this professional perspective.[114]

SUMMARY

The controversial treatments we have been discussing are intrusive in the sense that they involve a physical entry or intrusion into the body. ECT and psychotropic medications are commonly used, but psychosurgery must currently be considered experimental.

ECT has been used successfully with depressed patients, but the value of its use with other mental patients, notably schizophrenics, is uncertain. It has the advantage of working quickly and may help avoid the threat of imminent suicide by severely depressed patients. The exact process which ECT initiates in the body remains undefined.

A variety of side effects have been noted. Brain damage may result and there is wide agreement that it causes significant cognitive confusion and memory loss regarding events which occurred immediately before and after the ECT. Repeated use of ECT may cause a cumulative permanent damage to these functions.

The use of psychosurgery in the United States has been reduced in recent years and it is now widely considered experimental. It is thought to be effective with some patients suffering from depression, extreme aggressive tendencies, phobias, and some neuroses. A variety of serious side effects were associated with lobotomies. Newer, more localized surgery has resulted in fewer side effects although reduced intellectual capability and emotional blunting are still noted.

Psychotropic medications have proven beneficial to many patients. Antipsychotic drugs may reduce the symptoms of some psychoses. Antidepressant drugs are frequently prescribed for control of depression and other mood disorders. Antianxiety drugs are very widely prescribed for anxiety and adjustment disorders. Side effects are associated with their use, however.

Some have suggested that the invasive forms of therapy may do more harm than good to many patients and that the treatments should not be available. The availability of psychotropic medication is controlled by the Food and Drug Administration and is available only if it can be proven to be safe and effective. The use of ECT has been regulated in many areas and one community attempted to prohibit it. To the extent that these treatments show promise of success in some patients it is difficult to argue that they should be completely unavailable. On the other hand, a strong argument can be made that to ensure that patients are not misled about a treatment, they should elect to undergo the treatment only after a thorough and full understanding of the consequences of that decision.

The concept of informed consent is meant to ensure that patients may exercise autonomy by receiving medical information which is essential in deciding whether to accept treatment. Because of the substantial consequences associated with the invasive therapies, and the disagreement over their efficacy, it is particularly important that patients have a thorough understanding of these treatments before they consent to them. Information patients receive should include the benefits and risks associated with it, alternative forms of treatment and the consequences of none at all.

Many candidates for these treatments suffer from serious mental conditions likely to interfere with their ability to make fully informed decisions. Therefore, therapists should be careful to tailor the informed consent process to ensure that the goals of informed consent are met. Dealing with a patient during times of lucidity, repeating information concerning proposed treatment to patients over a period of several visits, and couching the information in terms the patients are likely to understand will help to ensure that patients give informed consent.

In some instances, treatment may be suggested for patients who have not given informed consent. Legally incompetent patients, for example, cannot give it. A guardian or next of kin may consent for these patients, but it should be the obligation of the guardian to do what is in the best interest of the patient. We argue that this treatment should follow what the patient would have wanted if that can be determined. A mental-health "living will" may be useful in such circumstances. When a determination cannot reasonably be made concerning what the patient himself would want, a guardian probably should consent to treatment which is consistent with what most patients similarly situated commonly do.

Involuntary patients are frequently candidates for one of the intrusive therapies. Difficult problems arise when therapists or hospital officials wish to give a patient one of the invasive therapies over his objection. We argue that when a truly competent patient refuses treatment, it is appropriate to force treatment only when a patient is a threat to himself or others.

A particularly difficult question is judging when someone is incompetent to make a treatment decision. The fact that a patient refuses treatment is, of course, in and of itself insufficient to justify forced treatment. Patients who can understand the choices available and the nature and consequences of the decisions, and are able to express a choice of treatments, should probably be considered competent to make the decision.

Those who would completely prohibit the use of invasive therapies and those who would rather freely give them to patients without full and adequate informed consent both express a well-meaning paternalism which suggests that patients really are not able to make these decisions for themselves. Indeed in many instances it may be difficult for patients to do so. The "autonomy" approach suggests that it is highly desirable, and possible, for most patients to make these decisions. As a result, some patients will make decisions which others believe foolish. The goal of autonomy is to develop ways of ensuring that adequate informed consent processes are developed and used with patients who have some impairment. Very little effort appears to have been made to develop such procedures. As research improves the invasive treatments, other research is needed which will ensure that these therapies can be used to protect the well being of patients as the patients themselves see their own interests.

NOTES

1. A number of states have placed substantial limits on the use of some invasive therapies, at least without the consent of the patient. California and Massachusetts are commonly cited as examples.

2. The proposition which was on the November 1982 ballot in Berkeley, California was opposed by many therapists and was approved by the voters. The proposition made the use of shock treatments on voluntary or involuntary patients a misdemeanor. The law was held unconstitutional by a state court. Northern California Psychiatric Society v. Berkeley, No. 556 778-3 (Cal. Super. Ct. Sep. 14, 1983), *aff'd*, 178 Cal. App. 3d 90, 223 Cal. Rptr. 609 (1st Dist. 1986).

3. Gonzales, Psychosurgery: Waiting to Make a Comeback?, 21 *J.A.M.A.* 2245 (1980).

4. Harper & Wiens, ECT and Memory, 161 *J. Nervous & Mental Diseases* 245–254 (1975).

5. Morrissey, Steadman & Burton, A Profile of ECT Recipients in New York State During 1972 and 1977, 138 *Am. J. Psychiatry* 618 (1981).

6. Though convulsions have been considered "disease" throughout the history of medicine, they were also recognized very early as a change agent. Induction of convulsion is considered by some to be the oldest surviving somatic treatment in Western psychiatry. In 1781, W. Oliver, the Physician Extraordinary to George III of England, inadvertently overdosed a patient with camphor, causing a convulsion, and in that doctor's opinion, improvement. A few isolated physicians followed his example, but it was not until the 1930s that these procedures began to be refined and applied with any consistency.

In Hungary in the 1930s, Ladislaus von Meduna observed that epileptics seldom manifested schizophrenia, hence theorized that if one could induce convulsions in schizophrenics, the schizophrenia would remit. Unfortunately, over time it has become clear that von Meduna was not correct. Von Meduna used metrazol, a derivative of camphor, to induce the convulsions, while in Austria Manfred Sakel used insulin shock. Other poison gases, such as fluorothyl (Indoklon) have also been employed, but have dropped out of use, primarily because of problems of control in their administration.

7. The history of ECT is interesting. While his contemporaries were working with pharmacological agents, Ugo Cerletti in Rome devised a means of inducing convulsions with electric shock.

> Some weeks later, the Police commissioner of Rome sent Cerletti such a suitable subject, a vagrant found wandering about the city's railroad station. "This subject was chosen for the first experiment of induced electric convulsions in man. Two large electrodes were applied to the frontoparietal regions, and I decided to start cautiously with a low-intensity current of 80 volts for 0.2 seconds. As soon as the current was introduced, the patient reacted with a jolt, and his body muscles stiffened; then he fell back on the bed without loss of consciousness. He started to sing abruptly at the top of his voice, then he quieted down.

> "Naturally we who were conducting the experiment were under great emotional strain, and felt that we had already taken quite a risk. Nevertheless, it was quite evident to all of us that we had been using too low a voltage. It was proposed that we should allow the patient to have some rest, and repeat the experiment the next day. All at once, the patient, who evidently had been following our conversation, said clearly and solemnly, without his usual gibberish: 'Not another one! It's deadly!'

> "I confess that such explicit admonition under such circumstances, and so emphatic and commanding coming from a person whose enigmatic jargon had until then been very difficult to understand, shook my determination to carry on with the experiment. But it was just this fear of yielding to a superstitious notion that caused me to make up my mind. The electrodes were applied again, and a 110 volt discharge was applied for 0.2 seconds."

> Although he never tells us what became of that historic first subject, Cerletti was confident enough to invent even more exotic experiments. In one test, he injected psychiatric patients with homogenized suspensions of cells from the brains of pigs that had been repeatedly shocked.

Quoted in Friedberg, Let's Stop Blasting the Brain, 9 *Psychology Today* 18 (Aug. 1975).

8. J. Friedberg, *Shock Treatment Is Not Good for Your Brain* (1976).

9. Blachly, Attitudes, Data, and Technological Promise of ECT, 14 *Psychiatric Opinion* 9 (1977); National Institute of Mental Health, *Electro-Convulsive Therapy: Consensus Development Conference* (1985).

10. Essman finds that within 6 to 10 seconds after ECT there is a reduction in cerebral glucose levels, in 30 seconds glycogen levels are decreased, and by 50 seconds there is a threefold increase in the lactate level. There are also indications of reduction of RNA in areas of the central nervous system and a decrease in overall protein synthesis. There is evidence of increased blood brain barrier permeability to norepinephrine (a neurotransmitter), and since this factor has been implicated in some theories of depression, this could explain the positive effects of ECT on that disorder. Essman, Neurochemical Changes in ECS and ECT, 4 *Seminars in Psychiatry* 67 (1972); Friedberg, ECT as Neurologic Injury, 14 *Psychiatric Opinion* 16

(1977). See J. Maxmen, *The New Psychiatry* (1985); NIMH Report, *supra* note 10.

11. Riddick & Meyer, The Efficiency of Automated Relaxation Training With Response Contingent Feedback, 4 *Behav. Therapy* 331 (1973).

12. Lambourn & Gill, A Controlled Comparison of Simulated and Real ECT, 133 *Brit. J. Psychiatry* 514 (1978). See J. Friedberg, *supra*, note 8.

13. "After a host of such reports in the early 1940s, Riese added two more human autopsy studies to the growing list and commented: 'In all observations of sudden death after electric shock reported so far, petechial hemorrhages, cellular changes and some glial proliferation stand out prominently, as an almost constant whole.'

"Pathologists have been especially interested in cases which discriminate between the direct effect of electricity and the mechanical and hypoxic effects of convulsive motor activity. Several of the earliest reports included cases where oxygen and curare had been administered. Then, in 1953, came a case which spoke for itself. Larsen reported a 45-year-old man who had been given four electroshocks in the course of five days. The ECT did not induce any convulsions and the subject died of pneumonia 36 hours after the fourth electroshock. When the brain was removed, fresh subarachnoid hemorrhage was found in the upper part of the left motor region—'at the site where an electrode had been applied.'

"By 1957, Impastato had summarized 214 electroshock fatalities, adding 40 more of his own. Brain damage was the direct and leading cause of death in victims under 40 years of age.

"The manifestation of such damages to the temporal lobes and other parts of the brain is amnesia. The memory loss is predominantly, though not entirely, retrograde. It is densest for the period during and prior to the shocks and may stretch back for years. It generally follows Ribot's Law for all pathologic amnesias: the new dies before the old, the exact opposite of normal forgetting." Friedberg, *supra*, note 10 at 17.

14. Quoted in Friedberg, *supra*, note 7 at 18.

15. Arnot, Observations on the Effects of Electric Convulsive Treatment in Man—Psychological, 36 *Diseases Nervous System* 499 (1975); Avery & Winokur, Mortality in Depressed Patients Treated with Electroconvulsive Therapy and Anti-depressants, 33 *Archives Gen. Psychiatry* 1029 (1976); Blachly, Attitudes, Data, and Technological Promise of ECT, 14 *Psychiatric Opinion* (1977).

16. Squire & Chase, Memory Functions Six to Nine Months After Electroconvulsive Therapy, 32 *Archives Gen. Psychiatry* 1557 (1975).

17. Squire, Slater & Miller, Retrograde Amnesia and Bilateral Electroconvulsive Therapy: Long-Term Follow-Up, 38 *Archives Gen. Psychiatry* 89 (1981). See generally Janis, Psychologic Effects of Electric Convulsive Treatments: Part 1: Post-Treatment Amnesias, 3 *J. Nervous & Mental Disease* 359 (1950).

18. Goldman, Gomer & Templer, Long-Term Effects of Electroconvul-

sive Therapy Upon Memory and Perceptual-Motor Performance, 28 *J. Clinical Psychology* 32 (1972).

19. "The significantly greater error scores obtained by the ECT's on both the Bender-Gestalt and the Benton after a relatively long time period since the last course of treatment suggest that ECT causes irreversible brain damage. Furthermore, it seems plausible that the cognitive impairment results from the cumulative damaging effect of each treatment, particularly in view of the significant correlations between number of ECT and both Benton number correct and error scores. Such ECT-produced structural changes would be consistent with the common clinical observation of progressive mental deterioration of epileptics, especially if untreated." *Id.* at 33.

20. J. Friedberg, *supra,* note 8.

21. Squire & Chase, Memory Functions Six to Nine Months After Electroconvulsive Therapy, 32 *Archives Gen. Psychiatry* 1557 (1975); Squire & Zouzounis, ECT and Memory: Brief Pulse Versus Sine Wave, 143 *Am. J. Psychiatry* 596 (1986) (use of brief pulse may reduce memory loss).

22. Friedberg, ECT as Neurologic Injury, 14 *Psychiatric Opinion* 16 (1977).

23. Memory Drug Piracetam Now Being Researched in U.S., 2 *Brain/ Mind Bull.* 3 (1977).

24. Cohen & Squire, Retrograde Amnesia and Remote Memory Impairment, 19 *Neuropsychologia* 337 (1981); NIMH Report, *supra,* note 9.

25. Ruff, A Case Report of Cognitive Impairment and Movement Disorder Associated with ECT, 137 *Am. J. Psychiatry* 1615 (1980).

26. Weiner, Whanger, Erivin & Wilson, Prolonged Confusional State and EEG Seizure Activity Following Concurrent ECT and Lithium Use, 137 *Am. J. Psychiatry* 1452 (1980); Weiner, Volow, Gianturco & Cavenar, Seizures Terminable and Interminable with ECT, 137 *Am. J. Psychiatry* 1416 (1980).

27. Abrams, What's New in Convulsive Therapy, in *New Dimensions in Psychiatry* 85–98 (S. Arieti and G. Chrzanowski eds., 1975); Annett, Effects of Right and Left Unilateral ECT on Naming and Visual Discrimination in Relation to Handedness, 124 *Brit. J. Psychiatry* 260 (1974). See J. Maxmen, *supra,* note 10.

28. Miller, Small, Milstein, Malloy & Stout, Electrode Placement and Cognitive Change with ECT: Male and Female Response, 138 *Am. J. Psychiatry* 384 (1981).

29. Annett, Effects of Right and Left Unilateral ECT on Naming and Visual Discrimination in Relation to Handedness 124 *Brit. J. Psychiatry* 260 (1974).

30. Blachly, *supra,* note 9. See J. Maxmen, *supra,* note 10.

31. Miller et al., note 28, *supra.*

32. *Id.*

33. Kendell, The Present Status of Electroconvulsive Therapy, 139 *Brit. J. Psychiatry* 265 (1981).

34. J. Beatty, *Biological Basis of Behavior* (1987); R. Ornstein, *The Psychology of Consciousness* (1977).

35. d'Elia, Rojotma & Widepalm, Comparison of Unilateral Dominant

and Ono-Dominant ECT on Verbal and Non-Verbal Memory, 53 *Acta Psychiatrica Scandinavica* 85 (1976).

36. Morrissey, Steadman & Burton, A Profile of ECT Recipients in New York State During 1972 and 1977, 138 *Am. J. Psychiatry* 618 (1981); Weiner & Power, The Use of ECT Within the Veterans Administration Hospital System, 21 *Comprehensive Psychiatry* 22 (1980).

37. May, Schizophrenia, A Follow-Up Study of Results of Treatment: Hospital Stay Over Two to Five Years, 33 *Archives Gen. Psychiatry* 481 (1933).

38. Arnot, Observations on the Effects of Electric Convulsive Treatment in Man—Psychological, 36 *Diseases Nervous System* 499 (1975); Blachly, Attitudes, Data, and Technological Promise of ECT, 14 *Psychiatric Opinion* 9 (1977).

39. For a thorough review of the use, benefits and risks of ECT see American Psychiatric Association, *Task Force Report: Electroconvulsive Therapy* (1978). A National Institutes of Health advisory panel recommended that ECT be used only with informed consent and with care to avoid side effects. The panel found that ECT is an acceptable form of treatment when used cautiously. National Institute of Mental Health, *Electro-Convulsive Therapy: Consensus Development Conference* (1985).

40. Salzman, The Use of ECT in the Treatment of Schizophrenia, 137 *Am. J. Psychiatry* 1032, 1041 (1980).

41. J. Maxmen, *supra*, note 10; Kendell, The Present Status of Electroconvulsive Therapy, 139 *Brit. J. Psychiatry* 265 (1981); Scovern & Kilman, Status of Electroconvulsive Therapy: Review of the Outcome Literature, 87 *Psychological Bull.* 260 (1980).

42. Weiner & Power, *supra*, note 36.

43. Morrissey, Steadman & Burton, A Profile of ECT Recipients in New York State During 1972 and 1977, 138 *Am. J. Psychiatry* 618 (1981).

44. Weiner & Power, *supra*, note 36.

45. Blachly, *supra*, note 9; Perry & Tsung, Treatment of Unipolar Depression Following Electroconvulsive Therapy: Relapse Rate Comparisons Between Lithium and Tricyclic Therapies Following ECT, 1 *J. Affective Disorders* 123 (1979).

46. Scovern & Kilman, Status of Electroconvulsive Therapy: Review of the Outcome Literature, 87 *Psychological Bull.* 260 (1980).

47. *Id.*

48. *Id.*

49. Coopen, Abou-Saleh, Millin, Bailey, Metcalfe, Burns & Arnold, Lithium Continuation Therapy Following Electroconvulsive Therapy, 139 *Brit. 1 J. Psychiatry* 284 (1981); Perry & Tsung, Electroconvulsive Therapy: Relapse Rate Comparisons Between Lithium and Tricyclic Therapies Following ECT, *J. Affective Disorders* 123 (1979); Salzman, The Use of ECT in the Treatment of Schizophrenia, 137 *Am. J. Psychiatry* 1032 (1980).

50. See note 49, *supra*; J. Maxmen, *supra*, note 10.

51. B. Martin, *Abnormal Psychology* (1977); Blaney, Contemporary The-

ories of Depression: Critique and Comparison, 86 *J. Abnormal Psychology* 203 (1977).

52. See Blaney, *supra,* note 51.

53. McCabe, ECT in the Treatment of Mania: A Controlled Study, 133 *Am. J. Psychiatry* 688 (1977); NIMH, Report, *supra,* note 39.

54. Mandel, Electroconvulsive Therapy for Chronic Pain Associated With Depression, 132 *Am. J. Psychiatry* 632 (1975).

55. Gonzalez, Psychosurgery: Waiting to Make a Comeback?, 244 *J.A.M.A.* 2245 (1980).

56. *Id.* See J. Maxmen, *supra,* note 10.

57. Psychosurgery was practiced even by the Inca Indians of Peru who "trephined" skulls. They would bore small holes in the skulls, apparently to release the evil spirits harbored within. Yet, some scholars suggest they actually were intending to work within an anatomical paradigm, and the evil spirits theory is simply cultural condescension. An excellent review of psychosurgery is E. Valenstein, *Great and Desperate Cures: The Rise and Decline of Psychosurgery and Other Radical Treatments for Mental Illness* (1986).

58. Flor-Henry, Psychiatric Surgery—1935–1973: Evolution and Current Perspectives, 20 *Canadian Psychiatric A. J.* 157 (1975). Of 39 patients who had undergone such an operation, a decrease in emotional excitability and aggressivity was apparent in 85 percent. Severely retarded patients did not do as well. Narabayashi used a stereotactic technique, in which the amygdaloid nuclei were destroyed with oil and wax. Similarly, lesions of the cingulate (portion of the brain) tended to reduce psychic and/or motoric hyperactivity, while temporal lobe surgery was employed to ease or reduce epileptic seizures. See Comment, Psychosurgery and the Involuntarily Confined, 24 *Vill. L. Rev.* 949 (1979).

59. E. Hitchcock, L. Laitinen & K. Vaernet, *Psychosurgery* (1972). PST focuses ultrasonic irradiation on part of the prefrontal white matter through the intact dura. The sonic beam in PST varies in size, but is generally about 20mm in diameter. It is aimed through the prefrontal areas with the assistance of a relatively simple stereotactic device developed specifically for this purpose. Selective therapeutic lesions are produced, but the blood supply is left intact and fiber tracts are undisturbed. See A. J. O'Callaghan and D. Carroll eds., *Psychosurgery: A Scientific Analysis* (1983).

60. National Commission for Protection of Human Subjects of Biomedical and Behavioral Research, *Report* (1976). See generally Plamondon, Psychosurgery: The Rights of Patients, 23 *Loy. L. Rev.* 1007 (1977).

61. Gonzalez, Psychosurgery: Waiting to Make a Comeback?, 244 *J.A.M.A.* 2245 (1980).

62. Trotter, Federal Commission OK's Psychosurgery, 7 *APA Monitor* 4 (1976), describes the following examples.

L.M. is an obese, 32-year-old unmarried and unemployed woman, inarticulate to the point of near muteness, with a history of over ten years of intermittent hospitalizations for what has been described as both "chronic schizophrenia" and "depression." When she was in her early 20s, L.M. began to have episodes of destructive rage and irrational speech and became unable to care for herself. She has had three psychosurgical operations (cingulotomies) without apparent success. Her parents indicate some moderate improvement after the first operation (their daughter talked to them for the first time in years), but it was short lived. There was no improvement after either of the subsequent operations. The patient is profoundly hypokinetic, cannot give any history, cannot be tested except with operant methods. She has had an undetermined number of shock treatments and is on many different drugs.

T.M. is a married woman of 37, also overweight (220 lbs.), with a similar diagnostic history of schizophrenia and depressive hallucinations. . . . She had her first psychosurgery (also a cingulotomy) at age 30 because of suicidal tendencies and reportedly felt tremendous relief. She was still suspicious, but no longer felt "as if encased in a plastic cube." . . . She and her husband made a trip West to seek the help of a neurosurgeon in California, from whom she received a "multiple target stereotaxic procedure" (bilateral lesions in the cingulum, amygdala and substantial innominata). This was in January 1975. Immediately afterwards, the patient reported that she was no longer suspicious, but still felt fearful. She went back to her psychiatrist in the East, who suggested one more cingulotomy. She received this third psychosurgical operation the following August, after which, except for one six-week regression, she reports being entirely well.

Previously, this patient had received 27 ECTs and 60 insulin coma treatments. Asked for her views of psychosurgery and whether she would recommend it to others, she says emphatically, "I would tell them to snap it up as quick as they could. It's a godsend, it is, I cannot say enough about them [the operations]. I don't know why they work or how they work, but they are a true godsend. They gave me back my life."

63. Trotter, Federal Commission OK's Psychosurgery 7 APA Monitor 4 (1976). Teuber and his colleagues examined 34 patients all who had undergone cingulotomy (removal of a small portion of the brain), an operation in which the cingulum received small lesions. The cingulum is a bundle of nerve fibers connecting the frontal lobes with the various structures of the limbic system, which is hypothesized to control emotional responses. A variety of syndromes were treated, but only two were significantly helped, and depression was the major predictive component. Of the seven patients with severe depression, five claimed full or partial relief. Most success was obtained in cases of persistent pain associated with depression; 9 of 11 such cases reported complete relief or near complete relief. Interestingly, the literature has tended to view severe obsessive-compulsives as good candidates for psychosurgery, but in the four such cases studied in depth for the commission, there was a total lack of treatment effect.

The use of bilateral anterior cingulotomy was also evaluated by a group of psychologists with the Massachusetts Institute of Technology. (Gonzalez, Treating the Brain by Cinguilotomy, 244 J.A.M.A. 2141 [1980].) Gonzalez reported that after the group reviewed the results of 137 patients undergoing this operation, it was found that there is a "minor but permanent functional deficit in patients who are over age 30 years at the time of surgery," that the operation had little therapeutic value for disorders other than intractable major depression and chronic pain, and that patients who did not improve with the first operation failed to improve following "one or two more."

Mirsky and Orzack evaluated 27 patients for the commission, and similarly found depression to be the only complaint to respond to three psychosurgical procedures. Paradoxically, it was observed that those patients who reported the greatest improvement also manifested the greatest evidence of cognitive loss.

64. Editorial, 6 *J. Med. Ethics* 115 (1980).

65. Trotter, Federal Commission OK's Psychosurgery 7 *APA Monitor* 4 (1976).

66. Gostin, Ethical Considerations of Psychosurgery: The Unhappy Legacy of the Pre-Frontal Lobotomy, 6 *J. Med. Ethics* 149 (1980).

67. See authorities cited in Plotkin, Limiting the Therapeutic Orgy: Mental Patients' Right to Refuse Treatment, 72 *Nw. U.L. Rev.* 461, 468–70 and notes 37–47 (1977).

68. *Id.*

69. These "major tranquilizer" drugs include three major chemical groups: chlorpromazine (Thorazine) and fluphenazine (Prolixin) are phenothiazine drugs, thiothixene (Navane) is a thioxanthene drug, and haloperidol (Haldol) is a butyrophenone drug. Hollister, Anti-psychotic Medications and the Treatment of Schizophrenia in *Psychopharacology* 121, 137 (J. Barchas, P. Berger, R. Ciaranello & G. Elliott eds. 1977). See M. Hersen & S. Breuning, *Pharmacological and Behavioral Treatment* (1986).

70. Kety, Genetic and Biochemical Aspects of Schizophrenia, in *The Harvard Guide to Modern Psychiatry* 93 (A. Nicholi ed. 1978). Dopamine is a neurotransmitter and it is thought that schizophrenia may result from an excess of dopamine in the brain or from dopamine receptors in the brain which are unusually sensitive. The psychotropic drugs, then, may prevent psychotic episodes by interfering with the action of dopamine.

71. Comment, Madness and Medicine: The Forcible Administration of Psychotropic Drugs, 1980 *Wis. L. Rev.* 497, 539. Some studies of chronic schizophrenics conclude that patients given antipsychotic medication improve more than patients given a placebo, other studies conclude the medication is less effective than placebos and still other studies conclude that it makes no difference whether patients are given placebos or antipsychotic medication. *Id.* at 539–40 and notes 184–88. See Brooks, The Constitutional Right to Refuse Anti-Psychotic Medications, 8 *Bull. Am. Acad. Psychiatry & L.* 179, 182–84 (1980). See generally Comment, Antipsychotic Drugs: Regulating Their Use in the Private Practice of Medicine, 15 *Golden Gate U. L. Rev.* 331 (1985).

72. K. Bernheim & R. Lewine, *Schizophrenia: Symptoms, Causes and Treatments* 123–24 (1979); E. Persad *Use of Drugs in Psychiatry* (1986).

73. Brooks states "a total catalogue of the side effects caused by antipsychotic medications, including the most and least common, would be a horrendous document." Brooks, The Constitutional Right to Refuse Anti-Psychotic Medications, 8 *Bull. Am. Acad. Psychiatry & L.* 179, 184 (1980).

74. Kane & Smith, Tardive Dyskinesia: Prevalence and Risk Factors, 1959 to 1979, 39 *Archives Gen. Psychiatry* 16 (1981); Wettstein, Tardive Dyskinesia and Malpractice, 1 *Behav. Sci. & L.* 85 (1983).

75. Fann, Davis & Jaworski, The Prevalence of Tardive Dyskinesias in Mental Hospital Patients, 33 *Diseases of the Nervous System* 182 (1972); Mills, Nordquist, Shelton, Gelenberg & Putten, Consent and Liability with Neuroleptics: The Problem of Tardive Dyskinesia, 8 *Int'l J. L. & Psychiatry* 243 (1986); Sovner, DiMascio, Berkouritz & Randolph, Tardive Dyskinesia and Informed Consent, 19 *Psychosomatics* 172 (1978). See Mukherjee, Rosen, Cardenas, Varia & Olarte, Tardive Dyskinesia in Psychiatric Outpatients: A Study of Prevalence and Association with Demographic, Clinical, and Drug History Variables, 39 *Archives Gen. Psychiatry* 466 (1982).

76. The most commonly prescribed antidepressant drugs are the tricyclics, such as Amitriptyline (Elavil) and Imipramine (Tofranil). These drugs are considered "mood elevators" and, in general, have been found to be effective in improving depression. The tricyclics produce an effect by increasing the amount of norepinephrine (NE) or seretonin available to neurons in the brain. This has led some researchers to suggest a primary role for NE and serotonin in the etiology of depression. Thomson, Side Effects and Placebo Amplification, 140 *Brit. J. Psychiatry* 64 (1982).

77. Discovery of the psychoactive properties of MAO inhibitors came in the early 1950s when they were being used in the treatment of tuberculosis. Some patients reported an emotional "lift" when undergoing treatment with these drugs, which led to their eventual use with clinically depressed individuals. MAO Inhibitors, such as Phenelzine (Nardil) or Tranylcypromine (Parnate) indirectly reduce the metabolism of NE and Seretonin, thus increasing the availability of these neurotransmitters. F. Shumer, *Abnormal Psychology* (1983).

78. Gelenberg, Prescribing Antidepressants, 9 *Drug Therapy* 95 (1979); Milkovich & van den Berg, Effects of Prenatal Meprobamate and Chlordiazepoxide Hydrochloride on Human Embryonic and Fetal Development, 291 *New Eng. J. Med.* 1268 (1974). See M. Hersen & S. Breuning, *Pharmacological and Behavioral Treatment* (1986).

79. F. Shumer, *supra*, note 77.

80. Milkovich & van den Berg, *supra*, note 78.

81. N. Carlson, *Psychology of Behavior* (1980); E. Persad, *supra*, note 72; Fieve, The Clinical Effects of Lithium Treatment, 2 *Trends in Neuroscience* 66 (1979). Accurate monitoring of blood concentrations is necessary to determine effective and nontoxic dosages. It has not been shown to significantly impair intellectual functioning or sexual responsivity or to diminish normal affective quality.

82. One potential problem which has received limited notice is the possibility that the prolonged use of these drugs may cause a patient to develop supersensitive dopamine receptor sites. This could actually exacerbate schizophrenic symptoms. The existence and seriousness of this phenomenon have

not been conclusively identified. Choninard, Jones & Annable, Neuroleptic-Induced Supersensitive Psychosis, 135 *Am. J. Psychiatry* 1409 (1978).

83. The incidence of malpractice claims in all psychotherapy is quite low. The frequency and cause of malpractice claims is described further in chapter 1.

84. Medicaid and Medicare payments would not cover all forms of treatment, and in fact may be specifically limited to discourage certain forms of treatment, the limitation on funding for abortion is an example.

85. See, e.g., Shapiro, The Right of Privacy and Heroin Use for Pain-killing Purposes by the Terminally Ill Cancer Patient, 21 *Ariz. L. Rev.* 41 (1979); Note, Antipsychotic Drugs: Regulating Their Use in the Private Practice of Medicine, 15 *Golden Gate U. L. Rev.* 331 (1985); Comment, Laetrile: Statutory and Constitutional Limitations on the Regulation of Ineffective Drugs, 127 *U. Pa. L. Rev.* 233 (1978). See generally Lee & Herzstein, International Drug Regulation, in *Annual Review of Public Health* (L. Breslow ed. 1986).

86. In California, for example, a very restrictive ECT statute was declared unconstitutional by unduly interfering with individual treatment decisions. Aden v. Younger, 57 Cal. App. 3d 662; 129 Cal. Rptr. 535 (4th Dist. 1976). The California legislature quickly passed an act that was less restrictive of voluntary ECT. An effort by the voters of Berkeley, California to ban ECT altogether was also declared unconstitutional. See note 2 *infra*.

87. U.S. v. Rutherford, 442 U.S. 544 (1979).

88. See Tenenbaum, ECT Regulation Reconsidered, 7 *Mental & Physical Disabilities L. Rep.* 148 (1983).

89. One who was clear what the cost had been for him was Ernest Hemingway.

> In December 1960, Hemingway underwent 11 shock treatments at the Mayo Clinic in Rochester, Minnesota. Three months later he was back for another series. His friend and biographer, A. E. Hotchner, described him at that time: "Ernest was even more infuriated with these treatments than the previous ones, registering even bitterer complaints about how his memory was wrecked and how he was ruined as a writer. . . ." Hotchner quotes Hemingway: "What these shock doctors don't know is about writers and such things as remorse and contrition and what they do to them. . . . What is the sense of ruining my head and erasing my memory, which is my capital, and putting me out of business? It was a brilliant cure but we lost the patient." One month after the second series of ECT, Hemingway killed himself.

Friedberg, *supra*, note 7 at 18.

90. American Psychiatric Association, *Task Force Report: Electro-Convulsive Therapy* (1978); National Institute of Mental Health, *Electro-Convulsive Therapy: Consensus Development Conference* (1985); Kendell, The Present Status of Electroconvulsive Therapy, 139 *Brit. J. Psychiatry* 265 (1981).

91. National Commission for the Protection of Human Subjects of Biomedical and Behavioral Research, *Report* (1976).

92. Trotter, Federal Commission OK's Psychosurgery, 7 *APA Monitor* 4 (1976).

93. Regarding the problems of informed consent in psychotherapy, see Note, The Doctrine of Informed Consent Applied to Psychotherapy, 72 *Georgetown L. J.* 1637 (1984).

94. Garvey, Freedom and Choice in Constitutional Law, 94 *Harv. L. Rev.* 1756 (1981); Kaufmann & Roth, Psychiatric Evaluation of Patient Decision-Making: Informed Consent to ECT, 16 *Soc. Psychiatry* 11 (1981); Macklin, Some Problems in Gaining Informed Consent from Psychiatric Patients, 31 *Emory L. J.* 345 (1982).

95. See Canterbury v. Spence, 464 F.2d 772 (D.C. Cir.), *cert. denied,* 409 U.S. 1064 (1972).

96. When a patient is unconscious and immediately requires medication, the emergency exception may legitimately be invoked; and when a patient is immediately and seriously dangerous to himself or others and cannot be controlled through less intrusive means, then medication may be justified without consent. In some instances temporary restraint or seclusion would be less intrusive.

97. The disclosure of the risks of a procedure may be upsetting to many patients, so the "therapeutic privilege" would appear to be relevant. This exception to the informed consent requirement cannot be broadly applied. All patients are likely to be distressed by hearing about the risks of a procedure they are about to undergo. Only when it is likely that the information will be so distressing that the patients' health will be seriously affected by it can the information be withheld. The fact that the information would cause the patient to refuse the treatment certainly cannot be the basis for withholding the information—such an exception would be contrary to the whole purpose of informed consent.

98. Canterbury v. Spence, 464 F.2d 772 (D.C. Cir.), *cert. denied,* 409 U.S. 1064 (1972).

99. Mitchell v. Robinson, 334 S.W.2d 11 (Mo. 1960).

100. See Sterling Drug, Inc. v. Yarrow, 408 F.2d 978 (8th Cir. 1969). See Note, A Common Law Remedy for Forcible Medication of the Institutionalized Mentally Ill, 82 *Colum. L. Rev.* 1720 (1982).

101. In fact some recent research suggests that many voluntary mental patients are at least somewhat incompetent to give informed consent to treatment. See C. Lidz, A. Meisel, E. Zerubavel, M. Carter, R. Sestak & L. Roth, *Informed Consent: A Study of Decisionmaking in Psychiatry* (1984); Appelbaum, Mirkin & Bateman, Empirical Assessment of Competency to Consent to Psychiatric Hospitalization, 138 *Am. J. Psychiatry* 1170 (1981).

102. See generally Meisel, The Expansion of Liability for Medical Accidents: From Negligence to Strict Liability By Way of Informed Consent, 56 *Neb. L. Rev.* 51, 113–21 (1977). The most effective methods of obtaining informed consent may be fairly informal processes. Munetz, Loren & Roth, Informing Patients About Tardive Dyskinesia, 42 *Archives Gen. Psychiatry* 866 (1985).

103. A number of problems would exist in implementing such a treatment will, such as determining the competency of the patient when the will was

drawn and determining when the will was revoked. Similar problems exist with living wills, and common testimentary wills. See Chodoff & Peele, The Psychiatric Will of Dr. Szsaz, 13 *Hastings Center Rep.* 11 (April 1983); Reinert, A Living Will for a Commitment Hearing, 31 *Hosp. & Community Psychiatry* 857 (1980); Szasz, The Psychiatric Will—A New Mechanism for Protecting Persons Against "Psychosis" and "Psychiatry," 37 *Am. Psychologist* 767 (1982). Other proposals include the durable power of attorney (effectively appointing a guardian in case of incompetence) and the "irrevocable treatment contract" or "Ulysses contract" (preventing the revocation of consent to treatment once consent has been given—the legality of such contracts is doubtful).

104. The Supreme Court, in Parham v. J. R., 442 U.S. 584 (1979), ruled that the decision of parents to voluntarily commit a minor child should be reviewed by an independent person (e.g., a physician) but that a judicial review of the parental decision to hospitalize was unnecessary. On the other hand, the Court has ruled that minors may exercise certain rights of privacy (e.g., obtaining an abortion or contraceptives) without the specific permission of their parents. It is not entirely clear when parents may make decisions for older minors in matters of great importance, e.g. when the effects of treatment are irreversible. Therefore, in some instances, parents may not be able to consent to psychosurgery, ECT or even psychotropic medication over the objections of an older minor.

105. There is strong reason to believe that minors over the age of 14 give consent much like adults, and that they possess the same ability to consider relevant information and to reason. Melton, Children's Participation in Treatment Planning: Psychological and Legal Issues, 12 *Prof. Psychology: Research & Prac.* 246 (1981).

106. An excellent review of legal restrictions is contained in S. Brakel, J. Parry & B. Weiner, *The Mentally Disabled and the Law* 357–67 (3rd ed. 1986). See Mills, the Rights of Involuntary Patients to Refuse Pharmacotherapy: What is Reasonable, 8 *Am. Acad. Psychiatry & L. Bull.* 313 (1980); Rhoden, The Right to Refuse Psychotropic Drugs, 15 *Harv. Civ. Rts. & Civ. Liberties L. Rev.* 363 (1980); Symonds, Mental Patients' Right to Refuse Drugs: Involuntary Medication as Cruel and Unusual Punishment, 7 *Hastings Const. L. Q.* 701 (1980).

107. Instances where ECT has been administered without adequate consent may be common. Even when consent is obtained, it may not be "informed" consent. Certainly the following consent forms that were administered to patients are inadequate, if not worthless. "'I understand,' the consent form reads, 'that I am giving the staff of Bryce Hospital authority to carry out routine procedures and treatment as necessary to bring about my return to home and good health. I further understand that in the event special or emergency measures as shall be deemed necessary by the staff of Bryce Hospital every effort will be made to explain the need to me and/or my nearest relative. In the event, however, that I am unable to comprehend and my nearest relative cannot be reached, I (or my nearest relative) consent

to such emergency psychiatric or medical treatment as shall be deemed necessary by the staff. . . .' Listed below are five categories—diagnostic tests, electroshock therapy, local anesthetics, general anesthetics and emergency surgery—with boxes beside them in which patients are asked to indicate 'yes' or 'no'. One patient, who signed the consent forms as 'Super Fly,' indicated 'yes' to diagnostic tests, local anesthetics, etc., but 'no' to ECT. He was shocked ten times. In another case, the consent form was signed by the ward psychologist." 6 *APA Monitor* 7 (1975).

108. Kaufman & Roth, Psychiatric Evaluation of Patient Decision-Making: Informed Consent to ECT, 16 *Soc. Psychiatry* 11 (1981). On the other hand, most patients who initially refuse treatment eventually accept it, but the refusal and subsequent delay in therapy apparently does little harm. Appelbaum & Gutheil, Drug Refusal: A Study of Psychiatric Inpatients, 137 *Am. J. Psychiatry* 340 (1980). See C. Lidz, A. Meisel, E. Zerubavel, M. Carter, R. Sestak & L. Roth, *Informed Consent: A Study of Decisionmaking in Psychiatry* (1984).

109. F. A. Rozovsky, *Consent to Treatment: A Practical Guide* (1984); Katz, Disclosure and Consent in Psychiatric Practice: Mission Impossible?, in *Law and Ethics in the Practice of Psychiatry* 91 (C. Hoffling ed. 1981); Parry, Legal Parameters of Informed Consent Applied to Electroconvulsive Therapy, 9 *Mental & Physical Disability L. Rep.* 162 (1985). Limitations also exist on the use of aversive therapies, token economies and behavior modification. For an excellent review of these issues see D. Wexler, *Mental Health Law: Major Issues* 213–56 (1981); Friedman, Legal Regulation of Applied Behavior Analysis in Mental Institutions and Prisons, 17 *Ariz. L. Rev.* 39 (1975).

110. Kaimowitz v. Michigan Dept. Mental Health, Cir. Ct., Wayne Co., Mich. reprinted in A. Brooks, *Law, Psychiatry and the Mental Health System* 902 (1974).

111. Kloss, Consent to Medical Treatment, 4 *Med. Sci. & L.* 89 (1964).

112. Professor Wexler has provided a particularly thorough analysis of the decision. D. Wexler, *Mental Health Law: Major Issues* 193–213 (1981).

113. The federal government (Health and Human Services and Food and Drug Administration) has proposed strict limitations on the use of prisoners as experimental subjects. See e.g., 21 C.F.R. [Code of Federal Regulations] §50.44 (1984).

114. For a general review of professional issues as they relate to treatment and legal rights see Gelman, Mental Hospital Drugs, Professionalism, and the Constitution, 72 *Georgetown L. J.* 1725 (1984).

CHAPTER 4
LICENSING
AND
MENTAL HEALTH CARE
DELIVERY

The mental health care delivery system,[1] is the means by which society determines what services will be available, their quality, who will receive them, their cost, and their financing. Mental health care delivery is rarely like a free, competitive market economy. A number of factors interfere with the operation of pure competition. For example, there is no free access to mental health markets (licensing is required), patients do not have complete knowledge of the various services available and their efficacy, and insurance and other third-party payers warp normal costing and demand principles. Even with the increased emphasis on promoting some competition-like aspects of health care, which started in the late 1970s, the system is far from a freely competitive market.

In reality, mental health care is a product of political, social, and economic forces. This chapter considers the interplay of these forces. Among the areas currently debated are licensing of professionals, hospital privileges, insurance reimbursement for services, and proposals for including mental health services in any plan for national health insurance.

LICENSING

Oliver Wendell Holmes once wrote that "if the whole *materia medica* . . . could be sunk to the bottom of the sea, it would be all the better for mankind—and all the worse for the fishes,"[2] a claim also made for the licensing of mental health practitioners.[3] Licensing is intended primarily to protect the public from inadequate or dangerous practitioners. Licensing also serves to protect the licensed profession from certain kinds of competition and promotes its respectability.[4] Licensing is double-edged: It may promote the public interest by improving the quality of care, but it may threaten it because entry into the profession is restricted, so that availability of services is reduced and prices are increased. Whether licensing actually serves the public interest, and if so, what form of licensing best serves it, thus continue to be important questions.[5] It is possible that the trend toward increased licensing will be reversed and that "deregulation" could even result in the abandonment of some current licensing statutes.[6]

Although the primary purpose of licensing is supposed to be public protection, these laws are seldom passed without the support of the group being licensed. The persons most likely to oppose licensure of a new group are those already licensed groups in similar professions. There are many reasons a profession may seek licensure: it is a means of protecting the public;[7] it is a formal recognition of the legitimacy and value of the profession; and it is a step along the route of being included both in a testimonial privilege (which is usually associated with licensed professions)[8] and in third-party reimbursement plans. Of course, other groups might oppose licensure to protect their own interests.[9]

Practicing without a license is generally a misdemeanor carrying a maximum penalty of a fine and a short jail term. Prosecution for unauthorized mental health practice is very infrequent and, unless a patient is seriously harmed, often does not result in significant penalties when it does occur.

Types of Licensing

State licensing activities take several forms. It may prohibit certain kinds of practice without a license (for example, using ECT or prescribing drugs). It may also limit the use of certain titles such as "psychologist" or "M.D." or "marriage counselor." Or the state may require registration in order to keep track of who is engaged in practice. It is common for a state that limits practice to licensees to also limit the use of the title associated with that profession.

There is no consistent name for these three forms of regulation. The limitation on practice is called a "licensing statute," but licensing is also used to include limiting the use of a title. Title regulation is often called "certification licensing," but that term is also used in some instances to refer to some master's-level licensing.[10] To avoid confusion, we will use "practice" laws or statutes to refer to limitation on practice, "title" laws to refer to limitations on the use of title, and "registration" laws to refer to the requirement for registration with the state. "Licensing" generally refers to the first two kinds of regulation.

The purpose served by each of these forms of regulation differs. "Practice" acts are intended to completely prohibit the incompetent from providing services. The theory is that the possibility of harm to the public is so great that it is necessary to prohibit them from practicing. Most states license a wide range of activities and professions ranging from physicians, psychologists, and attorneys to cosmetologists. Title laws are intended to provide information in that, by reserving certain titles or labels to those with minimal levels of competence and credentials, people can ascertain whether a practitioner has at least that level of quality. Although registration laws provide no direct consumer service, they do provide a method of keeping track of practitioners.

Professional Differences

Mental health professions have approached licensing in various ways. Interestingly, there is virtually no licensing in psychiatry (beyond the M.D. requirement) and psychiatrists as a group have not sought licensing authority. (Licensing must be clearly distinguished from board certification, which is voluntary and not required to practice a specialty or to use a specialty title.) Psychologists, on the other hand, have actively (and successfully) sought licensure. Social workers, marriage and family therapists, and counselors have more recently sought licensure statutes.[11] Some states have licensed a wide variety of other mental health professions, including psychiatric technician nurse (Arkansas), psychiatric technicians (e.g., California, Colorado), pastoral counselors (New Hampshire), "drugless healing" (e.g., Illinois, Washington), social psychotherapy (Texas), recreational therapist (Utah), and alcoholism and drug counselors (Virginia).[12]

Any physician may claim to be a psychiatrist, without special training or testing. In fact, it appears that less than half of those specializing in psychiatry have obtained certification.[13] The reasons are not entirely clear. It is perhaps related to the development of psychiatry within medicine. The medical profession has its own licensing system and a history of specialty practice without specialty licensing. It may also be that there has been little need for physician/psychiatrists to depend upon specialty licensing for recognition and third-party reimbursement.

Among professions, there has been a debate over multilevel licensing. Who should be included within licensing provisions and the qualifications for licensure? In psychology, for example, most states license only those with doctorates, and the issue has focused on the potential licensure or certification of master's-level psychologists.[14] In social work some states have agreed to license social workers with a bachelor's degree.[15] These debates are not generally whether the lower level degree should qualify the professional for the same license as the higher degree, but rather whether a holder of the lower level degree should be recognized by the state at all or permitted to engage in independent practice. There is often concern that multilevel licensing will confuse the public and weaken the prestige and respect of the higher level license. Such disputes have sometimes defeated licensing for the profession, or required a compromise that essentially provides for multilevel licensing. When it does occur, the lower levels are generally given a different title and are required to work under the supervision of a holder of the higher level license.

Licensure is a matter of state law. There is considerable variance from state to state on the professions that are licensed and on the details of the licensing law. Licensure is generally a statutory and regulatory matter and there are relatively few appellate cases dealing with mental health licensing.[16]

Requirements for Licensure

Although requirements vary considerably from state to state and from profession to profession within the same state, there are several common elements,[17] among them, completion of an academic degree, passage of a licensing examination, completion of supervised work experience or internship, and demonstration of good moral and ethical character.

Professions and states vary concerning the kind of education required for licensure.[18] Some type of accreditation is generally required for the institution granting an approved degree. An educational requirement for licensing requires the establishment of some standards to determine what constitutes adequate education. Without accreditation, diploma mills could grant meaningless degrees and effectively destroy the education requirement. Professional associations, such as the American Psychological Association or the National Association of Social Workers, usually have some system of educational accreditation.[19] In some states, however, the education requirement for licensure may be met without graduation from a professionally approved school.[20] Regional accreditation may be used to meet the educational requirement. The difficulty with regional accreditation is that it is not oriented toward the needs of one profession but rather toward an entire institution (e.g., a university) and therefore does not deal with the quality of the professional training program, and tends to have relatively low standards for approval.[21]

Another issue involving the education requirement is what types of training qualify for training requirement.[22] For example, while the Psy.D. or a Ph.D. in clinical psychology would qualify as training for licensure in psychology, would a Ph.D. in counseling or a Ph.D. or Ed.D. in education psychology? Generally these questions are left to the licensing board and its decisions are accepted so long as the board makes a decision consistent with its own policies and the state statute.[23]

Licensing examinations generally contain a written component which may be supplemented by an oral examination or practicum exam (patient diagnosis or counseling). These examinations are commonly written or administered by the state board which also provides for scoring them and determines what "passing" scores are.

The supervised work experience or practicum is meant to ensure that during the initial years of practice, the professional has the guidance necessary to deal with the complexities of practice. It is a transition period between the intense supervision that is supposed to be part of academic training and the relative lack of supervision of fully licensed practice. In addition, it serves the function of a "probationary" period in that gross incompetence or unethical conduct during the internship might result in the denial of a full license.

The character and fitness aspect of licensing protects the public from dishonest and unethical behavior. Serious acts of dishonesty, such as crimes of moral turpitude or failure to meet fiduciary responsibility, can be the reason for refusing to license an otherwise fully qualified applicant, but few applicants are denied on this basis, perhaps in part because many educational institutions would not accept such students into training programs,[24] and perhaps because the state licensing boards have not made great efforts to uncover prior dishonest behavior.

Licensing requirements may seem somewhat redundant: what is the need for an educational requirement if there is a licensing exam that could test the applicant's knowledge? Why have an internship when similar experience should have been provided as part of training? In fact, these provisions are intentionally redundant, in part, to provide checks on various parts of the process. Inadequately prepared applicants who somehow get through a training program may be stopped by the exam. In addition, examination results can affect the training programs; a number of exam failures from one school may indicate a need to increase the academic rigor of that program. The internship may expose seriously incompetent practitioners, or help to compensate for any weaknesses in the training program.

Licensing Boards

Licensing is done by state licensing boards, generally appointed by the governor, or other state and professional officials. The controlling majority of the boards are usually made up of the members of the regulated profession. In addition to responsibility for the examination and initial licensing function, most boards are charged with the duty of revoking licenses and imposing other forms of discipline (described below).[25]

Reciprocity

Licensure is controlled by each state, and generally a license is valid for practice only in the state which has granted it. There commonly are exceptions for emergency or short-term practice. Some states will recognize the license of another state as the basis for granting a license. As with licensing provisions themselves, reciprocity provisions vary widely.

License Renewal

After initial licensure, relicensing essentially becomes a registration procedure. A license holder may be required to provide information about type and location of practice, and to pay a fee. However, there are no license renewal examinations, or any serious review of professional competence. This is similar to the licensing provisions of all types, including those for lawyers. It means, however, that it is virtually impossible for licensing authorities to assure the continued competence of those relicensed.[26] This may in part be based on the assumption that once licensed, practitioners increase the level of competence in the areas in which they actually practice and therefore reexamination is unnecessary. It may also reflect the political reality that licensing statutes are developed by those in the licensed profession and they generally would not be very enthusiastic about having to take licensing exams throughout their careers.

Continuing education is viewed by some as one way of helping to ensure the continued competence of professionals. In some instances continuing education "credits" or hours are required to maintain a license. Although the success of compulsory continuing education is debatable, these courses should at least provide the opportunity for professionals to stay abreast of some of the latest developments in their areas of practice.[27]

Discipline and License Revocation

Licensing boards generally have an obligation to discipline, or to revoke the licenses of professionals who engage in misconduct or are unfit to continue practice. The bases for imposing discipline or revoking a license vary, but generally include incompetence to continue practice, unfitness because of alcohol or drug addiction, illegal activity which reflects on trust or professional standing, and serious unethical misconduct.[28] The board is usually empowered to promulgate regulations that specify the grounds for revoking licenses and to take a variety of disciplinary actions ranging from a private reprimand to suspension or revocation of the license.[29]

Professional discipline involves punitive action on behalf of the state, and the removal of a license is the taking of "property." Therefore a state licensing board must comply with constitutional due process requirements when disciplinary action is taken, which requires that the board hold a hearing at which the accused person may present and challenge evidence. To respond to the claims against them, practitioners must be given a fairly clear statement of the claims of misconduct. To avoid inadvertently engaging in prohibited activities, professionals must be given a reasonably clear understanding of the conduct that is prohibited. This does not, of course, require the specificity of a criminal code, but the law must give fair notice of what acts are prohibited.

A disciplinary proceeding is generally a formal hearing, held before the board or a hearing officer appointed by the board. It is common for the professional who is the subject of the hearing to be represented by an attorney, and to present witnesses and evidence to the board. A state attorney, or an attorney hired by the board, generally presents the evidence for discipline. Those seeking to impose discipline generally have the burden of proof.

Disciplinary actions against mental health practitioners are rare.[30] Most state boards are understaffed, many have no full-time professional staff members, and few have full-time investigators trained to discover unethical or incompetent practice. Boards almost always respond only to complaints filed with them, rather than seeking out incompetent practitioners. Most do not have the resources to conduct adequate investigations of complaints. Moreover, professionals are generally unwilling to file complaints against their peers, so patients may become the major source of complaints. As we have seen in malpractice cases, mistreated patients are likely to be reluctant to expose their mental health histories. In addition, because there is no single method of treating many mental health conditions, many patients may not know that they have been harmed or mistreated. The inability or unwillingness of the boards to deal aggressively with inadequate or unethical practitioners is a major weakness of most professional licensure.[31]

Ethics and Licensing

Licensing can be an important method of enforcing professional ethics and a serious breach may be the basis for revoking a license. Therefore, ethical codes are more than general statements of professional ideals; they become the basis for the continued right to practice. If codes of ethics are effective in protecting the public from dishonesty, inadequate service, or unfair advantage, then licensing is a method of fulfilling the profession's obligation to protect the public. Unfortunately, many professional codes of ethics are vague and often combine aspirational statements with minimum ethical standards. As a result, the ethical standards generally serve as the basis for board action only in the most outrageous cases of dishonesty (stealing from a patient or making fraudulent insurance claims for services not rendered) or taking advantage of a patient (sexual relations with a patient). It is important that codes of ethics make some clear distinction between the goals or aspirations of the profession, and the minimum level of professional conduct required of all practitioners.

Beyond Licensing

Licensing involves the minimum qualifications necessary to practice a profession. Higher standards may be established by groups for membership or special certification. For example, the American Board of Professional Psychology (ABPP) and the American Board of Psychiatry and Neurology have requirements for certification that extend well beyond those required by states to practice psychology or medicine. Such forms of certification are not part of the state licensing process.[32]

These forms of credentialing may be useful to other professionals when making referrals. They may also be useful to the public in selecting a therapist and to third-party reimbursement plans. Unfortunately, few people understand the significance of these credentials, and even when they do they may be misled by other groups with similar sounding names that impose much less stringent requirements for certification. Many of the functions of labeling licensing would be better served if the public were more aware of the importance of these special credentialing services, if misleading similar titles were prohibited and if the professions would make available to the public lists of certification boards with rigorous standards. Such a process might be opposed by those without the certification, but it would encourage practitioners to seek board approval.[33]

Hospital staff privileges are another form of credentialing, and are discussed later in this chapter.

Criticism of Licensing

Mental health licensing is criticized for unnecessarily limiting the supply of practitioners and thereby reducing the availability of and increasing the price of mental health services, for stifling innovation, for making it difficult for paraprofessionals to perform effectively, for decreasing geographic mobility and distribution of professionals, and for discriminating against groups that would find it most difficult to get the credentials necessary for practice (minorities and women) and that suffer most from an insufficiency of practitioners.[34] At the same time, licensure is criticized for being ineffective in eliminating the incompetent or harmful from practice.[35] Together these criticisms almost suggest that the licensing process is preventing the competent from practicing, and permitting the incompetent to practice.[36]

The criticisms, while probably overstated, do demonstrate some problems. Since the very purpose of licensing is to eliminate from practice those who are not of a minimum level of competence, the licensing process undoubtedly reduces the number of practitioners. This probably tends to increase prices somewhat, and makes services less readily available to some. To the extent it reduces the number of "unnecessary" practitioners, however, it may tend to reduce treatment that is not necessary or desirable.[37] Licensing may also somewhat inhibit innovation. On the other hand, claims of innovation may be an excuse for quackery. The real question is whether licensing reduces *effective* innovations more than it protects against ineffective or even dangerous ones. If licensing discourages the use of paraprofessionals, that is undesirable only if it prevents them from doing things that need not be done by professionals.

There are undesirable consequences of licensing, whether or not one agrees with all of the criticisms described above. The process is time-consuming, requires state resources, may suggest to the public greater competency than it actually assures, and will result in some incorrect decisions. The primary question is whether these costs are worth the benefits in improved mental health care and in the avoidance of quackery and fraud. This is a calculation that cannot be performed with precision, and trying to guess about it is the major source of debate about the desirability of mental health licensing.

Another question is whether licensing is successful in ensuring minimum levels of competence. An argument can be made that it does not. Few applicants are denied licenses because they are never able to pass the examination or because of character and fitness considerations. In reality, the educational requirement is probably the major requirement limiting licensure, and it may become even less effective if there are no rigorous accreditation standards. Another weakness in ensuring minimum competency—one shared with other professions—is that very few practitioners have their licenses revoked. There are few efforts to seek out unethical professionals and remove them from practice. Furthermore, the absence of relicensing provisions makes it unlikely that practitioners who become incompetent will be detected and their licenses revoked.[38]

We believe that some form of mental health licensure is desirable. In the absence of label licensing, mistakes about the quality of the professionals would be common. There are undoubtedly some procedures that are sufficiently dangerous that they should be undertaken only by qualified experts. There is a social, as well as an individual, interest in ensuring that mental health services are performed by competent professionals. The personal interest is clear— the individual wants effective treatment. Others also have an interest in ensuring competent mental health activities. For example, if the services are paid for by insurance or Medicare or Medicaid, there is a social interest in determining that reasonably competent services are provided. There is also a broad social interest in reducing antisocial activity, and to the extent that effective treatment may reduce it, competent treatment ought to be ensured.

Autonomy and Licensure

A more philosophical question of autonomy and public protection also exists. Those philosophically opposed to all licensing argue that individuals should be free to seek services from anyone of their choosing, whether or not the professional is approved by the state; the individual takes the risk (if there is one) of being harmed by an incompetent and the risk of not finding out enough about the professional to determine competency. Those favoring licensing argue that it is often unrealistic for a lay person to judge the competence of professionals and that society has a public safety interest in ensuring that those seeking mental health services receive competent treatment. This debate is one of perception (e.g., how dangerous is an incompetent practitioner) and one of values (how much should the government intervene to protect us from a very bad choice of practitioners).

Improving Mental Health Licensure

Several reforms could increase the overall efficacy of licensing:

1. The label "psychiatrist" should be limited to those with special training and recognized ability in psychiatry. It is likely that the public is currently misled about the qualifications of some claiming to practice psychiatry. At a minimum, title licensing of psychiatrists should be undertaken.

2. If practice licensing (limits on who can perform services) is to be undertaken, the services within the definition of the practice must be much more clearly set out either by statute or by regulation. The definitions now used are extremely broad and often worthless. For example, a proposed model licensing act for psychology defines the practice of psychology as rendering "any psychological service involving the application of principles, methods, and procedures of understanding, predicting and influencing behavior . . . ; the methods and procedures of interviewing, counseling, and psychotherapy; of constructing, administering and interpreting tests of mental abilities . . . ; and of assessing public opinion."[39] A model social work act defines the practice of social work as "service and action to affect changes in human behavior, a person's or persons' emotional responses, and the

social conditions of individuals, families, groups, organizations, and communities, which are influenced by the interaction of social, cultural, political, and economic systems."[40] These definitions apply to the activities of much of the population. They are so broad as to be worthless.

3. The educational requirements should be more clearly defined. For example, whether a counseling doctoral degree is sufficient for one to be licensed as a clinical psychologist should be rather clearly determined. This should be based not on labeling, but on content, and therefore could be most efficiently performed by the accreditation function.

4. The accreditation of educational programs should be strengthened. In the long run, maintaining an effective education requirement requires a dependable accreditation process that prevents diploma-mill operations. Most states do not depend on rigorous national professional accreditation to determine which educational programs provide sufficiently sound educational programs to fulfill licensing requirements. Few state boards are equipped to conduct full and adequate accreditation reviews within their own state, and none is able to conduct adequate reviews of programs outside their own states. As a result, education accreditation for licensure tends to be haphazard and without very high standards and this seriously weakens licensing educational requirements. Licensing should require graduation from an educational program accredited by the nationally recognized professional body.

5. The use of titles that are similar to label licensing titles should be prohibited. Thus, if use of the title "psychologist" requires a license, the use of terms such as "psychotherapist" or "psychocounselor" by those not licensed should also be prohibited. States should be particularly careful to avoid using similar titles for different, licensed professionals. For example, "certified psychologist" should not be used to designate a master's-level professional (required to practice under supervision) if "licensed psychologist" indicates a doctoral-level, independent practitioner. The similarity is likely to be confusing to the public and thereby defeat the purpose of title licensing.

6. The character and fitness reviews should be more thoroughly conducted, and boards should be less reluctant to use past dishonesty as the basis for denying state licenses. Licensure discipline in one state should generally be a disqualification for licensure in another state. Each profession should establish a central national registry of disciplinary action and complaints to detect the unethical practitioner who moves from one state to another.
7. State boards should be much more aggressive in seeking out the unethical or incompetent practitioner for discipline. Complaints to the board should be thoroughly investigated by experienced staff. The public should be reminded that the licensure board is available to receive complaints and the board should actively seek information from those who might have complaints. To the extent possible consistent with due process, the confidentiality of patients and clients with complaints should be recognized. This recommendation would unquestionably require the addition of staff and funding for state boards.
8. State boards should be more inclined to impose significant penalties for any serious breach of ethical rules and for incompetency.
9. Some form of relicensing should be required to demonstrate continued competency in the area of practice or subspecialization.
10. Efforts should be made to inform the public of various levels of certification that go beyond licensing. Professionally recognized diplomate or certification status should be explained to the public.
11. If clearly defined practice licensing is used, states should more vigorously prosecute the unauthorized or unlicensed practice of the profession. Such prosecutions now are extremely unusual.

Eliminate Licensing?

The current state of licensing has caused some to urge that mental health licensing in its present form be eliminated. Hogan has proposed that the state register mental health professionals and require that they make available to the public information, including experience and academic training, statement of ethical beliefs, proposed length of treatment, and results that are to be expected.[41] Such a proposal has the advantage of making available a maximum amount of information about a therapist, while allowing a significant form of competition to exist. However, it is certainly not realistic to expect most patients who need medical or mental health services to be able to carefully study the various therapists in order to choose the right or qualified ones. Certainly an argument can be made that in such times of need, many patients cannot conduct a "Consumer Report" review of the options available to them. Nor is it reasonable to expect that states could enforce compliance with claims made by therapists in these reports to the public. As a result fraud could easily become a significant problem.

A system of licensing that works well may serve both the professions and the public. The problem with the current system may be that it fully works neither in eliminating the incompetent and unethical, nor in providing the advantages of a freely competitive market. The compromises that have produced licensing have resulted in the worst of both worlds for the public; many of the costs of regulation are present but the potential benefits of licensure regulation are reduced by the weak licensing provisions currently enforced. We believe that, to best serve the public, licensing procedures should be significantly strengthened and restructured as described above.

OTHER LIMITATIONS ON PRACTICE

Mental health practice is also controlled by the regulation of hospital privileges and authority to prescribe drugs. Because services will ordinarily be provided only if they can be paid for, the reimbursement issue, described in the following sections, is also an important form of indirect regulation.

Hospital Privileges

Traditionally, authority to practice independently in hospitals and to admit patients to hospitals has been limited to physicians. Therefore, psychiatrists have been the only mental health professionals with hospital privileges, while other mental professionals can be called upon to assist in a hospital, they operate at least in theory under the direction of a physician. A mental health professional seeing a patient who needs hospitalization, of course, must refer the patient to a physician for admission. In a few areas of the country, however, limited hospital privileges have been granted to some nonphysician mental health professionals, while elsewhere the issue is a matter of hot debate.

Staff privileges are granted by each hospital according to its own criteria. However, hospital accreditation standards play a significant role in the process. Since 1951, the Joint Commission on Accreditation of Hospitals (JCAH) has been the major accrediting body for hospitals.[42] Although it is a voluntary accrediting body, many third-party payers (including federal health programs) depend on JCAH accreditation. The JCAH regulations have reflected the physicians' control of the policies of that organization. Until recently, the accreditation standards permitted hospitals to grant staff privileges only to physicians. Recently, however, the medical staff of the hospital has been redefined to include in addition "licensed individuals permitted by law and the hospital to provide patient care services independently in the hospital."[43] Several states have by statute provided that licensed psychologists and others may be granted staff privileges.[44]

Even without such specific statutory authority hospitals may be able to grant staff privileges to such professions. Not surprisingly, however, most hospitals have not immediately started to grant privileges to nonphysicians. Threats of antitrust lawsuits have in some cases encouraged the hospitals to consider it. (One basis for the antitrust claim is that refusal of privileges is a conspiracy to restrain trade by reducing competition through the refusal to let qualified professionals into the hospital "market.") Indeed the threat of antitrust action probably played a major role in the JCAH decision to amend its criteria.[45]

There are several reasons for these efforts to expand privileges. Without them, some mental health professionals claim treatment may be disrupted or interrupted when a patient enters the hospital. It is argued that if they could admit the patient to the hospital and continue to direct their care, treatment would improve. Others argue that the refusal to grant staff privileges reduces competition and thereby economically harms both patients and nonphysician mental health professionals.[46] At the same time, mental health training programs are now sufficiently complete to ensure adequate knowledge to direct the hospital treatment programs of some mental patients. Therefore, it is argued, it is unnecessary for a licensing physician to further ensure the qualifications of those trained for independent practice.

The nature of hospital practice, at least in larger hospitals, has changed. Physicians are now commonly limited to practicing only in their specialties. New methods of health care delivery may rely heavily on those with staff privileges and care providers. For example, preferred provider organizations (PPOs) may be structured around professionals with privileges at a particular hospital or set of hospitals. Without being part of the staff, mental health professionals may be excluded from these important new forms of health care. In addition, the hospital staff plays an important role in the governance of hospitals and in the assurance of quality care. It is argued that mental health professionals cannot fully participate in process without staff privileges.

There are also numerous arguments against permitting nonphysician staff privileges. For one, they are not licensed to perform a full range of services; for another, their philosophy of treatment may not be consistent with the medical models on which hospitals are typically structured. Others argue that their training programs are inadequate to prepare them for independent work in a hospital setting, and therefore the quality of care may be inferior to that which could be provided by physicians.[47] Physician control over staff admission policies is, of course, one practical reason that privileges have been rejected.

There is by no means complete agreement within the nonphysician mental health professions that staff privileges are desirable. Some claim such status would increase the public esteem and recognition of the professions, while others suggest that they would change the nature and focus of professional practice, education, and treatment approaches. Still others fear a continuing adversarial relationship with psychiatrists and other physicians within the hospitals.

JCAH accepting non-physician practitioners, the developing concept of limited staff privileges, and the increasing respect and public acknowledgment of a variety of mental health practitioners all suggest that the move toward hospital staff privileges for mental health professionals will probably continue. Hospitals will still be able to restrict staff privileges. They need not admit everyone with the licensing or academic credentials necessary for practice. They can require special levels of education, experience, and quality of practice; they may impose very high standards for nonphysicians; and they may narrowly define the kinds of activities that mental health professionals may perform, require substantial consultation with the physicians, and limit the participation of mental health professionals in staff governance.

Prescription Drugs

Currently, psychiatrists are the only mental health practitioners permitted to order prescription drugs for patients. All other physicians are also licensed to prescribe psychoactive drugs to patients whether or not those physicians have specialized training in psychiatry or neurology.

The control of prescription drugs is a matter of both federal and state law. Federal law establishes the basic regulation and approval of medication (including the classification of compounds as over-the-counter or prescription drugs); state law deals with the licensing of specific individuals permitted to prescribe medication.

In many ways, issues concerning the authority to prescribe drugs are similar to those raised about hospital staff privileges. The arguments for authorizing some nonphysician mental health professionals to prescribe psychopharmacological agents are that drugs have become an important part of psychotherapy; restrictions on the professionals permitted to prescribe drugs increase costs; and psychologists, social workers, and others should be able to integrate drug therapy with other forms of psychotherapy. Those in favor of limited prescription authority point to the authority granted to dentists and optometrists to use some prescription drugs and devices. Yet it is also argued that most current mental health programs lack adequate training in pharmacology to justify such authority and that most of these programs would find it philosophically contrary to their treatment approaches. Others claim that prescription authority might encourage mental health professionals to rely too heavily on drugs. Again, the political reality is that expansion of prescribing authority would face considerable opposition from physicians.

To date, there has not been much professional effort to obtain prescribing authority, in part because there is little likelihood of success in the near future. Unless there is a considerable increase in conditions for which there is a clearly effective drug therapy, it is unlikely that the nonpsychiatric professions will seek authority to prescribe drugs.

REIMBURSEMENT FOR MENTAL HEALTH SERVICES

Estimates are that at any time 15 percent to 20 percent of the population is in need of mental health services, and that a third of the population has experienced a mental disorder during their lives.[48] Despite this broad need, or perhaps in part because of it, the provision of mental health services has been very limited both in terms of reimbursement for service and in terms of the variety of professionals whose services are covered for reimbursement. We now briefly consider the coverage of mental health services by private insurers and the government, and the limitations on the mental health professional whose services will be covered by insurance or government programs.[49]

Provision of Mental Health Services

Following World War II there was dramatic growth in the health care insurance industry. Private health insurance became a standard employment fringe benefit. Although the tendency until the early 1980s was to expand coverage, mental health coverage has typically been minimal, with severe limits on coverage for inpatient days and even more limits on outpatient services.[50] By the 1980s, some benefit programs had substantially reduced previous coverage.[51] When health maintenance organizations (HMOs) were recognized and protected by Congress, they were required to provide comprehensive health care, with the exception that they could limit inpatient and outpatient services for mental health care.[52]

The reasons for this may have to do with the difficulty in determining when services are really necessary or when a patient is malingering or a mental health professional is providing unnecessary services. Mental health injuries may seem less real than observable physical injuries. Much mental health treatment is seen as general improvement or growth-oriented rather than curing a disease, and in that sense appears to be elective or even cosmetic. Some forms of therapy, e.g., traditional psychoanalysis, are very extended and quite expensive. Psychotherapy is criticized as being "insubstantial care for self-defined illnesses with no clear indication of starting or finishing and no way to judge effectiveness—whether there are results worth paying for."[53] These attitudes may explain why insurance companies and employers who purchase health insurance for their employees may not see mental health coverage as important or attractive.

Despite setbacks in other areas, coverage for mental illness may be increasing somewhat as a result of state legislative action and the changing nature of health care. A number of states have now passed mental health "parity" statutes.[54] These laws require that insurance carriers within the state provide mental health coverage on the same basis or to the same extent as physical coverage. The purpose of these statutes is to prevent unfair discrimination against those with mental illness. The Supreme Court has upheld the constitutionality of such statutes, and their popularity seems to be growing.[55]

As we shall see, several changes in delivery of health services, such as the emphasis on coverage of all medical care and not just hospital-based services (e.g., HMOs), may ultimately encourage greater coverage of some outpatient mental health services. If they can reduce the incidence of physical health problems or hospitalization, then there will be a strong economic incentive to provide them.

State and Local Government Programs

Governments have long accepted some responsibility for dealing with and caring for the mentally ill.[56] It has traditionally fallen to state and local governments to offer mental health facilities for patients detained through the involuntary civil commitment process and for some patients unable to pay. States generally fund a wide variety of mental health programs. While state and local governments maintain a major responsibility for providing mental health care to the indigent, since the 1960s the federal government has taken an increasingly larger role.

The Federal Government

The major health care programs of the federal government are Medicare and Medicaid, and a variety of specific health service programs directed in part toward mental health care. Medicare is part of the Social Security program that provides health care services for elderly and for the disabled. Funding for mental health services under Medicare has been extremely limited, and it has been particularly resistant to expanding mental health coverage. In this sense it has followed private health insurance. Because of substantial increases in the cost of the program, there has been little inclination to expand coverage.[57]

The traditional means of reimbursement for Medicare hospital expenses (the major portion of the program) has been on a "cost" basis so that in effect hospitals were paid on the basis of treatment costs. There was thus little incentive for hospitals and physicians to reduce costs. Medicare has moved toward a "prospective payment system" under which hospitals are reimbursed at a predetermined rate based on the condition or diagnosis of the patient and the location of the hospital. Medical conditions are placed in diagnostic related groupings (DRG), and hospitals are paid a flat rate for each admission based on the DRG as adjusted to take limited account of geographical factors. Hospitals receive the same amount for the admission regardless of the actual length of hospital stay or the efficiency or inefficiency of the hospital. The DRG system imposes strong economic incentives for hospitals to operate efficiently and to keep Medicare patient stays as short as possible. Because of the complexity of psychiatric diagnoses and conditions, DRGs in this area have been delayed. The use of DRGs may influence mental health care in a number of subtle ways. It will encourage hospitals to discharge mental patients as quickly as possible, perhaps thereby promoting deinstitutionalization. In the long run, it may also encourage the use of mental health professionals if providing mental health services to those hospitalized for physical ailments promotes early release from the hospital. The incentive toward efficiency may also encourage hospitals to use lower priced professionals (e.g., social workers, or para-professionals), instead of higher priced professionals (e.g., psychiatrists) to perform some services. The long-term effects of the prospective payment system and the use of DRG cannot yet be fully calculated.[58]

Medicaid is a cooperative federal-state effort to provide medical services for the indigent.[59] The federal government provides substantial funding and general regulations under which states operate their Medicaid programs. States have some latitude under Medicaid to decide who and what conditions will be covered to provide for the health care costs for the poor. The federal funding for mental health care is extremely limited under Medicaid. For example, it does not cover services to patients under 65 in an "institution for mental diseases."[60] Most states provide few Medicaid mental health services. Because states are permitted to define their programs within federal guidelines, the programs vary somewhat from one state to another.[61] Budget cuts and reallocations have had the effect of reducing further funds for Medicare, Medicaid, and related Social Security programs.[62]

The major federal involvement in efforts to provide mental health services came after World War II. During the war nearly 1.9 million men were rejected for military service because of mental problems.[63] In addition, descriptions of state mental hospitals as "snake pits," "human warehouses," and "houses of horror"[64] attracted considerable national attention. One account stated that these hospitals rivaled "the horror of the Nazi concentration camps—hundreds of naked mental patients herded into huge, barn-like, filth-infested wards, in all degrees of deterioration."[65] The National Mental Health Act of 1946 was passed to encourage research and investigation relating to the causes, diagnosis, and treatment of psychiatric disorders through the National Institute of Mental Health (NIMH).[66] In 1955 Congress established the Joint Commission of Mental Health and Illness, which reported its findings in 1961.[67] It noted the need for massive expenditures in the mental health field and argued for comprehensive care centers. President Kennedy, responding to the report, urged a "bold new approach" in the federal response to national mental health problems: reducing the number of institutionalized patients by 50 percent within ten years and replacing large mental hospitals with comprehensive community mental health centers. The Community

Mental Health Center Act of 1963 provided money to construct comprehensive mental health centers, later to be funded through the states.[68] Each community mental health center was to include inpatient, outpatient, and partial hospitalization services; 24-hour emergency services; and consultation and education services. To the extent possible they were also to engage in a broad range of diagnostic services, rehabilitation services, pre-care and after-care services, and education and research. It was hoped that these centers would provide equal access to quality services for the rich and poor alike.

By 1970, 450 community mental health services were in operation, but the growth was reduced as federal funding slowed somewhat and states demonstrated reluctance to fund the centers as planned. The centers, as well as the development of psychoactive drugs and an emphasis on deinstitutionalization, resulted in dramatic reduction in the number of patients in mental institutions.[69] Unfortunately, the release of patients from mental institutions was not accompanied by a sufficient increase in community based treatment facilities, housing, training, and educational and recreational programs. As a result deinstitutionalization too often was "a shift of patients from back wards to back alleys."[70]

In the late 1970s another presidential commission recommended a number of new service initiatives to provide mental health treatment for anyone who needed it regardless of income.[71] The commission's report essentially viewed mental health services as a right with a corresponding public responsibility for financing the services. The Mental Health Systems Act of 1980 was arguably the most comprehensive mental health legislation ever passed in the United States.[72] It coordinated a variety of mental health services and continued emphasis on community mental health centers. Special programs were provided for chronically mentally ill, children and adolescents, the elderly, minorities, and rape victims. Before much of this act could be implemented, its sponsor, President Carter, was replaced by President Reagan, and much of the act was repealed. Funds were cut for services and in place of specific programs, states were given "block grants" covering broad ranges of health services and mental health programs.[73]

Many view 1978 to 1980 as the high water mark of federal involvement with and concern for funding for mental health services. However, the process of deinstitutionalization was never accompanied by the planned community facilities nor were the promises of providing mental health services to all Americans who needed them fulfilled. Other federal programs have followed the same fate. Federal mental health interest has had an element of fadishness. There has been funding for problems of immediate public interest which subsides to be replaced by a new "in" problem, among them child and adolescent care, rape victim counseling, family violence, alcohol and drug dependence, and post-traumatic stress syndrome. Federal mental health services funding has not been consistent or pursued with any form of long-term planning.

Reimbursement for Professional Services

When mental health services are covered by government programs or private insurance the question often remains: which professionals may provide services and be reimbursed for them? In the past, most private insurance provided for billing by or through a psychiatrist. The major medical insurance company (Blue Cross & Blue Shield) strongly favored psychiatrists, perhaps because the company was closely tied to physicians.[74] This process probably tended to increase prices, and decreased the availability of services of psychologists and other independent providers.

Several factors are tending to increase the ability of nonpsychiatric mental health professionals to participate in reimbursement plans. Some states have passed "freedom of choice" legislation which gives consumers the right to choose from a range of mental health professionals which can be reimbursed by insurance.[75] The threat of antitrust action against reimbursement-only-through-psychiatrist provisions has reduced the number of such provisions in insurance contracts.[76] In addition, a number of new economic considerations provide incentives to use the least costly effective therapy. HMOs, preferred provider organizations (PPOs), and DRGs, for example, should encourage the use of psychologists, social workers, and other independently licensed professionals. In HMOs, for example, payment is based on a flat fee for providing all health needs rather than on a straight fee-for-service basis. Therefore, the incentives are to provide effective treatment at the lowest cost possible and this may encourage the use of nonphysician mental health providers whose fees tend to be lower than psychiatrists.[77]

In addition, new trends in health care are tending to de-emphasize in-hospital, physician-oriented treatment (which is of course the most expensive form of health-care) and emphasize services performed, often by nonphysicians, on an outpatient basis. On the other hand, these trends may harm nonpsychiatrist mental health providers, because physicians may increasingly serve as gatekeepers to more and more mental health care.[78] For example, PPOs may require referral through a primary physician and thereby limit the roles of others. If all health care must be initiated through an organization (PPO or HMO) to which only physicians have access, then mental health care *could* increasingly be initiated through physician contact and with some physician supervision. It is too early to determine what the ultimate role of these new forms will be, let alone what effect they will have on the provision of mental health care services.[79]

BENEFITS AND COSTS OF MENTAL HEALTH CARE

Efficacy of Therapy

Early studies of the efficacy of psychotherapy suggested that therapy was of little value.[80] Later studies with improved research methodology utilizing meta-analysis have demonstrated a general efficacy of psychotherapy. Smith, Glass and Miller reviewed 475 studies involving controlled evaluations of psychotherapy by considering "effect sizes" of psychotherapy.[81] They found that on average, a person after psychotherapy was better off than 80 percent of those who did not receive psychotherapy, while 9 percent of those who received psychotherapy were worse off than those who did not receive it. Their study was evaluated and amplified by Landman and Dawes, who came to similar conclusions.[82] The Office of Technology Assessment, a scientific study arm of Congress, reviewed the literature on psychotherapy outcomes. It too concluded that psychotherapy in general is effective.[83] Shapiro and Shapiro, using refined meta-analysis techniques devised by Smith, Glass and Miller, concluded that in general there is moderate positive effect found for psychotherapy.[84]

While evidence exists for some positive effects from psychotherapy generally, the more difficult question is what forms of therapy are most effective. One author counted 160 "brand names" of psychotherapy[85] and, as the Office of Technology Assessment noted, it is critical to know which types of psychotherapy in which setting are best for a patient. However, existing data do not, in most cases, answer these questions.[86] Although Shapiro and Shapiro found a modest superiority of cognitive and behavioral methods of psychotherapy and modest inferiority of psychodynamic and humanistic therapies,[87] these findings have been criticized.[88] While there has been some suggestion that for even severely disturbed patients intensive outpatient care is more effective than intensive inpatient care,[89] it is generally concluded that "the present evidence does not permit the identification of any procedures or techniques that are clearly ineffective or unsafe or that any are clearly more effective than others."[90]

In addition to the issue of the efficacy of various kinds of therapy, the question of comparative cost-effectiveness arises.[91] That is, determining how effective various therapies are per dollar cost of providing them. Several studies indicate that for most patients, mental hospitalization is less cost-effective than outpatient therapy.[92] The difficulty in establishing clear differences in the effects of different kinds of therapy makes it impossible to do a detailed cost-effectiveness analysis. The absence of these kinds of data is probably a major factor in the reluctance of government and private insurers to expand mental health care coverage. Because the most effective therapy may depend on the mental condition, age and status, feelings about therapy, and so on, a complicated series of studies will be necessary to determine which therapies are effective in what circumstances.

Mental Health Coverage and Health Care Costs

Another important question is the effect that providing mental health care coverage has on total health care cost. Reductions are likely in total costs if patients can be diverted from expensive hospitalization to less expensive outpatient care. One study found that the cost of *comprehensive* mental health care benefits was considerably less expensive than *selected* mental health benefits.[93] One reason for this may be that the former encourage outpatient care, the latter inpatient care. It is also possible that comprehensive services encourage early (and less expensive) treatment.

Providing mental health services may reduce total health care spending by reducing the use of physical health care services. There is considerable evidence that emotional factors may cause or aggravate physical disorders. From 6 percent to 86 percent of patients in general medical settings have been found to have psychological disorders.[94] Perhaps half of the patients with psychological disorders are seen by nonpsychiatric physicians.[95] For patients with health problems, providing mental health services can significantly reduce total medical services costs. While mental health care costs increase as a proportion of total health care costs, the mental health costs are offset by a reduction in general medical utilization. There is evidence that medical services utilization may be reduced for virtually all mental health diagnostic groups by providing psychotherapy.[96] The level of this reduction can be significant, perhaps ranging from 25 percent to 60 percent reduction in general medical utilization when mental health benefits are available.[97]

These data must be considered tentative, but they do suggest the very real possibility that increasing mental health services may reduce total health care costs. Additional studies concerning the effect of mental health services on total health care costs are continuing. Medicaid patients, for example, are being studied in selected areas. If the data reported above are confirmed, it is reasonable to expect that mental health services could be expanded as a way of reducing total health care costs.

Thus, while it is not yet possible to compare the efficacy or cost effectiveness of various kinds of mental health services, there is significant evidence for the following propositions:

1. In general, mental health care is effective in promoting change or improving the mental condition of patients ("curing" faster than without treatment).
2. Provision of comprehensive mental health services may be less expensive than providing selective (inpatient) mental health services only.
3. Providing mental health services reduces the demand for physical health care and thereby may reduce total health care costs.

Given these propositions it is somewhat surprising that coverage for mental services has been so limited. The explanation may lie in the historical development of private and governmental health care coverage, with its emphasis on hospital care. It may relate to the absence (until recently) of incentives to cut costs and provide efficient services, and it may relate to the fact that only recently have dependable data concerning the benefits of mental health care coverage been available. To the extent that new systems of physical care put an emphasis on keeping patients out of the hospital and reducing total health care costs, coverage for outpatient mental health care may become increasingly important.

COSTS AND UTILIZATION OF MENTAL HEALTH FACILITIES

The level and nature of mental health services has changed dramatically since World War II. There has been a significant increase in the number of mental health care episodes along with a substantial decrease in the percentage of mental health care episodes that involve mental hospital admission.[98] These changes are demonstrated by the fact that in 1955, there were 1.7 million such episodes in the United States, with more than 75 percent of these services being provided in inpatient facilities. By 1977, there were nearly 7 million patient care episodes of which only 27 percent were inpatient services.[99] Even controlling for population growth, the number of patient care episodes per 100,000 population tripled during the period. (These data do not include mental health care provided by partial care facilities such as halfway houses, private office practice, and general hospital medical services, and therefore probably considerably understate the true rate of mental health care episodes.) It appears that between 8 and 10 million people utilized mental health services in 1975, but it is estimated that the unmet need for additional services included 11 to 16 million people.[100]

The number of mental health care episodes in *state* mental hospitals decreased from 850,000 to 576,000 annually during this period.[101] This decline reflects the discovery of psychotropic drugs, restrictive involuntary civil commitment statutes, improved psychological rehabilitation techniques, increased use of community mental health services, and financial incentives to transfer long-term mental patients to nursing homes.[102] It also reflects the fact that hospitalization for mental conditions has shifted from mental hospitals to general hospitals. In 1965 there were 180,000 general hospital psychiatric in-patient episodes, while in 1979 there were approximately 1.2 million general hospital psychiatric admissions.[103] Thus the total number of mental health related hospital episodes may have increased even though the number of patients in mental hospitals has decreased.

Mental health care consumes a relatively small part (about 12 percent) of the total U.S. health care costs. Nearly 70 percent of the money spent on mental health care is for hospitalization. Ironically, while 70 percent of mental health care costs are for inpatient care, over 70 percent of the mental health care services are for outpatient treatment.[104] Total health care expenditures in the United States now constitute more than 10 percent of the gross national product, and the general rate of increase in health expenditure has exceeded the general rate of inflation. The federal government currently pays about 40 percent of health care expenditures, the largest component of which is hospital reimbursement.[105] Thus, there is a significant incentive to use outpatient mental health services as a means of reducing total health care costs.

It is the level of underutilization of mental health services, or the size of the unmet demand for those services, that is most notable. It is estimated that at any time 15 percent to 20 percent of the population is experiencing a mental or emotional problem of some significance.[106] It is apparent from the data reported above that only a relatively small proportion of that group will actually receive mental health treatment. Such underprovision has periodically been the focus of significant social and governmental concern.

THE PHILOSOPHY AND FUTURE OF MENTAL HEALTH CARE DELIVERY

The current substantial unmet need for services reflects the absence of reimbursement schemes. Government programs have provided some services for the indigent with serious mental problems and limited services for others. Private health insurance, usually provided through employers, has generally provided only minimal mental health benefits. Other services have been purchased directly by those needing them. Thus the determination of how much service will be available and who will get the services has depended on political considerations (government programs), employee benefits, and ability to pay for services. The medically indigent, middle and lower socioeconomic groups, often do not fare well under such a system because of the inability to privately purchase mental health services. The goal of making mental health services available to all Americans regardless of the ability to pay has largely gone unfulfilled.

Competition and Mental Health Care

Until recently, health care was becoming an increasingly regulated part of the economy. But during the last few years this trend has been reversed and there are now efforts to impose market-like discipline, intended to reduce costs while maintaining service. The increased applicability of antitrust laws, the use of DRGs for Medicare reimbursement, and the development of PPOs and HMOs have added elements of competition. The consequences of these changes, while far from certain, have the potential for substantially increasing the use of outpatient mental health services.

Efforts to reduce health care costs have sometimes resulted in the loss of mental health care services from insurance, but the potential for mental health care services to reduce total health care cost may ultimately encourage the provision of these services to the poor, and medically indigent lower and middle income families. In the absence of proof that one form of therapy is more effective than another, or that one class of mental health professionals is more effective than another, there may be a trend toward providing services through lower-cost rather than higher-cost professionals. Over the long run, the incentives to avoid inpatient care will undoubtedly increase.

There is a risk, however, that mental health services may become less available in the push to cut costs. If they continue to be viewed as nonessential extras and unrelated to physical health care costs, then these will be among the first to be cut. The reduction in government-funded mental health services and private insurance contracts suggests that mental health may be viewed as desirable but not essential or even important. Evidence concerning the overall health care cost with and without the inclusion of mental health care suggests that cutting mental health services may be costly in the long run. The challenge to those promoting mental health benefits is to continue to develop data demonstrating the cost-effectiveness of mental health services generally and of specific forms of therapy.

National Health Insurance

The most comprehensive form of government regulation of health care is national health insurance. The United States is the only major industrial country without such a program. Depending on one's point of view, this either represents one reason for the high level of quality of medical services available within the country or the reason for the high percentage of gross national product devoted to them. The United States has some elements of national health insurance.[107] The Medicare system, for example, provides general health coverage for the elderly; Medicaid for the indigent has similar elements. Government expenditures for health care may represent 40 percent to 50 percent of health care services.[108]

Although the broad universal coverage of national health insurance does not appear to be imminent in the United States, it is likely that the debate will continue. In addition, discussion continues about the desirability of expanding current federal health programs in ways that would, in effect, move the country closer to universal coverage.

National health insurance would not necessarily be comprehensive in terms of providing complete mental health coverage. In fact, some recent major legislative proposals have provided for very limited mental health coverage within a national health insurance program. The reasons for this exclusion are the same as those for limited coverage: it is difficult to define what conditions should be covered by the insurance or to determine when the patient is "cured" or no longer needs treatment; there traditionally has been relatively limited consumer demand for mental health coverage and thus mental health may appear to be optional or elective rather than essential; some mental health care is aimed at personal growth or education rather than "real" health care; and mental health care is commonly provided outside the hospital and therefore does not fit neatly within hospital-based insurance plans.

The arguments in favor of including mental health care within national health insurance are: mental health problems are as real and as painful as physical disease and those with mental conditions as surely deserve treatment as do those with physical conditions; the failure to provide for outpatient mental health services is likely to result in more expensive hospital treatment; providing good mental health services (especially outpatient care) apparently lowers total health care costs; and physical and mental conditions are related and should be considered together in treating the whole person.[109] If comprehensive mental health coverage proves to be an effective means of reducing total health care costs, then those services will probably be covered by future comprehensive national health insurance proposals. Otherwise the prospect for including broad mental health benefits under national health insurance will remain bleak.

If mental health coverage is to be included in government programs, mental health benefits will have to be narrowly and precisely defined. They should be defined in terms of the treatment of relatively significant mental distress or conditions and the prevention of these conditions when their development is likely. This definition, although imprecise, excludes general growth therapy, encounter groups, and education. While such activities may be worthwhile, classifying them as mental health care tends to trivialize the importance of serious mental health needs. Clearly defined treatment plans against which individual treatment can be measured or considered are also needed. Such an approach obviously has problems in terms of failure to recognize the individual differences among patients, but it is probably necessary for third-party payers to be assured that they are not being billed for unnecessary or experimental treatment.

SUMMARY

Licensing of mental health professionals, which is a matter of state law, is now found in virtually every state in the United States. The purpose of licensing is to protect the public from incompetent, and therefore dangerous, practitioners and from quacks. In practice, licensing also provides a formal recognition of the profession, tends to reduce the number of people admitted to practice, and protects professions from competition. Thus, while licensing has a potential for protecting the public, it also has a potential for harming it. State licensure laws may prohibit the performing of certain services without a license (practice laws), prohibit the use of a title or label without a license (title laws) or require the licensee to register with the state (registration laws).

There are substantial differences among mental health professions concerning the nature of licensing laws. Psychiatry is essentially without a license requirement, other than that of an M.D., and any physician can claim to be a psychiatrist. Psychology licensing varies considerably from state to state, but most states license doctoral-level psychologists, while a significant minority also provides some licensing or certification for masters-level psychologists. Social work generally recognizes various levels of licensing depending on educational level. In some states there are also licensing laws for marriage or family counseling.

The requirements for licensing ordinarily include the completion of an academic degree, passage of licensing examination, completion of supervised work experience, and demonstration of good moral or ethical character.

Once a license is granted, it is fairly uncommon for it to be revoked. There is generally no requirement for periodic retesting or recertification. State licensure boards are authorized, following appropriate hearings, to remove a license if they find a professional is incompetent to continue practice, unfit because of alcohol or drug addiction, engaging in illegal activity which reflects on trust or professional standing, or has engaged in serious professional misconduct. It is unusual for a state board to take strong disciplinary action against the holder of a license. Boards are seldom proactive and usually depend upon complaints from the public or other professionals to draw attention to the need for disciplinary action. Discipline may range from a private reprimand to license suspension or revocation. Strong disciplinary action is seldom taken.

A number of criticisms are leveled against licensing, including that it unnecessarily limits the supply of practitioners, resulting in fewer services at higher prices, that it stifles innovation, and that it limits the geographical distribution of mental health services. There is a basis for some of these criticisms.

The question that must be asked is whether the public gains sufficiently to justify the costs of licensing. We believe a number of reforms would strengthen licensing and help protect the public. Most of the suggestions we make in this chapter are intended to tighten licensing requirements. An alternative suggested by others is to eliminate licensing and replace it with a system of consumer information that would permit consumers to choose the kind of professional and the type of service desired. In a world of sophisticated consumers, this might be an appropriate system, but doubts can be raised about its practicality in today's world. The public, as well as individuals who seek therapy, have a stake in the quality of care available to those who need such services.

In addition to licensing there are a number of other limitations on mental health practice. These include the availability of hospital privileges and authority to prescribe medicines. Both have traditionally been the exclusive province of physicians, although in some areas of the country other mental health practitioners have gained limited hospital staff privileges. Recent revisions in the accreditation standards for hospitals permit hospitals to grant staff privileges to nonphysicians under some circumstances. The debate over hospital staff privileges for nonphysician mental health professionals is likely to continue, with the trend likely to be toward expansion of privileges. Less debate has occurred on the desirability of authorizing mental health professionals with appropriate training to prescribe medicines, but similar arguments can be anticipated.

Reimbursement for providing mental health services is an indirect means of regulating mental health care. It is estimated that between 15 percent and 20 percent of the population is in need of mental health services. Only a small portion of those needing the services will receive them. Private insurance and government programs such as Medicare and Medicaid generally provide only very limited coverage for mental health services. Even "comprehensive" health plans such as health maintenance organizations often do not provide full coverage for mental health services. The federal government as well as state and local governments directly provide some mental health services. A major effort to make mental health services available to everyone has been the community mental health center program. These programs were never funded as planned and that goal remains unfulfilled.

Limiting coverage for mental health services, particularly for outpatient services, may prove to be counterproductive. There is reason to believe that the availability of good outpatient services may reduce mental health hospitalization. It may also be that providing mental health services reduces the demand for physical health services, thereby reducing the total cost of health care. It has been difficult to demonstrate the efficacy of one form of psychotherapy over other forms. However, data do suggest that mental health care in general is effective.

Major proposals for national health insurance have provided relatively limited coverage for mental health, consistent with current government policies in Medicare and Medicaid.

The immediate future for adequate mental health care is not bright. The long-term outlook is somewhat brighter, although far from certain. To encourage adequate care, essential mental health services should be separated from individual growth or education goals, the efficacy of various forms of treatment should be demonstrated, treatment plans for various conditions should be articulated by the professions, the ability of mental health care to reduce total health care cost should be more clearly established, and the public should be made aware of the need for and benefits of mental health care.

NOTES

1. The term "system" is perhaps unwarranted if it implies the existence of a single, organized or integrated mechanism of providing mental health care services. In fact, the "system" is fragmented, inconsistent from part to part and full of holes in which some of those needing mental health services do not receive them.

2. O. W. Holmes, Sr., *Medical Essays* 203 (1892).

3. In fact, one critic of licensing quotes Holmes as part of his argument that professional entry requirements are arbitrary and harmful. D. Hogan, *The Regulation of Psychotherapists* 252 (1979) [hereinafter *The Regulation of Psychotherapists*]. The four volumes by Hogan on the regulation of psychotherapy is an extraordinarily complete and very useful review of licensure laws affecting psychotherapy. Although somewhat dated, volume 2 of the work, subtitled *A Handbook of State Licensure Laws,* provides a state-by-state and profession-by-profession summary of licensing regulation.

4. C. Gilb, *Hidden Hierarchies: The Professions and Government* (1966); Gross, The Myth of Professional Licensing, 33 *Am. Psychologist* 1009 (1978); Wallace, Occupational Licensing and Certification: Remedies for Denial, 14 *Wm. & Mary L. Rev.* 46 (1972).

5. For a history of the regulation of the mental health professions see

J. Ehrenwald ed., *The History of Psychotherapy: From Healing Magic to Encounter* (1976); H. Kendler, *A History of Psychology* (1987); Danish, Considering Professional Licensing from a Social and Historical Context, 9 *Counseling Psychologist* 35 (1980); Note, Regulation of Psychological Counseling and Psychotherapy, 51 *Colum. L. Rev.* 474 (1951).

6. In a few instances licensing statutes have been repealed or allowed to expire. See B. Fretz & D. Mills, *Licensing and Certification of Psychologists and Counselors* (1980); Hale, The Illusion of Effective Regulation, 35 *Clinical Psychologist* 10 (1981); Jackson & Branum, Licensing is Lovelier the Second Time Around, 2 *Prof. Prac. Psychology* 35 (1981).

7. Ideally, a profession is guided by a high sense of social responsibility. In return for a high level of self-regulation granted by society, the professions should ensure that only reasonably competent and ethical practitioners are permitted to practice, that monopoly-type profits are avoided, that the profession renders service only within its area of expertise, and that it does not restrict licensing for the purpose of promoting its own economic interests. See Sanford, The Criteria of a Good Profession, 6 *Am. Psychologist* 668 (1951).

8. Geiser & Rheingold, Psychology and the Legal Process: Testimonial Privileged Communications, 19 *Am. Psychologist* 83 (1964).

9. S. Gross, *Of Foxes and Henhouses: Licensing and the Health Professions* (1984).

10. See R. Schwitzgebel & R. K. Schwitzgebel, *Law and Psychological Practice* 222 (1980). In Kentucky, on the other hand, the state licensure board has recognized master's-level psychologists as certificands.

11. See Kern, State Regulation of Social Work, 10 *Val. U. L. Rev.* 261 (1976); Rutledge, State Regulation of Marriage Counseling, 22 *Fam. Coordinator* 81 (1973); Snow, Counselor Licensure as Perceived by Counselors and Psychologists, 60 *Personnel & Guidance J.* 80 (1981); Swanson, Moving Toward Counselor Licensure: A Statewide Survey, 60 *Personnel & Guidance J.* 78 (1981).

12. D. Hogan, *The Regulation of Psychotherapists* (vol. 2) 57–69, 97–110 (1979).

13. Levit, Sabshin & Meuller, Trends in Graduate Medical Education and Specialty Certification, 290 *New Eng. J. Med.* 545 (1974). See Taylor & Torrey, The Pseudo-Regulation of American Psychiatry, 129 *Am. J. Psychiatry* 34 (1972); Karson, Regulating Medical Psychotherapists in Illinois: A Question of Balance, 11 *J. Mar. J. Prac. & Proc.* 601 (1978).

14. See McMillan, Professional Standards and the Master's Level Psychologist, 4 *Prof. Psychology: Research & Prac.* 296 (1973); Wayne, An Examination of Selected Statutory Licensing Requirements for Psychologists in the United States, 60 *Personnel & Guidance J.* 420 (1982).

15. See Hardcastle, Public Regulation of Social Work, 22 *Soc. Work* 14 (1977).

16. In the relatively few appellate cases involving licensing, the major issues have been due process (did the state provide a fair hearing or clear

standards for discipline) or whether a degree meets the educational requirements for a license. E.g., Aronson v. Hall, 707 F.2d 693 (2d Cir. 1983);
Larkin v. Winthrow, 368 F. Supp. 796 (E.D. Wis. 1973), *rev'd*, 421 U.S. 35
(1975); Matter of Parting, 37 N.C. App. 302, 246 S.E.2d 519 (1978).

17. For a discussion of provisions contained in licensing statutes see
B. Fretz & D. Mills, *Licensing and Certification of Psychologists and Counselors*
(1980); D. Hogan, *The Regulation of Psychotherapists* (Vol. 2) (1979); Wayne,
An Examination of Selected Statutory Licensing Requirements for Psychologists in the United States, 60 *Personnel & Guidance J.* 420 (1982).

18. See generally Kiesler, The Training of Psychiatrists and Psychologists, in *Psychology and National Health Insurance* (C. Kiesler, N. Cummings
& G. VandenBos eds. 1980).

19. Ensuring rigorous educational requirements through accreditation
is a problem for many professions. This occurs because of the failure of the
profession to require professional accreditation (some mental health professions), the failure to deal adequately with foreign school graduates (medicine), or the failure of the accrediting agency to implement rigorous
standards. See generally Smith, Accreditation Revisited: ABA Reexamination
of Approved Law Schools, 27 *Wayne L. Rev.* 95 (1980).

20. Wiens & Menne, On Disposing of "Straw People," Or, An Attempt
to Clarify Statutory Recognition and Educational Requirements for Psychologists, 36 *Am. Psychologist* 390 (1981). States could choose to require
graduation from a fully accredited (professional association) program. Dra-
ganosky v. Minnesota Board of Psychology, 367 N.W.2d 521 (Minn. 1985).

21. See generally Goodstein & Ross, Accreditation of Graduate Programs in Psychology—An Analysis, 21 *Am. Psychologist* 218 (1966); Matarazzo, Higher Education, Professional Accreditation and Licensure, 32 *Am.
Psychologist* 856 (1977).

22. Fox & Barclay, The Foundation of Professional Psychology, 37 *Am.
Psychologist* 306 (1982); Kayton, Statutory Regulation of Psychologists: Its
Scope and Constitutionality, 33 *St. John's L. Rev.* 249 (1959); Wiens &
Menne, On Disposing of "Straw People," Or, An Attempt to Clarify Statutory
Recognition and Educational Requirements for Psychologists, 36 *Am. Psy-
chologist* 390 (1981).

23. Smith, Psychology and the Courts: Some Implications of Recent
Decisions for State Licensing Boards, 9 *Prof. Psychology: Research & Prac.*
489 (1978); Wallace, Occupational Licensing and Certification: Remedies
for Denial, 14 *Wm. & Mary L. Rev.* 46 (1972); Note, Due Process Limitations on Occupational Licensing, 59 *Va. L. Rev.* 1097 (1973). The difficulties
in adequately assessing competency are reviewed in J. Lloyd & D. Langsley
eds., *Evaluating the Skills of Medical Specialists* (1983).

24. B. Fretz & D. Mills, *Licensing and Certification of Psychologists and
Counselors* (1981).

25. Comment, Procedural Due Process and the Separation of Functions
in State Occupational Licensing Agencies, 1978 *Wis. L. Rev.* 833. For a

general review of licensing and special certification legal issues see L. Langsley ed., *Legal Aspects of Certification and Accreditation* (1983).

26. Small, Recertification for Psychiatrists: The Time to Act is Now, 132 *Am. J. Psychiatry* 291 (1975).

27. See Brown & Uhl, Mandatory Continuing Education: Sense or Nonsense?, 213 *J.A.M.A.* 1660 (1970). The continuing education requirements for a variety of professionals are set out in Jaschik, More States Are Requiring Professionals to Take Continuing-Education Courses, *Chronicle of Higher Ed.*, May 21, 1986, at 13, 16.

28. W. VanHoose & J. Kottler, *Ethical and Legal Issues In Counseling and Psychology* (1977).

29. Smith, Psychology and the Courts: Some Implications of Recent Judicial Decisions for State Licensing Boards, 9 *Prof. Psychology: Research & Prac.* 489 (1978).

30. Hogan reported that a survey of state boards of licensure revealed that on average they received only about one complaint per year per board. From the time of the establishment of state boards until 1972, only five licenses or certificates were revoked. D. Hogan, *The Regulation of Psychotherapists* at 260. During a one-year review, there were only 61 complaints of unethical conduct with the central office of the American Psychiatric Association, *Id.* at 334. Butler & Williams, Description of Ohio State Board of Psychology Hearings on Ethical Violations from 1972 to the Present, 16 *Prof. Psychology: Research & Prac.* 502 (1985) (only 11 ethical violations were determined by the Ohio board in 13 years). However, the number of complaints is increasing.

31. See generally J. Carlin, *Lawyers' Ethics: A Survey of the New York City Bar* (1966); Thackrey, Breakdown in Professional Self-Monitoring: Private Practice Announcement, 16 *Prof. Psychology: Research & Prac.* 163 (1985).

32. In a few instances membership in a specialty board may be accepted as the basis for licensing. For example, some states will accept ABPP as the basis for licensing.

33. See Wellner & Zimet, The National Register of Health Service Providers in Psychology in *The Professional Psychologist's Handbook* 185 (B. Sales ed. 1983). But see Clovis, The Boards—What Price Glory, 128 *Am. J. Psychiatry* 784 (1971).

34. E.g., D. Hogan, *The Regulation of Psychotherapists* 238–39 (1979).

35. E.g., S. Gross, *Of Foxes and Henhouses: Licensing and the Health Professions* (1984); Frieberg, The Song Is Ended but the Malady Lingers On: Legal Regulation of Psychotherapy, 22 *St. Louis U. L. J.* 519 (1978).

36. M. Gross, *The Psychological Society: A Critical Analysis of Psychiatry, Psychotherapy, Psychoanalysis and the Psychological Revolution* (1978); R. Reinehr, *The Machine that Oils Itself: A Critical Look at the Mental Health Establishment* (1975); Somers, Accountability, Public Policy, and Psychiatry, 134 *Am. J. Psychiatry* 959 (1977).

37. The story is told of the therapist who denied that he provided any

unnecessary therapy. He reported, "I don't put someone in therapy unless I absolutely need the money."

There exists a danger that if there are too many professionals they may unnecessarily place some people in extended treatment programs or extend treatment longer than necessary. Because much mental health treatment does not have clear, standard protocols, overtreatment is particularly a potential problem in psychotherapy.

38. Bernstein & LeComte, Licensure in Psychology: Alternative Directions, 12 *Prof. Psychology: Research & Prac.* 200 (1981).

39. American Psychological Association (Committee on State Legislation), A Model for State Legislation Affecting the Practice of Psychology, 22 *Am. Psychologist* 1095 (1977) (later revised).

40. National Association of Social Workers, *Legal Regulation of Social Work Practice* (1973). See also W. Nichols, *Marriage and Family Counseling: A Legislative Handbook* (1974).

41. D. Hogan, *The Regulation of Psychotherapists* 361–62 (1979).

42. See Zaro, Batchelor, Ginsberg & Pallak, Psychology and the JCAH: Reflections of a Decade of Struggle, 37 *Am. Psychologist* 1342 (1982). The JCAH was developed by the American Medical Association, the American Hospital Association, the American College of Surgeons and the American College of Physicians. The American Dental Association is now part of the JCAH structure. Lieberman & Astrachan, The JCAH and Psychiatry: Current Issues and Implications for Practice, 35 *Hosp. & Community Psychiatry* 1205 (1984).

43. Joint Commission on Accreditation of Hospitals, *Accreditation Manual for Hospitals* (1984).

44. California, Georgia, and the District of Columbia have led in the development of a statutory authority for psychologists to be given staff privileges. Currie, Legislative Initiatives in Hospital Practice, paper presented American Psychological Association (1983). Copeland, Hospital Privileges and Staff Membership for Psychologists, 11 *Prof. Psychology: Research & Prac.* 676 (1983).

45. Bershoff, Hospital Privileges and the Antitrust Laws, 38 *Am. Psychologist* 1238 (1983). See generally Virginia Academy of Clinical Psychologists v. Blue Shield, 624 F.2d 476 (4th Cir. 1980), *on remand,* 501 F. Supp. 1232 (E.D. Va. 1980), *cert. denied,* 450 U.S. 916 (1981); Dolan & Ralston, Hospital Admitting Privileges and the Sherman Act 18 *Hous. L. Rev.* 707 (1981); Drexel, The Antitrust Implications of the Denial of Hospital Staff Privileges, 36 *U. Miami L. Rev.* 207 (1982); Kissam, Government Policy Toward Medical Accreditation and Certification: The Antitrust Laws and Other Procompetitive Strategies, 1983 *Wis. L. Rev.* 1.

46. Bershoff, *supra,* note 45; Tanney, Hospital Privileges for Psychologists, 38 *Am. Psychologist* 1232 (1983).

47. See generally American Psychiatric Statement, Position Statement on Hospital Privileges for Psychologists, 125 *Am. J. Psychiatry* 1458 (1981). See also Elfant, Psychotherapy and Assessment in Hospital Settings: Ideo-

logical and Professional Conflicts, 16 *Prof. Psychology: Research & Prac.* 55 (1985) (involvement in hospitals may lead to "implicit identification with values and principles alien to the discipline of psychology").

48. The President's Commission on Mental Health reported that at any time about 15 percent of the population is in need of some form of mental health services. This was based on the commission's review in 1978. President's Commission on Mental Health, *Report of the President's Commission on Mental Health* (1980). More recently a study of mental conditions has revealed that over a six-month period, 17 percent to 23 percent of the population may suffer a psychiatric or emotional condition (based broadly on DSM-III categories). Myers et al., Six-Month Prevalence of Psychiatric Disorders in Three Communities, 41 *Archives Gen. Psychiatry* 959, 966 (1984) (the study was a careful review of conditions in three metropolitan areas). About one-third of the population (ranging from 29 percent to 38 percent) has experienced a psychiatric or emotional condition during their lifetimes (based broadly on DSM-III categories in three metropolitan areas). Robins et al., Lifetime Prevalence of Specific Psychiatric Disorders in Three Sites, 41 *Archives Gen. Psychiatry* 949, 952 (1984). The two articles cited in this note are part of an excellent, very large study of the prevalence of psychiatric conditions, based on NIMH epidemiological catchment area programs. Several articles in issue number 10 of volume 41 of the *Archives of General Psychiatry* describe the study. See W. W. Eaton & L. Kessler eds., *Epidemiologic Field Methods in Psychiatry: The NIMH Epidemiologic Catchment Area Program* (1985).

49. See Banta & Saxe, Reimbursement for Psychotherapy, 38 *Am. Psychologist* 919 (1983); Ruby, The Policy Implications of Insurance Coverage for Psychiatric Services, 7 *Int'l J. L. & Psychiatry* 269 (1984).

50. See R. H. Felix, *Mental Illness—Progress and Prospects* (1967); P. Margo, R. Gripp & D. McDowell, *The Mental Health Industry: A Cultural Phenomenon* (1978); T. McGuire, *Financing Psychotherapy: Costs, Effects and Public Policy* (1981).

51. The federal government, for example, in 1981 began cutting mental health benefits in its Federal Employees Health Benefits Program through Blue Cross and Blue Shield. Outpatient visits were limited to 50 annually, inpatient days were limited to 60 and co-payments were raised from 20 percent to 30 percent.

52. Health Maintenance Organization Act of 1973, Pub. L. No. 93-222 (1973). See Blonstin & Marclay, HMOs and Other Employee Health Plans: Coverage and Employee Premiums, 6 *Monthly Labor Rev.* 28 (1983).

53. McGuire, Markets for Psychotherapy, in *Psychotherapy: Practice, Research, Policy* 76 (G. R. VandenBos ed. 1980).

54. McGuire & Montgomery, Mandated Mental Health Benefits in Private Health Insurance, 7 *J. Health Politics, Policy & L.* 380 (1982).

55. Metropolitan Life Insurance Co. v. Massachusetts, 105 S. Ct. 2380 (1985). Heitler, Mandated Benefits: Their Social, Economic, and Legal Implications, 11 *L., Med. & Health Care* 248 (1983).

56. M. Levine, *The History and Politics of Community Mental Health* (1981); D. Mechanic, *Mental Health and Social Policy* (1969).

57. DeLeon & VandenBos, Psychotherapy Reimbursement in Federal Programs: Political Factors in *Psychotherapy: Practice, Research, Policy* (G. R. VandenBos ed. 1980); Ruby, The Policy Implications of Insurance Coverage for Psychiatric Services, 7 *Int'l J. L. & Psychiatry* 269 (1984).

58. See Binner, DRGs and the Administration of Mental Health Services, 41 *Am. Psychologist* 64 (1986); Taube, Lee & Forthofer, DRGs in Psychiatry: An Empirical Evaluation, 22 *Med. Care* 597 (1984). See also Goldman, Pincus, Taub & Reiger, Prospective Payment for Psychiatric Hospitalization: Questions and Issues, 35 *Hosp. & Community Psychiatry* 460 (1984).

59. The legislative purpose of Medicaid is to "enable each State . . . to furnish medical assistance on behalf of families with dependent children and of aged blind, or permanently disabled individuals, whose income and resources are insufficient to meet the costs of necessary medical services and rehabilitation. . . ." 42 U.S.C. §1396 (1982).

60. The Supreme Court has refused to prohibit this practice. For a discussion of the issues see Connecticut v. Heckler, 105 S. Ct. 2210 (1985).

61. Somewhat related to Medicaid is the Supplemental Security Income (SSI) program of Social Security. It provides a subsistence allowance to the disabled. 41 U.S.C. §1381 (1982). Inmates of *public* institutions do not generally receive SSI payments. When combined with very limited mental health coverage under Medicaid and Medicare, these limitations for inpatient mentally ill can be severe. This practice was challenged but upheld by the Supreme Court in Schweiker v. Wilson, 450 U.S. 221 (1981).

62. Changes in Medicare, Medicaid and Supplemental Security Income may reduce federal funds for mental health services by 25 percent.

63. D. Mechanic, *Mental Health and Social Policy* (1969).

64. F. D. Chu & S. Trotter, *The Madness Establishment* (1974).

65. A. Deutsch, *Shame of the State* (1948).

66. Pub. L. No. 79–487 (July 3, 1946).

67. The Commission was established through the Mental Health Study Act of 1955. The Commission's report was entitled *Action for Mental Health*.

68. Pub. L. No. 88-164 (Oct. 31, 1963). In the act, Congress envisioned the establishment of local or community "catchment areas" of between 75,000 and 200,000 persons.

69. M. Levine, *The History and Politics of Community Mental Health* (1981).

70. Borus, Issues Critical to the Survival of Community Mental Health, 135 *Am. J. Psychiatry* 1029 (1978).

71. President Carter appointed the President's Commission of Mental Health shortly after assuming office in 1977. Mrs. Carter was the honorary chairperson of the commission. It recommended a number of new service initiatives and sought to correct the imbalance between physical and mental health expenditures and services. It also supported reimbursement for mental health services provided by nonmedical professionals. It recommended the

establishment of the mental patient's Bill of Rights (perhaps its most enduring contribution).

72. Pub. L. No. 96-398 (Oct. 7, 1980).

73. Omnibus Reconciliation Act of 1981, Pub. L. No. 97–35 (1981). For a discussion of the problems with the mental health system, see Talbott, The Fate of the Public Psychiatric System, 36 *Hosp. & Community Psychiatry* 46 (1985).

More recently the Protection and Advocacy for Mentally Ill People Act of 1986 was enacted. It provides limited funds for states to provide advocacy services for people with mental illness and emotional disorders. Among other things, the advocacy is intended to protect these patients from neglect and abuse and to assist them in obtaining benefits. Pub. L. No. 99–319 (1986).

74. Dorken & Webb, Third-Party Reimbursement Experience: An Interstate Comparison by Insurance Carrier, 35 *Am. Psychologist* 355 (1980).

75. Most states now have some form of freedom of choice law, and many health insurance companies now support such laws. Cummins, Mental Health and National Health Insurance: A Case History of the Struggle for Professional Autonomy, in *Psychology and National Health Insurance: A Sourcebook* (C. Kiesler, N. Cummings & G. VandenBos eds. 1980); Tenney, Hospital Privileges for Psychologists, 38 *Am. Psychologist* 1232 (1983).

76. E.g., Blue Shield of Virginia v. McCready, 457 U.S. 465 (1982); Virginia Academy of Clinical Psychologists v. Blue Shield of Virginia, 624 F.2d 476 (4th Cir. 1980), *on remand,* 501 F. Supp. 1232 (E.D. Va. 1980), *cert. denied,* 450 U.S. 916 (1981). The antitrust aspects of these new forms of delivery are considered in K. Wing, *The Law and the Public's Health* 171–95 (2d ed. 1985); Batavia, Preferred Provider Organizations: Antitrust Aspects and Implications for the Hospital Industry, 10 *Am. J. L. & Med.* 169 (1984); Schmidt, Health Maintenance Organizations and the McCarran-Ferguson Act, 7 *Am. J. L. & Med.* 437 (1984).

77. Wiggins, The Psychologist as a Health Professional in the Health Maintenance Organization, 7 *Prof. Psychology: Research and Prac.* 9 (1976).

78. Turkington, Preferred Providers Please and Puzzle Private Practitioners, *APA Monitor* Feb. 1984, at 18. See Brady & Krizay, Utilization and Coverage of Mental Health Services in Health Maintenance Organizations, 142 *Am. J. Psychiatry* 744 (1985); Cheifetz & Salloway, Patterns of Mental Health Services Provided by HMOs, 39 *Am. Psychologist* 495 (1984).

79. Sank & Shapiro, Case Examples of the Broadening Role of Psychology in Health Maintenance Organizations, 10 *Prof. Psychology: Research & Prac.* 402 (1979) found very few staff positions for psychologists and fewer still in leadership roles.

80. Eysenck, The Effects of Psychotherapy: An Evaluation, 16 *J. Counseling Psychology* 319 (1952). See H. Eysenck, *The Effects of Psychotherapy* (1966); May, For Better or For Worse? Psychotherapy and Variance Change: A Critical Review of the Literature, 152 *J. Nervous & Mental Disease* 184 (1971).

81. M. Smith, G. Glass & T. Miller, *The Benefits of Psychotherapy* (1980).

Effect size is the mean difference between treated and control groups, divided by the standard deviation of the control group. Effect size is thus a standardized mean difference that can be used to compare several different rating systems, instruments, and therapies. It is therefore useful in reviewing a large number of studies of the consequences of therapy.

82. Landman & Dawes, Psychotherapy Outcomes: Smith and Glass' Conclusions Stand Up Under Scrutiny, 37 *Am. Psychologist* 504 (1982). See also Howard, Kopta, Krause & Orlinsky, The Dose Effect Relationship in Psychotherapy, 41 *Am. Psychologist* 159 (1986) (50 percent of patients of psychotherapy were improved measurably by the eighth session, 75 percent by the 26th session; there was not much of an increase beyond that).

83. Office of Technology Assessment, *The Efficacy and Cost-Effectiveness of Psychotherapy* (1980).

84. Shapiro & Shapiro, Meta-Analysis of Psychotherapy Outcome Studies: A Replication and Refinement, 92 *Psychological Bull.* 581 (1982).

85. Parloff, Psychotherapy Research Evidence and Reimbursement Decisions: Bambi Meets Godzilla, 139 *Am. J. Psychiatry* 718 (1982).

86. Office of Technology Assessment, note 83 *supra*; Banta & Saxe, *Reimbursement for Psychotherapy,* 38 *Am. Psychologist* 919 (1983).

87. Shapiro & Shapiro, *supra,* note 84.

88. McGuire & Frisman, Reimbursement Policy and Cost-Effective Mental Health Care, 38 *Am. Psychologist* 935 (1983).

89. Binner, Halpin & Potter, Patients, Programs and Results in a Comprehensive Mental Health Center, 41 *J. Consulting & Clinical Psychology* 148 (1973); Cassell, Smith, Gruenberg, Boan & Thomas, Comparing Costs of Hospital and Community Care, 23 *Hosp. & Community Psychiatry* 197 (1972).

90. Parloff, *supra,* note 85.

91. See T. McGuire, *Financing Psychotherapy: Costs, Effects and Public Policy* (1981).

92. Kiesler, Mental Hospitals and Alternative Care, 37 *Am. Psychologist* 349 (1982) (reviewing 10 studies where patients were assigned either to inpatient or to outpatient care; the outpatient care was consistently more positive than inpatient care). See studies cited in note 89, *supra.*

93. Cohen & Hunter, Mental Health Insurance: A Comparison of a Fee-for-Service Indemnity Plan and a Comprehensive Mental Health Center, 42 *Am. J. Orthopsychiatry* 146 (1972). Selective mental health benefits cost $13.80 per member, comprehensive benefits cost $3.88. If outpatient service results in even a minor reduction in inpatient services the cost savings can be quite substantial. Therefore, even though increased mental health services were provided under the comprehensive plan, the total cost was lower because of the reduction in inpatient services. For a review of studies regarding psychotherapy and medical care utilization see Jones & Vischi, Impact of Alcohol, Drug Abuse and Mental Health Treatment on Medical Care Utilization: A Review of the Research Literature, 17 *Med Care* 1 (1979).

94. Schlesinger, Mumford & Glass, Mental Health Services and Medical

Utilization, in *Psychotherapy: Practice, Research, Policy* (G. VandenBos ed. 1980). One implication of the Schlesinger study is that general health care costs may be increased if mental health services are not provided to those who need them.

95. Regeir, The Nature and Scope of Mental Health Problems, in *Primary Care: Variability and Methodology in Mental Health Services in General Health Care*, vol. 1 (Institute of Medicine, National Academy of Sciences, 1979).

96. Rosen & Wiens, Changes in Medical Problems and Use of Medical Services Following Psychological Intervention, 34 *Am. Psychologist* 420 (1979).

97. Schlesinger, Mumford & Glass considered 11 studies involving the use of medical utilization by those receiving psychotherapy. They found that following psychotherapy, patient medical utilization dropped approximately 25 percent. Schlesinger, Mumford & Glass, Mental Health Services and Medical Utilization, in *Psychotherapy: Practice, Research, Policy* (G. VandenBos ed. 1980). Cummings found that the availability of mental health services reduced general medical utilization for patients by up to 60 percent. Cummings, The Anatomy of Psychotherapy Under National Health Insurance, 32 *Am. Psychologist* 711 (1977). For a review of a number of studies suggesting that mental health services may reduce total medical care usage for a number of conditions, see D. Upton, *Mental Health Care and National Health Insurance* 113–27 (1983).

98. A "mental health care episode" is an admission to an inpatient facility or presence on the role of an outpatient facility.

99. M. Witkin, *Trends in Patient Care Episodes in Mental Health Facilities* (1980).

100. Kiesler, National Health Insurance Testimony to the House of Representatives in *Psychology and National Health Insurance: A Sourcebook* (C. Kiesler, N. Cummings & VandenBos eds. 1980).

101. Witkin, *supra,* note 99.

102. Okin, State Hospitals in the 1980s, 33 *Hosp. & Community Psychiatry* 717 (1982).

103. Kiesler, Mental Hospitals and Alternative Care, 37 *Am. Psychologist* 349 (1982).

104. Kiesler, Public and Professional Myths About Mental Hospitalization, 37 *Am. Psychologist* 1323 (1982).

105. DeLeon & VandenBos, Psychotherapy Reimbursement in Federal Programs: Political Factors, in *Psychotherapy: Practice, Research, Policy* (G. VandenBos ed. 1980).

106. See note 48, *supra.*

107. See generally K. Davis, *National Health Insurance* (1975); J. Feder, J. Holahan & T. Marmor eds., *National Health Insurance: Conflicting Goals and Policy Choices* (1980); C. Kiesler, N. Cummings, G. VandenBos eds., *Psychology and National Health Insurance* (1980); D. Upton, *Mental Health Care and National Health Insurance* (1983).

108. DeLeon & VandenBos, Psychotherapy Reimbursement in Federal

Programs: Political Factors, in *Psychotherapy: Practice, Research, Policy* (G. VandenBos ed. 1980).

109. See Burns, National Health Insurance: Inclusion of Mental Health Care and Clinical Psychology, 9 *Prof. Psychology: Research & Prac.* 723 (1978); Cummings, The Anatomy of Psychotherapy Under National Health Insurance, 32 *Am. Psychologist* 711 (1977); McSweeney, Including Psychotherapy in National Health Insurance, 32 *Am. Psychologist* 722 (1977).

CHAPTER 5
LEGAL ISSUES IN TESTING

Tests designed or administered by mental health professionals have become increasingly important decision-making tools, affecting many aspects of individuals' lives. "Tests" include a broad range of instruments, such as personality tests, ranging from the Minnesota Multiphasic Personality Inventory (MMPI), to projective tests such as the Rorschach; a wide variety of IQ, school placement, achievement, aptitude, and college admission tests; all manner of employment and disability-related tests; polygraphs and other "truth finding" tests; and tests administered for courts such as those to determine competency to stand trial. Even a partial listing begins to suggest the range of legal and social interests which they now touch. It is not surprising, therefore, that they are increasingly coming to the attention of the legal system.

Mental health professionals are involved in designing, validating, and administering tests, and interpreting their results. Each of these functions must be carefully and accurately completed for a test to be a dependable instrument on which to make decisions, and the failure of any of these functions may create legal and ethical problems for mental health professionals and others.

Many of the legal and ethical principles involving testing are considered elsewhere in this book.[1] In this brief chapter, we summarize a few of the legal and ethical issues concerning testing, some special problems with employment tests and IQ tests, and some future issues regarding the regulation of testing.

LEGAL ISSUES INVOLVING TESTING

The following are brief summaries of several legal issues involving tests.

Malpractice

Selecting an inappropriate test, incorrectly administering it or care-lessly interpreting it are potential forms of professional negligence. If someone is injured as a result, it is possible that professional lia-bility based on negligence (malpractice) may result. In the past mental health professionals have been protected from liability by several legal rules, including concepts of limited duty (professionals giving a test to someone for a third party, such as an employer, may owe a duty to the third party but not necessarily to the test-taker), the absence of a clear understanding of what tests were appropriate for what circumstances, and the difficulty in proving damages or causa-tion. Almost all of these protections against liability are being eroded by case law, statutes, and changing professional practices. The future probably holds somewhat greater malpractice liability for negligent testing.[2]

Defamation

Civil liability may also arise for defamation and similar harmful false-hood torts (making false, harmful statements about another). These torts include libel (written defamation), slander (oral defamation), false light (a privacy tort), and injurious falsehood.[3] The law of def-amation is complicated, but essentially a false statement made about another that harms the other's reputation, and that is made negli-gently or maliciously, may be defamatory.[4] Thus, making false, harm-ful statements about someone on the basis of bad testing may give rise to defamation liability. Often mental health professionals are pro-tected by limited common law or statutory "privileges" (not related to testimonial privileges to protect confidentiality) because they are providing information in legally protected relationships, such as to an employer. However, these privileges would ordinarily not apply if the false statement were made recklessly or with the knowledge that it was false. Although the rules concerning defamation are in flux, defamation liability arising out of testing is unlikely to become a major problem for mental health professionals.

Confidentiality

Special problems of confidentiality arise when tests are given for someone other than for the person taking the test, or when they are given to minors.[5] For example, school and employment testing raise problems as to who may have access to information revealed during testing. In addition to the test results, there conceivably may be an effort to obtain responses to specific test items or questions. If, for example, a student has been asked about drug use or sexual attitudes, parents might seek a child's answers to those specific questions. Similar problems may arise in court proceedings when communications are not covered by a testimonial privilege. While responses to specific questions have not been a subject of major legal problems yet, increased awareness of information contained in tests is likely to change this. Before a test is administered it should be clear to the professional, to the taker, and to the organization paying for the test, who will have access to what information. The confidentiality of test results and answers to specific questions remains a significant potential problem.

Open Records Laws

The federal government and most states now have freedom of information acts or open record statutes. These laws typically permit public access to most government records, and allow individuals the right to see and correct their own records held by government agencies. Personal privacy provisions in these laws will usually prevent the public from seeing test results of individuals. However, except where real harm would result, most people have the right to see their own records. Therefore individuals may have the right to see their own psychological test results and any written interpretations of those results if they are held by a state agency. Ordinarily open record laws do not apply to records held by private individuals or organizations. However, statutes that allow persons access to their own private medical records may apply to test results. Most laws contain exemptions to prevent a person from copying an actual test itself if to do so would compromise the security or future usefulness of the test, and to prevent access to psychological information that might be harmful.

Buckley Amendment

The Family Educational Rights and Privacy Act, commonly known as the Buckley Amendment, permits students or their parents access to a wide range of educational records.[6] Within limits this includes the right to the results of tests conducted by mental health experts and made part of school records. It should be emphasized that the Buckley Amendment applies to school records and not to those records held by individual practitioners or even other state agencies.

Demands to see records subject to open records laws or the Buckley Amendment may involve one of several exceptions. Therefore a mental health professional who is faced with a demand for tests or test results under these laws but does not believe the information should be released should immediately seek legal advice. Demands for the release of answers to specific test questions should be granted only after very careful review. Courts have generally been reluctant to order the release of individual test questions.[7]

Licensing

Licensing statutes in some states specify testing as one of the areas in which mental health professionals, particularly psychologists, are licensed. The implication is that the administration or interpretation of tests without a license may be prohibited. These laws are often vague, making it difficult to know what kinds of test administration are protected by the licensing statute.[8] There is very little legal authority on the question of whether a license is required to give or interpret mental health tests, and if so what license is required to give what tests. This is one area in which licensing statutes and regulations should be more explicit. In the meantime, mental health professionals should be aware that administering or interpreting tests without a license (or without supervision from another professional) may constitute the illegal practice of a profession.

Testimony in Court

Tests often form the basis of courtroom or hearing testimony by mental health experts. It is, of course, important to review the appropriateness of any tests on which testimony is based. The review should include the test's validation and technical studies. The professional should emphasize that expert opinions given in court are based on a number of factors, not only the results of one or two tests. A similar approach is advisable if experts are asked the reason for a particular question in a test or the meaning of a response to it. Single questions generally have no more meaning than a single piece of a jigsaw puzzle has meaning. Computer-generated interpretations of tests, such as MMPI, should also be described as only one basis for reaching a conclusion. Experts may find it advisable not to bring the test instrument to court at the time of testimony. If the instrument is available in court, it may encourage cross-examination about individual items. This issue should be raised with the attorney with whom the mental health expert is working.

Polygraph Examination and Hypnosis

In many states polygraph examinations and hypnosis are subject to special rules. For example, some states severely limit the use of polygraph examinations in employment testing.[9] Congress is also considering legislation that would limit the use of the polygraph. Many courts now limit the use of hypnosis with potential witnesses in criminal trials. In addition some states require special licensing or test procedures for polygraphers or hypnotists.

New Test Development and Experimentation

The process of developing new tests often requires extensive trials on human subjects. This is a form of human experimentation, although relatively risk free. Much of this experimentation is exempt from HHS federal regulation, although the Department of Education has adopted significant regulations which may affect experimental education testing.[10] Test subjects should understand the nature of their participation and be given the choice to refuse. Many tests have experimental items which are being validated for future use. Generally, we believe that test takers should be informed about such items but, to avoid impairing the validation process, the experimental items should not be specifically identified.[11]

Copyrights

Most standardized tests are copyrighted. The use or copying of these tests without permission of the owners of the copyright is a violation of the copyright law and would subject the person infringing the copyright to liability and penalties. A copyrighted test (it will be so designated somewhere on the test) should not be copied or read for administration or otherwise used without permission of the owner of the copyright.[12]

Contracts

In securing copies of a test or permission to use a test, conditions are often stipulated by the test owner. Generally, these conditions of use will amount to contractual obligations and mental health professionals should carefully observe the terms or limitations on use of the test. Failure to do so is likely to be seen as a breach of contract.

ETHICAL ISSUES

Sound ethical standards is a key to resolving most current legal problems with testing. An example of sound ethical testing standards is the American Psychological Association's Ethical Principles, which contain a particularly thorough and thoughtful series of principles concerning testing. What follows is a list of major provisions dealing with testing.[13] It is interesting that the principles not only require proper administration and interpretation by professionals, but also attempt to prevent others from misusing test results.

1. Professionals who are responsible for decisions or policies based on test results must have an understanding of the test, validation problems, and test research.[14] In the development, publication, and utilization of tests, profes-

sionals make every effort to promote the welfare and best interest of the client.

2. Professionals should guard against the misuse of tests and attempt to prevent misuse by agencies of which they are employees.[15]

3. Professionals must respect a client's right to know the results and interpretation of tests.

4. Professionals should make every effort to maintain the security of tests and should not reveal the contents of tests unless legally mandated to do so.

5. Professionals should "try to assure the appropriate use of assessment techniques *by others*" (emphasis added).

6. Clients have a right to a full explanation of the nature and purpose of tests.

7. In reporting results, professionals must report reservations that exist regarding validity or reliability or the inappropriateness of the norms for the person tested.

8. Professionals should make every effort to avoid and prevent the use of obsolete tests.

9. Computer generated test interpretation services are considered professional-to-professional consultation and professionals should make every effort to avoid misuse of assessment reports.

10. Professionals should avoid using, and discourage the use of, tests administered or scored by inappropriately trained or unqualified persons.

11. Those responsible for developing tests must utilize established scientific procedures and relevant ethical standards.[16]

EMPLOYMENT AND SCHOOL TESTING

No areas of testing have been so fraught with controversy and legal activity in recent years as employment and school (particularly IQ and placement) testing. Many of the difficulties have centered around the problem of racial or cultural discrimination. These are complicated issues only briefly outlined here.

Employment Testing[17]

Traditionally, employers were able to use whatever criteria they desired in hiring employees and were able to fire employees at will for virtually any reason.[18] Federal and state civil rights laws have limited employers' discretion in using such factors as race, gender, and physical disability. Part of the employment civil rights movement dealt with the issue of tests whose results could, in effect, be used to discriminate against one group or another.

The Civil Rights Act of 1964 provides that employment testing may not be conducted arbitrarily or capriciously.[19] In *Griggs v. Duke Power Company* the Supreme Court held that a violation of the civil rights act does not require that there be an intent to discriminate against minorities.[20] Rather, tests which have the effect of discriminating against minorities are illegal if they are unrelated to or do not measure job capabilities. If there is a disparate impact on minorities, the employer is required to demonstrate the relationship between employment tests and the job. In subsequent decisions, the Supreme Court has held that once a *prima facie* case of discrimination is proved, the burden shifts to the employer to articulate some legitimate, nondiscriminatory reason for the discrepancy. It has also held that employment tests must be carefully validated according to federal regulations, and that when a test is discriminatory there must be no alternative selection devices available that do not discriminate.[21]

These decisions were based primarily on federal civil rights law. In addition, the U.S. Constitution prohibits discrimination by any governmental unit including school boards, hospitals, and any other activity carried on by any kind of government agency.[22] Federal civil rights statutes and the Constitutional prohibition are not precisely the same and have not been applied by the courts in the same way. In *Washington v. Davis,* for example, the Supreme Court determined that for employment discrimination by governments to violate the Constitution, some purposeful or intentional discrimination must be demonstrated.[23] However, the purposeful conduct can be demonstrated indirectly. This is a somewhat higher standard than required to demonstrate a violation of the civil rights acts.

Central to demonstrating that an employment test can be legitimately used is the process used for validating the test. Federal regulations permit the use of criterion-related, content-related, or construct-validity studies.[24] Put very generally, construct validity measures the degree to which candidates have identifiable characteristics that have been determined to be important in successful performance of the job. Content validity compares performance on a test with general areas of skills or abilities. There has been some confusion in federal courts concerning which form of validation technique is appropriate in any given circumstances.[25] In general, a test is likely to be acceptable the more it: specifically measures the skills, characteristics, or talents essential to a position; tests all of the necessary skills; will eliminate unqualified applicants (as opposed to rank ordering those who are qualified); is validated for the populations among which it will be used.

Despite some difficulty, confusion, and inconsistencies in dealing with the questions of the type of validity by which test instruments should be judged, generally courts have focused on whether an employer has selected clear job-related skills and whether the test examines those skills, or whether it has been demonstrated to predict those who can do an adequate job. Test development and validation are the province of mental health professionals. Regulation of employment testing has encouraged the use of professionals to design and validate appropriate tests.

Educational Testing

Following the Supreme Court's *Brown v. Board of Education* decision,[26] which declared intentionally segregated schools to be unconstitutional, some schools used educational testing as a way of maintaining racial segregation. Other districts adopted track systems (a division of students along ability groupings as determined by IQ or similar tests) which effectively segregated classes, regardless of whether that was the intent. These programs relied heavily on IQ and similar tests and constitutional challenges to the existence of these programs began less than a decade after the *Brown* decision.[27] In *Hobsen v. Hansen,* for example, a federal court found that a track system and the standardized testing on which it depended violated the constitution because the classification into tracks was not done on fully valid bases.[28]

Legal attention to testing was accompanied by a professional debate concerning the use of standardized tests. The tests were seen as a legitimate way of improving education by permitting attention for the special needs of students. Yet the fear was expressed that minority children were being unfairly labeled as uneducable and placed in special classes. The bitterness of this professional debate is perhaps best illustrated by a statement by the Association of Black Psychologists which begins, "Psychological testing historically has been a quasi-scientific tool in the perpetuation of racism. . . . Under the guise of scientific objectivity, it has provided a cesspool of intrinsically and inferentially falacious data which inflates the egos of whites by demeaning Black people and threatens to potentiate Black genocide."[29]

While a number of cases have attacked educational placement of children based on IQ and similar tests,[30] none has attracted more attention than *Larry P. v. Riles*.[31] The case extended over nearly a decade. In addition to raising constitutional issues, it also depended on a variety of federal statutes that sought to guarantee full education opportunity for the mentally handicapped and that encouraged education for as many handicapped students as possible.[32] Although there were many aspects to the *Larry P.* case, the use of IQ tests to place children in educably mentally retarded (EMR) classes was at the center of the decision. The plaintiffs claimed that the IQ tests that were used resulted in the placement of a disproportionately large number of minority students in EMR classes, which worked to their disadvantage. Considerable testimony was presented both in favor of and opposed to IQ testing.[33] The court found that the tests violated federal law and the Constitution, and permanently enjoined their use. It further required that any intelligence tests given for educational placement or selection must yield the same pattern of scores for different groups of students, yield approximately equal means for all standardization sample subgroups, and yield scores which were correlated with relevant criterion measures. Essentially the court found that the tests were racially or culturally biased and that the differences between interracial group means on the tests had not been explained.

Interestingly, a somewhat similar suit, *PASE v. Hannon,* reached a contrary conclusion when the court determined that standardized intelligence tests (used with other criteria) were not racially biased against minorities in the placement of students in special classes.[34] In that case the judge personally reviewed each question on standard intelligence tests and "determined" himself that very few of them were racially or culturally biased.

It is not particularly unusual for federal courts in different parts of the country to reach different conclusions on a legal or factual issue. Indeed, the courts were faced with grossly divided professional opinion on the question of test bias. What is interesting is the way in which the courts treated tests.[35] In the *Larry P.* case, the court essentially required that IQ tests produce the same overall result for different racial groups, evidencing some misunderstanding about the purpose of tests. In the *PASE* case the judge intuitively decided whether specific test items were racially or culturally biased, a highly unreliable form of decision-making. Both cases illustrate a serious lack of judicial sophistication. Judges are not trained in the science of testing. When confronted with inconsistent information and differing expert opinion, it is perhaps not surprising that they resort to inappropriate methods of reviewing tests or reach flawed conclusions.

In part the difficulty with these tests has been their labeling as "intelligence tests." The question should not be whether they really measure some innate ability but rather whether they adequately measure whatever they are being used to determine (e.g., classroom placement). If in fact they measure the student's ability to participate reasonably well in regular classroom (i.e., if they are valid for this form of placement), then they should be considered adequate for the purpose of determining classroom assignment. The court of *Larry P.* dealt with this question to some extent but it was almost lost in the argument over cultural bias, IQ, and the reason for interracial disparities. If classrooms are culturally biased (e.g. standard English required), then valid, reliable tests are likely to reflect a similar bias. And the fact that over time some students may raise their IQ scores is not highly relevant to the issue of *current* classroom placement. (Of course, it would be relevant if a test given this year was used to determine placement ten years from now.) The issue of whether IQ differences arise from environmental effects, educational opportunity, or genetic differences is interesting but not centrally relevant when the issue is proper educational placement. Abuses occur when tests designed for one purpose are used for another; are poorly designed, administered, or interpreted; or are not given frequently enough to be the basis for current decision-making. Some cases have not adequately focused on these issues.

The legal furor over the use of IQ tests has reduced the educational dependence on them. In addition, federal policy favoring mainstreaming generally has reduced the necessity for them. IQ tests currently are combined with the number of other evaluations, many of them based on subjective judgments of teachers and counselors. This raises an additional question of whether subjective judgments are likely to be more accurate, reliable, or valid than judgments made from test scores. If placement is made on the basis of even more biased or unreliable factors, then disposing of the tests may be counterproductive. In the end, the question is not what the perfect system is, but what the best and most accurate system is. The potential for discrimination and judgment on the basis of improper factors is probably at least as likely to exist with subjective judgments as it is with standardized tests.

FUTURE REGULATION OF TESTING

The legal limitations on and increased regulation of some tests suggests public dissatisfaction with many forms of standardized testing. This is due in part to the excesses of some in making claims for these tests, or in using them inappropriately and without sufficient validation. Part of the reaction, however, is killing the messenger who brings bad news; tests have provided some information that we do not want, either individually or as a society.

Much of the regulation of testing has been beneficial. The emphasis on validating tests, for example, should be applauded. Other reforms seem destructive and appear almost to be aimed at destroying certain kinds of tests. The truth in testing law, passed in New York, that required the release of questions and answers of college entrance exams is an example.[36] There is perhaps a growing attitude that, like war and generals, testing is too important to be left to the behavioralist scientists.

The mental health professions should concentrate efforts on developing and enforcing ethical standards regarding testing. Licensing statutes should specify who is qualified to administer and interpret tests. Methods must be devised to provide courts with better scientific information and sharper thinking about the nature and consequences of tests. In the major cases noted above, the problem has not been the obtaining of some scientific information. The evidence presented was often seriously conflicting. More emphasis should be placed on whether a test actually does what it claims to do. Perhaps the emphasis in some cases on the racial or cultural differences in tests has overshadowed a central question: does a test improve or reduce the chance of making a correct decision? If a test is meant to assess the ability to conduct an activity that is itself directed or biased toward one culture, it does little good to change the test if the activity remains unchanged.

Arguments about testing are not likely to subside. Testing has become so critical to so many important decisions that it will continue to invite disputes. Among the challenges facing the law is to better understand the theory and practice of testing. Among the challenges facing the mental health profession is to better inform the public about testing. It is important that professionals adhere to the highest professional and ethical standards in developing, administering, and interpreting tests. As public interest in testing expands, legal regulation of testing will increase. This poses a potential threat that useful, effective, and efficient forms of assessment will be unnecessarily limited by well-meaning efforts to avoid harm from test abuse or to produce more socially acceptable results. However, regulation also has the potential for being a catalyst to improve testing and to eliminate the unethical and inept testers. The direction the law takes will in part depend on the quality of information courts and lawmakers receive from mental health professionals.

NOTES

1. See, for example, chapter 1 (malpractice and ethical principles), chapter 2 (confidentiality and privilege protections regarding tests), chapter 4 (licensing related to testing), chapter 6 (experimentation, education test development), chapter 8 (truthfinding process, including polygraph), chapter 10 (participation in the legal system), and chapters 11–19 (regarding tests used to assess competency and responsibility).

2. As noted in chapter 1, the clearer the standard of acceptable professional conduct and the more important an activity is to people's lives, the greater the probability of malpractice claims. Testing is becoming a more sophisticated enterprise, and perhaps mistakes are more noticeable. See C. Newmark ed., *Major Psychological Assessment Instruments* (1985). At the same time, testing in employment and other areas has become increasingly important; therefore it is possible that malpractice liability will increase on the basis of negligently administered or evaluated tests. However, it is not yet clear that the legal duty is to the applicant (as opposed to the employer)

in administering employment tests. See Kahn & Taft, The Application of the Standard of Care Doctrine to Psychological Testing, 1 *Behav. Sci. & L.* 71 (1983).

3. Each of the forms of harmful falsehoods has its own history, special elements that must be proved, and potential for damages. The law in these areas tends to be quite technical and complex. The interested reader is referred to W. P. Keeton et al., *The Law of Torts* (5th ed. 1984), libel and slander 771–848, false light 863–68, injurious falsehood 962–77.

4. Defamation and related concepts impose liability for speech. There is great concern, therefore, that this liability may violate the freedom of speech or freedom of the press. To protect such First Amendment interests, the Supreme Court requires that when a public official or public figure is defamed, he or she must demonstrate the statement made with malice, that is with knowledge that a statement is false, or reckless disregard of the truth.

5. These issues are considered more fully in chapter 2.

6. 20 U.S.C. [U.S. Code] §1232g (1982); 34 C.F.R. [Code of Federal Regulations] §99 (1985).

7. New York has adopted a "truth in testing" statute that is intended to permit test-takers to have access to information about the test and their performance on it. N.Y. Educ. Law §340 (McKinney's 1984 Supp.). But see Association of American Medical Colleges v. Carey, 482 F.Supp. 1358 (N.D. N.Y. 1980) (enjoining enforcement of the New York law).

8. The licensing statutes are described in chapter 4.

9. About 20 states have limits on the use of polygraph tests in employment. See chapter 8. The use of hypnosis with prospective witnesses is also considered in chapter 8.

10. These regulations concern student rights in research, experimental activities and testing. 49 Fed. Reg. 35,318 (1984) (to be codified at 34 C.F.R. parts 75, 76, and 98).

11. Chapter 6 contains a thorough review of issues related to the use of human subjects in research.

12. See Association of American Medical Colleges v. Carey, 482 F.Supp. 1358 (N.D. N.Y. 1980); Harcourt, Brace & World v. Graphic Controls Corp., 329 F.Supp. 517 (S.D. N.Y. 1971).

13. American Psychological Association, *Ethical Principles of Psychologists* (1981). Unless otherwise noted, the ethical statements noted in this section are from principle 8. The standards are paraphrased. The APA standards are stated in terms of the obligations of psychologists, but are referred to here as professionals because they should have wide applicability to mental health professionals. See also American Psychological Association, *Standards for Educational and Psychological Tests* (1974).

14. This provision is from 2e of the principles.

15. This provision is contained in principles 1c and 8.

16. See American Psychological Association, *Standards for Educational and Psychological Tests* (1974). Regarding computer scoring see Matarazzo,

Computerized Clinical Psychological Test Interpretations: Unvalidated Plus All Mean and No Sigma, 41 *Am. Psychologist* 14 (1986).

17. Other employment-related tests raise additional issues. For example, the use of polygraphs (Brown, Employment Tests: Issues Without Clear Answers, 30 *Personnel Administrator* 43, 50–51 [Sept. 1985]) and genetic tests (Murray, Genetic Testing at Work: How Should it be Used, 30 *Personnel Administrator,* 91 [Sept. 1985]) are examples of such tests. Polygraph testing is considered in chapter 8.

18. Labor union collective bargaining and similar contractual arrangements have had the effect of reducing "at will terminations" in many industries.

19. 42 U.S.C. $2000e (1982); 29 C.F.R. $1607 (1985).

20. Griggs v. Duke Power Company, 401 U.S. 424 (1971).

21. E.g., Connecticut v. Teal, 457 U.S. 440 (1982); Albemarle Paper Co. v. Moody, 422 U.S. 405 (1975); McDonnell Douglas Corp. v. Green, 411 U.S. 792 (1973). See Chamallas, Evolving Conceptions of Equality Under Title VII: Disparate Impact Theory and the Demise of the Bottom Line Principle, 31 *UCLA L. Rev.* 305 (1983); Norborg, A Warning Regarding the Simplified Approach to the Evaluation of Test Fairness in Employee Selection Procedures, 37 *Personnel Psychology* 483 (1984).

22. The provisions of the Fourteenth Amendment (prohibiting some forms of discrimination) apply only to governmental entities, those provisions do not apply to purely private actions. However, federal civil rights statutes do apply to private employers.

23. Washington v. Davis, 426 U.S. 229 (1976).

24. 29 C.F.R. $$1607.5, 1607.14 (1985). "Users may rely upon criterion-related validity studies, content validity studies or construct validity studies. . . . New strategies for showing the validity of selection procedures will be evaluated as they become accepted by the psychological profession."

25. See generally Equal Employment Opportunity Commission, *Guidelines on Employment Selection Procedures* (1970), and *Uniform Guidelines on Employee Selection Procedures* (1977); Anastasi, Evolving Concepts of Test Validation, in *Annual Review of Psychology* (M. Rosenzweig & L. Porter eds. 1986); Klieman & Faley, Assessing Content Validity: Standards Set by the Courts, 31 *Personnel Psychology* 701 (1978); Wollack, Content Validity: Its Legal and Psychometric Basis, 5 *Public Personnel Mgmt.* 397 (1976) (noting a number of cases in which judges misinterpreted or confused federal guidelines).

26. Brown v. Board of Education, 347 U.S. 483 (1954).

27. See generally Norwood v. Tucker, 287 F.2d 798 (8th Cir. 1961); Dove v. Parham, 181 F.Supp. 504 (E.D. Ark.), *aff'd,* 282 F.2d 256 (8th Cir. 1960); Shuttlesworth v. Birmingham Board of Education, 162 F.Supp. 372 (N.D. Ala.), *aff'd,* 358 U.S. 101 (1958).

28. Hobsen v. Hansen, 269 F.Supp. 401 (D.D.C. 1967), *aff'd, sub nom.* Smuck v. Hobsen, 408 F.2d 175 (D.C. Cir. 1969).

29. Jackson, On the Report of the Ad Hoc Committee on Educational

Uses of Test with Disadvantaged Students: Another Psychological View From the Association of Black Psychologists, 30 *Am. Psychologist* 88 (1975).

30. E.g., McNeal v. Tate County School District, 508 F.2d 1017 (5th Cir. 1975); Singleton v. Jackson School District, 419 F.2d 1211 (5th Cir. 1969), *rev'd in part on other grounds, sub nom.* Carter v. West Feliciana School Board, 396 U.S. 290 (1970).

31. Larry P. v. Riles, 343 F.Supp. 1306 (N.D. Cal. 1972) (preliminary injunction), *aff'd,* 502 F.2d 963 (9th Cir. 1974); 495 F.Supp. 926 (N.D. Cal. 1979).

32. Notably, federal law concerning education for the handicapped includes Education of the Handicapped Amendments, Pub. L. No. 93-380 (codified as 20 U.S.C. §1400 [1982]); and Education for all Handicapped Children Act, Pub. L. 94-142 (codified at 20 U.S.C. §1414 [1982]). Also relevant are the Civil Rights Act of 1964 (42 U.S.C. §2000 [1982]) and the Rehabilitation Act of 1973 (29 U.S.C. §701 [1982]).

33. A substantial number of behavioral scientists were involved on both sides of the case. Accounts of the experiences and feelings of mental health professionals and attorneys concerning the *Larry P.* and *PASE* decisions are fascinating. E.g., Condas, Personal Deflections on the *Larry P.* Trial and Its Aftermath, 9 *Sch. Psychology Rev.* 154 (1980); Cremins, *Larry P.* and the EMR Child, 16 *Ed. & Training Mentally Retarded* 158 (1981); Lambert, Psychological Evidence in *Larry P. v. Wilson Riles:* An Evaluation By a Witness for the Defense, 36 *Am. Psychologist* 937 (1981); Sattler, The Psychologist in Court: Personal Reflections of One Expert Witness in the Case of *Larry P. v. Wilson Riles,* 11 *Sch. Psychology Rev.* 306 (1982).

34. PASE v. Hannon, 506 F.Supp. 831 (N.D. Ill. 1980).

35. An interesting review of the cases is Bersoff, Testing and the Law, 36 *Am. Psychologist* 1047 (1981). See also Bersoff, Regarding Psychologists Testily: Legal Regulation of Psychological Assessment in the Public Schools, 39 *Md. L. Rev.* 27 (1979).

36. N.Y. Education Law §340 (McKinney 1984 Supp.). But see Association of American Medical Colleges v. Carey, 482 F.Supp. 1358 (N.D. N.Y. 1980).

CHAPTER 6
BEHAVIORAL RESEARCH AND THE USE OF LIVING SUBJECTS

James Thornwell, a private in the U.S. Army stationed in Germany, was given LSD without his knowledge or consent.[1] A group of researchers working on experimental "mind control" techniques thought that the drug might be a form of truth serum.[2] Instead it produced severe emotional disturbances which ultimately led to Thornwell's suicide. As part of another effort to determine the effects and value of LSD, a civilian Army employee was given LSD without his knowledge or consent and also committed suicide a short time later.[3] In a much different study, subjects told they would receive vitamin injections actually received epinephrine to maintain physiological arousal; the purpose of the study was to examine the effects of physical arousal.[4] In the Milgram obedience study, research subjects were told to administer what they thought were dangerous and even potentially lethal electric "shocks" to other "subjects," who were actually confederates of the researcher.[5] The test was to determine the subjects' response to authority, but they were told it was to test approaches to learning. The subjects were not, of course, informed that they might be put into a potentially very stressful situation in which self-esteem might be a victim. Other researchers replicated the study with children as young as six.[6]

These episodes suggest important legal and ethical issues regarding the use of humans in behavioral science research. While much research can be carried on with other animals or (infrequently) even with computer simulations, some research is impossible without experimentation on human beings. In this chapter we consider the circumstances in which it is appropriate to use human research subjects, the legal and ethical limits on their use, and special problems associated with consent to participation in behavioral research. Recently, there has been controversy about the use of animals. The special issues regarding their use are noted at the end of the chapter.

The history of experimentation on humans is a long one. Indeed, if experimentation is defined broadly enough, human experimentation is as old as the human species.[7] Although concern about human experimentation dates back centuries, the atrocities committed in Nazi Germany in the name of research served to emphasize the potential for substantial abuse of human subjects. Those atrocities were the basis for the adoption of international codes of conduct concerning the use of humans in research. The Helsinki and Nuremberg statements of ethics are perhaps the two best known codes. The Nuremberg principles were announced during the Nazis war-crimes trial to establish the basis of what is acceptable research and what research may be considered a crime against humanity.[8]

The Nuremberg principles emphasize consent by the subject, the importance of minimizing risks to them, and a determination that the benefits will outweigh the risks of the experiment. The principles provide that "voluntary consent of the human subject is essential," and that subjects have the right to withdraw from the experiment at any time. The experiments must be conducted by qualified people in a way that will avoid all unnecessary risks. Research should be terminated if it becomes too risky.[9]

Experience since World War II has demonstrated that unethical human experimentation can occur in free societies.[10] Live liver cancer cells were injected, without consent, into unsuspecting mental patients. In another instance, a cancerous tumor was transplanted into a woman, who ultimately died of the transplanted cancer, after being seriously misinformed about the purpose of the "transplant."[11] Serious ethical questions also have been raised about some behavioral science experiments, as the experiments described at the beginning of the chapter demonstrate.

REGULATION OF EXPERIMENTATION INVOLVING HUMANS

Human experimentation has increasingly focused on prior review of the experiments before they are undertaken to ensure that they are ethical and legal. Such review protects potential human research subjects, and it also protects scientific investigators, by providing an examination of their research so they do not inadvertently or carelessly undertake illegal or unethical research, which can incur civil (and in extreme cases criminal) liability.[12]

Autonomy and Regulation

The increased regulation is not without philosophical, ethical, and political controversy. It involves a complex conflict between autonomy and paternalism. Regulation interferes with both researchers' and subjects' autonomy by preventing them from entering into some research relationships. The principle of autonomy would suggest that if researcher and patient want to agree to conduct a highly risky experiment, they should be free to do so. Some argue that this autonomy should be permitted, without regulation. On the other hand, it is argued that this kind of "free market" approach has been insufficient in the past to protect subjects from harm and that some intervention is essential to protect research subjects from unscrupulous or unethical researchers.[13]

Ironically, during the time that autonomy of patients has been emphasized in treatment, the level of regulation of research has increased. These trends are not so inconsistent as they may seem. Much of research regulation is ultimately directed toward promoting autonomy by ensuring full informed consent to participation. Other regulation deals with those who cannot make decisions for themselves. Finally, some regulation is based on the proposition that researchers and subjects are not on equal footing and that a true free-agent subject relationship often does not exist. Neither the ideal of complete autonomy nor of complete protection can be fully implemented by regulating human research. Regulation represents a continuing compromise between these conflicting goals in an area of human experience sufficiently unlike normal endeavors to warrant special rules.

Reasons for Reviewing Research

Federal law requires prior review for studies funded by the federal government and for studies that involve unapproved drugs or devices.

Many foundations and funding agencies also commonly require similar reviews. Universities, hospitals, and other institutions often require that their faculty, students, and employees obtain approval of studies involving human subjects. Some journals also require prior ethics review for research results they publish. Finally, some investigators voluntarily seek such reviews as a matter of professional or personal ethics.

Federal Regulation

Generally, reviews of human experimentation are conducted in accordance with federal regulations.[14] Even reviews that are not required by federal law often follow the same requirements. There are two major federal regulations. One is for the Department of Health and Human Services (HHS) applied generally to federally funded research.[15] The other is for the Federal Food and Drug Administration (FDA) which applies to experiments with drugs and medical devices.[16] Although there is some difference between these two sets of regulations, notably in the area of prisoners and children, they are generally quite similar. The review is conducted by a local institutional committee, an Institutional Review Board (IRB), before the experiment is undertaken. On the basis of the criteria in the federal regulations, the IRB either grants approval for the project, requests modifications in it, or rejects it. Only in very unusual cases is there ethics review beyond the IRB.

Institutional Review Boards

An IRB is located in, and is part of, the institution conducting the experiment, or in which it takes place. The IRB is appointed by the institution, and must include members with experience in scientific investigation, training in law, and expertise in ethics. One or more members must not have any formal connection with the institution. The work of the IRB is subject to HHS regulations and institutions must periodically assure the department that their IRBs are conforming to the law. The FDA periodically audits IRBs.

There are several aspects to IRB review of proposals for experimentations on humans: (1) The IRB must determine whether the experiment should be permitted to proceed at all. This requires that the potential for benefit from the knowledge gained from the experiment exceeds the potential risk to the human subjects. (2) If such an experiment is justified, the IRB must then ensure that there are no unnecessary risks to the subjects of the experiment. (3) The IRB must also ensure that only subjects who have fully consented (or for whom full consent has been given) are included within the experiment. As part of this the committee must provide for a thorough informed consent procedure. (4) IRBs also have an obligation to continue the review of projects they have approved.[17] This continuing review usually includes periodic reports of progress from the investigator and the requirement that any substantial adverse reaction be reported immediately to the committee.[18]

Studies of IRBs indicate that there is great diversity in the actual operation of the committee and the rigor with which they review proposed experiments.[19] Some committees seldom require significant revisions and never reject a research proposal. Others almost always require some changes in protocols, especially in the area of informed consent. Few studies are completely rejected by IRBs. In fact, there is undoubtedly a bias in favor of approval.[20] The review by many committees is superficial, and some, in fact, apparently conduct their reviews by mail.[21] Others, probably the majority, are quite conscientious, and meet regularly. Such diversity and the absence of thorough review by some committees should be expected because of the decentralized nature of the review process—each institution has its own review committee. In addition, the membership of an IRB can be manipulated by an institution to virtually ensure approval of all proposed projects.[22] With an adequate system of audit and review by the FDA and HHS, many of the problems with IRBs could be corrected, but this federal review of IRBs is not sufficiently effective.

It is obvious from the above that the time it takes an IRB to review a proposed study varies considerably from one committee to another. Except in emergencies, review must be conducted before the human study is actually begun, and many funding agencies require that the study be reviewed before application for funding is complete. Therefore, researchers should contact the IRB as soon as possible to determine how much time review will take, what documents must be submitted, and the process of the committee. If the investigator has a deadline for an application, or for beginning the research, that should be clearly communicated to the IRB at the time application is made for approval of the research.

There are advantages to local review of experimentation in terms of the speed with which the review can be conducted and in the ability to apply local ethical standards to proposals. On the other hand, permitting institutions to appoint their own IRBs and the presence of several IRBs within urban areas invites manipulation and inconsistent reviews within the same city. An alternative approach would be to provide for local committees, which would review studies from all institutions within a small geographic area.[23]

INFORMED CONSENT

Voluntary consent to participate in an experiment is almost universally recognized as fundamental. Mere consent is not adequate, the consent must be based on sufficient information on which to make a proper decision.[24] An interesting question is the definition of human experimentation, and in particular when research begins and therapy ends. In fact, therapy and experimentation are not mutually exclusive concepts.[25] For informed consent purposes, research should be very broadly defined. Thus, if part of a treatment is experimental, special informed consent is warranted.

The technical requirements for informed consent in all human studies have been generally described in case law and statute. Perhaps the most helpful and complete guidelines concerning informed consent in experimentation are contained in the HHS regulations, which include the following basic elements:[26]

1. A statement of the nature of the research that the experimenter is proposing.
2. A statement of the benefits to the subject or to others.
3. A statement of the risks. It is often necessary to add an additional statement that all the risks may not be known because of the experimental nature of the procedure or drug. It is not just physical risks of injuries which must be disclosed to potential subjects. Psychological or emotional risks, legal and financial risks, pain, inconvenience, and risks to privacy should all be disclosed to a subject.

4. A statement of the extent to which confidentiality will be maintained.
5. A statement of the alternatives or standard forms of treatment which will be available to patients if they do not participate in the experiment. This, of course, is unnecessary in the case of nontherapeutic experiment where the experiment is not done in any way to directly benefit the patient.
6. An offer to answer any questions that the patient has about the procedure or experiment, and where additional information may be sought.
7. A statement that the patient, without penalty, may refuse to participate or may discontinue participation in the experiment at any time.
8. An explanation of whether any compensation or treatment will be available if there is injury. (This applies only to research involving more than minimal risk.)

In some circumstances other information should be provided to subjects. This information may include: risks (if any) to a fetus if the subject is pregnant; additional costs to the subject for participating in the experiment; consequences (*not penalties*) of a decision to withdraw before the procedures are completed; the sponsor of the research; circumstances that may require early termination of the experiment; a statement that new findings affecting a subject's willingness to continue will be communicated to the subject; and the number of subjects involved in the experiment. Subjects should be given copies of the consent form to keep.

With this information a patient theoretically has the data necessary to make a reasoned and informed decision. In identifying the risks for potential subjects it is important that a researcher not let the value of the experiment change the way the risks are described. The researcher must remember that the obligation is to put the interests of the patient first, and to avoid any form of conflict of interest in which the excitement for the research project might interfere with doing what is fair to the patient. When professionals seek to use their own patients or clients in a study, they must meet very high standards of candor and disclosure in discussing the research project with those patients.[27]

The informed consent process may be seen as something of a charade since many patients will participate in an experiment simply because they are asked to do so by their therapists or doctors and will pay little attention to the information in an informed consent.[28] It is undoubtedly true that there is a group of people who will pay little attention to complex consent documents. It is critical, therefore, that the consent process be noncoercive and that the language and format of the informed consent be structured to promote understanding. Generally, a written rather than oral informed consent should be used.

Much attention has been focused on the initial process of providing information to the subject and the subject's agreement to participate in the study. In a very real sense, however, the subject must continuously consent to participate in the study, and be permitted to withdraw without penalty from the experiment at any time.[29] This option should be emphasized in the informed consent process. Withdrawal, of course, represents a revocation of consent to further participation, and this right is at least as important as the initial right to informed consent. In many instances, subjects may not fully understand (or may ignore) information given to them when they enter the study; they may find it to be more painful or risky than they initially appreciated. Therefore, their decision to continue or to withdraw is "more informed" than the initial decision to participate.

The desire of an investigator to avoid losing data is not a valid reason to deny the right to withdraw from an experiment. Although federal regulations do not directly speak to the issue, the investigator should not attempt to exercise much influence over the subject who wishes to withdraw. Ironically the Milgram study described earlier suggests that subjects may be highly susceptible to, and easily coerced by, the authority of the investigator and therefore continue in the study. (Subjects in that study who asked to quit were requested or told to continue and many did continue even under very stressful conditions.)

LIABILITY FOR HUMAN EXPERIMENTATION

Liability for human experimentation is rare. Negligently conducted experiments or highly stressful experiments might subject the experimenter to liability for resulting injuries. Experimentation, theoretically, raises the possibility of special kinds of liability. For example, an experimenter could be liable for failure to conduct adequate studies (e.g., on animals) before human testing.

The use of an experimental technique to treat a patient implies that something other than the usual or standard treatment is being used on the patient. When deviating from the usual or standard form of treatment, experimenters have a special duty to obtain full and complete informed consent from the experimental subjects. If, having been given full information concerning the alternatives, subjects freely choose to accept an experimental treatment, then the choice of an experimental method by the subjects will protect the experimenter from liability for using an experimental rather than the standard treatment.[30]

At what point does a procedure stop being experimental, and become legally acceptable? A new approach starts as experiment, becomes a "new procedure," and then becomes "commonly accepted." It is experimental until there is sufficient data to tentatively establish its efficacy, and it should be considered accepted practice when "a significant number of the profession is now using it in ordinary practice."[31] Of course, this moment cannot be defined with precision. When practitioners have serious doubts about the acceptance of a new procedure they may use the informed consent to permit patients to accept a new or experimental therapy.

Several causes of action other than negligence may arise out of improper experimentation. For example, the observation of very private activity without consent or the release of information from therapy for research purposes may give rise to invasion of privacy claims. When a researcher, without consent, intentionally places a subject under considerable stress to test reactions, there is a possiblity of the intentional infliction of mental distress (also known as "outrage"). The incorrect reporting of information in a way that can be identified with an individual or small group may be the basis for a defamation claim. Each of these torts is a remote possibility in research, but when research is improperly conducted the possibility becomes less remote.

Another issue is whether an IRB's approval of an experimental protocol will insulate an experimenter from potential liability for harm to subjects. Such a review is not likely to totally insulate a researcher from liability. At the same time, if IRBs do not perform their obligations to protect human subjects by reasonably careful review of experimental protocols, members of the committee are potentially liable for their negligence.[32]

Not every injury directly resulting from an experimental procedure will lead to liability. Only if there is inadequate informed consent, negligence, or the commission of an intentional tort will liability be imposed.

SPECIAL ISSUES IN
BEHAVIORAL SCIENCE RESEARCH

Behavioral science research involving humans raises a number of special legal and ethical issues. These issues relate to the kinds of research conducted (e.g., questionnaire or observational research), the fact that most of it is limited-risk research, the techniques of some research (deception and randomization), and the payment of subjects.

Defining Research

Defining research is sometimes difficult. Examples of this difficulty are the public observation of a subject, the use of new treatment techniques, and chart studies (review of data contained in existing patient files or charts). Federal regulations define research very broadly, as "a systematic investigation designed to develop or contribute to generalizable knowledge."[33] Under this definition, public observation, questionnaires, and chart studies are research. It should be noted, however, that some of these (described below) are exempt from federal regulations. The approach taken in the federal regulations (HHS), is a broad definition of research with the special exclusion from regulation of some considered very low risk.

Observational Research

Observational research is commonly used in the behavioral sciences and its regulation has been the subject of debate. Some argue that because the researcher is not intervening in the lives of the subjects, little protection is necessary or required. Others have noted that, particularly in observational research where the observation is unknown to the subjects, there is potential for harming the subject. The most likely harm is from embarrassing conduct revealed outside the research.[34] It is reasonable to protect subjects of observational research when they could be identified from the data, and the observations involve sensitive conduct (e.g., illegal activity, sexual behavior, or drug use) potentially harmful to the subject if revealed. This is essentially the approach taken by the federal regulations.[35]

Another form of nonintervention research is the review of existing charts or other data about the subjects. When this information is gathered from public records, of course, there is little likelihood that it will involve an invasion of privacy. This is not so, however, when data from hospital or other health records are used. Federal regulations permit the exemption of these chart studies from careful review if the subjects cannot be publicly identified.[36] In theory, the ethical and legal obligations of the holder of the medical records will be sufficient to ensure no improper use. Mental health records may contain particularly sensitive information. The interest of patients in the privacy of their records is, we believe, strong enough to warrant review of research that will involve mental health files, even if the data taken from them will not be maintained in an identifiable form.[37]

Questionnaires and Interviews

Questionnaires and interviews raise many of the same issues. For the most part, this information gathering does not seriously interfere with a subject. The federal guidelines exempt from regulation questionnaire/interview research unless respondents can be identified from the data maintained, the information could be harmful if revealed, *and* the research involves a sensitive area of life such as drug abuse, sexual behavior, or illegal conduct.[38] Because subjects can choose whether or not to answer a researcher's questions, they are inherently protected provided that they understand they may choose not to answer any question.

Some questions may be highly embarrassing or upsetting to subjects even though answers may not be kept in a personally identifiable form. If there is a risk of such items in a questionnaire or an interview, the investigator should seek IRB review whether or not technically required by federal regulations.

Education Research

Research involving "normal education practices" is generally of very little known risk to the subjects. It is controlled by the instructional requirements of the institution in which it is conducted, and is so ill-defined and pervasive that it could be almost impossible to regulate very effectively. HHS regulations exempt this kind of educational research.[39]

Cognitive, diagnostic, aptitude, and achievement tests are much like questionnaires in terms of their invasiveness and level of risk. These tests are also exempt if the information taken from these resources cannot be identified to any individuals.[40]

The fact that the research described above is exempt from HHS regulation does not mean that it is not subject to other forms of regulation, say from state or local governments, the institutions in which the research is conducted, or a private organization funding it. In addition, other federal agencies have authority to regulate some forms of human studies. For example, the Department of Education has increased parents' ability to prevent the inclusion of their children in some forms of educational testing.[41]

Low-Risk Research

The exceptions to federal regulation involve extremely low risks to the subjects. Many forms of behavioral science research fall into these categories. Many other forms of research that must be reviewed by IRBs also involve minimal risks, and approval should be quick. For example, a research project to study the use of biofeedback to reduce the desire to smoke would be low risk. IRBs can often give quick approval (known as "expedited review") to such low risk experiments.[42]

New Drugs

Among the most rigorously reviewed and regulated forms of human research is the testing of new drugs and devices. These studies are regulated by the FDA.[43] FDA regulations, of course, apply to new psychotropic medicines as well as to other new drugs.[44] Before human testing, sufficient laboratory and animal studies must have been conducted to justify use of the compound on humans. The risk of serious injury is present in the testing of new drugs. Therefore, the use of experimental drugs is generally carefully reviewed by the IRB and the process of informed consent is more closely scrutinized than for most other forms of research.

Several phases of human testing are generally employed, usually by increasing the size of the groups administered the drugs. The drug is first tested on a small number of healthy humans to determine its toxicity, then, on a larger group to determine dosage and efficacy. Finally, a still larger group of patients is used to obtain a large pool of data to further establish efficacy, side effects, contraindications, and the like. IRBs must approve the use of the drug at each phase of testing.[45]

Payment for Participation

In some instances investigators are able to pay subjects. It is generally seen as appropriate if it compensates for their time, travel, or discomfort. It is not considered appropriate when it is the major, or undue, inducement to participation. Significant payment risks attracting to experiments those who are participating only for the money.[46] It would be socially unacceptable to use only the poor as research subjects.

Behavioral scientists sometimes wish to use payment as a means to induce subjects to complete an experiment. A researcher might withhold all payment if a subject fails to complete participation. Assume, for example, that in an adaptation to stress experiment a subject will be placed in five different stressful situations, one each day for five days. The study requires the researcher to compare the reaction to stress on the first and last day. The subject will be paid $100, but will receive it only upon completion of the fifth day. Although some

IRBs permit this process, it is inappropriate. The right to withdraw from an experiment is very important. The payment-upon-completion plan is inconsistent with the principle that a subject should be permitted to withdraw from an experiment *without penalty*. By dropping out on the fourth day, the subject is essentially penalized for the four days of time travel and inconvenience he or she has already put into the experiment. In addition, it may in effect be a form of undue inducement to participate in the last part of the experiment. In the example, if a subject finds participation in the stress study quite uncomfortable and does not want to proceed after the fourth episode, he or she will in effect receive $100 for participating in one episode (the last). Ordinarily, where a study has several parts, any payment should be prorated to reflect time and energy expended and discomfort endured until the time of withdrawal.

Randomization and Double Blind Studies

The regulation of human studies and the informed consent process need not interfere with good research practices such as the use of control groups, randomization (placing a subject in the treatment or control group on the basis of chance) or double blind (neither the subject nor the researcher knows which group a subject is in). It may be impossible to know before informed consent is obtained what experimental group a participant will be in. The subject can, however, be informed of, and consent to, the process of randomization or double blinding.[47]

DECEPTION

Deception usually involves misinforming subjects about the purpose or nature of a study, or about what they will experience. The subject therefore consents to one thing and experiences or participates in something different.[48] The justification given for deception is that some research could not be conducted without it. The Milgram study is an example of this. Theoretically, if the experiment is not risky, the deception will not be harmful because subjects can later be informed of the true nature of the experiment.

Deception is common in behavioral science research. In social psychology, for example, it is estimated that 20 percent of experiments involve deception.[49] Another study found that about 60 percent of the studies in *The Journal of Personality and Social Psychology* involve it.[50] These findings are consistent with those of other studies.[51] In fact, it appears that the professional concern about deception has not produced a reduction in its use in research studies.[52]

Some argue that deception is necessary to perform many kinds of behavioral research, that it is not invasive, and that subjects do not object to its use. Recent studies[53] confirm a number of older studies[54] indicating that many college students are not particularly concerned with deception or invasion of privacy in experimental studies. This may point to a different value system than IRBs and regulators employ[55] or it may represent students' expectation that deception will be employed in such research.

Others argue that the use of deception violates the fundamental principle of informed consent, and tends to bring behavioral sciences into disrepute and may make it difficult for those deceived to trust mental health professionals in the future. In addition, undergraduate subjects may be able to see through supposed deception, or even become inclined to engage in their own deception when they participate in experiments.[56]

Some professional associations have adopted specific standards dealing with deception. A particularly thorough set has been adopted by the American Psychological Association.[57] Examples of commonly stated ethical requirements for deception are: the research problem is of importance; the research objectives would not be obtainable without deception; the subject will be permitted to withdraw along with his or her data when the deception is revealed; the researcher will take responsibility to detect and remove stressful effects of the deception; and the reasons for the deception are so compelling that when subjects are informed, they can be expected to find it reasonable and suffer no loss of confidence in the integrity of the investigator. After an experiment requiring deception, the subject is supposed to be informed of the deception and the reasons for it and encouraged to discuss any negative feelings. In fact, this debriefing process may often be poorly done or not done at all. Ullman and Jackson's review of two major psychology journals showed that as late as 1980, only about half of the studies involving deception mentioned debriefing, and it was rarely reported for incarcerated criminals, juvenile delinquents, and psychiatric patients.[58]

Federal regulations do not speak directly of deception, perhaps because it is a particularly difficult and controversial subject. The regulations do permit IRBs to modify informed consent requirements or to waive the requirements of informed consent.[59] IRBs might use this section to approve deception, but it is stretching the concept of "not including" or "altering" elements of informed consent to permit misinformation in lieu of information. If the regulations are intended to permit deception, that should be specifically provided.

Deception is often discussed as though it were a single concept. It is not. There may be deception in the statement of the purpose of the experiment, concerning the identity of the equipment or participants used in the study, or about what the subject will experience. An example of deception of purpose is where subjects are told they will take an IQ test to determine the effect of light intensity on the outcome of exams, when the real purpose is to study the relationship between race and IQ. Deception as to equipment or participant takes place when a subject is hooked to a machine which the subject is told is an excellent lie detector; it is actually an empty box with a light on it, and it is operated by a confederate rather than a polygraph expert. An example of deception about what will be experienced is where the subjects are told they will be asked to sit in a quiet room and identify people, when in fact, the subjects are subjected to unexpected and excessive noise and light to study their powers of observation. Research deception often involves more than one of these, as where subjects are told they will be taking a written test to study openness on questionnaires. In fact, a staged "robbery" occurs to test the reliability of the subjects as eyewitnesses. This study involves all three kinds of deception.

Each form of deception carries its own risks.[60] In the case of differences in purpose or differences in identity of participants or equipment, most of the risk is that the subject will be associated with research which the subject finds objectionable, for example, the racial IQ study. To avoid that risk, it is possible to allow subjects to withdraw their data at debriefing if there is objection to the research. Avoiding the risk of harm when subjects will experience something other than that to which they have consented is much more difficult although some of the difficulties could be overcome using the modified informed consent procedure described below.

While reasonable people have disagreed about whether deception should be permitted, there is little doubt that it is now used extensively. Because its use does pose some risks to perceived trustworthiness of the behavioral science professions, and it does involve at least some invasion of values highly prized in our society, deception should be minimized.[61] A good first step would be rigorous adherence to ethical standards such as those established by the American Psychological Association. Deception should be used only if it is impractical to do research without it and the research should have a potential to be important to the advancement of science. The risks (including emotional or psychological risks) should be minimal. Special efforts should be made to permit subjects to easily opt out of the research while it is in progress, and to withdraw their data following debriefing. Debriefing should be required except in the most extraordinary cases.[62]

To implement protection of subjects, IRBs and other ethics committees should require written justification from researchers for use of deception. Alternatives should be explored fully.[63] Journals should not publish the results of research done unless the study has been approved by an IRB-type committee before the research is conducted, and unless debriefing has occurred. Thesis and dissertation committees should not approve proposals that do not include justification for any deception, and during oral examination, questions should be asked about the use of deception. Kelman suggests that some of the energy now used to create ingenious deceptions should be put into the development of new techniques which would allow subjects full participation in the research project.[64]

Investigators might consider using a special form of informed consent, indicating that the investigator might temporarily misinform the subject about some aspects of the experiment, with the assurance that it would be fully discussed at the close of the experiment. Subjects who are concerned about deception would then be able to decide not to participate. Subjects so informed might be looking for the deception, but it is likely that many subjects now look for it.

THE USE OF SPECIAL SUBJECTS

The research use of such groups as minors, students, prisoners, and mental patients raises special problems. The distinction between therapeutic and nontherapeutic experiments is important in considering these groups. "Therapeutic experiments" hold the real possibility that the subject will directly benefit from participation. For example, drug testing in which patients are given a drug that may be superior to the treatments currently available, would be a therapeutic experiment. A nontherapeutic experiment is one not likely to directly benefit the subject—say a drug given for research purposes to a healthy subject who could not benefit from it.

Students

The use of students in experimentation raises a number of issues, primarily whether the students have given free and voluntary consent to participation. When students are requested by one of their instructors to be subjects, it may be difficult for them to decline without feeling that their standing in class is in jeopardy. This may be a particular problem in graduate education and in medical schools, where there often is a fairly close working relationship between the faculty member and student and where a faculty member can have a substantial impact on the career of a student.

One solution is to refuse to permit students to participate in experiments conducted by faculty members in their school. In at least one instance, when an IRB imposed such a limitation on the use of medical students, students requested that the rule be withdrawn because they wished to be allowed to participate in medical experimentation as a learning experience. The students indicated that they were better able to assess the risks of participating in an experiment than the great majority of people and that they thought it was valuable for future physicians to have some feeling for what it was like to be an experimental subject. Their point was well taken and the ban on the use of medical students was dropped, although faculty were prohibited from directly soliciting their own students. It is also important that the institution make it clear that it is absolutely unethical for the faculty member to take a student's participation, or refusal to participate in an experiment, into account in grading or teaching the student.

It is common for students in undergraduate behavioral science classes to be required to participate in an experiment as part of a class assignment. Many of the human studies done by behavioral scientists are done on students taking introductory psychology courses. Aside from the thought that our view of human behavior may be based on the reactions of college sophomores, ethical questions are raised by requiring students who wish to take a class to participate in an experiment. This requirement may be justified on the basis that participation in the experiment is a learning process which, in part, helps students understand more about the nature of behavioral science research. It is also common for students to be given a choice of experiments and to permit students to withdraw from them after their participation has started. Some schools permit students to write a paper or to do a special project rather than participate. These provisions undoubtedly provide sufficient alternatives to students. However, it is important that the potential for abuse of students be recognized in any requirement that students act as human subjects as part of a class requirement. Careful monitoring and periodic review of these programs is essential if abuse is to be avoided.

Another issue occurs with education research. Students at all levels of education may be divided into various groups to test new methods of instruction or to compare the efficacy of various teaching and learning theories. It is not uncommon for these studies to be carried on without the consent or the knowledge of the students or their parents.[65] The rights of students to be involved in deciding whether or not to participate in an education experiment has received relatively little attention compared with the rights of patients to determine whether or not they wish to receive a new form of medical treatment.[66] As noted earlier, much of such research is exempt from HHS regulations, however there are ethical issues involved. Also, Department of Education regulations now permit parents to limit the kind of educational research a school may undertake with their children.[67] These regulations have the potential for significantly hindering many types of education and school-based research. Behavioral science and educational researchers should more carefully consider ethical issues in research involving students and develop appropriate guidelines.

Minors

Consent to treatment and to participation in experimental procedures has traditionally been given by parents or guardians for minors. But minors and their parents sometimes have conflicting needs or values which may interfere with treatment decisions. Because most states define majority at 18 or 21, the conflict in values between parents and adolescents may be significant. For these reasons some modifications are recognized in the parental-consent-for-minor rule. For example, mature minors may consent to an abortion without parental consent.[68] The voluntary admission of a minor to a mental institution must be reviewed by an independent professional.[69]

The consent of minors to participation in nontherapeutic experimentation is particularly difficult.[70] It is appropriate for people to decide for themselves that they will take risks to promote scientific knowledge. It is quite another matter for them to consent to *someone else* taking the risks. As Justice McReynolds said, "Parents are free to become martyrs themselves. But it does not follow they are free, in identical circumstances, to make martyrs of their children."[71] Parents may not fully appreciate the risks of a child's participation in a study, or they may not care enough to consider carefully the risks and benefits.[72]

The distinction between therapeutic and nontherapeutic experiments is of particular importance in human studies involving children.

As therapeutic experiments often benefit the child, their participation generally involves no serious ethical and legal problems. Nontherapeutic experiments present special problems in protecting the welfare and privacy of subjects, and several approaches can be used to protect minors from harm.[73] Such studies on minors should be undertaken only if they cannot reasonably be done on adults. In addition, minors should participate in the informed consent process to the fullest extent possible. Those 14 years and older can be involved fully in deciding whether or not to participate in a study. Even a child of 7 can often be involved in deciding whether or not to consent to an experiment. To be effective, the consent process must be carefully designed to be noncoercive.[74] Children should also understand that they may withdraw from the experiment at any time without penalty. Additional protections for minors can be provided by ensuring that the research has been carefully designed to remove unnecessary risks, by particularly careful preparation of those conducting the research, and by providing for easy termination if the risks appear greater than anticipated. A strong argument has been made that in nontherapeutic research, minors should be used as subjects only if there are only modest risks to them.[75]

HHS regulations implement many of the principles discussed above.[76] They require the IRB to provide for assent by the minor when that is reasonable, as well as for consent by the parent or guardian.[77] If the research is not therapeutic and is of greater than minimal risk, both parents (if available) must consent to the child's participation. Only research that is therapeutic or that involves only slightly more than minimal risk may be approved by the IRB. Nontherapeutic research involving significant risk must be reviewed by an HHS panel.[78]

With adequate precautions and preparation, research involving minors can be accomplished ethically by protecting their rights and interests and by engaging their participation in the informed consent process.

Mental Patients

The participation of mental patients in human research raises difficult problems because there are questions about their competency to consent to participate, they are vulnerable and dependent on others within an institution, and they may be more subject than others to emotional harm from experimentation. Despite these problems, institutionalized patients have in the past been extensively used in research. Consent either was not sought or was readily given when hospital staff members were acting as guardians.[79]

Mental patients must be divided into two groups: incompetent and legally competent. Guardians make legal judgments for patients who are legally incompetent and are thus empowered to consent to treatment or research with the obligation to make decisions in the best interest of the incompetent. When therapeutic experiments show promise of assisting an incompetent patient where other treatment or procedures would not, it may be in their best interest to be involved in the study. In most instances, however, participation in nontherapeutic experiments involving any risk would not be in the best interest of an incompetent and it is difficult to see the "best interest of the patient" justification for guardians to consent to the participation of an incompetent patient in a nontherapeutic experiment. (An exception would be where the patient, while competent, had expressed a desire to participate.) However, guardians have not been precluded from consenting to nontherapeutic research on behalf of their wards, perhaps on the theory that everyone has some moral obligation to participate in the advancement of knowledge since everyone benefits from it. Nor has the participation of incompetent mental patients thus far been limited to those conditions which particularly affect the incompetent.[80]

Consent for participation by incompetent patients raises the same issues discussed concerning minors. One particular difficulty is that legal guardians often have no close personal interest in the patient. The guardian may be a representative of a bank, law firm, or the institution in which the patient is housed. These guardians may see their obligation as primarily to care for the property and money of the incompetent, and they may grant the care facility a broad or blanket consent. Given the obligation of guardians to do what is best for the incompetent it is surprising that they normally would consent to nontherapeutic research involving more than minimal risk.

The usual rules regarding consent technically apply to the participation of competent mental patients. Yet the existence of a mental illness may impair mental patients' ability to consider whether or not to participate in an experimental procedure even if it does not make the patients legally incompetent.[81] More thorough and complete information must sometimes be given for a mental patient to make an informal decision regarding treatment.[82]

Determining competence to consent to research is sometimes difficult. If there is no formal determination of incompetence (as through a court proceeding) and if it is not obvious that the subject is in fact incompetent, the subject should be involved in the decision of whether or not to participate in the research. When competency is doubted, however, the next of kin or guardian should also be involved in the decision to participate.[83]

The dependence and vulnerability of institutionalized mental patients makes them particularly subject to coercive researchers. The use of prisoners in experiments, as we shall see, has been subject to close scrutiny because prisons are inherently coercive. Many mental institutions are at least as inherently coercive as prisons. Patients may find it extremely difficult to reject a request to participate, particularly if the request comes from a therapist or other caregiver. This argues for a special consent procedure to avoid coercion. For example, caregivers should not request the participation of their own patients. In addition, it should be easy for the patient to discontinue participation without penalty.

Mental patients may be at special risk because they may misunderstand the nature of what is happening. A patient may fear the EEG electrodes will destroy his brain.[84] Thus, even apparently harmless, noninvasive research should be carefully scrutinized and not carried out over the objection of even incompetent patients.

Federal regulation of research on mental patients is suprisingly modest. While special regulations covering minors and prisoners have been implemented by HHS, specific regulations have not been implemented for mental patients. The National Commission suggested a number of protections, but these have not yet been adopted. The failure of HHS and the FDA to implement regulations is disappointing in light of the special vulnerability of mental patients and the potential for abuse. Mental patients are arguably the group most in need of regulatory protection.[85]

Even in the absence of federal regulations, researchers may, of course, pay special attention to the needs of mental patients. And IRBs, in fulfilling their obligations to review the risk of proposed studies and to provide "additional safeguards" to protect particularly vulnerable subjects, may also require special protection for the mentally disabled.[86] For example, for competent mental patients the informed consent process could be structured to be noncoercive and to provide additional information. A patient advocate not associated with the research may be used to help patients understand their rights. For incompetent patients, policies should ensure that the best interest of the patient is in fact the basis for deciding whether or not to participate. Consent to nontherapeutic experiments involving more than minimal risk should be reviewed very carefully. Generally, incompetent patients should not be entered into studies in which they refused to participate while competent and if competence is restored they should be permitted to decide whether or not to continue in it. We believe that research should not be conducted on incompetents if it could be done with competent subjects. Finally, IRBs should be particularly careful in conducting periodic reviews of approved research.[87]

Prisoners

Prisoners may be used in research for two reasons. First, the behavior and condition of criminals is a matter of considerable interest. Second, as a carefully controlled, stable population, whose environment can be easily manipulated, prisoners are particularly attractive for human experimentation.[88]

Although prisoners are mentally capable of giving informed consent, the nature of the prison environment is inherently coercive. The inducements to participate in human experimentation might be such that free and voluntary consent in prisons is difficult. Fletcher, for example, suggests that it is impossible for prisoners to be free of undue pressure and states that those who have lost their freedom through imprisonment should not be asked to participate in hypocritical charade of "freely" giving up individual rights.[89] Others have responded that prison life is very closely controlled and prisoners typically do not have an opportunity to consider options, and therefore the chance to participate in an experiment offers a prisoner one of the few opportunities for "self-determination."[90] Others argue that by participating in an experiment a prisoner may gain a new sense of personal value through sacrifice, perseverance, and altruism and that association with the scientists conducting an experiment may be a most beneficial relationship for the prisoner.[91] Albert Sabin argued for "the Sabin bill of rights" which states that the right to volunteer for medical experiments "should not be denied to anyone because of service in the armed forces, imprisonment for a crime against society, unemployment, poverty, boredom, or even a sincere desire to help others."[92]

Substantial HHS regulations now apply to the use of prisoners in human studies.[93] The regulations try to promote free consent by ensuring that participation (or refusal) will not affect parole decisions and that participants will not be unduly tempted by a promise of improved living conditions. Procedures for the selection of participants must be fair. In addition, the research must be therapeutic, of minimal risk, or directed toward studies of particular relevance to prisoners. An IRB considering prisoner research must have on it a prisoner representative. FDA suggested similar regulations, but has indefinitely delayed their implementation.[94]

LOSSES FROM HUMAN EXPERIMENTATION

There are very few significant injuries caused by participating in non-therapeutic research.[95] Therapeutic research has more injuries associated with it because of the risks associated with treatment, such as experimental chemotherapy for cancer. Much of the debate over compensation for research injuries has centered on whether researchers and sponsors of research should be strictly liable for injuries. Currently, if injuries are caused by an intentional tort or the negligence of the researcher, then the investigator is liable for the injuries. Otherwise, unless other arrangements are made by contract or the consent of the parties, an injured subject will be responsible for paying for injuries. Federal regulations require investigators to tell subjects whether or not treatment and compensation will be available if there is injury.[96]

Some argue for imposing strict liability to cover all injuries caused by participation in nontherapeutic experimentation because, they claim, participation is a selfless act to advance knowledge and it is therefore inappropriate to further burden injured subjects with the cost of injuries; a compensation system will encourage participation by subjects; and the failure of such a system will impose particularly difficult burdens on poorer subjects.[97] Others argue that it would be unfair to researchers (especially those without government or foundation grants) by requiring that they purchase insurance; it would encourage subjects to file claims for trivial injuries; there are so few injuries that there is no need for a compensation system; and subjects and researchers should be free to agree on whether compensation will be provided for injuries. Compensation could, of course, be provided through government resources instead of private programs, but there has been no effort to move in that direction.

Of special interest in behavioral science research are emotional injuries.[98] These injuries are very difficult to assess and to evaluate, and yet they are likely to be the most common injury from behavioral research. Fortunately, they are seldom so serious as to be debilitating or disabling. Therefore, they generally produce little lost income or significant treatment expenses. The proper level of compensation for emotional suffering may be especially difficult to calculate. Behavioral researchers, in preparing human-studies protocols, should consider what will be done if the unexpected happens—if injuries are caused by their study.

EXPERIMENTATION INVOLVING ANIMALS

The traditional assumption by most scientists and ethicists has been that the interests of animals were of little or no importance in conducting research. In fact, ethical principles often require that research be first done on animals to avoid risk to humans.[99] This assumption has recently come under increasing vocal opposition. Some of the opposition has gone beyond vocal. A number of break-ins to free or liberate lab animals have been reported. One such event at the University of California-Riverside reportedly resulted in nearly $700,000 in damages. Antivivisectionists have opposed the cruel use of animals for decades. Until recently, most of the concern, however, has been directed at ensuring proper care and lodging for lab animals. Currently broader concerns are raised about the use of animals in experiments.[100] These concerns are directed both at the killing of animals in research projects and pain inflicted on animals. Some groups have identified the behavioral sciences as among the abusers of animals. Recent annual meetings of the American Psychological Association, for example, have seen vigorous demonstrations and protests against the use of animals in behavioral research.

The current animal rights movement represents a wide spectrum of views about the proper role of animals. At one extreme there is opposition to virtually all use of animals in research.[101] This position suggests that if humans are to benefit from research, then studies should be done on humans or through computer models of behavior. Other groups oppose research that will place animals under considerable stress or in great pain, but these groups do not clearly oppose the killing of animals for research. Still other groups oppose the use of certain kinds of animals, for example the use of pound animals, which are generally killed but instead sometimes sold to researchers at prices below those of animals bred for research purposes. Opposition to the use of these animals is based on the fact that they were once somebody's pet, albeit generally an abandoned pet.[102]

State laws regulating the use of animals have, in the past, commonly been limited to preventing unnecessary cruelty to animals and to requiring reasonable care and shelter. They are often very vague, leaving undefined such terms as unnecessary cruelty. They have not been of any significance in limiting research. Federal laws have been directed to requiring adequate care of animals that are part of federally funded research.[103]

One's view of the propriety of research on animals is essentially dependent on philosophical beliefs about the place of animals in the world and their place relative to man.[104] One view is that animals are created with rights equal to humans. Human dominance of animals is, in this view, nothing more than bullying by the stronger over the weaker.[105] This view would produce a virtually complete ban on all animal research (and produce vegetarians as well). On the other extreme is the view that animals are completely without rights, that is, humans have absolutely no obligation to animals. The infliction of pain or death is in this view of no more consequence than the "abuse" of a stone or crab grass.

There are, of course, many points of view between these extremes.[106] A common belief is that animals have interests to be considered, but of lesser importance than humans. This is not a single view, but a collection of views that weights the interest of animals differently and that may divide animals according to their intelligence, or some perceived special qualities. These philosophies permit some experiments using animals.

One general principle undoubtedly could claim wide support—that unnecessary physical or emotional discomfort or harm should not be inflicted on animals. (Many would add that unnecessary animal deaths should also be avoided.) The trick is determining what is "unnecessary." It is unnecessary if the researcher is inadequately prepared or if the research is poorly designed. It would also be unnecessary if the research provides no realistic hope for advancing knowledge, or if the research could be conducted without inflicting the pain. (The suggestion that much behavioral research could be conducted using computer models, however, is misleading because it is based on the erroneous assumption that good computer models exist for this kind of research.) Many would also impose a pain/benefit test on animal research. That is, the value of the information must exceed the pain to the animal. The difficulty, however, is valuing both the possible benefits from animal studies, and the pain to the animals. For the moment at least, this calculation is primarily left to the individual researcher. However, the animal rights movement may change this.

The animal rights movement may result in significant changes in the laws protecting animals.[107] The federal regulation of funded research involving animals has already been tightened, and the availability of pound animals has been reduced. Federal research grants have been threatened or terminated because of concern about pain inflicted on animals. It is entirely possible that state and local cruelty to animal laws could be expanded to include many forms of research. If these laws are enacted, behavioral research may be particularly vulnerable. Much biomedical research has a strong political appeal as having the potential for preventing or treating serious diseases (notably cancer and hereditary diseases). Most behavioral research does not have this appeal.[108] It is conceivable that Congress, state legislatures, or local governments faced with demand to do something about animal research, and not wanting to be accused of preventing the discovery of a cure for cancer, will turn to behavioral research as a safe way of meeting the political demand for action.

It is important that behavioral scientists inform the public of the reasons for the use of animals in behavioral research, and of the benefits of such research. Greater concern and professional debate about the issues raised, and the adoption of ethical principles where none exist, would help demonstrate a legitimate effort at self-regulation.[109] Student educational studies which endlessly replicate prior studies should be avoided if they produce significant physical or emotional pain in animals.[110] For example, studies demonstrating that mice will starve to death rather than cross painful electrically charged grids are not suitable student projects. The failure to reform unnecessarily abusive experimentation invites restrictive regulation. Animal researchers should be able to clearly state their personal philosophy of animal use and to justify clearly their experimental use of animals based on that philosophy.

SUMMARY

The long history of experimentation in humans has been punctuated by serious abuses of human subjects. The Nazi atrocities and the abuse of subjects in some experiments in the United States following World War II have resulted in regulation of human studies. This regulation includes the prior review of proposed studies by Institutional Review Boards (IRBs).

The increased regulation of experimentation is not without controversy. There has been concern that the regulation will interfere with important research and thereby retard knowledge. In addition, some commentators consider the regulation to be interference with the autonomy of researchers and subjects to agree to any studies they wish to undertake or in which they wish to participate.

Most review of research is intended to ensure that the benefits outweigh the risks of the study, that the risks have been minimized as much as possible, and that informed consent has been obtained. Informed consent is intended to protect subject autonomy by including in experiments only people who freely agree to participate. Information about the nature of the experiment and the risks and benefits of, and alternatives to, participation are at the heart of informed consent. Subjects should also be informed that there is no penalty for failure to participate and that they may withdraw from the study at any time.

Special issues arise in behavioral research. The issues include defining "research," and determining whether it includes observation studies, questionnaires, and education research. Federal regulations generally exempt these kinds of studies from regulation. Deception has been of particular concern in behavioral research. It has been ethically justified when the research is important, it could not be carried on without deception, it is of low risk, and the subject will be debriefed following the study. There is a substantial amount of deception used, some of which fails to meet these ethical principles. The use of deception usually means that the principles of informed consent have been violated, and this is the basis of much of the criticism of it. Some of the goals of informed consent could be achieved if subjects specifically consented to deception, in the same way some subjects now consent to participation in randomization or double blind studies.

Experimentation with students, minors, mental patients, and prisoners has been the subject of intense debate. The major difficulty with these groups is their inability to grant free consent to participation in experiments. Students may be unduly influenced by their instructor to participate in an experiment, children may be entered into an experiment by their parents inappropriately, and mental patients may be entered in an experiment by their guardians without proper controls. Particularly when nontherapeutic experiments are being performed, the participation by these individuals must be carefully examined.

HHS regulations now provide special protections for prisoners and minors. The regulations concerning prisoners are meant to ensure that they are not coerced into participation. The regulations concerning minors seek to ensure that they are involved in nontherapeutic experiments only if the risks involved are fairly low. Unfortunately, mental patients have not received similar protection from federal regulations. Researchers may take steps to help ensure the protection of mental patients by limiting the risks to which they are subjected, by recognizing that the mentally disabled may misunderstand what is done to them, and by permitting them to be involved in the consent process to the extent possible. The participation of mental patients should be terminated early if unusual stress or emotional pain is noted.

Few injuries result from human experimentation. If an injury is caused by negligence, or if the researcher has agreed to provide compensation, then the researcher may be subject to liability for the injury. Otherwise, research subjects are responsible for their own injuries. Strict liability is sometimes suggested as a method of providing compensation to subjects injured during research.

While the use of humans in research has received considerable attention, recently the use of animals has also been the subject of controversy. The animal rights movement has challenged the traditional position that scientists were free to conduct any form of research as long as they adequately cared for research animals. The behavioral sciences have been identified by some animal rights groups as among the worst abusers of animals. Some groups would essentially prohibit all use of animals, others would require a more thorough cost/benefit study before animals are used. This movement may result in more extensive federal, state, and local regulation of animal research. Behavioral scientists should be able to state their own philosophy regarding the use of animals and be prepared to justify clearly the animal use in any experiment.

Notes

1. Thornwell v. United States, 471 F.Supp. 344 (D. D.C. 1979).
2. J. Marks, *The Search for the Manchurian Candidate* 53–86 (1979).
3. Wecht, Medical, Legal and Moral Considerations in Human Experimentation Involving Minors and Incompetent Adults, 4 *J. Legal Med.* 27 (1976).
4. Marshall & Zimbardo, Affective Consequences of Inadequately Explained Physiological Arousal, 37 *J. Personality & Soc. Psychology* 970 (1979).
5. S. Milgram, *Obedience to Authority: An Experimental View* (1974); Gordon, Mental Distress in Psychological Research, 21 *Baylor L. Rev.* 520 (1969).
6. Shanab & Yahya, A Behavioral Study of Obedience in Children, 35 *J. Personality & Soc. Psychology* 530 (1977).
7. Eating the apple could be classified as the first human experimentation producing bad result. (Others might argue that the creation of Adam, or Eve, was the first.)
8. Nuremberg Military Tribunal, The Nuremberg Code, 2 The Medical Cases 181–82 (G.P.O. 1947). This code was used in United States v. Karl Brandt, et al., Trials of War Criminals Before Military Tribunals Under Control Law No. 10 (Oct. 1946–Apr. 1949).

For an excellent review of issues regarding human experimentation see J. Katz, *Experimentation With Human Beings* (1972).

There may still be a need for international control of some forms of human experimentation. Bassiouni, Baffes & Evrard, An Appraisal of Human Experimentation in International Law and Practice: The Need for International Regulation of Human Experimentation, 72 *J. Crim. L. & Criminology* 1597 (1981).

9. The Nuremberg principles are as follows:

1. The voluntary consent of the human subject is absolutely essential. This means that the person involved should have legal capacity to give consent; should be so situated as to be able to exercise free power of choice, without the intervention of any element of force, fraud, deceit, duress, overreaching, or other ulterior form of constraint of coercion; and should have sufficient knowledge and comprehension of the elements of the subject matter involved as to enable him to make an understanding and enlightened decision. . . .

2. The experiment should be such as to yield fruitful results for the good

of society, unprocurable by other methods or means of study, and not random and unnecessary in nature.

3. The experiment should be so designed and based on the results of animal experimentation and a knowledge of the natural history of the disease or other problem under study that the anticipated results will justify the performance of the experiment.

4. The experiment should be so conducted as to avoid all unnecessary physical and mental suffering and injury.

5. No experiment should be conducted where there is an *a priori* reason to believe that death or disabling injury will occur; except, perhaps, in those experiments where the experimental physicians also serve as subjects.

6. The degree of risks to be taken should never exceed that determined by the humanitarian importance of the problem to be solved by the experiment.

7. Proper preparation should be made and adequate facilities provided to protect the experimental subject against even remote possibilities of injury, disability, or death.

8. The experiment should be conducted only by scientifically qualified persons. The highest degree of skill and care should be required through all stages of the experiment of those who conduct or engage in the experiment.

9. During the course of the experiment the human subject should be at liberty to bring the experiment to an end if he has reached the physical or mental state where continuation of the experiment seems to him to be impossible.

10. During the course of the experiment the scientist in charge must be prepared to terminate the experiment at any stage, if he has probable cause to believe, in the exercise of good faith, superior skill and careful judgment required of him that a continuation of the experiment is likely to result in injury, disability, or death to the experimental subject.

10. Congress provided for the appointment of a national commission to consider issues related to human experimentation. See National Commission for the Protection of Human Subjects of Biomedical and Behavioral Research, *The Belmont Report: Ethical Principles and Guidelines for the Protection of Human Subjects of Research* (1978) [hereinafter cited as *The Belmont Report*]. Other reports issued by the commission regarding institutional review committees and research with children, prisoners and mental patients are cited throughout this chapter.

11. These and other ethically questionable human experiments are described in Beecher, Ethics and Clinical Research, 274 *New Eng. J. Med.* 1354 (1966).

12. See Gray, The Regulatory Context of Social and Behavioral Research, and Robertson, The Social Scientist's Right to Research and the IRB System, both in, *Ethical Issues in Social Science Research* 329, 356 (T. Beauchamp, R. Faden, R. J. Wallace, Jr., & L. Walters eds. 1982); Imber, Glanz, Elkin, Stotsky, Bayer & Leber, Ethical Issues in Psychotherapy Research, 41 *Am. Psychologist* 137 (1986).

13. For a summary of the debate concerning autonomy in human experimentation see Tancredi & Maxfield, Regulation of Psychiatric Research: A Socioethical Analysis, 6 *Int'l J. L. & Psychiatry* 17 (1983).

14. A review of the various policies and procedures of federal agencies

for the protection of human subjects is contained in National Commission for the Protection of Human Subjects of Biomedical and Behavioral Research, *Report And Recommendations: Institutional Review Boards,* Appendix 2 (1978) [hereinafter cited as *Institutional Review Boards*].

15. HHS regulations are at 45 C.F.R. [Code of Federal Regulations] §46 (1985) and include sections on the use of prisoners and of children.

16. FDA regulations are at 21 C.F.R. §50 (1985).

17. For the regulations concerning Institutional Review Boards see 45 C.F.R. §§46.103–46.108 (1984). See also Levine, The Institutional Review Board in *Institutional Review Boards,* Appendix 4; Robertson, The Law of Institutional Review Boards, 26 *UCLA L. Rev.* 484 (1979).

18. Robertson, *supra,* note 17, at 511.

19. B. Barber, J. Lally, J. Mararushka & D. Sullivan, *Research on Human Subjects* (1973); R. Levine, *Ethical and Regulation of Clinical Research* (1981); DuVal, The Human Subjects Protection Committee: An Experiment in Decentralized Federal Regulation, 1979 *Am. B. Found. Research J.* 571 (1979); A Survey of Institutional Review Boards and Research Involving Human Beings, in *Institutional Review Boards,* Appendix 1. See also Cowan, Human Experimentation: The Review Process in Practice, 25 *Case W. Res. L. Rev.* 533 (1975).

20. For a discussion of some extreme examples of IRB approval of research see Baumrind, Research Using Intentional Deception: Ethical Issues Revisited, 40 *Am. Psychologist* 165, 166–67 (1985).

21. See studies cited in note 19, *supra.*

22. The institution has control over appointment of the members of the IRB, subject to the requirement that there be some diversity of background and that at least one member not be affiliated with the institution. Therefore, an institution could appoint to the IRB members with a strong inclination to approve all proposed research projects.

23. See generally, regarding the work of, and problems with, IRB review of research, Schwartz, Institutional Review of Medical Research: Cost-Benefit Analysis, Risk-Benefit Analysis and the Possible Effects of Research on Public Policy, 4 *J. Legal Med.* 143 (1983).

24. But see Ozar, An Alternative Rationale for Informed Consent by Human Subjects, 38 *Am. Psychologist* 230 (1983). See also Appelbaum, Roth & Lidz, The Therapeutic Misconception: Informed Consent in Psychiatric Research, 5 *Int'l J. L. & Psychiatry* 319 (1982).

25. For a discussion of the problems in psychotherapy in drawing the distinction between therapy and research see London & Flerman, Boundaries Between Research and Therapy, Especially in Mental Health, in *The Belmont Report,* Appendix 15. See generally Levine, The Boundaries Between Biomedical or Behavioral Research and the Accepted and Routine Practice of Medicine, in *The Belmont Report,* Appendix 1.

26. 45 C.F.R. §46.116 (1985). The FDA requirements are similar, 21 C.F.R. §50.25 (1985).

27. See Dworkin, Must Subjects Be Objects?, in *Ethical Issues in Social*

Science Research 246 (T. Beauchamp, R. Faden, R. J. Wallace, Jr. & L. Walters eds. 1982).

28. See Lidz & Roth, The Signed Form—Informed Consent?, in *Solutions to Ethical and Legal Problems in Social Research* 145 (R. Boruch & J. Cecil eds. 1983).

29. See 45 C.F.R. §46.116 (8) (1985).

30. See Robertson, Legal Implications of the Boundaries Between Biomedical Research Involving Human Subjects and the Accepted or Routine Practice of Medicine, in *The Belmont Report*, Appendix 16.

31. Curran, Professional Negligence—Some General Comments, 12 *Vand. L. Rev.* 535, 541 (1959).

32. For a review of the potential civil liability of IRBs see, Bordas, Tort Liability of Institutional Review Boards, 87 *W. Va. L. Rev.* 137 (1984).

33. 45 C.F.R. §46.102(e) (1985) (HHS regulations).

34. See Wilson & Donnerstein, Legal and Ethical Aspects of Nonreactive Social Psychological Research: An Excursion Into the Public Mind, 31 *Am. Psychologist* 765 (1976).

35. 45 C.F.R. §46.101(b)(4) (1985) (HHS regulations).

36. 45 C.F.R. §46.101(b)(5) (1985) (HHS regulations). These same rules apply to the use of excess pathological specimens.

37. See generally Adams, Medical Research and Personal Privacy, 30 *Vill. L. Rev.* 1077 (1985); Steinberg, Social Research Use of Archival Records: Procedural Solutions to Privacy Problems, in *Solution to Ethical and Legal Problems in Social Research* 249 (R. Boruch & J. Cecil eds. 1983).

38. 45 C.F.R. §46.101(3) (1985). Strangely, the regulations exempt survey research unless it contains information that could harm the subject if released *and* the research deals with sensitive aspects of the subject's life. It would be more reasonable to substitute *or* for the *and*. In many instances there may not be much difference since sensitive information will usually be harmful if released.

39. 45 C.F.R. §46.101(1) (1985) (HHS regulations).

40. 45 C.F.R. §46.101(2) (1985).

41. Student Rights in Research, Experimental Activities and Testing, 49 Fed. Reg. 35,318 (1984) (to be codified at 34 C.F.R. parts 75, 76, and 98).

42. 45 C.F.R. §46.110 (1985).

43. The FDA regulations concerning the human testing of new drugs and devices are at 21 C.F.R. §50 (1985). If the research into a drug or device is funded through HHS, it will ordinarily also be subject to HHS regulations. HHS and FDA regulations are similar, except where prisoners or children are used as subjects.

44. The FDA regulations apply to new drugs and devices and to studies that will be submitted to the FDA as part of an application for a marketing permit.

45. For a description of the clinical testing of new drugs see E. Martin & R. Martin, *Hazard of Medication* 45–49 (1978).

46. A special kind of "payment" in behavioral science research is com-

pletion of course credit by participation in an experiment. That issue is considered below in the section dealing with students.

47. But see Brownell & Stunkard, The Double-Blind in Danger: Untoward Consequences of Informed Consent, 139 *Am. J. Psychiatry* 1497 (1982).

48. See generally R. Bausell, *Experimental Methods* (1986); Baumrind, Nature and Definition of Informed Consent in Research Involving Deception, in *The Belmont Report*, Appendix, 23.

49. See Bassford, The Moral Role Differentiation of Experimental Psychologists, 15 *Soc. Sci. & Med.* 27 (1981).

50. Gross & Fleming, Twenty Years of Deception in Social Psychology, 8 *Personality & Soc. Psychology Bull.* 402 (1982).

51. Approximately half of psychology undergraduates surveyed reported that deception had been used in experiments in which they had participated. Smith & Richardson, Amelioration of Deception and Harm in Psychological Research: The Important Role of Debriefing, 44 *J. Personality & Soc. Psychology* 1075 (1983). See Menges, Openness and Honesty v. Coercion and Deception in Psychological Research, 28 *Am. Psychologist* 1030 (1973).

52. Gross & Fleming, *supra*, note 50.

53. Keehn, To Do or Not To Do: Dimensions of Value and Morality in Experiments with Animals and Human Subjects, 15 *Soc. Sci. & Med.* 81 (1981); Lynch & Graves, Participants' Perceptions of Ethical Issues in Research with Humans, 52 *Psychological Rep.* 231 (1983).

54. Farr & Seaver, Stress and Discomfort in Psychological Research: Subject Perception of Experimental Procedures, 30 *Am. Psychologist* 770 (1975); Simmons, Client Attitudes Toward Release of Confidential Information Without Consent, 24 *J. Clinical Psychology* 364 (1968).

55. Forsyth & Pope, Ethical Ideology and Judgments of Social Psychological Research: Multidimensional Analysis, 46 *J. Personality & Soc. Psychology* 1365 (1984); Smith & Bernard, Why are Human Subjects Less Concerned About Ethically Problematic Research Than Human Subjects Committees?, 12 *J. Applied Soc. Psychology* 209 (1982).

56. Orne, On the Social Psychology of the Psychologist Experiment, 17 *Am. Psychologist* 776 (1962); Schultz, The Human Subject in Psychological Research, 72 *Psychological Bull.* 214 (1969).

57. American Psychological Association, Committee for the Protection of Human Participants in Research, *Ethical Principles in the Conduct of Research With Human Participants* (1973, 2d ed. 1982).

58. Ullman & Jackson, Researchers' Ethical Conscience: Debriefing From 1960 to 1980, 37 *Am. Psychologist* 972 (1982).

59. 45 C.F.R. §46.116(d) (1985) (HHS regulations). The IRB may alter or waive some of the requirements for informed consent only if minimal risk is involved, the rights and welfare of the subject will not be adversely affected, the research could not be carried on without the alteration, and whenever "appropriate" the subject will be provided with additional information after

participation. The FDA regulations for waiving informed consent are more restrictive. 21 C.F.R. §§50.20, 50.23, 50.27 (1985).

60. See Sieber, Evaluating the Potential for Harm or Wrong (parts I, II & III), *IRB: A Review of Human Subjects Research* Nov. 1982, Jan.–Feb. 1983, June 1983, at 1 (each issue).

61. The arguments against the use of deception are forcefully reviewed in Baumrind, Research Using Intentional Deception: Ethical Issues Revisited, 40 *Am. Psychologist* 165 (1985).

62. Smith & Richardson, Amelioration of Deception and Harm in Psychological Research: The Important Role of Debriefing, 44 *J. Personality & Soc. Psychology* 1075 (1983).

63. Geller, Alternatives to Deception: Why, What and How?, in *The Ethics of Social Research: Surveys and Experiments* 40 (J. Sieber ed. 1982).

64. Kellman, Humane Use of Human Subjects: The Problem of Deception in Social Psychological Experiments, 67 *Psychological Bull.* 1 (1967).

65. HHS regulations generally exempt from review educational research in educational settings. 45 C.F.R. §46.101(b)(1) (1985).

66. See DuVal, Educational Research and Protection of Human Subjects, 1977 *Am. B. Found. Research J.* 477.

67. Student Rights in Research, Experimental Activities, and Testing, 49 Fed. Reg. 35,318 (1984) (to be codified at 34 C.F.R. §§75, 76 and 98).

68. Akron v. Akron Center for Reproductive Health, 462 U.S. 416 (1983); Planned Parenthood of Central Missouri v. Danforth, 428 U.S. 52 (1976). *Cf.* Goss v. Lopez, 419 U.S. 565 (1975) (involving due process of children in public school discipline); Tinker v. Des Moines School District, 393 U.S. 503 (1969) (involving a child's freedom of expression in schools).

69. Parham v. J.R., 442 U.S. 584 (1979).

70. For a thorough review of the issues involved in the use of minors in human experimentation see National Commission for the Protection of Human Subjects of Biomedical and Behavioral Research, *Research Involving Children* (1977) [hereinafter referred to as *Research Involving Children*]. Included in the Appendix to the report is a study by the Survey Research Center of the University of Michigan indicating that there is substantial research on children. Projects which included at least 25 percent children represented about one quarter of all the research which passed through the Institutional Review Boards studied. Most of the research was "therapeutic," although about 30 percent was for other purposes, such as contributing to general scientific knowledge. Appendix 1 at 4–5.

71. Pierce v. Society of Sisters, 268 U.S. 510 (1925).

72. Ferguson, The Competence and Freedom of Children to Make Choice Regarding Participation in Research, 34 *J. Soc. Issues* 114 (1978); Glanz, Amos & Katz, Scientific Research with Children: Legal Incapacity and Proxy Consent, 11 *Fam. L.Q.* 253 (1977); Wiethorn & Campbell, The Competency of Children and Adolescents to Make Informed Treatment Decisions, 53 *Child Dev.* 1589 (1982).

73. See Langer, Medical Research Involving Children: Some Legal and Ethical Issues, 36 *Baylor L. Rev.* 1 (1984).

74. Bartholomew, The Ethics of Non-Therapeutic Clinical Research on Children, in *Research Involving Children*, Appendix 3.

75. See e.g., *Research Involving Children* at 12–18.

76. 45 C.F.R. §46.401–409 (1985). FDA differs from HHS regulations regarding children. FDA has not implemented special regulations protecting children.

77. The HHS regulations regarding children depend on the concept of "assent." Assent is defined in the regulations as "a child's affirmative agreement to participate in research. Mere failure to object should not, absent affirmative agreement, be construed as assent." 45 C.F.R. §46.402(b) (1985). The concept does not differ significantly from adult consent.

78. 45 C.F.R. §46.407 (1985).

79. See generally The National Commission for the Protection of Human Subjects of Biomedical and Behavioral Research, *Research Involving Those Institutionalized as Mentally Infirm* (1978) [hereinafter *Mentally Infirm*].

80. See generally Stanley & Stanley, Psychiatric Patients in Research: Protecting Their Autonomy, 22 *Comprehensive Psychiatry* 420 (1981).

81. The informed consent process is difficult to make effective even under the best of circumstances. There are even greater difficulties with mental patients. C. Lidz, A. Meisel, E. Zerubavel, M. Carter, R. Sestak & L. Roth, *Informed Consent: A Study of Decisionmaking in Psychiatry* (1984); Grossman & Summers, A Study of the Capacity of Schizophrenic Patients to Give Informed Consent, 31 *Hosp. & Community Psychiatry* 205 (1980).

82. Concerning informed consent for mental patient subjects see Annas, Glantz & Katz, The Law of Informed Consent in Human Experimentation: Institutionalized Mentally Infirm, in *Mentally Infirm*, Appendix 3.

83. Issues related to competency and consent are considered in chapters 3, 16, 18 and 19.

84. Siris, Docherty & McGlashan, Intrapsychic Structural Effects of Psychiatric Research, 136 *Am. J. Psychiatry* 12 (1979).

85. Much of the research involving mental patients may avoid IRB review because it involves observational research, questionnaires or tests, chart studies, or special demonstration projects. (45 C.F.R. §46.101 [1985]). See Tancredi & Maxfield, Regulation of Psychiatric Research: A Socioethical Analysis, 6 *Int'l J. L. & Psychiatry* 17 (1983).

86. 45 C.F.R. §46.111(b) (1985) provides, "Where . . . the subjects are likely to be vulnerable to coercion or indue influence, such as persons with acute or severe physical or mental illness, . . . appropriate additional safeguards [should be] included in the study to protect the rights and welfare of these subjects."

87. IRBs are required to conduct continuing review of approved research. At least once each year the IRB must review continuing research projects. 45 C.F.R. §46.109(e) (1985). The time period for review should be shortened when the research subjects are mental patients.

88. Issues involving the use of prisoners as subjects in experiments are reviewed in National Commission for the Protection of Human Subjects of Biomedical and Behavioral Research, *Research Involving Prisoners* (1976).

89. Fletcher, Human Experimentation: Ethics in the Consent Situation, 32 *L. & Contemp. Probs.* 620 (1967).

90. Hubbard, Individual Risks v. Societal Benefits, in *Experiments With Human Subjects* 135–38 (C. Freund ed. 1970) [hereinafter *Experiments With Human Subjects*].

91. Lsagna, Special Subjects in Human Experimentation, in *Experiments With Human Subjects* 262–275 (C. Freund ed. 1970).

92. Sabin, Individual Risk v. Societal Benefit, in *Experiments With Human Subjects* 127–29 (C. Freund ed. 1970).

93. 45 C.F.R. §46.301–.306 (1985).

94. 46 C.F.R. §35.085 (1981). The regulations which were suspended are subpart C of 21 C.F.R. §50.40 (1985).

95. A study of nontherapeutic research found no fatalities and that only .04 percent of participants suffered temporary disabilities and 1/93,000 permanent disability. Cardon, Dommel & Trumble, Injuries to Research Subjects: A Survey of Investigators, 296 *New Eng. J. Med.* 650 (1976).

96. 21 C.F.R. §50.26(a)(6) (1985); 45 C.F.R. §46.116(a)(6) (1985).

97. President's Commission for the Study of Ethical Problems in Medicine and Biomedical and Behavioral Research, *Compensating for Research Injuries: A Report on the Ethical and Legal Implications of Programs to Redress Injuries Caused by Biomedical and Behavioral Research* (1982).

98. Jacobs & Kotin, Fantasies of Psychiatric Research, 128 *Am. J. Psychiatry* 1074 (1972); Silverstein, Compensating Those Injured Through Experimentation, 48 *Conn. B. J.* 322 (1974).

99. The Nuremberg principles, for example, require that human experimentation be based "on the results of animal experimentation." Principle 3, Nuremberg Code, note 9, *supra*.

100. For a discussion of the kinds of experiments that many find objectionable see A. Rowna, *Of Mice, Models and Men: A Critical Evaluation of Animal Research* (1984). See also Note, Toward Legal Rights for Laboratory Animals?, 10 *J. Legis.* 198 (1983). A very thorough report on the use of animals is from the Congressional Office of Technology Assessment, *Alternatives to Animal Use in Research, Testing, and Education* (1986). That report suggests that in 1983 "at least 17 million to 22 million animals were used in research and testing in the United States."

101. See T. Regan, *All That Dwell Therein* (1982).

Perhaps because of increasing malpractice insurance premiums, some mental health professionals have suggested that experiments be performed on attorneys rather than rats. Proponents claim that lawyers are more plentiful than lab animals, that torture or abuse of attorneys would cause no public outcry, and that lab assistants are less likely to become attached to attorneys than to rats. In addition, they claim, there are some things rats just won't do.

102. D'Ver, The End of the Pound Dog, 10 *Lab Animal* 23 (1981).

103. A very good review of general animal cruelty law is contained in D. Favre & M. Loring, *Animal Law* (1983) at 121–66. See Curran, Biomedical Laboratories and Criminal Liability for Cruelty to Animals, 309 *New Eng. J. Med.* 1564 (1983).

104. See S. Clark, *The Moral Status of Animals* (1977); C. Hume, *The Status of Animals in the Christian Religion* (1957); Mulder, Who is Right About Animal Rights?, 29 *Lab. Animal Sci.* 435 (1981).

105. P. Singer comes close to adopting this position in *Animal Liberation: A New Ethics for Our Treatment of Animals* (1975) which begins, "This book is about the tyranny of human over nonhuman animals." (Preface, vii).

106. See generally the discussion of points of view concerning the moral status of animals in B. Rollin, *Animal Rights and Human Morality* (1981), and the works cited in note 104, *supra*.

107. See U.S. Dept. Health and Human Services, *NIH Guide Supplement for Grants and Contracts, Laboratory Animal Welfare* (June 25, 1985); Favre & McKinnon, The New Prometheus: Will Scientific Inquiry be Bound by the Chains of Government Regulation?, 19 *Duquesne L. Rev.* 651 (1981).

108. See Bannister, The Fallacy of Animal Experimentation in Psychology, in *Animals in Research* 307–17 (D. Sperlinger ed. 1981); Dresser, Research on Animals: Values, Politics, and Regulatory Reform, 58 *S. Cal. L. Rev.* 1147 (1985). The potential problems for behavioral researchers is suggested by the literature being handed out by animal rights groups in Washington, D.C. in 1986 which were especially critical of behavioral research. *"Behavioral Studies: These psychology experiments are perhaps the most atrocious and cruel.* Experimenters pull baby monkeys from their mothers at birth and put them with phoney 'monster mothers.' These surrogate mothers eject spikes, become red-hot, and turn into a variety of other horrifying creatures, all created by scientists with impressive PhDs. The baby monkey sadly tries to cling to his mother, no matter how much pain he must endure. The infant's determination is regularly monitored by the bemused researchers." (emphasis added) Distributed by People for the Ethical Treatment of Animals, P.O. Box 42516, Washington, D.C. 20015.

109. The ethical principles of the American Psychological Association provide for the welfare of experimental animals, noting that in the final analysis, "the animal's immediate protection depends upon the scientist's own conscience." The principles provide that researchers subject animals to pain, stress, or privation "only when an alternative procedure is unavoidable and the goal is justified by its prospective scientific, educational, or applied value." American Psychological Association, *Ethical Principles of Psychologists,* Principle 10 (1981). In 1985 the American Psychological Association adopted an additional comprehensive set of guidelines regarding the use of animals in experimentation and teaching. In addition to standards for the care of animals, the guidelines require a cost-benefit consideration between pain to the animal and value of the study.

110. H. McGiffin & N. Brownley, *Animals in Education* (1980). The new APA guidelines apply to animals used in teaching.

PART II

HUMAN BEHAVIOR
AND
THE COURTROOM

CHAPTER 7
JURY SELECTION AND ATTITUDE CHANGE IN THE TRIAL PROCESS

Empirical science has increasingly focused on the judicial system, and particularly on the study of factors influencing jury selection and the process and outcome of trials.[1]

Psychologists and other social scientists have joined forces with legal experts in this research effort, and a variety of approaches have been used in such investigations. However, a lack of consistency in the methodology employed, along with the growing recognition of the extreme complexity of the issues involved, has placed some limits on the ability to generalize from these studies to the actual courtroom.[2] A more in-depth look at the problems associated with this research will follow later in the chapter.

THE INFLUENCE OF INDIVIDUAL CHARACTERISTICS

Around 1935 scientific investigation of the courtroom process began. Early studies, such as those of Hewgill and Miller,[3] and others noted in Sales[4] and Nietzel,[5] demonstrated that statements were more likely to be accepted if they were attributed to a liked personality than a disliked one, or that jurors were more easily persuaded by sources perceived as trustworthy and expert.[6] Such early works laid the groundwork for a later increase in studies concerning characteristics of defendants, judges, jurors, attorneys, and witnesses.

In this discussion "defendant" refers to the defendant in a criminal trial. In some instances concepts discussed in this chapter apply to both the plaintiff and defendant in civil trials. However, caution must be exercised in generalizing too much research involving criminal trials to those involving civil trials. In criminal trials the focus is generally most clearly on the defendant, but in civil trials the focus may be both on the plaintiff and on the defendant. This may produce a more complex interaction, for example, of personality factors.

The Defendant and the Victim

Clarence Darrow once noted that "jurymen seldom convict a person they like or acquit one they dislike."[7] Yet, much is involved in the "liking" or "disliking" of a person. For example, Cook found that the amount of time the person actually looks directly at the other person or persons was related to whether or not a person was liked.[8] However, it cannot be clearly ascertained from Cook's findings whether or not deliberately changing the amount of looking behavior changes the degree to which one is liked, or whether more looking behavior occurs only when one already is liked. Cook's data tend to support the former idea.

Although the defendant's characteristics—such as trustworthiness, attractiveness, and the nature of the offense committed—were initially considered to have a rather straightforward effect on the jury, later studies have found these characteristics to interact highly with other elements of the case. For example, Sealy and Wain reported that out of such traits as being honest, trustworthy, frank, openly cunning, stable, and cooperative, only trustworthiness and honesty were found regularly to correlate with the defendant's being acquitted or convicted.[9] In theft cases, the perception of the main witness for the prosecution as trustworthy and the defendant as untrustworthy was highly correlated with guilty verdicts, with the perception of the witness as the best predictor of the initial verdict and that of the defendant as the best predictor of final verdict. In the case of rape, the perception of the victim as trustworthy was the best predictor of initial and final verdict both for the defendant against whom there was a strong case and for the one against whom the only evidence was the woman's accusation.

In examining the nature of the offense committed, in interaction with various personality variables of the victim, a number of studies have found that mock jurors tend to assign longer sentences to defendants if the *victim* is socially attractive than if he or she is socially unattractive. Yet Boor found that varying the intellectual competence of the victim of a swindle, theoretically in order to manipulate sympathy for the victim, did not change the severity of sentence imposed.[10] Singleton and Hofacre tested the effects of burglary and swindle victims' physical appearance, hypothesizing that defendants who victimize physically attractive individuals would receive longer sentences than those who victimize physically unattractive individuals. The hypothesis was not supported.[11] Two possible explanations for these contradictions are that physical attractiveness has a different effect than social attractiveness, that the attractiveness effect only operates when the offense is serious—e.g., rape.

From another perspective, Shaw and McMartin proposed that an equity principle operates whereby the jury's severity will be relaxed to the extent that the defendant has suffered.[12] In their research, when a defendant was injured in an automobile accident, mock jurors gave more lenient sentences than otherwise. Rumsey analogously proposed that if the defendant has experienced psychological suffering as a consequence of harm negligently inflicted on another, this would similarly incline jurors to be lenient.[13] His hypothesis that a remorseful defendant would receive a lighter sentence than a nonremorseful one was indeed supported. This suggests that Shaw and McMartin's equity principle does extend to psychological factors, and other research reviewed by Gerbasi, Zuckerman, and Reis, and developed in later studies, supports this concept.[14]

One experimental artifact in the above studies is that the defendants were presented as guilty before the facts of injury, remorse, and suffering were given. Hence, there is the perennial problem of generalization to the courtroom situation. Yet, it does appear that type of crime can contribute to the jury process, especially where this interacts with one or more personality factors of the defendant, the victim, or the witnesses.

Research traditionally has broken the personal characteristics of defendants into two areas, general attractiveness (physical and social) and demographics (background, race, and socioeconomic status). As stated previously, the attractiveness of the defendant has been found to interact highly with other elements of the case. For example, the nature of the offense committed strongly influences the attractiveness variable.[15] Juries are influenced toward leniency by the attractiveness of a defendant if the crime is unrelated to their attractiveness (for example, burglary), and attractive clients tend to win more money in civil cases.[16] Yet, they are actually harsher toward attractive defendants who are likely to have used their attractiveness as an integral part of their offense (for example, fraud). Also, while this attractiveness-leniency effect is true of *sentencing* (for which juries are not generally responsible), it does not have a marked effect on ratings of the perceived guilt of the defendant (the more frequent task of juries).[17]

Two other popular and controversial research topics concern the racial and socioeconomic status of the defendant. The defendant's race has previously received the most attention with somewhat contradictory findings reported. It has been traditionally thought that blacks not only have a higher probability of being convicted of a given crime than whites, but also that their sentencing is more severe.[18] Yet, McGlynn, Megas, and Benson found that longer sentences were often assigned to white males found guilty.[19] The explanation for these apparent contradictions may be that race and socioeconomic status are highly interactive. For example, an interaction has been found among the race and socioeconomic status of the defendant, and the seriousness of the crime committed.[20] What was previously considered a race factor is apparently a class factor, with courts responding to a popular class stereotype that people of lower socioeconomic status tend toward violence. In general, juries were harsher on lower class defendants regardless of race. Low socioeconomic status can perhaps be interpreted as an achieved rather than as an ascribed status. Unlike race, juries may see it as a reflection on the character of the defendant. Nonetheless, it is clear that for certain individuals, a bias based on race alone does exist and does effect their decision process as a juror.[21]

The complexity of the above findings point out the futility of seeking single predictors of a jury's decisions. Researchers would be prudent to investigate an interaction of variables that can be expected to affect a process rather than a single variable predictive of an individual decision.

The Juror

Many of the same demographic variables discussed in regard to the defendant have also been studied in relation to the juror. Again, they have been found to be highly interactive and complex.

Jurors' levels of education, race, age, and gender were found to modify the influence of their personalities, which had been defined in terms of socialization, empathy, and autonomy.[22] These personality variables had been chosen for their recognized role in a person's attitude toward social rules, and were found to be related to their behavior as jurors. Among other findings, males with higher socialization scores gave more guilty verdicts, whereas females with higher scores gave fewer; males with high empathy scores were found to give more not-guilty verdicts; and high autonomy scores were associated with more not-guilty verdicts, regardless of the sex of the juror.

Gender

Stephan demonstrated that jurors are less likely to convict a person of their own gender.[23] Frederick noted some inconsistent results regarding gender, yet concluded that in general women were a bit more likely than men to render guilty verdicts, to deliver more punitive sentences, and to be less active in deliberations.[24] Rumsey and Rumsey studied gender (using college undergraduates as subjects) in rape cases.[25] They found women more punitive here, both with respect to the verdict and in attributing more responsibility to the defendant. However, both men and women did assign approximately equal sentences.

These findings should be viewed in light of the fact that most criminal defendants are men.[26] Laird cites research that has shown women to be more susceptible to persuasion.[27] This may be less important than other factors since traditional status inequalities are generally carried into the courtroom, making it difficult for women to make an impact on jury verdicts.[28] This may at least partially account for Frederick's conclusion that women are less active in deliberations.

Age

Most researchers and practicing attorneys agree that the younger the juror, the less likely to convict or punish severely. This may reflect an ability to identify with the defendant, since on the average, defendants are younger than jurors. In summarizing his own, as well as other, research Zeigler states that the young, more than the old, show attitudes more in line with beliefs that are basic to our legal system.[29] He states these differences occur in "such matters as the inference of guilt from silence, the presumption of innocence, the predisposition of the young to break the law, the performance and prerogatives of the police, and the role of the grand juror vis-à-vis the district attorney."[30] Laird points out that younger people are more changeable and thus subject to greater persuasion.[31]

Socioeconomic Status

Socioeconomic status (SES) has been shown to be inversely related to probabilities of conviction.[32] Lower SES jurors are more conviction prone, especially if the juror is male. High SES males are acquittal prone particularly in the face of less telling evidence. Higher intelligence, or the ability to conceptualize, integrate, and abstract, is certainly in the defendant's favor, especially in more complex trials.[33] The less intelligent jurors, probably through an inability to detect biased messages in some situations, are more easily persuaded.[34] Additionally, individuals who have more developed reasoning are regarded as more likely to be in the defense's favor, since they generally require clearer proof and higher standards of responsibility.[35]

Authoritarianism

Investigators have also looked at the influence of jurors' belief systems, especially the dimension of authoritarianism.[36] The authoritarian personality has been characterized as having a conservative, rigid, and punitive attitude. Authoritarian jurors are harsher than other jurors toward criminal defendants. As such, they are more likely to return a guilty verdict and to impose a more severe punishment. Boehm indicated authoritarians, both at the time of verdict and at one-week followup, remembered significantly more details about the character of the offender and less facts about the case itself than others.[37]

More recent research indicates that authoritarians are more likely to vote to convict defendants of race and SES similar to themselves.[38] When the dissimilar defendant is of lower status, the poorer behavior was expected of him. This was determined by polling the individual mock jurors before deliberation. Lamberth, Krieger, and Shay went a step further and looked at predeliberation votes of individual jurors, as well as jury decisions.[39] The authoritarians were more likely to have voted guilty at the predeliberation stage, and more likely to have changed their vote at postdeliberation. Authoritarians tend to ally themselves with the power source. During the trial, the prosecution is usually seen as more powerful than the defense, thus the guilty predeliberation votes. Once deliberation starts, the power shifts to the majority jury opinion. Additionally, juries render more moderate decisions than do individuals, in that the time to deliberate is shorter.[40]

A related idea is the effect of personality type on group leadership and its relationship to the verdict. Authoritarian leaders are often strongly dominant, and while groups led by authoritarians often suffer from low morale and hostility, they do seem to be more efficient and to make fewer errors than groups led by democratic or *laissez-faire* leaders.[41]

Locus of Control

Another dimension concerns a juror's locus of control—whether individuals believe that they exercise a considerable amount of control over their lives (internal locus of control), or instead feel more as if life is basically controlled by environmental factors (external). Previous research has found "internals" to attribute more responsibility to the defendant than "externals."[42] This has also been found to be true of jurors who scored high on a Just World scale, which measures a person's acceptance of the Just World Theory,[43] which holds that people get what they deserve. Such a belief is correlated with harsher sentencing, and also with an internal locus of control.

Some have tried to apply locus of control research to the task of jury selection. However, it is difficult to assess a person's locus of control without administering such a test, and virtually all judges would forbid this. It is true that people in certain vocations are more likely to have these attitudes (e.g., military officers, high authoritarian; engineers, internal locus of control), and in this less refined way, such variables can be used to make an estimate in jury selection.

"Death Qualified" Jurors

"Death qualified" jurors are those potential jurors who are not against imposing the death penalty in a capital case. Jurors who are morally opposed to the death penalty, or others whose feelings about capital punishment would "prevent or substantially impair" their duties as a juror in capital cases, are excused "for cause" from serving on the jury.[44] Death qualified jurors therefore make up the entire jury in such cases.

Recent research indicates that attitudes of potential jurors toward the death penalty are part of a constellation of personality/attitudinal variables centering around the individual's subjective view of criminal justice, and death qualified persons are significantly more likely to be "more punitive, less sensitive to procedural and constitutional guarantees, less equable in . . . [their] evaluation of . . . [the defense] and more willing to ignore a judge's instructions about pretrial publicity."[45]

A growing body of evidence supports the hypothesis that death qualified jurors are biased in favor of the prosecution and conviction, regardless of the circumstances or evidence. Thus the social science data suggest that the fact that only death qualified jurors can sit on the jury of capital cases poses a serious threat to the defendant's right to trial by a representative cross-section of jurors.[46] Ironically, in the very cases in which we most want completely fair and unbiased jurors (capital cases), the rules provide for selecting what are, in effect, conviction-prone juries. The Supreme Court has made it easier to dismiss jurors who oppose the death penalty, and this may increase the level of the problem,[47] and approved the use of death qualified juries.

Lockhart v. McCree gave the Court an opportunity to review the social science data to determine if death qualified juries are conviction-prone, and if so whether such biasing violates the Sixth and Fourteenth Amendments.[48] The defendant sought a non-death qualified jury to determine guilt. The Court dismissed most of the behaviorial science studies as irrelevant or inadequate, and held that even if death qualified juries were more conviction-prone, that would not violate the Constitution. The Court noted that there is no right to a "cross-section" of the community on a jury, that even if there were such a right the systematic exclusion of those opposed to the death penalty would not remove a "distinctive group" and thereby prevent a jury from being a fair cross-section, and that the state has a significant interest in being able to select one jury to decide guilt and punishment.

The dissent characterized the majority's approach as "glib nonchalance ill-suited to the gravity of the issue presented and the power of respondent's claim." Most behavioral scientists would probably see the treatment of the studies as being "glib nonchalance" indeed. An additional problem with the death qualification process is that it focuses attention on the death penalty at the very beginning of the trial. There is evidence that consideration by jurors of the harshest verdict first tends to result in harsher verdicts.[49]

Colussi has proposed a two-jury system in capital cases wherein a non-death qualified jury would make the guilt determination and a death qualified jury would deliberate on the sentencing issue. Although this system would be fairer in determining guilt, the sentencing jury remains vulnerable to the "unfair" cross-section criticism.[50] Under the *Lockhart* case, states are free to adopt such a bifurcated system, but not required to do so.

The Attorney

While research dealing specifically with the role of attorneys has been sparse compared with that on the roles of defendant and the juror, there is some information available.

As with the defendant, such individual characteristics as the attractiveness, race, and gender of attorneys plays a rather complex, interactive role in whether juries like or trust them and ultimately believe them. McGuire and Bermant found that jurors were more likely to vote not guilty following deliberations when the defense attorney was male than when the defense attorney was female, however, a later study did not find the gender of the attorney to be a significant factor in most instances.[51] A more important variable may be the attorney's race. Jurors appear to have a predisposition against black attorneys which is evidenced in their verdicts.[52] This may reflect the belief that blacks are less educated and have a lower socioeconomic background.

Interpersonal characteristics of the attorney merit consideration. In general, the greater the perceived credibility of the attorney, the greater will be the persuasive impact.[53] Factors contributing to credibility include physical appearance, consistency, similarity to the jury, and characteristics of the presentation itself, which will be discussed later.

The "looking behavior" of attorneys has a significant influence on jury perceptions. It will come as no surprise to trial attorneys that experimental research suggests that an attorney, as well as a client, is well advised to make a significant effort to make eye contact with jurors during a trial. Cook summarizes evidence that overall, the more one person looks at another, the more the other person will feel that they are liked.[54] However, both pattern and amount of looking are important. Subjects prefer those who give long glances, and evaluate less favorably those who look the same amount but in frequent and short glances. Other research found that a continuous gaze was less well received than a more normal pattern of looking (approximately three-quarters of the time). These statistics apply to relatively short interactions.

Overall, the desired image for the attorney is one of "liked expert." For example, attorneys who badger witnesses or make use of deceit and trickery in getting their points across impress jurors with their expertise, yet at the same time lose their image of being fair and honest.[55] Attorneys should avoid arrogance and the unnecessary badgering of witnesses in order to maintain credibility and trustworthiness.

The Judge

The personality and style of the trial judge is similarly influential. How judges choose to orchestrate a trial has, of course, a heavy impact on its outcome. An individual, in a novel situation where expected and appropriate behaviors are unclear, will turn for cues to someone of higher status—i.e., the judge—for the cues to proper behavior. This is due in part to the degree to which juries rely on them for help. Judges' perceived status, knowledge of the law and legal proceedings, and control over the courtroom situation all make jurors look to them for guidance. Even the smallest of cues concerning a judge's opinion of the case is often picked up by jurors.

The Supreme Court noted the susceptibility of jurors to judicial influence as early as the 1890s and noted that the judge's "lightest word or intimation is received with deference, and may prove controlling."[56] Practicing attorneys are acutely aware of how the jury always looks to the judge for guidance and the research of Zeisel and Diamond lends support to this contention.[57] This recognition of a judge/jury influence process has developed primarily through cases focusing upon the prejudicial content of a judge's behavior, and this naturally includes nonverbal behavior.

Social scientists have found that human beings are likely to behave differently in an experimental situation than they would in real life because of heightened awareness and apprehension. Further, it has been established that an experimenter often unintentionally cues the subject in an effort to control the outcome of the experiment, and, in turn, the subject unconsciously searches for and responds to these cues.[58] Even the most subtle of cues are effective in guiding behavior, and it appears reasonable to assume that a judge is going to have as much power over a jury as an experimenter has over a subject.

The direct guidance given by a judge can range from an objective assistance to 'fatherly' direction, to dictatorial control, depending upon the personality of the particular judge. However, here too, judges are often walking a fine line. Jurors who consider them to be overly dominating may go against the judge's lead, in reaction to what they feel is a questioning of their ability to do their job.

Witnesses

The source of the information presented is another factor which influences the decision-making of a jury. Not surprisingly, a source who is trusted, liked, and/or respected exerts much more influence on a jury than one who is not. Many variables are involved in the gaining of such trust and admiration, particularly the role, perceived expertise, and behavior of the individual.[59] Two particularly influential types of witness are the expert witness and the eyewitness. (The eyewitness is discussed in chapter 9.)

The Expert Witness

It is not surprising that information is more persuasive if it is presented by someone perceived to be an "expert" on a communicated topic, and when the presenter provides supporting arguments and data.[60] In addition, the persuasive impact of expertness and argumentation is independent and additive. That is, the expertness of a person per se was enough to persuade a receiver regardless of accompanying arguments, but such persuasion tended to increase with an increase in argumentation. (Incidentally, the physical attractiveness of the source seemingly had no major effects here.)

Two notes of caution are in order.[61] First, there is evidence to suggest that the influence of expert testimony deteriorates with time. Apparently, the message becomes disassociated from the source of expertise. Thus, the anticipated and actual length of a trial becomes important. In a long trial, having the experts testify last should create the greatest impact. Secondly, attorneys can often successfully negate expert testimony by having an equally qualified "expert" give contradictory testimony. Faced with the conflicting opinions of two equally qualified witnesses, jurors usually disregard both with the assumption that each was unduly biased toward their respective positions.

Thus, characteristics of key participants in a trial do exert an influence on the outcome of a trial, though this influence is not always precisely defined. Such characteristics are not, however, the only source of influence in the trial process.

INFLUENCES WITHIN THE TRIAL PROCESS

Pretrial Publicity

The publicity from major trials often creates a genuine conflict between the right of a defendant to a fair trial by an impartial jury, and freedom of the press. The courts have long recognized the potential influences of pretrial publicity and occasionally allow a change of venue, when the extent of pretrial publicity has jeopardized the empaneling of an impartial jury.

Jurors are not disqualified "for cause'" simply because they have heard about a case, but only if they have been so influenced by pretrial publicity that they cannot set aside any tentative conclusions about the case, and therefore cannot fairly reach a conclusion based on the evidence presented. Generally, courts depend on jurors' self-reports about whether they can be impartial, a process that has obvious problems.

Behavioral scientists can measure the effects of pretrial publicity through telephone or personal interview surveys, much as is done in Gallup polls. Questions are directed not only at the respondents' levels of awareness of the issue, but also as to whether or not this has caused them to consolidate a belief on guilt or innocence. The judge may then use this data to rule on the change of venue issue. The difficulty comes when there is so much publicity that virtually no locale is really available.

Does pretrial publicity actually affect jurors? A review of five highly publicized trials found jurors asserting that they had approached the trial with an open mind and had given an honest verdict despite the publicity.[62] Also, most of the lawyers and judges involved in the trials agreed. However, this result has all of the typical contamination of self-reported data, especially the fact that people often report how they feel things "ought to be" rather than "as they are."

Most scholars suggest that pretrial publicity does affect juror verdicts, with the probability that the education of the juror is a crucial factor in the degree to which it is influential.[63] The more educated juror is affected less by it, which may indicate that if a jury is achieved that has not processed any pretrial publicity, it may simply be an uninformed, nonrepresentative section of the populace, a group that is also likely to be lower in intelligence than the general population. Until more definitive data become available, it is both logical and within the best interest of the defendant to continue to assume that substantial pretrial publicity does have a significant effect on a trial's outcome. Options, other than change of venue, for countering the effects of pretrial publicity include continuances (assuming that memories fade), lengthier and more specific voir dire, sequestration of juries, and clear instructions by the judge to disregard information heard about the case outside of court.

Inadmissible Evidence

Evidence which has been ruled inadmissible by a judge is not supposed to be considered by a jury in arriving at a verdict. Not surprisingly, however, jurors do not always disregard such information after it has been presented.[64]

While there is evidence that listeners generally are highly persuaded by conversations which they felt that they were not supposed to hear, the influence of inadmissible evidence is a more complex issue. There are indications that inadmissible evidence is most influential in cases involving weak or circumstantial evidence.[65] Yet even then a judge's instruction to disregard it may eliminate its biasing effect.[66] Other studies have produced contradictory results, suggesting that the nature of the information is the crucial factor in whether or not inadmissible evidence is used by a juror. For example, *proacquittal* inadmissible evidence did not have a substantial effect.[67] In addition, while coerced confessions are generally ruled inadmissible, it has been found that the means of coercion can determine whether or not a jury will use the confession in formulating a verdict. Confessions resulting from a promise of leniency were used by a jury, while those resulting from a threat of harm or punishment were not.[68]

Thus, just as in the issue of pretrial publicity, it is not yet clear whether or not jurors can disregard information that has already been received. The weight of evidence suggests they often cannot. An added danger is that some attorneys knowingly introduce inadmissible evidence that may irreparably influence a jury. Strict rules for determining the admissibility of evidence, outside of the hearing of the jury, at least help to minimize such abuse until a better understanding of its influence is obtained. Another option is the increased use of videotape to record potentially inadmissible evidence without the jury present. Then it is presented to the jury only if the judge rules it is admissible. Videotaping also enhances efficiency and flexibility in trials, yet does result in a similar retention of information, ability to detect deception, and most importantly, similar verdicts.[69]

Presentation of Evidence

How admissible evidence is presented affects how it is received by jurors. For example, jurors can often be "immunized" against later persuasion.[70] When one side presents anticipated arguments, and then refutes them, the jury is likely to build up a resistance to the other side's arguments. Whether this is due to a bolstering of the jurors' cognitive defenses, as McGuire posited, or to the exposition of weaknesses in the opposing position, as Hilgar, Atkinson, and Atkinson argued, research supports the wisdom of presenting anticipated arguments of the opposition along with evidence expected to defeat those arguments.[71]

Repetition is another important element in the presentation of evidence. When more than one witness presents the same information, a recapitulation of the facts should be included. Regardless of the modality of presentation, and regardless of whether repetitions are spaced weeks or minutes apart, repetition of statements can raise the rated truth-value of the statements.[72] Harkins and Petty found that messages are more persuasive when multiple sources present multiple arguments.[73] For example, several witnesses with a different argument for why the defendant is guilty will have more impact than a single witness presenting several arguments or several witnesses presenting the same argument. Guilt is the repeated message. This repetition is particularly true when note taking is discouraged or prohibited. Unfortunately, jurors are very commonly discouraged or prohibited from taking notes during trials, so repetition becomes important, especially in longer trials.

Opening Statements

From a psychological perspective, opening statements may serve to create thematic frameworks that guide jurors in their processing and interpretation of the actual testimony and evidence that is presented later in the trial.[74] Thematic frameworks not only affect the encoding and retrieval of information from memory,[75] but also the interpretation that is placed on that information.[76]

Pyszczynski, in a study with mock jurors, found some limiting conditions where this is true.[77] The promise of persuasive testimony by the defense to prove the defendant's innocence made jurors more sympathetic to the defendant's case even though such testimony was never entered as evidence. This was true only so long as the prosecution did not later remind the jury of the defense's unfulfilled promise; when so reminded, the jury was more likely to find the defendant guilty than if the promise had never been made. The promise did not influence the jury immediately, but rather influenced their inferences of guilt later in the trial. The reminder seems to have caused the jury to discredit the defense attorney and doubt the other aspects of his case.

In a study with mock jurors, Pyszczynski and Wrightman determined that when the defense attorney's opening statement was extensive, but not exaggerated, jurors were relatively unaffected by the testimony of the prosecution's first witness.[78] However, when the defense opening statement was brief, jurors were greatly influenced by the testimony and were inclined toward a guilty verdict. Jurors tend to be swayed somewhat by the first strong presentation encountered. Since the prosecution presents its opening statement first, it can create the initial thematic framework of guilt.

Although a thematic framework may influence the jurors' cognitive set, research on the effects of recency and primacy is in direct contradiction to the above. Simply stated, is a jury influenced more by the first set of information it receives or the last? At first glance it would seem to be basically a problem of the order of presentation. However, a closer look reveals that it is an issue of both order and the content.[79] In terms of gross order, referring to which side goes first in opening and closing argument and presentation of evidence, the side going last appears to have the advantage. As far as the influence of order, it is generally agreed that for the defense there is an advantage in using its strongest evidence at the end of the presentation. The prosecution should probably present its strongest evidence early. Laird appears to cover all the possibilities by stating that a case should be started and concluded with a strong witness since the jurors' maximum attention will be at the beginning and ending of the trial.[80]

It is evident that this issue is complex, and interaction with other variables appears to determine how order effect operates.

Perceived Consequences of a Verdict

Consistent with the presumption of innocence, most jurors say that they consider the punishment of an innocent person to be a more serious mistake than the acquittal of one who is guilty.[81] Such jurors will be more inclined toward leniency as the severity of the prescribed penalties for an offense increases. This severity-leniency hypothesis does not draw unanimous support from researchers and legal experts.[82]

Rendering a verdict and establishing a penalty are usually treated as two distinct parts of a trial. Thus, jurors are often unaware of specific penalties while they are deciding upon a verdict. Naturally, it is likely that jurors assume that conviction on a more serious offense will result in a more serious penalty despite their not knowing exactly what such a penalty would be. In most situations, more accurate information leads to better judgments, so from this perspective alone it would be worthwhile to consider more fully informing jurors of the results of their decisions, especially where there are different levels of charges on which the defendant can potentially be convicted. The Supreme Court has been concerned that telling jurors that appellate courts will review death sentences encourages juries to impose the death penalty too easily because they do not fully consider the seriousness of their decision.[83]

The Processing of Trial Information

The factors involved in the assimilation of trial information also influence a juror's decision-making. Persuasive information is generally considered to be processed by either of two models, the systematic view or the heuristic view.[84] In the systematic view, an individual processes the received information and actively looks for the validity of arguments and for overall conclusions. The heuristic view assumes listeners make rather little effort to process information. They rely instead on more easily accessible data, such as physical characteristics of the witnesses, or their emotional tone.

Research now indicates that the depth of the involvement of a listener may influence which of these approaches is used by a juror in reaching a decision.[85] Apparently, high involvement with a message leads recipients to employ a systematic information processing strategy. Low involvement leads to the use of a heuristic processing system. Obviously, a jury has full knowledge that it will be given time to discuss the trial information. This, along with research indicating that "a high level of arousal and interest was associated with [juror] participation," would suggest that jurors who more actively participate develop a state of "high involvement" with messages received.[86] Logically, then, the more active juror more often gives more attention to trial evidence than to unrelated characteristics of trial participants.

Instructions

Increasing attention is also being paid to the influence of the trial judge's charge to the jury, in which jurors receive instructions on applicable law, and the criteria for reaching a verdict. Both the timing and the content of these instructions influence a trial's outcome.

When the instructions are given can have an impact on jurors' verdicts. Jurors receiving instructions *before* the presentation of evidence view the defendant as less likely to have committed the crime than either those receiving instructions *after* the evidence or those receiving *no* instructions at all.[87] The implication here is that unless jury instructions are given at the beginning of a trial, a defendant may not be gaining their full benefit, if any benefit at all, of the presumption of innocence. In most states the timing of instructions is left to the discretion of the trial judge, so judges could reverse the usual process of giving instructions at the end of the trial, just before deliberation.

Unless instructions are given at the beginning of a trial, jurors will have no concrete criteria against which to process trial information properly. Given no guidelines, jurors are likely to turn to their own criteria, constructed from the media, attorneys' statements, personal experience, and the like. This has serious ramifications since information which is initially encoded into memory often has a predominant influence on later information.[88] It is thus very improbable that last-minute instructions will dislodge improperly processed information.

To remedy this situation, instructions could be given both before and after the evidence. In this way, the likelihood that jurors will process information according to desired criteria throughout the trial is greatly increased. At the same time, the juror will have his or her memory refreshed before the jury deliberates, and additional instructions not anticipated at the beginning of the trial can be given.

This issue is somewhat irrelevant though, if, as many legal experts and researchers now claim, jurors are unable to understand the instructions in the first place. For example, judges often tell juries that they must decide the evidence "beyond a reasonable doubt" in a criminal trial, and that they must look to a "preponderance of the evidence" in a civil trial. Usually this instruction is given with only a cursory explanation of what these terms mean, if any explanation is given at all. Simon and Mahan[89] and Graham, Meyer and McNiel[90] indicate these terms are not understood at all well. In testing for the comprehension of 14 standard jury instructions, only 39 percent of all ideas contained in the instructions were comprehended, and only a bit more than half of the ideas *essential* to the understanding of the law were understood. The results of a two-year study in 1981 sponsored by the National Institute of Mental Health and the Justice Department's National Institute of Justice similarly found that the average juror comprehends about half of the legal instructions given by a judge. A major problem is the language used in the instructions. Indeed, researchers found that by rewriting instructions in a clearer and simpler form, the comprehension rate for jurors rose dramatically. As a result of these and similar findings, a push is now underway toward standardized instructions which provide the judge with a concise, error-free explanation of the law, in language that can be understood by jurors.[91]

Another positive reform would be to allow jurors to take written copies of the instructions into deliberation with them. Some research has shown written instructions were consistently able to resolve confusion more quickly than oral instructions.[92] Further, it could help eliminate the potential for problems that develop because of an inability to accurately recall the instructions.

There is a disproportionate number of elderly people in jury pools. Subtle losses can occur from gradually developing impairments that can accompany aging.[93] As a result, the elderly can have difficulty taking in more than one essential feature of a message. That is, in a setting where there are many messages (a trial), some will either recall the source of the message (the speaker), or the content, but often not both.

Along somewhat similar lines, a person's judgment over a passage of time will be disproportionately influenced by information which remains the most available in memory.[94] Among other things, the vividness of the information appears to be important, in that it remains more available in memory for a longer period of time.[95] In this regard, emotion-charged words and intense arguments tend to be more effective than rational ones.[96] "A trial decision is the result of the effective exploitation of rational and especially emotional denominators of experience."[97] Thus a juror's decision may be unduly influenced by those arguments presented most vividly. This, unfortunately, encourages a dramatic (and often partial or prejudicial) presentation of facts, rather than an orderly and complete presentation by an attorney.

Deliberation

An early breakdown of activities during deliberation found the following: 50 percent of the time was spent on discussing opinions and personal experiences, either directly or indirectly related to the trial; roughly 25 percent was devoted to discussing procedural issues; 15 percent was spent on testimony; and 8 percent was used on instructions.[98] More educated jurors placed greater emphasis on matters of procedure and instruction, while those with only a grade school education were more interested in opinions, testimony, and personal experiences.

Personal experiences can include prior jury duty and the question arises about the effect of prior experience on subsequent cases. Some jurisdictions assume that prior experience has no impact on juror behavior. However, trends toward higher conviction rates by experienced jurors were found in a number of studies, although the differences were not significant.[99] Prior experience may not necessarily lead to higher conviction rates, but the strength of the previous cases relative to the current case may bias the verdicts.[100] If the second prosecutor presents a weaker case than his predecessor, the juror is more likely to find the second defendant not guilty.

Deliberation is subject to the principles of group process relating to conformity, since some form of unanimity is ultimately used in rendering most verdicts. One relevant phenomenon which often occurs during deliberation is termed "polarization," the tendency for jurors to shift their opinions even further in the direction of their initial position during deliberations. Apparently, once a position has been taken on an issue, any ensuing contradictory evidence will be disclaimed and even reacted to negatively, while any supportive evidence will be used to reinforce it. For example, one study found that counterarguments increased unfavorable thoughts about the person presenting them, resulting in decreased agreement with the position.[101] Favorable ideas, on the other hand, had the opposite effect.

The effects of polarization are indirectly evident in the low rate of verdict change reported by jurors. The Chicago Jury Project found that in 90 percent of their 225 case, the verdict was identical to the majority opinion on the first ballot.[102] This was supported by subsequent research which found that in all of the ten felony cases studied, the final outcome of the trial was the same as the majority vote on the first ballot.[103] In addition, 95 percent of these jurors had made what proved to be unalterable decisions after two ballots.

This resistance to change raises some interesting questions about the purpose of deliberation. Noting that 89 percent of the jurors they interviewed admitted to having reached a decision even before deliberation began, Bridgeman and Marlowe comment:

> First, largely on the basis of the evidence and testimony, the juror arrives at a conclusion regarding the defendant's guilt or innocence. A second phase ensues after the trial proper in which the juror seeks consensual validation for his or her judgment by learning the verdicts and arguments of the other jurors.[104]

If "validation" is the true role of deliberation, and if "validation rates" are at the reported 90 percent level, *predeliberation* processing becomes even more significant. It also strengthens the argument for jury instructions at the beginning of the trial.

DECISION RULES AND JURY SIZE

The Supreme Court has dealt with constitutional issues related to jury size and unanimous verdicts in criminal cases. In 1972, the Court upheld nonunanimous verdict rules for twelve-person juries in *Johnson v. Louisiana*[105] and *Apodaca v. Oregon*.[106] Yet, in *Burch v. Louisiana*[107] the Court required unanimous decisions in six-person jury cases. A closer look at the reasoning in *Burch* helps to explain the apparent inconsistency. In delivering the majority opinion, Justice Rehnquist noted,

> [T]his case lies at the intersection of our decisions concerning jury size and unanimity. As in *Ballew*, we do not pretend the ability to discern a priori a bright line below which the number of jurors participating in the trial or in the verdict would not permit the jury to function in the manner required by our prior cases. ... But having already departed from the strictly historical requirements of jury trial, it is inevitable that lines must be drawn somewhere if the substance of the jury trial right is to be preserved. ... [W]e think that when a State has reduced the size of its juries to the minimum number of jurors permitted by the Constitution, the additional authorization of non-unanimous verdicts by such juries sufficiently threatens the constitutional principles that led to the establishment of the size threshold that any countervailing interest of the State should yield.[108]

In *Ballew v. Georgia* the Court had established six to be the minimum number of jurors necessary to guarantee a person the constitutional right to a jury trial.[109] The Court looked to research that suggested between six and eight as the optimal jury size, but which also found that chances were much higher of convicting an innocent defendant if the jury size were less than six. In general, smaller size results in fewer hung juries and higher conviction rates, but lower conviction rates in lesser offenses. However, they also tend to reduce the recall of trial information and the probability that minorities will be present, and more easily overcome (or suppress) the extreme (defined statistically) biases of individual members.[110]

The *Ballew* decision supplements and clarifies an earlier ruling in which the Court had allowed as constitutional the use of juries having less than twelve persons.[111] As noted by Justice Rehnquist in *Burch*, the Court in *Williams* had ruled smaller juries as constitutional, "particularly if the requirement of unanimity is retained."[112]

Unanimity is currently required by local rule in federal cases, and in those at the state level using six-member juries. Nevertheless, state cases involving juries of more than six persons are allowed great flexibility in their decision rules. Some states have accordingly adopted such modifications as five-sixths, three-fourths, and two-thirds majority requirements for a verdict.

Proponents of nonunanimous decision rules claim that the resulting verdicts are quicker and less costly, that they produce fewer hung juries, and that they make jury fixing more difficult.[113] On the other hand, their opponents claim that they produce higher conviction rates, and as such are unfavorable to the defendant. Some evidence to support this latter notion has been found.[114]

PROBLEMS WITH RESEARCH

As we have noted, there are various methodological problems in this research area.[115] As one reviewer of this research points out,

> Procedures differ widely from one study to another, some relying on individual verdicts and others employing group deliberation. Dependent measures taken from subjects vary greatly from study to study (e.g., length of sentence, severity of the crime, evaluation of the defendant).[116]

Some critics argue that even if all variables were systematically controlled, the resulting data would still be tainted because of problems inherent in studying a "mock" courtroom process. Following the uproar caused by earlier attempts to monitor actual jury deliberations, social scientists have had to be content with laboratory replications of the courtroom process. Much of this mock jury research fails to closely approximate real courtroom procedures, usually employing written case materials to simulate the trial. These case materials are often brief and only rarely approach the complexity of most actual jury trials. Also, it has been commonplace to completely omit any analogue of many key trial elements, such as *voir dire*.[117] In addition, the "jurors" in such studies are often undergraduate college students, hardly representative of the typical jury pool.[118]

Even if variables were systematically manipulated within an ideal replication of the courtroom process, a major problem with this research would be that the lack of real-life consequences to a mock juror's decisions could bias results to some degree. This argument draws some subjective support from the observation that the actual trial process appears to induce an intensified caution and critical approach among the jurors.

Have the flaws just discussed concerning this research destroyed all applied value of the findings? Fortunately not. First, some solid and replicable data, as detailed earlier in this chapter, have been collected. One pragmatic application of great interest from this research is scientific jury selection, the subject of the next section. In spite of problems in research designs as noted here, scientific jury selection has been very successful in practice.

SCIENTIFIC JURY SELECTION

Attorneys have long attempted to get the most favorable jury for their clients using informal sets of beliefs as to what constituted a favorable juror. Most suppositions were based on the collective anecdotes of the profession, their own experience, intuition, and logic. However, some studies have concluded that attorneys are grossly ineffective in selecting favorable or eliminating unfavorable jurors, and it is suggested that attorneys who rely solely on this approach may be doing a disservice to their clients.[119] This may be changing with the advent of scientific jury selection.

Scientific jury selection is not scientific in the sense that it is based on clear, empirically derived data, but refers to procedures which borrow heavily from the related empirically derived data of the social and behavioral sciences to select a jury.[120]

Most agree that scientific jury selection first fully became visible in the winter of 1971–72 in the "Harrisburg Seven" trial.[121] In this trial, Philip Berrigan and seven co-defendants were tried by the federal government on conspiracy charges, including an alleged plan to kidnap Henry Kissinger. Former U.S. Attorney General Ramsey Clark headed a huge defense team, including several attorneys, and a phalanx of social scientists and student assistants, most of whom had volunteered their services. They collected enormous amounts of data on community attitudes, and jurors' background characteristics.

They used this to profile an "ideal juror" and then to select an actual jury through the process of *voir dire* and challenges. Despite strong evidence to convict, the jury was hopelessly hung, and the government decided the chances of success in retrial were not offset by the expense of another trial. In the following years, many similar, and usually successful, jury selections were carried out.

We will now look at how jurors are scrutinized and challenged in the *voir dire* process, and then consider methods and ethical issues of jury selection.

VOIR DIRE AND CHALLENGES

Voire dire literally means "to see; to say" or more figuratively, "to see what they will say." It is the process of questioning potential jurors by the attorneys (common in state trials) and the judge (more so in federal trials). This material and other background data is then analyzed to decide which potential jurors to accept and which to challenge. The rationale for *voir dire* is lodged in the Sixth Amendment to the United States Constitution, which states that "In all criminal prosecutions, the accused shall enjoy the right to a speedy and public trial, by an impartial jury of the State and district wherein the crime shall have been committed." The jury pool is commonly obtained from voter lists, though they are usually complemented by others such as motor vehicle registration and property lists.[122]

The attempt in *voir dire* is to get rid of any potential juror whose biases negate reasonable impartiality (challenges for cause) or are otherwise unfavorable to one side (peremptory challenges), and thus to obtain what each side considers a reasonable array of jurors.[123] It is in this latter regard that some have criticized jury selection as "unethical" and in need of control.

Attorneys also use *voir dire* to "educate" the jury.[124] Many questions (e.g., "Would all of you as potential jurors be able to clearly keep in mind that the defendant is innocent until proven guilty, and that the evidence must convince you beyond a reasonable doubt," etc.) are asked even though there is no real belief that someone will say "no," and thus be struck for cause. Attorneys at this point also may attempt to explain their case and to persuade jurors to accept their theory of the case. In a related vein Melvin Belli has suggested that potentially abhorrent or repulsive evidence (e.g., pictures of grisly murder scenes) be presented to the jury during *voir dire*.[125] The purpose is to defuse any later "shocking qualities," if these would negatively affect the case.

Potential jurors found to be biased can be dismissed through challenges. The whole initial panel of jurors can in fact be voided. For example, a challenge to the array may be based on any systematic and intentional exclusion of women or any racial group or social or economic class. Such exclusions are unconstitutional.[126] It is not necessary to show actual bias or harm, just systematic exclusion.[127]

Individual jurors may also be dismissed through a challenge for cause. An unlimited number of cause challenges may be used, provided the judge concurs with the attorney's assessment of bias.[128] Typical bases for a challenge for cause would be an economic or political interest in the trial's outcome, certain physical or mental disabilities, a family relationship to one of the attorneys or the parties involved, previous service on a jury that dealt with the same issue, or a strong bias or preconceived opinion that would jeopardize impartiality. Challenges for cause are not easily granted by most judges. Something more is required than general potential for bias. There must be some strong reason to believe that the juror will be significantly predisposed toward one result or another. Jurors who strongly oppose the death penalty are generally dismissed for cause in capital cases, as we have noted.[129]

Much of *voir dire* is intended to provide information on which peremptory challenges may be exercised by the attorneys. The peremptory challenge is a right to dismiss a potential juror without showing cause. The number of peremptories allowed to either side in both civil or criminal trials varies according to the jurisdiction and on the complexity or seriousness of the issues at trial, but is generally fixed by statute.[130]

Prosecutors and defense counsel alike have traditionally had wide discretion in the use of peremptory challenges. In *Batson v. Kentucky* the Supreme Court reduced prosecutors' latitude.[131] Batson, who was black, was convicted by a jury from which the prosecutor had used peremptory challenges to remove all (4) blacks. In the past the Court had permitted a challenge to this form of racially based strikes only if the defendant could show a pattern of racially biased strikes, a showing that proved to be extremely difficult.[132] This case was important because it allowed a defendant to show bias in his own case rather than requiring proof of a pattern of bias.

To establish improper exclusion of racial groups, the defendant must establish a *prima facie* case of purposeful discrimination, including that he is a member of a "cognizable racial group . . . and that the prosecutor has used peremptory challenges to remove members of the defendant's race." At that point the burden shifts to the prosecutor to demonstrate "a [racially] neutral explanationn for challenging the black jurors."[133] Claims that a juror would be partial to the defendant because they are the same race are not a sufficient explanation, nor is the prosecutor's assurance of good faith. Apparently, similar limitations will not apply to the defense.

Several pitfalls may be encountered in *voir dire.* Many prospective jurors view the questioning as a test of their suitability and may be unwilling to admit to bias or prejudice, which may lead the juror to lie either consciously or unconsciously.[134] One way an attorney may combat this problem is to ask open-ended questions that call for a narrative response from the juror rather than a yes-or-no answer. This type question not only provides the maximum amount of verbal response and valuable attitudinal insight, but also gives the attorney more opportunity to observe the nonverbal communication of the juror.[135]

Another problem area is the courtroom setting under which the jurors are questioned. In most jurisdictions, at least some of the *voir dire* consists of questions to the group as a whole.[136] Suggs and Sales suggest that, because of group pressures, both the group and individual-within-a-group styles of questioning are inadequate in producing honest self-disclosure. The questioning of an individual juror within a group is an improvement over the group technique, but is still conducive to a conformity factor. This idea seems to be borne out in actual court situations. A review of murder trials in Kentucky identified four different types of *voir dire* questioning procedures.[137] These types included: (1) questions by judge and attorneys of one potential juror at a time with the panel sequestered; (2) questions by judge and attorneys of the group followed by sequestered questions on specific topics; (3) questions by judge and attorney of the group, including questions of individual jurors on specific topics in open court; and (4) questions by judge and attorney of the group without individual questioning. Full sequestering resulted in more sustained challenges for cause than did any of the other types and thus would appear to improve the defendant's chances of receiving a fair trial.

TYPES OF SCIENTIFIC JURY SELECTIONS

Jury selections vary in their complexity, depending on the amount of money or volunteers available, the amount of inquiry allowed into jurors' backgrounds, the extent of *voir dire* that will be allowed, and the cost to clients if the trial decision were to go against them. We will break down the five potential stages that can be, though not always are, included in a jury selection.[138]

Community Survey

A questionnaire is administered to a representative sample of the jury pool in the location where the case is to be tried. Its purpose is to collect all information conceivable that may bear on the case, such as attitudes toward issues, facts, and the defendant; demographic characteristics; personality; and general attitude measures.[139] It is also used to assess the effects of pretrial publicity and provide cues as to how best to phrase questions during *voir dire*.[140] Further, it may provide counter-intuitive data, thus giving the attorney an edge in determining who is likely to be for or against the case.[141] From this data, the investigators usually develop a profile of the ideal juror for their side.[142] For example, in the conspiracy trial involving Nixon cabinet members, the "worst possible juror" for the defendants was identified as "a liberal Jewish Democrat, who reads the *New York Times* or *The Washington Post,* listens to Walter Cronkite, is interested in political affairs, and is well informed about Watergate."[143] The defense also tended to select persons low in education, socioeconomic status, and community participation. This profile makes understandable some of the critiques that say jury selection may be at least unethical, as their desired juror was the type of person least interested in or prepared to cope with the complex evidence and testimony in this trial. As with the next stage, this stage is expensive. For example, the jury selection portion of the trial of Joan Little cost about $35,000.[144]

Individual Information Investigation

This process involves gathering background material on actual jurors. One could directly interview them, their employer, neighbors, etc., but such an approach is not only expensive and, in some circumstances, illegal, but has not been proven effective.

Another technique, a "related others" information network, is a bit more efficient, especially in smaller towns, though again it is quite expensive. Family members or volunteers, called key informants, form a "core pool," and they are trained to circulate lists of potential jurors to friends and acquaintances in order to elicit whatever relevant background information is available.[145] Other sources available for gaining personal information about jurors include tax, property, credit, and police records.[146] Though costly, one can gain information about areas of a juror's life in which a judge would disallow questioning, and one also is able to move into the *voir dire* with some extra information. However, though perhaps within legal bounds, some find this stage of jury selection to be ethically dubious, not only because of the "intrusion into privacy" issue,[147] but also because this may be another instance where the exorbitant costs do not justify the information gained.[148]

Rehearsal

This process is carried out in some form with a "shadow jury," composed of persons hired to function as a jury. Whether the whole trial or only a small portion of it is rehearsed depends on the importance and complexity of the trial issues, available financial resources, and the preferences of the attorney and psychologist. Rehearsal provides the forensic psychologist with a chance to assess how different types of jurors will react to different types of argument and evidence. Additionally, it indirectly forces attorneys to actually role-play and self-observe their presentation. This is a most effective technique, but one which many attorneys ignore.[149]

An interesting new twist to the application of mock jury research was applied in a massive antitrust suit against the American Telephone and Telegraph Company. In that suit, lawyers for the plaintiff, MCI Communications, employed "practice juries" in the preparation of their case. Using evidence, but no witnesses, they prepared both sides of the case and delivered each in a 45-minute presentation that was a condensation of opening statements and closing arguments. Afterward, the mock jurors deliberated over a verdict as the attorneys watched and listened behind a one-way mirror. This clever application completely bypassed the issue of generalizability, held replication problems to a minimum, and applied many of the same techniques proven effective in scientific jury selection.[150] It was apparently effective in view of the $1.8 billion eventually awarded MCI.

Voir Dire Rating

Here, information gained through *voir dire* (and the background investigation) is compared with the desired juror profile, which has been generated from the general research literature, the consultant psychologist's and the attorney's relevant expertise, and information from the sample survey, if employed. Sheets with the critical demographic and attitudinal data are prepared for the final stage.

Decision Point

The difficulty here is that the complex array of data generated previously must now be collapsed into a series of yes-no decisions. Since there are limits to the number of peremptories available, these are interrelated decisions. To use a peremptory on someone means that a later potential juror, who is even more unacceptable, may have to be taken. There are also issues regarding the predicted power of a potential juror. For example, it might be worthwhile to strike someone who may be mildly negative to one's position but who may become influential, rather than striking a *more* negative person who is likely to be a passive participant in deliberations.[151]

Many of the early jury selections were extensive operations, involving many of the procedures described above. These selections were allegedly almost always successful. There are several possible reasons for this. First, the unsuccessful selections may never have been reported. Secondly, the fact that these selections were so thorough and extensive could be the primary reason for success. Thirdly, many of these trials, e.g., Harrisburg Seven, Gainesville Eight (these are not athletic teams), Angela Davis, and Mitchell and Stans, were political and involved conspiracy charges. These are notoriously difficult to successfully prosecute, which would contribute to the high rate of success here.[152]

It is probable that the use of stages 1 and/or 2 can at least somewhat increase the success rate over using only stages 3 through 5. However, at present, there are no data to support the hypothesis that there is any substantial or worthwhile increment in *success rate* from adding stages 1 and 2.[153] Also, a standard jury selection using only stages 3 through 5 is not likely to cost nearly as much as those using stages 1 and 2.

The junior author has up to now carried out 35 jury selections, 29 of which used only stages 3 through 5. Of these 29, all but four were "successful," and it was felt that even if stages 1 and 2 had also been employed in two of those which were lost, they still would not have been successful. The selections that did obtain more information using stages 1 and 2 were successful. Discussions with other persons doing jury selection also found no strong support for the idea that stages 1 and 2 provide a definitive and significant increment in success, but this is a point that needs more empirical data.

ETHICAL-LEGAL ISSUES IN JURY SELECTION

There are a number of controversial ethical-legal issues in jury selection and persuasion.[154] The overriding issue is whether scientific jury selection improperly "loads" the jury and, if so, is it actually unethical to do so. Jury selection as it is usually practiced tries to obtain the most favorable jury to the client; it does try to "load." However, this is within the concept of the adversary approach, and attorneys have always tried to use their intuition to get the most favorable jury. Only if the selectors are hired in a "friend of the court" status would they appropriately try to select an "impartial jury."

A related point is that scientific jury selection may give one party unfair advantage.[155] This is a problem. In theory, either side is free to hire any expert, but there is a probability that there will be inequity here because of ability to afford the processes described. It is, however, not the responsibility of the expert in an individual case to remedy such potential inequities. The system itself must exert the control.

There are two major approaches that would help to limit the abuse or inequities here. The first would be greater limitations on what may be covered in *voir dire,* and this is happening in many jurisdictions. A second is the greater use of already available legal remedies in protecting potential jurors from invasion of privacy or harassment. A third possibility would be to prohibit the use of experts in picking a jury. However, such an approach would be impractical and potentially unconstitutional. A final suggestion is to try to "even the match" by ensuring that those representing poorer clients have resources available to retain expert assistance.

JUROR SELECTION FACTORS

There are a number of factors a behavioral scientist may use to select jurors. Earlier in this section, several variables were detailed. From that discussion, there is the clear inference that those jurors who are authoritarian, have an internal locus of control, and who believe in a "just world" should be selected by the prosecution and struck by the defense in a criminal trial. In a civil trial, one can place this data within the most powerful axiom in this area, the "empathy rule," which simply states that one should pick those jurors who are most similar on most of the important variables to one's own side. The most relevant person on that "side" is the defendant or plaintiff, though the attorney's style, appearance, etc. (as noted in The Rehearsal Stage) are also quite important.

Another juror variable noted earlier was gender. Though some research suggests women will tend to favor the prosecution when the defendant is female, most research points to men as more likely to convict.[156] Most research also points to Republicans, Protestants, older people, business persons, higher socioeconomic groups, and peoples of Teutonic ancestry as more likely to favor the prosecution.[157] Obviously there are important variations within these overall categories. For example, one finds that while Southern Democrats and Republicans usually favor the prosecution, Northern Democrats, Independents, and some Northeastern Republicans tend to favor the defense.[158] Again, all of the above recommendations should be considered within the overall structure of the "empathy rule." In addition, there are going to be variations in response, based on particulars of the individual case, as well as on many as yet undetermined variables.[159]

Jurors are also selected on in-courtroom behavior during *voir dire*. Factors considered here are body language, amount and quality of eye contact, and other nonverbal modes of communication.[160] For example, crossing the arms or avoiding eye contact while being interviewed by the attorney suggests a negative attitude toward that side.[161] These phenomena are believed to be beyond the voluntary control of the individual and indications of anxiety.[162] Although some believe that specific nonverbal communications indicate specific covert behaviors, others feel this is patently absurd.[163] However, it is possible that there may, at times, be some sort of anxiety-produced response, indicating that further questioning on the topic at hand may prove fruitful. The psychologist may use the frequency of these nonverbal "signs" during questioning on neutral topics, such as background information, as a baseline against which later observations are compared; and a record may be kept of the frequency and type of each topic, when they occurred, and who was questioning the juror.[164] While this is an interesting area, there in fact have been few substantiated findings here, and the process is still far more an art than a science.

Possible group dynamics are also considered in the scientific selection of jurors in that each is considered with respect to the roles they are likely to assume during the deliberation process.[165] Of greatest importance for consideration are leaders, followers, negotiators, "hold-outs," and "isolates."[166]

Other sources of information used in selection are time series data on trial outcomes of particular types of crimes,[167] and records of jurors' past behavior.

SUMMARY

There is a consensus among most researchers and legal observers that the respect and perceived importance of the juror's task in an actual trial induces an intensified caution and critical approach, which overcomes some biases extraneous to the evidence of the case. Yet there are cases where such a view is not helpful, especially in cases where evidence is minimal, nebulous, or contradictory, making extraneous variables seemingly more important. Unfortunately, as one researcher points out, it is just such a case that is likely to go to trial, as cases with weak evidence are often dropped by the prosecution, and cases with strong evidence are often plea-bargained by the defense.[168] These biases are a major reason for the success of scientific jury selection.

Slowly but surely, then, the variables involved in the trial process are being uncovered, studied, and reapplied in the courtroom. Recent court decisions indicate that while the judicial system is richly based in precedent and tradition, it is not necessarily stagnant. Even the most fundamental of legal principles must remain open to scrutiny, as one last example demonstrates. Research has shown that criminal defendants who appear to be withholding evidence are more likely to be judged guilty than those who appear to answer straightforwardly.[169] This includes the manner in which the Fifth Amendment to the Constitution is invoked. Those defendants who invoked "the Fifth" on their own volition were judged more harshly than those who appeared to use it at the advice of their attorney. Thus, this frequently used principle of the legal system may paradoxically work *against* the defendant in some cases.

The factors influencing the trial process and jury selection therefore range from the great to the small, the expected to the unexpected, and the known to the unknown. With time, the proportion of the known should increase, aiding the first task of courtroom process, to find the truth.

NOTES

1. R. Hastie, S. Penrod & N. Pennington, *Inside the Jury* (1983); W. Loh, *Social Research in the Judicial Process* (1985); Lempert, Social Sciences in Court: On "Eyewitness Experts" and Other Issues, 10 *L. & Hum. Behav.* 167 (1986).

2. McCloskey, Egeth & McKenna, The Experimental Psychologist in Court: The Ethics of Expert Testimony, 10 *L. & Hum. Behav.* 1 (1986); Pennington & Hastie, Jury Decision-Making Models: The Generalization Gap, 89 *Psychological Bull.* 246 (1981).

3. Hewgill & Miller, Source Credibility and Response to Fear-Arousing Communications, 32 *Speech Monographs* 95 (1965).

4. B. Sales, *The Trial Process* (1981). See V. Hans & N. Vidmar, *Judging the Jury* (1986).

5. Nietzel & Dillehay, Psychologists and Voir Dire: A Strategy and Its Applications, paper presented at American Psychological Association (1979).

6. Strodtbeck & Lipinski, Becoming First Among Equals: Moral Considerations in Jury Foreman Selection, 49 *J. Personality & Soc. Psychology* 927 (1985).

7. Quoted in Stephan, Selective Characteristics of Jurors and Litigants: Their Influence on Juries' Verdicts, in *The Jury System in America* 97 (R. Simon ed. 1975).

8. Cook, Gaze and Mutual Gaze in Social Encounters, 65 *Am. Scientist* 328 (1977).

9. Sealy & Wain, Person Perception and Jurors' Decisions, 19 *Brit. J. Soc. & Clinical Psychology* 7 (1980).

10. Boor, Effects of Victim Competence and Defendant Opportunism on Decisions of Simulated Jurors, 100 *J. Soc. Psychology* 315 (1975).

11. Singleton & Hofacre, Effects of Victims Physical Attractiveness on Juridic Judgments, 39 *Psychological Rep.* 73 (1976).

12. Shaw & McMartin, Effect of Who Suffers in an Automobile Accident on Judgmental Strictness, 1 *Proc. 81st Ann. Convention of Am. Psychological A.* 239 (1973).

13. Rumsey, Effects of Defendant Background and Remorse on Sentencing Judgments, 6 *J. Applied Soc. Psychology* 64 (1976).

14. Gerbasi, Zuckerman & Reis, Justice Needs a New Blindfold: A Review of Mock Jury Research, 85 *Psychological Bull.* 323 (1977); Shaffer, Plummer & Hammock, Hath He Suffered Enough? Effects of Jury Dogmatism, Defendant Similarity, and Defendant's Pretrial Suffering on Juridic Decisions, 50 *J. Personality & Soc. Psychology* 1059 (1986).

15. Barnett & Field, Character of the Defended and Length of Sentence in Rape and Burglary Crimes, 104 *J. Soc. Psychology* 271 (1978).

16. Adney, Winning Through Effective Client Appearance, 15 *Trial Lawyers Q.* 51 (1983).

17. Weiten, The Attraction-Leniency Effect in Jury Research: An Examination of External Validity, 10 *J. Applied Soc. Psychology* 340 (1980).

18. H. Toch, *Legal and Criminal Psychology* (1961).

19. McGlynn, Megas & Benson, Sex and Race as Factors Affecting the Attribution of Insanity in a Murder Trial, 93 *J. Experimental Psychology* 90 (1976).

20. Stewart, Defendant's Attractiveness as a Factor in the Outcome of Criminal Trials, 10 *J. Applied Soc. Psychology* 348 (1980).

21. Gleason & Harris, Race, Socioeconomic Status and Perceived Similarity as Determinants of Judgments by Simulated Jurors, 3 *Soc. Behav. & Personality* 175 (1975).

22. Mills & Bohannon, Character Structure and Jury Behaviors, 38 *J.*

Personality and Soc. Psychology 662 (1980); Shaffer, Plummer & Hammock, *supra*, note 14.

23. Stephan, Selective Characteristics of Jurors and Litigants: Their Influence on Juries' Verdicts, in *The Jury System in America* (R. Simon ed. 1975).

24. Frederick, Jury Behavior: A Psychologist Examines Jury Selection, 5 *Ohio N. U. L. Rev.* 511 (1978).

25. Rumsey & Rumsey, A Case of Rape: Sentencing Judgments in Males and Females, 41 *Psychological Rep.* 459 (1977).

26. Stephan, Sex Prejudice in Jury Simulation, 88 *J. Personality* 305 (1974).

27. Laird, Persuasion: A Tool of Courtroom Communication, 19 *J. Hum. Behav.* 50 (1982).

28. Hans, Jury Selection in Two Countries: A Psychological Perspective, 12 *Current Psychological Rev.* 283 (1982).

29. Zigler, Young Adults as a Cognizable Group in Jury Selection, 76 *Mich. L. Rev.* 1045 (1979).

30. *Id.,* at 1083.

31. Laird, *supra*, note 27.

32. Morgan & Comfort, Scientific Jury Selection: Sex as a Moderator Variable of Demographic and Personality Predictions of Impaneled Felony Jury Behavior, 43 *J. Personality & Soc. Psychology* 1052 (1982).

33. M. Nietzel, *Psychological Consultation in the Courtroom* (1979).

34. Laird, *supra*, note 27.

35. Arbuthnot, Attributions of Responsibility by Simulated Jurors: Stage of Moral Reasoning and Guilt by Association, 52 *Psychological Rep.* 287 (1983).

36. T. Adorno, E. Frenkel-Brunswick, D. Levinson & R. Sanford, *The Authoritarian Personality* (1950). See also J. Monahan & L. Walker, *Social Science in Law: Cases and Materials* (1985); Shaffer et al., *supra*, note 14.

37. Boehm, Mr. Prejudice, Miss Sympathy and the Authoritarian Personality: An Application of Psychological Measuring Techniques to the Problem of Jury Bias, 1968 *Wis. L. Rev.* 734.

38. McGowen & King, Effects of Authoritarian, Anti-Authoritarian and Egalitarian Attitudes on Mock Juror and Jury Decisions, 51 *Psychological Rep.* 1067 (1982).

39. Lamberth, Krieger & Shay, Juror Decision Making: A Case of Attitude Change Mediated by Authoritarianism, 16 *J. Research Personality* 419 (1982).

40. McGowen & King, *supra*, note 38.

41. Gerbasi, Zuckerman & Reis, Justice Needs a New Blindfold: A Review of Mock Jury Research, 85 *Psychological Bull.* 323 (1977).

42. *Id*; Sosi, Internal-External Control and the Perception of Responsibility for Another Accident, 30 *J. Personality & Soc. Psychology* 393 (1974).

43. Lerner, The Desire for Justice and Reactions to Victims, in *Altruism and Helping Behavior* (J. Macauley & L. Berkowitz eds. 1970).

44. Wainwright v. Witt, 105 S.Ct. 844 (1985).

45. Fitzgerald & Ellsworth, Due Process v. Crime Control: Death Qualifications and Jury Attitudes, 8 L. & Hum. Behav. 31, 45 (1984); Thompson, Cowan, Ellsworth & Harrington, Death Penalty Attitudes and the Conviction Process, 8 L. & Hum. Behav. 85 (1984).

46. Colussi, The Unconstitutionality of Death Qualifying a Jury Prior to the Determination of Guilt: The Fair Cross-Section Requirement in Capital Cases, 15 Creighton L. Rev. 595 (1981–82); McCall, Sentencing By Death Qualified Juries and the Right to Jury Nullification, 22 Harv. J. Legis. 289 (1985).

47. Wainwright v. Witt, 105 S.Ct. 844 (1985).

48. Lockhard v. McCree, 106 S.Ct. 1758 (1986).

49. Greenberg, Williams & O'Brien, Considering the Harshest Verdict First, 12 Personality & Soc. Psychology Bull. 41 (1986).

50. Colussi, supra, note 46.

51. McGuire & Bermant, Individual and Group Decisions in Response to a Mock Trial, 7 J. Applied Soc. Psychology 220 (1977); the later study, Cohen & Peterson, Bias in the Courtroom: Race and Sex Effects of Attorneys on Juror Verdicts, 9 Soc. Behav. & Personality 81 (1981).

52. Cohen & Peterson, supra, note 51.

53. See Laird, Persuasion: A Tool of Courtroom Communication, 19 J. Hum. Behav. 50 (1982); Wells, Lawyer Credibility, 7 Trial 69 (1985).

54. Cook, Gaze and Mutual Gaze in Social Encounters, 65 Am. Scientist 328 (1977).

55. P. Ekman, Telling Lies (1985); M. Nietzel & R. Dillehay, Psychological Evaluations in the Courtroom (1986); Hayes, Applying Persuasive Techniques to Trial Proceedings, 24 S. Carolina L. Rev. 38 (1972).

56. Starr v. United States, 153 U.S. 614 (1894).

57. Zeisel & Diamond, The Jury Selection in the Mitchell-Stans Conspiracy Trial, 1 Am. B. Found. Research J. 151 (1976).

58. R. Rosenthal & V. Jacobson, Pygmalion in the Classroom (1968). See also T. Barber, LSD, Marijuana, Yoga and Hypnosis (1970); R. Bausell, Experimental Methods (1986).

59. Apple, Streeter & Krause, Effects of Pitch and Speech Rate on Personal Attributions, 37 J. Personality & Soc. Psychology 715 (1979); Erickson, Lind, Johnson & O'Barr, Speech Style and Impression Formation in a Court Setting, 14 J. Experimental Soc. Psychology 266 (1978). See Bausell, supra, note 58; Lempert, Social Sciences in Court: On "Eyewitness Experts" and Other Issues, 10 L. & Hum. Behav. 167 (1986).

60. Maddux & Rogers, Effects of Source Expertness: Physical Attractiveness and Supporting Arguments on Persuasion: A Case of Brains Over Beauty, 39 J. Personality & Soc. Psychology 235 (1980).

61. Hovland & Weiss, The Influence of Source Credibility on Communication Effectiveness, 15 Pub. Opinion Q. 635 (1951). See Lempert, supra, note 59; McCloskey, Egeth & McKenna, The Experimental Psychologist in Court: The Ethics of Expert Testimony, 10 L. & Hum. Behav. 1 (1986).

62. Cohen, Effect of Media: Survey of 5 Cases: Jurors Not Swayed, *Los Angeles Times,* Apr. 11, 1976.

63. R. Reissner, *Law and the Mental Health System* (1985); Carroll, Kerr, Alfini, Weaver, MacCoun & Feldman, Free Press and Fair Trial: The Role of Behavioral Research, 10 *L. & Hum. Behav.* 187 (1986); Gerbasi, Zuckerman & Reis, Justice Needs a New Blindfold: A Review of Mock Jury Research, 85 *Psychological Bull.* 323 (1971); Padawer-Singerr & Barton, Impact of Pretrial Publicity on Jurors Verdicts, in *The Jury System in America* (R. Simon ed. 1975).

64. W. Loh, *Social Research in the Judicial Process* (1985).

65. Sue, Smith & Caldwell, Effects of Inadmissible Evidence on the Decisions of Simulated Jurors: A Moral Dilemma, 3 *J. Applied Soc. Psychology* 345 (1973). See Teitelbaum, Sutton & Johnson, Evaluating the Prejudicial Effect of Evidence: Can Judges Identify the Impact of Improper Evidence on Juries?, 1983 *Wis. L. Rev.* 1147.

66. Wolf & Montgomery, Effects of Inadmissible Evidence and Level of Judicial Admonishment to Disregard in the Judgments of Mock Jurors, 7 *J. Applied Soc. Psychology* 205 (1977).

67. Thompson, Cowan, Ellsworth & Harrington, Death Penalty Attitudes and the Conviction Process, 8 *L. & Hum. Behav.* 85 (1984).

68. Kassin & Wrightman, Prior Confessions and Mock Jury Verdicts, 10 *J. Applied Soc. Psychology* 123 (1980).

69. Miller & Hewitt, Conviction of a Defendant as a Function of Juror-Victim Racial Similarity, 105 *J. Soc. Psychology* 159 (1978).

70. McGuire, The Nature of Attitudes and Attitude Change, in *Handbook of Psychology* (G. Kindney and E. Aronson eds. 2d ed. 1968).

71. E. Hilgard, R. Atkinson & R. Atkinson, *Introduction to Psychology* (1975); M. Nietzel & R. Dillehay, *Psychological Evaluations in the Courtroom* (1986).

72. Schwartz, Repetition and Rated Truth Value, 95 *Am. J. Psychology* 393 (1982).

73. Harkins & Petty, The Multiple Source Effect in Persuasion: The Effects of Distraction, 7 *Personality & Soc. Psychology Bull.* 627 (1981).

74. Pyszczynski & Wrightman, The Effects of Opening Statements on Mock Juror's Verdicts in a Simulated Criminal Trial, 11 *J. Applied Soc. Psychology* 301 (1981).

75. Dooling & Mullet, Locus of Thematic Effects in Retention of Prose, 97 *J. Experimental Psychology* 404 (1973); Zadny & Gerard, Attributional Intentions and Information Selectivity, 10 *J. Experimental Soc. Psychology* 34 (1974).

76. Brainerd, Kigma & Howe, On the Development of Forgetting, 56 *Child Dev.* 1103 (1985).

77. Pyszczynski & Wrightman, *supra,* note 74.

78. *Id.*

79. Walker, Thibant & Andreoli, Order of Presentation at Trial, 82 *Yale*

L. J. 216 (1972). See Vinson, How to Persuade Jurors, 72 *A.B.A. J.* 72 (1985).

80. Laird, Persuasion: A Tool of Courtroom Communication, 19 *J. Hum. Behav.* 50 (1982). See S. Kassin & L. Wrightsman eds., *The Psychology of Evidence and Trial Procedure* (1985).

81. B. Sales, *The Trial Process* (1981); Greenberg, Williams & O'Brien, Considering the Harshest Verdict First, 12 *Personality & Soc. Psychology Bull.* 41 (1986).

82. W. Loh, *Social Research in the Judicial Process* (1985); Greenberg et al., *supra,* note 81.

83. Caldwell v. Mississippi, 105 S.Ct. 2633 (1985).

84. Chaiken, Heuristic Versus Systematic Information Processing and the Use of Source Versus Cues in Persuasion, 39 *J. Personality & Soc. Psychology* 752 (1980).

85. *Id.* See also Bordens & Horowitz, Joinder of Criminal Offenses: A Review of the Legal and Psychological Literature, 9 *L. & Hum. Behav.* 339 (1985); Petty & Cacioppo, Issue Involvement Can Increase or Decrease Persuasion by Enhancing Message-Relevant Cognitive Responses, 37 *J. Personality & Soc. Psychology* 1915 (1979); Tanford, Penrod & Collins, Decision Making in Joined Criminal Trials, 9 *L. & Hum. Behav.* 319 (1985).

86. Bridgeman & Marlowe, Jury Decision-Making: An Empirical Study Based on Actual Felony Trials, 64 *J. Applied Psychology* 91 (1979).

87. Kassin & Wrightman, On the Requirement of Proof: The Timing of Judicial Instruction and Mock Jury Verdicts, 37 *J. Personality & Soc. Psychology* 1877 (1979).

88. Krull & Wyer, Category Admissibility and Social Perceptions: Some Implications for the Study of Person Memory and Interpersonal Judgments, 36 *J. Personality & Soc. Psychology* 841 (1978).

89. Simon & Mahan, Quantifying Burdens of Proof, 5 *L. & Soc. Rev.* 319 (1971).

90. Graham, Meyer & McNeil, *Understanding Jury Instructions* (1985) (unpublished manuscript).

91. Severence, Greene & Loftus, Toward Criminal Jury Instructions That Jurors Can Understand, 75 *J. Crim L. & Criminology* 198 (1984).

92. Forston, Sense and Non-Sense: Jury Trial Communications, 1975 *B.Y.U. L. Rev.* 601.

93. Salmon & Meyer, Neuropsychology and Its Implications for Personal Injury Law, in *Psychology in Product Liability and Personal Injury Law* (M. Kurke & R. Meyer eds. 1986).

94. Reyes, Thompson & Bower, Judgment Bias Resulting from Availability of Arguments, 39 *J. Personality & Soc. Psychology* 2 (1980); Tanford et al., *supra,* note 85.

95. Kassin, Eyewitness Identification, 49 *J. Personality & Soc. Psychology* 878 (1985).

96. Laird, *supra,* note 80.

97. Redmont, Persuasion, Rules of Evidence and the Process of Law, 4 *Loy. L.A.L. Rev.* 253 (1970).

98. James, Status and Competence of Jurors, 64 *Am. J. Soc.* 563 (1959).

99. M. Nietzel & R. Dillehay, *Psychological Evaluations in the Courtroom* (1986); Nietzel & Dillehay, Psychologists and Voir Dire: A Strategy and Its Applications, paper presented at American Psychological Association (1979).

100. Kerr, Severity of Prescribed Penalty and Mock Jurors' Verdicts, 36 *J. Personality & Soc. Psychology* 1431 (1978).

101. Petty & Cacioppo, *supra,* note 85.

102. H. Kalven & H. Zeisel, *The American Jury* (1966).

103. Bridgeman, & Marlowe, *supra,* note 79, at 96.

104. *Id.*

105. Johnson v. Louisiana, 406 U.S. 356 (1972).

106. Apodaca v. Oregon, 406 U.S. 404 (1972).

107. Burch v. Louisiana, 441 U.S. 130 (1979).

108. *Id.,* at 137.

109. Ballew v. Georgia, 435 U.S. 223 (1978).

110. W. Loh, *Social Research in the Judicial Process* (1985).

111. Williams v. Florida, 399 U.S. 78 (1970).

112. Burch v. Louisiana, 441 U.S. 130, 135 (1979).

113. Koehler, Civil Juries: Recent Legislation Allowing Non-Unanimous Verdicts, 18 *Washburn L. J.* 269 (1978).

114. Katnik, Statistical Analysis and Jury Size: Ballew v. State of Georgia, 56 *Den. L. J.* 659 (1979). See also Buckhout, Weg, Reilly & Trohboese, Jury Verdicts: Comparison of 6 v. 12 Person Juries and Unanimous v. Majority Decision Rules in a Murder Trial, 10 *Bull. Psychonomic Soc'y* 175 (1977).

115. Pennington & Hastie, Jury Decision-Making Models: The Generation Gap, 89 *Psychological Bull.* 246 (1981); See also R. Bausell, *Experimental Methods* (1986); Kelner, Jury Selection: The Prejudice Syndrome, 56 *N.Y. St. B. J.* 34 (1984).

116. Gerbasi, Zuckerman & Reis, Justice Needs a New Blindfold: A Review of Mock Jury Research, 85 *Psychological Bull.* 323, 324 (1977).

117. Hans, Jury Selection in Two Countries: A Psychological Perspective, 12 *Current Psychological Rev.* 283 (1982); Nietzel & Dillehay, *supra,* note 99; Weiten, The Attraction-Leniency Effect in Jury Research: An Examination of External Validity, 10 *J. Applied Soc. Psychology* 340 (1980).

118. Morgan & Comfort, Scientific Jury Selection: Sex as a Moderator Variable of Demographic and Personality Predictions of Impaneled Felony Jury Behavior, 43 *J. Personality & Soc. Psychology* 1052 (1982).

119. LaFitte, The Use of Social Science Techniques in the Jury Selection Process, 2 *Rev. Litigation* 199 (1982).

120. Hafemeister, Sales & Suggs, Behavioral Expertise in Jury Selection, in *Law and Mental Health: International Perspectives,* Vol. 1 (D. Weisstub ed. 1985); Rosenhan, Selecting a Jury, Presidential Address, presented at the annual meeting of the American Academy of Forensic Psychology (1981).

121. M. Saks, *Jury Verdicts* (1977); M. Saks & R. Hastie, *Social Psychology in Court* (1978).

122. Fidler, Social Science and Jury Selection: A Lawyer's View, paper presented at American Psychological Association (1981).

123. Frederick, Jury Behavior: A Psychologist Examines Jury Selection, 5 *Ohio N.U. L. Rev.* 511 (1978); Hafemeister et al., *supra*, note 120.

124. *Id.*; Hans, *supra*, note 117.

125. M. Belli, *Modern Trials* (1963).

126. Ballard v. United States, 329 U.S. 187 (1946).

127. Taylor v. Louisiana, 419 U.S. 522 (1975).

128. Buteyn, *People v. Williams*: Expansion of the Permissible Scope of *Voir Dire* in the California Courts, 15 *Loyola L.A. L. Rev.* 381 (1982).

129. Wainwright v. Witt, 105 S.Ct. 844 (1985).

130. See generally Dicker, Systematic Exclusion of Cognizable Groups by Use of Peremptory Challenges, 11 *Fordham Urb. L. J.* 927 (1982–83); Harper, Rethinking Limitations on the Peremptory Challenge, 85 *Colum. L. Rev.* 1357 (1985).

131. Batson v. Kentucky, 106 S.Ct. 1712 (1986).

132. Swain v. Alabama, 380 U.S. 202 (1965).

133. Batson v. Kentucky, 106 S.Ct. 1712 (1986).

134. P. Ekman, *Telling Lies* (1985); Suggs & Sales, Juror Self-Disclosure in the Voir Dire: A Social Science Analysis, 56 *Ind. L. J.* 245 (1981).

135. Perlman, Town v. Country: Is Trial Strategy the Same?, 19 *Trial* 68 (1983). See also Burke, *Voir Dire*—As a Game, As a Procedure, As a Pastime and As Intimacy, 58 *Fla. B. J.* 310 (1984).

136. Suggs & Sales, *supra*, note 134.

137. Neitzel & Dillehay, Psychologists and Voir Dire: A Strategy and Its Applications, paper presented at American Psychological Association (1979).

138. Hafemeister et al., *supra*, note 120; Lees-Haley, The Psychology of Jury Selection, 2 *Am. J. Forensic Psychology* 61 (1984); Schulman, Shauer, Coleman, Enrich & Christie, Recipe for a Jury, 6 *Psychology Today* 37 (1973). See generally V. Hans & N. Vidmar, *Judging the Jury* (1986).

139. LaFitte, The Use of Social Science Techniques in the Jury Selection Process, 2 *Rev. Litigation* 199 (1982).

140. Covington, State of the Art in Jury Selection Techniques, More Science Than Luck, 19 *Trial* 84 (Sept. 1983).

141. Lees-Haley, *supra*, note 138.

142. Covington, *supra*, note 140.

143. Zeisel & Diamond, The Jury Selection in the Mitchell-Stans Conspiracy Trial, 1 *Am. B. Found. Research J.* 151 (1976).

144. Frederick, Social Science and Jury Selection, paper presented at American Psychological Association (1981).

145. LaFitte, *supra*, note 139.

146. Covington, *supra*, note 140.

147. LaFitte, *supra*, note 139.

148. P. Keith-Spiegel & G. Koocher, *Ethics in Psychology: Professional Standards and Cases* (1985).

149. Rosenhan, Selecting a Jury, Presidential Address, annual meeting of American Academy of Forensic Psychology (1981).

150. *Id.* See B. Sales, *The Trial Process* (1981).

151. Zeisel & Diamond, *supra,* note 143. See also A. Ginger, *Jury Selection and Criminal Trials* (1980).

152. Shapley, Jury Selection: Social Scientists Gamble in an Already Loaded Game, 185 *Science* 1033 (1974).

153. Saks, Social Science and Jury Selection: A Consumer Advocate Position, paper presented at American Psychological Association (1981).

154. P. Keith-Spiegel & G. Koocher, *supra,* note 148; McCloskey, Egeth & McKenna, The Experimental Psychologist in Court: The Ethics of Expert Testimony, 10 *L. & Hum. Behav.* 1 (1986); See Frederick, Social Science Involvement in *Voir Dire*: Preliminary Data on the Effectiveness of "Scientific Jury Selection," 2 *Behav. Sci. & L.* 375 (1984).

155. Purwin, D'Agostino & Brown, Loaded for Acquittal? Psychiatry in the Jury Selection Process, 7 *U. W. L.A. L. Rev.* 199 (1975).

156. R. Simon, *The Jury System in America* (1975); Saks, *supra,* note 153.

157. Plutchick & Stewart, Jury Selection: Folklore or Science, 1 *Crim. L. Bull.* 3 (1965). See also Simon, *supra,* note 156; A. Ginger, *Jury Selection and Criminal Trials* (1980); Rosenhan, *supra,* note 149.

158. Plutchick & Stewart, *supra,* note 157.

159. Frederick, *supra,* note 144; Saks, *supra,* note 153; Rosenhan, *supra,* note 149.

160. Ekman, *supra,* note 134; LaFitte, The Use of Social Science Techniques in the Jury Selection Process, 2 *Rev. Litigation* 199 (1982).

161. Frederick, Social Science and Jury Selection, paper presented at American Psychological Association (1981); Ginger, *supra,* note 157.

162. LaFitte, *supra,* note 160.

163. Swanson & Wenner, Sensory Language in the Courtroom, 4 *Trial Dipl. J.* 13 (Winter 1982).

164. LaFitte, *supra,* note 160.

165. M. Saks & R. Hastie, *Social Psychology in Court* (1978). Hans, Jury Selection in Two Countries: A Psychological Perspective, 12 *Current Psychological Rev.* 283 (1982); LaFitte, *supra,* note 154.

166. LaFitte, *supra,* note 160.

167. Levine, Using Jury Verdict Forecasts in Criminal Defense Strategy, 39 *J. Mo. B.* 345 (1983). See generally Covington, Jury Selection: Innovative Approaches to Both Civil and Criminal Litigation, 16 *St. Mary's L. J.* 575 (1985).

168. Ugwvegbu, Racial and Evidential Factors in Juror Attribution of Legal Responsibility, 15 *J. Experimental Soc. Psychology* 133 (1979).

169. Ekman; *supra,* note 134; Shaffer & Sadowski, Effects of Withheld Evidence on Juridic Decisions, 5 *Personality & Soc. Psychology Bull.* 40 (1979); Tanford, Penrod & Collins, Decision Making in Joined Criminal Trials, 9 *L. & Hum. Behav.* 319 (1985).

CHAPTER 8
THE TRUTH-FINDING PROCESS
AND DECEPTION

Chris reported that he had discovered the mutilated and sexually molested bodies of his mother and eight-year-old sister when he returned home, but his coolness in recounting his discovery made the police suspicious, and he was taken to the station for further questioning. Late that afternoon Chris submitted to a polygraph exam, which he failed. After being informed of the results of the polygraph examination, and after intensive questioning, at 2:30 A.M. he confessed to having sexually molested and killed his mother and sister, though he refused to sign a written statement to that effect.

Is this episode an example of the effectiveness and practical utility of modern methods of detecting deception? Subsequent physical evidence gathered by a private investigator proved that Chris could not have committed the crime, and six months later someone else confessed to doing it. Why, then, did Chris confess orally and fail the polygraph exam, thus providing police with two of the most damning types of evidence against him? First, as will be shown later, the polygraph is not a measure of honesty *per se*; rather it measures psychophysiological arousal which can result from fear of being caught in a lie, as well as more general sources of arousal including anger, fear of being falsely accused, bereavement, and so forth. The polygraph is also likely to detect individual differences in physiological reactivity; that is, some people are simply more responsive to stress than others. Chris believed the polygraph was infallible, and he was naturally highly reactive physiologically since he had been up since six o'clock that morning, had come upon the dead and mutilated bodies of his mother and sister, and was now being doubted by police officers—people he highly trusted. These factors all contributed to his being labeled "deceptive" by the polygraph examiner. The officer's report that they now had "proof" that he was lying undoubtedly shocked his sense of reality, and his confusion was exacerbated by a hypnotic style interrogation. The oral confession came after Chris had been up for 18 hours, and only after the interrogating officer had him close his eyes, place his head on a chair in front of him, and imagine suggested scenes as "they could have been." These scenes included Chris's imagining how he might have killed and raped his mother and sister. All of this together produced the confession.

Both hypnosis and the polygraph are commonly used techniques for the detection of deception. Throughout history, there have been numerous attempts to discriminate liars from those telling the truth. Early attempts focused on trial by ordeal or by combat. Trial by ordeal was especially in vogue throughout the middle ages. For example, the ability to walk over hot coals without being burned was used to determine whether one was telling the truth. Interestingly, the extremities often become cold in emotional stress. Yogis who dazzle observers by walking barefooted across a bed of hot coals have changed and controlled their physiology so that the feet remain cool, thus lessening the chances of actually burning the flesh. These techniques have been observed in almost all cultures. Not long ago, Bedouin tribesmen would require questionable witnesses to lick a hot iron. If their tongue was burned, it was considered as evidence of lying. In a similar vein, the Chinese required potential witnesses to chew rice powder and then to spit it out. The statements made were considered untruthful if the rice powder was dry. Those suspected of lying in ancient Britain were forced to attempt to swallow a huge "trial slice" of dry bread and cheese, and if they could not do so easily enough in the judgment of the observers, they were considered to be lying. All of these tests are based on the belief in a critical assumption, in this case, that the flow of saliva is a direct indicator of stress and emotional disruption associated with deception.

CRITICAL ASSUMPTIONS

There are critical assumptions in most approaches to lie detection. The first is the assumption that those being tested know they are lying. The absence of deception does not necessarily imply truth. For example, a witness to a crime may truthfully believe A to have been the criminal, and yet be mistaken. The absence of deception is generally a necessary, but not necessarily a sufficient, condition for establishing truth. The second assumption is that someone who is lying is distressed physiologically or psychologically by the lying or the fear of being detected.

There is an implicit assumption in studying the detection of deception that the truth can be defined, so that some conceptions of truth that relate to the legal process should be examined. William James defined truth as that which is ultimately agreed upon. In the behavioral sciences, truth is defined in the short range as consensually agreed upon logical inferences, beyond which point it requires statistically replicated and validated data. From the perspective of the law, one definition provides three elements that consistently denote truth: (1) agreement of thought and reality, (2) consistency in communicability of the logical inferences in the thought, and (3) eventual verification by observation or data.[1] Thus, the concept of consistent multiple corroboration of facts is inherent in either discipline's conception of truth.

Another widespread assumption pertinent to deception detection is that the legal system is highly accurate in its judgments, so that any technique would have to be very accurate to augment it. Consider a situation in which 90 people are telling the truth and 10 are lying, while some newly devised test is able to discriminate liars from truthtellers with 90 percent accuracy. This would be a very high rate of accuracy, almost certainly better than any method now available. In this case (see Figure 1) 81 people who told the truth would be correctly identified as honest (Cell A). Of those who lied, nine would be detected (Cell D). These two cells combined yield the 90 percent "hit rate" or number of correct classifications. Cell B reflects the type 1 error (false alarms)—i.e., nine people who told the truth but would be labeled deceptive. Cell C reveals that one person who lied would be perceived by the test as having told the truth, a type 2 error ("misses").

Many critics of objective tests would note that nine innocent individuals out of a hundred may receive punishment, and then be inclined to reject the test as legally inadmissible, or even unethical. In doing so, they fail to consider a cherished assumption: that the legal system in its present form can do a better job. As is evident from other materials in this book, there are ample reasons to believe

Figure 1
Subject is *labeled*:

		truthful	dishonest
	truthful (n = 90)	cell A 90 × .90 = 81	cell B 90 × .10 = 90 − 81 = 9
Subject is *actually*:	dishonest (n = 10)	cell C 10 × .90 = 9	cell D 10 × .10 = 10 − 9 = 1

that the judicial system does not always achieve a high rate of discrimination between guilty and innocent. There simply is no hard evidence on the accuracy of our legal system in assessing the truth it purports to explore, and such data may be impossible to gather. In a recent seminar involving law and psychology students, the law students asked for "evidence" that psychologists are effective in several professional roles. After noting a variety of studies (of varying quality) to bolster their position, the psychology students turned this question around: what evidence did they have that the trial system "works" in determining truth. The best response that could be given to questions about whether the legal system works, was that "you have to have faith in the system." Some of the law students believed this was a reasonable response, while others believed that this was a powerful assumption that essentially leaves unanswered a critically important question about the legal system.

TRUTH-FINDING IN COURT

Detection of deception is important within the court system in many kinds of determinations. For example, defendants in criminal cases may feign insanity or incompetence in order to avoid prosecution or demonstrate "diminished capacity." Similarly, in civil cases plaintiffs may feign physical or psychological injury. In addition, individuals in other circumstances may attempt to present themselves in a favorable light—for instance in the case of a convict seeking to be released on probation.

Malingering,[2] within the mental health field, is "the voluntary production and presentation of false or grossly exaggerated physical or psychological symptoms."[3] Resnick remarked that "no other syndrome is as easy to define, but difficult to diagnose."[4] He differentiated among five types of malingering: (1) simulation, the feigning of nonexistent symptoms; (2) dissimulation, the concealment of existent symptoms; (3) pure malingering, the invention of a nonexistent disability; (4) partial malingering, the exaggeration of existent symptoms; and (5) false imputation, the ascription of true symptoms to a cause consciously recognized as unrelated to them. Any such acts are typically called faking or lying by laypeople.

There is considerable variability among the "symptoms" observed in malingerers, as there are many different motives for the deception and different resources available to the deceiver. Criminal defendants may fake auditory hallucinations or some other signs of overt psychosis.[5] Sierles reviewed previous research indicating that sociopaths and substance abusers frequently malinger.[6] The attempt here is apparently to shift responsibility for misdeeds to their implied illness. Very successful fakers may avoid prosecution altogether if they are judged incompetent to stand trial although, ironically, they may be incarcerated for quite some time if subsequently committed involuntarily on the basis of the same bizarre symptoms.

Conversely, Resnick has noted that sexual psychopaths confined indefinitely become adept at "faking good" in order to gain release.[7] Successful deception which hides existing mental health problems may also serve to gain special privileges or better living conditions.[8]

The incidence of malingering is uncertain, but it may be widespread in certain settings. In tort cases, for instance, in a high percentage of cases studied there is complete recovery after awards for physical injury, suggesting the possibility of malingering. Studies cited by Resnick indicate from 40 percent to 96 percent full recovery within two years of such awards.[9] Jones cites similar statistics.[10]

PSYCHOLOGICAL MEASURES OF DECEPTION

"If ever there is devised a psychological test for the valuation of witnesses, the law will run to meet it," wrote Wigmore in *Evidence* (1923). Wigmore probably should have added the words "valid and accurate" before "psychological test." Many psychological measures have been devised, and of these, a substantial number can be used for the evaluation of deception or the emotional state of witnesses. Those that are applicable vary markedly in their usefulness and in their ability to detect deception. Yet, in many cases they provide an accurate cue that the person is deceiving, even when other indices have missed the deception.

The MMPI

The most commonly administered psychological test is the Minnesota Multiphasic Personality Inventory (MMPI), a questionnaire composed of 566 self-reference statements to which persons must respond either true or false.[11] It incorporates several "validity scales," i.e., subscales whose purpose is to detect deviant test-taking attitudes. These validity scales are the "cannot say," L, F, and K scales, designed respectively to measure omission of items, presentation of the self in an overly favorable light (or "lying"), endorsement of items rarely endorsed by a normal group, and clinical defensiveness. Clinicians should examine both the raw scores and the pattern of scores on each of these subscales in order to determine whether the taker has responded in a direct and honest manner. With respect to detection of deception the validity scales assume prime importance. In interpreting these scales, such client characteristics as age, social status, and education level must be taken into account, because different raw scores are expected among different client groups.[12]

The MMPI validity scales were developed along with the clinical scales in the 1940s.[13] Most of the MMPI items were developed using "empirical validation." That is, out of a large pool of proposed items, only those correlated with certain observed subject characteristics were retained. The F scale items, for example, are those that were answered in the scored direction by 10 percent or less of the normal subjects used to standardize the test. K scale items were devised by comparing the abnormal-looking profiles of hospitalized patients with those of psychiatric patients whose profiles appeared normal. The items that best differentiated these two groups of profiles were retained in the K scale. The K scale is thought to tap relatively subtle defensive attempts to deny pathology. The L scale, on the other hand, taps more overt attempts to look good, often in an obvious, almost self-aggrandizing way. Since the initial release of the MMPI, the empirical bases for the validity scales have broadened as new research has attempted to use them in a variety of ways in detecting deception.

Several authors have reviewed the use of the MMPI in detecting deception. Grow, McVaugh, and Eno evaluated the effectiveness of 13 different techniques for analyzing MMPI responses in attempting to detect deception by asking 150 undergraduate psychology students to answer the questions both legitimately and according to a faking set, either "fake bad" or "fake good."[14] They cross-validated their findings on a clinical sample of 53 clients believed to fall naturally into one of these three categories. They found that 10 percent to 80 percent of the variance associated with faking could be accounted for by using various detection strategies including raw score cutoffs, F minus K ranges, sawtooth profile, and others.

The simplest way of assessing deception on the MMPI is merely to scrutinize the validity scales individually. MMPI scales are standardized so that scores above 70 correspond with significant indications of the relevant patient characteristics. Elevations on the L or K scales above 70 indicate lying or defensiveness respectively, although other interpretations are possible. For example, elevations on scale 6, which is sensitive to paranoid characteristics, may be seen in conjunction with a high score on K and the resulting profile might not be inaccurate for a person whose disturbance includes many paranoid features. Elevations around 70 on the F scale are often found in seriously disturbed persons, while much higher scores, perhaps 85 and beyond, are often associated with faking.

The most commonly used technique to assess faking appears to be the "F − K index," simply the raw score for K subtracted from the F raw score. Initially suggested by Paul Meehl this index has been used to detect both "faking bad" and "faking good," depending on the direction of the difference.[15] The cutoff scores or decision rules for this index have varied somewhat from one investigator to another. Ziskin reviewed the history of various F − K proposals and concluded that "these quantitative indices . . . appear to provide one method of detecting malingering for which research validation does exist."[16] The best decision rules for labeling a profile as valid or deceptive should depend on the base-rate for deception in the population being considered. Cutoffs used in a college counseling center would be inappropriately conservative in a forensic setting and would allow many deceptive profiles to go undetected. Recall the earlier discussion of type I and type II errors. A rule which is very conservative in order to improve the false alarms will also lead to more deceptive profiles slipping under the cutoff, thus worsening the miss rate. The point at which these types of errors are both minimized depends on the actual proportion of malingering subjects, a value which may be difficult to ascertain. Ziskin has suggested a fairly liberal cutoff rule in forensic settings, given the high rate of malingering attempts.

Other methods of assessing malingering have centered on the content of particular MMPI items. Such attempts focus on the inability of most malingerers to adequately predict which items they should endorse if they were really disturbed. Hence, the clinician may examine the "subtle versus obvious" items, those that most persons would know to endorse versus those that only a "real" disturbed person or a mental health professional would know should be answered in the scored detection. Koss, Butcher, and Hoffman have identified "critical items" that reflect basic symptoms patterns.[17] To the extent that subjects do not endorse these items, they might be judged not to have known disorder despite other characteristics of the profile.

Finally, a high number of unanswered items, indicated by a high "cannot say" score, should alert the clinician to examine the items left blank. One of the simplest methods to dissemble is simply not to answer items which might be revealing. In this circumstance it may be possible to validate the profile by asking the subject to answer the excluded items. One other recently proposed index may be mentioned, although lack of cross-validation makes it suspect. Lanyon and Lutz found that "defensive" felony sex offenders were best discriminated from "nondefensive" sex offenders by use of an L + K − F raw score index.[18]

The use of malingering indicators as described above is not foolproof. Rogers reviewed research suggesting that, under some circumstances, the MMPI may be successfully faked.[19] Research by Kroger & Turnbull indicates that faking is possible only when subjects take on a "role" and have accurate information about it.[20] To the extent that someone has prior experience with psychologically disturbed persons, they may have the knowledge needed to "fake bad" successfully. In many forensic settings, such experiences are more prevalent than in the population at large. On the other hand, a stereotypical view of good adjustment is accessible to almost everyone in society, and thus "faking good" may be more difficult to detect.

In summary, the MMPI scales provide several indicators of deception, based upon raw scores or difference scores on the validity scales and occasionally on clinical scales. These techniques are not foolproof; at times, undetected faking may occur. In addition, multiple indicators may give discrepant information. Despite these problems and the continuing debate over appropriate cutting points for identification of deception, most MMPI indicators have been cross-validated and have been generally accepted as useful. These indicators include the three validity scales, differences among scores on these scales (in particular, F − K), and comparison of scores on obviously versus subtly pathological items of the clinical scales.

Other Psychological Tests

Unlike the admissibility of hypnosis, the admissibility of test data as evidence has been little challenged.[21] This is true even though clinicians commonly disagree over interpretations of test results, and the use, especially, of projectives "has been said to violate the principle that scientific evidence is inadmissible unless substantial agreement among the experts has been demonstrated."[22] Of course, experts who present such data are open to cross-examination. A bibliography on psycholegal assessment presented almost 200 citations, some relevant to the use of the MMPI and other tests in detecting deception.[23]

Although MMPI research on detection of deception is more abundant, other tests too have been used as indicators of deception. While the MMPI is designed to measure "psychopathology," other psychological questionnaires are designed to measure more normal personality traits. The Cattell 16 PF Test is such a test,[24] and scales which tap both "faking good" and "faking bad" have been devised for it.[25]

These types of tests can be supplemented by focusing specifically on the potential attempts of clients to produce "socially desirable" responses. A commonly used test here is the Marlowe-Crowne Social Desirability Scale.[26] The choices in such tests are matched on their social desirability, so the clients' choices are not dictated by social desirability alone, but rather by their own personality patterns.

Several studies have examined deception and its detection using the Rorschach inkblot technique, with some studies concluding that deception could not be detected. For example, in one study 46 Fellows of the Society for Personality Assessment detected fewer than 10 percent of Rorschach protocols produced by normal subjects instructed to respond as if they were paranoid schizophrenics.[27] The success of these subjects in being labeled psychotic depended in part on the information they had received about the nature of paranoid schizophrenia. As noted earlier, it is easier to fake when the characteristics to be presented are well defined. Rogers and Cavanaugh noted that the more than 5000 research studies on the Rorschach raise many questions and, in general, fail to substantiate diagnostic validity of this instrument.[28] It is apparently more useful for generating broad descriptive hypotheses than specific, definitive, judgments. Their survey of forensic psychiatrists, however, indicated that the Rorschach was specifically requested by the referral source in a quarter of related evaluations.

Rogers concluded that all psychometric approaches are susceptible to dissimulation.[29] No test procedure alone can adequately protect against its occurrence, so that clinicians need to adopt a set toward its detection. We believe further protection could be afforded by the use of a good standard battery including the MMPI, Cattell 16 PF Test, and the Marlowe-Crowne. The use of interview indicators of deception, although not actually a psychological test, can be helpful in the detection of deception as well.

Resnick noted that professional criminals are skilled liars and suggested that clinicians acquire factual knowledge of the case beyond what the accused believes they possess.[30] This information may be gleaned from police reports and arrest records, probation reports, interviews with the arresting officer and witnesses, as well as discussions with family, parole officers, etc.[31] In addition, knowledge of specific symptom patterns for valid disorders as well as fabricated symptoms is crucial. Consider, for example, reported hallucinations. Valid hallucinations are usually associated with delusions, can be attributed to some psychic purpose, tend to be intermittent rather than continuous, are generally clear, involve more sensory modalities than audition (the most frequently faked type), can generally be ignored, even if they are commands, and tend to subside when patients carry out various coping strategies. Careful interviewing could establish that the subject does or does not fit the valid hallucination pattern.

Resnick also outlines a general approach to detecting malingering in criminal defendants.[32] A "mind set" to detect is important. Defendants should be evaluated soon after the crime, so that there is less time for them to develop a plan of deception. The clinician must explain the purpose of the examination, along with the lack of confidentiality. Despite the obvious difficulty this disclosure establishes, good rapport will still help to elicit the needed material. Open-ended questions and accurate note taking are important. Past psychiatric illness should be explored and later validated through examination of hospital records. A prolonged interview, a rapid series of questions, and certain leading questions reduce the ability to maintain a counterfeit account. If the question remains unresolved, psychiatric observation in a hospital setting may be ordered. It is one thing to present a plausible front for a few hours during an interview, it is much more difficult to keep it up during an extended period of observation in the hospital.

In addition, Resnick listed clues to malingered psychosis.[33] Some of these clues are visible from interview information and others from behavioral situations. Malingerers may overact their parts, may be eager to call attention to their illnesses, more commonly can feign the content than the form of schizophrenic thinking, may claim sudden onset of a delusion, and may tell a far-fetched story to fit the facts of the crime into the supposed illness. Often the reported symptoms will fit no known diagnostic category. Contradictions in the accounts of the crime are likely, as are nonpsychotic alternative motives for the crime. The style of malingerers tends to involve repetition of answers and slowness to respond, lack of perseveration, and stilted descriptions of the contents of auditory hallucinations. Malingerers are unlikely to show subtle signs of residual schizophrenia. Thus, knowledge of patterns of disorders, interview techniques, and constant surveillance of behavioral cues aid in detecting deception.

CUES OF DECEPTION

"Body Language," after the book of the same name, has been a popular topic in recent years. Its adherents claim to be able to tell much about a person from gestures, mannerisms, postures, and poses. For the most part these claims are based on single observations or speculative logic, and have usually not been verified by other researchers. Yet some solid research has been done, so at least a rudimentary knowledge of the significance of certain body movements, speech patterns, etc. is taking shape. It is now possible to discuss, with some qualifications, the behavioral correlates of deception.

A most comprehensive treatment of behavioral clues to deception is Ekman's *Telling Lies*.[34] This work reviews over 30 years of research by Ekman and others. Ekman describes three emotional experiences that commonly occur in those who deceive: (1) "detection apprehension," the fear of being caught; (2) "deception guilt," negative feelings associated with perpetrating a lie regardless of what is being covered up; and (3) "duping delight," the thrill of succeeding with one's deception. Behavioral clues to any or all of these feelings in the suspected liar would obviously be good evidence that deception is being attempted. In a more general sense, deception can involve the presentation of almost any behavioral evidence of emotion, particularly if it is inconsistent with the story being told.

Ekman cautions that there is no sign of deceit itself, only the attendant emotions that might betray it. Liars have expectations about what signs of emotion others will attend to, and it is these that they conceal or fabricate, while other signs of the "true" emotion remain. Unfortunately, "most people pay attention to the least trustworthy sources—words and facial expressions—and so are easily misled."[35]

Verbal and Voice Cues

In reviewing verbal clues to deceit, Ekman identifies two which have a considerable degree of utility. "*Slips of the tongue,*" first described in detail by Freud, are especially useful since they are, by definition, bits of information that are inconsistent with the story being told. This inconsistency is a fairly direct indicator that the speaker feels something different than what is overtly presented. Similarly, "tirades" often produce deception-specific information, as the deceiver may temporarily lose control of his or her actions and compromise the lie. A truly masterful liar will, of course, not commit either of these costly errors. Other verbal indicators are associated with an emotional experience, but do not point directly to conflict between expressed and felt emotions. Many speech errors, frequent pauses or hesitations, or indirect speech may all indicate that the story being told is not well rehearsed or they may indicate a variety of negative emotions. The utility of these clues varies with the circumstances (e.g., is this the first time the person has needed to recollect the story, or are negative emotions appropriate to the story?). Similarly, voice pitch raised, increased in volume, and made more rapid may be indicative of fear, excitement, or anger; and slower pace suggests sadness or boredom. The first triad of speech characteristics could be associated with detection apprehension and duping delight (lying) or with indignant anger at being accused (truth-telling), so again, interpretations of these sorts of clues depends greatly on the context in which they occur.

Cues from the speaker's vocal style have also been associated with deception. Maier and Thurber found that subjects could discriminate students role-playing as truth-tellers versus those playing deceptive from tape recordings alone.[36] Despite this intriguing result, the investigators were unable to determine which cues were most useful. Other subjects who were presented with visual cues did less well at discriminating, possibly because they attended to role-players' faces. High voice pitch, and many speech errors may be associated with lying.[37]

Facial Cues

Most people believe that clues to truth are to be found in the face of the deceiver; everyone has heard that it is difficult to "look someone in the eye" and tell an untruth. Most people in our culture have therefore learned to consciously maintain eye contact when deceiving. Burns and Kintz, for example, found that under some circumstances liars maintain more eye contact than the truthful.[38] This finding illustrates the difficulty of inferring deception from facial clues. The face is a very complex system for presenting information, and can be thought of as a multichannel communication system. Some of the available channels are under voluntary control and hence are useful for the deceiver who wants to "mask" the information he hopes to conceal. Other channels are not under voluntary control. Pupils increase their dilation as people attempt to deceive, a finding that holds for both genders.[39] Lying probably causes a general increase in autonomic responsiveness, and pupil dilation is just one concomitant feature of this pattern. On the whole, then, facial cues to deception are difficult to interpret because the deceiver is able to confuse the situation by giving conflicting signals.

Ekman's analysis of facial clues illustrates the difficulty most of us have in using such information.[40] He cites three types of information present in the face that indicate the speakers' "true" emotion, but all of these require special knowledge or training to be understandable. The first two of these signs are closely related, and are termed "*micro expressions*" and "*squelched expressions.*" They are both of short duration, perhaps a quarter second, but are specific to the felt emotion. In either case, the leaky expression is quickly wiped away or masked with another, typically a smile, in an effort to hide the experienced emotion. Given their short duration, these signs are easier to detect on film than live. "*Reliable muscle*" clues are more lasting, but again require special knowledge to interpret.

A number of investigators have demonstrated that some facial muscles are associated with parts of the motor cortex that exert strongly voluntary control. Other facial muscles are primarily innervated from parts of the brain which are intimately tied to "emotion centers." This latter type have been called "reliable" because they involuntarily produce parts of expressions associated with felt emotions, no matter what the speaker is doing with the rest of the face. The most reliable area of the face is the forehead, although some reliable clues are also found in the muscles surrounding the mouth. While all three of the above clues could be useful, most lie catchers do not, and perhaps cannot, use them unless specifically instructed. At the other extreme of subtlety are indicators such as tears, blushing, blanching, and trembling, which everyone can interpret without special knowledge. Somewhere in between are blinking and pupil dilation, both indicators of a wide variety of autonomic nervous system activities ranging from sexual arousal to disgust. Their interpretation is highly context dependent.

Body Cues

Body movements as cues to deception are somewhat easier to interpret because they are simpler and less prone to being masked voluntarily. It appears, for example, that deceivers tend to take positions further away from their target than would a truthful individual.[41] The work of a variety of investigators has led to the conclusion that extremes of hand or leg and foot movements are associated with deception.[42] That is, very frequent or very infrequent hand and leg movements are associated with the anxiety of lying, while truthful individuals fall in the middle range.

In examining cues from the body, Ekman describes three classes of hand gestures which may be observed. The most interesting of these he calls *"emblems."* An emblem is a gesture which has a specific and very clear meaning. There are reportedly about 60 emblems in common use in America and these include the "OK" sign, shrug, hitchhikers' thumb, and "the finger." Emblems can easily be compared with the story line to see if they agree. They appear in one of two ways when they are not wanted by the speaker: either a fragment of the emblem will be shown, or it will be given out of the usual up-front, presentation position. In any case, Ekman suggests that "the emblematic slip can be trusted as a genuine sign of a message that the person does not want to reveal."[43]

"Illustrators" are hand gestures used to punctuate speech and explain ideas difficult to put into words. People vary greatly in their use of illustrators, so prior knowledge of the speaker's habit is needed to interpret any changes. Two factors seem to account for the reduction in illustration when people deceive. They may either lack emotional investment in what they are saying or they may be having trouble deciding what to say. In either case, reductions in illustrators are associated with deception.

"Manipulators" are essentially grooming behaviors, some of which are not socially approved, such as cleaning the ears or smacking the lips. An increase in manipulators, often called fidgeting, is associated with a variety of negative emotions, and may indicate anxiety caused by deception. Unfortunately, such an increase may also indicate that the speaker is relaxed and comfortable; thus, this sign is somewhat unreliable. Other clues in the body, such as irregular or rapid breathing, sweating, or frequent swallowing, are probably difficult to fake,

but they are indicative of general arousal of the autonomic nervous system and are consequently vague as to what emotion is being experienced.

Age

Other researchers have found that many people become better deceivers with age.[44] This ability seems to result in part from improved control over some facial muscles, thus mixing-up the message where most people look for signs of deceit. Indicators which remain beyond the voluntary control of the elderly deceiver are generally not attended to. Another hypothesis is that speech clues such as pauses, indirect speech, and the like are very common in the elderly and hence are not likely to arouse suspicion.

Most of the above research needs to be replicated with a variety of populations and in different settings, and must be shown to be stable and consistent over time. Despite these limitations, there are some useful nonverbal cues for deception.

1. People become more sophisticated at deceiving as they age.
2. The ability to deceive ordinary people depends on control of some facial musculature since most people look to the face for deception cues in day-to-day interactions.
3. Ordinary people attend to the wrong aspects of the face, possibly because the "right" cues are very difficult to see. There are some good facial cues but they are rarely used.
4. Body cues are harder to fake or cover up than facial cues. This is especially true of emblematic slips and illustrators.
5. People tend to be motorically extremely active or extremely inactive when deceiving.
6. Auditory cues are more important than visual cues. This is especially true for slips of the tongue and tirades, but also for speech errors, indirect speech, and unusual pauses.
7. Deception is generally associated with increases in voice pitch, volume, and rate, though deception is not the only interpretation.
8. There are many indicators of autonomic nervous system arousal which could indicate anxiety associated with deception. These include fast or shallow breathing, sweating,

frequent swallowing, blinking, pupil dilation, tears, blushing, and blanching. In some circumstances these signs could be consistent with the story being told.

In any event, detecting deception using behavioral cues is clearly more a clinical art than a science. Labeling someone deceptive *solely* on the bases of such information is unsupported by empirical findings to date.[45]

HYPNOSIS

The lay public probably sees hypnosis as the major form of psychological truthfinding. It is also one of the most legally, ethically, and theoretically controversial techniques.

Nature and Effect of Hypnosis

There has even been a great deal of controversy as to what hypnosis actually consists of. Many would argue that the hypnotized person does indeed go into a "trance," defined as a qualitatively different state of consciousness. However, as yet, it has been difficult to find any consistently quantifiable correlates of this allegedly unique state. Orne[46] sees hypnosis as an extension of role playing. However, some studies tend to disconfirm this view at least in part.[47] Barber views hypnosis as a byproduct of previous attitudes and expectations, while still others argue that it is a heightened state of concentration and suggestibility in which clients suspend their belief systems.[48] Virtually all agree that dependence on the decisions of the hypnotist is a factor.

Responsivity to hypnosis appears to be a stable and measurable trait.[49] It is strongest in late childhood. About two-thirds of the normal population appears to be hypnotizable to some degree. However, only 5 percent to 10 percent are highly hypnotizable, and those persons tend to show evidence of hypnosis-like states even when not formally induced. Naturally, these differences in hypnotizability have implications for the use of hypnosis to detect deception. First, for many people these techniques are not applicable. Second, the risk that hypnosis may itself change a person's memory of an event will vary according to the hypnotizability of the subject and the extent to which hypnosis is formally induced. The highly hypnotizable subject may spontaneously alter his percepts or memories in the presence of hypnosis, and manipulated deception may easily occur for such subjects if hypnosis is carried out improperly.

The evidence as to whether individuals can be induced to commit antisocial acts is not totally clear. The weight of evidence is that they cannot be so induced when these acts are repugnant to their belief systems.[50] This finding is contrary to the popular view that the hypnotist has absolute control over the subject. In one study, O'Brien and Rabuck asked seven female college "volunteers" in three different experimental conditions to make a homosexual approach to a woman (actually a confederate of the experimenter) who would leave the building when the experimental subject did.[51] Subjects in Condition I were told to go up to this woman, claim they were attracted to her, and suggest going somewhere alone. This was done while they were under hypnosis. Subjects in Condition II were told to do the same thing, only this time the act was induced as a post-hypnotic suggestion, i.e., to be carried out after they had been released from the hypnotic state. The subjects in Condition III were also asked to do the same thing, this time as a waking suggestion, i.e., they were never hypnotized. Interestingly enough, the only subjects who carried out the suggested behavior were two people in Condition III, so it is probable they were simply going through a role they thought they should play. In any case, hypnosis clearly did not cause them to perform behaviors against their belief system.

Hypnosis in Detecting Deception

It has been asserted throughout both the legal and psychological literature that hypnosis can be helpful in assessing truth-telling, and also in expanding the memory of those testifying in court. Research does not support this view. Most deceivers strongly wish not to be discovered, and hypnotized subjects cannot be coerced to do something they strongly resist. Secondly, a number of authors have indicated that the process of hypnosis itself can be faked, that individuals can perform most if not all the behaviors that truly hypnotized subjects are capable of carrying out,[52] and that hypnotized subjects can willfully lie.[53] So any interrogation under hypnosis designed to detect deception is problematic.

In spite of these considerations, some have persisted in using hypnosis to detect deception. The common hypnotic method for trying to cut through possible deception is to first bring clients to a point of "deep hypnosis," suggest that they will be compelled to tell the truth (after first demonstrating to them the power of hypnosis by having them carry out several commands or "challenge suggestions"), and then ask the relevant questions.

Hypnosis has been useful in criminal investigations in ways other than in a direct assessment of deception, one of which is to enhance the recall of witnesses. The problems with using hypnosis for memory enhancement are significant. Nonetheless, it continues to be utilized for this purpose. There is evidence that other nonhypnotic techniques may be just as effective in eliciting memory details. So at this time, the unique advantages of memory facilitation by hypnosis are questionable. Hypnosis can be useful in some circumstances, when carefully used as one part of an investigation. Hypnosis does have one marked advantage over the nonhypnotic techniques, it is more impressive to most clients, thus facilitating their cooperation and concentration.

Because hypnosis can be useful in the investigative phase of crime, more and more police officers are being trained in it. This presents significant problems and though useful in certain instances, there are serious ethical issues.[54] Police officers do not have the extensive training in human behavior that provides the context from which one can validly and effectively judge the results of a hypnotic inquiry. When police officers do use hypnosis, it should be required that they receive some consistent consultant supervision by someone trained both in hypnosis and the broader aspects of human behavior and psychopathology. In any case, in this type of endeavor, the hypnotist helps to elicit further clues which then can be investigated in traditional fashion.

The junior author of this book has participated in numerous investigative operations in which hypnosis furthered the development of clues. A good example of a case in which it can be useful is the case of Virginia, a rape victim. Using a time-regression technique, Virginia was asked to return to the scene of the crime, and the details she had already provided were fed back to her in the hypnotic patter. She was eventually able to remember five of the six digits of the license plate on the car into which she had been forced by the rapist. The police were then able to arrest a suspect who was identified by the victim and who subsequently confessed to the crime.

Hypnosis and the Law

Hypnosis may enter the legal arena in several ways: as a defense for criminal acts supposedly committed by a hypnotized individual, as an investigatory device, or as an aid to the examiner in determining the subject's state of mind (either at the time of examination or at a previous time). Hypnosis may also be important in considering the admissibility of confessions induced by hypnosis or of evidence from a witness whose memory has been refreshed under hypnosis.[55]

Cases involving defendants allegedly hypnotized at the time they committed a crime are rare.[56] Although some debate continues as to the coercive power of hypnosis, both mental health professionals and courts have considered the likelihood of crimes being committed under hypnotic suggestion to be small and have not been persuaded by such a defense.

As pointed out earlier, the use of hypnosis as an investigatory device by law enforcement personnel has sparked much criticism. In such instances it is used supposedly to enhance memory about an event. However, the improper (or at times even the proper) use of hypnosis may alter the memory of the witness. Therefore, it must be used very carefully in investigations.

The topics of greatest relevance to detection of deception are the use of hypnosis as a scientific method to determine an individual's state of mind and to "refresh" or enhance the memory of witnesses. Under limited circumstances, the clinician may testify as an expert witness to the truthfulness of a statement made by a hypnotized individual or as to the individual's state of mind before the hypnotic examination.[57] The presentation of such evidence is highly unusual. The legal issues involved are whether the proper foundations have been laid for the presentation of hypnotic evidence and the reliability of the particular hypnotic techniques used.[58]

Without a proper foundation, courts will not admit related statements on an individual's state of mind. In *People v. Diggs*, such a foundation was held to include the establishment of the reliability of the method, the qualifications of the expert witness testifying, and the fact that scientific procedures were used in the particular case.[59] Most states use the Frye rule as the standard. According to *Frye v. United States*,[60] in order to admit the results of scientific or mechanical methods, "the thing from which the deduction is made must be sufficiently established to have gained general acceptance in the particular field in which it belongs."[61] This case itself referred to the use of the polygraph, but the same rule has been applied to hypnosis. The Frye rule tends to lead to the inadmissibility of hypnotic results related to detection of deception.

Courts have generally not permitted the use of hypnosis in the open courtroom.[62] Such use appears unnecessary and may influence a jury unduly. Confessions induced by hypnosis are highly suspect because they are not highly reliable, and yet confessions are powerful evidence. Whether hypnotic coercion of confession can indeed occur is related to the question of whether any forms of coercion may be induced by hypnosis. As in the latter case, the evidence is unclear. However, there appears to be more room for the effects of suggestion. Dickerson concludes that confessions resulting from the use of hypnosis should be inadmissible.[63] This issue is closely related to the admissibility of testimony from any witness who has been hypnotized.

A witness who has been hypnotized may not be completely reliable because during the hypnosis (in a highly suggestible state) the witness may have been inadvertently given information which the witness later remembers as "fact," or because the recollection of events under hypnosis may make the witness more certain of events than he or she should be, perhaps leading the jury to put too much credence in his or her testimony. Thus, the hypnosis of a witness during the investigative phase of a case may significantly influence the witness at trial. Such "refreshing" of memory has produced three types of response within the courts.[64] Many courts accept the logic of *Chapman v. State* and allow such evidence to be presented to the jury, allowing the fact finder to judge the credibility of the testimony.[65] Other courts, following the modern trend, adhere to the reasoning in *State v. Hurd* and allow it only if the procedures used comply with certain established safeguards to be discussed later.[66] A minority of courts follow the holding of *State ex. rel. Collins v. Superior Court*,[67] and exclude all such testimony on the grounds that hypnosis is a generally unreliable technique and does not meet the standard of the *"Frye* rule."[68]

One consideration behind the decision of whether to allow hypnotically refreshed testimony is the impact of such testimony upon a jury. It is often assumed that juries tend to weight too strongly the evidence gained through the use of hypnosis, thus inappropriately enhancing the witness' credibility. Even if juries do not know that hypnosis has been used, the hypnosis may make a witness appear to be more certain or sure of a fact. At least juries should be informed that hypnosis may have this effect.[69] Ironically, however, if the jury is told of the hypnosis of the witness, the jury may put excessive reliance on the evidence, based on the layperson's belief that hypnosis is likely to help assure reliability.

At a minimum, to assure reliability courts should follow the principles outlined in *State v. Hurd,* which referred in particular to the use of hypnosis to refresh memory.[70] According to the *Hurd* court, six procedures must be demonstrated for hypnosis to be accepted as reliable. (1) The investigation must be conducted by an experienced hypnotist. (2) The hypnotist must be neutral with respect to the case. (3) Any information given to the hypnotist prior to the session must be recorded. (4) Before hypnosis, the hypnotist should record the patient's recollection of relevant facts. (5) All contacts between the hypnotist and the client must be fully recorded. (6) Only the hypnotist and the client may be present at any sessions.[71] These safeguards are commonly referred to as the "Orne criteria" because they are largely based upon suggestions made by Orne.[72] While not all states have accepted these conditions, the trend is toward following them.

As a practical matter, quite apart from the legal difficulties with the use of hypnosis, its importance as a truthfinding tool is limited for the following reasons:

1. The client (suspect or witness) may not be hypnotizable. Only about 50 percent of the population will go into a reasonably "deep" hypnotic state, using a standard hypnotic administration.
2. The client may simply refuse to be hypnotized.
3. The client may attempt to fake being hypnotized. While an

experienced hypnotist will usually recognize this, a sophisticated client could possibly carry it off even then.

4. Even though clients are hypnotized, they may still persist in their deception, similar to the way subjects may persist in deception under "truth drugs."

Clearly, there are serious problems with the admissibility of hypnosis-generated evidence. There is much dependence on cues from the hypnotist, and it is quite clear that the testimony could be biased. We believe that it is inappropriate to accept hypnosis-generated evidence without strong qualification of that evidence.

If, in spite of all the problems, hypnosis is employed, the following precautions should be followed.

1. Obtain the consent of all those directly involved.
2. Obtain specific and written consent from the client.
3. Have the hypnotic consult performed by a well credentialed expert. A psychologist or psychiatrist who is board certified in either forensics and/or hypnosis, and who has some direct experience in the other specialty is recommended.
4. Make a recording of the session, preferably video.
5. Have the expert draw up a written report of the hypnosis proceedings, with comments on the client's level of hypnosis, veracity, and general level of psychological functioning.
6. Invite the client's attorney to be present (but absolutely silent and out of view) during the hypnotic interrogation, if it is legally permissible.

PHYSIOLOGICAL TRUTH-FINDING

Deception and the Eye

The mean diameter of the pupil increases as subjects attempt to deceive observers.[73] This would suggest that pupillography, or the mechanical measurement of pupil diameter of the eye, could have a place as a measure of deception. Pupilary response is promising because pupil diameter is a reasonably quantifiable measure, accessible, does not require a verbal response from the subject, and is probably less amendable to voluntary control by the deceiver than are other commonly used measures, such as respiration. However, no efficient and reasonably inexpensive apparatus is yet available for common usage.

Other measures of the eye might also eventually be useful in this area. Iridiology, which focuses on measuring the characteristics of the iris, is currently fashionable in some quarters as an indicator of various physical and psychological disorders. However, there is little scientific evidence that this is a valid procedure. It is possible that a more accurate and consistent observation of changes in the iris could produce indicators of deception that would be useful to future deception examiners.

In similar fashion, there is the possibility that changes in retinal color, which is quite variable and sensitive to emotional changes, could indicate deception. As yet, there has been little except anecdotal support for this approach, though it is interesting and has some promise.

Truth Drugs

The use of drugs to obtain the "truth" in criminal proceedings first emerged in the early 1920s in Texas. An obstetrician, Dr. Robert E. House, noted the remarkably self-disclosing verbalizations of a patient who had received scopolamine as an aid for the rigors of childbirth. Dr. House then obtained permission to aid in the interrogation of two prisoners in a Dallas jail, again using scopolamine. They had both vehemently asserted their innocence, and this continued under the "truth serum." Largely as a result of this, both were found not guilty in a subsequent trial. Dr. House believed that a client under scopolamine could not "create a lie" and the media quickly jumped in to promote the use of this new "truth serum." The use of such drugs increased in the early 1930s, and ever since then experiments have been attempted with a variety of drugs, including sodium amytal and sodium pentothal. But even in the early days there were words of caution, such as those uttered by Dr. W. Lorenz in 1932, "Much care must be exercised by the experimenter to evaluate the results. He must discriminate, if possible, what is the product of fantasy and what of fact."[74]

A particularly important pioneering study was carried out by Red-lich, Ravitz, and Dession,[75] who interviewed nine subjects under so-dium amytal to see if they could persist in "lies" while under the influence of the drug. The results were not so clear cut as they ex-pected, since some partially confessed, some fully confessed, and some persisted in lying throughout. They found that neurotics were most prone to confess under the drug, particularly if they had strong feelings of guilt and anxiety. These feelings were general, rather than being directly related to the specific lies themselves. As a result, per-sons with these unconscious self-punitive tendencies will confess not only to actual lies, but also to crimes they have never committed. This, along with other research, indicates that those individuals who are particularly guilt-ridden or prone to an intense fantasy life are likely to admit to crimes under drug interviews, often whether they have committed them or not.[76] On the other hand, psychopathic per-sons appear to be able to persist in their lies even to the point of drug-induced unconsciousness.

Fortunately, the law has generally reflected this research. Evidence obtained under a truth drug is considered unreliable and at best an opinion. Of course, if the person has not submitted voluntarily to the truth drug, there are important ethical problems and constitu-tional issues of self-incrimination, and the due process. There would also be serious questions of liability on the part of the examiner as a result of this intrusion into the individual's privacy. Even if the person voluntarily submits, the information appears to be of little value ex-cept as fantasy material, or at best a clue to a further investigation. Thus, under a truth drug there is a general disinhibition, and so a variety of thoughts and verbalizations emerge. It is true there is a freer expression of facts. Unfortunately, there is also a concomitant upsurge of fantasy, whim and dreamlike material.

Microwave Respiration Monitor

Respiration measurement has traditionally been considered one of the most effective functions measured by the polygraph.[77] Yet, full efficiency is seldom reached because of the mechanical device used in the polygraph examination to measure respiration—a piece of rubber tubing that stretches around the subject's chest. Unfortunately, this device is easily affected by bodily movement, there are problems in placement of the tubing, and there are difficulties keeping such a mechanical device in exact calibration.

The microwave respiration monitor (a microwave interferometer) sends a beam against the person's chest, and reads the return beam, much as a radar unit does. As a result, the above problems are eliminated. In addition, it better allows for measurement of some of the specific components of the respiration response, including amplitude of each inhalation and exhalation, deviations in breathing rate, and relative change in the volume of each breath. It can also be used at a substantial distance.

In addition, it does not require the subject to make a verbal reply. Finally, the instrumentation can be put into a small, portable package that can be attached to any standard polygraph. The utility of the information gathered is probably comparable to that obtained with the polygraph.

The Voice Analyzer

Deception may produce an increase in voice pitch, noticeable even to the observer who has no equipment of any sort.[78] This suggests that the voice may be another modality for detecting deception. The original systematic attempt to do this occurred in 1971 when the Dektor Counterintelligence and Security Company announced their voice analyzer, which they call the Psychological Stress Evaluator (PSE).

The PSE received a good response in the market, in part because of its portability and its apparently reliable measurement, and because it allows the covert or hidden assessment of a person's truth telling. In addition, particularly in the early years, this voice analyzer was used to diagnose truth telling on the basis of voices on an audiotape or television. This led to a rash of pronouncements as to whether or not important figures, such as the President, were telling the truth when they spoke publicly. It is now clear that such intermediary systems as tape recordings produce a marked loss of efficiency, and the probability of making a reliable (not to mention valid) assessment goes down. Also, it is now well agreed that unless a subject volunteers to participate in a structured interview, it is virtually impossible to discriminate lying from truth accompanied by stress. As with the polygraph, the major cue for deception is stress, which could be caused not only by a lie, but also by a response to a distracting internal thought, to physical pain, or even to cues or gestures from other individuals around the speaker.

Two major components, the glottal tone and the formant frequencies, make up the audible portion of the human voice.[79] The glottal tone occurs when moving air vibrates the vocal cords. When air in the various cavities of the head is agitated by the glottal tone, the formant frequencies then appear. Voice analyzers, however, focus on inaudible aspects of the human voice, referred to as muscle microtremors, which are frequency modulations (FM) that are superimposed on the audible voice frequencies. These minute oscillations in the vocal musculature occur at an approximate rate of 8 to 13 cycles per second. When a person is under stress, these microtremors are usually suppresed, though this would not be noticeable to anyone without special equipment.[80]

Several studies suggest that the voice analyzer is not nearly as effective as the polygraph or even behavioral observation in measuring deception. While it is effective at detecting high levels of stress, it is ineffective when the stress level is relatively low (which is of course the time when one really needs the machine).

Most agree that the PSE is reliable. For example, if you took a tape recording of any voice, and played this into five different PSEs, the readout from all five would be fairly similar. More important is the question of its validity. It consistently measures something, but does the resultant data have any significance or meaning to the area of deception? While psychophysiologic arousal as measured by the polygraph has a logical relationship to deception, the voice print adds the additional inferential step of relating changes in voice patterns to arousal and then to deception.

As yet, the use of voiceprints to detect deception seems to have received only minimal support in science and the legal system. Courts have allowed voiceprints as an adequate means of *identification* under certain conditions,[81] but have typically attached limitations to its use.[82] Courts do not accept it as a measure of *deception*. Although some companies such as Dektor have claimed their products are 95 percent to 99 percent accurate in identifying persons who are deceptive, claims such as this have not been substantiated in published scientific literature.[83] "There is little scientific evidence to support the reliability and validity of instruments that attempt to detect deception by means of voice analysis. In light of our present knowledge, reliance on this equipment by industry and by the judicial system is risky at best."[84]

In spite of the lack of usage and acceptance in the courts, and the rejection for general usefulness by the armed services,[85] the voice analyzer is increasingly used in the business sector, occasionally without the subject's awareness, which of course raises serious legal and ethical concerns.

THE POLYGRAPH: BACKGROUND

Cesare Lombroso first used standardized measurement of physiological functions to determine the honesty of a criminal suspect in 1875.[86] His technique used blood pressure and pulse changes, and was followed in 1914, by Vittorio Venussi who attempted to employ respiration to detect deception. The first person to use several measures at one time was William Marston. He separately measured muscle tension, blood pressure, respiration, and galvanic skin response (GSR). In 1927, John Larson refined this into a single instrument that continuously measured respiration, pulse rate, and blood pressure. The instrument was improved by Leonard Keeler, and he reintroduced the use of the GSR. He also made a number of other improvements, and the instrument he eventually settled on was dubbed the "Keeler Polygraph." It is the prototype for most modern instruments.

The modern field polygraph is a portable instrument which minimally records simultaneous changes in GSR, respiration, and cardiovascular activity. Some standard models measure only two physiological reactions, typically, respiration and cardiovascular activity. Laboratory polygraphs, which are generally more sensitive than field models, usually monitor a much larger number of physiological responses and may be linked to computer systems as well, allowing immediate analysis of relevant physiological data. It should be noted that most empirical research on the polygraph has been done with sophisticated laboratory equipment, whereas most actual "lie detection examinations" use less precise and less sophisticated equipment.

Innovations in the use of the polygraph have been rare in recent years, perhaps, in part, because in some states the measures that can be used are mandated by law. For example, an interesting refinement was suggested in 1945 by John Reid.[87] Since blood pressure measures can be distorted by unobservable muscle activity, he placed sensors in various parts of the client's chair to detect this activity. However, most polygraphers believe they can pick up this activity on their own, so unfortunately, it has not been integrated into the general practice of polygraphy.

Polygraph examiners are usually certified through training at a school of polygraphy, but few have any psychological or research training. Although some states have licensing laws for polygraphers, there is no single body of polygraph operators that trains, licenses, and monitors its members in the fashion of the ABA or APA.[88] Ironically, state laws occasionally mandate the type of measurement that is to be made, despite research indicating that newer or different measures are more valid. Clearly the above issues have been a major concern of the courts in granting admissibility to polygraph results in criminal proceedings.

Standard Procedure

Polygraphy subjects are asked to sit in a room designed to keep distractions to a minimum, on a straight backed chair with concave arms that keep their forearms stable. They are asked to look straight ahead, and not to make any unusual movements or to speak without reason. The standard measures are blood pressure, galvanic skin response (GSR), and respiration.

The measure of respiration is occasionally clumsy, requiring the placement of two stretchable rubber pneumograph tubes around the client's abdomen and chest. The stretching of these tubes caused by breathing changes the air pressure inside the tubes, which is transferred via a bellows to the recording pen.

The GSR, which taps the electrodermal response, is obtained from electrodes taped to the index and ring fingers. The GSR is recorded by administering a very small, though constant, voltage which measures the skin's conductivity of this current. There is good evidence that the GSR is the best single indicator of deception.[89] In fact, one study indicates that it may provide more accurate information when used alone than when used in conjunction with other measures.[90]

Blood pressure is measured by an inflated cuff placed around the client's arm. The pulsations of blood through the vessels cause increased pressure which is transferred to air pressure in cuff, and then to the recording pen. The number of strokes per unit of measurement indicates the pulse rate. While some polygraphers assert that changes in the entire band of strokes indicate changes in blood pressure, shifts in the cardiotracing are a function of the pressure on the cuff, which varies from time to time. Because the cardiomeasure is often a bit uncomfortable, substitute techniques such as a low pressure cuff or a tube that fits over the finger to measure the pulse and blood volume have been used.[91] These devices are more mechanically sophisticated, though more fragile, and they require a higher level of examiner sophistication.

Theoretical Assumptions of Polygraphy

It is inaccurate to refer to the polygraph as "the lie detector." It is more accurately described as a measure of emotional arousal, as it taps such physiological reactions as anticipatory anxiety, anger, or fear. Several theorists have pointed out that it is impossible to consistently and validly discriminate various emotional states into separate physiological patterns.[92] In other words, there is no unique physiological response to deception,[93] and it is apparent that the interpretation of emotional arousal is a complex task.[94]

The evidence is clear that the three critical variables in determining people's response to the polygraph are their overall confidence that the polygraph is able to detect lying, their fear of detection, and their general physiological responsiveness.[95] The last variable refers to novel or stressful stress stimuli. Put simply, some persons respond physiologically to almost any type of stimulus while others tend not to respond at all. Physiologically responsive subjects are more likely to be seen as deceiving than those whose physiological responses are more stable, even when the groups are matched on the degree of intent to deceive.[96]

Polygraphers realize that the subject's confidence in the instrument is critical, so they spend time in an attempt to demonstrate the potency of the technique. Apparently, the accuracy of polygraph detection varies directly with the quality of the pre-test demonstration.[97] General societal attitudes regarding the effectiveness of the polygraph indicate that people generally perceive the polygraph to be highly effective.[98] Collectively, the influence of general societal attitudes, as well as the specific attempts made by polygraphers to convince individuals of the polygraph's effectiveness, seem to play an important role in determining the accuracy of a single test.

A problem with this technique is that there are many innocent subjects who are physiologically labile and have high anticipatory anxiety about the procedure. Thus, they are seen as deceiving when they are not. Also, as in the case of Chris presented at the beginning of this chapter, a strong belief in the efficacy of the procedure can be used against an innocent person to induce a confession.

The novelty of the procedure to the subject is also important. Those who are undergoing their first polygraph are much more likely to show anticipatory anxiety, and thus be construed as deceiving even though they are not.[99] People are much less likely to "fail" a polygraph after they have undergone the procedure a few times.

The concept that fear of detection is critical suggests another important issue: can psychopaths, people who are theoretically without guilt or remorse about their antisocial behavior, beat the polygraph because of this lack of guilt? Most experts agree that the critical issue is not guilt, but the fear of detection,[100] and even the psychopath shows the situational anxiety which can be generated by the fear of being detected.[101] For example, Raskin and Hare found that they could detect deception regarding a mock crime when they used a prison population (which has a higher percentage of psychopaths), just as effectively as they could with a normal population.[102]

Evidence that psychopaths can frequently be detected by the polygraph has also been provided by Balloun and Holmes.[103] In an ingenious experiment, they induced certain subjects to cheat and thus could study an attempt to avoid detection in a "real crime." One half of their subjects were characterized as low on "psychopathy," the other half were characterized as high. Balloun and Holmes found no substantial differences in the ability to detect deception in these two separate groups.

Though in general psychopaths can be detected, there is other evidence that suggests it may be easier for them to avoid detection in certain circumstances. For one thing, the primary psychopath tends to be chronically underaroused psychologically and physiologically.[104] Waid and Orne found that innocent subjects who were physiologically labile were more likely to be detected as deceiving than were guilty subjects who were physiologically stable and nonreactive.[105] This suggests that psychopaths are less likely to be detected when lying than are others. It is also interesting that level of socialization seems a predictor. The most highly socialized subjects are more likely to be misclassified as deceivers than are those who are poorly socialized.[106]

Beating the Polygraph

There are several methods by which subjects may make their polygraph essentially unreadable, or even slant it so as to make them look honest when they are being deceptive:

1. Since there is good evidence that it is much easier to discover deception when clients are taking their first polygraph,[107] several "dry runs" of an actual polygraph can be administered to reduce the chances of detection.
2. Substantial information about what the polygraph involves and how it works would complement the "dry run" approach, by dispelling the concept that the apparatus is infallible, or nearly so.
3. Training in a relaxation response, using such techniques as progressive relaxation or autogenic training, can establish a relaxation response which can compete with anxiety that is intended to arise during the polygraph examination.
4. Biofeedback could be used to train the person to control the specific functions that are tapped in the polygraph exam. Dawson found that actors training in the Stanislavsky Method were unable to deceive polygraph examiners.[108] This finding suggests that the more long-range and specific approaches, such as biofeedback and progressive relaxation, are of more benefit, as any control of the critical physiological responses requires extensive training.

5. Clients can voluntarily induce physiological reactions (e.g., having a tack in their shoe and then pricking themselves on occasion). If done at random times it does not make them look more honest, but it does make the record very difficult to interpret. A related technique is to randomly flex the skeletal muscles, which effects the same results.
6. Lykken has argued that he can train clients to consistently beat the "control question" technique[109]—a combination of baseline or irrelevant questions with essential questions. Lykken suggests that training clients to discriminate the control questions and then at that time augmenting their physiological responses, possibly through some of the techniques mentioned earlier, will disrupt the record so as to make it basically uninterpretable.

Polygraphers do have some methods for recognizing these techniques. For one, sophisticated examiners attach muscle sensors that pick up any voluntary muscle flexing. Also a voluntary attempt to increase autonomic reactions leads to an abrupt increase and then a quick decrease in blood pressure, whereas actual lying is more commonly associated with an initial gradual increase and then a gradual decrease in blood pressure. Voluntary efforts to control autonomic reactions also change the breathing pattern so that a serrated tracing occurs, rather than the smooth tracing associated with normal breathing.

THE POLYGRAPH EXAMINATION

The polygraph examination usually consists of four stages: data collection, pretest interview, test administration, and post test interview.

Data Collection

During data collection polygraph examiners typically obtain a thorough knowledge of the specific background data in a case to formulate questions. This data gathering can prejudice examiners' eventual judgments, and many feel that their ultimate decisions about deception are based far too much on the case data, as opposed to information gained from the polygraph itself.[110] This is an essential weakness of much of the research establishing the "potency" of the polygraph. The polygraphers may show a high level of agreement with independent judges of case material, though it turns out that they have usually looked at the very same information the judges had. So the polygraph material was additional information, not the only information. Such research may demonstrate only that polygraph examiners can learn to imitate judges in their prior evaluations of background evidence.

The Pretest Interview

It is generally considered to serve five important functions.[111]

1. The pre-exam interview is primary in persuading the client that the polygraph is potent in detecting deception.
2. The pretest interview allows an estimate of the level of emotional lability that the polygrapher will have to face.
3. This is the place for developing the baseline questions, as opposed to questions relevant to the particular incident.
4. The client is told of the questions and their order, so that surprise is not an overwhelming issue.
5. The pretest interview is a time when a sophisticated and persistent polygraph examiner is often able to obtain confession. If it does not happen here, it can start to wear down clients so that they may confess later,[112] as in the case of Chris.

Controlling subjects' beliefs or "set" is a critical variable in any method of deception detection. The set operates to psychologically pressure the client to produce the truth. For example, when subjects were told that the psychological tests they were about to take had built-in scales that were effective in detecting lying, the subjects disclosed more personal information and admitted to less socially desirable behavior patterns than did those persons who were told nothing and were asked only to take the test and be honest in their responses.[113] Of perhaps greater significance, another group was only told that if there was any suggestion in the psychological test that they had lied, they would be given a lie detection exam. This group was even more self-disclosing and admitted to more socially undesirable patterns than did the other groups. It is probable that an even more powerful effect could have been generated if the person were placed next to an actual polygraph or was hooked up to it while taking the psychological test. In any case, manipulation of the set is critical in obtaining "honest" response patterns.

Test Administration

While other examination techniques have been used by polygraphers, the three techniques described below (irrelevant-question, control-question, and guilty-information or concealed-information) seem to be the most widely used and studied. They vary in sophistication, ease of use and accuracy. *The irrelevant-question technique* is traditional and straightforward. The examiner asks several irrelevant questions, such as "Do you live in Middletown?" as well as several relevant questions, e.g., "Were you the person who raped Nancy?" Responses to the irrelevant questions are thought to provide a baseline against which the other more relevant questions can be measured. However, it is extremely difficult to control for the emotional impact of the relevant questions, and anticipatory anxiety can easily occur during the irrelevant questions. This is the least sophisticated technique used, and an exam which only used this technique would be considered inadequate by most experts.

The control-question technique was reportedly originated by John Reid.[114] It is the most commonly used polygraph technique today.[115] Certain questions specifically relevant to the crime at hand are asked, as well as "control questions" designed to produce an emotional and/ or a deceptive response. Some examples of typical control questions are:

a) "Before you were 20 years of age, did you ever steal anything from anyone other than your parents?"

b) "During your teenage years, did you ever purposely hurt someone?"

The polygraph examiner presents these as questions regarding general honesty in behavior, and indicates that anyone who would admit to such misbehavior is probably a liar or criminal. This presentation is designed to induce all subjects to deny the control items, while knowing that they are lying, or at least are deeply concerned about their honesty. Note that while the polygrapher claims that only a guilty person would have done such things, he privately assumes that all subjects have done so. These are sometimes called "known lie" questions.

The examiner compares the subject's response to the assumed lie or control questions with questions specific to the matter at hand. If responses to control questions are stronger, it is assumed that the relevant items were answered truthfully, thus producing less arousal. If the relevant items produce stronger responses, it is believed that the subject has lied on these questions as well. The examiner generally comes to no conclusion when responses are about equal.

There are several assumptions made here. First, it is assumed that subjects are completely unable to tell which questions are controls and which are relevant. This point is critical, since everyone would be likely to experience some arousal to questions relevant to a crime they are accused of, whether correctly or incorrectly. Most experts agree that even moderately intelligent subjects can tell the specific and threatening relevant questions from the controls.[116] Second, subjects must believe that the device is infallible. If the technique is seen as fallible, then deceptive subjects may be bolstered in their belief that they can beat the polygraph, and hence not show indications of apprehension, while honest subjects may fear that the machine or operator could make an error implicating them in a crime they did not commit, thus inducing exactly the kind of arousal which the polygraph detects. Given the oft replicated finding in decision-making research that people consistently overestimate the likelihood of negative consequences, the honest subject who lacks blind belief in the polygrapher's method may be very likely to experience upset on the relevant questions.

The third major assumption is that all subjects will experience a considerable degree of emotional arousal to the control questions. It is very difficult, however, to determine the meaning of the control questions. For example, "did you ever purposely hurt someone" could be viewed by some subjects as referring to life-threatening bodily harm. Under these conditions many subjects would honestly answer "no," despite the intent of the examiner that they should lie. Other subjects interpreting such questions more liberally may include psychological discomfort as hurting. The examiner really never knows what question is being answered, or whether the yes or no he receives is a lie, though he assumes it to be so. Thus, the meaning of any emotional arousal associated with the control questions depends upon the subject's past behaviors and present attitudes, neither of which are known. The meaning of the control question is, in Fulkerson's terms, response determined.[117]

An analysis of the above assumptions for the control question technique would suggest that many subjects, honest or deceptive, would be very reactive to relevant questions, and thereby appear guilty. Limited research by independent investigators suggests that the technique does, in fact, have a strong "guilty" bias,[118] i.e., though it is effective in detecting deception, fully half of honest or innocent subjects are labeled liars.

A major suggestion to improve the control-question technique is to include control questions designed to elicit truthful answers, but which are otherwise similar to crime-relevant questions. Lykken has suggested fabricating imaginary "control crimes" that are as threatening as the real crime. At this stage, no research is available to indicate whether such proposals could strengthen the marginally adequate control question techniques.

Several tests, in general referred to as *the concealed-information tests,* depend on reactions to knowledge that only a guilty suspect could have.[119] The first such test, the card test, originated many years ago by Leonard Keeler, presents the client with stimuli that are all relevant to the general crime, though only one is specific to the crime at hand. For example, the murder suspect might be presented with a knife, a gun, and a hatchet, one at a time. Theoretically, only the guilty subject would know that a gun had been used, and would thus have a substantially larger reaction to it. There are problems in devising actual tests within this approach, and there are also problems in controlling for the types of information presented here, so it is seldom used by most polygraphers.

The *peak-of-tension* test, also originated by Keeler, is analogous to the card test. Rather than presenting different items, it presents a sequence of stimuli of the same type. For example, in an armed robbery, the alleged thief would be asked questions like "Did you steal fifty dollars . . . two hundred and fifty dollars . . . five hundred dollars

... etc?" This approach has many of the same problems as the card test. In addition, many subjects anticipate the critical item, and thus prepare themselves to lessen any kind of guilt response.[120]

The third and most sophisticated concealed information test is the *guilty knowledge test,* originated by Lykken.[121] It involves a multiple question, multiple choice format, wherein a guilty individual is presented a question and a series of five responses in which only one response offered by the examiner is critical. An innocent subject would only have a .20 probability of showing a fear of detection response, if indeed they made any differential response at all. The questions are analaogous to those in the peak-of-tension test—e.g., "When Nancy was raped, something was knocked off of the table next to you. Was it a glass of water? beer bottle? ashtray? glass figurine? or a vase of flowers?" If six of these five choice questions are used, the probability that an innocent subject would respond to all of the critical items is .00065 which is much lower than the probability of a guilty subject responding in that fashion. This technique has received strong experimental support for its validity.[122] However, possibly because it was not developed by a polygrapher, or there is added work required to set up this format, or it requires more detailed information about the crime, it has not been widely used by polygraphers.

The Post Test Interview

Here, results of the test are either shared with the subject, or the subject is informed that the results will be reported to a third party when they become available. The decision on whether or not the results are to be shared immediately with the subject is largely a function of the context in which the test was performed. Some strategies call for limited interrogation of the subject if the results suggest deception, and some strategies recommend further testing or interviewing if test results are inconclusive.

THE RELIABILITY AND VALIDITY
OF THE POLYGRAPH

Until recently, mental health professionals have not played a major role in polygraph research.[123] Most of the research that is available has been done in laboratory settings. In the typical experimental paradigm, subjects engage in a mock crime, and the polygrapher tries to discover deception in the responses to a series of guided questions. The fundamental problem with this research is its lack of generalizability. On one hand, subjects in experimental situations are not likely to demonstrate as much affective arousal as persons involved in real-life examinations. On the other hand, laboratory polygraphs are often more sensitive and sophisticated than field polygraphs, thus complicating the generalizability issue even further. Finally, while the polygraph has had its most widespread use in private industry in recent years, virtually all relevant research has been done in actual or simulated criminal contexts.[124] Again, generalizability may be an issue here.

There is significant evidence that the polygraph is a fairly reliable instrument, i.e., the same protocol (since different protocols from the same person are often read differently) is usually read in the same direction by different examiners. However, many of the studies that have primarily supported the reliability of the polygraph are tainted by the fact that virtually all of these people were trained by the same polygraph school.[125] At present, it does appear safe to say that polygraph interpretations are reliable across examiners at an acceptable rate, and at a high rate when these examiners have received similar training.

As regards validity, there are major problems: The consequences of being detected in deception are not similar in the laboratory and the real world; the mock crimes that are used in this research are not personal to the subject and they are often a bit contrived and lacking in a general sense of reality. Obviously, a person caught lying in the laboratory will not suffer the consequences that someone in the real world will. Generalizability is therefore affected.

What is more, it is frequently impossible to know the level or incidence of actual guilt, what Orne refers to as "ground truth."[126] While laboratory studies such as Balloun & Holmes deal adequately with this point,[127] they have difficulties with the points mentioned above. Conversely, the studies that adequately handle those points fall down here.

Although professional polygraphers have frequently reported accuracy rates of 98 percent to 100 percent, most empirical studies have found accuracy rates ranging from 64 percent[128] to 94 percent,[129] against chance rates of 50 percent. Bartol notes that most reports submitted by professional polygraphers claiming extraordinary success do not detail the methods and procedures used, nor the criteria used to decide accuracy rates.[130] He concludes that in most scientific studies of the polygraph, accuracy hovers between 70 percent and 85 percent.

The Congressional Office of Technology Assessment reviewed available research on the polygraph in their 1983 report, *Scientific Validity of Polygraph Testing*, and designated only 10 field studies as having met minimal standards for scientific research. These best studies would point to an overall accuracy rate near 70 percent, with a strong tendency to reach a judgment of deception. In several studies, half of the truthful subjects were wrongly labeled as deceptive.

Given a polygraph with validity estimates of approximately 70 or 75 percent, analysis of the errors made indicates that the ratio of false positives to false negatives may exceed 10 to 1.[131] That is, of the errors made, very few will involve the identification of a deceitful person as innocent (false negative); rather, most errors will result from falsely identifying an innocent subject as deceitful (false positive). Reported false positive rates have ranged from 17 percent[132] to 55 percent,[133] but such rates are difficult to assess beyond the context of an individual study, because they exist as a function of the base rate of deception in a given population and the validity of the test used.

Given the consistently low rates of false negative errors in polygraph studies, it has been generally accepted that attempts to mask deception will almost always fail. Some research supports this belief.[134] However, as we noted earlier, Lykken has shown that persons (particularly psychopaths) can be trained to mask deception.[135] Further, Waid and Orne report an interesting study on the effects of meprobamate, a tranquilizer, in masking decisions.[136] They conclude that tranquilizers do reduce electrodermal responses in deceitful subjects, and given the widespread abuse and availability of these drugs, they suggest that more care should be taken to ensure that they are not used to aid persons who wish to successfully deceive a polygraph examiner.

Certain field studies, such as those by Bersh[137] and Barland and Raskin,[138] have effectively detected deception. However there are two general problems with these studies. First, just as with empirical studies, while they are reasonably accurate in detecting deceivers, they have also shown high rates of classifying innocent subjects as deceptive (55 percent in the Barland and Raskin study). In addition, the data available in these studies are confounded by the fact that the criterion measure, a panel of judges who looked at the case material, overlaps substantially with the polygraph judges, who also unfortunately had the very same case material to look at. This can clearly lead to a judgment based on the case material as much as on the polygraph evidence.

An ingenious field study that handles this problem as well as the issue of "ground truth" was devised by Horvath.[139] Horvath managed to find a number of polygraph tests that had been given to people who later confessed their guilt, and another group of protocols from people who were later cleared of guilt when someone else confessed. Ten different polygraphers examined these charts and came up with an impressive reliability rate of 89 percent. Unfortunately, they were only able to show a 64 percent validity rate, and they perceived innocent subjects as guilty 49 percent of the time.

Another validity issue involves the polygraph machine itself. Although field polygraphers typically prefer measures of respiratory and cardiovascular activity, and some states require these measures as a minimum for "truth telling" instruments,[140] empirical research has consistently reported that measures of skin conductance (SCR or SRR or GSR) detect deception more accurately than other physiological measures.[141]

A similar situation exists in regard to the various examination techniques. The control-question technique remains the most widely used and researched technique, though it has repeatedly been attacked by critics who question its validity.[142] Meanwhile, other techniques have been demonstrated to have higher accuracy rates in laboratory study, but are not widely used in practice.[143]

Szucko and Kleinmuntz presented data to suggest that statistical analyses of polygraph protocols performed more accurately than did clinical interpretations, leading the authors to conclude that the prospects for improving clinical accuracy with the polygraph are not very promising, and that more attention should be paid to purely statistical interpretations.[144] In a 1984 rebuttal to this paper, Ben-Shakhar and Lieblich dispute the validity of the statistical procedures used by Szucko and Kleinmuntz, and argue that neither clinical nor statistical analyses of polygraph data are effective in determining deception.[145]

The controversy surrounding the validity of polygraph tests has prompted much debate, including Congressional hearings in 1983, which occurred in response to President Reagan's directive to expand the use of polygraph tests in government agencies. An analysis of polygraph testing was conducted by a scientific advisory panel commissioned by the congressional Office of Technology Assessment (OTA).[146] The panel concluded that despite the aura of technology surrounding polygraph tests, they are not infallible and that the substantial rates of false positives, false negatives, and inconclusives must be kept in mind.[147] The debate rages on, with a real need for improved and increased scientific research.

LEGAL ISSUES INVOLVING THE POLYGRAPH

There are several important legal trends concerning the polygraph. The most intense debate concerns employment testing and the courtroom admissibility of the results of polygraph examinations.[148] Because of increasing awareness of the problems with the polygraph, and in spite of heavy lobbying by professional polygraphers as well as industry representatives, many states have passed statutes precluding or limiting truth testing by employers or potential employers. Similar legislation is being considered by Congress. These statutes typically prohibit employers from requiring employees to consent to polygraph examinations "as a condition of employment or continued employment." Such language has led employers to argue that the statute is not violated if the employer makes it clear that regardless of the outcome of the exam, the employee's employment status is secure. To date, the courts have found such reasoning lacking in persuasion, as demonstrated in *State v. Berkey Photo,* where the court stated,

> We readily reject as did the County Court . . . the defendant's contention that its request was not a condition of employment or continued employment within the statutory contemplation. Surely the employee would understand that it was despite any formal assertion by the employer to the contrary and his understanding would be wholly realistic in view of the employment relationship.[149]

In spite of the trend by state legislatures to preclude polygraph use by private industry, the federal government is expanding the use of such tests for screening and investigative purposes. The Defense Department and several other departments and agencies apparently have plans to institute coerced polygraph screening programs that will ultimately create a "cyclical, but steady, proliferation of unwarranted and inaccurate polygraph testing in the government."[150] In response to OTA's conclusions after critically reviewing all the scientific literature relating to the validity of polygraph testing cited earlier in this chapter, Congress mandated a freeze on the Defense Department's polygraph plans for 1985 and 1986. However, unless legislation controlling the use of polygraph testing within the federal government is enacted, the immediate trend will probably be toward an ever-widening use of such tests with federal employees.[151]

Another legal trend appears to be that of state legislators, at the instigation of polygraphers, stipulating the different modalities that have to be part of the polygraph exam. This is especially interesting since Balloun and Holmes and others found the GSR to be the only standard modality that provided an effective detection of deception.[152] More importantly, when other modalities were added to the GSR, they detracted from the overall accuracy. It may also discourage polygraphers from working with newer techniques that offer significant promise in this area. In the cortical evoked potentials paradigm, for example, a discrete auditory or visual stimulus (a click or blip of light) is presented to the subject and the reactions in the various portions of the brain are mapped. A sophisticated computer analysis of this data can result in the representation of subtle changes that can indicate deception. However, this requires substantial time and sophistication, and so far has received little attention from polygraphers.

The most critical legal issue regarding polygraphy is the admissibility of polygraph into evidence. The case which is still the benchmark for law in this area is *Frye v. United States*,[153] where the court held that evidence obtained from a polygraph is inadmissible, and will not be admissible until the technique is generally accepted and established in the fields of psychophysiology and psychology.

While *Frye* has never been overturned, it has in varying degrees been undermined in some state and federal courts. A notable trend has been to allow polygraph evidence if there has been prior written agreement of *both* sides of a case.[154] Most states follow this, though in addition most require that the jury be admonished about some of the limitations of the polygraph. Also, the limitations of both the examiner and the polygraph are to be made available to the jury through cross examination. Burkey has been puzzled by the trend toward stipulation, "It is difficult to understand how the polygraph method is improved merely because the parties stipulate to be bound by it. Would the court approve a stipulation to be bound by the toss of a coin?"[155]

Some courts have noted the importance of the defendant's consent to permit the polygraph to be used. For example, in *Orange v. Commonwealth* the court held that the defendant must not only give permission to take the test, but in addition they must specifically agree to allow the results to be introduced, thus necessitating a two-part permission process.[156] Once defendants agree to take the test and allow the results to be used, they cannot withdraw the results if they are unfavorable.[157]

Perhaps the best example of the courts' struggle with the polygraph is in Wisconsin, where in 1933, and again in 1943, the state's Supreme Court refused to admit polygraph evidence at all, even if both parties had stipulated to its admission. In 1974, in *State v. Stanislawski,* the court decided the polygraph could be admitted with written stipulation by both parties and with some further limiting conditions.[158] Later, the U.S. Seventh Circuit Court of Appeals held that the stipulation portion of *Stanislawski* violated due process under the Fourteenth Amendment if the prosecutor has refused to stipulate to a polygraph test without explanation.[159] The Supreme Court of Wisconsin took issue with the interpretation of *Stanislawski* and decided that polygraph evidence is inadmissible in the state of Wisconsin whether a stipulation is made or not.[160]

Courts have continued to struggle with the acceptability of polygraph testimony. This has at times produced unusual or inconsistent cases. For example, in *United States v. DeBetham,* the *Frye* standards were undermined somewhat by the statement that the criterion for scientific acceptance can be polygraphy as well as psychophysiology and psychology.[161] Unfortunately, polygraphy is not a science, and has too often relied on anecdotal data and unsupported testimonials rather than sound experimental methodology. Polygraphy has not been fully open to new psychophysiological modalities nor to incorporating techniques such as the guilty-knowledge test, even in light of its demonstrated higher success rate.[162] Another example of court confusion regarding the polygraph is *United States v. Ridling* in which the court claimed that the scientific evidence substantiating the polygraph is already available, and that providing court-appointed polygraphers will protect clients from unqualified examiners.[163] It is true that while courts have voiced concern that juries may be too impressed with polygraph evidence, the question remains unresolved and some data suggest that they are able to put such data in perspective.[164] Nonetheless there is probably a trend toward admitting polygraph evidence where both parties have consented.

Two Supreme Court decisions, *Washington v. Texas*[165] and *Chambers v. Mississippi,*[166] are being used as precedents to further the admissibility of polygraph evidence. Both cases focus on the compulsory process clause of the Sixth Amendment, which allows the accused to call witnesses for courtroom testimony. For example, one court used this reasoning to reverse a trial court's decision to keep out unstipulated polygraph evidence.[167]

If courts permit the use of polygraph evidence, with the agreement of both parties, we suggest its use be subject to the following conditions:

1. The defendant must be allowed to refuse a polygraph examination without the refusal in any way suggesting guilt, in order not to violate his rights under the Fifth Amendment.
2. The examiner should possess a college degree, at least at the baccalaureate level, with a significant emphasis in human behavior (e.g., a major in psychology).
3. He or she should receive at least six months formal training in polygraphy under an experienced, competent polygrapher.
4. The examiner should have had at least three years experience as a specialist in the field of polygraph examinations.
5. The examiner should use measures and techniques (e.g., guilty knowledge test) which have the highest level of scientific support as to validity.
6. The examiner's testimony must be based on polygraph records that are available for cross-examination.
7. The use of evidence should be collaborative in nature, and not introduced as conclusive.

8. Jurors should be clearly cautioned by the judge regarding the validity of the polygraph so that it is not granted disproportionate weight by the jury.

SUMMARY

Lying or deception can occur in many different situations and for many different motives. Failures to detect deception may produce judgmental errors which are costly to society or to certain individuals. Consequently, there is a great deal of interest in any technique for detecting deception.

Psychological methods of detecting deception fall into three general groups. Use of objective personality tests constitutes the first group. These measures often rely on empirically derived scales embedded within the test which aim to detect deviant patterns of response, patterns which are not consistent with a "true" personality description of the individual taking the test. Generally, these approaches have demonstrated their utility in detecting deception.

A second group of detection strategies relies upon the clinical acumen of the examiner. Persons who try to deceive by feigning mental disorder or, conversely, by denying real pathology, are faced with a difficult task. The well-trained mental health professional is able to draw upon a knowledge of human behavior to demonstrate that the conditions reported by such persons are not consistent with known mental disorders, or that residual signs of disorder remain in someone attempting to deny pathology. This approach emphasizes interviewing skills, careful observation, and broad, expert knowledge. While this approach is probably quite useful, it is more a clinical art than a science, because it is difficult to gather data to demonstrate its utility.

The third psychological approach is based on behavioral indicators of emotion. Few people know what behavioral cues to look for, and the clues that are widely used by laypeople are probably of limited value. There is no specific pattern of behaviors that indicate lie-related emotions. Good liars go to great lengths to present a believable front, and it may be difficult to know what behaviors to attend to in trying to catch the deceptive person. Detection based on body language, verbal clues, and the like, is very difficult, unreliable, and to do even the minimally adequate job these unreliable indicators allow requires knowledge which few experts possess.

A variety of physiological measures of emotion have also been employed as tests of deception. All types of "lie detector" technologies are merely methods of measuring physical changes that accompany a wide range of emotions. Again, there is no specific universal pattern of physical change associated with lying or truth-telling, merely signs of emotionality.

The conventional polygraph has been widely used in criminal proceedings and employment screening. There are a variety of questioning techniques available to the polygraph examiner. Some of these, such as the relevant/irrelevant technique, common in employment screening, have not been shown to produce accurate distinctions between truthful and deceptive subjects. The control question technique, widely used in criminal investigations, often leads to the correct identification of deceptive persons but may label many truthful persons to be deceptive as well. Other techniques based on knowledge that only a guilty person would have could theoretically do a better job, but these techniques are not currently used by field polygraphers, and have not been evaluated in realistic settings. While the legal system has traditionally not admitted polygraph evidence because it is not scientifically acceptable, it is permitted where both sides of a case consent to the use.

A variety of other physiological detectors have also been developed. These include the Psychological Stress Evaluator (PSE), based on voice changes, and the Microwave Respiration Monitor, which senses changes in breathing. No adequate scientific validation of these techniques is yet available.

The potential threat to privacy posed by various "lie detectors" and the harm caused by a false determination of deception have naturally resulted in legal scrutiny of these devices. Private employers seem especially enamored of it as a screening device, and as a result, many states have managed to prohibit its use there. Some states have licensed polygraphers, and have even mandated what measures are to be used. The federal government may further limit the use of polygraph in employment.

Finally, hypnosis and drugs have been considered as methods to compel persons to tell the truth. Most research indicates that neither of these methods can get people to do something they want not to do. Guilty persons do not want to admit that their protestations of innocence are a sham, and neither hypnosis nor drugs is likely to induce them to confess. Persons who feel unusually guilty about unrelated matters may, while "under," confess to acts they did not commit. Because hypnosis is a heightened state of relaxation, it may be an effective aid to memory in persons who are voluntarily hypnotized, simply because anxiety impairs concentration and memory. If hypnosis reduces anxiety, the person may remember more. Unfortunately, because subjects are highly suggestible while hypnotized, their memories may be changed rather than improved.

One can think of any of these techniques, e.g., hypnosis and truth drugs, as methods of disrupting people's normal methods of deception. None of these truthfinding devices is even close to 100 percent effective. Indeed, most are far from that. Since the psychological set of a person toward a truthfinding technique is critical, each technique may have an impact on some people. But what has not yet been adequately tried is a combination of these types of approaches. For example, hypnosis could be combined with a drug. The result might be no better than either one of them alone, or it might be a cumulative effect, or even a geometric effect. One could also add in the techniques of either sensory or social deprivation. Under such conditions, people become extremely responsive to messages from anyone who then communicates to them. One could employ a significant period of sensory deprivation, followed by hypnosis and/or a truth drug. The effect would likely be very powerful. (All of these processes, of course, present serious legal problems when used without consent.)

Probably the most efficient and effective method would be to use a combination of physical and psychological tests, to be administered by an examiner with substantial training and experience in the study of human behavior. This would suggest that the clinical psychologist or psychiatrist who has had experience with these tests, and with forensic issues, would be the best person to examine and testify as regards the truth of testimony. Unfortunately, it is not likely that this suggestion will be instituted on any broad basis.

It is interesting to speculate about what would happen if an inexpensive device is eventually produced which validly detects deception at close to a hundred percent rate. Would there then be any need for standard courtroom and jury processes? In fact, since court and jury processes certainly do not reach this degree of certitude, would it not be an injustice to use them rather than the new and more certain method of detection? Would it be appropriate for employers (or even friends) to use the device daily to detect deception? It is probable that there would be much resistance to the use of such a machine. As seriously as we seek the truth, having it this close would not necessarily be ideal because of the level of control over people that it would permit. Perhaps, despite the Biblical promise, the whole truth would *not* set us free.

NOTES

1. Memphis Telephone Co. v. Cumberland Telephone and Telegraph Co., 231 F. 835 (6th Cir. 1916).

2. Pollack, Gross & Weinberger, Dimensions of Malingering, in *New Directions For Mental Health Services: The Mental Health Professional and The Legal System* (B. Gross & L. Weinberger eds. 1982).

3. American Psychiatric Association, *Diagnostic and Statistical Manual of Mental Disorders* 331 (3d ed. 1980).

4. Resnick, The Detection of Malingering Mental Illness, 2 *Behav. Sci. & L.* 21, 23 (1984).

5. *Id.*

6. Sierles, Correlates of Malingering, 2 *Behav. Sci. & L.* 113 (1984).

7. Resnick, *supra*, at note 4.

8. Gallucci, Prediction of Dissimulation on the MMPI in a Clinical Field Setting, 52 *J. Consulting & Clinical Psychology* 917 (1984); Gutheil, Forensic Assessment, in *Law and Mental Health: International Perspectives*, vol. 1 (D. Weisstub ed. 1986).

9. Resnick, *supra*, at note 4.

10. Jones, Malingering in an Industrial and Motor Accident Context, 14 *Austl. J. Forensic Sci.* 75 (1982).

11. R. Meyer, *The Clinician's Handbook* (1983); Newmark, The MMPI, in *Major Psychological Assessment Instruments* (C. Newmark ed. 1985).

12. See note 11, *supra*.

13. R. Colligan, D. Osborne, W. Swenson & K. Offord, *The MMPI: A Contemporary Normative Study* (1983).

14. Grow, McVaugh & Eno, Faking and the MMPI, 36 *J. Clinical Psychology* 910 (1980).

15. P. Meehl, *Clinical v. Statistical Predictions: A Theoretical Analysis and Review of the Evidence* (1954).

16. Ziskin, Malingering of Psychological Disorders, 2 *Behav. Sci. & L.* 39, 43 (1984).

17. Koss, Butcher & Hoffman, The M.M.P.I. Critical Items: How Well Do They Work?, 44 *J. Counseling & Clinical Psychology* 921 (1976).

18. Lanyon & Lutz, MMPI Discrimination of Defensive and Non-Defensive Felony Sex Offenders, 52 *J. Consulting & Clinical Psychology* 841 (1984).

19. Rogers, Towards an Empirical Model of Malingering and Deception, 2 *Behav. Sci. & L.* 93 (1984).

20. Kroger & Turmbull, Invalidity of Validity Scales: The Case of the M.M.P.I., 43 *J. Counseling & Clinical Psychology* 85 (1975).

21. Adelman & Howard, Expert Testimony or Malingering: The Admissibility of Clinical Procedures For the Detection of Deception, 2 *Behav. Sci. & L.* 5 (1984).

22. *Id.* at 16.

23. Ziegenfuss & Ziegenfuss, Psycholegal Assessment, Diagnosis and Testimony: A Bibliography, 10 *J. Psychiatry & L.* 503 (1982).

24. R. Meyer, *The Clinician's Handbook* (1983).

25. Krug, Further Evidence on 16PF-Distortion Scales, 42 *J. Personality Assessment* 513 (1978); Winder, O'Dell & Karson, New Motivational Distortion Scales for the 16PF, 39 *J. Personality Assessment* 532 (1975).

26. D. Crowne & D. Marlowe, *The Approval Motive: Studies in Evaluative Dependence* (1964).

27. Albert, Fox & Kahn, Faking Psychosis on the Rorschach: Can Expert Judges Detect Malingering?, 44 *J. Personality Assessment* 115 (1980).

28. Rogers & Cavanaugh, "Nothing but the Truth" . . . a Reexamination of Malingering, 11 *J. Psychiatry & L.* 443 (1983).

29. Rogers, Towards an Empirical Model of Malingering and Deception, 2 *Behav. Sci. & L.* 93 (1984).

30. Resnick, *supra,* note 4.

31. M. Maloney, *A Clinician's Guide to Forensic Psychological Assessment* (1985); Gutheil, *supra,* note 8.

32. Resnick, *supra,* note 4.

33. *Id.*

34. P. Ekman, *Telling Lies* (1985).

35. *Id.,* at 81.

36. Maier & Thurber, Accuracy of Judgment of Deception When Interviewers Watched, Heard or Read, 2 *Personnel Psychology* 23 (1968).

37. See notes 40–43, *infra.*

38. Burns & Kintz, Eye Contact While Lying During an Interview, 7 *Bull. Psychonomic Soc.* 87 (1976).

39. Heinveil, Deception and Pupil Size, 32 *J. Clinical Psychology* 675 (1976).

40. Ekman, *supra,* note 34.

41. Ekman, Friesen & Scherer, Body Movement and Voice Pitch in Deceptive Interactions, 16 *Semiotica* 23 (1976).

42. R. Mitchell & N. Thompson eds., *Deception: Perspectives on Human and Nonhuman Deceit* (1986); Mehrabian, Nonverbal Betrayal of Feelings, 5

J. Experimental Research in Personality 64 (1971); Schneider, & Kintz, The Effect of Lying Upon Foot and Leg Movement, 10 *Bull. Psychonomic Soc.* 451 (1977).

43. Ekman, *supra,* note 34, at 103.

44. Feldman, Jenkins & Papoola, Detection of Deception in Adults and Children Via Facial Expressions, 50 *Child Dev.* 350 (1979).

45. C. Bartol, *Psychology and American Law* (1983); Schachter, Amnesia and Crime: How Much Do We Really Know, 41 *Am. Psychologist* 286 (1986).

46. Orne, Implications of Laboratory Research for the Detection of Deception, 2 *Polygraph* 169 (1973).

47. D. Brown & E. Fromm, *Hypnotherapy and Hypnoanalysis* (1986); Greunewald, On the Nature of Multiple Personality: Comparison With Hypnosis, 32 *Int'l J. Clinical & Experimental Hypnosis* 170 (1984); Spanos, Radtke, Bertrand, Addie & Drummond, Disorganized Recall, Hypnotic Amnesia and Subjects' Faking: More Disconfirmatory Evidence, 50 *Psychological Rep.* 383 (1982).

48. T. Barber, N. Spanos & J. Chaues, *Hypnosis Imagination and Human Potentialities* (1974).

49. Spiegel & Spiegel, Uses of Hypnosis in Evaluating Malingering and Deception, 2 *Behav. Sci. & L.* 51 (1984).

50. D. Brown & E. Fromm, *Hypnotherapy and Hypnoanalysis* (1986); W. Edmonston, *The Induction of Hypnosis* (1986); Dickerson, Hypnosis: A Survey of Its Legal Impact, 11 *Sw. U. L. Rev.* 1421 (1979); Parrish, Moral Predisposition and Hypnotic Influence of "Immoral" Behavior: An Exploratory Study, 17 *Am. J. Clinical Hypnosis* 115 (1974).

51. O'Brien & Robuck, Experimentally Produced Self-Repugnant Behavior as a Function of Hypnosis and Waking Suggestion: A Pilot Study, 18 *Am. J. Clinical Hypnosis* 272 (1976).

52. Coe & Sarbin, An Experimental Demonstration of Hypnosis as Role Enactment, 71 *J. Abnormal Psychology* 404 (1966).

53. R. Udolf, *Forensic Hypnosis* (1983); Dickerson, *supra,* note 50.

54. Gravitz, Resistance in Investigative Hypnosis, 28 *Am. J. Clinical Hypnosis* 76 (1985); Sheehan & Tilden, The Consistency of Occurrences of Memory Distortion Following Hypnotic Induction, 34 *Int'l J. Clinical & Experimental Hypnosis* 122 (1986); Timm, The Effect of Forensic Hypnosis Techniques on Eyewitness Recall and Recognition, 9 *J. Police Sci. & Ad.* 188 (1981).

55. See Dickerson, *supra,* note 50.

56. Dickerson, *supra,* note 50; Edmonston, *supra,* note 50.

57. Dickerson, *supra,* note 50.

58. Comment, Hypnosis in Our Legal System: The Status of its Acceptance in the Trial Setting, 16 *Akron L. Rev.* 517 (1982–83).

59. People v. Diggs, 112 Cal. App.3d 522, 169 Cal. Rptr. 386 (1st Dist. 1980).

60. Frye v. United States, 293 F. 1013 (D.C. Cir. 1923).

61. Comment, *supra,* note 58 at 523.

62. Dickerson, *supra,* note 50; Comment, *supra,* note 58.

63. Dickerson, *supra,* note 50.

64. Ruffra, Hypnotically Induced Testimony: Should it Be Admitted?, 19 *Crim. L. Bull.* 293 (1983); Comment, Hypnosis—Should the Courts Snap Out of It?—A Closer Look at the Critical Issues, 44 *Ohio St. L. J.* 1053 (1983). See Wilson, Greene & Loftus, Beliefs About Forensic Hypnosis, 34 *Int'l J. Clinical & Experimental Hypnosis,* 110 (1986).

65. Chapman v. State, 638 P.2d 1280 (Wyo. 1982). See R. Udolf, *Forensic Hypnosis: Psychological and Legal Aspects* (1983); Harnisch, Hypnotically Refreshed Testimony: In Support of the Emerging Majority and *People v. Hughes,* 33 *Buffalo L. Rev.* 417 (1985); Note, Hypnotically Induced Testimony: Credibility versus Admissibility, 57 *Ind. L. J.* 349 (1982).

66. State v. Hurd, 86 N.J. 525, 432 A.2d 86 (1981). See Sprynczynatyk v. General Motors Corp., 711 F.2d 1112 (8th Cir. 1985) (establishing safeguards for the introduction of hypnotically enhanced testimony).

67. State ex rel. Collins v. Superior Court Moricopa County, 132 Ariz. 180, 664 P.2d 1266 (1982).

68. Frye v. United States, 293 F. 1013 (D.C. Cir. 1923). A very good statement of this position is State v. Mack, 292 N.W.2d 764 (Minn. 1980), although the court appeared to back away from the absolute position somewhat in State v. Ture, 353 N.W.2d 502 (Minn. 1984).

69. E.g., People v. Hughes, 59 N.Y.2d 523, 453 N.E.2d 484, 466 N.Y.S.2d 255 (1983); Adelman & Howard, Expert Testimony on Malingering: The Admissibility of Clinical Procedures for the Detection of Deception, 2 *Behav. Sci. & L.* 5 (1984).

70. State v. Hurd, 86 N.J. 525, 432 A.2d 86 (1981).

71. See Diamond, Inherent Problems in the Use of Pretrial Hypnosis on a Prospective Witness, 68 *Cal. L. Rev.* 315 (1980); Falk, Posthypnotic Testimony—Witness Competency and the Fulcrum of Procedural Safeguards, 57 *St. John's L. Rev.* 30 (1982–83); Note, Admissibility of Present Recollection Restored by Hypnosis, 15 *Wake Forest L. Rev.* 357 (1979); Note, The Use of Hypnosis to Refresh Memory: Invaluable Tool or Dangerous Device?, 60 *Wash. U. L. Q.* 1059 (1982).

72. Orne, The Use and Misuse of Hypnosis in Court, 27 *Int'l J. Clinical & Experimental Hypnosis* 338 (1979). See Roberts, The Abuse of Hypnosis in the Legal System, 3 *Am. J. Forensic Psychiatry* 67 (1982–83); Note, Pretrial Hypnosis and Its Effect on Witness Competency in Criminal Trials, 62 *Neb. L. Rev.* 336 (1983).

73. Heinveil, Deception and Pupil Size, 32 *J. Clinical Psychology* 675 (1976).

74. Lorenz, Criminal Confessions Under Narcosis, 31 *Wis. Med. J.* 245 (1932).

75. Redlich, Ravitz & Dession, Narcoanalysis and Truth, 107 *Am. J. Psychiatry* 586 (1951).

76. E.g., Freedman, Psychopharmacology and Psychotherapy in the Anxiety, 13 *Pharmakopsy* 279 (1980).

77. Horowitz, The Microwave Respiration Monitor, paper presented at American Psychological Association Convention (1973).

78. Mitchell & Thompson, *supra*, note 42; Ekman & Friesen, Constants Across Cultures in Face and Emotion, 17 *J. Personality & Soc. Psychology* 124 (1971).

79. Lambert, The Psychological Stress Evaluator: A Recent Development in Lie Detector Technology, 7 *U. Cal. Davis L. Rev.* 332 (1974).

80. Link, Lie Detection Through Voice Analysis, 5 *Polygraph* 163 (1976).

81. United States v. Baynes, 687 F.2d 659 (3d Cir. 1982); United States v. Williams, 583 F.2d 1194 (2d Cir. 1978), *cert. denied,* 439 U.S. 1117 (1979); United States v. McDaniel, 538 F.2d 408 (D.C. Cir. 1976); Comment, Voiceprint Identification: The Trend Toward Admissibility, 9 *New Eng. L. Rev.* 419 (1974).

82. R. Schwitzgebel & R. Schwitzgebel, *Law and Psychological Practice* (1980).

83. Hollien, Vocal Indicators of Psychological Stress, in *Forensic Psychology and Psychiatry* (C. Bahn & R. Rieber eds. 1980).

84. C. Bartol, *Psychology and American Law* 204 (1983). But see Comment, Lie Detector Evidence: New Mexico Court of Appeals Holds Voice-Stress Lie Detector Evidence Conditionally Admissible, 13 *N.M. L. Rev.* 703 (1983).

85. Link, *supra*, note 80.

86. J. Reid & F. Inbau, *Truth and Deception: The Polygraph Technique* (1966).

87. *Id.*

88. Bartol, *supra*, note 84.

89. Balloun & Holmes, Effects of Repeated Examination on the Ability to Detect Guilt With a Polygraphic Examination, 64 *J. Applied Psychology* 316 (1979); Waid & Orne, The Psychological Detection of Deception, 70 *Am. Sci.* 402 (1982).

90. Balloun & Holmes, *supra*, note 89.

91. Geddes & Newberg, Cuff Pressure Oscillations in the Measurement of Relative Blood Pressure, 14 *Psychophysiology* 198 (1977); Podlesny & Raskin, Effectiveness of Techniques and Physiological Measures in the Detection of Deception, 15 *Psychophysiology* 344 (1978).

92. H. Selye, *The Stress of Life* (1956); Lykken, Psychology and the Lie Detector Industry, 29 *Am. Psychologist* 725 (1974); Waid & Orne, *supra,* note 89.

93. D. Lykken, *A Tremor in the Blood* (1981). See Mitchell & Thompson, *supra,* note 42.

94. S. Feshbach & B. Weiner, *Personality* (1986); Saxe, Dougherty & Cross, The Validity of Polygraph Testing: Scientific Analysis and Public Controversy, 40 *Am. Psychologist* 355 (1985).

95. Axelrod, The Use of Lie Detectors by Criminal Defense Attorneys, 3 *J. Crim. Def.* 107 (1977); Waid & Orne, *supra,* note 89.

96. Waid & Orne, *supra,* note 89.

97. Bradley & Janisse, Accuracy Demonstrations, Threat and the Detection of Deception, 18 *Psychophysiology* 307 (1981).

98. Alpher & Blanton, The Accuracy of Lie Detection, 9 *L. & Psychology Rev.* 67 (1985); Gerow, Attitudes Towards the Use of the Polygraph, 6 *Polygraph* 266 (1977).

99. Balloun & Holmes, *supra,* note 89.

100. Reid & Inbau, *supra,* note 86; Podlesny & Raskin, *supra,* note 91.

101. R. Meyer, *The Clinician's Handbook* (1983); Hare, Twenty Years Experience with the Cleckley Psychopath, in *Unmasking the Psychopath* (W. Reid, D. Dorr, J. Walker & J. Bonner eds. 1986).

102. Raskin & Hare, Psychopathy and Detection of Deception in a Prison Population, 15 *Psychophysiology* 126 (1978).

103. Balloun & Holmes, *supra,* note 99.

104. R. Hare, *Psychopathy: Theory and Research* (1970); Hare, *supra,* note 101.

105. Waid & Orne, *supra,* note 89.

106. Waid, Orne & Wilson, Effects of Levels of Socialization on Eltodurmal Detection of Deception, 16 *Psychophysiology* 15 (1979).

107. Balloun & Holmes, *supra,* note 89.

108. Dawson, Physiological Detection of Deception, 17 *Psychophysiology* 8 (1980).

109. D. Lykken, *A Tremor in the Blood* (1981); Lykken, The Detection of Deception, 86 *Psychological Bull.* 47 (1979).

110. Horvath, The Effect of Selected Variables on Interpretation of Polygraphy Records, 62 *J. Applied Psychology* 127 (1977). See Lykken (1981), *supra,* note 109; Lykken (1979), *supra,* note 109.

111. Alpher & Blanton, *supra,* note 98; Reid & Inbau, *supra,* note 86.

112. Lykken (1979), *supra,* note 109.

113. Macciocchi & Meyer, unpublished paper, University of Louisville (1981).

114. Reid & Inbau, *supra,* note 86.

115. Alpher & Blanton, *supra,* note 98; Dawson, *supra,* note 108.

116. P. Ekman, *Telling Lies* (1985).

117. S. Fulkerson, chapter 2, in *A Cognitive Approach to Psychological Testing* (1974).

118. Barland & Raskin, Validity and Reliability of Polygraph Examinations of Criminal Suspects (Report No. 76-1, Dept. Justice, 1976); Horvath, *supra,* note 110.

119. Podlesny & Raskin, Effectiveness of Techniques and Physiological Measure in the Detection of Deception, 15 *Psychophysiology* 344 (1978).

120. Gustafson & Orne, Effects of Perceived Role and Role Success on the Detection of Deception, 49 *J. Applied Psychology* 412 (1965).

121. Lykken, *supra,* note 92; Lykken (1979), *supra,* note 109; Lykken, *supra,* note 93.

122. Davidson, Validity of the Guilty Knowledge Technique: The Effects

of Motivation, 52 *J. Applied Psychology* 62 (1968); Lykken, *supra,* note 92; Lykken, *supra* (1979), note 109; Lykken, *supra,* note 93.

123. Saye, Doughtery & Cross, The Validity of Polygraph Testing: Scientific Analysis and Public Controversy, 40 *Am. Psychologist* 355 (1985).

124. Hurd, Use of the Polygraph in Screening Job Applicants, 22 *Am. Bus. L. J.* 529 (1985); Sackett & Decker, Detection of Deception in the Employment Context, 32 *Pers. Psychology* 487 (1979).

125. Horvath, *supra,* note 110; Horvath & Reid, The Reliability of Polygraph Examiners Diagnosis of Truth and Deception, 62 *J. Crim. L., Criminology & Police Sci.* 276 (1971); Hunter & Ash, The Accuracy and Consistency of Polygraph Examiners Diagnosis, 1 *J. Police Sci. & Admin.* 370 (1973).

126. Orne, Implications of Laboratory Research for the Detection of Deception, 2 *Polygraph* 169 (1973).

127. Balloun & Holmes, *supra,* note 89.

128. Lykken (1979), *supra,* note 109.

129. Podlesny & Raskin, *supra,* note 91; Raskin & Podlesny, Truth and Deception: A Reply to Lykken, 86 *Psychological Bull.* 54 (1979).

130. C. Bartol, *Psychology and American Law* (1983).

131. Dawson, Physiological Detection of Deception, 17 *Psychophysiology* 8 (1980).

132. *Id.*

133. Barland & Raskin, *supra,* note 118.

134. Dawson, *supra,* note 131; Raskin, Scientific Assessment of the Accuracy of Deception: A Reply to Lykken, 15 *Psychophysiology* 143 (1978).

135. Lykken, The Detection of Deception, 86 *Psychological Bull.* 47 (1979); Lykken, The Psychopath and the Lie Detector, 15 *Psychophysiology* 137 (1978).

136. Waid & Orne, *supra,* note 89.
A wide variety of activities may help avoid detection of deception. In one study, pressing toes against the floor, biting the tongue and counting backward from 100 all worked to avoid detection of deception, and these techniques were themselves not detectable. Honts, Raskin & Kircher, Countermeasures and the Detection of Deception, paper presented to the American Psychological Association (1986).

137. Bersh, A Validation Study of Polygraph Examiner Judgments, 53 *J. Applied Psychology* 399 (1969).

138. Barland & Raskin, *supra,* note 118.

139. Horvath, *supra,* note 110.

140. Saks, Judicial Notebook, 15 *APA Monitor* 19 (1984).

141. Bradley & Janisse, Accuracy Demonstrations, Threat and the Detection of Deception, 18 *Psychophysiology* 307 (1981); Balloun & Holmes, *supra,* note 89.

142. Lykken (1979), *supra,* note 109; Ben-Shakhar, Lieblich & Bar-Hillel, An Evaluation of Polygraphers, 67 *Applied Psychology* 701 (1982).

143. Lykken, Psychology and the Lie Detector Industry, 29 *Am. Psychol-*

ogist 725 (1974); Podlesny & Raskin, Effectiveness of Techniques and Psychological Measures in the Detection of Deception, 15 *Psychophysiology* 344 (1978).

144. Szucko & Kleinmuntz, Statistical Versus Clinical Lie Detection, 36 *Am. Psychologist* 488 (1981).

145. Ben-Shakhar & Lieblich, On Statistical Detection of Deception: Comment on Szucko and Kleinmuntz, 39 *Am. Psychologist* 79 (1984).

146. Office of Technology Assessment, *Scientific Validity of Polygraph Testing* (1983). See Brooks, Polygraph Testing: Thoughts of a Skeptical Legislator, 40 *Am. Psychologist* 348 (1985); Katkin, Polygraph Testing, Psychological Research and Public Policy: An Introductory Note, 40 *Am. Psychologist* 346 (1985).

147. Saye, Doughtery & Cross, The Validity of Polygraph Testing: Scientific Analysis and Public Controversy, 40 *Am. Psychologist* 355 (1985). For the review by another government agency, see, Department of Defense, *The Accuracy and Utility of Polygraph Testing* (1984). The American Psychological Association in 1985 adopted a statement regarding polygraphs, noting that "scientific evidence is still unsatisfactory for the validity of psychophysiological indicators to infer deceptive behavior," and cautioning against the use of the tests except under very limited circumstances.

148. N. Ansley, *Quick Reference Guide to Polygraph Admissibility, Licensing Laws, and Limiting Laws* (1983). See D. Lykken, *A Tremor in the Blood* (1981); Bureau of National Affairs, *Polygraphs and Employment* (1985); Lykken, *supra,* note 143.

149. State v. Berkey Photo, 150 N. J. Super. 56 374 A.2d 1226 (1977). See Nagle, The Polygraph in Employment: Applications and Legal Considerations, 14 *Polygraph* 1 (1985); Hartsfield, Polygraphs, 36 *Labor L. J.* 817 (1985).

150. Brooks, *supra,* note 146 at 353. There have been a series of federal hearings on the use of the polygraph by employers and by government agencies. For a review of a number of these see, Office of Technology Assessment, *Scientific Validity of Polygraph Testing: A Research Review and Evaluation* (1983). See Zafran & Stickle, Polygraphs in Employment: A State Survey, 33 *Clev. St. L. Rev.* 751 (1986).

151. *Id.* See Note, National Security Directive 84: An Unjustifiably Broad Approach to Intelligence Protection, 51 *Brooklyn L. Rev.* 147 (1984).

152. Balloun & Holmes, *supra,* note 89.

153. Frye v. United States, 293 F. 1013 (D.C. Cir. 1923).

154. State v. Valdez, 91 Ariz. 274, 371 P. 2d 894 (1962).

155. Burkey, Privacy, Property and the Polygraph, 18 *Labor L. J.* 79 (1967). Some have accepted this logic. E.g., State v. Biddle, 599 S.W.2d 182 (Mo. 1980); State v. Grier, 307 N.C. 628, 300 S.E.2d 351 (1983), *later appeal,* 314 N.C. 59, 331 S.E.2d 669 (1985); Note, Stipulation Cannot Make Polygraph Results Admissible, 47 *Mo. L. Rev.* 586 (1982). See Raskin, The Polygraph in 1986: Scientific, Professional, and Legal Issues Surround-

ing Application and Acceptance of Polygraph Evidence, 1986 *Utah L. Rev.* 29.

156. Orange v. Commonwealth, 191 Va. 423, 61 S.E.2d 267 (1950).

157. People v. Houser, 85 Cal. App.2d 686, 193 P.2d 937 (1948).

158. State v. Stanislawski, 62 Wis.2d 730, 216 N.W.2d 8 (1974).

159. McMorris & Israel, 643 F.2d 458 (7th Cir. 1981).

160. State v. Dean, 103 Wis.2d 228, 307 N.W.2d 628 (1981).

161. United States v. DeBetham, 348 F.Supp. 1377 (S.D. Cal. 1972), *aff'd,* 470 F.2d 1367 (9th Cir. 1972), *cert. denied,* 412 U.S. 907 (1973).

162. D. Lykken, *A Tremor in the Blood* (1981); Lykken, The Detection of Deception, 86 *Psychological Bull.* 47 (1979); Lykken, Psychology and the Lie Detector Industry, 29 *Am. Psychologist* 725 (1974).

163. United States v. Ridling, 350 F.Supp. 90 (E.D. Mich. 1972). The Eighth Circuit expressed disapproval of this decision, United States v. Alexander, 526 F.2d 161 (8th Cir. 1975).

164. Cavoukian & Heslegrabe, The Admissibility of Polygraph Evidence in Court, 4 *L. & Hum. Behav.* 117 (1980). See Alpher & Blanton, The Accuracy of Lie Detection: Why Lie Tests Based on the Polygraph Should Not Be Admitted Into Evidence Today, 9 *L. & Psychology Rev.* 67 (1985).

165. Washington v. Texas, 388 U.S. 14 (1967).

166. Chambers v. Mississippi, 410 U.S. 284 (1972).

167. State v. Dorsey, 87 N.M. 323, 532 P.2d 912 (N.M. Ct. App.), *aff'd,* 88 N.M. 184, 539 P.2d 204 (1975). (Regarding later statute, see, Tafoya v. Baca, 103 N.M. 56, 702 P.2d 1001 [1985].)

CHAPTER 9
EYEWITNESS TESTIMONY

Eyewitness testimony is so highly regarded by the legal system that if the only witness to a crime fails to make an identification, or picks the wrong person out of a lineup, the investigation might well cease at that point. Yet witnesses usually do make an identification in a lineup. It has been estimated, depending on the country and the jurisdiction involved, that from 60 percent to 80 percent of people who are asked to view a lineup will make an identification. Unfortunately, this may be as great a tribute to social psychology as it is to good police work.

Since the justice system depends so heavily on eyewitness identification it is most important that it be accurate. Yet the value and accuracy of eyewitness identification is being increasingly challenged in the psychological and legal literature.[1] Prosecuting attorneys have indicated that they regard eyewitness identification as relatively accurate and that judges and juries appropriately emphasize its importance.[2] Defense attorneys, on the other hand, feel that eyewitness identifications are often inaccurate and are overemphasized.

Potential problems with eyewitness identification have been known for some time. During the trial of Adolf Block in 1924, 22 witnesses who made a positive and unqualified identification were proven to be in error. In *Fry v. Commonwealth,* the accused was identified by eight people, five of whom were unequivocal in their identification.[3] Though such surety is common, it is especially interesting here, as in this case the robber was wearing "big brown goggles," a peaked cap, and overalls. Even though 30 witnesses testified positively that Fry was at home in another state when the robbery occurred, he was convicted of the robbery. The case was reversed on appeal, the appellate court saying that although the prosecution witnesses were probably being honest, though mistaken (and the research would support this contention), the verdict of the jury was against the weight of the evidence.

The problem is hardly new. In 1927, Felix Frankfurter, then a law professor and later a member of the Supreme Court, wrote "What is the worth of identification testimony even when uncontradicted. The identification of strangers is proverbially untrustworthy."[4]

The interesting phenomenon is the power of any eyewitness identification, even when contradicted. Wall reports numerous cases where heavily contradicted eyewitness identification was still accepted by a jury.[5] One jury believed the comments of nine supposed eyewitnesses, many of whom openly admitted they could have been mistaken, rather than accepting the completely uncontradictory testimony of 40 respected and disinterested alibi witnesses. However, another study examined the weight which jury members gave to various types of evidence by examining audiotapes of the deliberation process. This study showed that when eyewitness testimony was available, regardless of whether it had been discredited, jury members placed greater weight on circumstantial evidence (such as money found in the accused's automobile) than they did when eyewitness testimony was unavailable.[6]

Even families and close friends have been known to frequently misidentify corpses. Worse, imposters have passed themselves off as children or spouses for years. While these are rare occurrences, they have been documented. Even trained observers such as police officers make such mistakes; this is very likely subconscious rather than malicious as the officers may badly want a conviction in a case.[7]

We will later examine how specific aspects of a lineup and related procedures can result in error, but will first examine some psychological sources of error. From a perusal of the psychological literature one could infer that virtually any eyewitness testimony may suffer from questionable accuracy. Loftus reasonably points out that this does not mean that eyewitness accounts cannot be reliable; the difficulty is that we generally do not know when and to what extent reports may be incorrect or impaired.[8] Conditions of lying aside, witnesses are probably seldom if ever aware of the inaccuracy in their own testimony.

In fact, although the U.S. judiciary employs the witness' level of confidence as one of five criteria used to assess the trustworthiness of eyewitness testimony, the relationship between witness accuracy and confidence has been found to be unreliable and often quite low.[9] The correlation depends on a number of factors, some concerning the nature of the event to be remembered, situational stress, opportunity to observe the event and persons involved, familiarity with the target; and some concerning social or forensic influences such as lineup procedures and methods of interrogation.[10] In general, it seems that the accuracy/confidence relation is more valid under conditions that are conducive to accurate identification of suspects. Under low optimal conditions, the correlation between confidence and accuracy approaches zero.

Unfortunately, jurors usually place a great deal of importance in the perceived confidence of a witness and the eyewitness' expressed certainty has been shown to greatly effect how people perceive witness credibility under cross-examination.[11] Although jurors do alter their rate of belief in eyewitness testimony depending on conditions under which a witness has viewed an event, their compensation tends to be inadequate and they are generally more overbelieving of witnesses testifying about events perceived under low optimal conditions. Witness confidence does not appear to be altered as conditions change, although their accuracy changes drastically.[12]

The law cannot lag behind scientific fact and common knowledge forever.[13] Skillful use of psychological knowledge and techniques are needed to place in context the mistakes made by "reliable eyewitnesses" and therefore make these errors less harmful to the truth finding process. A systematic use of psychological expertise may drive some eyewitness testimony out of court, or perhaps make eyewitnesses more careful of identification. Therefore it is more important to note specific physical and psychological variables relevant to assessing the performance of an eyewitness.

BASIC RESEARCH VARIABLES
IN EYEWITNESS IDENTIFICATION

Perception refers to the functioning of sensory organs; the auditory and visual senses are especially relevant. Information remembered is, of course, subject to the vagaries of any sensory defect that may be present.

Vision

Glaucoma, color blindness, near and far-sightedness are widely known and appreciated. There are many other defects which are less obvious and less commonly considered. Visual performance may be affected by dark adaptation, level of illumination, and length of exposure to the stimulus. Individuals with a history of brain damage, high blood pressure, stroke or other cerebrovascular disorders should be considered as likely candidates for visual field cuts and blind spots. Also, simple aging causes deficits in vision, as it does in all other senses.

Hearing

Obviously, even young witnesses may suffer from impaired hearing. As Lipscomb long ago noted, tests of college freshmen who have listened to a great deal of hard rock music indicate that many of them can hear no better than a person aged 65.[14] Judgments resting on hearing alone tend to be more accurate than those based on visual cues alone, while judgments resting on the two combined are, as might be expected, superior to judgments made on either alone.

Speed and Distance

Judgments of speed from the center of the visual field are less accurate than those made on the basis of peripheral vision. In applying this to the courtroom, Lezak notes that a witness who was looking directly at the subject may often provide less reliable testimony than a witness whose judgment was made from the corner of the eye.[15]

Time

Time judgments show a wide range of variation for different individuals and under different conditions, and judgment is usually accurate only up to periods of 5 or 6 seconds. For longer periods, passage of time is judged in terms of external cues which themselves vary in reliability. Furthermore, perception can be easily disrupted by drugs. Additionally, cyclic alterations of blood chemistry resulting from diseases such as diabetes and emphysema, or even from aging, affect mental efficiency and in turn compromise perception.[16]

Attention

Attention and set also affect the reliability of perception. As we view the world around us we do not register every event that we are exposed to. The intensity of a directly registered stimulus does not have a regular relationship to its actual intensity in nature.[17]

When exposed to an ambiguous stimulus, a person's perception of that situation is influenced by previous experience with similarly ambiguous stimuli. An example of this is the popular drawing of a woman which appears in many introductory psychology texts and which can be perceived as either a very elderly or a young lady. The image perceived is determined from the type of drawings (young or old ladies) that have been previously shown to the subjects. The effects of a lineup or of having a witness look at a photograph of a suspect can be seen as an analogous process. Thus, people generally see what they expect to see. The unfamiliar, the vague, or the unexpected are converted to the familiar and reorganized, or are ignored and not registered at all.[18]

Miller's early research still has relevance to this issue in terms of the limited information-processing capability from which we all suffer.[19] Substantial accuracy and clarity of perception occur only in a narrow perceptual field. At these times, peripheral material is fuzzy and frequently is not registered at all. The converse also holds, if the witness was busy trying to attend to everything, it is quite improbable that the discrete details from the scene will be recalled. Thus, a person's manner of attending as well as the expectancy can influence perception.

Experience, Learning, and Stereotype

Observers' ages, gender, and backgrounds powerfully color their perception of another person or situation. For example, young people tend to view anyone more than a quarter of a century older than themselves as "old," an observation painfully familiar to most parents. Similarly, age estimates may be artificially close to the age of observers. Frequently observers will perceive the subject in the same terms as themselves, and this effect can be powerful enough to override sex differences. Also, observers have typically been found to use terms and focus on details that are more relevant to their own sex, irrespective of the sex of the subject.

More recently, research on the effect of age of the witness tends to call for a certain level of caution concerning eyewitness testimony of elderly witnesses compared with that of young adults. Yarmey holds that elderly witnesses may be more likely to be affected by such things as unconscious transference and negative stereotypes which influence misidentification of peripheral figures, such as innocent bystanders.[20]

Courts have been cautious in dealing with children as witnesses and experimental evidence supports this caution. Several authors point out the improbability of obtaining adequate testimony from children under six and the need for lawyers to elicit information from any child with a minimal distortion, especially since children are inferior in memory performance and more susceptible to suggestion to the degree they are younger.[21]

As a general matter, women appear to be more accurate than men as eyewitnesses. However, in research studies, men were more accurate witnesses when violent crime was involved in the observation.[22] It may be that women are more familiar with certain types of information and men are more familiar with other types.

Training also affects perception and any prior training of the witness should be considered in evaluating the testimony. Although trained persons do not perceive more accurately overall, they do tend to perceive more accurately those aspects which they have been trained to look for.[23] Verines and Walker compared perceptually untrained people with police officers.[24] The police did not in toto perceive more details than the untrained sample. Yet, they did perceive more crime-related details, such as a person striking at someone else, a hand holding a gun, or a police car. Training influences perception by selectively directing it to "relevant" details.

Race

Stereotypes combined with the effects of unique life experiences represent learning variables which also may affect perceptual accuracy.[25]

Dark skin as a stereotype exerts a powerful effect on perception. Se-cord's early research indicated that there is a tendency to attribute undesirable qualities to people with darker skins. Prejudiced whites show that skin color does contaminate judgments, yet blacks also tend to attribute more positive attributes to lighter skinned people. For instance, Allport exposed his subjects to a drawing of a subway car scene in which a white man holding a razor was facing a black man. At a later followup inquiry, 50 percent of the subjects (of both races) stated that the black man had held the razor.[26]

Wall included cross-racial identification ("the witness and the per-son identified are of different racial groups") as one of 12 "danger signals" in accepting an eyewitness identification.[27] It has been as-sumed by most researchers that persons of one race are at a disad-vantage in recognizing someone of another race.[28] Reviewing the research in this area, Lindsay and Wells noted that the majority of studies present at least partial evidence in support of this belief.[29] In ten out of thirteen studies, whites were better than blacks at identi-fying other whites, and blacks were better than whites at identifying other blacks. Yet, the size of this difference was shown to be rather small. Incorrect identifications apparently occurred about 10 percent of the time for same-race identification and no more than 25 percent of the time for cross-race identification, indicating about 15 percent greater accuracy for same-race identification. However, Lindsay and Wells criticized these studies for not using the forensic paradigm (involving staged crimes), but rather having relied on the classic memory paradigm of the laboratory, where optimal and controlled viewing conditions were available.

Lindsay and Wells have presented a study along with an interesting argument which suggests that eyewitnesses of a different race from the suspect may be preferable. In their study, a theft was staged and Caucasian and Oriental witnesses were asked to identify a Caucasian thief from a photo spread. Caucasians correctly identified the thief 83 percent of the time, while Oriental eyewitnesses correctly iden-tified the thief 77 percent of the time. However, when viewing a photospread containing a picture of a person who resembled the thief (an innocent suspect) Caucasians identified this person as the thief 45 percent of the time, while Orientals identified this person only 15 percent of the time. Lindsay and Wells hold that cross-race identifi-cation is more informative about the guilt or innocence of the subject

and thus better evidence. Overall, the authors say that any relationship that exists between race and identification accuracy is weak and
inconsistent.[30] They call for research which addresses the extent to
which triers of fact differentially weight cross-race identifications.

Physical Appearance

Lezak[31] and Cook[32] demonstrate the positive effects of smiling behavior and increased "looking behavior." Physiognomic qualities,
such as the distance between the eyes, height of the forehead, or
thickness of the lips, also influence perception. Features which are in
the average range are usually perceived as "good" while extremes in
either direction tend to be associated with negative perceptions.

Personality

Work originated by Jerome Bruner and his colleagues suggests that
around 80 percent of the population functions with a synthetic style
as opposed to an analytic approach to the world.[33] In a synthetic
style, an individual attempts to integrate a broad range of perspectives
into a total impression with limited regard for detail. An analytic
style is more concerned with detail, to the exclusion of a whole or
integrated perception. Since most people are synthetic in orientation,
most eyewitnesses may be relatively poor at constructing a detailed
and accurate account of events.

Stress

Emotions also influence perceptions. States of anxiety have provided
a particular research focus. States of high anxiety particularly impair
perceptual efficiency by creating blind spots, blurring impressions,
and by increasing the likelihood of blocks and distortions.[34] Buckhout, in a study of Air Force flight crew members, found significantly
diminished accuracy in reading dials and detecting other information
signals under stress.[35] Under severe stress, the arousal of the sympathetic nervous system is likely to further distort already disrupted

perceptual performance. Furthermore, anxious people are not only more likely to interpret what they see as threatening, but are also quite capable of making implausible inferences by forming erroneous perceptions from already incomplete impressions. Of course, the legal system often relies on eyewitness testimony that depends upon the recall of events witnessed under considerable stress. Obviously, witnessing a crime or a serious accident is likely to produce considerable stress in the observer.

Sleep

Of all body states, including medication, sleeplessness is particularly prone to produce perceptual distortions. If a witness has been without sleep for 24 hours, any report is likely to be unreliable.[36] If sleeplessness persists for 36 hours or more, delusional and hallucinatory material may well occur.

Memory

As with perception, details in memory become blurred and are recombined into new syntheses. In addition, only a small percentage of material originally perceived ever remains available for recall. Once on the stand, a witness may be unable to retrieve much of what was seen and may fill in without being aware of any deception. Spontaneously retrievable information is probably as little as 10 percent and rarely more than 40 percent of the actual learned material. Also, most importantly in relation to the legal process, forgetting occurs in the first day, or even minutes, after witnessing the initial event.

Though memories can persist, they do not remain unchanged. People often modify inconsistencies by fabricating the missing details. Buckhout cites the case where a journalist fabricated the instance of a naked woman who became stuck on a newly painted toilet seat.[37] Later, when the reporter visited the locale of the alleged event, several witnesses recalled not only embellished details of the event, but also their own role in it.

Pressures created by observations that are inconsistent with their own value system may lead witnesses to reconstruct an event. This tendency was termed cognitive dissonance by Leon Festinger. Memories that represent dissonant cognitions are also less accessible, and are particularly subject to reconstruction. Hence, personality characteristics, sex, age and socioeconomic status, and personal values and attitudes can all act upon the quality of the recalled material.[38] In particular, as already noted, stress is likely to disrupt memory processing, and stress is an almost inherent quality in those real-world situations that will later require eyewitness identification.[39]

In addition, a witness may be socially pressured to remember exact details which are not actually available, and the details can be manipulated by the questioner.[40] In this manner, rather impossible positive identifications have been made. During the Sacco and Vanzetti trial, a woman testified that she could positively identify Sacco, a stranger, as he drove approximately 60 to 80 feet from her. She even described in detail such minute things as his hands, the color of his shirt, and his face, all after viewing him for a matter of seconds.[41] A poll of the jurors in that case showed that at least two were greatly impressed by her identification and others were not particularly critical.

APPLIED RESEARCH IN EYEWITNESS IDENTIFICATION

General Research

Robert Buckhout's pioneering and innovative studies are still influential today. In one research study, Buckhout staged an "assault" on the campus of the California State University at Hayward.[42] A student actor "attacked" a professor in front of 141 witnesses; another confederate of the same age was on the scene as a bystander and the entire incident was videotaped. Sworn statements were then taken from the witnesses as to what happened and descriptions of the assailant were obtained.

The results were as would now be expected: the descriptions were quite inaccurate. The duration of the attack was overestimated by almost 250 percent. The average weight of the attacker was 14 percent too high and his age underestimated by more than two years. Only the height estimate was accurate and this is probably attributable to the fact that the subject was of average height, as people often cite "facts" based on the average person when uncertain.

Buckhout then waited seven weeks and presented a set of six photographs to each witness individually under four different experimental conditions. There were two kinds of instructions: low-bias, in which witnesses were asked only if they recognized anybody in the photographs, and high-bias, in which witnesses were reminded of the attack incident. In the high-bias condition they were told that authorities had an idea who the suspect was and were asked to find the attacker in one of two arrangements of photographs, all well-lit frontal views of young men including the attacker and the bystander. In the unbiased picture spread all six portraits were neatly set out with about the same facial expression and similarly clothed. In the biased spread the attacker was shown with a distinctive laughing expression and his picture was positioned at an angle relative to the rest.

Only 40 percent in the low-bias condition identified the suspect correctly and even the professor who was "attacked" picked out an innocent man. The highest proportion of correct identifications, 61 percent, was achieved only with a combination of a biased set of photographs and biased instructions. Subsequent testings were made with the same picture spreads with groups who had not seen the original incident but who instead had the assault described to them. They were then asked to pick the most likely perpetrator, and under the biased conditions they too picked the photo of the assailant. This, and a series of other similar studies, established substantial questions about the first stage of the eyewitness identification sequence.[43]

Elizabeth Loftus logically extended this area of research by examining the role of the interrogator upon the accuracy of eyewitness reports.[44] Loftus and her colleagues showed 56 undergraduates a videotape of a classroom disruption by eight "demonstrators." The confrontation between the demonstrators and the class was noisy but nonviolent, and then ended with the demonstrators peacefully leaving the classroom. When the tape ended the student observers were divided up into two groups. The subjects in the first group were asked to fill out and hand in a questionnaire. The questions were worded in an active-aggressive manner. The second group of subjects were also given a questionnaire to complete, but here the same information was requested in a relatively mild fashion.

One week later all of the subjects were asked to answer a series of twenty questions about the disruption to see if their descriptions of the incident had changed significantly during that week. Examples of some of the questions asked were:

1. The incident could be described as quiet ——, noisy——.
2. Would you describe the incident as peaceful——, violent——?
3. Do you recall if the demonstrators were pacifist——, belligerent——?

The results indicated a significant difference in the descriptions of the incident between the two groups. The first group of subjects, who were questioned about the event in an aggressive manner, recalled the incident as being noisier, more violent, and in general, more aggressive than were the students who were subjected only to a mild interrogation. The data strongly suggest that the first investigator to interrogate a witness can substantially color the way a witness sees or reports an incident.

Other specific studies by Loftus have shown that by simply changing one word in an interrogation situation, the relevant reports by an eyewitness may be modified.[45] For example, subjects were shown films of traffic accidents and were asked, "about how fast were the cars going when they hit each other?" Other subjects were in exactly the same situation, but the words "smashed into" were substituted for "hit." When the word was "hit," the estimates of speeds in miles per hour at collision were 34.0; when the word was "smashed," the average estimate was 40.8. When queried about the incident a week later, more than twice as many subjects in the "smashed" condition (no pun intended) reported having seen broken glass, even though there was none. Other research notes that these rather small cues can significantly influence time perception, a particularly important issue where premeditation is at question.

The trend of these findings has been confirmed in a simulated courtroom setting by Lipton.[46] Eighty subjects watched a film which first depicts a peaceful scene in a Los Angeles park, after which a man is suddenly shot and robbed. They then testified in a courtroom setting about what they saw either immediately or one week later. Lipton found that while unstructured testimony tends to be quite accurate though somewhat incomplete, testimony that was structured by questions from an attorney was more complete yet less accurate. Lipton additionally found that a delay of a week between eyewitness's observation and subsequent testimony adversely affects both the quantity and the accuracy of testimony.

More recently, on the basis of the realization that eyewitness testimony is the final segment in a series of events, the effects of new information on original memories have been studied.[47] The witness originally views an incident, is questioned by the police or lawyers, may view mugshots or lineups, and finally, in court, answers questions about the incident or identifies a suspect. As a result of their research, Hall and others offer two general principles that seem to govern changes in recollection that occur between the segments in the series. For changes to occur, the subject must not notice discrepancies between an original event and the misinformation that follows, and the memory for an original event must be activated, and thus rendered accessible to the influence of post-event experiences.

Christiaansen, Sweeny and Ochalek conducted post-event information research by having subjects witness a suspect. Later they were given more information.[48] When told that the suspect had committed an act requiring strength, subjects tended to give descriptions of a heavier person. Informed that the suspect had run away, subjects gave estimates of a lighter person. Similar manipulation of old man vs. young man yielded changes in estimated age. This post-event information closely parallels information a witness may elicit from the police concerning what a suspect has done.

Photograph Identification

Another stage of the eyewitness identification is the actual identification of a suspect. The witness may be shown a photograph, or be asked to witness a lineup. (Or, worse, a showup—a presentation of the suspect alone to the eyewitnesses, with no alternative choices from which to make a decision.) Photograph identification can consist either of one picture (as in a showup) or a number of photos (as in a lineup). Photo identification is obviously the least preferable type of identification.[49]

Another problem with photo identification is the effect it can have on the later identification of a suspect. Studies have shown that witnesses are better at recognizing faces than correctly identifying where they have viewed them.[50] In some cases a process described as unconscious transference may occur where a witness recognizes someone and places him or her at the scene of a crime when actually they were familiar because they had been seen in another setting.[51] A similar process may occur when witnesses recognize someone they had formerly seen in a photo array. Gorenstein and Ellsworth found that choosing an incorrect photograph from an array adversely affected a witness' performance on a later identification task.[52] The witness tended to identify the person in the previously chosen photograph rather than the actual perpetrator of a staged crime. A photo of this person had not been provided in the original photo array. The experimenters concluded that there is both a familiarity effect (I've seen this person before) and a commitment effect (I've identified this person before) operating. Christiaansen also found that viewing mugshots before a lineup often leads people to falsely identify persons seen only in mugshots,[53] and as in some other areas of eyewitness identification, confidence in one's judgment does not appear to be highly related to accuracy.[54]

The Lineup

The lineup is also problematic. A well conducted procedure can result in reasonably accurate pretrial identification, but it is fraught with danger. The police may be suggestive to the witness, usually without clear conscious intent. Prior to an identification procedure, the officer may say, "We've got the man." Lineups occasionally make the accused obvious by the clothes worn or by other aspects of appearance. Another problem occurs when a number of witnesses to the same crime view the lineup concurrently, as the pressure on any witness who is unsure is easy to imagine. Inadvertent events can also be suggestive to a witness. For example, the suspect could have been noticed in the company of a police officer before the lineup.

Buckhout and his associates have carried out a series of research studies over the years that have consistently demonstrated the problems with lineups.[55] For example, they report research which showed a film of a purse snatching in which the face of the young black male offender was visible for only a few seconds. Six photographs, including the attacker's, were shown to one group, and although 90 percent of the people in this group tried to make an identification, only 25 percent were correct. They next showed another group six photos of innocent men, but this time the interviewer simulated what can happen in a real-world situation when a police officer believes a certain person is guilty. That is, by the interrogator's smile, one photograph was subtly emphasized. In this group 80 percent attempted an identification, and 38 percent picked the photograph that had been accompanied by the smiling behavior. Buckhout and Ellison also reported several such real-world incidents.[56]

In accord with the research of Malpass and Divine[57] and Loftus,[58] and others,[59] several recommendations can, if followed, go a long way toward making for a fair and effective lineup.

1. It should consist of at least five people.
2. Everyone should be as similar in appearance as reasonably possible, including their clothing.
3. The suspect should be allowed to have an attorney present during the lineup, and to choose where to stand.
4. Witnesses should not view the suspect (or photographs of the suspect), or speak to each other before or during the lineup.
5. Distinctive but peripheral cues, such as a gold earring in a male, should be eliminated.
6. If any person in the lineup is spoken to, a similar statement or request must be made to all.

Even if these rules are rigidly followed, subtle cues may still operate. In addition, it may be useful to caution witnesses that it is entirely possible that the real criminal is *not* in the lineup. Wells has conducted research on the concept of a relative-judgment process.[60] The term relative-judgment refers to the tendency of witnesses to choose *someone* from a lineup, usually the member who most resembles the witnesses' memory of the suspect relative to other lineup members. Wells notes that cautioning witnesses that the offender may not be present would not totally eliminate relative judgment. His research does, however, support the idea that first utilizing a lineup in which the suspect is not present provides a means of assessing a witness' proneness to relative-judgment processing.[61]

Voice Identification

While most identifications by an eyewitness are made visually, some are made by voice recognition. Though early studies[62] suggest that this procedure is in some instances very accurate, more recent studies suggest it is reasonably accurate, only under certain conditions.[63] Hammersley and Read had subjects either listen to or converse with a voice for five minutes, and then asked them to pick out the voice from among 26 saying the same test phrase.[64] They found that passive recognition of a voice was very poor. However, recognition of a conversational partner was good—good enough, they conclude, to be used effectively in a forensic situation if the witness has talked with the person for more than a few minutes.

PROCEDURES TO ENHANCE IDENTIFICATION

Some research concerning efforts to enhance witnesses' memory has been done.

Hypnosis

The use of hypnosis to enhance or induce eyewitness testimony seems to rest upon the old trace theory of memory, assuming its permanence. Judicial acceptance of hypnotic memory is now limited because of the distortions and confabulations that may occur.[65] These distortions tend to show the influence of post-event information on a reconstructive process.

A set of safeguards to prevent the improper use of hypnotically refreshed memories was established by Orne as outlined in *State v. Hurd*.[66] However, no adequate evidence exists for dramatic improvement in accurate memory as a result of hypnosis. This is particularly true when there is a lack of substantial independent corroboration and the hypnotized witness either did not recall at all or recalled only poorly a memory before the hypnosis. Smith points out the increased suggestibility of hypnotized witnesses and their tendency to agree with the interrogator, and the risk that the eyewitness will be changed rather than enhanced by hypnosis.[67]

Other Techniques

From studies of the effect of hypnosis, Smith suggests the possibility of the use of nonhypnotic procedures of memory enhancement. She outlines three nonhypnotic factors which may lead to memory improvement: (1) encouraging witnesses to accept memories with less certainty during memory retrieval; (2) restatement of already known components of the event via a guided memory procedure;[68] (3) repeated testing sessions that allow for occurrence of experimental hypermnesia.

Yuille also conducted research aimed at increasing the accuracy of witnesses without biasing.[69] He required subjects to make a written report of their observations of a staged crime, and reported an improvement in accuracy of later memory that was less susceptible to distortion from post-event suggestions. Geiselman et al. found that various cognitive retraining procedures were helpful here.[70]

As stated previously, mug shots as a type of postevent information can cause an impairment in identification. When utilizing a traditional linear search of mug files, as the number of faces increases the errors in identification increase. Researchers have attempted to utilize various witness-computer interactive search systems to reduce such effects, with good results.[71]

THE LAW AND EYEWITNESS IDENTIFICATION

In 1967, the Supreme Court established constitutional procedures governing evidence of eyewitness identification in criminal trials.[72] In *Wade v. United States* the Court made the rather sweeping statement that "the influence of improper suggestion upon identifying witnesses probably accounts for more miscarriage of justice than any other single factor. . . . perhaps it is responsible for more such errors than all the other factors combined."[73] These decisions affect only cases where police set up a pretrial confrontation between an eyewitness and the defendant. Yet, they may have a more direct bearing than more famous cases.[74] In *Wade,* the Supreme Court recognized the need for counsel in the identification procedure. *Gilbert v. California* mandated an exclusionary rule regarding testimony concerning pretrial identifications made without benefit of counsel. *Stovall v.*

Denno makes overly suggestive identifications violation of the Constitution's guarantees of due process.

These three landmark decisions were greeted as the solution to a serious problem. However, although procedures have certainly improved, in practice they have turned out to be somewhat disappointing. Loopholes have taken away a great amount of protection for the accused. In *Wade,* while the suspect is afforded the right to counsel in identification proceedings, this may take effect only late in the investigative process. Since many of the problems with lineups occur before this point, *Wade* is inadequate. *Stovall* does not take into account less obviously successful cues that research suggests could have a powerful effect.

A further exception to *Wade* and *Gilbert* occurred when the Court allowed in-court identifications, despite improper pretrial ones, if the prosecution could show by "clear and convincing" evidence that the witness' identification in court was independent from the improper identification. This exception shows a lack of appreciation of the problems that Buckhout and others note are associated with eyewitness identification. There is no way to establish that an in-court identification is based on one confrontation rather than another. Some lower courts have determined that all a witness needs to show is that there had been a good opportunity to view the accused at the time of the offense.[75] An additional problem is that *Wade* did not give counsel any specific rights at the lineup. The attorney can only observe the procedure for suppression and appellate purposes, and cannot really have a significant impact on the details of the lineup.

Along with efforts to improve pre-trial identification procedures and to strengthen safeguards protecting the accused, there have been attempts to amend the tendency of a jury to accept eyewitness testimony uncritically. For example, the current position with respect to the accuracy of eyewitness identification is derived from a 1972 U.S. Supreme Court decision, *Neil v. Biggers.*[76] The Court listed the following five factors to be considered in determining accuracy: (1) the opportunity of the witness to view the criminal at the time of the crime; (2) the witness' degree of attention; (3) the accuracy of the witness' prior description of the criminal; (4) the level of certainty demonstrated by the witness at the time of confrontation; and, (5) the length of time between the crime and the confrontation. Since 1972, lower courts appear to have adopted the *Biggers* standards of eyewitness accuracy to the point of even rejecting due-process concerns.[77]

Several studies have been conducted on the above factors. For example, the opportunity to view the assailant has been interpreted by courts to refer to the amount of time that a witness had to observe the criminal. One of the earliest and most reliable continuing findings to be documented in the psychology of eyewitness testimony is that, in general, eyewitnesses tend to overestimate the length of time of events.[78] Studies have also been conducted dealing with the degree-of-attention factor. One interesting study using staged thefts showed that the accuracy of eyewitnesses' memories for trivial, peripheral details (e.g., whether there was a window in the room where the theft occurred) were negatively correlated with their accuracy in identifying the thief from a photo lineup.[79] That is, eyewitnesses who accurately identified the thief averaged fewer correct answers on a test of peripheral details than did eyewitnesses who identified an innocent person. Thus, the normal practice of attorneys who attempt to discredit eyewitnesses for failing to notice such peripheral details ends up influencing the jury to come to invalid conclusions. As previously stated, the confidence factor has been the subject of numerous studies which indicate that eyewitness certainty is unrelated to eyewitness accuracy.[80] This is true regardless of whether or not confidence is assessed at the stage of lineup identification or at the stage of cross-examination during mock trials.[81]

Because of the recent expansion in the number of studies done in the area of eyewitness reliability and the apparent contradictory results of some of these studies, several recent reviewers have attempted to explain these various findings and account for the conflicting results.

Deffenbacher, for example, reviewed 21 studies dealing with the effects of stress on the subsequent reliability of the eyewitness' report.[82] Ten of these studies produced results suggesting that the higher the arousal level, the more accurate the eyewitness. The remaining studies suggested just the opposite. Deffenbacher attempts to account for these findings by applying the Yerkes-Dodson Law. This law assumes that for every task there is an optimum level of arousal. Levels of arousal that are either too little or too great will impair performance on that task. Deffenbacher argues that in those studies where higher arousal levels increased accuracy, the arousal level used was actually rather low considering the complexity of the task. In the studies with the opposite pattern, he argues that the arousal level was considerably higher, and so lower levels of arousal were more optimal. Although interesting, this argument has not gone without criticism.[83]

Efforts have also been made to improve the eyewitness testimony process within the trial itself. One such effort is exemplified by the Devlin Committee's report, which called for specific courtroom procedures to deal with eyewitness testimony. This committee made the following recommendations:

The trial judge should be required

   a. to direct the jury that it is not safe to convict upon eyewitness evidence unless the circumstances of the identification are exceptional or the eyewitness evidence is supported by substantial evidence of another sort; and

   b. to indicate to the jury the circumstances, if any, which they might regard as exceptional and the evidence, if any, which they might regard as supporting the identification; and

   c. if he is unable to indicate either such circumstances or such evidence, to direct the jury to return a verdict of not guilty.[84]

These responses to the hazards involved in eyewitness testimony seem like they would be helpful, although the effect of the latter recommendations is yet to be determined.

Several researchers believe that, beyond the controls on identification procedures designed to protect the accused, the law would benefit by allowing expert testimony by psychologists concerning the validity of eyewitness testimony.[85] On the other hand, some do question whether psychologists are indeed ready to offer this type of help.[86]

Courts' reaction to this proposal has been mixed. However, studies assessing the effects of expert psychological testimony on juror behaviors have been fairly positive. A study conducted by Wells, et al. sought to test the effect of psychological "advice" on subject-jurors by presenting videotaped cross-examinations of eyewitnesses to two groups of subjects.[87] One group had previously viewed a videotape of a psychologist being questioned by a "defense attorney" regarding the nature of eyewitness memory; the other group had not. The main points made by the psychologist were the possibility of faulty identification ("15 percent to 85 percent of witnesses may choose a wrong person from a lineup") and the low correlation found between eyewitness accuracy and confidence. The expert testimony served to eliminate the jurors' overbelief in eyewitness testimony and reduced their reliance on confidence as a measure of accuracy.

A similar study by Loftus presented a transcript describing a trial where the major piece of evidence was an eyewitness report.[88] Half of the subjects read an account including expert psychological testimony concerning the reliability (or unreliability) of eyewitness testimony, the other half did not. The expert psychological testimony reduced the percentage of guilty verdicts, and increased the amount of attention, and perhaps increased the scrutiny given to eyewitness testimony during jury deliberations. Some studies suggest that expert testimony concerning eyewitness reliability increases jurors' scrutiny of other evidence as well.[89]

Although expert testimony would appear to have potential for reducing the overbelief phenomenon, many judges have disallowed such testimony for a variety of reasons. Some feel that the introduction of expert testimony compromises the integrity of the jury as the finder of facts, with the right to determine for itself the validity of certain evidence.[90] Others believe the evidence is irrelevant since the issue is not the reliability of eyewitnesses generally, but of a particular witness or witnesses who have not been studied. Still others have held that expert testimony on eyewitness memory is inappropriate in that the subject is not beyond the common knowledge of jurors, violating one of the four criterion set down for use of expert testimony in *United States v. Amaral*.[91] In light of research findings concerning the overbelief of eyewitness accounts by jurors, however, it is clear that the nature of eyewitness memory is, in many cases, beyond common knowledge. Further, while some courts have held that trial judges must constantly deal with problems of identification and are therefore in no need of expert testimony in this area, at least one study indicates otherwise.[92]

Yarmey and Jones examined the general knowledge about eyewitness reliability held by potential jurors and legal professionals, as well as a group of experimental psychologists considered experts in this area.[93] The study found that the legal professionals (which included judges) did not have a significantly greater overall degree of knowledge on these matters than did the potential jurors, although both groups were significantly less informed than the sample of expert psychologists. These results suggest that judges may not be in any better position than the jurors themselves as far as being able to guide or direct the jury. One criminal court judge commented, "this questionnaire has forced me to answer questions limited to factors that would never normally occur to me." It is likely that jurors considerably overestimate the accuracy of eyewitness identification.[94]

Nonetheless, few courts have provided that a party must be permitted to introduce experts on the issue of eyewitness reliability. The few decisions that have permitted this testimony have been narrow in scope. For example, the California Supreme Court ruled that expert testimony on specific psychological factors that could have affected the accuracy of an eyewitness identification is not per se inadmissible; however, it will not be needed in an ordinary case.[95] This court stated that expert testimony will be admitted only when an identification is a key element of the prosecution's case, but is not substantially corroborated by other evidence. This court also emphasized that the expert is to testify to the "scientific record" as it is relevant to specific factors in that particular case, and to avoid expressing any personal opinions.

Another general concern expressed by judges is based on the criterion set forth in the *Amaral* decision which requires that the value of expert testimony must outweigh its prejudicial effect. This is a valid concern, as juries may be overwhelmed by expert testimony and place a disproportionate amount of weight on it. Wells, Lindsay, and Tousignant also believe that expert psychological advice should be presented early in the trial so that its benefits can be used during (rather than after) the eyewitness testimony.[96]

Twining has pointed out that what takes place in open court represents only a small part of the legal process, and he therefore recommends taking a broader perspective on the problem.[97] Only a small minority of cases ever reach the stage of being contested in court and the outcomes of contested cases are heavily influenced by events and decisions that have occurred before trial.

Upon this basis, it can be argued that psychologists could enter the legal process at a number of stages, especially during the pretrial process. For example, they may be employed as consultants to law enforcement personnel, attorneys, and judges in addition to a possible role as expert witnesses.

SUMMARY

While eyewitness identification is assumed to be among the most reliable and persuasive evidence by both laypersons and the legal system, experimental evidence suggests that it can be problematic in a number of respects. Such issues become very important since the justice system often depends so heavily on this evidence.

Eyewitness testimony has been proven to be powerful, even when directly contradicted by other reliable testimony. Also, it has been traditionally accepted in the justice system (and it has a certain face validity to most jurors) that the more confident an eyewitness is in his or her testimony, the more valid it is. However, it appears that this holds true only under certain conditions—where visibility, appearance, etc. markedly facilitate accurate identification.

A variety of factors affect the accuracy of an eyewitness identification, among them distance from and speed of the object, time of day and visibility conditions, presence of distracting events, physical appearance of the object perceived, and differences in race and age between the perceiver and the perceived. Also, time elapsed between the perception, first reporting, and present report is important, and any events that interfere with the processing of the event into long-term memory, e.g., hypnosis, are relevant.

The pioneer work of Robert Buckhout with staged "crimes" pointed out how often witnesses to the same event produced contradictory testimony, and it emphasized the role of a biased perceptual set in producing incorrect identifications. Elizabeth Loftus, another research pioneer, logically extended this area to prove that variables in the interrogation situation critically influence the eyewitness report.

While most of the research has focused on eyewitness identification, similar problems in related areas such as photograph identification, voice identification, and lineups have also been found. Since lineups are often critical to criminal investigations, the accuracy of such a procedure is critical, and is markedly enhanced if several recommendations are followed:

1. The lineup should be sufficiently large, with five being a reasonable minimum.
2. Everyone in the lineup should be as similar in appearance as reasonably possible, including clothing.
3. The suspect should be allowed to have an attorney present during the lineup, and to choose where to stand in the lineup.
4. Witnesses should not view the suspect (or photographs of the suspect), or speak to each other before or during the lineup.
5. Distinctive but peripheral cues, such as a gold earring in a male, should be eliminated.
6. If any person in the lineup is spoken to, a similar statement or request must be made to all.

Procedures such as witness-computer interactive systems for identification, nonhypnotic memory improvement exercises, and hypnosis have all been used to enhance the accuracy of eyewitness identification. There is no solid evidence, however, that hypnosis is especially helpful here. Courts are also inclined to find that the use of hypnosis taints any related testimony, though the safeguards suggested by Orne and adopted in *State v. Hurd* help to minimize the suggestibility factor.

In 1967, The Supreme Court established constitutional procedures governing eyewitness evidence in criminal trials; *Wade v. United States* recognized the need for counsel in the identification procedure, *Gilbert v. California* mandated an exclusionary rule regarding testimony about pretrial identifications made without benefit of counsel, and *Stovall v. Denno* made overly suggestive identifications a due-process violation. Unfortunately, there was some ambiguity in each decision. In *Neil v. Biggers* the Court identified five factors to serve as the basis for determining the accuracy of eyewitness identification.

A variety of research studies have been directed at these issues. The result of these studies, as well as the information described throughout this chapter, can (and, we believe, often should) be made available to the jury through the testimony of an expert witness. Courts have ordinarily limited such testimony, apparently believing it is unnecessary, or fearing that jurors will be unduly influenced, even though studies seem to suggest that they can reasonably deal with such testimony.

Given the critical nature of eyewitness testimony, and the diversity of related factors and issues, this topic should continue to be of central interest to both law and the behavioral sciences.

NOTES

1. See E. Loftus, *Eyewitness Testimony* (1979); W. Loh, *Social Research in the Judicial Process* (1985); A. Yarmey, *The Psychology of Eyewitness Testimony* (1979); Brown, Deffenbacher & Sturgill, Memory for Faces and the Circumstances of the Encounter, 62 *J. Applied Psychology* 311 (1977); Buckhout, Eyewitness Identification, 231 *Sci. Am.* 23 (1974); Einhorn & Hogarth, Confidence in Judgment: Persistence in the Illusion of Validity, 85 *Psychological Rev.* 395 (1978); Lempert, Social Sciences in Court: On "Eyewitness Experts" and Other Issues, 10 *L. & Hum. Behav.* 167 (1986); Lezak, Some Psychological Limitations on Witness Reliability, 20 *Wayne L. Rev.* 117 (1973); Loftus, Expert Testimony and the Eyewitness, in *Eyewitness Testimony: Psychological Perspectives* (G. Wells & E. Loftus eds. 1984); Loftus, Silence is Not Golden, 38 *Am. Psychologist* 564 (1983); McCloskey, Egeth & McKenna, The Experimental Psychologist in Court: The Ethics of Expert Testimony, 10 *L. & Hum. Behav.* 1 (1986); Wells & Leippe, How Do Triers of Fact Infer the Accuracy of Eyewitness Identifications? Using Memory for Peripheral Detail Can Be Misleading, 66 *J. Applied Psychology* 682 (1981); Wells & Turtle, Eyewitness Identification: The Importance of Lineup Models, 99 *Psychological Bull.* 320 (1986); Woochen, Did Your Eyes Deceive You? Expert Psychological Testimony on the Unreliability of Eyewitness Identification, 29 *Stan. L. Rev.* 969 (1977).

2. Brigham & Wolfskiel, Opinions of Attorneys and Law Enforcement Personnel on the Accuracy of Eyewitness Identification, 7 *L. & Hum. Behav.* 337 (1983). See generally, J. Marshall, *Law and Psychology in Conflict* (1966).

3. Fry v. Commonwealth, 259 Ky. 337, 82 S.W.2d 431 (1935).

4. F. Frankfurter, *The Case of Sacco & Vanzetti: A Critical Analysis for Lawyers & Laymen* (1961).

5. P. Wall, *Eyewitness Identification in Criminal Cases* (1975).

6. Saunders, Vidmar & Hewitt, Eyewitness Testimony and the Discrediting Effect, in *Evaluating Witness Evidence: Recent Psychological Research and New Perspectives,* (S. Lloyd-Bostock & B. Clifford eds. 1983).

7. Buckhout, Personal Values and Expert Testimony, 10 *L. & Hum. Behav.* 127 (1986); Wall, *supra,* note 5; Loftus, *supra,* note 1; Loftus, *Experimental Psychologist as Advocate or Impartial Educator,* 10 *L. & Hum. Behav.* 63 (1986).

8. Loftus, *supra,* note 1; *supra,* note 7.

9. See Deffenbacher, Eyewitness Accuracy and Confidence: Can We Infer a Relationship?, 4 *L. & Hum. Behav.* 243 (1980); Einhorn & Hogarth, *supra,* note 1; Leippe, Effects of Integrative Memorial and Cognitive Processes on the Correspondence of Eyewitness Accuracy and Confidence, 4 *L. & Hum. Behav.* 261 (1980); Yarmey & Jones, Is the Psychology of Eyewitness Identification a Matter of Common Sense?, in *Evaluating Eyewitness Evidence: Recent Psychological Research and New Perspectives* (S. Lloyd-Bostock & B. Clifford eds. 1983); Wells & Murray, Eyewitness Confidence, in *Eyewitness Testimony: Psychological Perspectives* (G. Wells & E. Loftus eds. 1984); Kassin, Eyewitness Identification: Retrospective Self-Awareness and the Accuracy-Confidence Correlation, 49 *J. Personality & Soc. Psychology* 878 (1985).

10. Deffenbacher, *supra,* note 9; Deffenbacher, Bothwell & Brigham, Predicting Eyewitness Identification from Confidence: The Optimality Hypothesis, paper presented to the American Psychological Association (1986); Fox & Walters, The Impact of General Versus Specific Expert Testimony and Eyewitness Confidence Upon Mock Juror Judgment, 10 *L. & Hum. Behav.* 215 (1986).

11. Wells & Murray, *supra,* note 9.

12. Lindsay, Wells & Rumpel, Can People Detect Eyewitness Identification Accuracy Within and Across Situations?, 66 *J. Applied Psychology* 78 (1981).

13. Lezak, Some Psychological Limitations on Witness Reliability, 20 *Wayne L. Rev.* 117 (1973); Loftus, *supra,* note 7.

14. Lipscomb, High Intensity Sounds in the Recreational Environment: Hazard to Young Ears, 8 *Clinical Pediatrics* 63 (1969).

15. Lezak, *supra,* note 13.

16. Buckhout, Eyewitness Identification, 231 *Scientific Am.* 23 (1974); Hayflick, Molecular Aging, in *Handbook of Clinical Gerontology* (L. Carstensen & B. Edelstein eds. 1986); Zarit & Zarit, Molar Aging, in *Handbook of Clinical Gerontology* (L. Carstensen & B. Edelstein eds. 1986).

17. Biglan, VanHasselt & Simon, Visual Impairment, in *Handbook of Development and Physical Disabilities* (V. VanHasselt, P. Strain & M. Hersen eds. 1986); Brown, Deffenbacher & Sturgill, Memory for Faces and the Circumstances of the Encounter, 62 *J. Applied Psychology* 311 (1977).

18. Biglan et al., *supra,* note 17; Lezak, *supra,* note 13.

19. Miller, The Magical Number Seven, Plus or Minus Two: Some Limits on Capacity for Processing Information, 63 *Psychological Rev.* 180 (1955).

20. Yarmey, Age as a Factor, in *Eyewitness Memory, Eyewitness Testimony: Psychological Perspectives* (G. Wells & E. Loftus eds. 1984).

21. Cohen & Harnick, The Susceptibility of Child Witnesses to Suggestion, 4 *L. & Hum. Behav.* 201 (1980); Melton, Children's Competency to Testify, 5 *L. & Hum. Behav.* 73 (1981); Thompson & Myers, Inferences and Recall At Ages Four and Seven, 56 *Child Dev.* 1134 (1985).

22. Yarmey & Kent, Eyewitness Identification by Elderly and Young Adults, 4 *L. & Hum. Behav.* 359 (1980).

23. Lezak, *supra,* note 13.

24. Verines & Walker, Policemen and the Recall of Crime Details, 81 *J. Soc. Psychology* 217 (1970).

25. Secord, Stereotyping and Favorableness in the Perception of Negro Faces, 59 *J. Abnormal & Soc. Psychology* 309 (1959).

26. Buckhout, *supra,* note 16.

27. P. Wall, *Eyewitness Identification in Criminal Cases* (1975).

28. Brigham & Barkowitz, Do They All Look Alike? Experience, Attitudes, and the Ability to Recognize Faces, 8 *J. Applied Soc. Psychology* 306 (1978).

29. Lindsay & Wells, What Do We Really Know About Cross-Race Eyewitness Identification, in *Evaluating Witness Evidence: Recent Psychological Research And New Perspectives* (S. Lloyd-Bostock & B. Clifford eds. 1983).

30. *Id.*

31. Lezak, *supra,* note 13.

32. Cook, Gaze and Mutual Gaze in Social Encounters, 65 *Am. Sci.* 328 (1977).

33. Bruner, The Course of Cognitive Growth, 19 *Am. Psychologist* 1 (1964); J. Bruner, R. Olver & P. Greenfield eds., *Studies in Cognitive Growth* (1966).

34. Foa & Kozak, Emotional Processing of Fear, 99 *Psychological Bull.* 20 (1986); Luzak, *supra,* note 13.

35. Buckhout, *supra,* note 16.

36. J. Gackenbach, *Sleeping and Dreams: A Sourcebook* (1985); Lezak, *supra,* note 13.

37. Buckhout, *supra,* note 16.

38. Lipton, On the Psychology of Eyewitness Identification, 62 *J. Applied Psychology* 90 (1977). See Brainerd, Kingma & Howe, On the Development of Forgetting, 56 *Child Dev.* 1103 (1985); Elkin & Leippe, Physiological Arousal, Dissonance and Attitude Change, 51 *J. Personality and Soc. Psychology* 55 (1986).

39. Chatterjee, The Effects of Distraction Stress on Information Processing Performance, 3 *Behaviorometric* 74 (1973).

40. Lipton, *supra,* note 38.

41. P. Wall, *Eyewitness Identification in Criminal Cases* (1975).

42. Buckhout, *supra,* note 16.

43. Brown, Deffenbacher & Sturgill, Memory for Faces and Circumstances of the Encounter, 62 *J. Applied Psychology* 311 (1977); Buckhout, *supra,* note 7; Buckhout & Ellison, The Line-Up: A Critical Look, 11 *Psychology Today* 82 (1977); Wall, *supra,* note 41.

44. Loftus, Altman & Geballe, Effects of Questioning Upon a Witness' Later Recollections, 3 *J. Police Sci. & Ad.* 162 (1975); Loftus, *supra,* note 7.

45. E. Loftus, *Eyewitness Testimony* (1979); Loftus, Expert Testimony and the Eyewitness, in *Eyewitness Testimony: Psychological Perspectives* (G. Wells & E. Loftus eds. 1984); Loftus, Silence is Not Golden, 38 *Am. Psychologist* 564 (1983).

46. Lipton, *supra,* note 38.

47. Hall, Loftus & Tousignant, Postevent Information and Changes in Recollection for a Natural Event, in *Eyewitness Testimony: Psychological Perspectives* (G. Wells & E. Loftus eds. 1984).

48. Christiansen, Sweeny & Ochalek, Influencing Eyewitness Descriptions, 7 *L. & Hum. Behav.* 59 (1983).

49. N. Sobel, *Eye-Witness Identification* (1972); Jenkins & Davies, Contamination of Facial Memory Through Exposure to Misleading Composite Pictures, 70 *J. Applied Psychology* 164 (1985).

50. Brown, Deffenbacher & Sturgill, *supra,* note 43.

51. Loftus, Impact of Expert Psychological Testimony on the Unreliability of Eyewitness Identification, 65 *J. Applied Psychology* 9 (1980).

52. Gorenstein & Ellsworth, Effect of Choosing an Incorrect Photograph on Later Identification of an Eyewitness, 65 *J. Applied Psychology* 616 (1980).

53. Christiansen, Sweeny & Ochalek, *supra,* note 48.

54. Brown, Deffenbacher & Sturgill, *supra,* note 43; Loftus (1984), *supra,* note 45.

55. Buckhout, *supra,* note 16; Buckhout & Ellison, *supra,* note 43.

56. Buckhout & Ellison, *supra,* note 43.

57. Malpas & Devine, Measuring the Fairness of Eyewitness Identification Lineups, in *Evaluating Witness Evidence: Recent Psychological Research and New Perspectives* (S. Lloyd-Bostock & B. Clifford eds. 1983); Malpass & Devine, Research on Suggestion in Lineups and Photographs, in *Eyewitness Testimony: Psychological Perspectives* (G. Wells & E. Loftus eds. 1984).

58. Loftus (1984), *supra,* note 45.

59. Wells & Turtle, Eyewitness Identification: The Importance of Lineup Models, 99 *Psychological Bull.* 320 (1986).

60. Wells, The Psychology of Lineup Identifications, 14 *J. Applied Soc. Psychology* 89 (1984).

61. *Id.* See also Lindsay, Confidence and Accuracy of Eyewitness Identification from Lineups, 10 *L. & Hum. Behav.* 229 (1986).

62. McGehee, The Reliability of the Identification of the Human Voice, 17 *J. Gen. Psychology* 249 (1937).

63. Bull & Clifford, Eyewitness Voice Recognition Accuracy, in *Eyewitness Testimony: Psychological Perspectives* (G. Wells & E. Loftus eds. 1984); Hammersley & Read, The Effect of Participation in a Conversation on Recognition and Identification of Speakers' Voices, 9 *L. & Hum. Behav.* 71 (1985).

64. Hammersely & Read, *supra,* note 63.

65. Orne, Soskis, Dinges & Orne, Hypnotically Induced Testimony, in *Eyewitness Testimony: Psychological Perspectives* (G. Wells & E. Loftus eds. 1984); Smith, Hypnotic Memory Enhancement of Witness: Does It Work?, 94 *Psychological Bull.* 387 (1983). See W. Edmonston, *The Induction of Hypnosis* (1986); Nogrady, McConkay & Perry, Enhancing Visual Memory: Trying Hypnosis, Trying Imagination, and Trying Again, 94 *J. Abnormal*

Psychology 195 (1985); Orne, Scientific Status of Refreshing Recollection by the Use of Hypnosis, 253 *J. A.M.A.* 1918 (1985).

66. State v. Hurd, 86 N.J. 525, 432 A.2d 86 (1981).

67. Smith, *supra*, note 65.

68. Malpass & Devine, *supra*, note 57.

69. Yuille, A Critical Examination of the Psychological and Practical Implications of Eyewitness Research, 4 *L. & Hum. Behav.* 335 (1980).

70. Geiselman, Fisher, MacKinnon & Holland, Eyewitness Memory Enhancement in the Police Interview, 70 *J. Applied Psychology* 401 (1985).

71. Lenorovitz & Laughery, A Witness-Computer Interactive System for Searching Mug Files, in *Eyewitness Testimony: Psychological Perspective* (G. Wells & E. Loftus eds. 1984).

72. Stovall v. Denno, 388 U.S. 293 (1967); Gilbert v. California, 388 U.S. 263 (1967); Wade v. United States, 388 U.S. 218 (1967).

73. Wade v. United States, 388 U.S. 218, 219 (1967).

74. N. Sobel, *Eyewitness Identification* (1972).

75. United States ex. rel. Phipps v. Follette, 428 F.2d, 912 (7th Cir. 1970).

76. Neil v. Biggers, 409 U.S. 188 (1972).

77. United States ex. rel. Kirby v. Sturges, 510 F.2d 397 (7th Cir. 1975); Haberstroh v. Montanye, 493 F.2d 483 (7th Cir. 1974); State v. Henderson, 285 N.C. 1, 203 S.E.2d 10 (1974).

78. Wells & Murray, What Can Psychology Say About the *Neil v. Biggers* Criteria for Judging Eyewitness Accuracy?, 68 *J. Applied Psychology* 347 (1983); Note, Admission of Expert Testimony on Eyewitness Identification, 73 *Calif. L. Rev.* 1402 (1985).

79. Wells & Leippe, How Do the Triers of Fact Infer the Accuracy of Eyewitness Identification? Using Memory for Peripheral Detail Can Be Misleading, 66 *J. Applied Psychology* 682 (1981).

80. Loftus, *supra*, note 7; Malpass & Devine, *supra*, note 57; Kassin, *supra*, note 9.

81. Wells & Murray, *supra*, note 78; Wells & Turtle, *supra*, note 59.

82. Deffenbacher, Eyewitness Accuracy and Confidence: Can We Infer a Relationship?, 4 *L. & Hum. Behav.* 243 (1980).

83. McCloskey & Egeth, What Can a Psychologist Tell a Jury?, 38 *Am. Psychologist* 550 (1983).

84. Wells & Loftus, *supra*, note 1.

85. Fishman & Loftus, Expert Psychological Testimony on Eyewitness Identification, 4 *L. & Psychology Rev.* 87 (1978); Hosch, A Comparison of Three Studies on the Influence of Expert Testimony on Jurors, 4 *L. & Hum. Behav.* 297 (1980); Loftus (1984), *supra*, note 45; Loftus (1983), *supra*, note 45; Wells, Lindsay & Tousignant, Effects of Expert Psychological Advice on Human Performance in Judging the Validity of Eyewitness Identifications, 4 *L. & Hum. Behav.* 275 (1980). Even instructions to juries on the subject might be helpful. Katzev & Wishart, The Impact of Judicial Commentary

Concerning Eyewitness Identifications on Jury Decision Making, 76 *J. Crim. L. & Criminology* 733 (1985).

86. McCloskey & Egeth, *supra,* note 83; McCloskey, Egeth & McKenna, The Experimental Psychologist in Court: The Ethics of Expert Testimony, 10 *L. & Hum. Behav.* 1 (1986).

87. Wells, Lindsay & Tousignant, *supra,* note 85. See generally Deffenbacher, Bothwell & Brigham, Predicting Eyewitness Identification from Confidence: The Optimality Hypothesis, paper presented to the American Psychological Association (1986); Fox & Walters, The Impact of General Versus Specific Expert Testimony and Eyewitness Confidence Upon Mock Juror Judgment, 10 *L. & Hum. Behav.* 215 (1986).

88. Loftus, Impact of Expert Psychological Testimony on the Unreliability of Eyewitness Identification, 65 *J. Applied Psychology* 9 (1980).

89. Hosch, *supra,* note 85.

90. A large number of decisions have refused to permit expert testimony regarding the reliability of eyewitness identification, e.g., United States v. Smith, 563 F.2d 1361 (4th Cir. 1977), *cert. denied,* 434 U.S. 1021 (1978); United States v. Fosher, 449 F. Supp. 76 (D. Mass. 1978); Pankey v. Commonwealth, 485 S.W.2d 513 (Ky. 1972). See generally Comment, Do the Eyes Have It? Psychological Testimony Regarding Eyewitness Accuracy, 38 *Baylor L. Rev.* 169 (1986).

91. United States v. Amaral, 488 F.2d. 1148 (9th cir. 1973). See also Loftus & Monahan, Trial By Data, 35 *Am. Psychologist* 270 (1980).

The criteria for permitting expert testimony on the reliability of eyewitnesses, announced in *Amaral,* are: (1) the probative value of the expert testimony must outweigh the "costs" of the testimony, including prejudicial effects, waste of court time and confusion; (2) the testimony must present information beyond the understanding of the lay people on the jury; (3) the witness presenting the evidence must be qualified as an expert; and (4) the testimony must be consistent with accepted scientific theory.

92. Comment, Unreliable Eyewitness Evidence: The Expert Psychologist and the Defense in Criminal Cases, 45 *La. L. Rev.* 721 (1985). See Johnson, Cross-Racial Identification Errors in Criminal Cases, 69 *Cornell L. Rev.* 934 (1984).

93. Yarmey & Jones, Is the Psychology of Eyewitness Identification a Matter of Common Sense?, in *Evaluating Eyewitness Evidence: Recent Psychological Research and New Perspectives* (S. Lloyd-Bostock and B. Clifford eds. 1983).

94. Brigham & Bothwell, The Ability of Prospective Jurors to Estimate the Accuracy of Eyewitness Identifications, 7 *L. & Hum. Behav.* 19 (1983). See Deffenbacher & Loftus, Do Jurors Share a Common Understanding of Eyewitness Behavior?, 6 *L. & Hum. Behav.* 15 (1982); Rahaim and Brodsky, Empirical Evidence Versus Common Sense: Juror and Lawyer Knowledge of Eyewitness Accuracy, 7 *L. & Psychology Rev.* 1 (1982).

95. People v. McDonald, 37 Cal.3d. 351, 690 P.2d. 709, 208 Cal. Rptr. 236 (1984). See State v. Chapple, 135 Ariz. 281, 660 P.2d 1208 (1983);

Holt, Expert Testimony on Eyewitness Identification: Invading the Province of the Jury?, 26 *Ariz. L. Rev.* 399 (1984); Comment, Unreliable Eyewitness Evidence: The Expert Psychologist and the Defense in Criminal Cases, 45 *La. L. Rev.* 721 (1985).

96. Wells, Lindsay & Tousignant, Effects of Expert Psychological Advice on Jurors in Judging the Validity of Eyewitness Identifications, 4 *L. & Hum. Behav.* 275 (1980).

97. Twining, Identification and Misidentification in Legal Processes: Redefining the Problem, in *Evaluating Witness Evidence: Recent Psychological Research and New Perspectives* (S. Lloyd-Bostock & B. Clifford eds. 1983).

CHAPTER 10
THE MENTAL HEALTH
PROFESSIONAL
IN THE LEGAL SYSTEM

The mental health professional may assume a number of roles within the legal system. Indeed, mental health professionals' participation has increased considerably in recent years, and it appears that it will continue to become more important in the future. In this chapter we discuss the role as expert witness, a function quite different from everyday mental health practice. Also, we explore other functions in the trial process, such as consultant for jury selection or presentation of evidence, and outside the trial process, such as provider of treatment or assessment services.

EXPERT, CONSULTANT, ADVOCATE, OR
COURT-ORDERED THERAPIST

No matter how educated or experienced an expert witness, individuals should not take more than one of the following roles in the same case: expert witness, consultant, therapist, and advocate.[1] While any one of these roles is proper for a mental health professional, accepting more than one role in the same case, or even blurring the role boundaries, is inappropriate.

Pressure to take more than one role in a single case usually comes from the mental health professional or from one of the attorneys in the case. In the extreme, the unsuspecting professional may soon be agreeing (1) to testify as an expert witness, (2) to suggest theories of defense, (3) to offer advice on how to make the client more presentable to a jury, and (4) to help select a jury.

A closer look at these roles will make clear the reasons why they should not be combined. The professional called as an expert should not "represent" or become an advocate for the party that retains him or her. As an expert witness the person is present to assist the jury with questions for which special knowledge is required. In that sense, the "client" is the court. For this reason, expert witnesses may not be paid a fee contingent on the outcome of the case. As Shapiro notes,

> whenever one testifies in court, . . . one should not consider oneself an advocate for the patient, for the defense, or for the government. One is an advocate only for one's own opinion. When the expert witness allows himself or herself to be drawn into a particular position, because of a feeling that the patient needs treatment, that the patient should be incarcerated, or that society needs to be protected, the credibility and validity of one's testimony invariably suffers.[2]

It would be an abuse of process, as well as a way of diminishing the value of their testimony, for expert witnesses to use their unique role in order to advocate anything other than professional opinions. Further, we believe that accepting these multiple roles would be unethical, though the various codes of ethics of the professions do not deal very specifically with this issue.

The role of consultant in forensic cases is also a common one. The "client," in this case, is the side that retained the consultant. Jury selection, preparation of direct and cross-examination questions, review of treatment records, procurement of appropriate expert witnesses, recommendations for packaging and sequencing of evidence, courtroom jury monitoring, and other consultant functions may be performed. However, even here the forensic consultant must maintain some distance from the advocacy role taken by the attorneys.

Keeping professional distance from the advocacy process is one of the most challenging tasks faced by the consulting forensic specialist. A client may perceive professional detachment as coldness and lack of care about the case, but that risk must be taken to ensure the best possible consulting opinions.

The role of advocate is sometimes, but rarely, taken legitimately by forensic specialists. It is important for the forensic professional to make it clear when an advocate role has been taken. Otherwise, juries or the media may mistake statements intended only to advance a cause for a reasoned, responsible professional opinion. Use of expertise to promote a particular view that is not scientifically supported generally would be considered unethical.

Of course, when mental health professionals are appointed by the court, they cannot act as consultant or advocate for any party. They can be an advocate, however, for the scientific merit of their conclusions. If they are expected to provide treatment pursuant to a court order, professionals must avoid any other role that would compromise the appearance of neutrality. In some instances it would be acceptable to serve as a "neutral" expert, but it is unlikely that any other role would be appropriate.

Thus, as an expert witness, the primary allegation is to the opinion rendered to the court; as a consultant, to provide the best information rendered to the client; and as an advocate, to promote a cause or point of view. Each of these roles has limits and, in our opinion, one should neither take more than one role per case nor blur the role boundaries. In difficult cases of this sort, consultation with a professional colleague can be especially helpful. But if doubt still persists, the old adage "If in doubt, don't" is the wisest course.[3]

THE EXPERT WITNESS

The law requires of witnesses, "some qualification which will make them worth listening to."[4] The value of expert witnesses is that they have special knowledge or understanding that the jury does not. Therefore, expert witnesses may express opinions, as well as present facts, which might not be observable by the layperson.[5]

Qualification

Determination of what qualifies someone as an expert witness appears deceptively simple, at least in the Federal Rules of Evidence. Federal Rule 702 states:

> If scientific, technical, or other specialized knowledge will assist the trier of fact to understand the evidence or determine a fact in issue, a witness qualified as an expert by knowledge, skill, experience, training,

or education, may testify thereto in the form of an opinion or otherwise.

Thus, five areas of qualification for an expert witness are: knowledge, skills, experience, training, *or* education. "In one unusual case
a person who used LSD 100 times was qualified to express his 'expert'
opinion as to the identity and effects of that drug."[6] Experience alone
here permitted the admission of "expert" testimony. These rules establish the minimum qualification for permitting someone to express
conclusions as an expert. They do not, of course, establish the weight
the jury should give to the expert's testimony.

In regard to the forensic mental health and behavior expert witness,
Maloney lists the standard basis for establishing expertise, (1) education; (2) relevant experience, including previous diagnostic and intervention work, and positions held; (3) research and publications,
including books and articles; (4) knowledge and application of scientific principles; and (5) use of specific tests, procedures, and measurements.[7]

Physicians and Mental Health Professionals as Experts

It has been only recently that most mental health professionals have
been allowed to testify as experts. Traditionally, physicians were the
only "qualified" experts in the area of mental health issues. Physicians
were considered qualified, however, to testify in all areas of medicine,
including psychiatry.

This was taken to the extreme; as in a dispute over a mental health
issue when an experienced psychologist or social worker was not allowed to testify, but the testimony of an obstetrician or proctologist
was accepted because he or she was a physician.[8] This era has passed,
and psychologists, social workers and other mental health professionals now regularly testify. The current position generally accepted
by courts is that "a lack of medical training alone cannot disqualify
a witness from testifying on a mental condition relating to a psychiatric disorder."[9] This reflects a recognition of the level of training and
knowledge of nonphysician mental health professionals and a modification of the rules of evidence concerning the minimum qualification of expert witnesses. The weight that should be given to

testimony of various experts may vary depending on the jury (or judge) and on the nature of the testimony presented. Psychologists are not generally experts about the administration of drugs; psychiatrists are similarly seldom expert in the evaluation of psychological test data. Such testimony by psychiatrists should be easily impeachable by more sophisticated and detailed cross-examination, especially for those psychiatrists who use computer-generated reports from psychological tests such as the MMPI, the Cattell 16 PF test, and the Millon tests.

The Board Certified Forensic Expert

A relatively new and positive option is the development of board certification in forensic psychology and psychiatry. Both of these board certifications came about in the late 1970s. Both boards (American Board of Forensic Psychology, which is a sub-board of the American Board of Professional Psychology, and American Board of Forensic Psychiatry) make rigorous evaluations of candidates' work samples and then examine their overall awareness of and ability to function in the forensic area. This is in addition to requiring a number of years of experience in the area before they are even able to enter into candidacy for the board. These individuals are particularly qualified for most expert witness situations in the area of mental health and human behavior. Some caution, however, is necessary about experts claiming board certification that sounds similar to these, but which is much less rigorous.

General Principles for Case Preparation

Expert witnesses can take a number of additional measures to ensure that their procedures are ethical, appropriate and expert.[10] The first set of suggestions refers to general issues with which most professionals in these areas would concern themselves; the second set deals with preparation of the specific case in forensic area, prior to testimony; and the third set of suggestions focuses on the active courtroom appearance. These suggestions are stated in terms of recommendations for mental health experts. However, they also suggest principles for attorneys and courts in preparing and using such experts.

General Recommendations

The general suggestions for taking care of cases in order to make an expert and ethical presentation are:

1. Avoid taking any case in which you do not have a reasonable degree of expertise. If you are trying to branch into a new area make sure that you receive appropriate background education and supervision. It is also appropriate to inform the client, in a nonthreatening fashion, that this is a new area for you, and the other limits they can expect from your participation.

2. Have a clear (preferably, written) contract with your client. The contract should include the issue of compensation.

3. Take meticulous notes of your encounter with the client, and of other related events. This is especially true in diagnostic cases, as these often will have implications in the forensic area or in other decision-making agreements. Make sure that when you return to the case after a lengthy period of time that you will be able to clearly reconstruct what went on between you and the client, and that you can report clearly what the client told you. Additionally, it is worthwhile to record your overall impressions at the time in which you first summarized the data in your own mind.

4. Make sure your history is a thorough one, and that you have looked at all of the potential issues that are possibly relevant.

5. Even though mental health experts who are called by one party should be an advocate for their opinions and not for that party, they still must operate within the adversary legal system. Therefore, you should not discuss the case with anyone other than the court or the party for whom you have conducted an evaluation without the knowledge or permission of the court or that party.

Case Preparation

While the above mentioned principles are important for any professional who is involved in the mental health or forensic areas, there are several other suggestions that are important to follow if you expect to eventually become directly involved in the judicial process:

1. Take some time to observe courtroom procedures in general and try to observe various mental health professionals in the role of an expert witness.
2. To the degree possible, know what questions to expect when you enter the courtroom. Make sure you have discussed with the attorney ahead of time what kinds of questions will be asked and make sure the attorney understands what type of testimony you will be providing. If at all possible, do a complete dry run of the process and ask the attorney to attempt to anticipate the type of cross-examination that will be given, and again, if possible, do a dry run of the cross-examination.
3. Make sure your opinions and inferences are clearly elaborated and thought through well before going into the courtroom.
4. Make sure that all of your data are well organized, and make the decision as to which data you want to have available when you are on the stand. Remember that whatever you have with you will be open to scrutiny by opposing counsel. And you will need to decide whether you want to have all pieces of data there with you, including your work product notes. This is also a good time to rescore any objective and projective tests to make sure you have not made a mistake, which if the opposing counsel discovers it and makes it public, it is likely to call into question your entire testimony.
5. Prepare your testimony in language that will be meaningful to the court. Remember that jurors are going to be put off by jargon, or will misunderstand, and thus not give proper weight to your testimony.
6. Be ready to give a thorough overview of all the examination devices that you will be referring to. In the courtroom you may be asked about the reliability and validity of these

devices, or how they were derived, or what they are pur-
ported to measure. You should be ready to answer this in a
crisp and efficient fashion, in a language that people will
find understandable and useful.
7. Make sure ahead of time of the role you will take in the
courtroom situation and communicate this to the attorney
who has brought you into the case.
8. When you are close to actually presenting the case in
court, make sure you can be comfortable with your knowledge of the client. This may entail bringing the client in
for visits shortly before the court testimony. In many court
cases the professional may do the evaluation years before
actually going into court. In such a case you really ought
to see the client again, if at all possible.

Courtroom Presentation

The following suggestions are useful when it actually comes to
the point of presenting testimony in the courtroom.[11]

1. Be honest in all of your testimony. If you do not know
the answer, state that, and offer to give related information that may clarify the question. But do not try to answer questions when you really do not know the answer.
Aside from the ethical issues involved, it is likely that you
will be tripped up later in the cross-examination.
2. Do not be afraid to admit limitations in your expertise or
in the data that you have available. If the cross-examining
counsel presents a relevant and accurate piece of data, acknowledge this in a firm and clear fashion. Do not avoid
this, and do not put yourself into a defensive position.
3. Acknowledge, by eye contact, the person who has requested your statement, be it the judge or one of the attorneys. But at the same time, as much as possible,
maintain eye contact with the jury.
4. Avoid the three classic errors of the expert witness: becoming too technical, too complex in discussion, or too
condescending and simplistic in approach. Any of these
approaches is likely to lose the attention of the jurors,
and may also turn them against you and the content of
your testimony.

5. Try to avoid long and repetitive explanations of your points. If at all possible, keep your responses to two or three statements. If you feel more is needed, try to point out that you cannot fully answer the question without elaborating.

6. Do not answer questions that you do not really understand. If you are uncomfortable with the wording of the question, ask to have it restated and if need be, describe your problems with the question as originally posited.

7. Listen carefully to what is asked in each question before you answer. If there is a tricky component to the question, acknowledge that and then try to deal with it in a concise fashion. If the attorney has made an innuendo that is negative to the case or to you, respond, if you feel it is appropriate, without becoming adversarial. Keep your response unemotional. This *may* be a good time to bring in a bit of humor. (However, the use of humor requires *great* caution.)

8. If you feel the attorney has misstated what you have just said, take the time to unemotionally clarify what you actually did say.

9. Be prepared to be questioned about the issue of fees. Attorneys may ask questions like, "How much are you being paid to testify for this client?" You need to correct that and state that you were asked to do an evaluation, then gave your full and honest opinion to the best of your knowledge, and that it was then up to the attorney to decide whether he or she wanted to go ahead and use you in the courtroom. Also, make sure that you state that you are not being paid for your testimony, but that you are being paid for the time that you put into this trial, no matter what testimony would emerge from that time spent. For that reason, you probably will look better to the jury if you charge by the hour rather than charging a flat fee for a case.

10. Be professional in both your dress and demeanor. Informal dress is seldom appropriate in a courtroom. Reasonably conservative attire is likely to make a more positive impression on the jury. Similarly, your demeanor should be professional and you should avoid becoming involved in any kind of tirades or acrimony.

11. Do not personalize your interactions with an attorney

who is attempting to disrupt you. If you become emotional and make any kind of personal attack you will likely taint the value of your testimony. There may be times when you do need to express some emotion in giving an opinion, but make sure the emotion is properly placed on the opinion and not as a defensive or attacking response toward the court, jury, or a cross-examining attorney.

Cross-Examination

There are a variety of ways in which the cross-examining attorney will attempt to challenge the testimony of the expert witness.

1. One target for examination is the expert's qualifications. Two questions concerning qualifications are: (a) whether a witness is sufficiently qualified to be permitted to testify as an expert, and (b) the "weight" that should be given to the expert's opinion. Presumably, the more highly qualified the expert, the greater the weight. The expert's experience in the area and the level of relevant education are common targets. More often, the critique is directed toward the specialization that is important in this particular case. For example, an expert clinical psychologist may have had little involvement in the area of neuropsychology, and yet the critical point in the case may involve a neuropsychological issue. This, of course, would appropriately reduce the credibility of the expert.
2. Another common way to challenge the expert witness is through contradictory testimony from other experts in the field. These experts may testify in the trial, or it may be via a book or article submitted as written authority. A favorite approach is to attempt to lead the witness down the garden path by asking if such-and-such a source is authoritative, etc., and then presenting the contradictory testimony from that source. So, when an expert is asked if this book or person is authoritative, it may be wise to make the disclaimer that, "Dr. _____ does write in this field. Other experts might agree with some of the things he says, but he's not my authority [or the only authority]."

3. A third technique is to attack the procedures that are used by the expert witness. A classic instance is the discovery that the expert spent a very short period of time with the client. An expert who so cavalierly comes to such an important decision should be vulnerable in the cross-examination.

   The particular tests used in an evaluation are also important. For these reasons, most mental health expert witnesses prefer to use a variety of objective psychological tests in their examination. It is debatable whether having the tests computer-scored and interpreted adds something to the testimony.

   Projective tests can of course be used in court but they are much more vulnerable to cross-examination. A sophisticated attorney may pull out an ink blot and ask for the expert's response, or a typical response, and then try to get a statement from the expert as to what is the appropriate idea here or what can be made of a response the client made. This is one of those times when it is very critical for the expert witness to communicate that the opinions and inferences have been based on a variety of data.

4. Another area in which the expert witness can be impeached is through bias. For example, by attacking the expert witness as a "hired gun," and asking a variety of questions as to how the individual has been paid. As noted elsewhere, it is probably wise for the expert to bill on an hourly basis. Also, the expert should be prepared to note that it was his or her evaluation that was paid for, not any outcome or particular slant to the testimony, and that it was stated up front, "I will make my evaluation and give you my honest opinion."

   Another aspect here is attacking the expert as a "professional witness," one who spends virtually his or her entire career in going from courtroom to courtroom. People who do a lot of forensic work are vulnerable to this characterization, and need to be ready to present a picture of how they become involved in court cases, and why they appear commonly.

   Another potential bias here is any special relationship to the client. If there is any sense in which the expert is a friend of the client, or is doing the client a "favor," the expert's testimony is likely to have little positive impact on the jury.

5. Expert witnesses are ocassionally cross-examined on their
    own personal vulnerabilities or deficiencies. Any general
    indications of instability or relevant deviation in the his-
    tory of the expert witness may be brought out if they can
    be discovered.

6. Attorneys may also try to challenge the process of deriving
    the inference or opinion. They may try to introduce at
    least apparently contradictory data or they may just simply
    ask "Isn't this alternate idea *possible*?" It is important for
    the expert witness not to become too defensive here. There
    may be a reasonable admission that other interpretations
    are possible. The expert witness needs to define that we are
    in a world of probabilities, possibly stating something to
    the effect that "Yes, almost anything is possible, but I feel
    that the bulk of evidence supports the opinion I have ren-
    dered."

7. An excellent way to impeach an expert witness is to dis-
    close prior reports or transcripts of court testimony given
    by, or publications of, the same expert which are contra-
    dictory to the present testimony. The expert should be
    aware of this possibility, and experts who publish a great
    deal are even more vulnerable. They need to be able to rea-
    sonably explain this situation, e.g., that opinions do
    change over time and that they may have made a statement
    some time before in a book with which they do not wholly
    agree now, or they need to point out why the earlier com-
    ments do not exactly apply here. Again, defensiveness is a
    bad strategy here. Openness can be the best method of
    handling this type of attack.

Expert witnesses should remember that at its root, cross-examination is a process of searching for the truth by challenging the ideas
and conclusions of the expert.[12] In this sense, it compresses into a
short time the long process of challenge to publication and research.
Cross-examination is not a perfect process of truth-finding. The presentation of information to a lay jury may in a few instances cause
obfuscation through cross-examination. Some attorneys unfairly
badger or attack witnesses. The fact that some attorneys try these
tactics, however, does not mean that they have succeeded; such tactics
often backfire. Juries probably resent the use of trickery on credible
experts. If a mental health expert has drawn reasonable conclusions

based on full examination, and has avoided exaggerated statements and emotional responses to cross-examination, the expert will have succeeded in making his or her point to the jury. We emphasize that a dry run or practice cross-examination may be helpful, particularly for the expert that has not testified before. It may also be instructional to review Ziskin, *Coping With Psychiatric and Psychological Testimony*, a very important reference in describing methods of discrediting mental health testimony.[13]

The Fraudulent Expert

There have been several instances in recent years of individuals claiming professional credentials they did not actually possess, and then fraudulently practicing that profession.[14]

In one case, two methods of falsely establishing credentials were involved. The first was to claim a real credential he did not possess, e.g., claiming he had received a Ph.D. from the University of California in addition to an M.B.A. from the "Wharton School of Finance." Neither the Wharton School of Business nor the University of California system were able to report that he received any degree. It was also discovered that he had been licensed in psychology in Illinois, but that the license had subsequently been revoked. He still was licensed in Missouri, but that license had been gained by reciprocity from Illinois. He claimed various types of licenses in several other states. It was distressing to find out that he had been allowed to sit for licensure in Kentucky; it was comforting to find out that he had failed the examination.

A second more subtle technique for establishing credentials was to claim memberships and authorships with titles that were similar to, but not the same as, the genuine journal, society, etc. For example, authorships were claimed in the *Journal of American Psychiatry* and *The Annals of Forensic Psychology*, among others. Though these may sound real, and impressive, a search by the qualified library staff could not establish the existence of these journals. Other claims throughout the vita were similarly unverifiable.

Although some cases of successful misrepresentation may be virtually undetectable, their number can be reduced by a more active and vigorous self-monitoring within the mental health professions.

Of possibly greater importance is the education of attorneys on the importance of checking the credentials of expert witnesses, especially those experts who do not have solid local reputations and affiliations that would make such misrepresentation improbable. Such cases also support the need for quality certification procedures, over and above state licensure, such as carried out by the American boards in forensic psychology and psychiatry, as well as ways of making the results of such certification visible, clear, and accessible within the legal arena and to the public.

Reforms

There are a number of problems with the present use of expert witnesses in trials. For example, some experts are distressed at the spectre of cross-examination. Others are concerned that lay juries are inadequate to choose between conflicting complex scientific opinions. Still others worry that sometimes it is impossible to find scientific experts willing to testify in court, requiring them to make decisions with inadequate information.

Many reforms have been proposed, perhaps the most interesting the use of "blue ribbon" juries to decide complex scientific questions. Under this proposal, a small panel of experts would decide complex scientific issues and those decisions would be given to the regular jury as facts. Although there currently is no apparent momentum toward adopting "blue ribbon" juries, they could in the future serve a valuable function in very complex cases.

Another plan to avoid the use of conflicting experts is that parties be prohibited from calling experts and instead the judges appoint one or more "impartial" experts to testify concerning scientific matters. There are constitutional problems with completely eliminating the right of defendants to call expert witnesses. Many courts already have, at least in theory, the ability to call "impartial" experts in appropriate cases (while parties can still call their own experts). We believe that courts should make much greater use of existing authority to appoint experts.

There is sometimes a serious problem when an expert testifies in a way that is beyond accepted scientific opinion. The jury may then be confronted with grossly conflicting opinions and be unable to determine that one has gone beyond accepted scientific authority. One proposal that meets some of the objectives of a "blue ribbon" jury is to provide one or more "impartial" experts that would be presented to the jury if any expert witnesses testified to matters that were beyond accepted scientific knowledge. As a practical matter such a reform could be quite expensive and difficult to implement except in the most serious cases. The professional certification, described earlier, of those with special training and experience in forensic sciences related to mental health is a most positive step and may in the long run be a form of credentialing that will help identify to juries those with particular expertise in forensic mental health.

OTHER ROLES IN THE LEGAL SYSTEM

Mental health experts perform many other roles in the legal system. These roles range from serving as expert witness in administrative proceedings to providing treatment pursuant to court order. Regardless of the role the mental health expert is playing, several principles discussed in the previous section are important. First, the professional should clearly understand the role he or she is playing in the legal process and what is expected in terms of professional services. Second, it is critically important that the mental health professional avoid conflicting roles. Again this ordinarily means that the professional can assume only a single role in a case. Mental health professionals seldom act as private therapists when participating in the legal system. As a result, the professional should understand the limits of confidentiality and ensure that the patient also understands these limits. The issue of compensation should be settled early.

Administrative and Other Hearings

Mental health experts may participate in such administrative hearings as workers' compensation and Social Security disability proceedings. They may also serve similar roles in private dispute-resolution mechanisms such as arbitration. These proceedings have many of the aspects of trial although they tend to be more informal and are, of course, not tried before juries. Most of the advice given in the previous sections also apply to these proceedings.

Evaluation Reports

In some instances, mental health professionals provide evaluation reports to courts. These reports are received by the court, but the mental health professional may not be required to testify. Some presentence investigations and some child disposition reports are of this nature. It is important that these reports be complete and carefully worded.

Treatment Subject to Court Order

A criminal defendant, as a condition of release, may be required to seek or continue mental health treatment. In other circumstances, such as child custody, courts may require that therapy be undertaken. In these circumstances it is essential that the mental health professional understand what is expected in terms of treatment; that is, what the court will require to be accomplished before the patient is "released" from therapy. It may make a substantial difference whether the professional is expected to continue treatment until the defendant is "cured," is unlikely to perform further antisocial acts, has received "the usual" course of therapy, or would receive no further benefit from it.

Certain forms of therapy may not be available when conducted subject to court order. For example, extremely aversive therapies may be considered cruel and unusual punishment and thereby prohibited by the Constitution. As long as treatment is not extremely intrusive, painful, or embarrassing, and yet provides potential for benefit to the patient, it is unlikely it will be considered cruel and unusual punishment. If, however, questions concerning the propriety of any therapy might be raised, the professional should inform the court of the treatment plan before it is begun.

Courts often require periodic reports of the progress of therapy. It is important that the nature of these reports be carefully identified before treatment is undertaken. In most cases, the professional should clearly inform the defendant of the obligations of the therapist to the court. This information might include the fact that the usual rules regarding confidentiality will not apply to the treatment. If there is any question concerning the confidentiality rules that will apply, these should be clearly established with the court prior to treatment.

Mental health professionals should exercise caution in the language that they use in making reports to courts (or for that matter in testifying as expert witness). In particular, language that inadvertently suggests or implies dangerousness or sexual deviation may be misinterpreted and result in very unfortunate legal decisions.[15]

Legislative Process

Mental health professionals can perform a very valuable role to society by becoming involved in the legislative process. Unfortunately, mental health professionals have not traditionally been sufficiently involved with legislative bodies in developing statutory law. Fortunately, however, this is changing. Mental health professionals should take every opportunity to act as participants in developing statutes and regulations.

SUMMARY

Mental health professionals are playing increasingly important roles in the legal system. It is thus critical that they understand what they are expected to do in this capacity and that they avoid accepting conflicting roles. As expert witnesses, professionals are obligated to give the court their best opinions concerning scientific matters and to reasonably defend those opinions. A professional may act as consultant, owing an obligation to the client to provide the best advice concerning the case. In very rare circumstances, the professional may become an advocate for the client.

In preparing to testify as experts, mental health professionals should avoid taking cases in which they do not have a reasonable degree of expertise. They should have clear contracts with their clients, take careful notes of contacts with their clients, and do thorough histories. They should also fully prepare for case presentations by understanding court procedures, carefully organizing relevant data and opinions, reviewing all of the data gathered concerning clients, and preparing for cross-examination. In testifying, they should be honest in all of their testimony, not exceed the limits of their expertise, give relatively short but precise answers to questions, listen carefully to the questions asked by the attorneys, correct attorneys that misstate what the professional has testified, and not become emotional or angry. Cross-examination may challenge an expert's qualifications, examinations, conclusions, impartiality, and prior inconsistent statements. The professional should understand that just because an attorney attacks an expert does not necessarily mean that the expert's testimony will be discredited in the eyes of the jury.

A number of reforms in the way evidence from experts is presented to courts have been suggested. These suggestions include the use of "blue ribbon juries" or "impartial" experts. It is unlikely that either of these will become the standard method of establishing points of scientific evidence. At a minimum, however, it would be useful to provide a mechanism of informing juries when expert witnesses have exceeded the bounds of reasonable scientific authority.

Mental health professionals play a number of roles other than that as expert witnesses in court. They may serve as expert witnesses in administrative hearings and in private dispute resolutions. They may also provide treatment pursuant to court direction or court order. In these circumstances the purposes and limitations on treatment should clearly be stated from the beginning. If reports of progress will periodically be made to the court, this should be described both to the professional and to the client. Rules regarding confidentiality should be especially clear to the therapist and to the client.

Regardless of the roles they play in the legal system, mental health professionals should clearly understand what the role is and the purpose to be served in that role. They must carefully avoid assuming conflicting roles. The usual rules concerning the control of therapy and confidentiality of information supplied by clients are dramatically altered as part of a legal process. Therefore, it is particularly important that the rules regarding confidentiality and authority be established with precision.

NOTES

1. Barrett, Johnson & Meyer, Expert Witness, Consultant, Advocate: One Role Is Enough, 6 *Bull. Am. Acad. Forensic Psychology* 5 (1985); Kargon, Expert Testimony in Historical Perspective, 10 *L. & Hum. Behav.* 15 (1986).

2. D. Shapiro, *Psychological Evaluation and Expert Testimony* 77–98 (1984). For a somewhat different view see Diamond, The Psychiatrist as Advocate, 1 *J. Psychiatry & L.* 5 (1973) (suggesting that it is appropriate for the expert to use the status of expert witness as the basis for advocating law reform).

3. See D. Shapiro, *Psychological Evaluation and Expert Testimony* (1984); McCloskey, Egeth & McKenna, The Experimental Psychologist in Court: The Ethics of Expert Testimony, 10 *L. & Hum. Behav.* 1 (1986); Silber, Ethical Relativity and Professional Psychology, 29 *Clinical Psychologist* 3 (1976). See also Halleck, Responsibility in Psychiatry and Law, in *Law and Mental Health: International Perspectives,* vol. 1 (D. Weisstub ed. 1986); Loftus, Experimental Psychologist as Advocate or Impartial Educator, 10 *L. & Hum. Behav.* 63 (1986); Pollack, Psychiatric Consultation for the Court, 1 *Bull. Am. Acad. Psychiatry & L.* 267 (1973); Shlensky, Psychiatric Expert Testimony and Consultation, 24 *Med. Trial Tech. Q.* 38 (1977).

4. J. Wigmore, *Evidence in Trials at Common Law* 880 (Chadburm ed. 1979).

5. *Id.* See generally Woocher, Legal Principles Governing Expert Testimony by Experimental Psychologists, 10 *L. & Hum. Behav.* 47 (1986).

6. Belli, The Expert Witness, 18 *Trial* 35, 36 (1982).

7. M. Maloney, *A Clinician's Guide to Forensic Psychological Assessments* (1985).

8. See generally Loftus, Ten Years in the Life of an Expert Witness, 10 *L. & Hum. Behav.* 241 (1986) (describing the legal and professional controversy surrounding the acceptance of psychological expert testimony); Wilk, Expert Testimony on the Rape-Trauma Syndrome, 33 *Am. U. L. Rev.* 417 (1984).

9. Jenkins v. United States, 307 F.2d 637 (D.C. Cir. 1962) (en banc). In the *Jenkins* case, amicus curial briefs were submitted by the American Psychological Association (supporting the recognition of psychologists as experts) and the American Psychiatric Association (opposing such recognition of psychologists). A summary of the briefs is presented in C. Bartol, *Psychology and American Law* 110–111 (1983).

See e.g., United States v. Riggleman, 411 F.2d 1190 (4th Cir. 1969); People v. Davis, 62 Cal.2d 791, 402 P.2d 142 (1965); Rollins v. Virginia, 207 Va. 575, 153 S.E.2d 622 (1966); Perlin, The Legal Status of the Psychologist in the Courtroom, 4 *Mental Disability L. Rep.* 194 (1980); Woocher, Legal Principles Governing Expert Testimony by Experimental Psychologists, 10 *L. & Hum. Behav.* 47 (1986). The consequences of psychological testimony are considered in Wells, Expert Psychological Testimony: Empirical and Conceptual Analyses of Effects, 10 *L. & Hum. Behav.* 83 (1986).

10. See T. Blau, *The Psychologist as Expert Witness* (1984); M. Maloney, *A Clinician's Guide to Forensic Psychological Assessments* (1985); R. Meyer, *The Clinician's Handbook* (1983); J. Monahan & L. Walker, *Social Science in Law* (1985); D. Shuman, *Psychiatric and Psychological Evidence* (1986); D. Shapiro, *Psychological Evaluation and Expert Testimony* (1984); Buckhout, Personal Values and Expert Testimony, 10 *L. & Hum. Behav.* 127 (1986).

11. See generally M. Nietzel & R. Dillehay, *Psychological Consultation in the Courtroom* (1986); R. Sadoff, *Forensic Psychiatry: A Practical Guide* (1975); Bank & Poythress, The Elements of Persuasion in Expert Testimony, 10 *J. Psychiatry & L.* 173 (1982); Brodsky, The Mental Health Professional on the Witness Stand: A Survival Guide, in *Psychology in the Legal Process* 269 (B. Sales ed. 1977); Gutheil, Forensic Assessment, in *Law and Mental Health: International Perspectives,* vol. 1 (D. Weisstub ed. 1986).

12. Bazelon, Psychiatrists and the Adversary Process, 230 *Sci. Am.* 18 (June 1974).

13. J. Ziskin, *Coping With Psychiatric and Psychological Testimony* (3d ed. 1981). This is an impressive work that reviews a variety of approaches to mental health testimony. It includes examples of direct-examination and cross-examination, clinical reports and depositions. (Two volumes plus supplements, published by Law and Psychology Press, P.O. Box 9489, Venice, CA.)

14. Johnson & Meyer, The Fraudulent Forensic Psychologist: A Need for Professional Monitoring, 5 *Bull. Am. Acad. Forensic Psychology* 16 (1984).

15. For a general discussion of mental health treatment pursuant to a court order, or related to court proceedings, see Smith & Meyer, Workings Between the Legal System and the Therapist, in *Exhibitionism: Description, Assessment, and Treatment* 311–38 (D. Cox & R. Daitzman eds. 1980). See also Gutheil, *supra,* note 11; Halleck, *supra,* note 3.

PART III

BEHAVIORAL SCIENCE
AND
SOCIAL-LEGAL POLICY

CHAPTER 11
CRIMINAL RESPONSIBILITY AND THE INSANITY DEFENSE

The criminal law functions as a statement of the minimum obligations of conduct imposed by the state upon individuals. The violation
of these norms may result in the imposition of some form of punishment. The law, however, has recognized that some people may be so
mentally ill that it is in some sense unfair or futile to hold them
accountable for their conduct. This is consistent with the traditional
fundamental concept of the criminal law, free will; one should be
punished only if one chooses freely to do wrong. The theory is that
at some point mental illness interferes with this free will to the extent
that it is impossible for a person to be able to freely choose to do
right or wrong.

The insanity defense has received considerably greater attention
than is justified in terms of the frequency of its use by criminal defendants. One observer noted that "focusing on insanity is like wor-
rying whether the violin is out of tune in the band playing on the
deck of the *Titanic*."[1] One reason for the attention to insanity is that
this defense is often associated with criminal trials that attract wide
public interest, but, more fundamentally, the insanity defense raises
basic questions about the meaning of criminal responsibility and free
will. These concepts are at the foundation of the criminal justice
system, and the insanity defense requires that we examine some of
the assumptions on which that system is built.

Although commonly thought of as a defense to homicide, the insanity defense may be used against any charge.[2] Its successful use
precludes convicting defendants of crimes, or punishing them, even
though it is clear that they did prohibited acts. The mere existence
of mental illness in a defendant does not preclude conviction of a
crime unless it profoundly affected the defendant at the time the

crime was committed. The insanity defense, then, depends on basic concepts of criminal responsibility.

CRIMINAL RESPONSIBILITY

We have noted that the concept of free or responsible choice has traditionally been the foundation of the criminal law. Generally, all adults are presumed by the law to be responsible for their criminal acts. Hence, an individual who chooses to harm another is presumed culpable. However, the Anglo-American legal tradition has developed an exception to this theory of criminal liability:

> Blameworthiness or moral guilt is necessarily based upon a free mind voluntarily choosing evil rather than good; there can be no criminality in the sense of moral shortcoming if there is no freedom of choice or normality of will capable of exercising a free choice.[3]

The Anglo-American system of jurisprudence thus recognizes two elements within a criminal act: the *actus reus,* the actual, voluntary performance of the prohibited criminal act, and the requisite ingredient of criminal culpability, the *mens rea* (evil mind) or intent. The nature of the intent required varies from crime to crime, ranging from premeditation and malice to negligence and carelessness. It is defined as an element of the offense, generally by statute. (A few minor crimes impose strict liability.) This two-part analysis has been recognized from English common law. Blackstone expressed the concept.

> To make a complete crime cognizable by human laws, there must be both a will and an act. . . . So that, to constitute a crime against human laws, there must be, first, a vicious will; and, secondly, an unlawful act, consequent upon such vicious will.[4]

This theoretical link between criminal liability and free choice has been recognized by the United States Supreme Court:

> The contention that an injury can amount to a crime only when inflicted by intention is no provincial or transient notion. It is as universal and persistent in mature systems of law as belief in freedom of the

human will and a consequent ability and duty of the normal individual to choose between good and evil.[5]

Justice Cardozo observed that all law in western civilization is "guided by a robust common sense which assumes the freedom of the will as a working hypothesis in the solution of [legal] problems."[6]

If the concept of *mens rea* assumes rational choice, persons deprived of such capacity cannot have the *mens rea* to commit a crime. As one modern expression of this principle stated, "a person is not guilty of an offense unless he acted purposely, knowingly, recklessly or negligently, as the law may require, with respect to each material element of the offense."[7]

Punishment of a criminal offender may serve society in several ways. It implements and publicizes the community's concepts of morality, it protects society from further wrongdoing through the incarceration of the offender, it serves to deter the individual punished and others from doing similar wrongs, it may in some instances be used to rehabilitate the offenders and to allow their return to society as more useful citizens, and it may express a formal social retribution.[8]

The punishment of certain of the mentally disabled may not serve society in the same ways. For instance, if some mentally disabled do not have the capacity to make rational choices or understand either the law or the nature of their actions, the threat or actual imposition of criminal punishment may not have any significant deterrent effect on their behavior.[9] The criminal justice system has released a small group of mentally disabled from any criminal liability on the ground of "insanity." Broadly defined, the legal concept of insanity (and it is important to distinguish between legal insanity and the term as used by other professions) refers to diminished mental ability at the time of the crime which dismisses an offender's criminal responsibility.[10]

HISTORICAL PERSPECTIVE

In the distant past only the act was considered, with intention counting for naught. By the time of the Mosaic law, intent was held to be of some moment, as it was also in ancient Rome.[11] The medieval period brought a return to the standard of strict accountability. Yet in the midst of this relapse, recognition of insanity as a defense was developing in uncertain form.[12] Literature of that period reflected this development. Insanity was recognized by Shakespeare's day as a condition of exculpation. In *Hamlet,* for example, Ophelia is given a Christian burial despite having committed suicide, on the grounds that she was insane at the time of her death.[13]

There is evidence that the law was still quite strict in the eighteenth century.[14] In *Arnold's Case,* in 1724, Lord Tracy was ready to recognize the defense only if the defendant "doth not know what he is doing, no more than an infant, than a brute, or a wild beast,"[15] and Coke was only slightly more liberal in his attitude toward the lunatic when he wrote that to exempt him from responsibility for crime "there must be a total deprivation of memory and understanding."[16] Other commentators, such as Blackstone, were not so strict, and by the latter half of the eighteenth century Mansfield was already talking of the legal test of an unsound mind as being based on the ignorance of the difference between right and wrong.[17] This was the state of the law when the first of the modern rules, the M'Naughten rule, was enunciated in England. That rule has played a central role in the insanity defense for more than a century.[18]

On January 20, 1843, in Middlesex, Daniel M'Naughten, attempting to assassinate the Prime Minister, mistook his target and hit Edward Drummond, who later died of the injuries. At the trial, an insanity defense instruction was given to the jury.[19] M'Naughten was found not guilty.

Because of the political nature of the crime, the House of Lords was quite concerned over the assassin's acquittal. They therefore called the judges together to answer the abstract question of law: when would an acquittal because of insanity be justified? All of the judges except one agreed on a test of criminal insanity. It was a bit more restrictive test than that given by the trial judge:

> to establish a defense on the ground of insanity, it must be clearly proved that, at the time of the committing of the act, the party accused was labouring under such a defect of reason, from disease of the mind, as not to know the nature and quality of the act he was doing; or if he did know it that he did not know he was doing what was wrong.

It was further pointed out that the right/wrong test was not the ability to tell right from wrong in the abstract, but "in respect to the very act with which he is charged."[20]

LEGAL TESTS FOR INSANITY IN THE U.S.

Several major tests for legal insanity have had significant influence in the law of the United States.

The M'Naughten Rule

The oldest, and still an influential concept, is the M'Naughten rule. It is still the test used by several states (although the American Law Institute rule described below has replaced it in a number of jurisdictions).[21] Some states have supplemented the M'Naughten rule with a variation of the "irresistible impulse" rule (described below).

The Durham Rule

As a result of dissatisfaction with the M'Naughten rule the District of Columbia Federal Court of Appeals attempted to formulate a new and improved rule in 1954 in *Durham v. United States*.[22]

The D.C. Circuit Court of Appeals, in an opinion by Judge David Bazelon, pointedly criticized the M'Naughten rule and its variations. The court felt that the rule's narrowness made it "impossible [for mental health experts] to convey to the judge and jury the full range of information material to an assessment of defendant's responsibility." The new test, known as the Durham rule, provided for the defense of insanity if the criminal act was a "product" of mental disease or defect.[23] The test was immediately hailed as a great step forward by legal scholars. Unfortunately for its proponents, the Durham rule was not greeted with such enthusiasm in the courts,[24] and it was dropped by the circuit which had formulated it, in the 1972 case of *United States v. Brawner*.[25]

Model Penal Code and Substantial Capacity

When the D.C. Circuit decided to discontinue using its Durham rule, it replaced it with the rule proposed by the American Law Institute (ALI) in the Model Penal Code.[26] The occasion for this change was the murder trial of Archie Brawner.[27]

The Model Penal Code rule is:

> A person is not responsible for criminal conduct if at the time of such conduct, as a result of mental disease or defect, he lacks substantial capacity either to appreciate the criminality [wrongfulness] of his conduct or to conform his conduct to the requirements of the law.

The rule has a caveat to it which raises a number of questions:

> The terms "mental disease or defect" do not include an abnormality manifested only by repeated criminal or otherwise anti-social conduct.[28]

The exception appears to be aimed at preventing the psychopath, sociopath, or antisocial personality from being included within the insanity defense. The reason for excluding this disease or defect is not clear if the defendant is in fact lacking the capacity to conform his conduct to the law. Furthermore, the exception requires that the abnormality be "manifested *only* by . . . antisocial conduct." Since the psychopath (or anyone with any other serious "abnormality" for that matter) is likely to demonstrate *some* manifestation of that abnormality other than repeated antisocial conduct, there is a question of whether the "antisocial" exception can ever technically apply to anyone. Despite these questions, the exception has generally been accepted with the rule. There is, however, some reluctance to fully embrace the caveat. The D.C. Circuit, for example, adopted it as a rule of application by the judge to avoid miscarriage of justice, but not for inclusion in the instructions to the jury.[29]

The majority of jurisdictions in the United States adopted a combined cognitive (know right from wrong) and volitional (unable to conform conduct to the law) tests in substantially the language of the ALI test.[30] Following the insanity acquittal of John Hinckley, there has been a significant move to narrow the defense by eliminating the volitional test.

States have been given considerable freedom in adopting insanity tests. Since 1897, the Supreme Court has largely refused to speak on the subject of insanity. Although the Court suggested in 1895 that the insanity defense is important in ensuring fair criminal trials,[31] in recent years the Court has adamantly refused to prescribe or proscribe any legal tests of insanity used in the federal or the state courts.[32]

Irresistible Impulse

Some jurisdictions provide a variation of the "irresistible impulse" insanity defense as a supplement to the M'Naughten defense. This broadens the general insanity defense so that a person "may avoid criminal responsibility even though he is capable of distinguishing between right and wrong, and is fully aware of the nature and quality of his act provided he establishes he was unable to refrain from acting."[33] An irresistible impulse is generally defined as a behavioral response that is so strong that the person could not resist it by will or reason. It is not necessarily indicative of psychosis or "insanity."[34] The "irresistible impulse" is a "volitional" test of insanity.

Exoneration for an irresistible impulse was recognized as early as 1872, but the application to criminal law was only by way of dictum. In a suit for recovery on an insurance contract where the insured had committed suicide the Supreme Court found for the plaintiff. Justice Hunt observed that if the case had been a criminal case, the defendant "would have been entitled to a charge, that upon proof of the facts assumed, the jury must acquit him."[35] The ALI test has an irresistible impulse test built into it in the "unable to conform his conduct to the requirements of the law" section.

GUILTY BUT MENTALLY ILL

Growing dissatisfaction with the current insanity rules, and the popular belief, contradicted by substantial data, that many dangerous criminals escape conviction because of lenient insanity defense rules, have led to a search for alternatives to the insanity defense. One proposal is that the defense be supplemented or even replaced by a "guilty but mentally ill" rule. Under this approach mentally ill defendants are convicted of a crime, but so long as they remain mentally ill they serve the sentence in a mental health facility. When they are no longer mentally ill, they may serve the remainder of their sentences in prison.

DIMINISHED CAPACITY

Although not technically an insanity defense, most states in some cases permit defendants to present evidence that they did not have the mental capacity to form the specific belief, intent or state of mind that is required for the conviction of a crime.[36] This "diminished capacity" defense may be used even when the insanity defense could not be used (e.g., because the defendant had sufficient mental capacity to distinguish right from wrong). Diminished capacity might be used when a defendant could tell right from wrong, but did not have sufficient mental ability to premeditate or plan a murder. Under such circumstances the defendant might be convicted of a lesser offense.

CRITICISMS OF THE INSANITY DEFENSE

The learned and popular literature concerning the insanity defense includes a considerable amount of negative commentary. The criticisms relate to the following: the popular feeling that the defense is widely and successfully misused; the concepts of insanity and mental illness; the difficulty in obtaining dependable expert evidence on which courts may base decisions; the absence of any clear understanding of the meaning of the insanity defense; and the practical effect of the defense for the defendant.

Criticism of the insanity defense intensified following John Hinckley Jr.'s successful use of the defense against charges of shooting President Reagan and others. The response was similar to that following the original M'Naughten verdict. Both the public outcry and the proposed legislation following the Hinckley verdict reflect misconceptions about the insanity defense.

One popular fallacy deserves special attention. It is widely believed that a large percentage of criminals are acquitted each year because they plead insanity. The defense is actually rarely used and even more rarely successful. Of two million Americans tried for misdemeanors and felonies in 1978, only 1625 were adjudged insane. Comparable figures are found in studies conducted in Illinois and Wyoming. The extent of the confusion regarding the insanity defense was illustrated in Wyoming, where college students estimated that 37 percent of those indicted for a felony pleaded the insanity defense and of those, 44 percent of those were successful.[37] In fact only 0.5 percent pleaded insanity in Wyoming that year and only one plea was successful. Given the base rates of serious mental disturbances it is surprising that the figures are not higher. It appears that the few highly publicized cases in which the defendant was acquitted have distorted the public's awareness of the insanity defense's success rate. Moreover, most cases involving this defense receive considerable media attention whether or not the defense is successful. Interestingly, other critics claim that the defense is too difficult and restrictive and is therefore unavailable to some defendants.

The insanity defense undoubtedly has a somewhat greater impact than is indicated by the number of not guilty by reason of insanity verdicts. A few criminal defendants may not be brought to trial because the prosecution believes an insanity plea would succeed. In other cases the insanity defense may play a role in plea bargaining between the state and the defendant.

Others have contended that the insanity defense may not be beneficial to a defendant. Edward Wise, for example, develops the argument that the M'Naughten rule is only a special case of general defense, i.e., a justifiable failure to be aware that one is breaking the law. Hence, its unique function is not to exempt from punishment, but to ensure that the mentally ill are indefinitely restrained.[38] The successful use of the insanity defense does not, of course, actually guarantee that the defendant will be indefinitely restrained. Many defendants found not guilty by reason of insanity do spend considerable time in a mental institution.

Regardless of whether one attributes humane or self-serving motives to society's use of the insanity defense, it is currently difficult to defend the proposition that the successful insanity defense is always beneficial to the defendant. It is highly probable that the defendant will be placed in a mental hospital and the large majority remain there for years.[39] Considering the inadequate care and treatment in some state mental hospitals and the increased mental health services in prisons, the availability of professional assistance may not be markedly different between the two systems. Moreover, it is dubious whether the avoidance of the criminal stigma is worth the stigma of being classed as insane. Of course, in capital cases, the defense may serve to avoid the death penalty.

One of the most fundamental criticisms is aimed at the concept of insanity itself. Even the idea that mental "illness" or "disease" is the source of abnormal behavior has come under attack.[40]

> The concept of illness, whether bodily or mental, implies deviation from some clearly defined norm. . . . What is the norm deviation from which is regarded as mental illness? This question cannot be answered easily. But whatever this norm might be, we can be certain of only one thing: namely that it is a norm that must be stated in terms of psychosocial, ethical and legal concepts.[41]

Critics of the mental disease concept have argued that the classification of mental illness is somewhat arbitrarily based upon a behavior which those in authority find discomforting or unusual.[42] The claim that mental illness is a myth is, of course, decidedly a minority position. There is, however, broad disagreement within the mental health professions about the nature and classification of many forms of mental illness. Even when there is agreement on the theoretical nature of mental illness, professionals may disagree about the nature or existence of the illness in a specific individual. There are two major sources of substantial variance in a mental illness classification or decision: The observed behavior and the judgment of the observer.

The subjective nature of "insanity" substantially reduces the reliability of expert testimony on which the insanity defense depends. A variety of other factors make it difficult to obtain dependable expert evidence. For example, the expert is required to determine what the mental state of the defendant was at the time the crime was committed. This determination often must be made weeks or months after the crime, an extremely difficult assignment for the behavioral scientist. It is often difficult to obtain agreement among mental health professionals regarding the mental state or condition of a person at the time he is examined; the difficulties in obtaining consistent and clear assessments of a condition which may have existed at some time in the past are considerably greater.[43]

Another difficulty is that mental health experts vary with respect to the behaviors which are observed, the test results which are obtained, the theories which are held, and the behaviors which are deemed crucial in the decision. It is readily apparent that until these sources of variance are reduced, and until additional clarification is made as to the nature of the testing and judgmental processes, there will be large degrees of disagreement as to whether individuals are mentally disabled.

The selection process for insanity defenses makes the psychological judgments even more difficult. Experts are not dealing only with the extremes of "normal" and "abnormal" behavior. Often symptoms are borderline, because the obviously insane would not generally stand trial, and those who did not have some history of bizarre or peculiar behavior would not be likely to be successful with an insanity defense.

Another problem is that no highly reliable methods have been developed for detecting the faking of symptoms, and the possibility of such malingering may be a central concern in the insanity trial. A related problem involves feedback. With the present relationship between the expert witnesses and institutional systems, examiners often do not receive any feedback on the adequacy of their decision, and therefore it is doubtful that they will adjust or improve their predictions.

The issue of whether the individual was responsible for his criminal actions is a dilemma for the expert witness. Although the expert may not be asked whether a defendant was legally insane, he may well be asked whether the defendant possessed the mental capacity to conform his conduct to the law or to know right from wrong. Halleck asserts:

> To be useful to the courts in an insanity trial the psychiatrist must make a judgment as to the responsibility of an offender for a particular act. Yet, there is no body of fact or theory in the behavioral sciences which offers the psychiatrist any guidance in this task. Rather, assignment of responsibility primarily involves philosophical considerations. In this area every citizen has an opinion and it is unlikely that the psychiatrist's training or experience makes him more of an expert.[44]

Halleck believes that most of the disagreements between experts are over these philosophical issues and not over the nature of disorder or the choice of type of treatment. It is undoubtedly true that experts' general political and social orientations play important roles in their assignment of responsibility.

The criteria of right/wrong, or knowing or appreciating the nature or criminality of the act has been equally confusing to expert witnesses. One complaint has been that social conventions and unsupported theoretical belief systems, and not scientific data, are the basis for evaluating the degree of "knowing." Thus, in making this value judgment the expert is of little value.[45] Others have stated that practically without exception the mentally ill understand the moral and legal implications of their crimes,[46] and therefore the rule has no real function. In any case, it has been clear from the outset that the "knowing" tests of the ALI rule and M'Naughten are weak because they force a total emphasis on cognitive issues. The "irresistible impulse" concept or the ALI's "capacity to conform one's conduct" test (volitional tests) are efforts to avoid the cognitive emphasis, but they are not easily understood and applied. Again, these concepts are not subject to clear definition and scientific application, once more leaving the potential for value judgments to play a substantial role in the evaluation. As we shall see, the volitional test has recently been criticized as being so unclear as to be unworkable in practice.

At trial there is often conflicting testimony about a defendant's mental condition. The great uncertainty about the meaning of insanity, the absence of any clear and fully accepted mental health theory regarding insanity (and "free will"), the difficulty of performing mental-health assessments of criminal defendants which provide a clear basis for a decision regarding insanity, and the fact that professionals must determine what the mental condition of the defendant was long before the examination took place all contribute to differences of opinion among experts.

This conflict is bewildering to laypeople and sometimes leaves the impression that an attorney can find an expert to say just about anything. In fact an attorney may have a client examined by a number of experts until one is found who will testify to what the client needs,[47] and a prosecutor may talk to a number of experts to find one who is likely to be philosophically "right" for the prosecution's case. There are "hired gun" experts who will essentially mold their testimony to whatever the party hiring them needs. The conflicting testimony from experts undoubtedly contributes to the cynicism of much of the public regarding the insanity defense, the legal system, and the mental health profession.

CRIMINAL RESPONSIBILITY, FREE WILL, AND BEHAVIORAL SCIENCE

The problems described above often result from an inability of the law, despite repeated efforts, to clearly and precisely define insanity and the related concepts. The absence of clarity regarding basic concepts in the insanity defense results from more than simple sloppiness in defining terms; it also results from a fundamental confusion regarding some of the foundations of criminal law. There is no longer a clear understanding of what it means for someone who has committed an act to be "blameworthy" or "responsible" for his conduct. Behaviorists may view the actions of all people as being determined by environments and heredity. The concept of "free will," on which the criminal law was founded, has little meaning in such a formulation—all impulses on which a person acts are seen as "irresistible" in the sense that the heredity and environment of the person produce an action.[48]

Punishing some people because they voluntarily "chose" to commit a crime and finding others not guilty by reason of insanity because they did not have free will is, in the behaviorist's view, drawing a distinction that does not exist. The criminal law still depends essentially on the concept of free will. In such a construct, the insanity defense makes sense—when people are so afflicted that they are no longer free agents it is irrational to punish them for wrongly exercising a free will they no longer possess. Experts who do not depend on the notion of free will will continue to have problems providing useful advice and probative evidence to a system grounded in this concept.

One justification for making the mentally disabled a special exception is said to be that they lack the capacity for self-control. At best, this is unfortunate wording, since they clearly do not lack the capacity to learn the necessary discriminations in order to comply with the laws. The effectiveness of rewards and punishments in training the mentally disabled is reflected in the recent work with behavior modification programs in mental institutions. Obviously, they tend to learn more slowly than most people and to respond to different reinforcers. In some cases they may not be able to develop the same level of comprehension as to the "whys" of laws that normals can, but still the discriminations required by most laws are certainly not beyond their learning capacity. Hospitalized psychotics can manipulate the amount and type of information they provide to caretakers, and recognize that this manipulation has value in the decisions concerning their situation.

The ultimate theoretical justification for excluding only the "insane" from the punishment process is not clear and accounts for much of the difficulty in formulating a precise and theoretically clearly defensible insanity defense. In truth, however, rationalization of the insanity defense may depend upon, and have to wait for, a reexamination of the free will basis of the criminal law.

STUDIES OF THE INSANITY DEFENSE

The insanity defense is an area of law to be extensively investigated in major research projects. Simon[49] conducted mock trials using transcripts from two trials which were reduced to 60–90 minutes. Jurors were selected in the usual manner (they were not volunteers) and they were told by the judge that this research on the judicial process was of great interest to him. Although every attempt was made to be realistic, even these minor changes could conceivably have led to their findings being different from those which occur during an actual trial.

The effect of three different insanity instructions was investigated. The success of the insanity defense was markedly better in one trial than the other one, but the different instructions had surprisingly little effect. However, as expected, the M'Naughten rule led to slightly fewer not guilty decisions than either the Durham rule or the juries receiving no instructions at all for evaluating insanity; these latter two groups were quite similar in this result. On the basis of expert advice, model testimony was constructed. In comparison to the typical testimony, this model was more detailed, particularly about the defendant's background, and was more in layman's language. Again, somewhat surprising was the finding that model testimony was no more effective than testimony from an actual trial. Also, whether or not the judge informed the jury that a not guilty by reason of insanity verdict would automatically mean commitment was not found to be significant in the decision. Before any instructions from the judge, though, the large majority of jurors believed that innocence by insanity resulted in institutionalization. (The *Lyles* case, supported by the *Brawner* decision,[50] would clearly permit such institutionalizing at least for a period of observation, but could not guarantee institutionalization for an extended period of time. The Supreme Court has held that NGRI defendants may be civilly committed for a period which exceeds the maximum prison sentence for the crime with which they were charged.)[51]

The effect of social status and background upon juror deliberation was also studied. Blacks were more likely than any other group to vote NGRI. In general, jurors of relatively high status were less likely to accept an insanity plea. Contrary to lawyers' folklore, attitudes toward mental illness, psychiatry, and several other related areas had no apparent effect on the jury's decision. However, more definitive research on this issue is needed.

Klein and Temerlin used the same research design to investigate the consequence of conflicting psychiatric testimony upon jury decisions about insanity.[52] An additional change from the previous work was that the jury listened to an interview with the defendant, who either had many of the characteristics of a psychotic or seemed quite well adjusted. When there was conflicting psychiatric testimony or no such testimony at all, the jurors demonstrated a strong trend toward judging the defendant sane, regardless of whether the interviewee was psychotic or normal. In fact, the majority favored insanity only when both psychiatrists testified that the defendant was insane and the interviewed person was apparently insane at the time. In light of the fact that so often there is conflicting testimony, this research may have important implications for the practicality of using an insanity plea.

Pasewark, Pantle and Steadman studied individuals in the New York State criminal system who were acquitted of crimes by reason of insanity between 1971 and 1976. They were particularly interested in the effects of some attributes of the accused in leading to a verdict of NGRI.[53] They found that whites are about four times as likely to be successful in pleading NGRI as are blacks and about six times as successful as Puerto Ricans. They also noted that persons NGRI were significantly older than a comparison group of accused felons. Of the NGRI group, 62 percent were over 30 while the mean age at the comparison group was 23 years. Attribution theory would suggest that the stereotype that depicts mature Caucasians as law abiding motivates jurors to attribute some criminal acts by those individuals to mental disorders rather than to criminal intent. Since minorities may not be thought of in such terms, it is easier for jurors to attribute criminal acts to them. Pasewark et al. also found that, when analyzed county by county, the NGRI pleas were not entered more frequently in populous counties. They did note, however, that the "more brisk" the criminal justice business in a county, the less likely it was that the NGRI plea would be entered. This may relate to the large number of cases handled through plea bargaining. Plea bargaining is most frequent in areas in which caseloads far exceed judicial capacity and the NGRI defense is unlikely in such an harried environment.[54]

ASSESSMENT OF CRIMINAL RESPONSIBILITY

Evaluation of defendants pleading NGRI have varied considerably on the basis of the prior experience of the evaluator. Various clinicians administer different tests, draw different conclusions, and emphasize different portions of their evaluations, so it is not surprising that different opinions concerning insanity often result.

Cavanaugh has suggested certain basics for criminal responsibility evaluations.[55] He suggests a minimum of three or four separate interviews with the defendant in varied settings, following which the evaluator should review all clinical and police records. A pre-trial conference with lawyers from each side is suggested to ensure that the potential expert witness is clear on which aspects of the defendant's behavior and thought are relevant to the insanity question. Finally, clinical and correctional staff who are in closest contact with the accused should be interviewed.

Rogers, Dolmetsch, and Cavanaugh reported the development of an empirical approach to assess criminal responsibility that appears promising.[56] The instrument they developed, the Rogers Criminal Responsibility Assessment Scales (RCRAS) may introduce more objectivity into insanity evaluations. The instrument assesses 5 areas relevant to a legal definition of insanity: (1) the client's reliability, (2) evidence of organic brain disturbances, (3) evidence of psychopathology, (4) cognitive control, and, (5) behavioral control.

A hierarchical decision model based on the ALI rule is built into the instrument. This model requires the clinician to examine the variables named above and translate these into elements of the ALI standard. Following this transformation of psychological data into legal constructs, a specified decision process leads to a summary judgment as to responsibility.

Interrater agreement, or the degree to which independent evaluations of identical information agreed, was fairly high (rho = +.82). When applied to a group of defendants already classified as criminally insane by a team of forensic specialists, the RCRAS classified them in accordance about 92 percent of the time. Rogers et al. appear to have effectively melded law and behavioral science. They began with the best legal definitions of insanity available and set out to discover means of empirically defining the elements of those definitions. Thus the clinician using the RCRAS may be better able to evaluate precisely those aspects of his client which are pertinent to the insanity defense.

ALTERNATIVES TO THE PRESENT SYSTEM

Some proposals for change of the insanity defense involve only minor modifications of the present system. Other changes would result in the elimination of expert testimony in insanity cases or abandonment of the defense altogether.

Evidentiary Changes

One modification would bar all testimony from mental health experts, on the basis that such evidence is confusing to the jury.[57] A criticism of this suggestion is that behavioral scientists are in fact trained to do many things which may assist the jury. Their elimination would mean the elimination of this organized source of information and would simply result in the jury having less information.[58]

Other potential modifications include the elimination of the "advocacy" type mental health expert witnesses and their replacement by court-appointed, impartial expert witnesses and the elimination of adversary cross examination of experts. Prohibiting the parties (particularly the defense) from calling their own experts could violate a defendant's constitutional right to call witnesses, and eliminating cross examination would surely be unconstitutional. In addition, inasmuch as there are often widely divergent views on insanity questions, it is reasonable to conclude that the primary effect of a court-appointed witness system would be to withhold information from the jury. It might, however, be appropriate in many cases to have a court-appointed expert who would testify in addition to experts called by the parties. This can be done according to present law in many areas, but seldom is. Juries could be expected to place greater weight on the "neutral" expert. Preventing cross examination of experts might make testifying more comfortable for the expert, but it would permit the conclusions and opinions of the expert to go unchallenged.

In a few jurisdictions the prosecution has the obligation of proving the absence of insanity beyond a reasonable doubt. It is suggested that a lower standard of proof be used. Most states now provide that the burden of proving insanity is shifted to the defendant. Congress has by statute now provided that in federal criminal cases the defendant has the burden of proving the insanity defense.[59]

Complete Elimination

Some have advocated completely abandoning the insanity defense and related concepts. Their basic justification is that individual responsibility must be preserved throughout society or that there are more efficient means to handle the issue of lessened responsibility. The American Medical Association supported eliminating the insanity defense. Attempts to completely abandon both insanity as a defense and the requirement of *mens rea* may also violate constitutional due process.[60] So long as the criminal law is based on the concept of free will or *mens rea*, a defendant must have an opportunity to demonstrate its absence. (The *mens rea* defense is discussed below.)

Redefinition of Insanity

A number of suggestions short of completely abandoning the insanity defense have been made. One such approach is to eliminate the concept of "mental illness" and substitute for it more specific and testable criteria for insanity. The general goal would be to find scientifically established concepts, such as IQ scores, which are closely related to an individual's level of functioning. Silverman has proposed the development of the concept of psychological trauma as a substitute for mental illness.[61] Such concepts will have to prove their utility to the scientific community before they become incorporated into the law. While the concept of "mental illness" may be inadequate, there has as yet been no adequate resolution of this issue toward any new concept accepted by a substantial majority. The development of the RCRAS, mentioned above, may be a positive step.

Disposition and Sentencing

Another alternative is currently followed in a number of European countries.[62] It relates to the disposition or sentence rather than to the issue of guilt or innocence. This is, in reality, a form of abolition of insanity as a defense. This alternative does not purport to relate directly to the elements of the offense (in particular the requirement of intent), and the lack of responsibility, but explicitly gives the court or the jury the power to reduce the penalty for the offense. The Italian Penal Code, for instance, permits a sentence below the statutory minimum if at the time of the offense the person was in such a state of mind that his volition and capacity for understanding his acts were diminished. This type of system relieves the triers of fact from making the formal all-or-nothing choice of insanity in cases where it would be reasonable to rather seek a middle ground.

Another, related, effort to remove psychiatric evidence from the trial is the "bifurcated trial." Under this procedure, in effect, two trials would be held. The first would determine whether a defendant were guilty, the second to determine if the defendant should be exonerated because of mental illness. Although bifurcation has been tried by several states, it raises important questions, often makes the criminal process more complex, and does not necessarily eliminate all psychiatric evidence from the first trial.[63] It has not been widely accepted.

Guilty But Mentally Ill

Another approach which has gained considerable support recently is the "guilty but mentally ill" rule,[64] first introduced by statute in Michigan in 1975.[65] Sparked by public displeasure over the release of dangerous inmates of mental institutions,[66] the Michigan legislature adopted the rule that those who were adjudged to be mentally ill at the time the crime was committed could be convicted and would serve in a mental institution the time prescribed by statute for the crime.[67] A growing number of other states have adopted some form of this concept.

This reform does not necessarily completely eliminate the insanity defense. A jury may find a defendant guilty, not guilty, not guilty by reason of insanity, or guilty but mentally ill. A defendant found guilty but mentally ill is convicted of the crime, and is sentenced as anyone else convicted of the crime. So long as the defendant is mentally ill, the sentence is served in an institution where he can receive therapy. After mental health is restored, the remainder of the sentence may be served in a regular penal institution. The defendant must be released at the expiration of the sentence unless the state commences civil commitment proceedings.

The purpose of the guilty but mentally ill verdict may be to ensure that mentally ill guilty defendants receive treatment, or it may be an effort to reduce the successful use of the insanity defense by offering jurors a compromise verdict. Preliminary data from Michigan do not suggest that the number of insanity verdicts has been reduced, but the long-term effects are not clear.[68]

Mens Rea Approach

Goldstein, Katz, and others have suggested the possibility of abolishing all the current rules for determining insanity. The requirement of proof of *actus rea*, and *mens rea*, or intent necessarily includes some elements of the defense of insanity.[69] The Reagan administration proposed a similar change in federal criminal law following the Hinckley verdict. The Idaho law would eliminate insanity, but permit evidence that the defendant did not have the required *mens rea*. The complete elimination of the insanity defense raises some difficult constitutional questions unless the state then permits evidence on the question of *mens rea*.[70]

We noted earlier that *mens rea* is an essential element of most crimes and its absence generally precludes finding the defendant guilty. The insanity defense in some instances is a special way of demonstrating that the defendant could not have had the requisite *mens rea* because of mental illness. Therefore elimination of this insanity defense might leave many of the same issues to be considered as part of *mens rea*.

Eliminating the insanity defense and depending on a *mens rea* defense might, in theory, result in the conviction of some severely disturbed defendants. Suppose a delusional person kills his wife, after hearing voices suggesting that she is poisoning their son with brain waves, and the defendant believes that God has therefore commanded him to kill her. He probably has the *mens rea* to be convicted of murder, even first degree murder.[71] Yet, no clear purpose would be served by his conviction; the law probably cannot hope to have much of a deterrent effect in such situations and prison is not likely to have a rehabilitative influence on him.

As a practical matter, it is unlikely that abolition of the insanity defense, with a corresponding emphasis on *mens rea*, would have a profound effect on criminal justice. The scope of evidence regarding *mens rea* which would be permitted in such trials is not clear. In the long run, courts might permit testimony from psychotherapists regarding *mens rea* or intent.[72] This testimony might not vary dramatically from the evidence currently presented regarding insanity.[73] Juries may well be expected to acquit of serious crimes defendants who technically have the requisite *mens rea*, but who are manifestly insane. Also, some defenses, such as defense of others in the example above, might be expanded to include defendants who now use the insanity defense. In addition, the diminished capacity defense would probably become more widely used.

The prosecution has the obligation of proving *mens rea* beyond a reasonable doubt, a burden it does not have in most jurisdictions regarding the insanity defense.[74] Therefore, if emphasis is placed on the mental state of the defendant in a *mens rea* defense, some defendants might technically find it easier to win acquittal.

Eliminating the Volitional Test

Several scholars and professional groups have proposed that the volitional test (whether defendants were unable to conform their conduct to the requirements of the law) be eliminated, leaving only a cognitive test (whether defendants were unable to appreciate the wrongfulness of their conduct).[75] Both the American Bar Association and the American Psychiatric Association have supported this proposal.[76] The APA noted that it is very difficult for mental health experts to apply the volitional test in determining whether defendants were able to control their behavior. "The line between an irresistible impulse and an impulse not resisted is probably no sharper than that between twilight and dusk."[77] Mental health experts have less difficulty determining whether a defendant understood the nature and wrongfulness of an act (the cognitive test). This reform is the one to have received the greatest attention, and has been adopted in several jurisdictions, and for federal criminal trials.[78]

Eliminating the volitional test might reduce part of the conflicting and confusing expert testimony in some cases. Eliminating the volitional test does not seem fully consistent, however, with the fundamental policy of punishing only those who choose to do wrong. Among all the defendants who could not conform their conduct to the law, the cognitive-test would exonerate only those who were unable to do so because they could not *understand* that what they were doing wrong. Surely others who cannot control their actions for other reasons are as blameless (assuming some free will construct) as those who did a prohibited act not knowing it was wrong.

The positions of the ABA and APA appear to be based primarily on the proposition that experts are unable to give accurate and useful information regarding the volitional test. The appropriate reform might therefore be to maintain the volitional test as part of the insanity defense, but to prohibit mental health experts from testifying concerning it. The jury would then be faced more squarely with the question of whether or not the defendant should be held responsible for his action. It is true, given the free-will basis of the criminal law, that this is more of a normative than scientific judgment. It may therefore be appropriate for juries to face this question of volition without confusing scientific evidence.

Justification for Changing the Insanity Defense

The anachronistic dependence on free will as the basis for criminal law makes difficult the use of rational scientific theory to reform the insanity defense. Professor Michael Moore proposes an insanity defense based on the absence of "practical reasoning."[79] His concept of responsibility arises from the ability of someone to select rationally a course of conduct in pursuit of goals or desires. He proposes a "soft" free will or autonomy philosophy in which people are responsible for their acts as long as they have a choice; what caused them to make the choice is unimportant for responsibility. Moore sees the criminal law as legitimately based on this soft free will concept and apparently accepts "just deserts" (someone is punished because he deserves it) as the reason for punishment. However, if someone deserves punishment for making a bad choice, then the reasons he made the choice cannot be ignored. He is not morally blameworthy unless in some way he could really exercise some choice.[80] This elegant soft free will analysis is inconsistent with strong behaviorism, as Moore recognizes.[81] (He refers to it as Skinnerian "radical behaviorism".) Thus even soft autonomy cannot be the basis of the criminal law, and for a rational insanity defense, if behaviorism accurately describes human behavior.

One alternative is to judge proposed reforms against the other reasons for punishment: retribution,[82] deterrence (specific and general), restraint, and rehabilitation. It is not clear that any of the proposed reforms, including the abolition of the defense, would have a major impact on the efficacy of the criminal justice system in terms of these reasons for punishment.

In most instances, a general societal sense of retribution is not present when the insanity defense is successful. Where such a sense of retribution is present it is likely to be associated with the victim of the crime (e.g., a national leader) or the details of the crime (e.g., dismemberment of a body). Convicting of a crime those whose conduct is related to profoundly disturbed minds is not likely to increase society's sense of successful retribution. Even if that sense of retribution is more fully satisfied in some instances, it is questionable whether this is an adequate reason to convict the insane.

The deterrence of the criminal law may be somewhat reduced by the insanity defense if the defense consciously or subconsciously leads people to believe that they can escape punishment by pleading this defense. The public's gross overestimation of the successful use of insanity may affect deterrence, although it is doubtful that the possibility of successfully using the defense seriously affects the decision of very many people to engage in criminal conduct. In terms of deterrence, correcting the misunderstanding about the success rate of the insanity defense may be more important than reform. Paradoxically, if the discussion of insanity defense reforms contributes to the impression that the defense is widely and easily abused, the reform effort itself may be reducing the deterrent effects of the criminal law.

If deterrence is seen as the primary goal of the criminal law, then the insanity defense might be based on the "cop at the elbow" test: would the defendent have committed the crime if apprehension was certain. In such instances it is apparent that the criminal law cannot serve as a deterrent. The release of one defendant from criminal responsibility on this basis, however, may reduce the general deterrence of the criminal law.

The restraint function of punishment (removing the dangerous from society) is often accomplished as successfully through post-NGRI civil commitment as it would be through conviction of a crime. Some dangerous persons spend more time incarcerated through civil commitment than they would have spent if convicted of a crime. The Supreme Court has indicated that it is constitutionally permissible to keep NGRI defendants committed longer than the maximum prison term for the crimes with which they were charged.[83] Theoretically, because the civil commitment system uses absence of dangerousness as the primary criterion for release while the penal system does not, the civil commitment system could be more effective in ensuring appropriate restraint of a mentally ill, dangerous defendant.[84] In fact, it appears that on the average NGRI defendants and those convicted of similar crimes spend similar lengths of time institutionalized, although it does differ for specific categories of offenses. In addition, there is some evidence that post-institutional arrest rates are similar for NGRI and those convicted of similar offenses.[85] It is unlikely that any of the proposed insanity defense reforms would contribute much to improving the restraint of dangerous criminal defendants.

The rehabilitative function of the prison system has not been a great success.[86] The "rehabilitation" mentally disordered offenders often need most is mental health treatment. Such treatment may be limited at either a prison or a state mental hospital, but it may more likely be available at a hospital than at a prison. The guilty but mentally ill verdict proposal might increase the diversion of the mentally disturbed to treatment facilities, but other proposed reforms are aimed at reducing the number of successful NGRI defenses. If successful, the effect would probably be to divert a few mentally disturbed defendants from the civil commitment system to the prison system.

The effects of many of the proposed reforms are highly speculative. It is doubtful, however, that any reform which could be widely adopted would, as a practical matter, have any dramatic effect on the criminal justice system. In terms of the underlying basis of the criminal law, or the purposes of punishment, none of the proposed reforms clearly commands support. Real reform of the insanity defense undoubtedly will await a rethinking of the basis of the criminal law.

SUMMARY

"Insane" criminal defendants are generally not responsible for their criminal conduct. This is consistent with the general concept of criminal responsibility in which a person must both do a prohibited act (*actus reus*) and have a certain level of "evil" mind or intent (*mens rea*). The insanity defense is generally a complete defense to a criminal charge and has historically been fairly narrowly defined. The traditional formulation of the insanity defense has been the M'Naughten rule which requires that criminal defendants possess such a "disease of the mind, as not to know the nature and quality of the act they were doing" or be unable to distinguish right from wrong. The more modern approach is the American Law Institute's Model Penal Code which provides that the insanity defense may be used when the defendant "as a result of mental disease or defect . . . lacks substantial capacity either to appreciate the criminality of his conduct or to conform his conduct to the requirements of the law."

There have been a number of important criticisms of the insanity rule. One is that the concept of insanity does not have any meaning to behavioral scientists. There is even disagreement about whether the medical model of mental illness is meaningful. It is also difficult for experts to testify in insanity defense trials and there is a suggestion that in many cases insanity is "in the eye of the beholder" because the concept of insanity is so nebulous and bound to philosophical issues.

Some behavioral scientists argue that the process of establishing blameworthiness on the basis of free will or irresistible impulse is based on a model of human conduct which is misguided. For example, behaviorists view the actions of people as being determined by their heredity and environment. The concept of free will on which most of criminal law is based has little meaning in such a model and mental illness cannot be viewed as interfering with the ability of someone to exercise "free" choice or free will.

Experimental studies involving the insanity defense suggest that there may have been too much concern about the precise formulation of the insanity defense because the statement of the defense to a jury does not seem to make a substantial difference in terms of the probability of successfully using the insanity defense. It also appears that where there is conflicting expert testimony, jurors tend to reject the insanity defense.

A variety of alternatives have been suggested, ranging from dropping the insanity defense altogether to tinkering with the evidence that can be presented to the jury. It has also been suggested that the insanity defense might be used only to determine what should be done with a defendant after conviction of a crime or that jurors might be given the option of returning a verdict of "guilty but mentally ill" under which the defendant would be convicted of a crime but would serve his sentence receiving treatment for the mental illness. The momentum now appears to be toward dropping the "volitional" test for insanity.

The insanity defense has been a point of controversy for more than a century. In terms of its practical importance it does not deserve such attention. It is successfully used in a small percentage of criminal proceedings. However, it raises fundamental questions about the concept of criminal responsibility. It has not been precisely defined in terms that are easy for behavioral scientists and attorneys to comprehend and use intelligently. When it is used it often results in a jury being presented with a variety of bewildering expert testimony. Thus it is easy to predict that insanity defense will continue to be a matter of serious debate.

Despite all of the disagreements and criticism of the insanity defense, however, it is likely to endure in some form. Although it is sometimes difficult to state precisely why, or to understand the scientific basis for it, most people feel that there is something unfair and unproductive about convicting someone of a crime who does not know what he is doing or who cannot exercise some control (whatever that may mean) over his actions. The development of a sound theoretical basis for the defense would seem to be essential to formulating a clearly understood and workable insanity defense, and this may in turn have to await a reexamination of the free will basis of the criminal law.

NOTES

1. Arthur Miller quoted in 70 *A.B.A.J.* 44 (1984).
2. The more serious the offense, of course, the more attractive the insanity defense. The defense became increasingly common as the number of capital offenses increased. See Halpern, The Fiction of Legal Insanity and the Misuse of Psychiatry, 2 *J. Legal Med.* 18, 20 (1980).
3. Sayre, Mens Rea, 45 *Harv. L. Rev.* 974, 1004 (1932).
4. 4 *Blackstone's Commentaries* 21 (4 Lewis ed. at 1427–28 1898).
5. Morissette v. United States, 342 U.S. 246, 250 (1952).
6. Steward Machine, Co. v. Davis, 301 U.S. 548, 500 (1937).
7. Model Penal Code, Proposed Official Draft, Section 2.02 (1) (1962).
8. Hall, Psychiatry and Criminal Responsibility, 65 *Yale L. J.* 761, 765 (1955–56). The reasons for punishment are more fully considered in the next chapter. See generally L. Freedman ed., *By Reason of Insanity* (1983).
9. See United States v. Freeman, 357 F.2d 606 (2d Cir. 1966). The court there queried: "[H]ow is deterrence achieved by punishing the incompetent? Those who are substantially unable to restrain their conduct are, by definition, undeterrable and their 'punishment' is no example to others; those who are unaware of or do not appreciate the nature and quality of their actions can hardly be expected to rationally weigh the consequences of their conduct." *Id.* at 615.
10. The possible circularity of the definition of insanity is readily appar-

ent when insanity may relieve one of responsibility for a crime, and is defined in terms of the absence of a mental state necessary to establish criminal responsibility.

11. C. Mercier, *Criminal Responsibility* 25–26 (1926); D. C. Picquet & R. Best, *The Insanity Defense: A Bibliographic Research Guide* (1985).

12. See Quen, Anglo-American Criminal Insanity, An Historical Perspective, 2 *Bull. Am. Acad. Psychiatry & L.* 115 (1974).

13. Although Ophelia's insanity seems obvious to readers of the play, we can gather that the availability of the insanity defense in Shakespearian times may have been less attributable to one's mental condition as to his social position, as the following remarks of the gravediggers illustrate:

(2nd Clown). Will ye ha' the truth on 't? If
this had not been a gentlewoman,
she should have been buried out o'
Christian burial.

(1st Clown). Why, there thou say'st. And the
more pity that great folks should
have the countenance in this world
to drown or hang themselves more
than their even Christian.

W. Shakespeare, *Hamlet,* Act V, Sc. 1, Ll. 25–31.

14. N. Walker, *Crime and Insanity in England* (1968).

15. Quoted in United States v. Smith, 404 F.2d 720, 725 (6th Cir. 1968).

16. Quoted in Walker, *supra,* note 14 at 77.

17. 4 *Blackstone's Commentaries*, note 4 *supra.*

18. For an excellent review of the insanity defense in the nineteenth century see R. Smith, *Trial by Medicine: Insanity and Responsibility in Victorian Trials* (1981).

19. Daniel M'Naughten's Case, 8 Eng. Rep. 718 (1843). Lord Chief Justice Tindal gave the following charge:

"The question to be determined is, whether at the time the act in question was committed, the prisoner had or had not the use of his understanding, so as to know that he was doing a wrong or wicked act. If the jurors should be of the opinion that the prisoner was not sensible, at the time he committed it, that he was violating the laws of both God and man, then he would be entitled to a verdict in his favour."

20. *Id.*

21. Spring, The End of Insanity, 19 *Washburn L. J.* 23, 28–29 (1979).

22. The defendant in the *Durham* case was charged with housebreaking. He had been in and out of trouble with the law for a six-year period, and had suffered apparent emotional problems over the same period. During several commitments he was diagnosed as having a psychopathic personality, but at the trial, using the M'Naughten rule, he was convicted. The Court of Appeals reversed the conviction. Durham v. United States, 214 F.2d 862 (D.C. Cir. 1954).

23. *Id.*

24. In its home jurisdiction, it was found necessary to define "mental disease or defect," and any court using the rule was plagued with who could say the otherwise criminal act was the "product" of the disease. One was also left with the thorny problem of what constitutes a "mental disease or defect." Is it psychosis (a lack of reality testing), and if so, does this become a *de facto* defense? Does it exclude all neuroses and character disorders? Besides being limited in its home jurisdiction, its soundness was questioned in no fewer than 13 appellate cases, including in the Supreme Court of the United States in the concurring opinion of Justice Black in Powell v. Texas, 392 U.S. 514, 546 (1968).

25. United States v. Brawner, 471 F.2d 969 (D.C. Cir. 1972).

26. *Id.* at 979.

27. Archie Brawner went to a party where he was involved in a fight, announced he would come back to kill, and did so, firing five times through a metal door. Mr. Brawner appears to be neither an exemplary citizen nor very sane. Interestingly enough, both the defense and the prosecution expert witnesses agreed that Brawner was mentally ill. Diagnostic labels varied, but in general they agreed he was an epileptic, and in addition he was diagnosed as an "explosive personality disorder." The experts on both sides also agreed that his epilepsy *could* have been accentuated by alcohol (he had been drinking excessively that morning) or by a blow on the head received during the fight. The defense and the prosecution experts however differed on whether or not Brawner had fired his gun because of his disability.

The D.C. Court of Appeals decided to drop the Durham rule in favor of the ALI rule because, "The ALI rule is eclectic in spirit, partaking of the moral focus of M'Naughten, the practical accommodation of the 'control rules' (a term more exact and less susceptible of misunderstanding than 'irresistible impulse' terminology), and responsive, at the same time, to a relatively modern, forward-looking view of what is encompassed in 'knowledge.'" *Id.* at 979.

As for Brawner, the court did not seem to be convinced of his lack of blameworthiness under any rule or definition. In any event, rather than reversing the conviction, the court remanded the case for the trial judge to determine whether a new trial should be ordered in the interests of justice in the light of the new rule propounded.

The court failed to come to final conclusions regarding several crucial issues. For example, it wrestled with the idea of dropping the medical model, which would have eliminated the albatross of the illness or disease concept. The court suggested it was considering dropping the model but felt it could not because the consequences of such a change were highly speculative. *Id.* at 969.

28. American Law Institute, *Model Penal Code, Proposed Official Draft* 401 (1962).

29. United States v. Brawner, 471 F.2d 969 (D.C. Cir. 1972).

Another interesting issue is whether amnesia can be the basis for mitigation of responsibility. Hermann, Criminal Defenses and Pleas in Mitigation

Based on Amnesia, 4 *Behav. Sci. & L.* 5 (1986); Rubinsky, Amnesia and Criminal Law: A Clinical Overview, 4 *Behav. Sci. & L.* 27 (1986).

30. Spring, The End of Insanity, 19 *Washburn L. J.* 23, 28–29 (1979).

31. Davis v. United States, 160 U.S. 469 (1895).

32. E.g., Newsome v. Commonwealth, 366 S.W.2d 174 (Ky. 1962), *cert. denied,* 375 U.S. 887 (1963).

33. Pennsylvania v. Walzack, 468 Pa. 210, 360 A.2d 914, 929 (1976).

34. The irresistible impulse insanity defense received some public attention in the popular book and movie, *Anatomy of a Murder.* The apparent misuse of the defense in that work of fiction may have attributed to a general misunderstanding of the concept.

35. Mutual Life Insurance Co. v. Terry, 82 U.S. 580 (1873).

36. See Arenella, Diminished Capacity and Diminished Responsibility Defenses: Two Children of a Doomed Marriage, 77 *Colum. L. Rev.* 827 (1977); Lewin, Psychiatric Evidence in Criminal Cases for Purposes Other Than the Defense of Insanity, 26 *Syracuse L. Rev.* 1051 (1975). See generally Clark, Clinical Limits of Expert Testimony on Diminished Capacity, 5 *Int'l J. L. & Psychiatry* 155 (1982).

37. Pasewark & Seidenzahl, Opinions About the Insanity Plea and Criminality Among Mental Patients, 7 *Bull. Am. Acad. Psychiatry & L.* 199 (1979). Similar misconceptions have been noted among legislators and the public at large. See Jeffrey & Pasewark, Altering Opinions About the Insanity Plea, 11 *J. Psychiatry & L.* 29 (1983). See *infra,* note 54.

38. Wise, Criminal Responsibility, 2 *Mich. Acad.* 3 (1969).

39. Judicial Conference of the District of Columbia, *Report of the Committee on Problems Connected with Mental Examination of the Accused in Criminal Cases Before Trial* 170 (1964).

40. T. Szasz, *Insanity* (1986); Szasz, The Myth of Mental Illness, 15 *Am. Psychologist,* 113 (1960). See Lassen, The Psychologist as an Expert Witness in Assessing Mental Disease or Defect, 50 *A.B.A. J.* 239 (1964). For a general discussion of related philosophical issues see Weinberg & Vatz, The Mental Illness Dispute: The Critical Faith Assumptions, 9 *J. Psychology & L.* 305 (1981).

41. Szasz (1960), *supra,* note 40 at 114.

42. L. Ullman & L. Krasner, *A Psychological Approach to Abnormal Behavior* (1975).

43. This difficulty has led to the suggestion that the defense should be abolished. See B. Wooton, *Crime and the Criminal Law* (1963). But see Note, The Insanity Defense: Effects of Abolition Unsupported by a Moral Consensus, 9 *Am. J. L. & Med.* 471 (1984).

44. Halleck, The Psychiatrist and the Legal Process, 2 *Psychology Today* 25 (1969).

45. Leifer, The Psychiatrist and Tests of Criminal Responsibility, 19 *Am. Psychologist* 825 (1964).

46. Halleck, *supra,* note 44, at 26.

47. The practice of having the defendant examined by a number of ex-

perts is not without risks. The prosecution may be able to obtain the adverse reports and even call the expert as its own witness. State v. Carter, 641 S.W.2d 54 (Mo. 1982), *cert. denied,* 461 U.S. 932 (1983).

48. Even if not expressed in terms of "free will" the criminal law generally presumes the ability to choose to commit or not commit a crime. See generally Wexler, An Offense-Victim Approach to Insanity Defense Reform, 26 *Ariz. L. Rev.* 17 (1984) (suggesting the need for new analytical approach to insanity).

Professor Moore has suggested an interesting "soft free will" concept as the basis for the criminal law. See notes 79 to 81 and accompanying text, *infra.*

49. R. Simon, *The Jury and the Defense of Insanity* (1967). See Pasewark, Randolph & Bieber, Insanity Plea: Statutory Language and Trial Procedures, 12 *J. Psychiatry & L.* 399 (1984) (three different insanity tests resulted in no significant changes in the outcome of insanity cases).

50. United States v. Brawner 471 F.2d 969 (D.C. Cir. 1976); Lyles v. United States, 254 F.2d 725 (D.C. Cir. 1957).

51. Jones v. United States, 463 U.S. 354 (1983). See Pogrebin, Regoli & Perry, Not Guilty by Reason of Insanity: A Research Note, 8 *Int'l J. L. & Psychiatry* 237 (1986) (generally defendants who successfully raise the insanity defense do not spend fewer days in confinement than if they had been convicted of the crime).

52. Klein & Temerlin, On Expert Testimony in Sanity Cases, 149 *J. Nervous & Mental Disorders* 435 (1969).

53. Pasewark, Pantle & Steadman, Characteristics and Disposition of Persons Found Not Guilty by Reason of Insanity in New York State, 1971–1976, 136 *Am. J. Psychiatry* 655 (1979). See Steadman, Insanity Acquittals in New York State, 1965–1978, 137 *Am. J. Psychiatry* 321 (1980).

54. Phillips, Insanity Plea in Connecticut, 1970–72, summarized in 41 *Dissertation Abstracts Int'l* 697 (1980). See Pasewark & McGinley, Insanity Plea: National Survey of Frequency and Success, 13 *J. Psychiatry & L.* 101 (1985). The public also seriously misunderstands the legal test for insanity. Hans & Slater, "Plain Crazy": Lay Definitions of Legal Insanity, 7 *Int'l J. L. & Psychiatry* 105 (1984).

55. Rogers, Dolmetsch & Cavanaugh, An Empirical Approach to Insanity Evaluations, 37 *J. Clinical Psychology* 683 (1981).

56. *Id.* See generally T. Grisso, *Evaluating Competencies: Forensic Assessments and Instruments* (1986).

57. Liefer, *supra* note 45, at 830. For a review of several of the reform proposals see Herman, Assault on the Insanity Defense: Limitations on the Effectiveness and Effect of the Defense of Insanity, 14 *Rutgers L. J.* 241 (1983); Slovenko, Disposition of the Insanity Acquitee, 11 *J. Psychiatry & L.* 97 (1983); Wexler, *supra,* note 48.

58. For a debate regarding the role and function of mental health experts see Dix, Mental Health Professionals in the Legal Process: Some Problems of Psychiatric Dominance, 6 *L. & Psychology Rev.* 1 (1980); Hoffman &

Browning, Mental Health Professionals in the Legal Process: A Plea for Rational Application of Clinical Methods, 6 *L. & Psychology Rev.* 21 (1980). See Howard & Clark, When Courts and Experts Disagree: Discordance Between Insanity Recommendations and Adjudications, 9 *L. & Hum. Behav.* 385 (1985).

59. Comprehensive Crime Control Act of 1984, Pub. L. No. 98-473, 98 Stat. 1837 (1984); Comment, Recent Changes in Criminal Law: The Federal Insanity Defense, 46 *La. L. Rev.* 337 (1985).

60. American Medical Association, *The Insanity Defense in Criminal Trials and Limitation of Psychiatric Testimony* (approved Dec. 6, 1983). See generally N. Morris, *Madness and the Criminal Law* (1982); Szasz, The Insanity Pleas and the Insanity Defense, 40 *Temple L. Q.* 271 (1967); Teplin, The Criminality of the Mentally Ill: A Dangerous Misconception, 142 *Am. J. Psychiatry* 593 (1985).

The efforts by some states to eliminate the insanity defense have been held to be unconstitutional. E.g., Sinclair v. State, 116 Miss. 142, 132 So. 581 (1931); State v. Strasberg, 60 Wash. 106, 110 P. 1020 (1910). The U.S. Supreme Court has not recently clearly indicated whether or not the insanity defense is constitutionally required. See Robitscher & Haynes, In Defense of the Insanity Defense, 31 *Emory L. J.* 9, 51–59 (1982). More recently the abolition of the insanity by a state withstood constitutional challenges in the state courts. State v. Korell, 690 P.2d 992 (Mont. 1984).

61. Silverman, Determinism, Choice, Responsibility and the Psychologist's Role as an Expert Witness, 24 *Am. Psychologist* 5 (1969).

62. Dix, Psychological Abnormality as a Factor in Grading Criminal Liability: Diminished Capacity, Diminished Responsibility, and the Like, 62 *Crim. L., Criminology & Police Sci.* 313, 321 (1971).

63. Robitscher & Haynes, In Defense of the Insanity Defense, 31 *Emory L. J.* 9, 18–26 (1982). See I. Keilitz & J. Fulton, *The Insanity Defense and Its Alternatives* (1984); Louisell & Hazard, Insanity as a Defense, The Bifurcated Trial, 49 *Calif. L. Rev.* 805 (1961).

64. During the nineteenth century in England "not guilty by reason of insanity" was changed to "guilty but insane." This change had little effect because the two verdicts were determined to have the same meaning. Robitscher & Haynes, In Defense of the Insanity Defense, 31 *Emory L. J.* 9, 14 (1982). See Sherman, Guilty but Mentally Ill: A Retreat From the Insanity Defense, 7 *Am. J. L. & Med.* 257 (1981).

65. Comment, Guilty But Mentally Ill: Historical and Constitutional Analysis, 53 *J. Urban L.* 471 (1976).

66. Inmates of mental institutions were being released pursuant to the Michigan Supreme Court decision in *People v. McQuillan,* 392 Mich. 511, 221 N.W.2d 569 (1974). McQuillan had been adjudged not guilty by reason of insanity to the charge of assault with intent to commit rape and was subsequently incarcerated into a health facility for an indefinite time. At no point had a hearing been held to determine his present sanity and he thereupon brought an action to have the commitment order vacated. The court

held that the Fourteenth Amendment guarantees a "not guilty by reason of insanity" defendant a hearing to determine his present sanity prior to any deprivation of liberty. Pursuant to this case a number of sanity hearings were held in which a number of inmates were determined sane. A few that were released committed violent crimes thereafter and this sparked public outcry. The legislature responded with this statute. Now, a jury in Michigan to award a guilty but mentally ill verdict must find beyond a reasonable doubt that the defendant is guilty of the charge, that the defendant was not insane at the time the offense was committed, and that he or she was mentally ill at the time of the offense.

67. Mich. Comp. Laws Ann. §768.36 (1982). See People v. McLeod, 407 Mich. 632, 288 N.W.2d 909 (1980).

68. See Slobogin, The Guilty But Mentally Ill Verdict: An Idea Whose Time Should Not Have Come, 53 *Geo. Wash. L. Rev.* 494 (1985); Weiner, *American Medical News*, Aug. 6, 1982 at 3.

69. Goldstein & Katz, Abolish the Insanity Defense—Why Not?, 72 *Yale L. J.* 853 (1963).

70. See note 60 *supra.*

71. See Arnella, Reflections on Current Proposals to Abolish or Reform the Insanity Defense, 8 *Am. J. L. & Med.* 271, 276–77 (1982).

72. For a discussion of the evidence which might be permitted, see Insanity Defense Barred in Ohio, 68 *A.B.A. J.* 531 (1982).

73. Some courts have indicated, when the defendant has chosen not to plead the insanity defense, it is proper to limit psychiatric testimony regarding intent. See State v. Bouwman, 328 N.W.2d 703 (Minn. 1982). There might be less reluctance to admit such evidence if the insanity defense were not available. See Hendershott v. People 653 P.2d 385 (Colo. 1982), *cert. denied,* 459 U.S. 1225 (1983).

74. Most states either permit the prosecution to prove the sanity of the defendant with less than "beyond a reasonable doubt" standard, or require the defendant to prove insanity.

75. See Bonnie, The Moral Basis of the Insanity Defense, 69 *A.B.A. J.* 194 (1983).

76. The American Bar Association's position is described at 51 U.S.L.W. 2476–77 (1983); American Psychiatric Association, *Statement on the Insanity Defense* (1983). The National Commission on the Insanity Defense, *Myths and Realities: A Report* (1983), (a project of the Mental Health Association) recommended that both cognitive and volitional elements be maintained. See Rodriguez, LeWinn & Perlin, The Insanity Defense Under Siege: Legislative Assaults and Legal Rejoinders, 14 *Rutgers L. J.* 397 (1983) (proposals for legislative reform of the insanity defense are based on myths); Wexler, Redefining the Insanity Problem, 53 *Geo. Wash. L. Rev.* 528 (1985).

77. American Psychiatric Association, *Statement on the Insanity Defense* 11 (1983).

78. E.g., Pub. L. No. 98-473, 98 Stat. 1837 (1984).

79. M. Moore, *Law and Psychiatry: Rethinking the Relationship* 217–45

(1984). Practical reasoning is the ability to rationally select a course of conduct in pursuit of goals or wants.

80. Moore emphasizes that the cause or reasons for someone selecting a course of conduct are not important, that people can legitimately be held responsible for their conduct regardless of what caused the choice, so long as they possess practical reasoning. Consider three examples suggested by Moore. Because of a strong gust of wind, (1) a man's hand is thrown upward, (2) the man becomes cold and shivers, (3) the man becomes cold and puts on a jacket. Moore suggests the man should be held responsible for the third, but only the third action. But why, if that responsibility is based on just deserts? It is true that in putting on the jacket there is more brain activity (practical reasoning) than in the other two examples. But it is also true that there is substantial brain activity in the shivering example. The act of shivering is an effort by the body to warm itself as surely as is putting on the jacket. The only difference in a moral (or responsibility) sense is that the person could choose not to put the jacket on, he could not choose not to shiver. But, of course, from a behavioral/deterministic point of view this is not a real difference because the man could no more "choose" not to put on the jacket than he could "choose" not to shiver. Both are determined (at least in a moral sense) by the man's background and experience. Nor is it an answer to say that other people would have chosen not to put on the jacket, therefore it is a matter of individual moral blameworthiness, unlike shivering; other people, with other physical make-ups, would not have shivered (chosen not to shiver?). To say to the determinist that the man justly *deserves* punishment for putting on the jacket because he "chose" to put on the jacket, but does not *deserve* punishment because he did not choose to shiver, is to draw the moral distinction between an irresistible impulse and an impulse not resisted, a difference the determinist does not recognize.

When just deserts or other form of moral blameworthiness becomes the basis for imposing punishment, the reasons for the choice or the causes of the choice, are important. Those without "practical reasoning" should be excused from responsibility on the basis that they cannot make rational choices among alternatives and therefore cannot fairly be held accountable for the decision they make. When the issue is moral blameworthiness, or *just* deserts, for the behavioral/determinist the difference between those with and without practical reasoning is not of great importance.

81. Moore, *supra,* note 79, at 425.

82. Although retribution is generally listed as reason for punishment, there is a serious question whether this is legitimate. See generally C. Bartol & A. Bartol, *Criminal Behavior* (1986); J. Wilson & R. Herrnstein, *Crime and Human Nature* (1985).

83. Jones v. United States, 463 U.S. 354 (1983). See Pogrebin, Regoli & Perry, Not Guilty by Reason of Insanity: A Research Note, 8 *Int'l J. L. & Psychiatry* 237 (1986) (generally defendants who successfully raise the insanity defense do not spend fewer days in confinement than if they had been

convicted of the crime); Note, Commitment Following Insanity Acquittal, 94 *Harv. L. Rev.* 605 (1981).

84. In fact, the ability to accurately predict dangerousness is somewhat limited. However, since there appears to be a considerable debate over prediction of dangerousness, the civil commitment system may be particularly careful not to release dangerous patients. One study suggests that successful insanity defendants resemble general psychiatric patients more closely than prisoners. Mullen & Reihehr, The Mentally Ill Offender: A Comparison of Prison Inmates, Forensic Psychiatric Patients and General Psychiatric Patients, 9 *J. Psychology & L.* 203 (1981).

85. Pantle, Pasewark & Steadman, Comparing Institutional Periods and Subsequent Arrest of Insanity Acquittees and Convicted Felons, 8 *J. Psychology & L.* 305 (1980).

86. See F. Allen, *The Decline of the Rehabilitative Ideal: Penal Policy and Social Purpose* (1981); Bartol & Bartol, *supra*, note 82.

CHAPTER 12
PUNISHMENT

Most societies punish deviant or unacceptable behavior for reasons ranging from a desire to placate the gods[1] to a desire to help the offender.[2] As an alternative, some societies may choose to "treat" deviant behavior or to ignore it. Treatment and punishment are not necessarily mutually exclusive goals. The rehabilitative ideal, which was the center of much penal theory during the 1960s and 1970s, was treatment as well as a rationale for punishment. Generally, however, treatment and punishment are considered alternative approaches, treatment commonly associated with a medical model and punishment with a legal model.[3] Lawyers and behavioral scientists define punishment differently. "Punishment" in behavioral theory is a response which tends to reduce targeted behavior. In this chapter we use the term as it is commonly used in the law, meaning disabilities imposed by the government for misconduct.

Our society is currently becoming somewhat more punitive. Prison sentences have grown in length and frequency; the death penalty has returned; and rehabilitation has lost favor. This approach has resulted in a serious problem of overcrowded prisons, and the need for substantial additional resources to implement our decisions to punish. Many prisons are under federal court order to reduce crowding. During the last several years, the number of people in prison has increased significantly.[4] By 1982 the United States was annually spending $9 billion a year on corrections and about $35 billion on the criminal justice system, and it is not clear that society is getting its money's worth.[5]

In this chapter we examine the society's use of punishment, the need to balance it with other important social goals, alternatives to prison, and the imposition of the death penalty. We believe that the current system of punishment does not have clear goals, is often inconsistent and ineffective, is excessively expensive, and generally does not serve society well. Pouring substantial additional resources into the system is unlikely to serve any strong social purpose, and is likely to divert resources from other important public services. Of particular concern is the use of long prison terms.

TYPES OF PUNISHMENT

Misconduct may harm both individuals and society. The civil law provides a variety of actions for misconduct which harms individuals. The primary focus of these civil remedies is to provide compensation to individuals who are injured. A secondary purpose of civil law, however, is to punish offenders through economic loss. Criminal law seeks to protect the interests of society as a whole. The same act may give rise to both civil liability and criminal punishment.

The forms of punishment available include loss of freedom, fines, corporal punishment, capital punishment, and restitution. In the United States, fines and imprisonment are defined for most all crimes. Misdemeanors usually result in the imposition of fines, although a short jail sentence (less than one year) is sometimes imposed. Felonies carry with them the potential for incarceration for longer periods of time and the imposition of substantial fines. The loss of freedom often takes place outside an institution—parole and probation, for example. Probation may be given by a judge in lieu of incarceration; parole is usually the release from prison before the expiration of a prison term. In addition, state governors and the President (for federal criminals) can pardon a crime or commute a sentence from one form of punishment to a lesser form. Capital punishment is less commonly used than imprisonment or fines, but it is available in most states for some homicide offenses. Until relatively modern times, corporal and capital punishment were the major forms of punishment. Although corporal punishment is virtually unused in the United States, some have proposed reinstating some forms of it.

There has been increasing use of restitution-type punishment where the criminal is required to make efforts to directly "repay" or provide services to the individuals harmed or to society. This form of punishment appears to be increasing at least for relatively minor crimes, and has the advantage of benefiting the victim. Stigma is not ordinarily listed as a form of punishment, but conviction of a crime and imprisonment can be significant disabilities. The problems of the "ex con" in terms of social acceptance and employment are well known. Thus stigma is itself a form of punishment.

PURPOSES OF PUNISHMENT

The purposes of punishment are generally identified as retribution, deterrence, removal from society, and rehabilitation. The central reason for punishment changes from time to time. In the 1960s, for example, it was common to hear that retribution was unacceptable, and that rehabilitation should be the primary objective. During the 1980s, that position was probably reversed; today it is common to hear that retribution and restraint are the reasons for punishment and rehabilitation is identified as a failure.[6]

We will discuss the purposes of punishment under the following categories: retribution, just deserts, general deterrence, specific deterrence, prevention of wrongdoers from profiting from misdeeds, removal from society, rehabilitation, and statement of social values. Deterrence, removal, and rehabilitation are all intended to reduce antisocial conduct or to improve the criminal and are regarded as utilitarian. Retribution is generally not.

These goals are not entirely consistent. Pursuing one goal may make it more difficult to achieve another. There are, of course, many other social goals in addition to establishing effective punishment and these may conflict with implementing an effective system of punishment. Any system of punishment, therefore, requires a balancing of conflicting goals.

Retribution

Retribution is characterized by a desire to strike back at one who has caused harm. (A related concept, just deserts, often confused with retribution, is considered in the next section.) It is commonly said that a distinction must be drawn between private revenge and retribution, the imposition of punishment through a careful fact-finding and sentencing process is more calculating than private revenge is likely to be. At the same time, retribution does resemble social revenge.

An important function of the early criminal law was to avoid blood feuds by providing an alternative. Perhaps in this sense retribution is utilitarian in that it avoids private revenge seeking. If punishment is a legitimate surrogate for private revenge, victims' desire for retribution should have a substantial impact on the punishment imposed. In fact, within limits, it is not uncommon for the victims to have a significant say in the degree to which prosecution is undertaken. It is somewhat unusual, for example, for prosecutors to seek severe punishment when the victims are satisfied with a lesser punishment.

Beyond the private revenge feature of retribution, there is often a strong social feeling of anger and retributiveness from those who were not directly harmed by a crime. This represents a general fear of the effects of crime, but it may also reflect a frustration by those who struggle to obey the rules of society against those who do not similarly limit themselves.

With the renewed interest in retribution a fundamental question remains unanswered: is it a legitimate basis for punishment? The fact that victims or society feels anger or a sense of retribution does not necessarily justify acting on that anger. In part, the question of retribution is whether society should seek to overcome these emotional responses, or whether it should become the basis for social action.

Just Deserts

Retribution emphasizes a society's right to strike back; just deserts emphasizes the wrongdoer's deserving punishment whether or not there is any feeling of social retribution. It is sometimes argued that society has a moral obligation to impose punishment on criminals, not for utilitarian purposes but as a matter of promoting moral justice. The just deserts theory holds that punishment may legitimately be imposed even if the punishment neither serves a utilitarian purpose nor satisfies any social sense of retribution.

The basis for the just deserts approach may come from religious doctrine (although religions often promote forgiveness as well as vengeance) or from a fundamental moral principle (therefore provable only by intuition). Such a position is, of course, difficult to prove or disprove, but some of us do not have a strong intuitive feeling that "just deserts" requires punishment, or that it requires any particular form or severity of punishment. Some argue that it springs from a concept of mutual obligations or the "social contract."[7] This theory again depends on a belief in a social contract that carries with it the right or even obligation to inflict pain or injury on a member of the group who breaks the rules. However, a social contract would more appropriately require the repair of damage by someone who broke the rules than pure punishment.

The just desert concept probably fits best when based on free will theory of behavior. Someone is morally blameworthy, and therefore justly deserving punishment, if the person has freely chosen to do wrong. If a choice is "determined" in a strong behavioral sense, then it is difficult to consider the person to be *morally* blameworthy, and therefore difficult to justify just deserts. Thus, just deserts are not compatible with a strong determinist/behavioral view of human behavior.[8] As we saw in the chapter dealing with the insanity defense, using free will as a basis for criminal law and punishment is fraught with difficulties.

The just desert theory tends to emphasize the crime rather than the criminal. It is important under this theory that the "punishment fit the crime." Yet there is no clear understanding of what this means. It surely does not literally refer to "an eye for an eye." But what, then, is a "just desert" for a criminal who blinds someone in an assault? And does not the justice of the punishment perhaps fairly depend upon the individual or the factors which lead to the assault?

General Deterrence

Members of society fear criminal activity and want it stopped. The use of punishment to dissuade others from engaging in antisocial activity is a reason for imposing punishment. Deterrence may be general—to make an example of the criminal and thereby dissuade others from engaging in the activity—or specific—to dissuade the criminal himself from engaging in the criminal activity in the future.[9]

The question with general deterrence is whether the threat of punishment, or the punishment of one person, can dissuade another from engaging in unacceptable behavior. Such a theory requires that potential criminals consider the probability and disutility of punishment, and that the result of this calculation will dissuade them from the undesirable activity. At best, this is possible for some crimes and for some potential criminals. Crimes of passion or with a very high payoff or low probability of apprehension are unlikely to be significantly affected by general deterrence.

It is unreasonable to expect general deterrence to prevent all criminal activity. Some people will engage in antisocial acts regardless of the threat of punishment; others will not, even without any threat of punishment. On the other hand, some people, and some crimes, will be deterred by the threat of punishment. The issues are the degree to which deterrence can prevent criminal activity and the costs of the deterrence.

Another unresolved question is whether an increase in the severity of the threatened punishment can increase the effectiveness of the deterrent. The increase in punishment severity in recent years seems to assume such a link, but whether it actually exists is not clear.

Apprehension is central to general deterrence. Deterrence is difficult if there is little likelihood of being caught. The actual level of apprehension for serious crimes is a serious problem. It is estimated that only 12 to 20 out of 100 felonies result in an arrest and that less than 5 out of 100 felonies result in the imprisonment of the perpetrator. (Obviously the rate of apprehension and conviction varies considerably from one type of crime to another.)[10]

Specific Deterrence

Those who are punished for a crime might be expected to be less likely to commit the crime in the future. Specific deterrence could be effective because criminals calculate the risks of engaging in criminal activity, much like general deterrence with the added power of having seen the punishment itself. Or it might work as a kind of operant conditioning in which the illegal behavior is avoided without calculation.

It is unlikely that specific deterrence works very effectively as a form of operant conditioning. Punishment is not imposed uniformly (every time the target conduct occurs), nor is the punishment likely

to rapidly follow the undesired behavior. Again, the issue of apprehension becomes crucial.

Preventing Profit from Misdeeds

Without punishment wrongdoers would profit from their misdeeds
and this encourages some people to engage in illegal conduct. Punishment then may be viewed as a way of removing the profit from
crime. This is really a hybrid of the deterrence and just deserts position. Profiting from misconduct is wrong because it may encourage
wrongdoing; removing this profit deters crime. This kind of profit is
also unjust enrichment and may be viewed as fundamentally morally
wrong. The question is whether punishment can be effective in removing an unjust enrichment and in deterring such conduct. Apprehension again is a critical factor.

Removal

Society can be protected from crimes if we can restrain those who
are likely to commit them. Removal is based on the belief that those
who have been caught in the past would be likely to commit them in
the future. Because a relatively small number of people commit the
vast majority of crimes, we could theoretically reduce the crime rate
substantially by incarcerating or otherwise removing from society
that small number of people. Therefore, restraints on their freedom
protects society.

The legitimacy of imprisonment depends on: (1) the accuracy of
our prediction of which criminals are likely to be antisocial in the
future, (2) the proposition that those who have committed serious
crimes in the past will do so in the future, (3) the ability to release
these people when, but only when, they are no longer socially dangerous and (4) the ability to apprehend those with criminal propensities.[11]

Rehabilitation

Rehabilitation may be seen as a disease model of crime. The purpose
of punishing criminals is to reform or cure them of their antisocial

impulses. Psychotherapy, behavior modification, counseling, and skills training are among the techniques of rehabilitation. Rehabilitation should be more humane than other forms of punishment, but in reality being viewed as "sick" does not necessarily result in more humane treatment or less stigma than being considered criminal.

The rehabilitative ideal has faded dramatically in recent years. It fell out of favor primarily because it did not seem to work. In fairness, the rehabilitative ideal may not really have been given a true test. It was seldom, if ever, fully implemented. It may have failed not because of outcome, but because of costs. To fully implement a therapeutic environment would have been extremely expensive and well beyond most states' resources.

Statement of Social Values

The criminal law is one way of stating what conduct society finds unacceptable and of implementing broadly held social values. By providing punishment for their violation, society may emphasize and describe the importance it places on adherence to the values. It is a way of saying, "we absolutely don't want this conduct."

The system of punishment may perform this function, but if so, it is an expensive and confusing way of delivering the message. Actually, there are often inconsistent sentences in which relatively minor crimes end up being punished more severely than very serious ones. The Supreme Court recently found constitutional states' use of the criminal law to enforce social morals (the case involved sodomy). This case may encourage the development of punishment as a strong statement of social values.[12]

Crime Victims: Protection and Satisfaction

Protecting and satisfying crime victims may become a new goal of the criminal justice system, although it has not traditionally been a goal of punishment or criminal justice.[13] Of the goals discussed above, only one, retribution, is remotely directed toward the satisfaction of the victim.

Concern for the victim can be divided into two general parts: reducing the trauma of participating in the criminal justice system, and using the system to help the victim.[14] The first works to ensure that the victim is not further harmed by the system. It includes scheduling court hearings as conveniently as possible for the victim, and limitations on the cross-examination of victims (e.g., in rape cases) to avoid embarrassment. Promoting victims' interests range from providing for court-ordered restitution and other economic recovery for the victim, to the victim's participation in establishing the punishment.[15] The latter approach may be a form of "emotional compensation," permitting the victim to work through a certain level of anger and frustration. Economic compensation can be provided through direct payments from the criminal, other forms of restitution (e.g., services) from the criminal, or payments from the government.[16]

The civil law of torts has traditionally been the vehicle for compensating individuals for wrongs, with the criminal system dealing with the public interest in the wrongs. For a variety of reasons (notably, too few rich people go into crime), the tort system has not been particularly effective as a mechanism for compensating the victims of crime. The use of the criminal system as a mode for compensation is an interesting return to the common roots of torts and criminal law.[17] It is conceivable that the flexibility of the punishments and dispositions possible in the criminal law will provide a more satisfactory compensation for crime victims than the tort system has.

A Clear Purpose?

Does any clear, consistent purpose for punishment appear from this? Probably not. The problems we examine in the remainder of the chapter reflect the fact that we do not have clearly identified, consistent goals which we seek and reasonably expect to accomplish through punishment. The result is a hodgepodge of rules and practices that may have produced a system of punishment that is very expensive and may not be very effective.

IS THE CURRENT SYSTEM EFFECTIVE?

There is no definitive answer to the question of punishment effectiveness. First, as we have seen, we are uncertain of the goal against which we should measure effectiveness. This fact is made worse because some of the goals of punishment are inconsistent. For example, the desire to rehabilitate a criminal may conflict with our desire to impose retribution, and the "just desert" concept might require a much different prison term than a removal principle would dictate.

General and specific deterrence, preventing wrongdoers from profiting from misdeeds, removal, and rehabilitation are all aimed at reducing the overall crime rate, although they use different mechanisms to achieve this goal. Are they successful?

The question of the effectiveness of deterrence is whether more crimes would be committed if the threat of punishment were not present or of a different form. The question of removal is whether those imprisoned would commit additional crimes during the period of incarceration had they not been imprisoned. (In part, of course, the last question depends on whether you count as "crimes" those incarcerated commit against other prisoners while they are in prison.)

There is some reason to think that the threat of punishment is not a very effective deterrent. For example, prison has been described as an ineffective deterrent because it inflicts "chronic pain" as opposed to "acute pain." Punishment is often considerably removed in time from the offense.[18] In addition, because the probability of arrest and conviction is fairly low for many crimes, punishment is uncertain at best.[19]

Surely the threat of punishment does deter some people from some kinds of crime, but we know very little about the effectiveness of deterrents.[20] More precise questions should be asked: For what crime will the threat of fine or prison prove to be a significant deterrent? Does the length of imprisonment have any significant deterrent impact? Can the threat of punishment have an effect on the more serious crimes, particularly those involving personal injury, or do these occur without rational premeditation?[21] The threat of punishment undoubtedly has some deterrent effect for some crimes, even though this has not been adequately demonstrated or measured. However we cannot assume that increasing the intensity of punishment significantly affects most rates of crime.[22] The public does not have great faith that punishment is effective in deterring crime; nearly 80 percent believe that the law enforcement system does not deter crime.[23]

In reality the "removal" function of punishment may not be very effective. Theoretically, incarcerating the few criminals who are responsible for most of the crimes would drop the crime rate. Unfortunately, there is no reason to believe that our society has had great luck in apprehending and convicting these people or in successfully identifying them from among all the criminals arrested or in incarcerating them while they are still dangerous.[24] The persistent felon statutes discussed later in this chapter are meant to identify and imprison these career criminals, but these programs probably fail to recognize persistent felons soon enough or precisely enough to have an impact on the crime rate. One estimate is that the current use of punishment may affect the crime rate by less than 5 percent.[25]

The rehabilitative function of our system of punishment is now widely considered to be a failure.[26] Punishment as treatment probably reached its zenith in the 1950s and 1960s, but it held a place in punishment theory throughout this century. Some prisoners have been reformed and "improved" while in prison. It now appears, however, that many others have not been rehabilitated, and that still others were more debilitated than rehabilitated.[27] The potential for learning the business of crime and for becoming associated with serious criminals while in prison is well known. As we have noted, the rehabilitative ideal may never have been given a fair test because it was never fully implemented or funded. Interestingly, the public indicates that rehabilitation should be the primary emphasis of prison.[28]

It is particularly difficult to determine whether retribution and just desert goals are fulfilled. In part, this determination depends on one's estimation of what deserts are just and whether society and the victims of crimes are satisfied with punishment. However, the wide disparity in sentencing given to similar defendants for committing the same crime suggests that deserts are not even equal, let alone just. There appears to be great dissatisfaction among some segments of the public and some victims about the punishments meted out. Generally, the criticism is that the punishment is too light. About 80 percent of the population believes that local courts do not deal harshly enough with criminals.[29]

The low arrest and conviction rate for felons also interferes with the retribution and just deserts aspects of the criminal justice system. In the overwhelming majority of crimes, society's desire for retribution will go unsatisfied because no one will be apprehended. The concept of just deserts may also break down where the chance of apprehension is so small that punishment resembles a lottery rather than a systematic imposition of well-deserved justice.

Does our system of punishment serve any purpose? In truth, it probably serves all of the purposes we have discussed to some degree, in some cases. But the criminal justice system, as a whole, does not serve them very well. Even if all of the other problems could be solved, the difficulty in apprehending and convicting felons would undoubtedly destroy the ability of the system to meet its objectives. The low rate of apprehension then becomes a critical link in establishing an effective system of punishment. Assuming the current system of punishment is at least partly successful, the question remains, whether the successes of the current system are worth its costs. In addition to direct costs, such as the prison system, there are substantial indirect costs—lost potential productivity, family welfare, and other support costs.

SPECIAL ISSUES RELATED TO PRISONS

Imprisonment, and prison release programs, such as probation and parole, are currently the centerpiece of the punishment for serious crimes in the United States. In this section, we consider some of the important issues related to the use of prison and prison release programs.

Jails, prisons, and dungeons have been used for centuries to hold defendants awaiting trial and political prisoners. Imprisonment as a form of punishment is relatively recent. Around the time of the American Revolution, Pennsylvania Quakers used prison sentences as an alternative to the common forms of severe corporal and capital punishments.[30] The purpose was to permit a period of personal and biblical reflection. Unfortunately, over the years, such reflection has proved to be less beneficial for most prisoners than it was for the thoughtful Quakers who devised them.

From these humanitarian beginnings, prisons have become large institutions which are still expanding. At the end of 1983, 438,830 inmates were incarcerated, an increase of 5.9 percent during 1983. Prison population increased about 12 percent both in 1982 and in 1981.[31] The rapid expansion in the number of prisoners in recent years is related to longer penalties being imposed for a number of crimes, an increase in the number of crimes carrying significant prison terms, and an increase in the population 16 to 30 years old which commits much of the crime (although this population is now declining). It is estimated that in 1982, $9 billion was spent on corrections in the United States.[32]

The dramatic increase in prisoners has resulted in serious overcrowding. Although the Supreme Court has indicated that at least some overcrowding does not violate the Constitution,[33] prison conditions have become so bad that many prisons are under federal court orders to reduce crowding or improve facilities. Generally, federal courts are concerned that conditions violate the Eighth Amendment prohibition on cruel and unusual punishment.[34] It was estimated that 500 prison beds would have to be added weekly in the United States just to accommodate the rate of increase in prisoners which occurred in 1983.[35] In addition to the problem with federal courts, of course, the current overcrowding is likely to make it more difficult for prison officials to control prisoners and undoubtedly increases the possibility of violence and riots.

Despite popular discussions of "country club" prisons, they are immensely unpleasant places, which deny normal social interaction and almost any sense of privacy. In addition, they are replete with substantial intimidation and oppression by other inmates and some prison officials, sexual and other physical assaults, long periods of idleness, no opportunity for normal sexual activities and so on.[36] Beyond the immediate pain of incarceration, there is the disruption of what is often an already fragile family life, and employment and social relationships. In prisons, in fact, violence by inmates is a form of brutality, which we would not directly inflict upon prisoners in the name of punishment.

Given the costs of imprisonment, are too many criminals sent to prison and kept there too long? Public opinion believes just the opposite.[37] Public opinion notwithstanding, the current levels of incarceration are costly and may be counterproductive. Prison terms probably provide only a modest deterrent to crime, are of limited value as restraint, are not effective as rehabilitation, and are often not very satisfying as retribution or just deserts.

A strong argument can be made for reducing the length of prison terms.[38] Prison sentences are generally stated in terms of minimums and maximums with some discretion left to parole boards about when release should occur. The average minimum sentence imposed for all felonies is 4.3 years, the average maximum 8.6 years.[39] For property offenses the average minimum is 2.7, the average maximum 5.6 years, although parole usually results in release before the full sentence is served. These lengthy terms are probably not worth the costs. It is very doubtful that they provide a much stronger deterrent effect or opportunity for rehabilitation than do shorter terms. Long terms remove criminals from circulation, but may not do so in relationship to the potential for committing additional offenses. Longer periods may or may not better serve interest of retribution and just deserts.

A closely related subject is the issue of mandatory sentences, which require that a fixed or minimum prison term be imposed by the judge. The vast majority of states have some offenses for which there is mandatory sentencing, ranging from auto theft to murder, but most involve physical violence, drugs, or firearms.[40]

Mandatory prison terms are part of a larger issue of the degree to which individual differences should be taken into account in sentencing. The difficulty with nonuniform sentences is that sentences may be imposed on the basis of whim or factors (such as race) that are inappropriate in the decision process. A number of studies have indicated that the seriousness of the offense and the defendant's prior criminal record are the most important elements in determining the length of sentences, but a significant portion of variance in sentences is unexplained.[41] The failure to consider individual difference in sentencing, however, is likely to result in another kind of unfairness: individuals will be needlessly incarcerated. Futhermore, in one sense punishment is "unequal" even with uniform sentences because some offenders have more to lose through lengthy incarceration than do others.

A number of sentencing reforms have been tried within the last two decades which permit some discretion by the judge while eliminating as many of the inappropriate considerations as possible. Sentencing guidelines and presumptive sentences are examples. With presumptive sentence, a standard sentence is expected to be imposed except when special, clearly enunciated factors are present. Sentencing guidelines range from a form of presumptive sentence to a more complex table providing suggested sentences. A combination of relevant factors give a sentence or range within which the sentence should fall.[42] Such innovations are preferable to mandatory sentencing because of the limited flexibility they provide in taking individual differences into consideration.

Probation and parole provide for community-based supervision of the offender. Probation is usually granted by a judge at the time of sentencing (although under "shock" probation the defendant may spend a short time in prison and then be released on probation status). Parole is generally granted by a review board after the offender has been incarcerated. The parole or probation is usually contingent upon the offender's meeting a number of conditions. The violation of parole or probation may result in the offender's return to prison.

Probation and parole have the advantage of providing some limitation on freedom (thereby meeting deterrence and retribution/just deserts goals), and providing for some state supervision and guidance (fulfilling rehabilitation objectives). It has the potential disadvantages of not being as effective a form of removal or deterrent as a full prison sentence would be. It has the advantages of not desocializing offenders by removing them from normal society, permitting them to continue employment and being less expensive than incarceration. In the case of parole, it also represents an intermediate step between imprisonment and complete freedom.

Probation and parole are frequently used. There are about three offenders under supervision (approximately 1.5 million adults at any given time) for each one person confined.[43]

Several criticisms of parole and probation are legitimate. Judges and parole boards often have insufficient information on which to make these difficult decisions, which are essentially predictions of future behavior. There are often too few parole officers to adequately supervise the conditions of parole or probation. Periods of parole or probation are sometimes excessively long, thereby providing for unnecessary interference with the release of the offender from all state control, and additional expense to the state.

Despite these problems, supervised release from custody is essential. It is unlikely that the incarceration of the vast majority of those on parole would serve any purpose and in many cases would be harmful. Programs should provide for more adequate supervision of offenders, and for a better process for selecting those to be placed on probation or granted parole. Current selection processes may result in the release of a large number of dangerous felons.[44]

LIMITS ON PUNISHMENT

The Constitution of the United States, and the constitutions of many states, impose limitations on the kinds of punishment that may be imposed. The most important limitation is the Eighth Amendment's prohibition on cruel and unusual punishment.

The prohibition of cruel and unusual punishment in Anglo-American law can be traced to the Magna Carta of 1215. The English Bill of Rights of 1689 contained a specific prohibition on cruel and unusual punishment. The Eighth Amendment was added to the Constitution with little debate. Thus, it is difficult to determine precisely what the framers meant by the prohibition on cruel and unusual punishment. They took language from English law which was imprecise.[45]

The meaning of "cruel and unusual" thus remains somewhat unclear. Taken literally punishments would be prohibited only if they were both infrequently applied and also cruel. Under such a reading of the Eighth Amendment, extremely barbarous tortures could be imposed as long as they were inflicted with sufficient frequency not to be "unusual." It is more likely that the amendment prohibits punishments which are unreasonable *or* barbarous.

Cruelty is a subjective concept. Therefore it is a difficult task to determine what standards should be used to determine which punishments are cruel. Should only those punishments which were considered cruel at the time of the adoption of the Eighth Amendment be unconstitutional? Part of the answer to the question depends upon a broad question of constitutional interpretation: whether the Constitution should be interpreted as intended by those who wrote it or whether it should be interpreted in light of the needs and ideals of today. If the intent of the framers is viewed as critical, the question is whether the framers intended the term "cruel and unusual" to be interpreted only by the standards of the 1780s, or whether they intended "cruel and unusual" to be a flexible doctrine. The Supreme Court has said that the concept of cruel and unusual punishment is an evolving standard of constitutional law and that punishments that are considered cruel and unusual change as society changes.[46] It is, of course, somewhat difficult to know just what the "evolving" standards of cruel and unusual punishment are.

Several groups or types of punishment are generally accepted currently as cruel and unusual:

1. Barbaric and inhumane treatment. This limitation probably would apply to severe corporal punishment and other torture.[47] At least some limited corporal punishment is permitted by the Eighth Amendment. The Supreme Court has rejected, for example, the claim that all corporal punishment in schools violates the Eighth Amendment.[48]

2. Pointless or irrational harm or pain.[49] Punishment that serves no purpose is unreasonable and therefore cruel and unusual.

3. The conditions of incarceration must be reasonably humane. This is currently the source of considerable litigation. Although the Supreme Court has ruled that some overcrowding of prisons does not constitute cruel and unusual punishment, at some point overcrowding or unsanitary conditions are so severe that they become cruel and unusual.[50] Similarly, the failure to provide basic human needs such as nutrition and some medical care to prisoners is cruel and unusual.[51]

4. Status Crimes. Punishing someone for having a certain status or disease may violate the Eighth Amendment. Thus convicting one of being a drug addict is unconstitutional.[52] It is, however, constitutional to convict someone of acts related to addiction, such as possession or dispensing drugs or being in public in a drugged condition.[53] In many instances the state may choose to require treatment of a status if it is in the public interest. Thus civil commitment and mandatory drug treatment programs provide treatment rather than punishment and therefore do not necessarily violate the Eighth Amendment. The distinction between punishment and treatment may become important for constitutional purposes.[54] Whether this distinction between punishment and involuntary treatment is sensible is a matter of opinion. Involuntary treatment and punishment both involve loss of freedom and incarceration, and both are likely to result in a social stigma.

5. Extreme disproportionality. Punishments that are extremely disproportionate to the severity of the crime may violate the Eighth Amendment. It is in this area that much of the debate concerning cruel and unusual punishment

now rages. The Supreme Court has been particularly sensitive to Eighth Amendment claims where the death penalty is involved.[55]

There is considerable disagreement on the issue of whether prison terms must be proportional to the seriousness of the crime committed. The imposition of a life sentence for a parking violation is inconsistent with the Eighth Amendment, but beyond that consensus is difficult. The Court's decision in two cases involving life sentences under persistent felon statutes demonstrate this. In both cases, the defendants had been convicted of relatively minor property offenses. In the first case, the defendant was given a life sentence with the possibility of parole after 12 years had been served.[56] In the second case, a life sentence without the possibility of parole, although clemency or a pardon was possible from the governor.[57] The Court upheld the former sentence but struck down the latter as violating the Eighth Amendment.

In determining the proportionality of a sentence, three factors should be considered: (1) the harshness of the sentence in light of the seriousness of the crime, (2) sentences imposed in the same jurisdiction for more serious crimes, and (3) the sentences imposed in other jurisdictions for the same crime. The Court has held that great deference should be given to legislatures and to trial judges in setting the length of prison terms. It therefore appears that the Supreme Court will permit prison terms of great length even for relatively minor felonies except in extreme circumstances.

The Court's reluctance to strike down long prison terms for relatively minor crimes appears inconsistent with the review of other punishment. It has fully accepted the concept of proportionality regarding capital punishment. There is no reason to believe that the Eighth Amendment includes a proportionality principle only for capital crimes. It is also clear that significant (or brutal) corporal punishment violates the Eighth Amendment, and yet prisons are often a harsh and brutal environment. The Court has upheld life sentences for three felonies involving the theft of less than $300[58] and a forty-year sentence for possession of marijuana.[59] It is likely that many offenders, given a choice, would prefer relatively severe corporal punishment, which the court would find cruel and unusual, to the very long prison sentence the Court permits. The Court undoubtedly is concerned that proportionality reviews of prison sentences would overwhelm the federal courts because so many long sentences would be appealed on constitutional grounds. However, the "evolving standards" of cruel and unusual punishment should take into account the real brutality of extended prison terms and consider how such punishments can be permitted when other punishments which are cruel and unusual might be chosen instead.

A second system of justice exists for juvenile offenders. The juvenile justice system established in the United States near the turn of the century was meant to avoid the harshness of the adult criminal system and to establish a new approach for juveniles.[60] The system of juvenile justice is considered in chapter 13.

OTHER ISSUES RELATED TO PUNISHMENT

Persistent Offender Statutes

Persistent offender, habitual offender, or recidivist statutes have been enacted in nearly every state. These statutes provide for extended sentences, sometimes life sentences, for repeat offenders. In addition to being sentenced for the most recent criminal conviction, the offender receives an augmented or additional sentence for being a persistent offender. The provisions of the statutes vary from state to state in terms of the offenders who qualify, sentence imposed, and the procedures followed.[61] The purpose of these statutes is to remove from society those who repeatedly commit crimes. In fact, most states now provide for habitual offender statutes to take effect after a second felony conviction.[62] The theory is that this will remove the relatively small number of people who commit most of the criminal offenses.[63]

Unfortunately, persistent offender laws do not properly identify dangerous criminals or do not do so quickly enough, and may incarcerate others much too long. Many of the statutes provide for long incarcerations even after conviction for very minor property offense felonies. Two persistent felon prison term cases considered by the Supreme Court illustrate this problem. The Supreme Court upheld a life sentence, with the possibility of parole, for an offender who had been convicted of three felonies: fraudulent use of credit cards

($80), forged check ($28.36), and false pretenses ($120.75).[64] In another case, the Court struck down a life sentence *without* parole for an offender who had committed nonviolent, relatively minor property offenses.[65] The citizens of Texas and South Dakota were probably not much safer for having sentenced these two criminals to life, and yet the states were paying a significant price to hold them.

If persistent felons statutes are to be effective, they must be limited to serious offenses involving some real threat to the public. This is not to say that offenders, even those who commit relatively minor felonies, should not have been punished for their misdeeds, but life sentences for them make little sense. States often use persistent felon statutes against fairly old prisoners. In one of the cases noted above, for example, the offender was 36 years old when he was sentenced. The reduction in crime resulting from imprisoning many people older than 30 or 35 is probably minimal. The logic of sentencing many persistent criminals to extremely long prison terms, often extending well beyond the time when the offender will be 40, is not clear.

If these statutes have any chance of working, they probably need to be able to identify persistent offenders early and to incarcerate them during the high crime years, but not after the likelihood of substantial criminality has passed. This requires that states consider juvenile offenses as the basis for adult persistent offender sentencing.

Preventive Detention

The purpose of preventive detention is to hold suspects while they are awaiting trial or appeal so that they do not commit additional crimes during this time. Preventive detention relies on at least two premises: (1) that it is appropriate to hold suspects or others who are not finally convicted of a crime for which they can be imprisoned and (2) those who will commit additional crimes while awaiting adjudication can be predicted with reasonable certainty.

The arguments against the concept of preventive detention are that it violates the Eighth Amendment which provides, "Excessive bail shall not be required." When preventive detention is imposed, there is no bail and by definition, it is argued, that is excessive bail. It is argued that bail should be used only to ensure that the defendant will not flee. The purposes of requiring release on bail are to permit the defendant to help prepare a defense and go about ordinary daily life, and to respect the innocence of those accused. It also prevents authorities from using incarceration pending trial as a means of forcing a guilty plea or as a "chip" in plea bargaining. Preventive detention violates a principle fundamental to American law, the assumption of innocence. If one is truly innocent until proved guilty, there can be no more basis for holding one accused of a crime than there could be of plucking someone off the street at random to hold. Another argument is that preventive detention invites official abuse by encouraging the filing of charges in order to detain someone.[66]

Arguments in favor of preventive detention are that it is an effective way to deal with slow judicial processes and to protect the public from offenders likely to commit antisocial acts. It is also argued that while the Eighth Amendment prohibits excessive bail, it does not require that bail be granted; therefore, preventive detention does not violate the Eighth Amendment. Proponents of preventive detention note that it is much like civil commitment, and can be justified on the same basis; it prevents unnecessary harm to citizens. It is different than random incarceration of citizens because before preventive detention can be implemented, it must be likely that the defendant has committed a serious crime and is likely to do so while awaiting trial.

Even if preventive detention can be justified philosophically (a position we do not accept) it is based on the ability to predict who is likely to commit crimes pending trial. It is possible that these predictions can be made with some greater accuracy than civil commitment predictions of dangerousness, which are notoriously bad. Nevertheless, it is likely that there will be substantial errors in these predictions.

Preventive detention, even for juveniles, has been approved as constitutional by the Supreme Court.[67] The revision of the federal criminal code now permits preventive detention in federal cases.[68]

Probation and Parole

A number of issues concerning the current use of probation and parole were considered above. The public perception is that too many dangerous criminals are released too soon and that these criminals then commit additional crimes.[69] There is some evidence that a significant number of those on probation commit additional serious crimes.[70] Despite these concerns, given the large increase in prison populations, it can be argued that most offenders will have to be released earlier in their sentences. The alternatives are to build and operate a large number of additional prisons, to convict fewer people or to reduce the length of sentences imposed.

Many other questions remain unanswered. Among them, can judges and parole boards adequately predict which prisoners are dangerous, which need or deserve a prison sentence and which should be released? Are probation and parole implemented reasonably fairly, or do inappropriate factors play major roles in these decisions? Are the systems effective in protecting society from further criminal acts by offenders, in helping parolees make the adjustments from prison to normal social life, and in helping to return offenders to productive life? Are there sufficient parole officers to adequately supervise released offenders? Would there be any significant difference in society or in offenders if they were released conditionally into the community without supervision and without the restrictions normally imposed? Finally, are these systems worth the resources devoted to them? Because of the importance of parole and probation these questions deserve serious additional study.

Victimless Crimes

What acts or conditions are appropriate to punish? The Constitution clearly prohibits punishment for some acts (printing unpopular opinions, holding certain religious beliefs). Within the broad range of acts for which the Constitution would permit punishment, the question remains: What acts *should* be punished? Much of the debate on the appropriateness of criminal sanctions has centered on the "victimless" crimes or activities to which any "victim" has voluntarily agreed. These crimes typically include consensual adult sex offenses (such as prostitution, fornication, and sodomy).[71] Victimless crimes are considered as part of the chapter dealing with sexual variations (chapter 14).

Behavior Modification

Major questions concerning the use of behavior modification in prisons may arise from the ends or goals of the behavior modification, and from the means used to achieve those ends.[72] There is ultimately the question of the degree to which it is appropriate for society to change or manipulate prisoners, whether it is proper for the state to force or coerce participation in a behavior modification program designed to make a change the prisoner finds undesirable. For example, suppose a behavior modification technique is developed to reduce violent reaction to stress or to change sexual orientation, but a prisoner does not want the change. Does the commission of a crime give society sufficient authority to make personality changes involuntarily? Obviously the purpose of correctional institutions and punishment is to change the criminal. On the other hand, there are dangers associated with using conviction of a crime as the basis for making involuntary personality changes. At a minimum, we should require that the changes to be made be directly related to the criminal conviction. It would be inappropriate, for example, to use conviction for speeding as a basis for a behavioral modification program aimed at sexual preference. Only for the most serious offenses should involuntary changes be considered. In addition, the more closely tied behavior is to basic religious or political beliefs, the more likely it is inappropriate for the government to try to change the prisoner involuntarily. Thus, someone convicted of stuffing a ballot box should not be given behavioral modification to make him completely apolitical, nor should a snake handling religious group be instilled with an inordinate fear of snakes.

For the moment, these issues are more theoretical than real. As behavioral modification becomes increasingly sophisticated and effective, however, they will have to be faced. In addition to the legal questions there is the issue of whether it is ethical for behavioral scientists to participate in programs which make psychological changes that the patient does not want.

The means used to achieve modification also raise important issues. Two techniques, aversive therapy and token economies, have already been the source of controversy. Aversive therapy is the imposition of unpleasant stimuli to unwanted behavior for the purposes of reducing the likelihood that the subjects will engage in them. For example, administering a painful electric shock every time someone tries to steal something may ultimately extinguish the desire to engage in the theft.

Aversive therapy is probably included in what most people think of as punishment. The state is freer to involuntarily impose painful conditions on prisoners than it is with mental patients. Nevertheless, there are some limits. The involuntary administration of drugs that cause the sensation of suffocation and drowning or that cause violent vomiting, as punishment or as conditioning agents, with prisoners appears to violate the Eighth Amendment.[73] It is likely that somewhat less dramatic forms of aversive therapy would pass Eighth Amendment muster and be permitted, even when used involuntarily with prisoners.

Token economies seek to encourage and reward appropriate behavior and thereby provide positive reinforcement and encourage target behaviors. Points or "tokens" are provided for engaging in the desired behavior, such as going for a period of time without violent outbursts, completing an assigned task without supervision, or reading a book. The tokens or points can then be exchanged for privileges or goods that the subject views as valuable, such as a special kind of food, television time, visits from friends, or increased privacy. Token economies have been used in mental institutions and prisons, and their use has raised some difficult legal issues.[74] It is probably reasonable to expect their use to increase, and they might be particularly useful in promoting the ability to work with others in groups.[75]

As long as the ends they promote are appropriate, token economies in prisons should raise relatively few legal issues. Most of the problems in mental hospitals are not present in prison settings because of the reduced legal rights of prisoners. There is, however, an obligation to provide basic humane conditions in prisons. Therefore, requiring prisoners to earn tokens for basic necessities would probably not be permissible. Since prison authorities can manipulate so much of the environment, however, there should be little difficulty in finding attractive privileges to establish a token economy system.[76]

Behavior modification techniques may be used while an offender is in the community, perhaps as part of a probation or parole arrangement. Particularly when specific antisocial behavior is the target of change, community-based therapy may be desirable if adequate control can be maintained over the offender to ensure that the target behavior is not rewarded in the community.

Much behavior modification can probably legally be imposed even over the objection of an offender. With the completely voluntary consent of a prisoner, almost any form of behavioral modification program would be permitted. The prisoner who wishes to change violent propensities or a sexual preference can consent to treatments which may do that and may even agree to aversive therapies. The question, of course, is what constitutes voluntary consent within a prison setting. Is there voluntary consent, for example, where release from prison on parole depends upon the consent to therapy? The inherently coercive atmosphere of prison has resulted in a limitation on the use of consenting prisoners to human experimentation,[77] and elimination, in one case, of consent to psychosurgery.[78] Even if consent to behavioral modification is coerced by the prison setting, does that make it invalid? Not necessarily. The level of coercion that would make behavior modification illegal is not yet clear. Behavior modification is probably more likely to succeed with a consenting individual who wants to change. Some coercion is, perhaps, inevitable but consent to any behavioral modification that can properly be conducted only with consent should be free of any seriously coercive elements.[79]

BEHAVIORAL PRINCIPLES FOR MAXIMIZING THE EFFECTIVENESS OF PUNISHMENT

Several principles for maximizing the use of punishment can be distilled from behavioral science research. We will outline them here, but note that many of them would be difficult or impossible to implement given the realities of the criminal justice system. These principles are generally based on laboratory research. The degree to which the results apply to complex human situations is not entirely clear.[80]

A. *Certainty and Timing*
  1. Punishment should be delivered to all, or a very high proportion, of the behavior to be eliminated and should not appear to be random or infrequent.
  2. No unauthorized or uncontrolled means of escape from punishment should be permitted.

3. Punishment should occur soon after the undesired behavior.

B. *Intensity and Duration*

4. The initial punishment should be as great as reasonably possible.

5. Continuation of the unacceptable behavior should also bring punishment at the highest reasonable levels.

6. Duration of punishment, within limits, may increase effectiveness somewhat. However, long periods of punishment should be avoided to prevent habituation and adaption.

C. *Alternatives and Positive Reinforcement*

7. An alternative to the punished behavior should be available and rewarded. Punishment simply decreases the probability of a behavior and does not itself ensure positive acceptable behavior.

8. Punishment should not be associated with the presentation of reinforcement. The punishment may signal forthcoming reinforcement and therefore the subject may work for punishment.

9. All reinforcement should be removed from the target behaviors so that the same behavior does not receive both reward and punishment.

10. Where a behavior is acceptable in some situations but unacceptable in others, a clear distinction must be drawn between when it is and is not permissible.

D. *Undesirable Behavior*

11. Care should be taken to avoid promoting undesirable behavior which may be associated with punishment such as an increase in aggression, imitation of the act of punishing, substitution of new undesirable behaviors for the behavior being punished and suppression of non-target behaviors as well as the target behavior.[81]

We emphasize that although these principles are generally supported by laboratory research, some caution must be exercised in assuming that they can be applied correctly to the criminal justice and corrections system.[82] Considerable research remains to be done

on the application of these principles to complex human corrections.[83]

REFORMS AND ALTERNATIVES

A fair review of the system of punishment in the United States would
probably conclude that it is at best marginally effective. In truth, the
current system is a tangle of poorly defined and conflicting goals. The
centerpiece of the system, prison, provides rehabilitative opportunities for some, but it also desocializes and brutalizes others. A deterrent effect probably exists, but it may be limited particularly for
more serious crimes. The removal of many criminals from society may
have a rather modest effect on the crime rate. Given the gross disparity in the treatment of similar offenders and the small percentage
of offenders who are punished at all, the system seriously fails to
provide just deserts to criminal offenders. The desire for retribution
is at least partially met by the current system, but only the victims
of the relatively few criminals apprehended and convicted may feel a
sense of satisfaction.

The price of the current system of punishment, as we have noted,
is substantial. A variety of reforms have been proposed. The alternatives and reforms we consider in this section are not long-run solutions, but rather ways of modestly increasing the effectiveness of
punishment or of saving resources. A real long-term reform undoubtedly awaits a new approach to punishment, and probably a new approach to crime. For example, a change in the "free will" basis of
criminal law would undoubtedly have a substantial impact on the
foundations of punishment.

The rate of apprehension and conviction is a key to successfully
meeting most of the goals that are set for punishment. With a 100
percent apprehension rate almost any of the goals would have a
chance to succeed, but of course there probably would be little need
for punishment where apprehension was certain. Nobody disagrees
that criminals should be caught, but implementing this is obviously
extremely difficult. Given the importance of apprehension, a strong
argument can be made for diverting some resources from punishment, particularly prisons, to programs which may increase the rate
of apprehension.

Changes in the Use of Incarceration

Reducing the number of offenders in prison would reduce costs. Perhaps most effective would be to reduce the length of prison terms. Except for holding offenders with a high probability of committing additional serious crimes, little purpose is served by very lengthy prison terms. This would reduce the cost of imprisonment and reduce the likelihood of desocialization. Shorter prison terms could, of course, legitimately be coupled with a supervised release program. The number of crimes involving significant incarceration could also be reduced. Very short-term incarceration, sometimes called "shock probation," may be appropriate. Under such a system, an offender is placed in a prison for a short time, perhaps two to six weeks, as a way of emphasizing the seriousness of his or her conduct and the undesirability of prison life. Following the shock probation the offender is then paroled.

Other Limitations on Freedom

Some lesser restrictions on freedom may be adequate to accomplish some of the purposes of prison. Supervision of an offender in the community may be only 10 percent of the cost of imprisonment in a maximum security institution. Probation, parole, and limited release programs are efficient. In addition, or in lieu of them, short terms of incarceration, such as on weekends or during evenings, can also be used.

Electronic monitors may be a way of ensuring that limits on the freedom of movement are observed. Some jurisdictons are already experimenting with requiring offenders to wear an electronic ankle bracelet that sends a radio signal ensuring that prisoners stay home or wherever they are sentenced to be.[84]

Victims and Restitution

Reforms must consider the victims of crime. Complaints by victims that an offender got off too easy seem to be a strong argument for blocking reforms and for increasing the intensity of punishment. In addition, the system of punishment has traditionally done little to restore or compensate victims for the injuries they have suffered. Tailoring punishment to the needs of victims might aid the victims while reducing the costs of punishment. Ordering offenders to pay the victims substantial sums to cover their injuries has two problems. First, not enough wealthy people go into crime to make the suggestion practical, and second, compensation may not be seen as adequate punishment. On the other hand, requiring offenders to perform substantial, even long-term, services for victims or for others may be seen as some real punishment. A number of jurisdictions, including the federal government, require the consideration of some restitution as part of the sentencing process.[85]

The form of restitution must be carefully considered. A victim might be understandably reluctant to have a burglar polishing the family silver. One alternative is to have the victims and the offenders negotiate an agreement as part of the sentencing process. The agreement details how restitution will be made. Of course the agreement must be confirmed by the court. In some situations, it is appropriate to add public-service obligations.

There are several advantages to such victim–offender agreements. They permit victims to be part of the sentencing process and to work through a certain level of anger and frustration, and they provide at least some compensation to the injured victim. They require offenders to deal with the victims on a continuing basis, and offenders may learn the consequences of their antisocial conduct. In some instances offenders may also realize that they are ultimately going to have to deal with victims and therefore be more understanding of their feelings. Such agreements also reduce the cost of incarcerating some offenders. It would make "paying a debt to society" a more meaningful concept than is prison. On the other hand, restitution agreements may vary dramatically depending on the victim's level of sophistication in negotiation and feelings of retribution. Thus, punishment for the same crime may vary considerably depending on who the victim is. Such agreements do not remove offenders from society and they may commit additional crimes.

Concern for the victims is an important, relatively recent, part of the criminal justice system. The concern expresses itself in efforts to make the criminal process easier on victims when they file complaints or appear in court, in victim compensation systems funded by the state, in greater involvement of victims in the sentencing or disposition of offenders (including in the plea bargaining process), and in encouraging the use of restitution. This increased concern for victims is a positive recognition that crime harms individuals as well as society, and that civil remedies have generally been inadequate to provide any meaningful help to the victims of crime.[86] Considering victims often complicates the system. For example, victims may make plea bargaining agreements more difficult to complete, and an extremely vindictive victim may cause problems in making reasonable parole and probation decisions.[87]

It remains to be seen whether this interest in the problems of the victim can be sustained as a part of the criminal justice system. It could become an important basis for punishment and one of the purposes of the criminal justice system.

Noninstitutional Rehabilitation

Many of the rehabilitation programs, ranging from behavior modification to completion of high school courses, can be carried out in the community. Sentencing orders or orders for release can specify the rehabilitation programs in which the offenders agree to participate. These noninstitutional approaches are generally less expensive and desocializing than prison.

Corporal Punishment

Corporal punishment, including flogging, branding, brutalization, dunking, and stocks and pillory, was common until the nineteenth century.[88] There are now proposals that it be reinstated. One advocate describes the punishment of the future involving the use of painful electric shock.[89]

The advantages claimed for corporal punishment are that it meets retributive needs, provides a reasonable form of deterrence, is less expensive than prison, is less disruptive of families, and is ultimately more humane than prison. The arguments against it are that it is barbaric and cruel and unusual, and that it is not severe enough. There may be some validity to the argument that a return to moderate corporal punishment is more humane than a moderate prison term. It is likely that, given the choice, many convicts would opt for it rather than prison terms. Prisons are fairly brutal places with substantial assaultive "corporal punishment" by other prisoners. Prison terms may also be more likely than corporal punishment to disrupt the lives of offenders.

When used with other alternatives to prison, corporal punishment might provide an element of retribution that would make a reduction in prison terms more palatable to victims and to society. One danger is that it is a first step down the road to brutality. The inclination to demand longer and longer prison sentences does suggest that possibility.

Considering the Alternatives

The alternatives we have discussed, used in combination, will probably be as effective as the prison sentence, if not more so. They should be considerably less expensive. Long prison terms should be given only in special circumstances, such as when there is strong probability of repeated serious antisocial acts. Short prison terms or shock probation can be coupled with supervised release programs. If retribution or just desert goals must be met moderate corporal punishment could be used in some cases. In addition, a strong victim restitution and community service program should be used routinely. Incarceration might also have to be used for those who might try to escape from community based programs by running away. Increasingly, electronic devices will make it possible to keep track of defendants to minimize this problem. These alternatives are not new, but too limited use has been made of them in the past.

The Long Run

What are the long-term reforms? The treatment, or crime-as-disease, method as recommended, for example, by Dr. Karl Menninger, offered a major new approach.[90] Its popularity is clearly waning, because successful treatment techniques do not exist and the approach was oversold. It is possible that if successful treatment techniques were developed, the treatment alternative could become dominant. Of course, if treatment is to replace punishment, our society must be willing to abandon, or find alternatives for, the need for retribution and imposition of just deserts.

An alternative approach could conceivably be a real effort to eliminate some of the social swamps that breed criminality. This appears highly unlikely.[91] Nevertheless, the efforts to reduce child abuse and unemployment, for example, if successful, might reduce the need for punishment.

Another possibility is that the "victims" approach will be adopted. We have noted a substantial victims movement, and there is a clear trend toward greater concern for the victim in the criminal justice system.[92] It is conceivable that this will become more than a temporary fad, and will exercise greater influence on the criminal justice system. The system, in that case, could become more and more oriented toward providing emotional and economic compensation for the victim. Such an approach would be a dramatic change of emphasis of the system.

A CAPITAL IDEA: DEATH OR LIFE?

Death has been the punishment of choice throughout much of human history, indeed man has shown a remarkable ingenuity in finding ways of administering capital punishment.[93] The death penalty has become a hotly debated topic in the United States, and executions are again occurring with sufficient regularity that they are no longer headline stories. In the last decade the Supreme Court has decided more cases challenging capital punishment than any other form of punishment. Public opinion now currently favors capital punishment by a wide margin,[94] and it is likely that capital punishment will be more commonly used in the next few years.

Capital Punishment and the Supreme Court

The Supreme Court began in 1972 what has turned out to be a long series of capital punishment cases. In *Furman v. Georgia* the Court decided that the death penalty was cruel and unusual punishment as it was then administered.[95] At that time, juries or judges were often permitted to impose the death penalty without any guidelines or standards, resulting in nonuniform application of death penalties against the outcasts of society, unpopular groups, minorities, and the poor. The nine justices issued ten opinions (one was *per curium*, which did little more than announce the results of the case) which ran 243 printed pages. The strength of philosophical and legal disagreements engendered by the death penalty is illustrated by the opinions of the Supreme Court in *Furman*.[96] The Court did not decide that the death penalty itself was unconstitutional, only that the way it was being applied was unconstitutional. At the time of the *Furman* decision, there had been no executions in the United States for five years even though the death penalty existed in 41 jurisdictions at the time.

After *Furman*, states began adopting new capital punishment statutes and the Court held that the death penalty was not *per se* unconstitutional.[97] Following that the court decided a number of cases which establish a narrow road for states to follow. States cannot allow juries or judges complete discretion in imposing death, but mandatory death penalties are unconstitutional.[98] The defendant must be permitted to present any aspect of his or her character in mitigation.[99] The Court permits states to allow judges rather than juries to impose death sentences after considering special mitigating and aggravating circumstances.[100] The Court also held that imposing the death penalty for a rape or kidnapping in which the victim was not killed violates the Eighth Amendment because it is disproportionately severe to the crime.[101] Prisoners cannot be executed while incompetent.[102]

As a result of these principles, and a number of other rather technical rules,[103] the Supreme Court and other federal courts have been required to hear a large number of capital punishment cases raising federal constitutional issues. There is evidence that the Court may be tiring of this process and wishes to avoid hearing some of these appeals in the future.[104]

Thus, states are free to impose capital punishment for homicides if they set standards for the sentencing authority about when the death penalty should be imposed, but they must permit aggravating and mitigating factors to be considered in determining whether the death penalty is imposed in any individual case. States have considered a wide variety of mitigating and aggravating circumstances.[105] Examples of aggravating circumstances are prior convictions, hideous method of murder, and multiple murders. Examples of mitigating circumstances are diminished capacity, age of the offender, and presence of mental disturbance.

A most interesting aspect of the aggravating factors, notably in Texas, is the dangerousness of the offender. The death penalty may be imposed if the offender will likely commit serious crimes in the future. States that rely on predictions of future dangerousness as a major basis for imposing capital punishment are basing a critically important decision on predictions that are notoriously inaccurate. Even making less critical decisions on the basis of predictions of dangerousness has been vigorously criticized. Making life and death decisions on that basis is little more than a deadly game of chance. The American Psychiatric Association among others has argued that psychiatrists should never be permitted to offer a prediction concerning long-term dangerousness in capital cases and that even if psychiatrists do make such predictions, they should not be permitted to do so unless they have conducted a psychiatric examination of the defendant.[106] The Supreme Court has disregarded this advice.

In *Barefoot v. Estelle,* the Court held that it is appropriate for mental health experts to testify in capital cases about long-term dangerousness. "The suggestion that no psychiatrist's testimony may be presented with respect to defendant's future dangerousness is somewhat like asking us to disinvent the wheel. . . . It makes little sense, if any, to submit that psychiatrists, out of the entire universe of persons who might have an opinion on the issue, would know so little about the subject [of dangerousness] they would not be permitted to testify."[107] The Court missed the point. The reason psychotherapists are permitted to testify about predictions of dangerousness is that they are presumed to have special expertise in such predictions. If they are no better than any one else predicting dangerousness, there is no reason to let them testify. When psychotherapists make the predictions of dangerousness without a personal clinical evaluation, they often will have a very limited information base on which to make the prediction—probably making the prediction even less dependable. Ethical standards implicitly require psychiatric examinations prior to testimony concerning long-term dangerousness.[108] Incorrect predictions of dangerousness are not harmless. They are likely to appear to jurors to have special expertise and thus the predictions may well be seriously misleading. Despite the Court's confidence in cross-examination and other testimony, the presentation of unreliable evidence concerning dangerousness is more likely to confuse than to help the jury.

The psychiatric testimony presented to the jury in *Barefoot* shows how a jury can be misled. Barefoot was convicted of murdering a police officer. He had five prior arrests for nonviolent offenses. Neither of the two psychiatrists who testified for the prosecution had examined Barefoot, but both diagnosed him as a sociopath and told the jury that such a person would commit violent acts in the future. One of the psychiatrists claimed that his predictive accuracy was "100% and absolute" and the other claimed accuracy within a reasonable psychiatric certainty. The jury found that it was probable that Barefoot would commit acts of violence in the future and he was sentenced to death. Barefoot was executed by Texas.

Among the most interesting, and even bizarre, events surrounding predictions of death in Texas has been the testimony of Dr. James Grigson, variously known as "Dr. Death" and "The Killer Shrink." Dr. Grigson has testified in a number of capital cases. His testimony illustrates the difficulty in presenting expert testimony to courts on complicated matters. Dr. Grigson's testimony has been described as follows, "His testimony in these cases is remarkably similar. He describes the five part, all-purpose examination he conducts and then states his opinion that, based on that exam, the defendant is sociopath. He then describes and defines sociopathy and explains that it is (a) incurable and (b) not a mental illness of any sort. He postulates a scale of one to ten and places the victim at ten [or eleven]. He speaks with certainty. When asked by the defense lawyer if he is ever wrong about such judgments, he acknowledges that he is sometimes wrong, 'but,' he continues 'in this case, I'm not.'"[109]

Experts may present testimony outside acceptable professional limits without the jury ever fully being aware of that fact. Good witnesses, confident and unshakable in their views, can seriously mislead a jury. Cross-examination and rebuttal experts are sometimes not enough. Dr. Grigson's testimony is out of touch with the very discipline which is the basis for making him an expert witness.[110] Yet, this is the kind of testimony which the Supreme Court has permitted.

The Capital Punishment Debate

The debate over capital punishment has been intense, thorough, and inconclusive.[111] In the following paragraphs we briefly describe the most commonly discussed issues concerning capital punishment.

Deterrence, Removal, and Just Deserts

The death penalty has most commonly been justified on the basis that it deters homicide. Over the years, increasingly complicated statistical analyses have been used in an effort to determine whether the death penalty is more of a deterrent than other serious punishments. Initial efforts compared crime rates in similar states that did and did not have capital punishment or compared crime rates before and after abolition of capital punishment. Generally, no consistent differences were found which could be attributed to capital punishment.

In the 1970s, regression analysis was used to examine deterrence rates. Economist Isaac Ehrlich presented evidence that capital punishment was a deterrent.[112] It was suggested that each execution resulted in seven or eight fewer murders. Other researchers raised serious questions about Ehrlich's conclusions and about the methodology he had employed.[113] The result of the more complex statistical studies is to leave the deterrent effect of capital punishment very much in doubt. Both sides can claim some reputable data to support the proposition that capital punishment is or is not a deterrent. If it is a deterrent, it is probably a subtle one.

It is, of course, impossible to conduct a legitimate prospective social experiment to determine whether capital punishment is or is not a deterrent.[114] The likelihood is that the battle of data will wage back and forth without any clear conclusion.

Whatever the deterrent effects of capital punishment, it is obviously successful in removing offenders from society.[115] It does little good, however, to remove an offender who will not commit additional serious crimes. As we have seen, that is an ability in which we cannot have much confidence.

The argument is sometimes made that by taking others' lives murderers deserve to give up their own lives. This "eye for an eye" argument is seldom made for other crimes. Whether capital punishment is a "just" desert is very much a matter of who is defining just.

Antisocial Offenders

The argument is made that some people cannot live in society and it is unlikely that any therapy will improve them very much. It is unfair to warehouse these offenders for the rest of their lives in overcrowded and brutal prisons. Such confinement, the argument continues, can serve no useful purpose. The legitimacy of such a condition depends upon the legitimacy of several propositions, including (1) the criminals will remain antisocial and violent throughout their lives, (2) there is not now and will not be any help for them, and (3) we can distinguish those who meet the first two conditions from those who do not. None of the propositions can be established with great confidence. In addition, the premise that it is more humane and fair to kill offenders than to imprison them is on shaky grounds. Given the choice, it is likely that most of those sentenced to death would choose life imprisonment over capital punishment.

Costs

It is sometimes claimed that maintaining a prisoner for life is too expensive and we could reduce costs somewhat through capital punishment. Interestingly, just the opposite may be true. "Today, considering all the costs—including the financial expense and wear and tear on our courts and prisons—a system of capital punishment is considerably more expensive than a criminal justice system without capital punishment."[116]

Government as Teacher

The government can act as a powerful teacher. This is an argument that cuts both ways in the capital punishment debate. Proponents claim that the government should teach that it is wrong to kill and the government can demonstrate this by imposing a particularly strong penalty against those who take the lives of others; the failure to do so demeans human life by failure to give an adequate protection. The opponents of capital punishment, on the other hand, argue that when the government executes a criminal it is teaching that even cold-blooded, calculated killing of human beings is acceptable. The brutalizing lesson is that killing is a way to solve problems; through abolition of the death penalty, the government will teach an increased reverence for human life.

Unequal Application

A central reason the Supreme Court struck down the death penalty in the early 1970s was that it was applied unequally, and was particularly harsh against minorities. The purpose of the law after the *Furman* case was to remove the tendency toward unequal treatment. There is evidence, however, that the race of the offender and the victim continues to be an important factor in the persons sentenced to death.[117] Thus far the data must be based on capital sentences, not the number of sentences carried out. We can only speculate what the data will show concerning those who are actually executed. With sentencing authorities permitted to consider individual differences, it is likely that race will continue to be a factor in capital sentencing. Of course, it is likely to be a factor in all sentencing. Arguably it is now less true in capital cases than in other cases because of the substantial review which death sentences receive. The question is as yet unanswered whether sentencing discrimination is troubling enough to be a strong argument against the imposition of the death penalty. The Supreme Court has agreed to decide whether current application of capital punishment is reasonably equal.[118]

Mistakes

The criminal justice system makes mistakes. If substantial numbers of executions take place, it is almost inevitable that an innocent person will be executed sooner or later. It may also be true that the imposition of capital punishment makes it extremely difficult for the system to discover and admit a mistake and that execution discourages uncovering and admitting error.

Our Conclusion

The authors somewhat disagree with one another about whether capital punishment should be used. In reviewing the learned, and not so learned, debate concerning capital punishment, as well as our own arguments for and against it, we are struck by Clarence Darrow's statement that such questions "are not settled by reason; they are settled by emotion. When they are settled, they do not stay settled, for the emotions change."[119]

SUMMARY

Society has become more "punishment oriented" in the recent past. The result has been a dramatic increase in prison populations and a return to capital punishment. The increase in punishment has created a crisis in the prisons with severe overcrowding, an increase in resources demanded for prisons, and federal court orders against many states. This is a particularly good time, therefore, to rethink the methods of, reasons for, consequences of, and alternatives to our current system of punishment.

We generally use two forms of punishment: imprisonment and fines. Corporal and capital punishments, which were of major importance in the past, currently play a relatively small role. Restitution to victims and community service and alternative sentences are now being used increasingly.

It is commonly said that the purposes of punishment are retribution, deterrence, removal and rehabilitation. Other goals of punishment are to provide just deserts, to prevent wrongdoers from profiting from their misdeeds, to assist the victim, and to be a dramatic statement of social values and social policies. These are often inconsistent and even conflicting goals. Our society has not clearly identified and pursued any coherent punishment goals.

Probably all of the goals of punishment have been accomplished to some limited degree, but none is accomplished to any great extent.

Central to the failure to meet these goals is the relatively low rate of apprehension and conviction for many serious crimes. Accomplishing any of the goals requires a much higher rate of apprehension than is currently possible.

Prison was seen in the eighteenth century as a reform movement away from capital and cruel corporal punishments. We believe that too many people are sentenced to prison terms that are much too long. The purpose of these long terms is often not very clear, but the consequences for desocialization of the prisoners, for the families of prisoners, and for society can be significant. For every person who is incarcerated, three are on a supervised release program. The cost of these programs is typically about 10 percent of keeping a prisoner incarcerated. Sentencing authorities, usually judges, have traditionally been given great latitude in sentencing individual offenders. The result has been grossly unequal sentencing, which is justifiably criticized. The use of sentencing guidelines and presumptive sentences may help reduce the disparity while permitting the individual offender's circumstances to be considered.

The Eighth Amendment prohibits the use of cruel and unusual punishment. There has been a significant debate about the meaning of that constitutional phrase. The Supreme Court has taken the position that it is an evolving concept that changes as the values and practices of society change. For the moment, cruel and unusual punishment includes inhumane and barbaric torture, pointless or irrational harm or pain, unreasonable conditions of incarceration, status crimes, and extreme disproportionality between the seriousness of the crime and the severity of the punishment. The Supreme Court has indicated that the states have very wide latitude in setting even severe sentences for relatively insignificant crimes.

Other areas in which legal questions have arisen about punishment are: persistent felon laws, which provide for longer prison sentences after conviction of multiple felonies; preventive detention, which permits holding of some offenders in jail while they are awaiting trial based on a prediction that they will commit other crimes while released; punishment for victimless crimes or crimes to which there is consent; use of behavior modification techniques; and the question of whether behavioral science principles can be useful in structuring a successful system of punishment.

Some reforms in the current system of punishment should result in increased effectiveness of the system, or reduce the costs of punishment. The rate of apprehension is probably difficult to improve, and yet it is a critical variable in the effectiveness of the system. We suggest that there should be a substantial reduction in the length of many prison terms with an increase in the use of probation, parole, and other limited release programs, and the use of "shock probation." Other methods of limiting freedom, such as limiting movement or part-time incarceration, should also be considered. The increased emphasis on restitution and public service for offenders has much to recommend it, as it focuses some attention on the victim and requires that the offender take affirmative steps to repay a debt to the victim or society in a positive way. It may also force the victim and the offender to deal with the emotions and conflicts related to the crime. On the other hand, it runs the risk that the offender will commit additional crimes while completing the rehabilitation, or flee from the area. Many rehabilitation programs can be operated as successfully outside a prison as inside. Corporal punishment is little used, but it might be reinstated as a way of providing inexpensive and short duration punishment. Questions exist about whether it is cruel and unusual punishment and whether it will lead to a return to brutal and barbaric physical punishment.

In the long run, more thorough reform of the system of punishment will be necessary. No such reform is immediately on the horizon. Although rehabilitation and attacking the social causes of crime are not currently alternatives to a system of punishment, it is conceivable that they may become that.

Capital punishment is making a comeback in the United States. The Supreme Court has ruled that capital punishment is not cruel and unusual punishment, although it may become that if applied in an arbitrary or disproportionate manner. States must provide sentencing authorities with guidelines for imposing capital punishment, and the sentencing authority must consider mitigating circumstances that would preclude the death penalty. Some states use future dangerousness as a basis for opposing the death penalty, although such predictions are probably highly inaccurate.

The debate over the death penalty continues. After much statistical analysis it is still impossible to say with certainty whether or not it is a deterrent. Among other issues in the debate are whether death is a just desert, it models aggressive and barbaric behavior, it is applied unequally, and the possibility of mistakes that cannot be corrected. A substantial majority of Americans favor the death penalty and it is likely that it will be used with increasing frequency in the immediate future.

NOTES

1. H. Barnes, *The Story of Punishment* 38–48 (2d ed. 1972); H. Oppenheimer, *The Rationale of Punishment* (1913).

2. See K. Menninger, *The Crime of Punishment* (1968).

3. "If a doctor were called on to treat typhoid fever, he would probably try to find out what kind of water the patient drank, and clean out the well so that no one else could get typhoid from the same source. But if a lawyer were called on to treat a typhoid patient he would give him thirty days in jail, and then he would think that nobody else would ever dare to drink the impure water. If the patient got well in fifteen days, he would be kept until his time was up; if the disease was worse at the end of thirty days, the patient would be released because his time was out." M. Levin, *Compulsion* (1956).

4. Between 1974 and 1983, the number of state and federal prisoners increased from 229,721 to 438,830, an increase of more than 90 percent. Bureau of Justice Statistics, *Prisoners in 1983* (1984).

5. Bureau of Justice Statistics, *Justice Expenditures and Employment, 1982* (1985).

6. E.g., American Friends Service Committee, *Struggle for Justice* 146 (1971); J. Murphy, *Retribution, Justice and Therapy* (1979).

7. J. Murphy, note 6, *supra* at 77–115 (1979).

8. See the material in the previous chapter dealing with criminal responsibility, especially the discussion of the interesting book M. Moore, *Law and Psychiatry: Rethinking the Relationship* (1984).

9. See J. Gibbs, *Crime, Punishment and Deterrence* (1975).

10. Most crimes do not result in arrests. In 1982, for example, only about 20 percent of serious crimes *reported* were cleared by arrest. Bureau of Justice Statistics, *Sourcebook of Criminal Justice Statistics—1984* 515 (1985) (based on FBI data). When the number of felonies committed, as opposed to those reported, is considered, the rate of arrest is even lower. One study in New York indicated that only 3.6 percent of felons are convicted and only 0.3 percent are sent to prison for more than a year. H. Zeisel, *The Limits of Law Enforcement* 18 (1982).

11. See Cohen, Selective Incapacitation: An Assessment, 1984 *U. Ill. L. F.* 253.

12. Bowers v. Hardwick, 106 S. Ct. 2841 (1986).

13. There have been national commissions on the issue. E.g., U.S. Department of Justice, *The Criminal Justice Response to Victim Harm* (1984); President's Task Force on Victims of Crime, *Final Report* (1982); A.B.A.

Criminal Justice Section, *Guidelines for Fair Treatment of Victims and Witnesses in the Criminal Justice System* (1983).

14. Two important federal laws are intended to assist victims. Victim of Crimes Act of 1984, Pub. L. [Public Law] No. 98-473 (1984); Omnibus Victim and Witness Protection Act of 1982, Pub. L. No. 97-291 (1982). Kolibash, the Prosecutorial Perspective: The Victim and Witness Protection Act of 1982, 87 *W. Va. L. Rev.* 71 (1984). In addition, many states now have crime victims statutes. See Gittler, Expanding the Role of the Victim in a Criminal Action: An Overview of Issues and Problems, 11 *Pepperdine L. Rev.* 117 (1984).

The tradition here is relatively modern. In colonial days, as well as into the first part of the nineteenth century the victim was responsible for the prosecution of many crimes. As might be expected under such a system, restitution to the victim was an important part of such a system. McDonald, Towards a Bicentennial Revolution in Criminal Justice: The Return of the Victim, 13 *Am. Crim. L. Rev.* 649 (1976).

15. Davis, Kunreuther & Connick, Expanding the Victim's Role in the Criminal Court Dispositional Process: The Results of an Experiment, 75 *J. Crim. L. & Criminology* 491 (1984). See Keve, The Therapeutic Uses of Retribution, in *Offender Restitution in Theory and Action* 59 (B. Galaway & J. Hudson eds. 1978).

16. R. Meiners, *Victim Compensation* (1978); Harland, Monetary Remedies for the Victims of Crime: Assessing the Role of Criminal Courts, 30 *UCLA L. Rev.* 52 (1982).

17. See generally Epstein, Crime and Tort: Old Wine and Old Bottles, in *Assessing the Criminal* (R. Barnett & J. Hansel eds. 1977).

18. G. Newman, *Just and Painful* 133–36 (1983).

19. See note 10 *supra*.

20. See Panel on Research on Deterrent and Incapacitation Effects, *Deterrence and Incapacitation: Estimating the Effects of Criminal Sanctions on Crime Rates,* 19–63 (1978).

21. Goldman, Beyond the Deterrence Theory: Comments on Van Den Haag's "Punishment" as a Device for Controlling the Crime Rate, 33 *Rutgers L. Rev.* 721 (1981).

22. National Research Council, *Punishment and Deterrence* (1978); H. Zeisel, *The Limits of Law Enforcement* 53–68 (1982).

23. Bureau of Justice Statistics, *Sourcebook of Criminal Justice Statistics—1982* 244 (1983) (data from Louis Harris and Associates). However, another survey indicated that the public was about equally divided on the question of whether or not prison sentences deter crime. *Id.* at 251 (data from Research and Forecasts, Inc.).

24. National Research Council, *Punishment and Deterrence* (1978); Cohen, Selective Incapacitation: An Assessment, 1984 *U. Ill. L. F.* 253. About 61 percent of male state prisoners had been incarcerated before. Bureau of Justice Statistics, *Examining Recidivism* (1985).

25. S. Van Dine, J. Conrad & S. Dinitz, *Restraining the Wicked* (1979). See H. Zeisel, *The Limits of Law Enforcement* 53–68 (1982).

26. E.g., N. Morris, *The Future of Imprisonment* 13 (1974); American Friends Service Committee, *Struggle for Justice* 146 (1971); Martinson, What Works? Questions and Answers About Prison Reform, 35 *The Public Interest* 22 (1974).

27. The federal Sentencing Reform Act of 1984 (P.L. 98-473, Chapter II of Title II (1984)) abandons rehabilitation as the primary purpose of sentencing. It also attempts to provide for a more uniform length of sentences for crimes and emphasizes the use of restitution to the victims of crimes.

28. Bureau of Justice Statistics, *Sourcebook of Criminal Justice Statistics—1984* 223 (1985) (data from Louis Harris and Associates).

29. The perception of leniency was noted across ethnic groups, socio-economic levels and regions of the country. Bureau of Justice Statistics, *Sourcebook of Criminal Justice Statistics—1984* 226–27 (1985) (data made available through the Roper Opinion Research Center).

30. H. Barnes, *The Story of Punishment* 104–31 (2d ed. 1972). The Massachusetts Colony also used prison-like sentences, to a lesser degree.

31. Bureau of Justice Statistics, *Prisoners in 1983* 1–2 (1984). This increase cannot be attributed to deinstitutionalization of mental patients. Steadman, Monahan, Duffee, Hartstone & Robbins, The Impact of State Mental Hospital Deinstitutionalization on United States Prison Populations, 1968–1978, 75 *J. Crim. L. & Criminology* 474 (1984) (it did not appear that deinstitutionalization of mental patients was a significant factor in the increase of prison populations).

32. Bureau of Justice Statistics, *Justice Expenditures and Employment, 1982* (1985).

33. Rhodes v. Chapman, 452 U.S. 337 (1981).

34. Generally the basis for federal court intervention in state prisons is that the conditions are so bad in the prisons that they violate the Eighth Amendment's prohibition on cruel and unusual punishment. By 1984 about 40 states had prisons under court order, were operating under consent decrees or were in litigation regarding prison conditions. Bureau of Justice Statistics, *Prisoners in 1983* 3 (1984).

35. Bureau of Justice Statistics, *Prisoners in 1983* 5–6 (1984). See Westerfield, A Study of the Louisiana Sentencing System and Its Relationship to Prison Overcrowding, 30 *Loyola L. Rev.* 5 (1984).

36. H. Barnes, *The Story of Punishment* 170–81 (2d ed. 1972).

37. Bureau of Justice Statistics, *Sourcebook of Criminal Justice Statistics—1984* 226–27 (1985) (from National Opinion Research Center).

38. An American Bar Association report suggests that sentences are frequently excessive. American Bar Association Standing Committee on Association Standards for Criminal Justice 18.45–18.53 (2d ed. 1980).

39. Bureau of Justice Statistics, *Report to the Nation on Crime and Justice* 76 (1983).

40. *Id.* at 72.

41. Panel on Sentencing Research (National Research Council), *Research on Sentencing: The Search for Reform* 69–123 (1983).

42. These reforms are considered in the documents in H. Gross & A. von Hirsch eds., *Sentencing* 303–35 (1981).

43. Bureau of Justice Statistics, *supra,* note 36.

44. Probation and parole may not be effective in removing the dangerous from society. One study suggests that almost two-thirds of felons placed on probation were rearrested. J. Petersilia, S. Turner, J. Kahan & J. Peterson, *Granting Felons Probation: Public Risks and Alternatives* 20–25 (1985).

45. For modern reviews of the history of the Eighth Amendment see R. Berger, *Death Penalties* 29–76 (1982); Granucci, "Nor Cruel and Unusual Punishments Inflicted": The Original Meaning, 57 *Cal. L. Rev.* 839 (1969); Note, The Cruel and Unusual Punishment Clause and the Substantive Criminal Law, 79 *Harv. L. Rev.* 635 (1966).

There was some opposition to the Eighth Amendment because the language was "too indefinite." During the Congressional debate, Mr. Livermore noted "it is sometimes necessary to hang a man, villains often deserve whipping, and perhaps having their ears cut off; but are we in future to be prevented from inflicting these punishments because they are cruel?" 1 *Annals of the Congress* 754 (J. Gales ed. 1789).

46. See Solem v. Helm, 463 U.S. 277 (1983); Rummel v. Estelle, 445 U.S. 263 (1980); Trop v. Dulles, 356 U.S. 86, 101 (1958).

47. See Weems v. U.S., 217 U.S. 349 (1910); *In re* Kemmler, 136 U.S. 436 (1890) (limited by Gregg v. Georgia, 428 U.S. 153 [1976]); Jackson v. Bishop, 404 F.2d 571 (8th Cir. 1968).

48. Ingraham v. Wright, 430 U.S. 651 (1977).

49. See Rummel v. Estelle, 445 U.S. 263, 293 (1980) (Powell dissenting); *In re* Kemmler, 136 U.S. 436 (1890); Wilkerson v. Utah, 99 U.S. 130, 135 (1879) (limited by Gregg v. Georgia, 428 U.S. 153 [1976]).

50. Rhodes v. Chapman, 452 U.S. 337 (1981).

51. Estelle v. Gamble, 429 U.S. 97 (1976); Ruiz v. Estelle, 650 F.2d 555 (5th Cir. 1981).

52. Robinson v. California, 370 U.S. 660 (1962).

53. Powell v. Texas, 392 U.S. 514 (1968).

54. Allen v. Illinois, 106 S. Ct. 2988 (1986).

55. E.g., Enmund v. Florida, 458 U.S. 782 (1982); Coker v. Georgia, 433 U.S. 584 (1977) (plurality opinion). See Nevares-Muniz, The Eighth Amendment Revisited: A Model of Weighted Punishments, 75 *J. Crim. L. & Criminology* 272 (1984).

56. Rummel v. Estelle, 445 U.S. 263 (1980). See Harris & Wethern, Application of the Proportionality Doctrine to a Punishment of Imprisonment, 35 *Mercer L. Rev.* 681 (1984).

57. Solem v. Helm, 463 U.S. 277 (1983).

58. Rummel v. Estelle, 445 U.S. 263 (1980).

59. Hutto v. Davis, 445 U.S. 947 (1980) (granting *cert.* and reversing in light of Rummel v. Estelle).

60. G. Simonsen & M. Gordon, *Juvenile Justice in America* 20–25 (1979); U.S. Department of Justice, *Criminal Justice Information Policy: Privacy and Juvenile Justice Records* (1982); Shichor, Historical and Current Trends in American Juvenile Justice, 34 *Juv. & Fam. Ct. J.* 61 (1983).

61. See Schwartz, Eighth Amendment Proportionality Analysis and the Compelling Case of William Rummel, 71 *J. Crim. L. & Criminology* 378, 393 (1980).

62. K. Krajik & S. Gettinger, *Overcrowded Time: Why Prisons are So Crowded and What Can be Done* (1982).

63. Katkin, Habitual Offender Laws: A Reconsideration, 21 *Buffalo L. Rev.* 99 (1971).

64. Rummel v. Estelle, 445 U.S. 263 (1980) (sentenced under the Texas habitual offender statute).

65. Solem v. Helm, 463 U.S. 277 (1983) (the Court struck down the sentence as unconstitutional, a violation of the Eighth Amendment. Helm was sentenced under a South Dakota habitual offender statute).

66. "There's the King's Messenger. He's in prison now, being punished: and the trial doesn't even begin till next Wednesday: and of course the crime comes last of all."

"Suppose he never commits the crime?" asked Alice.

"That would be all the better, wouldn't it?" the Queen responded. . . .

Alice felt there was no denying that. "Of course it would be all the better," she said: "but it wouldn't be all the better his being punished."

"You're wrong. . . ." said the Queen. "Were you ever punished?"

"Only for faults," said Alice.

"And you were all the better for it, I know!" the Queen said triumphantly.

"Yes, but then I had done the things I was punished for," said Alice: "That makes all the difference."

"But if you hadn't done them," the Queen said, "that would have been better still; better, and better, and better!" Her voice went higher with each "better" till it got quite to a squeak. . . .

Alice thought, "There's a mistake somewhere—" Dershowitz, On Preventive Detention 309, in A. Goldstein & J. Goldstein, *Crime, Law and Society* (1971), quoting Lewis Carroll.

67. Schall v. Martin, 467 U.S. 253 (1984). The Court noted that all states permit preventive detention of juveniles.

68. The Bail Reform Act of 1984 (P.L. 98-473, Chapter I of Title II [1984]), permits that federal judges to hold without bail (preventive detention) those charged with felonies who pose a danger to the community. For a review of early cases concerning detention, see Serr, The Federal Bail Reform Act of 1984: The First Wave of Case Law, 39 *Ark. L. Rev.* 169 (1985).

69. Bureau of Justice Statistics, *Sourcebook of Criminal Justice Statistics— 1983* 258, 268, 270 (1984).

70. J. Petersilia, S. Turner, J. Kahan, & J. Peterson, *Granting Felons Probation: Public Risks and Alternatives* (1985) (study suggesting that a significant number of felons on probation commit crimes while on probation).

71. In Bowers v. Hardwick, 106 S. Ct. 2841 (1986), the Supreme Court indicated that states may constitutionally enforce victimless crimes. That case involved a Georgia statute that made consensual sodomy a felony, as it applied to private homosexual conduct.

72. Friedman, Legal Regulation of Applied Behavior Analysis in Mental Institutions and Prisons, 17 *Ariz. L. Rev.* 39 (1975). See J. Metson, *Punishment and Its Alternatives: A New Perspective for Behavior Modification* (1984); Schopp, Punishment as Treatment and the Obligations of Treatment Providers, 7 *Int'l J. L. & Psychiatry* 197 (1984) (in some instances treatment providers are obligated to punish).

73. Knecht v. Gillman, 488 F.2d 1136 (8th Cir. 1973); Mackey v. Procunier, 477 F.2d 877 (9th Cir. 1973).

74. See D. Wexler, *Mental Health Law* 213–56 (1981).

75. See *Social Psychology in Treating Mental Illness: An Experimental Approach* (G. Fairweather ed. 1964).

76. See generally T. Ayllon & N. Azrin, *The Token Economy: A Motivational System for Therapy and Rehabilitation* (1968); Friedman, Legal Regulation of Applied Behavior Analysis in Mental Institutions and Prisons, 17 *Ariz. L. Rev.* 39 (1975); Wexler, Reflections on the Legal Regulation of Behavior Modification in Institutional Settings, 17 *Ariz. L. Rev.* 132 (1975).

77. 45 C.F.R. §46.301–06 (1983).

78. Kaimowitz v. Michigan Dept. of Mental Health, Civil Action No. 73-19434-AW (Cir. Ct. Wayne County, Mich. July 10, 1973), reprinted in A. Brooks, *Law, Psychiatry and the Mental Health System* 902–24 (1974).

79. Ferracuti, Human Rights and Correctional Treatment, 7 *Int'l J. L. & Psychiatry* 215 (1984) (treatment of prisoners should be offered but not imposed).

80. Moffit, The Learning Theory of Punishment, 10 *Crim. Just. & Behav.* 131 (1983).

81. Newsom, Favell & Rincover, Side Effects of Punishment in *The Effects of Punishment on Human Behavior* 285–311 (S. Axelrod & J. Apsche eds. 1983).

82. See Houter, Punishment: From the Animal Laboratory to the Applied Setting in *The Effects of Punishment on Human Behavior* 13–44 (S. Axelrod & J. Apsche, eds. 1983).

83. See generally G. Walters & J. Grusec, *Punishment* (1977).

84. Lock 'Em Up? There's No More Room!, 60 *A.B.A. J.* 1351, 1352 (1983).

85. Victims and Witnesses Protection Act of 1982, Pub. L. No. 97-291, 96 Stat. 1242; C. Abel, *Punishment and Restitution: A Restitutionary Approach to Crime and the Criminal* (1984).

86. E.g., President's Task Force on Victims of Crime, *Final Report* (1982); R. Reiff, *The Invisible Victim* (1979); Gettler, Expanding the Role of the Victim in a Criminal Action: An Overview of Issues and Problems, 11 *Pepperdine L. Rev.* 117 (1984); Keisel, Crime and Punishment: Victim Rights Movement Presses Courts, Legislatures, 70 *A.B.A. J.* 25 (1984);

Kolibash, The Prosecutorial Perspective: The Victim and Witness Protection Act of 1982, 87 *W. Va. L. Rev.* 71 (1984).

87. See Davis, Kunreuther & Connick, Expanding the Victim's Role in the Criminal Court Dispositional Process: The Results of an Experiment, 75 *J. Crim. L. & Criminology* 491 (1984); Hagan, Victims Before the Law: A Study of Victim Involvement in the Criminal Justice Process, 73 *J. Crim. L. & Criminology* 317 (1982); Henderson, The Wrongs of Victim's Rights, 37 *Stan. L. Rev.* 937 (1985).

88. H. Barnes, *The Story of Punishment* 56–67 (2d ed. 1972).

89. A defendant (Jefferson) is found guilty of burglary in the first degree, his first offense, and told "'you will be taken immediately to the Punishment Hall to receive five shock units. Court dismissed.'" (Apparently the judge knows that the defendant will not appeal the guilty verdict.) The victim is directed to a spectator's room, then the defendant is seated in a specially designed chair. The technician sets the machine at the appropriate pain level, turns the dial to five, and presses the button. Jefferson receives five painful jobes of electricity to his buttocks. He screams loudly, and by the time the punishment is over, he is crying with pain. After that the defendant is free to go. The offender's wife runs to him crying "'I'm so glad it's over! Thank goodness you weren't sent to prison.'" Presumably, the victim leaves also satisfied. G. Newman, *Just and Painful* 42–43 (1983).

90. See K. Menninger, *The Crime of Punishment* (1968).

91. The suggestion that society reduce crime by removing the root causes, of course, is not new. A fairly recent, interesting effort to demonstrate that some of the money spent on the current criminal justice system would better be spent on early intervention in adverse social and economic conditions of children is, H. Zeisel, *The Limits of Law Enforcement* 18–87 (1982).

92. J. Hudson & B. Galaway, *Victims, Offenders, and Alternative Sanctions* (1981); Aynes, Constitutional Considerations: Government Responsibility and the Right Not to Be a Victim, 11 *Pepperdine L. Rev.* 63 (1984); Goldstein, Defining the Role of the Victim in Criminal Prosecution, 52 *Miss. L. J.* 515 (1982); Harrington, The Victim of Crime, 26 *So. Texas L. J.* 153 (1985); Kelly, Victims' Perceptions of Criminal Justice, 11 *Pepperdine L. Rev.* 15 (1984); Comment, Victim Restitution in the Criminal Process: A Procedural Analysis, 97 *Harv. L. Rev.* 931 (1984).

93. H. Barnes, *The Story of Punishment* 231–64 (1972).

94. Bureau of Justice Statistics, *Sourcebook of Criminal Justice Statistics—1984* 241–42 (1985) (sources: The Roper Poll and The Gallup Poll). Interestingly, capital punishment is now favored by the same margin it was favored in 1953. In 1965 a majority of those responding opposed the death penalty. *Id.* at 241. Murder is the only crime for which a majority supported the death penalty. *Id.* at 263.

95. Furman v. Georgia, 408 U.S. 238 (1972).

96. The private deliberations of the Court also apparently reflected fundamental disagreements. B. Woodward & S. Armstrong, *The Brethren: Inside the Supreme Court* 204–20 (1979).

97. Gregg v. Georgia, 428 U.S. 153 (1976). See R. Berger, *Death Penalties: The Supreme Court's Obstacle Course* (1982).

98. Roberts v. Louisiana, 431 U.S. 633 (1977); Woodson v. North Carolina, 428 U.S. 280 (1976).

99. Bell v. Ohio, 438 U.S. 637 (1978).

100. Baldwin v. Alabama, 105 S. Ct. 2727 (1985); Spaziano v. Florida, 468 U.S. 447 (1984).

101. Eberheart v. Georgia, 433 U.S. 917 (1977); Coker v. Georgia, 433 U.S. 485 (1977).

102. Ford v. Wainwright, 106 S. Ct. 2595 (1986).

103. See e.g., Caldwell v. Mississippi, 105 S. Ct. 2633 (1985), *later proceeding*, 481 So.2d 850 (Miss. 1985) (prosecution cannot tell jury that it is not the final word on the death penalty because its decision will be reviewed by appellate courts); Beck v. Alabama, 447 U.S. 625 (1980) (requiring that juries be permitted to consider lesser included offenses); Gardner v. Florida, 430 U.S. 349 (1977) (failure of state to strictly follow its own rules).

104. See e.g., Rumbaugh v. McCotter, 105 S. Ct. 3544 (1985); Glass v. Louisiana, 105 S. Ct. 2159 (1985); Wainwright v. Adams, 466 U.S. 964 (1984) (Marshall, dissenting in all cases). The Court was even called upon to decide whether states providing for death by lethal injection violate federal law because the substances have not been approved by the Food and Drug Administration for killing people. (The Court rejected the claim.) Heckler v. Chaney, 105 S. Ct. 1649 (1985). Special Project, Capital Punishment in 1984: Abandoning the Pursuit of Fairness and Consistency, 69 *Cornell L. Rev.* 1129 (1984). However, the Court continues to be called upon to decide a wide variety of capital punishment issues. For example, it has held that a defendant in an interracial capital case has the right to have prospective jurors questioned about racial violence (Turner v. Murray, 106 S. Ct. 1683 [1986]); to impose capital punishment the defendant must have killed, attempted to kill or intended that lethal force be employed (Cabana v. Bullock, 106 S. Ct. 689 [1986]); states must provide indigent defendants psychiatric expertise in capital sentencing hearings when the defendant's mental condition and dangerousness are issues (Ake v. Oklahoma, 470 U.S. 68 [1985]).

105. See H. Bedau, *The Death Penalty in America* 32–38 (3d ed. 1982).

106. See Amicus Curiae Briefs, American Psychiatric Association, Barefoot v. Estelle and Estelle v. Smith.

107. Barefoot v. Estelle, 463 U.S. 880 (1983).

108. See generally Amicus Curiae, American Psychiatric Association in Barefoot v. Estelle 18–25 (1983).

109. W. Winslade & J. Ross, *The Insanity Plea* 168 (1983).

110. For an excellent review of Dr. Grigson's testimony and the problems with it, see Dix, Participation by Mental Health Professionals in Capital Murder Sentencing, 1 *Int'l J. L. & Psychiatry* 283 (1978).

111. For an intriguing debate of capital punishment see E. van den Haag & J. Conrad, *The Death Penalty: A Debate* (1983); Greenberg, Against the American System of Capital Punishment, 99 *Harv. L. Rev.* 1670 (1986); van

den Haag, The Ultimate Punishment: A Defense, 99 *Harv. L. Rev.* 1662 (1986).

112. Ehrlich, The Deterrent Effect of Capital Punishment: A Question of Life and Death, 65 *Am. Econ. Rev.* 397 (1975); Ehrlich, Deterrence: Evidence and Inference, 85 *Yale L. J.* 209 (1975).

113. E.g., Bowers & Pierce, The Illusion of Deterrence in Isaac Ehrlich's Research on Capital Punishment, 85 *Yale L. J.* 187 (1975); Klein, Forst & Filatov, The Deterrent Effect of Capital Punishment: An Assessment of the Evidence, in *The Death Penalty in America* (H. Blau ed. 1982); Zeisel, A Comment on 'The Deterrent Effect of Capital Punishment' by Phillips, 88 *Am. J. Sociology* 167 (1982).

114. See Zeisel, The Deterrent Effect of the Death Penalty: Facts v. Faith, in *The Death Penalty in America* 116, 117–21 (3d ed. H. Bedau ed. 1982). Among other studies of deterrence and the death penalty are Bailey, Disaggregation in Deterrence and Death Penalty Research: The Case of Murder in Chicago, 74 *J. Crim. L. & Criminology* 827 (1983); Decker & Kohfeld, A Deterrence Study of the Death Penalty in Illinois, 1933–1980, 12 *J. Crim. Just.* 367 (1984); Forst, Capital Punishment and Deterrence: Conflicting Evidence, 74 *J. Crim. L. & Criminology* 927 (1983); McFarland, Is Capital Punishment a Short-Term Deterrent to Homicide? A Study of the Effects of Four Recent American Executions, 74 *J. Crim. L. & Criminology* 1014 (1983).

115. Professor Bartels has demonstrated, tongue-in-cheek, that capital sentences have a perfect "special deterrence" effect—those offenders sentenced to death do not commit the same crime again. Bartels, Capital Punishment: The Unexamined Issue of Special Deterrence, 68 *Iowa L. Rev.* 601 (1983).

116. Nakell, The Cost of the Death Penalty in *The Death Penalty in America* 241 (3d ed. H. Bedau ed. 1982).

117. In reviewing death sentences from four states, the probability of a death sentence when white kills black is about .01, when black kills white it is about .18. Bowers & Pierce, Racial Discrimination and Criminal Homicide Under Post-Furman Capital Statutes, in *The Death Penalty in America* (3d ed. H. Bedau 1982). See Special Project, Capital Punishment in 1984: Abandoning the Pursuit of Fairness and Consistency, 69 *Cornell L. Rev.* 1129 (1984).

118. McClesky v. Kemp, 54 USLW 3866 (S. Ct. 1986) (granting *cert.*).

119. Darrow quoted in *Capital Punishment: Hearings Before Subcommittee No. 3 of The Committee on the Judiciary,* House of Representatives, 92d Cong., 2d Sess. 19 (1972).

CHAPTER 13
JUVENILE JUSTICE: DELINQUENCY, ABUSE, AND CUSTODY

Todd, a ten-year old, has broken into a neighbor's house and stolen some silver. Upon investigation it appears that he has been skipping school. His father deserted the family when Todd was seven, and Todd's mother often leaves him alone for several days at a time while out of town; she sometimes punishes him by beating him rather severely with a stick. Todd's parents have recently filed for divorce, and are both seeking custody of Todd.

What should be the legal system's response to Todd? Like many who appear in juvenile courts, he is both victim and victimizer. Todd's situation raises a number of questions concerning the appropriate forms of social intervention.

1. Should Todd be criminally responsible for the theft? If not, should the law excuse this conduct or use it as a basis for intervening in Todd's life?
2. Should the state take any action to punish Todd (or his parents) because he is not attending school?
3. What action should be taken against Todd's father for leaving the family?
4. Is his mother's leaving Todd alone for several days child neglect? If so, what action should be taken against her or to protect Todd?
5. Are the severe beatings a form of abuse? If so, what action should be taken?
6. Who should be awarded custody of Todd in the divorce?

What other person should have visitation rights? Who should be obligated to provide the financial support?

These are among the different questions that face the juvenile system in dealing with the problems of minors. Mental health professionals are often involved with the judicial system in trying to resolve them. The law's approach to the problems of minors ultimately reflects society's view of children, a view that has changed dramatically during the last hundred years or so. At one time children were little more than the chattels of their parents, who were free to treat their children in almost anyway they chose, unless death resulted. During the nineteenth century there was a notable change in this attitude. At the turn of the century Illinois passed the first act to control dependent, neglected, and delinquent children.[1] Although some constitutional questions were raised about these early statutes, by 1917, juvenile court legislation had been adopted by virtually all states.[2]

The purposes of the juvenile laws are to permit state intervention into the lives of victimized or delinquent children to prevent harm and to permit guidance that might prevent a life of antisocial activity. The juvenile system was founded on two assumptions: troubled and delinquent juveniles had different needs than adult criminal defendants, and juvenile courts could operate in a therapeutic mode to "treat" children.[3] The juvenile courts were to act as a kindly, knowledgable parent that the child often did not have.

The watchword in juvenile decisions was to be the "best interest of the child." In practice, the theory has not worked perfectly. Much lip service is paid to the fact that the best interest principle is the guiding principle of juvenile courts. While it is one principle of juvenile court decisions, it is certainly not the only one. In determining custody, for example, the best interest of the child generally becomes the guiding principle only when the rights of potential custodians are essentially equal. In the area of delinquency, some suggest that juveniles have the worst of both the criminal justice system and the juvenile system.

Cases arising in the juvenile justice system may be divided into three general groups: delinquency, involving criminal behavior and "status" offenses; custody, determining who should have the responsibility for caring for and raising a child; and abuse and neglect, involving parents or guardians that are not properly caring for a child. We consider these in order.

JUVENILE DELINQUENCY

The principal reform of the juvenile justice system was removing juveniles from the adult criminal justice system and placing them within a strong rehabilitative system of their own. In many ways these reforms represented a crime-as-disease approach to juvenile delinquency. The idea was to treat juveniles for the problems that were causing the antisocial activity, thereby helping them grow out of their problems. The questions of fault and retribution were to be less important than the needs of the juveniles. In addition, reforms were meant to help juveniles avoid the brutality of the corporal and capital punishment then being imposed and to prevent juveniles from becoming imprisoned with hardened adult offenders who might serve as "professors of crime." The records and proceedings of juvenile court were to be private, thus preventing juveniles from developing a criminal record that could stigmatize them for life.[4] The juvenile system also provided a way of dealing with children who were wrong-doers, but who were below the age (about seven) of common-law criminal responsibility. Before the development of juvenile courts, in most states children under seven were not responsible for their crimes, those fourteen or over were responsible, and there was a rebuttable presumption that those between seven and fourteen were not responsible.[5]

There are two different but related groups of juvenile offenders: delinquents and "status offenders." Delinquency proceedings deal with the events that would have been criminal had they been committed by an adult. Delinquency proceedings have many of the aspects of an adult criminal trial, although the labeling of events is somewhat different. Adults are "arrested," juveniles are "taken into custody," there is "sentencing" of adults, and "disposition" of juveniles. Status offenders are juveniles who are in need of supervision because of some condition (e.g., truancy).

Delinquents

Throughout the juvenile process there is emphasis on diversion from the quasi-formal juvenile justice system to community treatment, social services, or prevention programs.[6] A diversion is most likely to occur by the police, who may decide to warn juveniles, reprimand them, or take them home. Perhaps one half of the potential delinquency cases are diverted by the police.[7] Many additional juveniles are diverted by the court prior to formal juvenile hearings.[8] A diversion reduces overloaded courts and may speed the process of resolving the juvenile's problems while lowering the cost of the system. However, research has not yet demonstrated a clear drop in recidivism because of diversion.[9] When it operates properly, diversion decisions are made with the individual needs of the juvenile in mind. However, these decisions are often made with little information about the juvenile and with an eye toward avoiding the inconvenience or cost of an official hearing.[10]

If a juvenile is not diverted to a nonjudicial process, a formal petition is filed alleging delinquency based on the findings of a preliminary inquiry. The hearing or "trial" is generally held in two stages, first the adjudication stage to determine whether the juvenile is a delinquent (guilty), followed by a disposition stage. Pending these hearings, the juvenile is ordinarily released into the custody of his parents or another responsible adult. However, most states permit juveniles to be held pending trial, as a form of preventive detention, if there is a reason to believe that the juvenile is dangerous or may leave the jurisdiction of the court. The Supreme Court has upheld this procedure as constitutional.[11]

The adjudication of someone as a delinquent may result in incarceration or other loss of liberty, and the stigma of being a juvenile delinquent. Therefore, despite the therapeutic ideal of the juvenile court system, courts have recognized juvenile delinquency proceedings as quasi-criminal.[12] As a result, juveniles have many, but not all, of the constitutional rights of an adult criminal defendant.[13] For example, juveniles have the rights to fair notice of the charges, to an attorney, to refuse to answer questions, and to proof of "guilt" beyond a reasonable doubt; they do not have the right to a jury trial.[14]

If after a hearing/trial the judge finds that the juvenile has committed a criminal act, the juvenile is judged to be a delinquent. The disposition decision is made, often after a separate hearing. There is heavy reliance upon social and psychological needs, although age plays a significant role.[15] Alternatives include reprimand; fine; educational direction; restitution; or placement in a training school, industrial school, detention center, or foster home. The length of incarceration in a juvenile facility varies from jurisdiction to jurisdiction, and it may last until the juvenile reaches the age of majority.[16] Most states allow decisions about when juveniles should be released to be made by the agency to which the child is sent.[17] The jurisdiction of the juvenile court is usually terminated when the juvenile reaches the age of majority. In some instances, juveniles may be incarcerated longer in a juvenile facility than they would have been if they were convicted of the same offense as an adult. Theoretically this is justified by the fact that the commitment is for the purpose of treatment and care, and it may take longer than the adult criminal sentence to fully rehabilitate the juvenile.

Some of the difficult issues in disposition are illustrated by socioeconomic status (SES). A higher-SES offender is likely to be able to demonstrate family and therapy resources which would not require institutionalization, while a lower-SES juvenile would not be able to demonstrate such support and thus is more likely to be institutionalized.[18]

Making disposition decisions on socioeconomic factors poses a dilemma. While it appears inappropriate to make incarceration decisions based on such factors, it would be destructive to unnecessarily institutionalize upper and middle class juveniles because it is necessary to institutionalize disadvantaged juveniles. Thus, the sentencing disparity involves a conflict between the values of wanting to avoid unnecessary or potentially harmful incarceration and the desire to be fair to all children regardless of socioeconomic status.

In some circumstances, the jurisdiction of the juvenile courts may be waived so that the juvenile may be tried as an adult criminal. This usually occurs when a serious offense has been committed and the juvenile is a recidivist or near the age of majority.[19] This waiver may be of critical importance because if juveniles are waived to adult courts, they may be sentenced to long prison terms, or perhaps, even receive the death penalty.[20] The waiver must follow a hearing to determine whether it is appropriate to send the child to adult court.[21] A juvenile waived to criminal court also loses the protection of the confidentiality afforded to juvenile records.

Status Offenders

A second group of juveniles subject to the jurisdiction of the juvenile courts are the "status offenders," juveniles in need of supervision because of conditions such as incorrigibility, truancy, or drug addiction. Status offenders account for perhaps 50 percent of the juvenile caseload in the country. The average period of commitment of juveniles to correctional institutions is 9.9 months; those held for status offenses remain an average of four to five months longer than minors charged with criminal delinquency.[22] Status hearings are considered less like criminal trials than are delinquency hearings, so status offenders are not guaranteed all of the constitutional rights a delinquent has.[23] Convicting an adult of a status crime violates the Constitution.[24] In theory the therapeutic nature of the juvenile system differs sufficiently from the adult criminal system to justify juvenile status offenders, although there is some authority that even this may be unconstitutional.[25] Status offenders are subject to the jurisdiction of juvenile courts and may be placed in juvenile facilities. Federal law now strongly discourages states from placing status offenders with juvenile delinquents in correction facilities, but they may be placed in community-based shelter facilities.[26]

The reality of the juvenile offender system is that a number of the goals of the system have not been met and that the primary goal of a therapeutic and rehabilitative system was probably unrealistic. Nevertheless, the juvenile system has resulted in a number of important reforms including preventing most juveniles from being incarcerated with adult offenders, protecting some information about juveniles from public disclosure, and avoiding some of the relatively harsh punishments of the adult prison system. On the other hand, the system may make it difficult to identify early and to incarcerate individuals who will commit a number of crimes during adolescence and early adulthood. The system has also resulted in some juveniles having the worst of both worlds—the absence of some protections of the criminal justice system for minor crimes plus the real possibility that they will be tried as adults for serious crimes.

A major advantage of the juvenile offender system is that it has separated juveniles from adult offenders. The criminal justice system should draw an additional line, keeping relatively young offenders (particularly, perhaps, those below the age of 14) away from the older juvenile offenders. At the same time, it should be clear that juvenile offenses are "warnings" and will be considered crimes for the purpose of sentencing should the offenders be guilty of criminal offenses after reaching the age of the majority. This might permit earlier identification and removal of adult offenders from society based on their juvenile record. The separation of delinquents, status offenders, and abused and neglected children should continue to be encouraged.

CHILD CUSTODY

Perhaps 1.2 million children each year are involved in custody proceedings as a result of divorce cases.[27] It is estimated that by 1990 one-third of the children in the United States will have divorced parents.[28] Other custody decisions arise when children have been seriously neglected or abused by their parents and must be removed from their parental homes or infrequently when both parents are killed.

The Best Interests of the Child

It is not literally correct that custody is assigned on the basis of what is best for the child. In fact, the primary principle in child custody is that parents have the right to the custody of their own children. There is a parental interest in child rearing that is part of the constitutional right of privacy. Absent a clear and convincing showing that the parents of the child are seriously inadequate, the custody of a child, as a matter of a constitutional law, stays with the parents.[29]

A hypothetical case illustrates these points. In a situation where the parents of a newborn are marginally adequate as parents but there are an aunt and uncle who would make wonderful parents and are willing to take the child, the clear best interest of the child might be to go with the aunt and uncle. However, the law will not operate in the best interest of the child in such a case. Even if the parents obtain a divorce, and a court must make the custody decision, custody will undoubtedly be awarded to one of the parents. In a few special circumstances custody has been awarded to someone other than the parents. In one unusual case a father had temporarily abandoned a child to the grandparents and a state court permitted the child to stay with the grandparents because of the emotional attachment to them plus questions raised about the father's "Bohemian lifestyle."[30]

The best interest of the child does become the guiding principle when the parties have an approximately equal legal claim to possession of the children, where there is serious misconduct or parental inadequacy, or where there are extraordinary circumstances.

The best interest of the child is, however, a vague standard which results in a great deal of judicial flexibility. This vagueness raises the possibility that decisions may be made on the basis of factors not identified. One writer has suggested that with no workable guidelines, judges are left to the criteria of their own consciences, shaped by the values of the culture in which they themselves were raised.[31]

The effect of shifting societal beliefs is demonstrated by the changing presumption concerning which parent should have custody. In the nineteenth century, although divorces were unusual, custody was ordinarily awarded to the father, who was better able to financially support the children (at that time the noncustodial parent ordinarily had no obligation of financial support).[32] With urbanization, fathers increasingly worked outside the home and mothers became much more clearly responsible for child raising. Therefore the presumption shifted and mothers became the preferred custodial parent. This was particularly true for children of "tender years" whose custody was almost always given to mothers.[33] Financial support was commonly split from custody, however, so that fathers continued to provide it.[34] Most recently, the tendency has been to drop any custody presumption in favor of one gender or the other,[35] although there is probably still a de facto presumption working in favor of the mother at least when young children are involved.

Studies of the desirability of one parent or the other have been somewhat ambiguous or contradictory.[36] The Uniform Marriage and Divorce Act lists several factors which may be used in determining what will be the best interest of the child:

1. The wishes of the child's parent or parents.
2. The wishes of the child.
3. The interaction and interrelationship of the child with his parent or parents, his siblings, and any other person who may significantly affect the child's best interest.
4. The child's adjustment to his home, school, and community.
5. The mental and physical health of all individuals involved.[37]

The act also cautions that courts should not consider anything regarding the conduct of a proposed custodian that does not affect the relationship to the child.[38]

These guidelines are difficult to apply with any precision when comparing the fitness of two relatively normal people. Particularly difficult custody issues arise when there are conditions that are ordinarily inappropriate for legal decision making, but which may have some effect on the suitability on one of the people seeking custody. The question is not whether such conditions make the person unfit as a parent, but whether they may make one of the parties a little less desirable than the other. Examples are the mental and physical health of the parent, interracial marriage of one of the parents, homosexuality, illegal heterosexual relationships, religious fanaticism, and absence of any religious beliefs. All of these have been part of some custody decisions in the past. Although the Supreme Court has recently permitted even race to be considered in custody decisions,[39] the trend seems to be away from permitting consideration of the above unless there is some reason to believe that it will adversely affect the child.[40]

Most custody decisions are really made not by courts, but by the parents as part of the divorce agreement or settlement. Although the courts must approve these custody decisions, it is unusual for them to upset the agreement arrived at by the parties. In fact the tendency has been toward promoting or encouraging the parties to come to custody agreements between themselves. In one sense, such a process is likely to be in the best interest of children. Parents are more likely to adhere to custody arrangements that are mutually acceptable to them. On the other hand, custody is but one among many issues which the divorcing parents must negotiate and compromise,[41] so that it may easily become a bargaining chip in resolving these other matters.

Considerable attention has been given to the concept of "psychological parent" in custody decisions.[42] According to this doctrine a custody decision should be made on the basis of *emotional* rather than *biological* parent-child relationships. The argument is made that the child needs at least one psychological parent for successful life adjustment and that this parent must be a reliable, accepting adult who is present on a daily basis. Therefore legal custody should be awarded to the adult who is most likely to fulfill such a role and this decision should be made as quickly as possible to avoid a disruption in the child's upbringing.[43]

Joint Custody

The relatively new concept of joint custody has gained considerable acceptance.[44] There are two types of joint custody, one in which both parents assume equal roles in making important decisions concerning the child but one parent is granted physical custody. In the second type of joint custody, parents take turns caring for the child.[45] There are a number of positive features of joint custody. It provides an opportunity for the child to have the support and closeness of two parents and for both parents to remain deeply involved with the child. It may reduce the win-lose aspects of divorce custody decisions. On the other hand, there are a number of risks associated with it. It may result in inconsistent decisions and guidance from the parents, a feeling of perpetually being uprooted, a general feeling of instability, and a sense of being torn between the parents.[46]

A number of commonsense criteria have been suggested by the courts and commentators for the appropriate use of joint custody. These include that the parents physically live close to each other, have long-term plans to stay at the same location, be able to manage the financial arrangements necessary to arrange the joint custody decision, be fit to fulfill the role of parents, and be committed to the joint custody arrangement. Joint custody should be acceptable to the child, and there should be a sufficiently nonhostile relationship between the parents to permit them to work together and to be relatively flexible in sharing responsibility. Finally, there should be a fair amount of agreement concerning child rearing and of the rules for the operation of joint custody, and both parents should be seen by the child as a source of security and love.[47]

A significant problem in some cases of joint custody arrangements has been the shuttling of a child between the mother's house and the father's house. One alternative to this arrangement, not yet part of joint custody arrangements, is to shuttle the parents rather than the child. Under this joint custody plan, the child would always live in the same house and the parent with immediate custody would live in that house with the child. Such an arrangement should decrease the level of disruption for the child, although it would increase those levels for the parents substantially.

Visitation and Support

Where custody is granted to one parent only, it is customary to grant the noncustodial parent visitation rights. (Visitation is formally ordered by the court, but it is usually negotiated between the parties as part of the divorce settlement.) The advantage of visitation rights, of course, is that it gives the child a continuing loving relationship with both parents and the possibility of support and parental guidance from both parents.[48]

Frequently, however, there are problems with visitation rights. Legal problems arise when the custodial parent refuses normal visitation rights or where the noncustodial parent does not strictly adhere to the schedule for visitation. In addition, conflict between parents may create loyalty conflicts in the child, thus producing stress on everyone involved.[49] In some respects visitation rights can be small-scale joint custody arrangements, and often too little careful consideration is given to the type of visitation that will be permitted. If the parents' child rearing ideas are dramatically different or if the divorce is particularly nasty, visitation rights may be accompanied by serious problems. Mediation efforts between the parents to establish clear rules regarding visitation have been encouraged to reduce these problems.

Again, the best interest of the child is not the only basis on which visitation decisions can be made. Parents have a continuing interest in being able to visit and see their children. Except when a parent is unfit, engages in serious misconduct, or there are other extraordinary circumstances, visitation will be granted if the noncustodial parent wishes to have those rights. However, where visitation results in harm, including serious psychological trauma to a child, visitation may be limited or terminated.[50] These are generally rather extreme situations. Behavioral science studies regarding potential harm from poor visitation, and research identifying the best forms of visitation plans are somewhat limited.[51]

Usually, but certainly not always, the noncustodial parent is required to help provide child support. Although support is paid to the custodial parent, it is an obligation due to the child and is not meant to be a form of alimony. The failure to pay court ordered child support, not an infrequent problem, may result in the court's seizing assets and wages, or even incarceration. Recently stiffer state and federal laws have been enacted in an effort to pursue delinquent parents.[52]

Theoretically, visitation and child support are not directly related. In practice they often are. However, the noncustodial parent is not legally privileged to stop support payments when there is an interference with normal visitation rights.

Parental Childnapping

A growing problem has been childsnatching by the noncustodial parent. States traditionally have not given full recognition to the child custody decisions of other states, so it has been possible to snatch a child, remove the child to another state, go to court in the second state, and obtain a different custody decree.[53] In addition, childsnatching, as opposed to kidnapping for ransom, traditionally has not been considered a serious crime and state and federal efforts to capture childsnatchers are often quite weak. Another problem has been that federal authorities and the states have not cooperated with each other in investigating and extraditing childsnatchers.[54] Recent changes in state and federal laws are aimed at resolving some of these problems.[55] For example, the Federal Parental Kidnapping Prevention Act of 1980 increases the federal role in enforcing childsnatching laws and in preventing the courts of one state from granting custody decrees that are inconsistent with those of another state.[56] In addition, courts are beginning to award civil damages to parents whose custodial rights have been interfered with through child stealing. Damages for loss of companionship and for cost of recovering a child (e.g., attorney fees, court costs, and travel expenses) are also being awarded.[57]

A somewhat related problem occurs when the custodial parent seeks to take a child from the state of the child custody order or a considerable distance from the parent with visitation rights. In the first case, some legal complications may occur in reviewing or making modification in the custody and support decrees, but these difficulties can usually be arranged to ensure the continuity of some court jurisdiction over the custody arrangement. The more difficult problem occurs when the noncustodial parent no longer will have access to the child because of the removal of the child to another area. Preventing the move would be unfair to the custodial parent, while permitting the move creates a hardship for the noncustodial parent. Recent cases preventing the removal of the child from the area have been the exception, but the issue is not yet fully settled. When such a move occurs, the visitation rights should be modified to make continued visitation reasonably convenient. For example, the court might order less frequent, but longer, visits to the noncustodial parent.[58]

Rights of Grandparents

There has been some move to provide grandparents with visitation rights as part of a divorce decree. Grandparents have an understandable interest in seeing grandchildren, and may contribute to the development of a child especially during times of stress.[59] However, their importance as child rearers, and their traditional legal rights, are considerably less than those of parents.[60] Adding grandparents' rights to the already extremely complex custody problems associated with divorce is likely to further complicate custody matters. Statutes which give grandparents legal visitation rights should be very carefully considered. The political realities may be that these statutes will become more common in the future; there is currently considerable support for the concept in states and from commentators.[61]

CHILD ABUSE AND NEGLECT

The problem of child abuse and neglect is not a small one. It is, of course, impossible to obtain accurate figures about the incidents of child abuse, but in the United States there is informed speculation that annually three million children or more are subject to abuse or neglect. Well over a million reports of child abuse or neglect are received by social service agencies each year, although a majority of these reports cannot be confirmed as actually having been abuse or neglect.[62] Child abuse or neglect may result in serious criminal penalties for those harming the child and may also result in the loss of the custody of the children or make the parents subject to other authority of the juvenile courts. Most child abuse cases are handled exclusively through informal, nonjudicial intervention, civil process and the juvenile courts; prosecution is ordinarily limited to the most serious forms of abuse or neglect. However, even milder forms of abuse are violations of the law and subject to criminal prosecution at the discretion of the local prosecutors and child protective service agencies.[63]

Major legal concern about child abuse is relatively recent. Ironically, early formal legal intervention primarily resulted from the efforts of the Society for the Prevention of Cruelty to Animals and had to be prosecuted under animal protection laws.[64] Child abuse and neglect went from a virtual nonissue to the focus of national political concern in a very short period.[65] Now all states have child abuse and neglect, and reporting laws.

Definition of Abuse and Neglect

Despite recent efforts to refine them, the definitions of child abuse and neglect are extremely broad and generally vague. In most states abuse includes physical harm, serious emotional injury, and sexual molestation or exploitation. Neglect often includes failure to provide adequate food, shelter, clothing, medical care, education, support and supervision.[66] The absence of clarity regarding what is abuse increases uncertainty about what is permitted and what must be reported to protective service agencies, creates confusion in the enforcement of the law, results in some under-reporting of abuse, causes unnecessary disruption of many families through false reports of abuse, and diverts resources of social service agencies away from the most serious abuse.

In most states the definitions of child abuse and neglect are broad enough to permit state interference with parental decision-making concerning such areas as schooling, child supervision, and decisions not to provide certain medical care or mental health care. Some of these areas of parental decision-making are constitutionally reserved to parents. For example, courts have permitted parents to provide for educational training of their children which most people would think unwise or even unreasonable.[67] Courts have been extremely reluctant even to order medical care for minors unless the absence of the care will be life-threatening. In some cases even rather grave threats to health have been insufficient for courts to order treatment over the objections of the parents.[68] Many child abuse laws appear to permit the state to interfere with child rearing in areas constitutionally reserved to parental decision making. Thus, these laws may be so broad as to be unconstitutional.

Abuse Reporting Statutes

All states now require that professionals report to social service agencies known or suspected child abuse. In most states mental health professionals have the obligation to report abuse no matter where the information comes from. Failure to report abuse may lead to civil or criminal liability.[69]

Abuse, State Intervention, and Custody

Informal handling of child abuse and neglect cases is preferred by courts and by most social service agencies. Therefore, a very small percentage of cases result in formal court adjudication and removal of custody from parents.

A relatively small proportion of the abuse and neglect that occurs is reported to child protective agencies. Of the reports that are received, it appears that nearly 60 percent cannot be confirmed and are essentially dropped, perhaps with some informal advising of parents or guardians.[70] If abuse or neglect is discovered, and it does not immediately seriously threaten the welfare of the child, the social services worker will usually try to informally arrange for family counseling.[71] In emergency situations, where the child's health is immediately endangered, the child is removed from the home on a temporary basis.

Upon discovery of abuse or neglect, the state may file in juvenile court a petition alleging parental abuse or neglect. The purpose of the hearing is to remove custody from the parents or otherwise protect the child. A court hearing follows after adequate time for the parents to prepare for it. Because very important parental rights are involved, the Supreme Court has held that "clear and convincing evidence" is required before parental rights may be terminated.[72] Strangely, however, the Supreme Court has held that parents are not constitutionally guaranteed the right to counsel during hearings.[73] Most states do provide counsel for indigent parents who cannot pay for attorneys themselves. In addition, a guardian *ad litem* is appointed by the court to represent the child's interest in the hearings. After the state, the parents and the child (through the guardian) present evidence and arguments concerning abuse or neglect, and if the state bears its burden by demonstrating abuse or neglect by clear and convincing evidence, the parents may be determined to have abused or neglected the child. A dispositional hearing is then held to determine what course of action should be taken. Among the alternatives are permitting the juvenile to stay with the parents but requiring informal supervision or formal counseling or therapy, temporarily removing the juvenile from the parental home to a foster home or to a state facility, placing the juvenile in a facility for mental health treatment, or—the most drastic and infrequently used step—terminating parental rights.[74] If parental rights are terminated the juvenile may be placed for adoption, with a legal guardian, or in long-term foster care.[75] As noted earlier, in addition to this civil process, criminal charges of abuse or neglect may also be filed against the parents.

There has been criticism of the traditional emphasis on retaining the family intact and avoiding criminal prosecution and removal of custody from abusing parents. Some authors urge more vigorous prosecution or removal of abused children from families. Williams, for example, claims that "keeping the abused child at home and treating the parents is often the most damaging placement for the child. In many instances, society's resources will be more profitably spent on facilitating adoption."[76] Others have proposed very early intervention to prevent any abuse. Such programs might be initiated during pregnancy.[77]

Identifying and Treating Abuse and Neglect

The goals of early identification of child abusers and of children who are abused are to provide treatment for the family rather than punishment. These goals depend on the ability of professionals to identify the children and their abusers, to treat abusers, and to assist children who have been abused or neglected. Physical abuse has often been difficult to identify accurately. Many other forms of neglect and emotional abuse are even more difficult to identify. Behavioral checklists, developmental deficiencies, and comprehensive psychological assessments have been suggested as means of establishing neglect or emotional abuse.[78] However, no standard, reliable, and accurate assessment is yet identified. Even studies attempting to identify the types of children who are likely to be subject to abuse,[79] and parents who are likely to become abusers[80] have been somewhat inconsistent and inconclusive. Treatment techniques that are highly effective remain to be fully developed both for parents who are abusers and for children who have been subject to abuse.[81] Given the large number of abusers who were once abused themselves, both forms of treatment are important.

There have been few adequate studies of the effectiveness of treating abusing parents. Blythe reviewed 16 studies (the bulk of available studies).[82] Half of these were single-case studies. Most of the studies contain various design flaws, so the vital question of the effectiveness of the treatment in avoiding further abuse cannot be resolved. In general the studies showed changes in parental behavior in the desired direction. However, research on treatment must be more carefully designed to answer the relevant questions about effective treatment.

Williams examined research on abusive parent recidivism rates with and without intervention.[83] Despite widely differing results in early reports, recent methodologically sounder studies have found consistent rates of recidivism of approximately 45 percent to 85 percent. Official reports of repeated cases of abuse are much lower, around 25 percent. Even with intervention, recidivism apparently remains high. Continued moderate to severe abuse occurred in about 50 percent of abusive parents.[84] Blythe cites studies that do indicate positive treatment-induced changes in abusive parents. However, it appears that these changes may often be insufficient to prevent further abuse.[85] Additional research may reveal more successful techniques or the particular circumstances (e.g., voluntary treatment as opposed to coerced intervention) in which techniques are successful. In addition, it is suggested that very early, primary intervention may be the most successful form of treatment. For example, Gray notes a program that begins with the collection of psychosocial data on expectant mothers. Interventions included prenatal classes, hospital policies promoting strong parent-child bonding, and regular postnatal contacts.[86] Additional research is also needed on the long-term effectiveness of such approaches and other preventive intervention.[87]

THE CHILD AS WITNESS

Many cases of abuse, particularly sexual abuse, depend primarily on the testimony of the child. There has apparently been a fairly strong assumption by the public that virtually all reports of abuse by a child are factual. Indeed, a few medical and mental health professionals assert, without any supporting empirical data, that this is true.[88] Some have even gone so far as to argue that a later retraction of a report of abuse is clear evidence that it actually occurred.[89]

The following hypothetical case suggests some of the difficulties. Tim, a four year old child of divorced parents, in his father's custody, testifies that his mother sexually abused him by fondling him during a visit. He says the events occurred about a year and a half ago. Tim's father has been very unhappy about the visitation arrangement since the divorce, which was quite acrimonious. The age of the child may also be the cause of some concern about his ability to tell the truth. It is not clear whether inconsistencies in the child's story are the result of his age or of fabrication. Tim is the only possible witness against his mother. If he is not a reliable witness, his mother, if guilty, will avoid punishment. On the other hand, there are possible bases for believing that the child is not reliable. It is possible that the father (who has custody and wants to eliminate the mother's visitation rights) has suggested the incident to the child. Should Tim be permitted to testify at all? If so, what weight should be given to his testimony?

Despite the assumption that children's evidence is highly reliable, there are some data that question this credibility.[90] In addition, research in developmental psychology is relevant to the reliability of child witnesses. Children gradually develop a sense of morality, and thus the ability to reflect upon truthtelling. Most experts see a conscience (or "superego") emerging most clearly about ages 6 to 8, although there are individual differences. Children, especially younger children, are prone to be easily suggestible and to readily engage in and to report fantasies. They are especially vulnerable to suggestion and to coercion from significant others. Children will, on occasion, use deception to please others or to retaliate against someone who has made them unhappy.[91]

The possibility that children may misunderstand, fantasize, be highly suggestible and use deception (without the benefit of a fully developed conscience), demonstrates that they cannot be assumed always to be accurate and completely reliable witnesses. However, they may often be the best, or only, witnesses to what occurred. To complicate matters further, children may be harmed by the process of presenting evidence through investigation and an extended legal process.[92] In addition, children may be unable or extremely reluctant to describe accurately and precisely what occurred. Therefore, it is essential to give some consideration of potential harm to the child witness.

Unfortunately, the goal of protecting the child witness and the goal of challenging testimony that is not entirely dependable are often inconsistent. For example, in recent years, anatomically correct dolls have been used in the investigation of sexual abuse. They may be of help in permitting the child to more easily describe what happened. However, there are potential problems with such a technique. Dolls are a traditional source of fantasy behavior so the propensity of children to be suggestible and to engage in fantasy may be heightened by the use of such dolls.

Some courts have tried to limit the harm to children testifying in abuse cases by permitting them to testify in nonthreatening surroundings rather than a courtroom and out of the presence of the accused, by permitting their testimony to be presented by videotape recording rather than in person to the jury, and by limiting cross-examination of the child.[93] These protections, however, may make it more difficult for the accused to have a fair trial, particularly if the major evidence is the testimony of the child. In a sexual abuse case this may be particularly difficult for the defendant because the heinous nature of the crime may make a successful defense difficult. The conflict of important values, fair trials and protecting children, has not been adequately resolved. The development of additional truth-finding techniques with children will be important.

MENTAL HEALTH PROFESSIONALS AND THE JUVENILE JUSTICE SYSTEM

Mental health professionals play a number of central roles in juvenile custody and disposition decisions. Frequently, they are the effective decision-makers because they provide for diversion or disposition outside of the judicial system, their recommendations are routinely followed by courts, and they provide the information on which judicial decisions are based. The informal nature of the proceedings and the absence of a jury tend often to reduce the level of cross-examination. The activities of the mental health professional in the juvenile justice process and testimony given is likely to be out of the range of public scrutiny.[94]

Recommendations made in chapters 10 and 14 generally apply to mental health professionals who work in the juvenile system. However, there are complications. One is the lack of a single "defendant." In many juvenile cases the juvenile, the parents and the interactions between them are all important and relevant. Interested parties may include one or two state agencies, the court, the parents, and one or more juveniles. It is therefore critical that it be clear to everyone who the mental health professional's client is and what the professional's responsibility to each of the parties is. The rules concerning confidentiality should be particularly clear to everyone before an evaluation or treatment is undertaken.[95]

Mental health professionals must have a very clear understanding of their roles. It may be an adviser to one of the parties, an "impartial" expert witness, an investigator, a provider of services, a decision-maker, or some other role. We have noted (chapter 10) the dangers of the mental health professional assuming more than one role in the legal system in a single case. In juvenile cases, assuming multiple roles may appear to be appropriate or even natural. The emphasis on treatment rather than on punishment and the principle of the best interest of the child may, for example, make the juvenile justice system appear quite analogous to therapy in private practice. In private practice it would be normal to both evaluate and treat a client and the client's family. However, despite the therapeutic ideal of the juvenile system, virtually all the juvenile justice proceedings are in some way adversarial. Furthermore, juvenile court jurisdiction may extend for years—for example, in a custody case incident to divorce. Therefore the possibility of a potential conflict of interest becoming a real conflict of interest exists when a professional assumes more than one role in any juvenile case.

Professionals may assume the role of mediators, an unusual role for them in the legal system. Mediation is sometimes used in custody disputes, for example. Here the effort is to get the parties to agree to a solution acceptable to everyone that serves the interest of the juvenile.[96] Such a system has the advantage of increasing the likelihood that all the parties can live reasonably comfortably with the arrangement while at the same time providing an expert to help facilitate communication and to help protect the interests of the child. Although this form of mediation is of less value in abuse and delinquency cases, mental health experts may in fact serve as informal mediators during the process of diverting juvenile cases from the courts. Again, role clarification is important, and it should be clear whether the professional's obligation is primarily to help the parties come to an agreement or to develop a plan that is best for the child.

SUMMARY

Although there has been much criticism of the juvenile justice system in recent years, there have also been some positive aspects of the system such as the separation of juveniles from adult offenders and the relative confidentiality of juvenile proceedings. The central ideal of an informal hearing in which a juvenile could be helped through counseling and advice by a fatherly (or motherly) judge has not commonly been realized in delinquency cases. The absence of full due process rights and the concept that juvenile courts may maintain jurisdiction over delinquents until the juvenile becomes an adult often do not particularly favor the juvenile. A more workable system might be to treat juveniles as adult offenders except that the disposition following conviction would be different. Within limits the confidentiality of these proceedings could be maintained for juveniles, and absolute separation of juveniles from adult prisoners should be continued.

In the area of custody we should not delude ourselves that the best interest of the child is really the major guiding principle of determining who should have custody of a child. Many other factors, including the parental constitutional right of privacy in child rearing play important and even dominant roles. Custody agreements arrived at between parties to a divorce probably should be more carefully reviewed to ensure that they are workable and that the best interests of the child are in fact protected.

Current definitions of child abuse and neglect are so broad and vague as to be nearly useless. Perhaps this reflects the fact that as a society we have not come to terms with the issue of just how far we are willing to let parents go before interfering with what they are doing to a child. It is sometimes argued that children belong to their parents, not to the state. On the other hand, juveniles also belong to themselves. The decision-making ability of adolescents suggests that it would be reasonable to allow them a greater decision-making authority. In fact, the law has begun to recognize this principle. For example, adolescents may decide whether or not to have an abortion; many states permit juveniles to consent to treatment of venereal disease or for some forms of counseling or medical treatment; the wishes of a juvenile are often taken into account in awarding custody. In short, the law seems to be very slowly moving toward holding juveniles more responsible for their misconduct and recognizing a greater competency at an earlier age than the common law traditionally provided.

NOTES

1. G. Simonsen & M. Gordon, *Juvenile Justice in America* 20–25 (1979).

2. *Id.,* Einhorn, Child Custody in Historical Perspective: A Study of Changing Social Perceptions of Divorce and Child Custody in Anglo-American Law, 4 *Behav. Sci. & L.* 119 (1986); Fox, Juvenile Justice Reform: A Historical Perspective, 22 *Stan. L. Rev.* 1187 (1970); Shichor, Historical and Current Trends in American Juvenile Justice, 34 *Juv. & Fam. Ct. J.* 61 (1983).

3. See U.S. Department of Justice, *Criminal Justice Information Policy: Privacy and Juvenile Justice Records* 14 (1982).

4. See references in notes 1 and 2 *supra*.

5. Department of Justice, note 3 *supra*; P. Piersma, J. Ganousis, A. Votenik, H. Swanger & P. Connell, *Law and Tactics in Juvenile Cases* (1977); Feld, Criminalizing Juvenile Justice: Rules of Procedure for the Juvenile, 69 *Minn. L. Rev.* 141 (1984).

6. U.S. Department of Justice, *Diversion of Youth from the Juvenile Justice*

System: Project Orientation Resource Handbook 3–9 (1980). See R. Jenkins, P. Heidemann & J. Caputo, *No Single Cause: Juvenile Delinquency and the Search for Effective Treatment* (1985).

7. H. Sandhu & C. Heasley, *Improving Juvenile Justice* 37 (1981).

8. G. Simonsen & M. Gordon, *Juvenile Justice in America* 375–76 (1981).

9. Severy & Whitaker, Juvenile Diversion: An Experimental Analysis of Effectiveness, 6 *Evaluation Rev.* 753 (1982).

10. See Department of Justice, note 6 *supra*.

11. Schall v. Martin, 467 U.S. 253 (1984). See Comment, The Supreme Court and Preventive Detention of Juveniles: A Principled Solution to a Due Process Dilemma, 132 *U. Pa. L. Rev.* 95 (1984).

12. *In re* Gault, 387 U.S. 1 (1967).

13. See S. Davis, *Rights of Juveniles* (2d ed. 1983); Feld, Criminalizing Juvenile Justice: Rules of Procedure for the Juvenile Court, 69 *Minn. L. Rev.* 141 (1984).

14. See generally McKeiver v. Pennsylvania, 403 U.S. 528 (1971); *In re* Winship, 397 U.S. 358 (1970).

15. Gottfredson, Chandler & Cohen, Legal Aim, Discretion and Social Control, 21 *Criminology* 95 (1983).

16. U.S. Department of Justice, *A Comparative Analysis of Juvenile Codes* 71 (1980); Fost, Fisher & Coates, Indeterminate and Determinate Sentencing of Juvenile Delinquents: A National Survey of Approaches to Commitment and Release Decision-Making, 36 *Juv. & Fam. Ct. J.* 1 (1985).

17. U.S. Department of Justice, *Standards for the Administration of Justice* 436 (1980).

18. D. West, *Delinquency: Its Roots, Careers and Prospects* (1982).

19. See Schornhorst, The Waiver of Juvenile Court Jurisdiction: *Kent* Revisited, 43 *Ind. L. J.* 583 (1968).

20. The Supreme Court has not precluded the use of capital punishment with juveniles. Eddings v. Oklahoma 455 U.S. 104 (1982). Because of the length of trials and appeals in capital cases, it is unlikely that anyone would be executed while still a juvenile. However, criminals may be executed for crimes committed when they were juveniles.

21. Kent v. United States, 383 U.S. 541 (1966).

22. Quinn & Hutchinson, Status Offenders Should Be Removed from the Juvenile Court, 7 *Pepperdine L. Rev.* 923, 924–30 (1980).

23. For example, the level of proof required to adjudicate a juvenile a status offender may be only clear and convincing, as opposed to the beyond a reasonable doubt standard required for delinquency. See *In re* Winship, 397 U.S. 358 (1970).

24. Robinson v. California, 370 U.S. 660 (1962).

25. Gesicki v. Oswalt, 336 F.Supp. 365, 371 (S.D. N.Y. 1971), *aff'd per curiam*, 406 U.S. 913 (1972). See J. Murray, *Status Offenders: A Sourcebook* (1983).

26. Juvenile Justice and Delinquency Prevention Act of 1974, 42 U.S.C. §5601 (1982).

27. U.S. Department of Commerce, *Statistical Abstract of the United States: 1985* 80 (1984). See Clingempeel & Reppucci, Joint Custody After Divorce: Major Issues and Goals for Reform, 91 *Psychological Bull.* 102 (1982); Wallerstein, Child of Divorce: An Overview, 4 *Behav. Sci. & L.* 105 (1986).

28. Clingempeel & Reppucci, note 27 *supra*.

29. Santosky v. Kramer, 455 U.S. 745 (1982).

30. Painter v. Bannister, 258 Iowa 1390, 140 N.W.2d 152, *cert. denied*, 385 U.S. 949 (1966). Apparently, the boy's father took him before a California court seeking permanent custody (during a summer visit). The court awarded custody to the father when the grandparents did not make an appearance in the California courts. R. Slovenko, *Psychiatry and Law* 377 (1973). See Garrison, Why Terminate Parental Rights?, 35 *Stan. L. Rev.* 423 (1983).

31. Comment, Child Custody: Best Interests of the Child versus Constitutional Rights of Parents, 81 *Dick. L. Rev.* 733 (1977). See R. Marafiote, *The Custody of Children: A Behavioral Assessment Model* (1985).

32. Clingempeel & Reppucci, note 27, *supra*; Howell & Toepke, Summary of the Child Custody Laws for the Fifty States, 12 *Am. J. Fam. Therapy* 56 (1984).

33. Howell & Toepke, note 32, *supra*.

34. Fischer, Mothers Living Apart From Their Children, 32 *Fam. Relations* 351 (1983).

35. For a discussion of recently adopted custody standards see, Freed & Walker, Family Law in the Fifty States: An Overview, 17 *Fam. L. Q.* 369, 431–33 (1985).

36. Compare, e.g., Gasser & Taylor, Role Adjustment of Single Parent Fathers With Dependent Children, 25 *Fam. Coordinator* 397 (1976); Lamb & Lamb, The Nature and Importance of the Father-Infant Relationship, 25 *Fam. Coordinator* 379 (1976); Parke & Sawin, The Father's Role in Infancy: A Re-Evaluation, 25 *Fam. Coordinator* 365 (1976); Pederson, Does Research on Children Reared in Father-Absent Families Yield Information on Father Influences?, 25 *Fam. Coordinator* 459 (1976); Santrock & Warshak, Father Custody and Social Development in Boys and Girls, 35 *J. Soc. Issues* 112 (1979); Shinn, Father Absence and Children's Cognitive Development, 85 *Psychological Bull.* 295 (1978).

37. Uniform Marriage and Divorce Act, §402 (1970, 1971 & 1972 amends.).

38. *Id.*, Comment at 21.

39. Palmore v. Sidoti, 466 U.S. 429 (1984). For an interesting commentary see Silverberg & Jonas, *Palmore v. Sidoti*, Equal Protection and Child Custody Determinations, 18 *Fam. L. Q.* 335 (1984).

40. E.g., *In re* Marriage of Carney, 24 Cal.3d 725, 157 Cal. Rptr. 383, 598 P.2d 36 (1979) (involving physical disability); Christian v. Randall, 33

Colo. App. 129, 516 P.2d 132 (1973) (involving a transexual); Moore v. Moore, 577 S.W.2d 613 (Ky. 1979) (involving sexual liaison outside of marriage); Kramer v. Kramer, 26 Md. App. 620, 339 A.2d 328 (1975) (denying custody because of significant emotional and substance abuse problems).

Among the most common questions is whether homosexuality of one of the parents is the basic for denying custody or visitation rights. Courts have not been consistent in answering the question. The trend, however, has been toward not considering sexual preference unless it is reasonably clear that it would adversely affect the child. Bagnall, Gallagher & Goldstein, Burdens on Gay Litigants and Bias in the Court System: Homosexual Panic, Child Custody, and Anonymous Parties, 19 *Harv. Civ. Rts.—Civ. Liberties L. Rev.* 497 (1984); Rivera, Queer Law: Sexual Orientation Law in the Mid-Eighties (Part II), 11 *U. Dayton L. Rev.* 275 (1986); Comment, Assessing Children's Best Interests When a Parent Is Gay or Lesbian: Toward a Rational Custody Standard, 32 *UCLA L. Rev.* 852 (1984); Comment [Annual Review], Homosexual Parent and Custody, 8 *J. Juv. L.* 291 (1984).

41. Scheiner, Musetto & Cordier, Custody and Visitation Counseling: A Report of an Innovative Program, 31 *Fam. Relations* 99 (1982).

42. J. Goldstein, A. Freud & A. Solnit, *Beyond the Best Interests of the Child* (rev. ed. 1979).

43. *Id.*

44. See generally Folberg, Joint Custody—The Second Wave, 23 *J. Fam. L.* 1 (1984); Kelley, Further Observations on Joint Custody, 16 *U.C. Davis L. Rev.* 762 (1983); Robinson, Joint Custody: An Idea Whose Time Has Come, 21 *J. Fam. L.* 641 (1983); Schwartz, Toward a Presumption of Joint Custody, 17 *Fam. L. Q.* 225 (1984); Note, Joint Custody: The Best Interests of the Child, 18 *Tulsa L. J.* 159 (1982).

45. Howell & Toepke, Summary of the Child Custody Laws for the Fifty States, 12 *Am. J. Fam. Therapy* 56 (1984).

46. See generally Atkinson, Criteria for Deciding Child Custody, 18 *Fam. L. Q.* 1 (1984); Robinson, Joint Custody: Constitutional Imperatives, 54 *Cin. L. Rev.* 27 (1985); Steinman, Joint Custody: What We Know, What We Have Yet to Learn, and the Judicial and Legislative Implications, 16 *U.C. Davis L. Rev.* 739 (1983).

47. The New Jersey Supreme Court established important criteria to ensure that joint custody operates smoothly. Beck v. Beck, 86 N.J. 480, 432 A.2d 63 (1981). Abarbanel, Shared Parenting After Separation: A Study of Joint Custody, 49 *Am. J. Orthopsychiatry* 320 (1979) (a study of several cases of joint custody suggested that it was generally positive); Grief, Fathers, Children and Joint Custody, 49 *Am. J. Orthopsychiatry* 311 (1979); Robinson, Joint Custody: An Idea Whose Time Has Come, 21 *J. Fam. L.* 641 (1983); Twiford, Joint Custody: A Blind Leap of Faith?, 4 *Behav. Sci. & L.* 157 (1986).

48. Clingempeel & Reppucci, Joint Custody After Divorce: Major Issues and Goals for Research, 91 *Psychological Bull.* 102 (1982).

49. Blau, An Evaluative Study of the Role of the Grandparent in the Best

Interests of the Child, 12 *Am. J. Fam. Therapy* 46 (1984); Hoorwitz, The Visitation Dilemma in Court Consultation, 64 *J. Contemp. Soc. Work* 231 (1983).

50. E.g., Lewis v. Lewis, 260 Ark. 691, 543 S.W.2d 222 (1976); Donaldson v. Donaldson, 198 Kan. 111, 422 P.2d 871 (1967). See Ryback v. Cobb County Dept. of Family and Children Services, 163 Ga. App. 165, 293 S.E.2d 563 (1982) (involving grandparent visitation).

Additional problems arise when the custodial parent wishes to move to another location in a way that will effectively eliminate visitation rights. Courts have been divided on the degree to which the custodial parent may remove a child. Compare, Carpenter v. Carpenter, 220 Va. 299, 257 S.E.2d 845 (1979); Pamperine v. Pamperine, 112 Wis.2d 70, 331 N.W.2d 648 (1983); Groh v. Groh, 110 Wis.2d 117, 327 N.W.2d 655 (1983). This matter is discussed briefly below.

51. Hoorwitz, The Visitation Dilemma in Court Consultation, 64 *J. Contemp. Soc. Work* 231 (1983).

52. In 1984 the Federal Child Support Enforcement Amendments were adopted. (Pub. L. No. 98–378). The law is technically an amendment to the Social Security Act. It provides for mandatory withholding of wages, expedited procedures for enforcing support obligations, withholding of support payments from tax refunds, and a variety of other provisions to encourage payment of support obligations.

Many states have adopted the Uniform Reciprocal Enforcement of Support Act to ensure that support decrees from one state can be easily enforced in other states. Fox, The Uniform Reciprocal Enforcement of Support Act, 4 *Fam. L. Rep.* 4017 (1978). See generally Freed & Walker, Family Law in the Fifty States: An Overview, 17 *Fam. L. Q.* 369 (1985).

53. See Lansing & Sherman, Legal Response to Child Snatching, 7 *J. Juv. L.* 16 (1983).

54. Note, Child Snatching: Remedies in Federal Courts, 41 *Wash. & Lee L. Rev.* 185 (1984).

55. All states have now adopted the Uniform Child Custody Jurisdiction Act to discourage removal of child to another state for the purpose of obtaining an inconsistent decree from the second court. In addition, states have increased penalties for, and cooperation concerning, childnapping. See Freed & Walker, Family Law in the Fifty States: An Overview, 17 *Fam. L. Q.* 369 (1985).

56. 28 U.S.C. §1738A (1982).

57. E.g., Lloyd v. Loeffler, 539 F. Supp. 998 (E.D. Wis.), *aff'd*, 694 F.2d 489 (7th Cir. 1982); Wood v. Wood, 338 N.W.2d 123 (Iowa 1983); Plante v. Engel, 124 N.H. 213, 469 A.2d 1299 (1983).

58. See note 50 *supra*.

59. Blau, An Evaluative Study of the Role of the Grandparents in the Best Interests of the Child, 12 *Am. J. Fam. Therapy* 46 (1984); Brummer & Looney, Grandparents Rights in Custody, Adoption, and Visitation Cases, 39 *Ark. L. Rev.* 259 (1985); Zablotsky, To Grandmother's House We Go:

Grandparent Visitation After Stepparent Adoption, 32 *Wayne L. Rev.* 1 (1985).

60. Notably, there is no constitutional privacy rights residing in grandparents that is comparable to the parental childrearing privacy rights.

61. Virtually all states give grandparents some rights to *petition* for visitation rights, but these rights vary greatly from state to state. Freed & Foster, Family Law in the Fifty States: An Overview, 17 *Fam. L. Q.* 365, 432 (1984). See Freed & Freed, Grandparents Visitation: Vagaries and Vicissitudes, 23 *St. Louis L. J.* 643 (1979); Note, Grandparents' Statutory Right to Petition for Visitation: Vermont and the National Framework, 10 *Vt. L. Rev.* 55 (1985); Note, Visitation Rights of a Grandparent Over the Objection of a Parent: The Best Interest of the Child, 15 *J. Fam. L.* 51 (1979).

62. U.S. Study on Child Abuse and Neglect, *National Study of the Incidence and Severity of Child Abuse and Neglect* 39–41 (1981). The number of reported children may now be approaching two million.

63. Abuse may also give rise to civil liability, despite traditional common-law immunities. For discussions of liability for one form of abuse, see Note, Incest: The Need to Develop a Response to Intra-Family Sexual Abuse, 22 *Duq. L. Rev.* 901 (1984); Note, Tort Remedies for Incestuous Abuse, 12 *Golden Gate U. L. Rev.* 609 (1983).

64. C. Cross, *Child Abuse and Neglect* (1984). See D. Finkelhor, *Child Sexual Abuse* (1985).

65. B. Nelson, *Making Child Abuse an Issue* (1984).

66. J. Giovannoni & R. Becerra, *Defining Child Abuse* (1979); Besharov, State Intervention to Protect Children: New York's Definition of "Child Abuse" and "Child Neglect," 26 *N.Y.L. Sch. L. Rev.* 723 (1981); Wald, State Intervention on Behalf of "Neglected" Children: A Search for Realistic Standards, 27 *Stan. L. Rev.* 985 (1975).

67. Wisconsin v. Yoder, 406 U.S. 205 (1972); Pierce v. Society of Sisters, 268 U.S. 510 (1925).

68. E.g., *In re* Phillip B., 92 Cal. App. 3d 796, 156 Cal. Rptr. 48 (1st Dist. 1979), *cert. denied sub nom.,* Bothman v. Warren B., 445 U.S. 949 (1980) (but see *In re* Cheryl H., 153 Cal. App. 3d 1098, 200 Cal. Rptr. 789 [2d Dist. 1984]); Friedrichsen v. Niemotka, 71 N.J. Super. 398, 177 A.2d 58 (1962); Ewald, Medical Decision-Making for Children: An Analysis of Competing Interests, 25 *St. Louis U. L. J.* 689 (1982).

69. See Fraser, A Glimpse at the Future: A Critical Analysis of the Development of Child Abuse Reporting Statutes, 54 *Chi.-Kent L. Rev.* 641 (1978); Newberger, The Helping Hand Strikes Again: Unintended Consequences of Child Abuse Reporting, 12 *J. Clinical Child Psychology* 307 (1983); Smith & Meyer, Child Abuse Reporting Laws: A Time for Reconsideration, 7 *Int'l J. L. & Psychiatry* 351 (1984). See generally Coleman, Creating Therapist-Offender Exception to Mandatory Child Abuse Reporting Statutes—When Psychiatrist Knows Best, 54 *Cin. L. Rev.* 1113 (1986).

70. U.S. Study on Child Abuse and Neglect, *National Study of the Incidence and Severity of Child Abuse and Neglect* (1981).

71. The great vagueness and discretion present in the social response to abuse and neglect invites uncertain responses to abuse and neglect. In part, this uncertainty results from the emotions, and the varied and sometimes suppressed reactions to these emotions. Prygoski, Of Predispositions and Dispositions: An Attitudinal Study of Decision-making in Child Abuse and Neglect Cases, 21 *Houston L. Rev.* 883 (1984).

72. Santosky v. Kramer, 455 U.S. 745 (1982); Armstrong, Termination of Parental Rights, 8 *J. Juv. L.* 442 (1984).

73. Lassiter v. Department of Social Services, 452 U.S. 18 (1981).

74. U.S. Department of Justice, *A Comparative Analysis of Juvenile Codes* 71 (1980).

75. U.S. Department of Justice, *Standards for the Administration of Juvenile Justice and Delinquency Prevention* 344–46 (1980).

76. Williams, Child Abuse Reconsidered: The Urgency of Authentic Prevention, 12 *J. Clinical Child Psychology* 312, 315 (1983).

77. Gray, Prevention of Child Abuse and Neglect, in *Child Abuse and Neglect: A Medical Reference* (N.S. Ellerstein ed. 1981).

78. E.g., Browne & Finkelhor, Impact of Child Sexual Abuse: A Review of the Research, 99 *Psychological Bull.* 66 (1986); Caplan, Watters, White, Parry & Bates, Toronto Multiagency Child Abuse Research Project: The Abused and the Abuser, 8 *Child Abuse & Neglect* 343 (1984); Kinard, Mental Health Needs of Abused Children, 59 *Child Welfare* 451 (1980); Lutzker & Rice, Project 12-Ways: Measuring Outcome of a Large In-Home Service for Treatment and Prevention of Child Abuse and Neglect, 8 *Child Abuse & Neglect* 519 (1984); Wolfe & Sandler, Training Abusive Parents in Effective Child Management, 5 *Behav. Modification* 320 (1981).

79. E.g., Caplan et al., *supra*, note 78; Green, Child Abuse by Siblings, 8 *Child Abuse & Neglect* 311 (1984); Starr, Child Abuse, 34 *Am. Psychologist* 872 (1979).

80. Caplan et al., *supra*, note 78; Howze & Kotch, Disentangling Life Events, Stress and Social Support: Implications for the Primary Prevention of Child Abuse and Neglect, 8 *Child Abuse & Neglect* 401 (1984); Junewicz, A Protective Posture Toward Emotional Neglect and Abuse, 62 *Child Welfare* 243 (1983); Shapiro, A CWLA Study of Factors Involved in Child Abuse, 59 *Child Welfare* 242 (1980).

81. For examples of preliminary efforts at demonstrating effective treatment techniques see A. Goldstein, H. Keller & D. Erne, *Changing the Abusive Parent* (1986); Crimmins, Bradlyn, St. Lawrence & Kelly, A Training Technique for Improving Parent-Child Interaction Skills of an Abusive-Neglectful Mother, 8 *Child Abuse & Neglect* 533 (1984); Crozier & Katz, Social Learning Treatment of Child Abuse, 10 *J. Behav. Therapy & Experimental Psychiatry* 213 (1979); Denicola & Sandler, Training Abusive Parents in Child Management and Self-Control Skills, 11 *Behav. Therapy & Experimental Psychiatry* 263 (1980); Wolfe & Sanders, Training Abusive Parents in Effective Child Management, 5 *Behav. Modification* 320 (1981).

82. Blythe, A Critique of Outcome Evaluation in Child Abuse Treatment, 62 *Child Welfare* 325 (1983).

83. Williams, Child Abuse Reconsidered: The Urgency of Authentic Prevention, 12 *J. Clinical Child Psychology* 312 (1983).

84. *Id.*

85. Blythe, *supra,* note 82.

86. Gray, Prevention of Child Abuse and Neglect, in *Child Abuse and Neglect: A Medical Reference* (N.S. Ellerstein ed. 1981).

87. *Id.* See Williams, Child Abuse Reconsidered: The Urgency of Authentic Prevention, 12 *J. Clinical Child Psychology* 312 (1983).

88. Faller, Is the Child Victim of Sexual Abuse Telling the Truth? 8 *Child Abuse & Neglect* 473 (1984).

89. Summit, The Child Abuse Accommodation Syndrome, 7 *Child Abuse & Neglect* 177 (1983).

90. E.g., Goodwin, Sahel & Rada, Incest Hoax: False Accusation, False Details, 6 *Bull. Am. Acad. Psychiatry & L.* 269 (1978); Sgroi, Sarnacki & Canfield, Validation of Child Sexual Abuse, in *Handbook of Clinical Intervention in Child Abuse* (S. Sgroi ed. 1982).

91. See generally G. Craig, *Human Development* (1986).

92. Mrazek, Sexual Abuse of Children, 21 *J. Child Psychology & Psychiatry* 91 (1980).

93. See Bulkley, Evidentiary and Procedural Trends in State Legislation and Other Emerging Legal Issues in Child Sexual Abuse Cases, 89 *Dick. L. Rev.* 645 (1985); Garnett, Children as Witnesses: Competency and Rules Favoring Their Testimony, 12 *Colo. Law.* 1982 (1983); Note, A Comprehensive Approach to Child Hearsay Statements in Sex Abuse Cases, 83 *Colum. L. Rev.* 1745 (1983); Note, The Testimony of Child Victims in Sex Abuse Prosecutions: Two Legislative Innovations, 98 *Harv. L. Rev.* 806 (1985); Developments, Defendants' Rights in Child Witness Competency Hearings: Establishing Constitutional Procedures for Sexual Abuse Cases, 69 *Minn. L. Rev.* 1377 (1985).

94. Lyman & Roberts, Mental Health Testimony in Child Custody Litigation, 9 *L. & Psychology Rev.* 15 (1985).

95. D. Skafte, *Child Custody Evaluations* (1984).

96. See generally Cornblatt, Matrimonial Mediation, 23 *J. Fam. L.* 99 (1984); Musetto, The Role of the Mental Health Professional in Contested Custody: Evaluator of Competency or Facilitator of Change, 4 *J. Divorce* 69 (1981); Pearson & Thoennes, Mediation in Custody Disputes, 4 *Behav. Sci. & L.* 203 (1986); Trombetta, Custody Evaluation and Custody Mediation: A Comparison of Two Dispute Interventions, 6 *J. Divorce* 65 (1982).

CHAPTER 14
LEGAL RESPONSES TO
SEXUAL VARIATIONS

A behavioral scientist, "Dr. X," took a law school criminal law course. The class was considering the legal distinction between adultery and fornication. (In fornication neither of the participants is married to anyone, in adultery one of the participants is married to someone else.) Dr. X was called upon to explain the difference. "I'm sorry, I don't know," he replied. "I've tried them both and I can't tell any difference at all." Perhaps this story illustrates some differences between law and the behavioral sciences in dealing with sexual variations. Unlike the behavioral sciences, the law has traditionally sought to reduce the "undesirable" by making criminal sexual conduct other than "standard" intercourse between those married to each other. The recent trend has been toward decriminalizing consensual sexual activity although, as we shall see, the Supreme Court may have signaled a return to a more repressive approach. In modern times the legal system appears to have assumed that behavioral scientists are especially well qualified to deal with sex offenders. Perhaps this results from the place of sexual conflicts in traditional psychodynamic theory, or because of a public perception that sex offenders must be emotionally disturbed.

A traditional part of the study of law and psychiatry and law and psychology has been sexual psychopath laws and sex offenses. In this chapter we briefly review social response to sexual variations, sexual offenses, and sexual psychopath laws. We conclude with a very short consideration of a philosophical question raised by sex offenses: when should the law interfere in consensual conduct between adults by punishing "victimless crimes"? Many of the issues discussed in this chapter are related to matters discussed in more detail in other parts of the book.[1]

SEXUAL OFFENSES

From early society, some sexual conduct has been considered as anti-social or criminal. Over the centuries, among the social reasons for trying to eliminate it have been to protect victims from sexual assaults, express society's strong sense of morality, promote health by avoiding the spread of venereal diseases or the transmission of genetic defects, and placate the gods.[2] The religious fear of divine punishment for sexual misconduct is not limited to ancient cultures, the story of Sodom and Gomorrah is still told, and in fact, a major type of sex offense ("sodomy") is named for the Biblical story.[3] Today the same reasons may be given for the punishment of some kinds of sexual conduct, although the emphasis is now on protecting victims of sexual assaults. The general trend has been toward more strictly or vigorously prohibiting nonconsensual conduct and removing or reducing criminal sanctions for consensual conduct.

Sexual offenses may be classified according to consent and violence, in the form of a matrix.

	Consent	*No Consent*
Non-Violent	fornication sodomy prostitution	exhibitionism (indecent exposure) child exploitation statutory rape
Violent	consensual sado-masochism	rape some child abuse

"No consent" includes apparent consent that is not legally binding, such as the consent of a child or a profoundly mentally retarded person. Arguably some sex offenses are not included in the matrix, such as zoophilia (sex with animals), depending on one's definition of victims and consent. These activities are, however, generally criminal. Other laws once considered sex-related, such as those prohibiting contraception and abortion, are now largely unconstitutional.[4]

Rape, Sexual Assault, and Child Molestation

Forcible rape and sexual molestation of children are now treated as the most serious sexual offenses. Traditionally rape has been defined as male-female sexual intercourse resulting from force or the threat of force by the male. It required only minimal "penetration," not completion of the sexual act. "Statutory rape" is consensual intercourse where the female is under age or mentally incompetent and therefore cannot give legally binding consent. In most jurisdictions these traditional offenses have been expanded and are often merged as varying degrees of seriousness of the crime of "sexual assault."[5]

Modern definitions of sexual assault include several offenses, such as forcible or violent assault (rape), sexual relations without consent and sexual relations with a child. Forcible assault now generally includes the use of force or threat of force by anyone (no longer limited to males) against anyone else (male or female). It may involve the penetration of vagina, anus, or mouth with penis or other object. Thus many of the new definitions of rape include involuntary homosexual acts and sodomy.

A second form of sexual assault is to have sexual relations with someone incapable of giving consent. Consent to sexual activity by someone not capable of giving consent is generally a less serious crime than the use of force. This usually involves a question of age, although other forms of incompetency such as severe mental disability may also preclude the ability to consent.[6] The age of consent ranges from 12 to 21, although most states tend to set the age of consent between 14 and 16. Another trend has been for states to set greater levels of severity for relations with younger children.[7]

Another expansion of the concept of forcible assault has been the recognition of "marital rape." Traditionally there could be no rape between partners to a marriage because the marriage provided consent to sexual contact. Several states, however, now have abandoned this concept.[8] Sexual assault may also involve fondling of the body. The fondling, if it involves a child, may be a form of child abuse and sexual assault.

A number of reforms of sexual assault laws are being considered. One interesting reform has been the criminal prohibition in at least one state against sexual relations between psychotherapists and their patients.[9] Other reforms of rape and sexual exploitation laws have been designed to encourage the reporting and prosecution of these crimes. An example of these laws are rape shield provisions that eliminate or greatly restrict the ability of the defense to inquire about the previous sexual activity of the victim. Since the issue of consent is central in a prosecution for rape, broad questioning about past sexual conduct was often permitted. Rape shield laws prevent this often embarrassing questioning.[10] Other laws permit the victims of child molestation to testify away from the courtroom, sometimes on video tape and with limited cross-examination.[11]

Reforms of these laws have not been without their critics. There is some fear, for example, that limits on the questioning of victims will result in the unfair conviction of some defendants. In many prosecutions for sexual assault the case essentially comes down to the word of the defendant against the word of the accused. Therefore, the defendant may wish to present evidence of considerable prior sexual activity by the victim as indirect evidence of consent. Concern has been expressed that these limits on the defense in rape and child molestation cases, as well as the very great public concern about these crimes, make it difficult for the defendant to obtain a fair trial.[12] There are other objections to the breadth and vagueness of laws, particularly child molestation laws. Uncertainty about the scope of these laws invites uneven and ineffective application of the laws. One other interesting criticism is that child protective laws unfairly discriminate against children by refusing them the right to choose to engage in sexual activity with older people.[13] The merit of such a position essentially depends upon the ability of youngsters to knowledgeably consent to sexual activity. There appears no inclination to ease sexual abuse laws by permitting young children to legally consent to sexual activity.

Rape and sexual molestation of children are serious felonies, carrying substantial prison terms. The Supreme Court has held that the states may not impose the death penalty for rape, but life imprisonment is permitted.[14] The question of treatment for serious sexual assault or child molestation is debated by mental health professionals.[15] The law has given limited consideration to providing treatment instead of punishment for serious sex crimes. However, treatment may be provided during imprisonment. Perhaps the most controversial approach for serious sex offenders has been castration, which has been seen variously as a punishment and treatment for these offenses; but this treatment has been heavily criticized and may be unconstitutional as cruel and unusual punishment. The use of "chemical castration" is now being promoted as a response to some sex offenses.[16]

Exhibitionism

Exhibitionists are the largest single group of apprehended sex offenders, accounting for more than one third of all sex offenders, and as a group they have among the highest rates of recidivism.[17] The likelihood of arrest and the tendency toward recidivism mean that a significant number of exhibitionists are seen by mental health professionals.[18]

To a mental health professional, exhibitionism is the display of one's genitals, for the purpose of obtaining sexual gratification through the exhibition, to an audience that is probably unwilling to view it. Criminal laws concerning "indecent exposure," "public lewdness," and "public indecency" make these activities illegal, although the statutes typically involve a good deal more than the activities of exhibitionists, among them such displays of genitals as nude sun bathing, erotic dancing, and public urination. Women may be charged with indecent exposure even though they are generally not thought by mental health professionals to be exhibitionist. The common-law offense of indecent exposure required "the intentional exposure of the person in a public place and in the presence of others." Many state statutes generally follow the common law, although some specify which body parts will be considered indecent if exposed. Some states require that the exposure be likely to cause affront or alarm, others do not.[19]

Indecent exposure is generally a misdemeanor, although the penalties for violation vary considerably from one jurisdiction to another. Some states provide for much greater penalties if the exposure is committed under "aggravating" circumstances, such as exposure to minors, or for repeat offenders. Under aggravated circumstances, the crime may be defined as a felony and a significant prison term may be imposed.

It is not at all unusual for someone charged with or convicted of indecent exposure to be given the alternative of seeking some form of therapy rather than going to jail. The real penalties for conviction of indecent exposure extend, of course, considerably beyond those imposed by law. The social stigma attached to it, for example, may result in difficulty in obtaining employment or being certified for a profession. For this reason indecent exposure charges are often dropped, or amended to another charge such as disorderly conduct, if the exposure did not involve aggravated circumstances, if the case did not involve a true exhibitionist, or if the defendant agrees to seek therapy.

The issue of the dangerousness of those convicted of indecent exposure repeatedly appears in one form or another in the legal system. For example there is some popular feeling that exhibitionism may be one step on the road toward more violent sexual offenses such as sexual assault. Most exhibitionists, however, are not dangerous and have no intention of further sexual contact with the victims beyond the exhibition. The exhibitionist is typically passive-dependent and obsessive and is often quite schizoid. A few subtypes of exhibitionists may be dangerous but this is generally infrequent. There is no reason to believe that exhibitionists move from this conduct to more violent or more dangerous sexual offenses.[20] Modern clinical studies generally characterize indecent exposure or lewd conduct as a social nuisance rather than as dangerous activity. The harm to the victim is ordinarily described as minimal.[21]

Confusion, uncertainty, and inconsistency regarding indecent exposure statutes and their enforcement illustrate the lack of any clear understanding of the public policies which these statutes are meant to promote. Undoubtedly, the statutes are based in part on a desire by the public to avoid having to look at naked bodies in public places. But this would not explain why jurisdictions prosecute as indecent exposure nudity in places where it is generally understood that nudity will occur. Where the nudity is consensual, only the strongest form of interest in public morality could justify the interference by the legal system.

Homosexuality

Consensual homosexual conduct has traditionally been illegal under state sodomy statutes. A number of states still explicitly prohibit homosexual conduct, but about half the states have removed criminal sanctions from private homosexual activity.[22] The constitutional right of privacy protects some forms of private sexual conduct or procreative decisions.[23] The Supreme Court has refused to apply the constitutional right of privacy to private homosexual conduct,[24] and other courts have been badly divided on the question.[25] Strong arguments have been made by commentators that if the constitutional right of privacy has any meaning, it must protect such a fundamental personal question as sexual preference when the conduct involved is in private.[26]

In 1986 the Supreme Court specifically held that the right of privacy does not protect private homosexual conduct. In *Bowers v. Hardwick,* the Court upheld a Georgia statute making consensual sodomy ("sexual act involving the sex organs of one person and the mouth or anus of another") a felony.[27] The major basis of the decision was that the right of privacy does not include homosexual activity (as evidenced by the fact that most states had sodomy laws when the Bill of Rights and Fourteenth Amendment were adopted), and therefore there is no constitutional protection for that activity. (The Court ruled that the issue of heterosexual sodomy, which was also prohibited by the Georgia law, was not yet before the Court.)

In a final paragraph that received little immediate attention, but which may be significant in the long run, the Court said that "majority sentiments about the morality of homosexuality" could be the rational, constitutional basis for the prohibition against sodomy.[28] Presumably the Court was referring to a political majority as evidenced by the fact that the Georgia statute had been passed and not repealed. This approach would seem to approve the constitutionality of a broad range of nondangerous victimless crimes, including heterosexual sodomy which the Georgia statute also appears to make illegal.

There were reports that Justice Powell, the "swing vote" in the 5-4 decision, changed his vote some time after the conference. (Justices are free to do so.) In a concurring opinion he noted that a prison sentence, or at least "one of long duration," for consensual sodomy would raise a serious cruel and unusual punishment question.[29] He did not explain the basis for his belief that some punishment, but not much, is constitutionally permitted for the crime. Furthermore, given the Court's great reluctance to review the length of prison sentences for "proportionality" to the seriousness of the crime,[30] there is no assurance that the Court would not permit a lengthy sentence for it.

A strong dissent would hold that the right of privacy included private, consensual sexual conduct in the home. Quoting Holmes, the dissenters found it "revolting to have no better reason for a rule of law than that . . . it was laid down in the time of Henry IV."[31]

It is unlikely that this case will have significant, direct impact. Very few criminal charges are made for private, consensual sodomy even in the 24 states (and D.C.), which have such laws. However, the indirect impact may be significant in signaling a return to criminalization of victimless crimes, in reducing the scope of the constitutional right of privacy, and in promoting antihomosexual attitudes and laws.

Laws prohibiting homosexual conduct usually are misdemeanors. They are virtually unenforced and are essentially unenforceable. The few arrests that are completed are usually made in public facilities such as restrooms or for solicitation or prostitution-related activity. Homosexual conduct in public, of course, is subject to laws concerning lewd conduct.

The legal response to homosexuality extends well beyond the issue of criminalizing private or public homosexual activity to include issues of whether public benefits or public employment can properly be denied someone because of sexual preference and whether private discrimination based on homosexuality should be legally prohibited.

The ability of the government to refuse employment or benefits to homosexuals is not yet fully clear. It appears that the government probably can discriminate on the basis of sexual preference when there is strong reason to do so. For example, the armed services have been permitted to discriminate because of special security considerations and living arrangements.[32] On the other hand, schools cannot dismiss teachers based on their advocacy or support for gay interests.[33] The AIDS epidemic may expand the government's legitimate interest in some of this discrimination.[34]

Government discrimination is probably not very effective in achieving its purposes. It cannot hope to detect most of the people who are not open about their sexual preference and therefore it serves to penalize only those who are honest. Ironically, such discrimination probably increases the possibility of security blackmail by increasing the penalty for public disclosure of homosexuality. The Supreme

Court's decision upholding criminal sodomy laws may encourage states to pass such laws and to discriminate on the basis of sexual preference.

Federal civil rights laws do not include sexual preference as one of the prohibited forms of private discrimination. A few state and local laws do prohibit such discrimination, however.[35] The basis of these laws is that homosexuality is, like race or gender, unrelated to most jobs or housing and therefore decisions made on that basis are arbitrary, unfair, and invidious. In most areas of the United States there has not been a broad public support for these antidiscrimination laws.

Where public discrimination is prohibited but private discrimination is permitted, it is sometimes difficult to draw a line between private and public decisions. For example the decision to refuse to recognize a gay student group by a university which receives substantial public funds has been open to legal challenge.[36] In addition, several professional schools, notably law schools, have refused permission for private and public employers who discriminate against homosexuals to recruit at the schools.[37]

The treatment of homosexuality by mental health professionals raises ethical issues when homosexuals seek to become heterosexual in orientation. The DSM III no longer recognizes homosexuality as a mental illness but does consider the difficulties in living with a sexual orientation as a mental condition.[38] Two types of ethical issues may arise. If it is almost impossible to change sexual orientation, then claiming to provide that treatment would be nearly fraudulent. Although treatment to change sexual orientation is difficult and success cannot be guaranteed, it apparently has some chance of working with highly motivated patients.[39] A second ethical question is more fundamental: is it appropriate to try to change sexual orientation? If homosexuality is not a mental illness, and is a legitimate human condition, one argument goes, then professionals should help homosexuals understand and be comfortable with their sexuality, not try to hide it or change it. The other side of the argument is that if someone strongly wishes to change orientation, perhaps because living in society as a heterosexual is more likely to be comfortable, then it is appropriate for a therapist to work with the homosexual to achieve this goal.[40]

SEXUAL PSYCHOPATH LAWS

Sexual psychopath laws provide for the long term incarceration of persons determined to be "sexual psychopaths," "sexually dangerous persons," or "mentally disordered sex offenders." Typically those subject to such laws are committed to a hospital or psychiatric facility and held there until they are determined by the medical staff of the institution to have been cured. Some of these laws provide for an indeterminate incarceration which may continue until the death of the person. In some ways these laws are like involuntary civil commitment statutes, although more directly tied to criminal sexual offenses.[41]

A number of such laws have been passed, often in response to brutal sex crimes. It is estimated that about half the states have had such laws. They have been promoted both as providing for humanitarian treatment of sex offenders and as protecting the public from sex maniacs.[42]

Sexual psychopath laws often fail to provide clear or sensible definitions of the persons subject to them. One state, for example, defines the concept as the existence of "such condition of mental instability or impulsiveness of behavior, or lack of customary standards of good judgment, or failure to appreciate the consequences of his act, or any combination of any such conditions as to render such a person irresponsible for his own conduct with respect to sexual matters and thereby dangerous to other persons."[43] Another jurisdiction defines a sexual psychopath as "a person, not insane, who by course of repeated misconduct on sexual matters has evidenced such lack of power to control his sexual impulses as to be dangerous to other persons because he is likely to attack or otherwise inflict injury, loss, or other evil on the objects of his desire."[44] All definitions do, however, generally involve a person who has some mental disorder and who is perceived as being dangerous because of the disorder, or who has committed certain sex crimes.

Sexual psychopath statutes usually provide for a hearing to determine whether a person ought to be committed. Psychiatric evidence is taken at the hearing to determine whether the person is suffering from a mental disease and is sexually dangerous. The defendant may be represented by counsel at these hearings and may cross-examine the expert witnesses, and present witnesses of his own. If it is determined that the person is a sexual psychopath, he will generally be committed to a hospital or psychiatric facility. There may be provisions for periodic review of the patient's condition by the court, but generally the staff at the hospital or psychiatric facility will determine whether the person is cured and can safely be released.[45]

Although sexual psychopath laws are generally meant to be civil rather than criminal in nature, courts have realized that like criminal convictions they involve incarceration and serious stigma. Some states provide that a person may be subject to the psychopath laws instead of the criminal sex laws; others provide that the sexual psychopath laws may be applied in addition to the imposition of criminal penalties. Some of these states do at least permit time spent in an institution pursuant to a sexual psychopath commitment to be subtracted from the prison term imposed for the criminal charge.

In 1986, in *Allen v. Illinois,* the Supreme Court considered the rights of those subject to sex psychopath laws.[46] The Court emphasized the difference between treatment and punishment when evaluating the applicability of constitutional rights. Allen was incarcerated under the Illinois Sexually Dangerous Persons Act, and claimed a violation of his right to avoid self-incrimination because the Court ordered him to submit to two psychiatric examinations and these were the basis for determining him to be a sexually dangerous person.

The Court noted that the right to avoid self-incrimination does not apply to civil cases,[47] and held that this was in fact a civil case. This was true even though the Illinois sex psychopath law requires proof of a criminal sexual assault, provides a jury trial with many of the rights of a criminal trial, establishes a "beyond a reasonable doubt" standard of proof, and permits the person to be incarcerated in facilities within a maximum-security prison. The majority found that this was a civil process based on the following: in addition to having committed a criminal act the person must also have a mental disorder and be dangerous, the person is released if no longer dangerous, and the purpose of the law is to provide treatment rather than punishment.

The dissent emphasized the great loss of liberty, the stigma and the criminal trial-like aspects of sex psychopath laws. It noted dangers in permitting states to establish "civil" actions like the sex psychopath statutes. The state might create "an entire corps of 'dangerous person' statutes to shadow its criminal code." By claiming commission of criminal offenses, findings of mental disorders and predictions of "criminal propensities," and a goal of "treatment" (rehabilitation) the state could thereby confine people in maximum-security institutions (prisons) for indeterminate periods as *civil* offenders. "Constitutional protections for criminal defendants would be simply inapplicable . . . [T]he result would be evisceration of criminal law and its accompanying protections."[48]

Sexual psychopath laws have been severely criticized in recent years. They are often poorly conceived and badly written statutes passed in response to a highly publicized serious sex crime. Criminal sex offenses, sentencing alternatives, and involuntary civil commitment statutes are adequate to deal with the problems that sexual psychopath laws were meant to solve.[49]

SEX, THE LAW, AND VICTIMLESS CRIMES

The traditional criminalization of much consensual sexual conduct between adults vividly raises the issue of "victimless crime"—those activities which are solitary or which directly involve only someone who has voluntarily consented to the activity. Traditional sex offenses classified as victimless crimes include prostitution, fornication, sodomy, and pornography offenses. Other victimless crimes include possession and use of narcotics, gambling, and self-protection laws (mandatory seat belt use or motorcycle helmet requirements).

In one sense, of course, these crimes are not absolutely "victimless" because they are not completely without effect on others. For example, it is possible that prostitution may encourage infidelity which may lead to the break up of marriages and families, and promiscuity does lead to higher levels of venereal disease which increase the cost of insurance and social programs, and viewing pornography may demean women or increase the chance of violence. Indeed, virtually everything anyone does has some indirect effects on someone else. One argument for criminalizing victimless crimes, then, is that these crimes in fact indirectly produce some victims and that we all have an interest in the health and welfare of each other. A second reason for making such victimless activities criminal offenses is to guide people away from engaging in conduct that is physically or morally harmful to themselves and to provide a clear statement of what society considers acceptable and good. A third reason for criminalizing victimless activities is that society has an interest in establishing a common moral climate. By engaging in immoral conduct a person tears at the moral fabric of society even if it involves no one else. Thus, to retain a moral and cohesive society, there is a social interest in prohibiting this conduct.[50]

The primary arguments against trying to criminalize these consensual or victimless activities are claims of autonomy and practicality. In a free society, citizens should be able to choose what to do with themselves so long as it does not significantly affect others. The claim that there is a social interest in every harm to oneself or indirect harm to another is basis enough to destroy all of the freedoms that the society should protect. As to the use of the criminal law to enforce one group's moral code on others, there is serious doubt that this is a legitimate function of the law in a free society. The practical argument is that it is impossible to enforce other people's morals (Prohibition is often cited as an example), and such efforts will only add money to the coffers of organized crime, turning many citizens into criminals and inviting unequal and arbitrary enforcement of the law. Such offenses may even trivialize the criminal law because they deal with petty events and because so many people almost routinely violate them.[51]

The decision to criminalize or punish activities carries with it real costs to society. Thus, when society decides to criminalize or punish activities these costs must be offset by substantial benefits if our criminal justice system is to be rational. Criminalization of consensual events requires that law enforcement agencies, courts, and correctional facilities use some of their limited resources to enforce and to punish violations of the victimless crimes. These are resources that probably must be diverted from other more serious events, including the apprehension and conviction of serious criminals. Even assuming that there are benefits from laws against consensual activity, the question remains whether the benefits are worth the costs of these laws.

MENTAL HEALTH PROFESSIONALS AND SEX OFFENDERS

Mental health professionals often play an important role in the legal system in evaluating and treating people charged with sex offenses.

Professionals should recognize the very great differences among the kinds of sex crimes and among the types of persons charged with them. A number of people charged with sex offenses are sent for evaluation to mental health professionals before the case is tried or even before formal charges are placed. The professional should clearly understand the purpose of the referral. Often it is for the purpose of determining whether the person should be diverted from the criminal system to therapy, or whether the charges should be dropped. Therapists may also be involved in the trial, or in evaluation after trial but before sentencing. In any of these settings the probability of dangerousness and recidivism will be of considerable concern. Because of a common misperception that all sex offenders are dangerous or may progress to more dangerous activities, mental health experts should be very cautious to avoid leaving an incorrect impression concerning dangerousness. It may be necessary to emphasize the absence of violent tendencies in some offenders, such as the exhibitionists.

One area in which mental health professionals are increasingly asked to serve is in the assessment of alleged child sexual abuse. For example, professionals may be asked to assess the ability of a child to truthfully testify in court or to help determine whether the sexual abuse actually took place. These assessments are of great importance involving very serious criminal charges. Because of the current national sensitivity to child abuse, and particularly to sexual abuse, any suggestion (even inadvertent) of abuse may have profoundly serious consequences for the parents. In many of these cases professionals should honestly and carefully explain the difficulty of reaching reliable and definite conclusions about what happened to a child. In other settings, such as custody cases, professionals should be extraordinarily careful to avoid suggestions of child abuse unless evidence exists for such a conclusion. In addition, professionals should be aware of the obligation to report abuse to the state once the likelihood of abuse has been established.

Mental health professionals may also be involved in providing therapy to persons charged with sexual offenses. Many of these defendants will enter therapy with a significant degree of coercion. The therapist should recognize this and be prepared to deal with it as well as with the possibility that the patient may feign a cure. The Eighth and Fourteenth Amendments may not permit the use of certain kinds of treatment, such as extreme aversive therapy, if the treatment has been court-ordered. A therapist concerned about whether a treatment is within the limit of the law should contact the court and explain the proposed treatment. The limits on confidentiality in such settings should be clearly explained to the defendant/patient. It should also be clear that the professional is obligated to make periodic reports to courts or to others.[52]

Mental health professionals should exercise great caution in the language that is used in making reports to, or testifying before, attorneys and courts. Technical language or analogies may mean something quite different to those untrained in behavioral science than it does to mental health professionals. For example, the statement that "because his victims are often children and young women, it is often considered that the exhibitionist is at least very similar to the pedophile. The dynamics of the disorders bear several similarities," may cause a lay person to assume that the exhibitionist is, or is likely to become, a pedophile or child molester. Such a conclusion by a judge or jury may have very serious consequences for the defendant. Therefore, the professional should take great pains to avoid language which may be misunderstood.

REFORMS OF SEX OFFENSES

The current status of sex offenses is a hodgepodge of inconsistent and even irrational laws and regulations. As we noted earlier, the trend has been to make sex offense statutes more precise, to eliminate consensual offenses and to more vigorously pursue nonconsensual offenses. We believe that these have been positive trends, but that they have been only partially successful.

Several additional steps would help to rationalize the system of sex offenses. First, the purposes of the laws must be very clearly stated and then drafted to ensure that the laws do not inadvertently or unnecessarily limit individual autonomy beyond achieving those purposes. Broad purposes of "setting a good moral climate" as the basis for the criminal law should, we believe, be viewed with skepticism. Second, once the goals are established, the most efficient and effective method of achieving the goal, consistent with other social objectives, should be established. Third, it should be determined whether the laws in pursuit of the goals can realistically be enforced. If they cannot, then little purpose is likely to be served by the criminalization, but the significant social costs are likely to result. Four, if the laws can be reasonably well enforced, lawmakers must determine whether the social costs of the laws will be less than the benefits to be derived from them. Laws that cannot be enforced, or can be enforced only at unacceptably high social costs, should be recast or discarded. These steps are more likely to lead to laws that are consistent and rational and that do not cost society more than they are worth.

NOTES

1. Of particular relevance are chapters 10, 11, 12, and 13, and those parts of chapters 1 and 2 dealing with confidentiality, ethics, and child abuse reporting.

2. See R. E. L. Masters & E. Lea, *Ax Crimes in History* (1963).

3. The Biblical story of the destruction of Sodom and Gomorrah appears at Genesis 18:20–19:26. The cities were destroyed after the Lord heard an outcry over the sin (particularly sexual excesses) there. Abraham apparently could not find even ten good men there. An interesting form of plea bargaining between the Lord and Abraham is recounted, Genesis 18:23–32.

4. See Roe v. Wade, 410 U.S. 113 (1973); Griswold v. Connecticut, 381 U.S. 479 (1965).

5. Kneedler, Sexual Assault Law Reform in Virginia—A Legislative History, 68 *Va. L. Rev.* 459 (1982).

6. Brongersma, Aggression Against Pedophiles, 7 *Int'l J. L. & Psychiatry* 79, 80–81 (1984), but see Finkelhor & Araji, Explanation of Pedophilia, 22 *J. Sex Research* 145 (1986).

7. For example, compare Model Penal Code §213.2 regarding sex with a female under 10, with the offense of sex with a person under 16 when the actor is 4 years older than the victim.

8. E.g., State v. Smith, 85 N.J. 193, 426 A.2d 38 (1981); Note, Forcible Rape in Washington: Criminal and Civil Sanctions, 19 *Gonz. L. Rev.* 363 (1983–84); Note, The Marital Rape Exemption, 52 *N.Y.U. L. Rev.* 306 (1977); Note, The Marital Rape Exemption: Legal Sanctions of Spouse Abuse, 18 *J. Fam. L.* 565 (1980).

9. "Any person who is or holds himself or herself out to be a therapist [physician, psychologist, social worker or other person providing psychotherapy services] and who intentionally has sexual contact [any intentional touching relating to sexual arousal or sexual humiliation] with a patient or client during any treatment, consultation, interview or examination is guilty of a . . . misdemeanor." Wis. Stat. Ann. §940.22 (West Supp. 1985).

10. Regarding rape shield rules of evidence and rape shield laws, see Federal Rules of Evidence 412; Tanford & Bocchino, Rape Victim Shield

Laws and the Sixth Amendment, 128 *U. Pa. L. Rev.* 544 (1980). See generally S. Katz & M. Mazur, *Understanding the Rape Victim* (1979); Berger, Man's Trial, Woman's Tribulation: Rape Cases in the Courtroom, 77 *Colum. L. Rev.* 1 (1977).

11. Problems associated with protecting and the reliability of children who may have been the victims of sexual abuse are discussed in chapter 13.

12. See generally Rudstein, Rape Shield Laws: Some Constitutional Problems, 18 *Wm. & Mary L. Rev.* 1 (1976); Tanford & Bocchino, note 10 *supra.*

13. Brongersma, Aggression Against Pedophiles, 7 *Int'l J. L. & Psychiatry* 79 (1984). See Abel, Becker & Cunningham-Rather, Complications, Consent, and Cognitions in Sex Between Children and Adults, 7 *Int'l J. L. & Psychiatry* 89 (1984); Constantine, The Sexual Rights of Children: Implications of a Radical Perspective, in *Children and Sex* (L. Constantine & F. Martinson, eds. 1981).

14. Coker v. Georgia, 433 U.S. 584 (1977).

15. E.g., Abel, Blanchard & Becker, An Integrated Treatment Program for Rapists, in *Clinical Aspects of the Rapist* (R. Rada ed. 1977); Lanyon, Theory and Treatment of Child Molestation, 54 *J. Consulting & Clinical Psychology* 176 (1986); Longo, Administering a Comprehensive Sexual Aggressive Treatment Program in a Maximum Security Setting, in *The Sexual Aggressor: Current Perspectives on Treatment* (J. Greer & I. Stuart eds. 1983); S. Verdun-Jones & A. Keltner eds., *Sexual Aggression and the Law* (1983).

16. For a review of the issues see Comment, the Use of Depo-Provera for Treating Male Sex Offenders: A Review of the Constitutional and Medical Issues, 16 *Toledo L. Rev.* 181 (1984). See Demsky, The Use of Depo-Provera in the Treatment of Sex Offenders: The Legal Issues, 5 *J. Legal Med.* 295 (1984); Ortmann, The Treatment of Sexual Offenders: Castration and Antihormone Therapy, 3 *Int'l J. L. & Psychiatry* 443 (1980); Note, Castration of the Male Sex Offender: A Legally Impermissible Alternative, 30 *Loy. L. Rev.* 337 (1984).

17. P. Gebhard, J. Gagnon, W. Pomeroy & C. Christenson, *Sex Offenders: An Analysis of Types* (1965); Gigeroff, Mahr & Turner, Sex Offenders on Probation, 32 *Fed. Probation* 18 (1968).

18. Smukler & Schiebel, Personality Characteristics of Exhibitionists, 36 *Diseases Nervous System* 600 (1975).

19. For a general review of indecent exposure laws and exhibitionism see Smith, Legal Stand Toward Exhibitionism, in *Exhibitionism: Description, Assessment, and Treatment* (D. Cox & R. Daitzman eds. 1980).

20. Smith & Meyer, Workings Between the Legal System and the Therapist, in *Exhibitionism: Description, Assessment, and Treatment* (D. Cox & R. Daitzman eds. 1980).

21. *Id.*

22. For a review of state statutes prohibiting consensual homosexual conduct see Note, The Right of Privacy and Other Constitutional Challenges

to Sodomy Statutes, 15 *Toledo L. Rev.* 811, 868–75 (1984). Most Western countries have removed criminal penalties for consensual sodomy.

23. E.g., Akron v. Akron Center for Reproductive Health, 462 U.S. 416 (1983); Planned Parenthood v. Danforth, 428 U.S. 52 (1976); Roe v. Wade, 410 U.S. 113 (1973); Griswold v. Connecticut, 381 U.S. 479 (1965).

24. In Doe v. Commonwealth's Attorney for Richmond [Doe v. City of Richmond], 425 U.S. 901 (1976), the Supreme Court affirmed a lower court upholding the constitutionality of a Virginia sodomy statute that prohibited private, consensual homosexual activity. The Court issued no opinion in reaching its decision, so the basis of the decision remains unclear, and a matter of debate even among members of the Court. Compare the opinions of Justice Brennan in Carey v. Population Services, 431 U.S. 678 (1977) (note 17 at 694), and Justice Renquist in the same case, *id.* note 2 at 718 (Renquist, dissenting). Subsequently the Court was evenly divided in affirming that it was unconstitutional for a state to discharge a teacher for advocating, promoting or openly practicing homosexual activities. National Gay Task Force v. Board of Education, 470 U.S. 903 (1985) (equally divided court). Bowers v. Hardwick, 106 S. Ct. 2841 (1986) (upholding the constitutionality of a criminal statute prohibiting sodomy, applied in this case to homosexual sodomy, even if conducted in private between consenting adults) is discussed *infra.*

25. E.g., Striking down consensual sodomy (or similar) statutes, State v. Saunders, 75 N.J. 200, 381 A.2d 333 (1977); People v. Onofre, 51 N.Y.2d 476, 415 N.E.2d 936, 434 N.Y.S.2d 947 (1980), *cert. denied,* 451 U.S. 987 (1981); Commonwealth v. Bonadio, 490 Pa. 91, 415 A.2d 47 (1980) (but see State v. Walsh, 713 S.W.2d 508 [Mo. 1986]). E.g., upholding consensual (or similar) statutes, Baker v. Wade, 769 F.2d 289 (5th Cir. 1985), *cert. denied,* 106 S. Ct. 333 (1986); Dronenburg v. Zech, 741 F.2d 1388 (D.C. Cir. 1984) (dealing with military regulations requiring the discharge of homosexuals); Doe v. Commonwealth's Attorney of Richmond, 403 F. Supp. 1199 (E.D. Va. 1975), *aff'd mem.,* 425 U.S. 901 (1976).

26. E.g., L. Rice, *Legalizing Homosexual Conduct: The Role of the Supreme Court in the Gay Rights Movement* (1984); Lasson, Civil Liberties for Homosexuals: The Law in Limbo, 10 *U. Dayton L. Rev.* 645 (1984); Rivera, Our Straight Laced Judge: The Legal Position of Homosexual Persons in the United States, 30 *Hastings L. J.* 799 (1979); Note, Survey on the Constitutional Right to Privacy in the Context of Homosexual Activity, 40 *U. Miami L. Rev.* 521 (1986).

27. Bowers v. Hardwick, 106 S. Ct. 2841 (1986).

28. *Id.*

29. *Id.,* Powell concurring.

30. E.g., Hutto v. Davis, 454 U.S. 370 (1982) (refusing to strike down a sentence of 40 years for possession of marijuana); Rummel v. Estelle, 445 U.S. 263 (1980) (refusing to strike down a sentence of life imprisonment for three theft offenses involving less than $300).

31. Bowers v. Hardwick, *supra,* note 27, Blackmun, dissenting.

32. E.g., Rich v. Secretary of the Army, 735 F.2d 1220 (10th Cir. 1984); Beller v. Middendorf, 632 F.2d 788 (9th Cir. 1980), *cert. denied,* 452 U.S. 905 (1981). But see Berg v. Clayton, 591 F.2d 849 (D.C. Cir. 1978); Matthews v. Marsh, *Civil No. 82-0216 P* (D.C. Maine 1984), *vacated and remanded,* 755 F.2d 182 (1st Cir. 1985) (reversal based on new information not available at trial). See Rivera, Queer Law: Sexual Orientation in the Mid-Eighties (Part II), 11 *U. Dayton L. Rev.* 275 (1986).

33. National Gay Task Force v. Board of Education, 470 U.S. 903 (1985) (affirming 10th Cir. by an equally divided Court). The circuit court decision is at 729 F.2d 1270 (10th Cir. 1984). For a review of teacher cases see Rivera, Queer Law: Sexual Orientation in the Mid-Eighties (Part I), 10 *U. Dayton L. Rev.* 459, 514–35 (1984).

34. Leonard, Employment Discrimination Against Persons With AIDS, 10 *U. Dayton L. Rev.* 681 (1984). See generally Comment, Preventing the Spread of AIDS by Restricting Sexual Conduct in Gay Bathhouses: A Constitutional Analysis, 15 *Golden Gate L. Rev.* 301 (1985).

35. A number of such laws are discussed in Meeker, Dombrink & Geis, State Law and Local Ordinances in California Barring Discrimination on the Basis of Sexual Orientation, 10 *U. Dayton L. Rev.* 745 (1984).

36. E.g., Gay Student Services v. Texas A & M University, 737 F.2d 1317 (5th Cir. 1984), *appeal dismissed,* 105 S. Ct. 1860 (1985); Gay Alliance of Students v. Matthews, 544 F.2d 162 (4th Cir. 1976); Gay Students Organization v. Bonner, 367 F. Supp. 1088 (D.N.H.), *modified,* 509 F.2d 652 (1st Cir. 1974).

37. In response to several law schools' refusal to permit military recruiters to use law school recruiting facilities (because the military discriminates on the basis of sexual preference), the military threatened to cancel all military contracts with the universities with which the law schools are associated. In the summer of 1984, the military decided to limit the threat of contract cutoffs to those law schools only, rather than to all other units in the universities.

38. Spitzer, The Diagnostic Status of Homosexuality in DSM-III: A Reformulation of the Issues, 138 *Am. J. Psychiatry* 210 (1981). See Duffy & Rusbult, Satisfaction and Commitment in Homosexual and Heterosexual Relationships, 12 *J. Homosexuality* 1 (1986) (found that satisfaction and commitment are comparable, although sample may have been biased).

39. E.g., W. Masters, V. Johnson & R. Kolodny, *Human Sexuality* (1982); Meyer & Freeman, A Social Episode Model of Human Sexual Behavior, 2 *J. Homosexuality* 123 (1977); McConaghy, Sexual Deviations, in *International Handbook of Behavior Modification and Therapy* (A. Bellack, M. Hersen & A. Kazdin eds. 1982). See generally Abramowitz, Psychological Outcomes of Sex Reassignment Surgery, 54 *J. Consulting & Clinical Psychology* 183 (1986).

40. See W. Redd, A. Porterfield & B. Anderson, *Behavior Modification* (1979); Davison, Not Can, But Ought: The Treatment of Homosexuality, 46 *J. Consulting & Clinical Psychology* 170 (1978); Sturgis & Adams, The

Right to Treatment: Issues in the Treatment of Homosexuality, 46 *J. Consulting & Clinical Psychology* 165 (1978).

41. S. Brakel, J. Parry & B. Weiner, *The Mentally Disabled and the Law* (3d ed. 1986). See Humphrey v. Cady, 405 U.S. 504 (1972); Specht v. Patterson, 386 U.S. 605 (1967).

42. Dix, Determining the Continued Dangerousness of Psychologically Abnormal Sex Offenders, 3 *J. Psychiatry & L.* 327 (1975); Granucci & Granucci, Indiana's Sexual Psychopath Act in Operation, 44 *Ind. L. J.* 555 (1969); Note, the Plight of the Sexual Psychopath: A Legislative Blunder and Judicial Acquiescence, 41 *Notre Dame Law.* 527 (1966).

43. Minn. State $526.09 (West 1975).

44. D.C. Code Ann. $22-3503 (1981).

45. For a general review of these laws see R. Slovenko, *Psychiatry and Law* 191–98 (1973); Annot. [Commitment of Sexual Offenders], 96 American Law Reports 3d 842 (1980).

46. Allen v. Illinois, 106 S. Ct. 2988 (1986).

47. French v. Blackburn, 428 F. Supp. 1351 (M.D. N.C. 1977), *summarily aff'd*, 443 U.S. 901 (1979).

48. Allen v. Illinois, *supra,* note 46.

49. N. Kittrie, *The Right to Be Different* 169–209 (1973 ed.).

50. See P. Devlin, *The Enforcement of Morals* (1965); H. L. A. Hart, *Law, Liberty and Morality* (1963); H. Packer, *The Limits of the Criminal Sanction* (1968).

51. For a brief summary of the arguments on both sides see E. Schur & H. Bedau, *Victimless Crimes: Two Sides of a Controversy* (1974).

52. Regarding the special concerns and issues when mental health professionals provide diagnosis or treatment of sex offenders, see Smith & Meyer, Workings Between the Legal System and the Therapist in *Exhibitionism: Description, Assessment, and Treatment* 311–38 (D. Cox & R. Daitzman, eds. 1980).

CHAPTER 15
THE PSYCHOPATH

The legal system is concerned with the adoption and enforcement of rules. A disorder characterized by rule-breaking should be of particular interest to the law. Surprisingly, the legal system has paid little attention to the antisocial personality. The psychopath, sociopath, or antisocial personality, presents a number of issues for the law and for mental health experts working with the legal system: (1) Because the psychopath may have difficulty following rules, psychopaths come to the attention of the legal system more frequently than the average citizen.[1] The intended deterrence of the criminal law or torts may be less effective with psychopaths. (2) The question of criminal responsibility is raised—i.e., is psychopathy a condition which should relieve a criminal defendant of responsibility for his actions? The applicability of the insanity defense raised by the ALI's Model Penal Code initially appears to preclude psychopathy as a basis for the insanity defense.[2] (3) Within the corrections system the psychopath also presents special issues of treatment and release. If psychopaths do not benefit from the same kinds of correctional "treatment," rehabilitative efforts of the penal system may not be effective with psychopaths. Therefore, decisions to release psychopaths on probation or parole may be complicated by the difficulty of determining whether a long term change has been achieved. Similarly, questions arise about the treatment of juveniles with psychopathic tendencies. Can the juvenile system, which is based on an ideal of guidance or treatment, have any realistic meaning or application to psychopathic juveniles? (4) The legal system depends heavily on the presentation of honest testimony. Do pychopaths possess characteristics which should limit or preclude their presenting sworn testimony? (5) Are psychopaths "fit" parents, and should the disorder be a factor in child custody cases? (6) Should psychopaths be precluded from obtaining licenses in professions in which honesty and reliability are critically important?

CONFUSION OF TERMS

The term "psychopath" is confusing. It may have different meanings to mental health professionals than it does to attorneys or the public. To enhance the confusion, the same mental health concept may also be labeled "sociopath" or "antisocial personality." All three terms are used by the courts and can be found in the professional literature.[3] "Antisocial personality" is the current nomenclature of the diagnostic manual of the American Psychiatric Association (DSM-III), although a previous edition used the term "sociopath." In using "antisocial," the DSM-III relies on a life history of violations of social norms and rules, including activities such as thefts and vandalism, substance abuse, running away from home, truancy, frequent casual sexual relations, physical aggressiveness, repeated debt defaults, impulsivity, and other behaviors which frequently violate the rights of others.[4]

"Psychopath" in much of the legal literature, and certainly in the popular press, sometimes refers to the dangerously mentally ill. Thus, "sexual psychopath laws" refers to statutes relating to dangerous, mentally disturbed sex offenders. These offenders may be psychotic or severely neurotic, but they are not generally primary psychopaths. In the press mass murderer David Berkowitz ("Son of Sam") was a "psychopathic killer" or a "psychopathic maniac."

Unfortunately, the current DSM-III term, "antisocial personality," may serve to confuse matters further. To many the term connotes a leather-jacketed street punk or motorcycle gang member. It also carries a vague connotation of malice, meanness, or willfulness of misconduct, which may be misleading. The danger of this kind of confusion is that the term will be used one way by the mental health professional and be misunderstood and used inappropriately in the legal system. In some ways "sociopath" was a preferable term.

Perhaps we need a new term which does not carry with it common meaning and connotations, but the use of still another new term for the same concept would probably serve only to confuse matters even more. We will use the psychopath, sociopath, and antisocial personality interchangably, although we will rely on the older term, "psychopath."

DIAGNOSTIC DESCRIPTION

The psychopath is a subgroup of the "Personality Disorders" in the DSM-III.[5] The antisocial personality disorder is defined as "a personality disorder in which there are a history of continuous and chronic antisocial behaviors in which the rights of others are violated, persistence into adult life of a pattern of antisocial behavior that began before the age of 15, and failure to sustain good job performance over a period of several years."[6]

Psychopaths are not psychotic, they are not delusional, and usually they are not poor at making interpersonal contacts. They may not be able to maintain relationships over time but they are often very good at initiating them.

Cleckley has listed the main features of psychopathy.[7] His list is based primarily on clinical experience, and distilled from his elegant and detailed case histories.

1. Superficial charm and good intelligence
2. Absence of delusions and other signs of irrational thinking
3. Absence of nervousness or neurotic manifestations
4. Unreliability
5. Untruthfulness and insincerity
6. Lack of remorse or shame
7. Antisocial behavior without apparent compunction
8. Poor judgment and failure to learn from experience
9. Pathologic egocentricity and incapacity for love
10. General poverty in major affective reactions
11. Specific loss of insight
12. Unresponsiveness in general interpersonal relations
13. Fantastic and uninviting behavior with drink and sometimes without
14. Suicide threats rarely carried out
15. Sex life impersonal, trivial, and poorly integrated
16. Failure to follow any life plan

Psychopathy has proved to be a relatively highly reliable diagnostic category,[8] and mental health professionals indicate a belief that it is a meaningful concept.[9] However, there is considerable disagreement about the traits which describe the psychopath. Gray and Hutchinson surveyed psychiatrists in Canada. They presented their sample a list of 29 referent concepts typically used to describe the psychopath.[10] Respondents were requested to rank the 10 concepts they considered most meaningfully descriptive in order of meaningfulness. No clear overall characterization emerged. However, the most frequently rated, "Does not profit from experience" was selected by 71.4 percent of the psychiatrists (chance level for this array is 34.5 percent). The ten most selected traits were:

1. Does not profit from experience
2. Lack of sense of responsibility
3. Unable to form meaningful relationships
4. Lack of control over impulses
5. Lack of moral sense
6. Chronically a recurrent antisocial
7. Punishment does not alter behavior
8. Emotionally immature
9. Unable to experience guilt
10. Self-centered

Not only was there no significant patterning of traits, but also no theoretical school was dominant. The clearly agreed upon descriptive concept in this sample was that the psychopath does not profit from experience.

PRIMARY AND SECONDARY PSYCHOPATHY

A refinement in the conceptualization of psychopathy has come from the differentiation of the primary and the secondary[11] or neurotic psychopath.[12] Secondary psychopaths show overt behavior patterns that are psychopathic, but unlike primary psychopaths they show substantial anxiety. Most definitions assume a low level of anxiety in the psychopath.

Lykken has defined the primary psychopath according to three characteristics that correlate well with the one factor that virtually all of Gray and Hutchinson's sample agreed on: "does not profit from experience."[13] A variety of studies have supported this differentiation.[14]

Blackburn did a cluster analysis of this data from 79 male offenders.[15] They found 4 profile types that accounted for 80 percent of the sample. Two of the types were the primary and secondary psychopath, and the other two were not at all like the psychopath, again pointing to the problems in studying psychopathy via a sample of criminals. Consistent with other theorists, Blackburn found the primary psychopaths to be extroverted but not neurotic, whereas with the secondary psychopaths the reverse was true. Not surprisingly, both types were high on an impulsivity dimension.

Although it may appear from the description of the antisocial personality disorder that these individuals would always eventually come into contact with the law, this may not be so. Primary sociopaths are more likely than others to find themselves incarcerated, because they engage in more frequent and more severe antisocial behavior than secondary sociopaths or nonsociopaths.[16] It appears that among psychopaths, as anxiety increases antisocial behavior decreases, whereas the opposite is true for nonpsychopaths.[17] These results also lend credence to the distinction of psychopaths along an anxiety dimension. There is not uniform support for the proposition that primary psychopaths manifest lower levels of anxiety.[18]

It is important to distinguish between the psychopath and others who commit antisocial acts. The DSM-III term, antisocial personality, invites confusion of these groups. Both the secondary ("neurotic") and the primary psychopath are quite different from those individuals who are antisocial because they grew up in a delinquent subculture. These delinquent individuals are normal in relation to the subculture they were reared in; they follow (often almost totally) the rules and mores of this group. They are as conformist as the good middle class, middle management person. The point is, not all criminals are psychopaths.

There has been considerable discussion of the "cause" of psychopathy. Explanations are offered based on genetic theories, brain disorder theories, cognitive theories, and social learning theories.

Psychoanalysts have not given much theoretical attention to the psychopath, compared with that given to various forms of neurosis and even psychosis. This is not surprising, considering the demands of that therapeutic approach. In psychoanalysis the patient must be willing to introspect about life history and sources of conflict, persist in a high number of therapeutic contacts over a long duration (usually at considerable expense), have a concern about the quality of interpersonal relationships and commitments, develop restraint (to the degree possible) and form significant and especially reflective decisions about life situations. There is obviously not a very good match between the demands of psychoanalysis and the characteristics of the psychopath. There has been some psychoanalytic theorizing that the psychopath was fixated at the phallic stage of development, hence the aggression into the environment. These theories speak of the psychopath's unconscious need for punishment.[19] Little research has been garnered to support these theories, and the latter point concerning latent guilt and the need for punishment may be more relevant to the neurotic psychopath than to the primary psychopath.

BRAIN DISORDER AND PSYCHOPATHY

The possibility of physiological or anatomical brain disorder has been discussed as the cause of psychopathy since the recognition of the syndrome. Such disorders should be subject to observable and communicable measurement, but actual scientific measurement has been problematic.[20]

Scientific measurement is complex where a brain disorder is asserted. The earliest attempt came when phrenologists thought they had solved the problem by charting head bumps, an early and inefficient development, but similar in concept to the brain-mapping studies later carried out by Wilder Penfield and others. Autopsies are possible with animals immediately after they manifest a behavior, but, of course, with humans such studies are impossible. Brain assessment techniques for live subjects are not yet precise enough to identify brain disorders associated with psychopathy.

The standard measure of brain disorder, the electroencephalogram (EEG), is often still inadequate to determine abnormalities, although computer scoring of analogue data has improved techniques. The problem with EEG analysis is illustrated by Ostrow and Ostrow's study of criminality and psychopathy.[21] They obtained EEGs on 440 convicts, and then designated a subgroup of 69 psychopaths using the criteria of a lack of empathy, impulsivity, and inability to accept social limitations. (This designation of a subgroup is a desirable methodological step that is often missing in studies.) Half of this psychopathic subgroup had abnormal EEGs, which would seem to offer strong support for a brain disorder hypothesis, yet 80 percent of the schizophrenics and 56 percent of the homosexuals also had abnormal EEGs. More surprisingly, 65 percent of the conscientious objectors in the sample also had abnormal EEGs. The problem is that even among "the normal" population, using any sign of EEG abnormality to indicate disorder, there are significant percentages, usually from 15–20 percent, of EEG abnormalities or "disorders."

Therefore, we must look at specific EEG abnormalities, and here there is some evidence for the brain disorder hypothesis, at least as regards the impulsive and highly aggressive psychopath. Hill found that 14 percent of the impulsive and aggressive psychopaths he studied showed abnormal slow-wave activity in the temporal lobes, and 8.2 percent of the murderers who would not fit the extremely aggressive and impulsive psychopath definition also manifested this disorder.[22] But only 2.8 percent of the other population of criminals and 2.0 percent of normals show this disorder. Hare notes this and similar research to develop the theory that the dysfunction is in the temporal lobes and limbic system (the areas considered to be the central regulators for emotional and motivational behavior).[23] The limbic system is particularly involved in the regulation of fear-motivated behaviors, and lesions in analogous areas in cats significantly lessen their ability to inhibit behaviors.

Another pattern of EEG abnormality, the positive spike phenomenon, has been shown to occur in extremely impulsive and aggressive psychopaths in rates as high as 45 percent while the incidence in the normal population is only approximately 1 percent.

Despite the EEG abnormalities, which are generally tied to aggressive behavior, there is currently little evidence to demonstrate a correlation between physical brain disorders and most psychopaths.

GENETIC THEORIES

As with most areas of psychopathology, there is a substantial question of the degree to which psychopathic behavior is genetically determined. Unfortunately, the guiding paradigm has often been to look for a single physical or genetic cause to explain virtually all the behavior, but human behavior is more complex than that.

This biological-determinism approach has had a long history. It was particularly evidenced in the school of phrenology, and still enamors some researchers. From Pinel's diagnosis of *manie sans délire* at the end of the eighteenth century and Pritchard's definition of "moral insanity" in 1835, there was an effort to discover genetic or "innate determinants" of the psychopath. A similar effort was evident in Koch's concept of "psychopathic inferiority" in 1888. The idea reached its zenith in the Italian school led by Lombroso at the beginning of this century.[24]

In order to separate the effects of environment and genetics, studies using genetically identical twins and fraternal twins raised apart have been developed. One of the first twin studies studied a sample of Bavarian prisoners with twins and found that 77 percent of the identical pairs were concordant for criminality, but only 12 percent of the same sex fraternal pairs were concordant.[25] Rosenthal reviewed a number of other similar studies.[26] There were varying results, but the general trend was to support the notion of a genetic component. In general, more recent research has continued to find this genetic factor to be important but not causal,[27] although findings have not been uniformly positive.[28]

These studies have shared a major defect, at least as regards any inferences to the genesis of the psychopathic personality: these are not studies of psychopathy, but of criminality. Other studies carry an even more specific error; they equate psychopathy with violent behavior.

In addition, these studies suffer other problems. One is the definition of psychopathy, though progress toward a more operational definition has been made.[29] Also, studies of separated identical twins are fraught with methodological problems. Recently it has become apparent that past determinations of fraternal versus identical twins have not always been accurate, and avoidance of confounding environmental influences has not always been well controlled.

Much interest in the last 20 years has focused on the relationship of an extra *y* (male) chromosome as a cause of antisocial behavior. This is an area where interchanging the terms psychopath and antisocial personality leads to confusion. Most of these studies have focused on the effects on aggressive behavior. Early investigations led to an enthusiastic belief that a clear explanation for many extreme assaultists had been found.[30] But reviews of this research, and further work, suggest that the *xyy* is of little explanatory value.[31] It may be implicated in a Lincolnesque Syndrome—persons who are tall, with relatively gaunt features and high cheekbones. As the term for the syndrome indicates, not everyone with this disorder makes it to prison, and indeed one may as likely find such men on a basketball court as in prison.

Researchers have also tried to identify functional characteristics which are associated with psychopathic or violent behavior. One such factor may be intelligence. Those with lower IQ scores are more inclined to criminality. While there is fierce debate here, most agree that at least some factors that contribute to IQ are inherited, and some would argue the great majority of IQ is so determined. Kunce and his colleagues describe some interesting findings regarding violent criminals.[32] They compared WAIS (IQ) profiles of 15 violent and 15 nonviolent criminals. They found one difference that discriminated the two groups. The violent criminals had a significantly lower mean score in abstract thinking ability. A second factor is body build, which is clearly genetically influenced. There is evidence that the mesomorph (the build of a powerful athlete) is more prone to acting-out behavior, and probably to psychopathy in general. Thirdly, brain dysfunction can be inherited and, as discussed elsewhere in this chapter, this has been implicated in some forms of psychopathic behavior. Again, caution must be exercised in implying any cause and effect relationship, especially regarding the lower score on the WAIS similarities subtest because this has not been a consistent research finding.

Though these may be contributing factors,[33] many respected investigators assert that it is clear that there is no single genotype involved in criminality, let alone psychopathy.[34] Indeed it is the view of many that while multiple genetic factors may contribute in a specific case, the role of heredity is less than that of the environment.

SOCIAL PSYCHOLOGY, LEARNING THEORY, AND THE PSYCHOPATH

Some data suggest that much psychopathic behavior can be explained on the basis of social learning theory.[35] The prototype of the various learning theory approaches is a 1957 study by Lykken,[36] who differentiated a group of criminal subjects into primary psychopaths, secondary psychopaths, and "normal" criminals. He then presented them with a "mental maze" consisting of a sequence of 20 choice points; at each choice point the subject had a choice of four levers, one of which was a correct choice and denoted as such by a green light. If the green light flashed, the subject moved on to the next choice of four. At each choice point an incorrect lever gave off a strong electric shock if pulled. Learning the sequence of correct levers was the overt task; avoidance of the punishment levers was the latent task.

There was no significant difference between the three groups on the overt task. But, on the avoidance task, the primary psychopaths were very poor at learning to avoid the punishing shock, whereas the secondary psychopaths and normal criminals did learn to avoid it at reasonably similar rates. Although the findings have been replicated,[37] some questions have been raised about the validity of the conclusions of these studies.[38]

A variation by Schachter and Latane with a replication of the Lykken study is of particular interest.[39] When the investigators injected adrenaline into the primary psychopaths, they performed at least as well or better than normals on the avoidance task.

Schmauk's variation also produced another finding of interest: primary psychopaths respond like normals when a tangible reinforcer such as money is used, but they do not learn the required response to either electric shock or directions and social reprimand. In fact, under the tangible reward condition, the primary psychopaths did slightly better than normals or secondary psychopaths, and this differential response was reflected in measurements of anxiety, arousal, and awareness. This suggests that if one presents a punishment to primary psychopaths that is within their value system, they may learn the response. Physiological measures of arousal, such as heart rate or electrodermal response, would then be an efficient means of determining what is in fact noxious or punishing to the psychopath. This, as well as other research, suggests that the ability to learn is not the issue, but rather it is the reduced tendency to respond.[40]

The above suggests the importance of social-learning variables, a view most clearly stated by Ullman and Krasner.[41] The psychopath is one who has trouble forming close attachments to people over time, and in addition does not respond to standard systems of rewards and punishments. Two types of parental behaviors often found in the background of psychopaths not surprisingly foster these patterns. Hare gives evidence that "one of the best predictors of adult psychopathy is having a father who was himself psychopathic, alcoholic, or antisocial."[42] The second pattern is of parents who administer rewards and punishments with such inconsistency that it is impossible for the child to develop a clear role. The child does not learn to respond to anything more than quite concrete reinforcements.[43] One prisoner who was incarcerated for theft typified this. As an adolescent he had stolen a TV which his parents found in his room. They proceeded to give him a lengthy lecture on how bad stealing was, the idea of sin, etc. That evening after dinner, the family gathered in the living room around the new TV set he had provided, where it remained to be enjoyed by all.

Ullman and Krasner have described this pattern, based on social learning theory.

> Case histories of people later called psychopaths who came from broken and/or extreme lower-class homes frequently indicate that they had been recipients of very severe physical punishment. The child had learned, quite rationally, that people are anything but positive reinforcers. Staying away from others and avoiding trouble would thus be very reasonable behavior. It is also likely that inconsistency, that is, punishment based on the adults' shifting moods rather than on the child's objective behavior, is involved. The result is twofold. First, the child's behavior is inconsequential; it seems that no matter what he does, if he interacts with people he will be punished. In this regard extreme punishment and extreme indulgence have similar eventual consequences. Second, whereas the inconsistent *overindulged* pattern leads to reinforcement of escape through apology and ingratiation, the inconsistent *brutally punished* pattern leads to avoidance by physical distance. Again the behavioral results are identical: when one's own behavior fails to serve as a meaningful stimulus for others, the consequences for the person are much the same whether the others have been seemingly too kind or too mean. Other people do not become effective secondary reinforcing stimuli for this individual.[44]

Widom's research further supports a notion that the primary psychopath develops a cognitive system (which internalizes the behaviors) that is markedly different in meaning and value loading from that of secondary psychopaths and normals.[45]

This social learning theory suggests that (1) Persons subjected to such parental behavior do not know how to respond to standard interpersonal stimuli. As we discuss in the next section, they may be starved for meaningful stimuli. (2) Basic trust, the foundation for committed interpersonal involvement, is absent or suppressed. (3) The psychopathy may be directed toward violence if there is a parental model for such behavior, and/or if violent or antisocial behavior is rewarded. (4) The psychopath responds to stimuli that do not have the same values for normals, hence are labeled "impulsive."[46]

THE PSYCHOPATH AND CONDITIONABILITY AND STIMULATION

Findings that point to lowered emotional arousal in the psychopath lead to the issue of conditionability, whether or not a clear brain malfunction is involved. Eysenck has written extensively of the differences among persons as to conditionability and relates these to genetic endowment.[47] Eysenck conceives the primary psychopath as low on neuroticism (anxiety) and high in extroversion, a view supported by the research of Witkin.[48] Psychopaths may be slow to develop operant and classically conditioned responses, and it may take more intense stimuli to create a response, which fits with the low emotionality concepts already noted. Eysenck views the secondary psychopath as having both high extroversion and high neuroticism, but Witkin's work would suggest they are significantly lower on extroversion than the primary psychopath.

The conditionability of the various bodily systems of psychopaths is not clear, except for skin conductance. Whereas there have been mixed results in finding more resistance in conditionability for psychopaths in such things as heart rate and blood pressure, a number of studies have found that psychopaths exhibit significantly less electrodermal activity upon the threat of shock or other aversive stimuli than do normals.[49] This again correlates with the notion that psychopaths have lowered states of emotional arousal and responsivity,[50] or even different autonomic patterning.[51]

A refinement of the conditionability hypothesis is found in Quay's theory that the psychopath is in rather constant need of stimulation and has only a minimal tolerance for sameness, a condition that in normals peaks in early adolescence.[52] This would fit with the findings that psychopaths have lowered state of emotional arousal. Quay, however, also emphasizes cognitive aspects, suggesting that all organisms strive for an optimal level of cognitive stimulation. He feels the psychopath adapts more quickly to stimuli, hence needs even more stimulation, and is thus

> unable to tolerate routine and boredom. While he may engage in antisocial, even vicious, behavior his outbursts frequently appear to be motivated by little more than a need for thrills and excitement. . . . It is the impulsivity and the lack of even minimal tolerance for sameness which appear to be the primary and distinctive features of the disorder. . . . The basic hypothesis is that psychopathic behavior represents an extreme of stimulation-seeking behavior and that the psychopath's primary abnormality lies in the realms of basic reactivity and/or adaptation to sensory input of all types.

Quay's findings have been amplified and supported by a number of other researchers including Skrzypek[53] and Ridgeway and Hare.[54] Wiesen[55] found that students low on the MMPI psychopathy scale found a cessation of visual and auditory stimulation to be reinforcing, whereas those high on the scale, hence higher in "psychopathy," found an increase in stimulation to be reinforcing. There have been problems with this research, notably the use of only MMPI scores to define the population. Yet, Quay's hypothesis continues to offer a promising insight concerning psychopathy. Widom offers some indirect data that mildly contradict Quay's ideas, but the great majority of relevant evidence is supportive.[56]

TREATMENT OF THE PSYCHOPATH

Proposed treatments for the psychopath span a wide range of alternatives. Some emphasize the need for imposition of a new control system, while others see control only as an initial means to allow involvement in more traditional therapies.[57] Rotenberg offers some interesting ideas on using techniques like systematic desensitization.[58] He also suggests how one might get "into the system" of the psychopath but does not present data, or explain exactly how you get the psychopath to stay interested in treatment. Similarly, Parlour discusses behavioral treatments for psychopaths but seems to assume a high control over the psychopath's behavior, as well as their willingness to respond.[59]

All plans for treatment of the psychopath encounter difficulty with control. The problem is that there is an underlying issue generally not adequately considered: the primary psychopath is simply not interested in being treated. A therapist's control of tangible positive reinforcers may permit some control, because the psychopath's interest switches to regaining control of the reinforcers, and hence the desired behaviors may be produced. But when the treatment is consequently "successfully terminated," control is returned to the psychopath and this may just reinforce a pattern of manipulation.

This is a rather grim picture, but it appears warranted, as the literature produces little evidence of long-term behavior change in the primary psychopath. Occasionally researchers refer to some of the successful treatment programs carried out with delinquents, but these programs appear less successful with older offenders, and in fact these programs are always more effective with the "subcultural socialized" delinquent who is not a primary psychopath.

The critical view of control presents two major problems. The first has already been suggested: while it is possible to gain control of the behavior within the specific setting, such as a prison or hospital, it is very difficult to set up generalization to the outside world, especially with a psychopath. Theoretically, if control is thorough enough, long enough, and then a proper graduation or weaning period is established, the desired generalization effect will occur. There is reasonable theory in support of this, but it has not been effectively demonstrated, particularly with primary psychopaths.

The other problem is simply the gaining of the level of control to significantly influence psychopaths' behavior. It is axiomatic that, the greater the level of control, the greater the initial impact. But it is also true that the greater the control, the more other cognitive variables, such as degree of resentment, must be considered. Gaining a substantial degree of control is important, and is often not easy.

The treatment picture can look pretty bleak, but this view has been challenged. There is a growing body of literature behind the efficacy of positive reinforcement with sociopaths. While it appears that sociopaths have great difficulty in avoidance learning, the evidence on learning via positive reinforcement seems to be increasing.[60]

Templeman and Wollersheim, after working extensively with psychopaths in prison, also came to the conclusion that therapeutic change is possible.[61] They suggest, when working with psychopaths it is important to remember that they are: not a homogeneous group and each individual may therefore require a different treatment; in general more likely to be motivated by tangible rewards than physical punishment; likely to respond to positive reinforcement (but the reinforcement must closely follow the behavior); may respond well to verbal feedback; and often seek constant and very high levels of stimulation.

Templeman and Wollersheim report adequate success in therapy using cognitive-behavioral techniques. Specifically, rational-emotive therapy, problem solving training,[62] and self-instruction techniques[63] have been reported as being beneficial.

LEGAL ISSUES

Insanity Defense

Many legal issues related to the psychopath have remained relatively unexplored. One issue, however, has received some attention: the question of whether the psychopath may use the insanity defense in criminal proceedings. Two issues are involved, is psychopathy a mental disease or defect (i.e., a form of "insanity"), and is it a condition of sufficient severity to excuse criminal conduct?

The Model Penal Code has a caveat to the insanity defense that initially appears to exclude the psychopath from using it. "The terms 'mental disease or defect' do not include an abnormality manifested only by repeated criminal or otherwise anti-social conduct."[64] This caveat may not technically exclude very many psychopaths because few abnormalities are "manifested *only*" by antisocial conduct,[65] but it is generally read as excluding them.

There is no clear reason to specifically preclude psychopathy from consideration as a mental disease and courts have been divided over the use of the caveat. Some courts have been troubled by the possibility of completely excluding psychopaths from the insanity defense.[66] It is sometimes wrongly suggested that psychosis should be the only basis for an insanity defense, and such a position would exclude all personality disorders including psychopathy. A more serious difficulty is that psychopathy is not likely to be seen as so serious as to remove responsibility. This is particularly true when the condition is described only in terms of social history, which is the basis of the DSM-III diagnosis.[67]

The insanity defense requires that the mental disease prevents defendants from appreciating the wrongfulness of their conduct or from conforming their conduct to the requirements of the law. Psychopaths undoubtedly can ordinarily appreciate the wrongfulness of their actions. Whether they can conform their conduct to the requirements of the law is more difficult. Because the condition is associated with the reduction of social control, some view the condition as making it impossible for one to conform his conduct to social norms; others may feel that it is nothing more than the absence of any real desire to control conduct.

The existence of evidence of physical disorders or manifestations of psychopathy would undoubtedly, in the eyes of courts, increase the "legitimacy" of psychopathy as a mental disease or defect. Mental conditions with a physical basis seem more "real." The rationale for such a position is not clear in terms of the effect of the condition on the behavior of defendants or on the "voluntariness" of their actions. Even though some correlation is found between psychopaths and brain abnormalities, it is not clear that the abnormalities cause the psychopathy.

In practice it is unlikely that jurors would be inclined to find a defendant not guilty by reason of insanity because of psychopathy. The psychopath just does not seem "sick" enough. The ability to function well and to fully understand what is happening will make the psychopath appear to be a scoundrel who simply chooses to do bad things. Even the "antisocial personality" label is likely to suggest a flawed character who chooses to disobey social rules.

Determining whether a defendant could not resist or chose not to resist committing an antisocial act is as difficult with the psychopath as with many other criminal defendants. We are dealing more with a question of moral blameworthiness based on free will concepts than with a question of scientific fact.

Subjecting psychopaths to the criminal justice system currently may be the only practical way of limiting or controlling their antisocial activity. Unlike many other insanity defendants, most psychopaths would not be subject to the involuntary civil commitment process. The long-term prospects for successful treatment of many psychopaths appear to be rather bleak. How then should the penal and juvenile systems deal with psychopaths? Treatment of psychopaths may be difficult because the psychopath often is not interested in treatment, may feign a "cure" to obtain release, and often reverts to old behaviors after release. Some promising treatment techniques have been described and may appropriately be used in prison or juvenile settings.

Sentencing and Release Decisions

The legal system should be aware of the special characteristics of psychopaths. For example, to effect rehabilitation, it may be necessary to exercise greater control over the psychopath than over others. There should be particularly careful review of whether real changes have been achieved; specifically the possibility of feigning rehabilitation should be considered. The failure to learn from experience may argue for the incarceration of psychopaths for the purpose of treatment at a fairly early point (e.g., first conviction), even for nonviolent crimes. For repeat offenders, the realistic possibility of continued repeated antisocial acts should be faced. This may suggest extended sentences, not to promote treatment, but to protect society from repeated antisocial conduct. Habitual offender statutes in many states, which provide for long prison terms after conviction of several serious crimes, may imperfectly serve this purpose. The existence of psychopathy is a legitimate factor to be considered in sentencing and disposition decisions.

There are limits on the use of a "status" as the basis for convicting someone of a crime. Thus, it is unconstitutional to convict one of the *status* of being a drug addict.[68] The conviction of a crime generally carries with it a concept of moral blame, and status is more in the nature of having a disease than choosing to act improperly. There is no similar prohibition of convicting one of *behavior* associated with a status—e.g., of convicting an addict of possessing illegal drugs, or convicting an alcoholic of public intoxication.[69] Is it proper to make release decisions based on the status of being a psychopath? The legal system recognizes differences between appropriate factors to be considered in sentencing and release decisions, and conviction of a crime. Sentencing and release decisions relate to the concepts of rehabilitation and protection of society. Therefore, the status of drug addiction would be a legitimate consideration in sentencing and probation decisions because it would relate to the ability of the prisoner to meet the conditions of probation, to avoid additional antisocial activity, and to demonstrate rehabilitation. Similarly, making a psychopath guilty of a status crime would be improper, but taking that status into account in making sentencing and release decisions—after a defendant has been convicted of another crime—is reasonable and consistent with the purposes of the penal system.

Child Custody

Several characteristics of primary psychopaths suggest that they are not likely to be good parents. Its presence is not one of the limited number of conditions which makes one parent completely "unfit," in a legal sense, to be a parent, but it is a legitimate factor to be considered in custody cases.

Psychopaths as Witnesses

Characteristics of the psychopath which are commonly recognized include untruthfulness or reduced sense of responsibility and lack of remorse or moral sense. These are, of course, not highly prized qualities in a witness. They suggest one who may be inclined to fabricate if it is to his benefit, and who may escape detection.[70]

The courts are extremely reluctant to disqualify anyone from testifying. Even convicted perjurers are not completely precluded from presenting testimony. Courts have been willing, however, to permit the jury to be given important information concerning a witness's truthfulness and honesty. For example, the jury may be told of a witness's conviction of a crime involving dishonesty. The jury may then take this into account when determining the witness's credibility.

Is the psychopathy of a witness a condition about which the jury should be informed? To justify the disclosure, the relationship between psychopathy and dishonest testimony should be established, the determination or diagnosis of psychopathy should be reasonably reliable and valid, and the information should not be unduly inflammatory or misleading to the jury. There is a relatively high diagnostic reliability reported for psychopathy. The level and nature of dishonesty associated with the condition should be more clearly identified, but the correlation between dishonest testimony and psychopathy appears as strong as it is between dishonest testimony and prior convictions (which generally may be disclosed to the jury). There are undoubtedly some circumstances in which the disclosure to a jury of psychopathy could be inflammatory—e.g., some instances in which a criminal defendant is a witness in his own case. However, it would not ordinarily be more inflammatory or misleading than disclosure of prior conviction of crimes. When psychopathy is clearly identified, therefore, disclosure of that to the jury, to establish the veracity of the witness, is theoretically justified.

However, a practical problem arises; an endless round of expert witnesses testifying that a particular witness is or is not psychopathic would be burdensome. Whether a witness has been convicted of a crime is a matter of fact; whether he is a psychopath is at least in part a matter of opinion. In many cases an extended debate over the psychopathy of a witness would not be worth the effort it would involve.

Professional Licensing

Psychopaths are likely to exploit those who trust and depend upon them. Clients of psychopathic professionals are at some risk of being exploited. It is unlikely that large numbers of psychopaths seek licensure in the learned professions in which trust and honesty are important, but if they are licensed they have the capacity for significant harm to the public. Therefore licensing authorities should be aware of the antisocial personality. There may be some reluctance to refuse licenses on account of psychopathy as a "status," although licenses may be denied or revoked because of, say, drug addiction. The psychopathic professional may be as dangerous to the public as the professional who is an addict.

Thus, it would be difficult to deny a professional license on the basis of diagnosis of psychopathy alone, and unaccompanied by prior misconduct. By definition a psychopath will have a history of anti-social conduct, but in some instances it may not have been adequately recorded in official records. It is likely that a psychopath applying for a professional license will have a life history of antisocial or dishonest conduct, some of which will be documented. Most licensing author-ities make at least limited investigations to determine character and fitness to practice. Any suggestion of a pattern of antisocial conduct over a number of years should alert licensing authorities to the pos-sibility of an antisocial personality, and where appropriate they should investigate the possibility of psychopathy. If psychopathy is confirmed, it should be possible to deny the license. Professional schools also have an obligation to notify licensing authorities of con-duct which may indicate psychopathy. When a determination of psy-chopathy is combined with misconduct while licensed, the authority should revoke the license. The denial or revocation of a license be-cause of a mental condition is harsh, but it is even harsher to invite antisocial conduct by psychopathic professionals on trusting and un-suspecting clients and patients. Furthermore, by definition the con-dition is tied to a pattern of past antisocial conduct which may justify disciplinary action.

In any instance in which legal or social decisions are taken in part on the basis of psychopathy, of course, the issue of accurate diagnosis of the condition is critical. Suspicion, or "armchair" diagnosis cannot be the basis for determining psychopathy.

SUMMARY

The psychopath, sociopath, and antisocial personality refer to the same condition which is often misunderstood in the legal system. There has been some confusion about these terms. We have used the terms interchangeably to refer to the condition described in the DSM-III as the antisocial personality.

The diagnosis of psychopathy is a valid one, at least as compared with other standard diagnostic terms. It is a meaningful and reliable term, in the sense that as long as some clarity of definition is made, people will agree on the diagnosis. The primary psychopath should be differentiated from the secondary or neurotic psychopath, and from the standard criminal or delinquent. There is an increasing agreement as to the factors that comprise this syndrome, including failure to profit from experience, superficial interpersonal relationships, high need for novel stimuli, impulsivity, and failure to respond to standard social controls.

Researchers are not agreed on the etiology of psychopathy, but there are indications that a mixture of genetic and environmental factors have an impact on the specific case.

Mental health practitioners have generally been unable to motivate the psychopath into effective treatment. A variety of innovative procedures has been suggested, but often the psychopath does not take an interest in these. Behavioral control procedures are effective in the immediate sphere, but generalization has not yet been demonstrated, and the cost of gaining the required level of control is expensive in many dimensions.

Because psychopaths engage in repeated episodes of antisocial behavior, they may be of special concern to the legal system. Yet, for the most part these problems have not received much attention from the law. One issue has received some consideration: whether psychopaths may use the insanity defense in criminal cases. The Model Penal Code insanity defense excludes mental conditions "manifested only" by repeated antisocial conduct. There is disagreement among courts and commentators concerning the issue. We see no strong reason to completely exclude psychopaths from using the insanity defense, although it is unlikely that many juries would believe that the condition is serious enough to warrant exculpation from criminal responsibility. As a practical matter, therefore, the insanity defense will not often allow psychopaths to avoid criminal convictions.

Sentencing and release decisions should take into account the special characteristics and problems of the psychopath. This may, in fact, argue for relatively early incarceration of the psychopath with a plan for rehabilitation which includes gaining substantial control over the psychopath. For repeat offenders, with whom treatment has been unsuccessful, the realistic possibility of continued antisocial acts must be faced and extended sentences considered to protect society. In all release decisions involving psychopaths, the serious problem of feigning successful treatment to gain release must be explored.

Psychopaths are not likely to be good parents. While this is not a reason to routinely take children away from parents with antisocial personalities, it is a legitimate factor to be considered in child custody decisions.

The legal system depends upon witnesses to present honest testimony. Jurors could legitimately be told of the psychopathy of a witness so they may assess the weight to be given to the psychopath's testimony. In reality there might be some difficulty determining whether a witness is a psychopath or not. A prolonged battle of expert witnesses over the psychopathy of other witnesses would be impractical. In some circumstances, however, the psychopathy of a crucial witness would be important enough to ensure that the jury receives the information.

Psychopathic professionals may be expected to take advantage of trusting and dependent patients and clients. Licensing boards should be aware of the risk which psychopaths present to the public and should specifically consider psychopathy if any pattern of antisocial conduct is suggested by a character and fitness investigation. Professional schools should also consider the significant harm which psychopathic professionals can inflict on patients and clients. Psychopathy confirmed by prior misconduct is a legitimate basis for denying a license.

In short, the legal system should pay more attention to the psychopath and the problems the psychopath presents for it.

NOTES

1. Psychopathic criminals commit more crimes than other offenders (Hare & Jutai, Criminal History of the Male Psychopath: Some Preliminary Data, in *Prospective Studies of Crime and Delinquency* [K. Van Dusen & S. Mednick eds. 1983]).They are also more prone to recidivism (Ganzer & Sarason, Variables Associated with Recidivism Among Juvenile Delinquents, 40 *J. Consulting & Clinical Psychology* 1 [1973]; Quinsey, Warneford, Pruesse & Link, Released Oak Ridge Patients: A Follow-Up Study of Review Board Discharges, 15 *Brit. J. Criminology* 264 [1975]), and more violent (Hare & McPherson, Violent and Aggressive Behavior by Criminal Psychopaths, 7 *Int'l J. L. & Psychiatry* 35 [1984]). Although the antisocial conduct of psychopaths suggests they will often come to the attention of the criminal justice system, not all criminals are psychopaths. The term "criminal personality" is not a DSM-III category, but describes a variety of personalities who come to the attention of the criminal justice system. See R. Meyer & P. Salmon, *Abnormal Psychology* (1983); J. Petersilia, P. Greenwood & M. Lavin, *Criminal Careers of Habitual Felons* 74–75 (1978).

2. American Law Institute, *Model Penal Code* §4.01 (Tent. Draft No. 4, 1956).

3. Courts in the United States have used all three terms. There are approximately 400 cases in which the term "psychopath" (not including "sexual psychopath") appears in federal cases and state appellate courts. "Sociopath" appears in approximately 250 cases, and "antisocial personality" in approximately 450 cases. See Slovenko, The Psychopath: Labeling in South Africa, 5 *Crime, Punishment and Corrections* 9 (1976). But see Schlesinger, Distinctions Between Psychopathic, Sociopathic, and Anti-Social Personality Disorders, 47 *Psychological Rep.* 15 (1980).

4. American Psychiatric Ass'n, *Diagnostics and Statistical Manual of Mental Disorders* 320–21 (3d ed. 1980) (DSM-III).

5. DSM-III states, "Personality *traits* are enduring patterns of perceiving, relating to, and thinking about the environment and oneself. It is only when *personality traits* are inflexible and maladaptive and cause either significant impairment in social or occupational functioning or subjective distress that they constitute "*Personality Disorders.*" DSM-III at 305.

6. *Id.* at 317–18.

7. H. Cleckley, *The Mask of Sanity* (4th ed., 1964).

8. An important study on the issue of diagnostic reliability is Spitzer et al., Quantification of Agreement in Psychiatric Diagnosis: A New Approach, 17 *Arch. Gen. Psychiatry* 83 (1967). They checked for diagnostic reliability of standard diagnostic categories, and controlled for differential base rates and different ratios of deviance between the major diagnostic categories. They found the highest level of agreement (.88) with the psychopathic personality, and the next highest agreement of .85 was with brain dysfunction (1.0 would indicate perfect agreement). Interestingly enough, the lowest index of agreement (.42) was found with psychoneurotic reactions. Hence, from the perspective of reliability, a psychopathic diagnosis does have utility. See Hare, Twenty Years of Experience with the Cleckley Psychopath, in *Unmasking the Psychopath* (W. Reid, D. Dorr, J. Walker & J. Bonner eds. 1986).

9. Gray and Hutchinson were able to survey approximately 70 percent of the registered psychiatrists in Canada, and as yet no one has been able to do a better job from a research design perspective. Gray and Hutchinson, The Psychopath Personality: A Survey of Canadian Psychiatrists' Opinion, and *Can. Psychiatric A.J.* 45 (1964). The major question asked was "Do you think the diagnosis of psychopathic personality is ever a meaningful one in psychiatry?" While 10.7 percent did not feel the concept was meaningful and 5.6 percent had no opinion, a rather substantial 83.7 percent stated that it was a meaningful concept.

10. *Id.*

11. Karpman, On the Need of Separating Psychopathy Into Two Distinct Clinical Types: The Symptomatic and the Idiopathic, 3 *Crim. Psychopathology* 112 (1941); Lykken, A Study of Anxiety in the Sociopathic Personality, 55 *J. Abnormal & Soc. Psychology* 6 (1957).

12. The problem with the term "neurotic psychopath" is that it suggests a neurotic process modifies a more basic psychopathic process, whereas most theorists would see the neurosis as primary. For example, there is evidence that the neurotic psychopath can develop meaningful interpersonal relationships and may show remorse for offenses committed, but at the same time does engage in antisocial and often aggressive patterns of behavior.

13. Lykken, *supra*, note 11.

14. Fagan & Lira, The Primary and Secondary Sociopathic Personality: Differences in Frequency and Severity of Antisocial Behaviors, 89 *J. Abnormal Psychology* 493 (1980); Lykken, *supra*, note 11; Schmauk, Punishment Arousal, and Avoidance Learning in Sociopaths, 76 *J. Abnormal & Soc. Psychology* 325 (1970).

15. Blackburn, An Empirical Classification of the Psychopathic Personality, 127 *Brit. J. Psychiatry* 456 (1975).

16. Fagan & Lira, *supra*, note 14.

17. *Id.*

18. Blackburn, Cortical and Autonomic Arousal in Primary and Secondary Psychopaths, 16 *Psychophysiology* 143 (1979).

19. F. Alexander & H. Staub, *The Criminal, the Judge, and the Public: A Psychological Analysis* (rev. ed. 1956). See Kegan, The Child Behind the Mask: Sociopathy as Developmental Delay, in *Unmasking the Psychopath* (W. Reid, D. Dorr, J. Walker & J. Bonner eds. 1986).

20. Reid & Bottinger, Genetic Aspects of Antisocial Disorders, 1 *Hillside J. Clinical Psychiatry* 87 (1979). But see J. Beatty, *Biological Basis of Behavior* (1987).

21. Ostrow & Ostrow, Bilaterally Synchronous Paroxysmal Slow Activity in the Encephalograms of Non-Epileptics, 103 *Nervous & Mental Disease* 346 (1946).

22. Hill, EEG in Episodic Psychotic and Psychopathic Behavior: A Classification of Data, 4 *EEG and Clinical Neurophysiology* 419 (1952).

23. R. Hare, *Psychopathy: Theory and Research* (1970).

24. It was claimed that the criminal was a born "type" who had clear "stigmatizing" facial features which were signs of degeneracy and discernibly different from those of normal people. Among the signs of the degenerate criminal were a cleft palate, a low forehead, unusual shaped head or nose, protruding ears, high cheekbones, and a scanty beard. These features were a direct throwback to the savage caveman. Lest the reader's mirror cause him too much anxiety, it must be clearly stated that, Hollywood type-casting notwithstanding, this theory has been almost universally abandoned. L. Ullman & L. Krasner, *A Psychological Approach to Abnormal Behavior* (1975).

25. J. Lange, *Crime as Destiny* (1931).

26. D. Rosenthal, *Genetic Theory and Abnormal Behavior* (1970).

27. S. Mednick & K. Christiansen, *Biological Basis of Criminal Behavior* (1977).

28. Rimmer & Jacobsen, Antisocial Personality in the Biological Relatives of Schizophrenics, 21 *Comprehensive Psychiatry* 258 (1980).

29. Schulsinger, Psychopathy: Heredity and Environment, 2 *Life History Research in Psychopathy* (M. Roff, L. Robins & M. Pollack eds. 1970).

30. Jacobs, Brunton, & Melville, Aggressive Behavior, Mental Sub-normality, and the XYY Male, 208 *Nature* 1351 (1965).

31. Ullman & Krasner, *supra*, note 24.

32. Kunce, Ryan, & Eckelman, Violent Behavior and Differential WAIS Characteristics, 44 *Consulting & Clinical Psychology* 42 (1976).

33. D. Rosenthal, *Genetic Theory and Abnormal Behavior* (1970).

34. Martin, *Abnormal Psychology: Clinical and Scientific Perspective* (1977). Witkin, Criminality in XYY and XXY Men, 193 *Science* 547 (1976).

35. Schmauk, Punishment Arousal and Avoidance Learning in Sociopaths, 76 *J. Abnormal & Soc. Psychology* 325 (1970). A more recent replication of the work of Lykken & Schmauk is Newman & Kosson, Passive Avoidance Learning in Psychopathic and Nonpsychopathic Offenders, 95 *J. Abnormal Psychology* 252 (1986).

36. Lykken, *supra*, note 11.

37. Schmauk, *supra* note 35.

38. Fulkerson & Finkelstein, If Psychopaths Exist, Do They Show Avoidance Learning?, (unpublished manuscript) (1983). See A. Finkelstein, *An Investigation of Avoidance Learning and Stimulation—Seeking in the Psychopathic Disorder* (doctoral dissertation, Univ. of Louisville) (1979).

39. Schachter & Lantane, Crime, Cognition, and the Autonomic Nervous System, in *Nebraska Symposium on Motivation* 221–275 (M. Jones ed. 1964).

40. Gendreau & Suboski, Classical Discrimination Eyelid Condition in Primary Psychopaths, 77 *J. Abnormal & Soc. Psychology* 242 (1971).

41. Ullmann & Krasner, *supra*, note 24.

42. Hare, *supra*, note 23.

43. This is consistent with the research followed from Lykken through Schmauk, see notes 14 to 35, *supra*. The various factors that may produce psychopathy are reviewed in Patterson, Performance Models for Antisocial Boys, 41 *Am. Psychologist* 432 (1986).

44. Ullmann & Krasner, *supra*, note 24 at 553.

45. Widom, Interpersonal and Personal Construct Systems in Psychopaths, 44 *Clinical & Consulting Psychology* 614 (1976).

46. See generally D. Doren, *Understanding and Treating the Psychopath* (1987); D. Levin, *Pathologies of the Modern Self* (1987).

47. H. Eysenck, *The Dynamics of Anxiety and Hysteria* (1957).

48. Witkin, *supra*, note 34.

49. Thorp, Maltzman, Syndulko, & Ziskind, Autonomic Activity During Anticipation of an Aversive Tone in Noninstitutionalized Sociopaths, 17 *Psychophysiology* 123 (1980).

50. Hare, *supra*, note 24; Blackburn & Lee-Evans, Reactions of Primary

and Secondary Psychopaths to Anger-Evoking Situations, 24 *Brit. J. Clinical Psychology* 93 (1985).

51. Steinberg & Schwartz, Biofeedback and Electrodermal Self-Regulation in Psychopathy, 85 *J. Abnormal Psychology* 408 (1976).

52. Quay, Psychopathic Personality as Pathological Stimulation Seeking, 122 *Am. J. Psychiatry* 180 (1965). See White, Labouvie & Bates, The Relationship Between Sensation-Seeking and Delinquency: A Longitudinal Analysis, 22 *J. Research in Crime & Delinq.* 197 (1985).

53. Skrzypek, Effect of Perceptual Isolation and Arousal on Anxiety, Complexity Preference and Novelty Preference in Psychopathic and Neurotic Delinquents, 74 *J. Abnormal & Soc. Psychology* 321 (1969).

54. Ridgeway & Hare, Sensation Seeking and Physiological Response to Auditory Stimuli, 18 *Psychophysiology* 613 (1981).

55. A. Wiesen, *Differential Reinforcing Effects of Onset and Offset of Stimulation on the Operant Behavior of Normals, Neurotics, and Psychopaths* (1965) (doctoral dissertation, Univ. of Florida).

56. Widom, Interpersonal Conflict and Cooperation in Psychopaths, 85 *J. Abnormal Psychology* 330 (1976).

57. Vaillant, Sociopathy as a Human Process, 32 *Archives Gen. Psychiatry* 178 (1975). More recent work is reviewed in D. Doren, *Understanding and Treating the Psychopath* (1987).

58. Rotenberg, Psychopathy, Insensitivity, and Resensitization, 6 *Prof. Psychology: Research & Prac.* 283 (1975).

59. Parlour, Behavioral Techniques for Sociopathic Clients, in *Contemporary Issues in Abnormal Psychology and Mental Illness* 179–187 (T. Burke ed. 1977).

60. Bennett, Treatment Implications From a Review of the Literature on Sociopaths, 25 *Corrective & Soc. Psychiatry & J. Behav. Tech.* 134, 135 (1979). Regarding treatment of younger patients see A. Kazdin, *Treatment of Antisocial Behavior in Children and Adolescents* (1985).

61. Templeman & Wollersheim, A Cognitive-Behavioral Approach to the Treatment of Psychopathy, 16 *Psychotherapy: Theory, Research & Prac.* 132 (1979).

62. D'Zurilla & Goldfried, Problem Solving and Behavior Modification, 78 *J. Abnormal & Soc. Psychology* 107 (1971).

63. D. Meichenbaum, *Cognitive Behavior Modification* (1977).

64. American Law Institute, *Model Penal Code* §4.01(2) (Tent. Draft No. 4, 1955).

65. See United States v. Freeman, 357 F.2d 606, 625 (2d Cir. 1966).

66. Compare United States v. Freeman, 357 F.2d 606 (2d Cir. 1966); United States v. Currens, 290 F.2d 751 (3d Cir. 1961) (adopting caveat); with Wade v. United States, 426 F.2d 64 (9th Cir. 1970); United States v. Smith, 404 F.2d 720 (6th Cir. 1968) (rejecting the caveat).

67. Uelmen, The Psychiatrist, the Sociopath and the Courts: New Lines for an Old Battle, 14 *Loy L.A. L. Rev.* 1 (1980). See Smith, The Psychopath as Moral Agent, 45 *Phil. & Phenomenological Research* 177 (1984).

68. Robinson v. California, 370 U.S. 660 (1962).

69. Powell v. Texas, 392 U.S. 514 (1968).

70. See generally Davidson, How Trustworthy is the Witness?, 2 *J. Forensic Med.* 14 (1955).

CHAPTER 16

COMPETENCY:
CAPACITY TO STAND TRIAL,
ABILITY TO MAKE A WILL,
AND GUARDIANSHIP

Incompetency is arguably the most powerful concept encountered in mental health law. By declaring persons incompetent we remove some or all decision-making authority from them. They can then be subjected to unwanted institutionalization, involuntary treatment, loss of control of their property, and loss of the ability to exercise many other important legal rights. Thus, incompetency presents a greater potential loss of control than do criminal punishment, civil commitment, and involuntary treatment. Its legal power, the potential for abuse, and the vague standards that are often used to define it may make incompetency a major mental health civil rights issue of the future.

The common concept in incompetency is that the law will not permit some people to make certain decisions because of their mental inabilities.[1] Competency is a legal concept, like insanity, that does not have any perfectly corresponding mental health concept. In fact, "incompetency" is not a single doctrine in the law; it has several different meanings.[2] Three kinds of competency are of particular importance in the law: capacity to stand trial, to make a will, and to manage one's own affairs (guardianship). In this chapter we concentrate on these three forms and consider the issue of whether competency is a useful legal concept.

STANDING TRIAL

A comatose patient is charged with having robbed a bank. The comatose patient would be at a great disadvantage if the trial on the charge were held while he is still unconscious. Such a trial would be a travesty, essentially a trial in absentia. Similar disadvantages would be experienced by a criminal defendant who was seriously impaired, even though not completely unconscious.

Incompetency to stand trial probably began to develop as a way of protecting the profoundly mentally ill from the harsh realities of early common law. The legal proceedings could not go on until the defendant entered a plea, thus the refusal to plead would bring matters to a halt. When a defendant refused to plead, heavier and heavier rocks were placed on the defendant until he agreed to plead or was killed. This practice, harsh enough when applied to the competent, was even crueler when applied to the mentally ill.[3] In modern times, competency is required for the more subtle reasons of due process.

Standards for Incompetency

The United States Supreme Court held in *Dusky v. United States* that the defendant must have "sufficient present ability to consult with his lawyer with a reasonable degree of rational understanding," and a "rational as well as a factual understanding of the proceedings against him."[4] Merely finding that the defendant is oriented as to time and place and has some recollection of the events that gave rise to the criminal charges is not enough. This standard is a very general statement, but it requires two broad kinds of competency. The first is an understanding of the charges and proceedings the defendant faces. The Court required that this be a "rational" as well as a factual understanding, apparently meaning that the defendant must be able to appreciate the potential consequences to him of the trial and be able to consider the effects of such decisions as taking the stand. The second aspect of the *Dusky* requirement is that the defendant be able to consult with his attorney. The Court held that the constitution requires only that this consultation be held to "a reasonable degree of rational understanding." Therefore the defendant does not have to be perfectly competent, only "reasonably" so.

Basis for Incompetency

Incompetency may be caused by a variety of problems, including emotional, mental, or physical conditions. One study found that 83 percent of the determinations of incompetency to stand trial were based on the gross diagnostic categories of psychosis and mental retardation.[5]

A criminal defendant must be competent throughout the criminal process. (Competency to stand trial is related to criminal trials and ordinarily is not relevant in civil proceedings.) The defendant must also be competent to make an effective confession, to plead guilty, and to be sentenced. Indeed someone convicted of a capital offense who becomes incompetent after sentencing cannot be executed while incompetent. In *Ford v. Wainwright* the Supreme Court held that the cruel and unusual punishment provision of the Eighth Amendment prohibits the state from executing a prisoner who is incompetent.[6] There is a long history of not executing the incompetent. Reasons given for not executing incompetents include that they cannot participate effectively in any last-minute appeals, it is inhumane and cruel, it provides no deterrence to others, it does not have retributive value, and it prevents the condemned from making a final religious peace.

The Court was divided on, and left somewhat unclear, the standards for determining incompetency to be executed and the hearing process that a state must employ. Justice Powell suggested that the proper standard is whether prisoners "are unaware of the punishment they are about to suffer and why they are about to suffer it." There was fairly broad agreement that the "hearing" must be before a neutral decision-maker and the prisoner must have the right to present evidence and arguments, but it appears that the hearing need not be before a judge, but may be before an impartial officer or board. The Court noted the importance of expert information from psychotherapists in reaching these decisions, but did not detail the constitutional requirements regarding such evidence.

An interesting question is whether amnesia can be the basis for the finding of incompetency to stand trial. Defendants who are completely unable to remember their activities during the time of the alleged crime are obviously at a very substantial disadvantage in presenting a defense. However, some courts have rejected amnesia as the basis for an incompetency claim.[7] A much better approach has been to determine whether the memory loss includes an area that is critical to the defense. One court adopting this approach established a very useful set of guidelines to determine whether amnesia made the defendant incompetent.[8]

Consequences of Incompetency

A defendant who upon examination is found to be competent may be taken to trial. A defendant found incompetent to stand trial may be held for a short time to determine if competency can be regained. If it is regained, the trial and other criminal processes may proceed. If not, defendants are civilly committed or released. A defendant who is tried even though incompetent is considered improperly convicted and the conviction should be reversed.

An interesting question is whether a defendant needs to be "more competent" to plead guilty or to waive certain rights than to go to trial. Some have argued that enhanced competency should be required to waive important rights or to plead guilty.[9] However, the consequence of such a rule would be to remove from some marginally competent defendants the right to plea bargain and it would require those least able to do so to take their case to a trial court. Requiring this form of enhanced competency would therefore appear to serve neither the interests of the criminal defendant nor of the state.[10]

Incompetency, Insanity, Civil Commitment, and Psychosis

There is considerable confusion among mental health experts about these concepts. This confusion extends even to those who testify in incompetency proceedings.[11] For that matter, it appears that even some trial judges and attorneys confuse these concepts.[12]

Incompetency and psychosis are not identical. While some incompetent defendants may be psychotic, other conditions such as mental retardation also may cause it. At the same time, not all psychotic patients are incompetent. For example, a schizophrenic patient whose delusional system does not significantly interfere with the ability to consult with an attorney or prepare a defense is competent to stand trial. Psychosis may have some relevance to the issue of competency, but it is not determinative of it one way or another.

Incompetency and the insanity defense are decidedly different concepts. They differ in terms of relevant time, standards, consequences,
and procedures. Insanity concerns the mental state of the defendant
at the time the crime was committed; incompetency involves the mental state of the defendant at the time of trial. Broadly stated the
standard for incompetency is whether the defendant can reasonably
assist with and participate in the trial, the standard for insanity is
whether the defendant at the time of the crime knew what he or she
was doing (or could conform conduct to the standards of the law).
The consequence of a successful insanity plea is that the defendant
is found not guilty; the consequence of being found incompetent to
stand trial is that the trial is delayed and the defendant can be tried
once competency is restored. Incompetency is not a defense to the
crime; insanity is. There are also a variety of procedural differences
including the time at which the issue can be raised, who can raise it,
and burden of proof. Incompetency is, in some ways, of greater practical importance than sanity. One study found that there were ten
times as many persons committed for incompetency to stand trial as
held following successful pleas of not guilty by reason of insanity.[13]

Involuntary civil commitment generally deals with the issue of
whether, because of mental illness, someone will be dangerous in the
future. Incompetency deals with the question of whether someone is
currently able to reasonably participate in the trial process. Someone
civilly committed is not necessarily charged with a crime and may be
fully competent to participate in the legal process, while someone
incompetent to stand trial may not be dangerous to anyone. Although
civil commitment and incompetency are different concepts, there is
some evidence of leakage between the two systems. Someone found
not competent to stand trial may be civilly committed for a period
to determine if competency can be restored. Incompetency to stand
trial may sometimes be used to restrain someone who could not be
held under the increasingly stringent commitment processes.[14]

Procedures

The question of incompetency to stand trial may be raised at any time
during the criminal process by any participant. Most often the defense
raises this issue; other times the prosecution or the judge does. In-

deed, a trial judge may be constitutionally required to raise the issue if no one else does and if the defendant appears to be seriously handicapped.[15] The court must conduct an investigation of the defendant's competency if any bona fide question is raised about it.

Once the issue is raised, the defendant is usually sent to a mental institution for an evaluation period, usually of 30 to 90 days. Following the period of assessment there is a hearing at which the mental health experts present their report, often in the form of conclusions. In most states the hearing is before a judge who makes a determination of competency, almost always following the recommendations of the mental health experts.[16] The burden of proof of incompetency varies depending on the jurisdiction.[17] At the end of the hearing the defendant is held for trial if competent, returned to the mental institution to regain competency, held pending a civil commitment hearing, or (rarely) released because incompetence is not likely to be restored in the foreseeable future.

The incompetency process may significantly interfere with a number of rights of criminal defendants. If competency is questioned, bail is often denied and the defendant (despite the presumption of innocence) must endure the very restrictive environment of a mental institution. In addition, the right of self-incrimination may be compromised because information disclosed by the defendant in the course of evaluation by mental health experts in some instances may be used against him or her at trial. The process may take considerable time and thereby jeopardize the right to a speedy trial. Perhaps most important, those found incompetent to stand trial may be held in a mental hospital for a considerable time to try to restore their competency. These commitment criteria are considerably less stringent than those for civil commitment, and if defendants are found incompetent they may be held longer than if they had been convicted of the crime and sentenced to prison.[18]

Assessment of Incompetency

A number of instruments have been developed to assist mental health experts examine a defendant who may be incompetent, and to report findings to courts. These instruments may be useful places to begin but they should not be the sole method of evaluation. Most of these instruments have not been fully validated and in some instances their reliability has been questioned.[19]

Two widely discussed instruments are the Competency Screening Test (CST)[20] and the Competency Assessment Instrument (CAI).[21] The CAI is an attempt to structure and standardize the competency interview procedure. It is expressed as a set of 13 ego functions covering the scope of law-related competencies required of defendants if they are to effectively cope with legal proceedings. These include appraisal of available defenses, understanding court procedure, appreciation of charges and penalties, and capacity to testify. The client is evaluated on a scoring system of totally incompetent to totally competent.

The CST is a sentence completion technique. It consists of 22 sentence stems such as "When I go to court the lawyer will ——" "If Jack has to try his own case, he ——" "If the jury finds me guilty, I ——" Answers are scored with a 0, 1 or 2, with higher scores indicating higher levels of competency.

These and other tests reported below have a number of advantages. They help focus on relevant issues concerning the ability to participate in the trial rather than on misleading concepts such as the insanity defense or dangerousness. However some commentators have noted that the validity and reliability of these tests has not been fully demonstrated.[22]

A number of other tests and checklists have been suggested. Examples of these suggestions include: the MMPI, which did not prove to be particularly effective;[23] an instrument by Bukatman, Foy, and DeGrazia who produced a set of six "factual" and seven "inferential" criteria for trial competency as well as a screening interview for competency evaluation;[24] and a Courtroom Apperception Test that follows the same format as the Thematic Apperception Test: a picture is shown to the patient, who is asked to respond with a story.[25] These approaches have not been widely accepted and each has problems associated with it.

The effort to develop new or refined instruments continues. Some of these are modifications of the CST and CAI. For example, the Fitness Interview Test (FIT) is a revision and expansion of the CAI and is intended to cover all possible grounds for a finding of incompetence to stand trial.[26] The Interdisciplinary Fitness Interview (IFI) is designed to consider incompetency from an explicitly functional perspective—that is, to judge competency from the context of the particular criminal charges and trial facing the defendant. It uses interdisciplinary interviews of both mental health and legal professionals.[27] Shatin suggests a brief version of the CST involving only five items and indicates a high correlation with the full CST.[28] A somewhat different approach is being taken by Burling and Saylor who are developing an instrument, the Court Competency Inventory (CCI), by determining factors that characterize defendants who are incompetent. The CCI is 15 items—depicting role playing situations—and is intended to assess both legal and social competence.[29] These new tests still must be more carefully examined and refined and none yet represents a single, generally accepted instrument.

Disposition of Those Found Incompetent

Defendants found incompetent are not automatically released from custody, but are most often placed in mental institutions to try to restore their competency or to be processed through the civil commitment system. This practice invites abuse; the potential exists for holding the people for long periods only because they were charged with crimes (not convicted) and were unable to stand trial. In the past, it appears these kinds of abuses were common. For example, one study showed that defendants found incompetent were hospitalized for an average of 4.3 years,[30] and another study found that over half of the incompetents referred to a mental hospital never left.[31]

This practice of holding defendants for an indefinite period was sharply curtailed by the U.S. Supreme Court in *Jackson v. Indiana*.[32] Jackson was charged with a robbery offense that amounted to about nine dollars. Because he was a deaf-mute with a mental deficiency, he was unable to participate in his defense or understand the proceedings against him and thus incompetent to stand trial. The trial court, as was customary in such circumstances, committed him to a mental institution until his competency was restored. The Supreme Court held that this approach violated the Constitution, and that the state must either release an incompetent defendant, start civil commitment proceedings, or hold the defendant for a relatively brief period to determine if competency can be restored. The Court emphasized that an incompetent defendant "cannot be held more than the reasonable period of time necessary to determine whether there is a substantial probability that he will attain that capacity [to stand trial] in the foreseeable future. . . . Furthermore, even if it is determined that the defendant probably soon will be able to stand trial, his continued commitment must be justified by that progress toward that goal."[33]

Unfortunately, the *Jackson* Court did not define the length of a "reasonable period of time." Several years after this decision, one review of state statutes demonstrated that maximum "reasonable" treatment extended to five years, with a year or more not being uncommon, and many states' statutes providing no limit on the length of treatment.[34] Certainly many of these statutes undoubtedly exceed the limits provided by the Constitution. Proposals for reform generally would limit treatment to three to six months.[35]

The facts in the *Jackson* case illustrate a potential bind for states. Jackson was not competent to be tried and probably would not be competent to be tried for *any* crime in the foreseeable future. The state could not long hold Jackson unless he could be committed through involuntary civil commitment. Therefore, he could probably not be involuntarily incarcerated, and could not be tried for crimes he might commit in the community. He would therefore appear to be able to commit additional crimes without risking punishment. The threat of this occurring is more theoretical than real. First, it is possible that Jackson could be placed in a protective setting pursuant to a guardianship proceeding. Second, the "threat" could be present only from nondangerous people who are therefore not subject to civil commitment. Third, there are only a small number of people who would fit in the Jackson category. In addition, the state may assist Jackson on a voluntary basis through the social services system, perhaps reducing the likelihood of additional dangerous activity.

An area of controversy has been the restoration of competency to stand trial through the use of psychotropic drugs, which some patients may wish to take voluntarily.[36] Some commentators have objected to even the voluntary use of medicine to induce competency, referring to it as an "artificial competency."[37] Although there is not a unanimous agreement, most courts favor permitting the trial of someone whose competency is maintained through the use of drugs.[38] Since the purpose of the drug is to move the defendant toward "normal" functioning, or at least to enhance competency to participate in the trial process, it generally makes sense to permit the use of psychotropic drugs to enhance competency.

On the other hand, side effects of the medicine may cause the defendant to make a negative impression on the jury during the trial. For example, some drugs may make the defendant look lethargic or uninterested in the proceedings, or if the defendant takes the stand to testify, he may have slurred or disjointed speech. One imperfect solution is to inform the jury that the defendant is taking medicine which may cause adverse effects.[39] Of course, even if the reason for taking the medication is not given, the information that the defendant is taking this kind of drugs may itself have a negative impact on the jury.

A much more controversial issue is whether defendants may be required, over their objections, to take medicine to restore competency. There is conflicting opinion by commentators and courts on this subject. The opinions sound much like the issue of whether involuntary mental patients can be given treatment over their objections. The state has an important interest in restoring sufficient competency to be able to conduct trials. Yet if people are competent to decide to refuse treatment (some may be competent to make personal decisions but not sufficiently competent to stand trial), the fact that they are charged with a crime should not be sufficient reason to impose involuntary treatment.[40] In addition, it would be an invitation to serious abuse to establish a system in which someone could be *charged* with a misdemeanor and thereby be required to undergo invasive therapies. Under such a system we could expect that some people would be charged with crimes, even minor misdemeanors, for the purpose of requiring them to undergo involuntary treatment.

In many cases, of course, someone incompetent to stand trial will also be incompetent to make personal decisions. In those circumstances, a guardian should be permitted to make the decisions concerning treatment. An interesting, but largely unexamined, question is whether the best interests of incompetent mental patients facing serious charges are to remain incompetent for some time rather than to have competency restored so that trials can be held.

Incompetency to Stand Trial in Reality

A number of studies describe the actual operation of incompetency to stand trial.[41] Not surprisingly, practice is not fully consistent with legal theory. One reason is that incompetency is sometimes used for some purpose other than concern about the defendant's ability to participate in a trial.[42] For example, the defense may use it as a means to delay the trial while the evaluation occurs, as a means to seek information for an insanity plea, or as a means of gaining a plea bargaining chip. Prosecutors or courts may use it as a way to deny bail to the defendant, to avoid speedy trial regulations, to obtain information from or about a defendant, or to find an alternative to involuntary civil commitment.[43]

As civil commitment has become more difficult, there is reason to believe that some people who might formerly have been incarcerated through involuntary commitment are now being charged with the crime and sent through incompetency procedures instead. Thus, criminal charges may be filed, resulting in civil incarceration because of incompetency to stand trial. In one study of people who were found incompetent, in 72 percent of the cases criminal charges were dismissed after release from the mental hospital. More than half of the defendants found incompetent had been charged only with misdemeanors and about 30 percent of the charges were for disturbing the peace.[44] This misuse of incompetency may account for the fact that the number of competency evaluations has been increasing.[45]

A relatively small number of defendants whose competency to stand trial is brought into question are actually found incompetent. A review of ten studies found that between 1.2 percent and 77 percent of those evaluated were actually found incompetent, or across all ten studies only 30 percent of those referred were found incompetent to stand trial.[46] The small percentage of actual incompetence may again be related to the misuse of incompetency to achieve other purposes, or it may be related to confusion over the standards for determining incompetency.

When the defense claims that a defendant is incompetent, he has generally been charged with a serious crime.[47] There is no reason to believe that those incompetent to stand trial are more likely to commit serious crimes than minor crimes. However, those charged with serious crimes have a greater incentive to use incompetency and they are likely to receive closer attention from the legal system. (Of course such crimes as securities fraud or embezzlement are not likely to be committed by those who are incompetent.) If incompetency to stand trial is being misused as a means of civil commitment, we may see a reversal of the relationship between the type of offense and referral for incompetency evaluation. The data discussed earlier concerning the increasing number of incompetency evaluations associated with misdemeanors may be evidence of this trend.

The majority, perhaps the vast majority, of mental health experts apparently confuse incompetency to stand trial with other concepts.[48] Somewhat more surprising, many attorneys and judges also do not understand competency or confuse it with mental illness generally. One study, for example, found that only 10 of 28 attorneys had any knowledge of the legal criteria that were the basis for incompetency to stand trial.[49] Another study found that many attorneys who had clients evaluated for competency did so for reasons that had little to do with legal criteria.[50]

Confusion among mental health experts concerning the criteria for incompetency is particularly alarming, because they often testify in conclusory terms, stating that the defendant is or is not competent to stand trial. In turn, judges tend to rely almost exclusively on this testimony.[51]

Reforms

The very loose standards for determining incompetency, the misuse of the concept in the criminal system, and the confusion about the standards for finding incompetency create a system which invites inconsistent, unfair, and incorrect application of the law. Reform of the process seems fully warranted. A number of fairly simple changes could significantly improve the system.[52]

A major improvement would ensure that mental health experts (as well as trial judges) fully understand the reason for incompetency evaluations and the criteria for incompetency to stand trial. Before the evaluation occurs, the legal standard should be clearly described in writing for the experts, informing them of several specific questions that they will be asked concerning the ability of the defendant to understand and participate in the criminal process. For example, they might be asked: Is there significant impairment in the ability of the defendant to understand specific elements of the crime with which he is charged? (The legal elements of the crime should then be described.) If so, in what way is this impairment likely to affect his functioning at trial?

Interdisciplinary teams of mental health professionals are not uncommon in incompetency evaluations. This concept should be expanded by including on the team one attorney familiar with the standards for incompetency and with the nature of the crime and possible defenses to it, in order to ensure that the legal standards are at the center of the evaluation.

Evidence revealed in a competency evaluation should be available for the competency hearing but not for any use at the trial, thus avoiding the problem of the defendant's having to give up Fifth Amendment rights in order to raise the issue of competency. It would also avoid the problem of an incompetent or marginally competent defendant confessing without fully understanding implications of his or her statement.

The continued development of testing instruments is important. Initial efforts that have been made to adapt the instruments to deal with the individual aspects of the trial of the defendant should be encouraged. Additional information concerning the validity and reliability of the testing instrument is also important.

Wherever possible, competency evaluations should be done outside of an institutional setting, thus permitting the defendant to be released on bail, reducing the cost of institutionalizing the defendant, and removing the incentive for misuse of these proceedings as replacement for involuntary civil commitment. There is evidence that only a very small proportion of the time that a defendant spends in a hospital is actually used for evaluation.[53]

The maximum time that the defendant can be held waiting the return of competency should be sharply limited and defined by statute, not exceeding three months. To the extent possible, defendants should be permitted to be released into the community during this period; the least restrictive alternative form of treatment should be employed. Incompetents should never be held longer to regain competency than they would likely be held if convicted of the offense.

Anyone determined to be incompetent should have some means of having the criminal charges reviewed carefully, thus minimizing the possibility that someone is wrongly accused and incarcerated without actually having committed any crime. Some have suggested that a "provisional trial" be held in which an incompetent would receive a full trial and, if found not guilty, released; if found guilty and still incompetent, the verdict of the provisional trial would be set aside and the defendant retried when competent. (Those evaluating competency could continue their evaluation during the trial to determine whether or not the defendant actually was incompetent during this time.)[54] If there were a reasonable expectation that competency could be restored following the provisional trial, the state could incarcerate the defendant for some period (perhaps three months) in an effort to effect that restoration. Because of the provisional trial, there would be a fair degree of confidence that the state was not incarcerating a completely innocent person. This proposal has much merit, but it is probably politically impossible. The thought of an incompetent defendant being found guilty following a full trial and then having that verdict set aside because of incompetency is likely to cause public uproar. This would be true particularly if it were unlikely that the incompetent would ever regain competency and therefore had to be released from custody or considered for ordinary civil commitment.

An alternative to the provisional trial is to provide an enhanced pretrial hearing. The purpose would be for a judge (not a jury) to determine whether there is clear and convincing evidence that the incompetent defendant was guilty of the crime. If so, the judge would determine the sentence under the usual criteria. If there were a reasonable likelihood that competency could be restored, the defendant could be held for some period. That period should be the shorter of three months or the length of the sentence that the court determined would likely be imposed. If there were not clear and convincing evidence that the defendant committed the crime, he or she would be released, subject to possible reindictment if competency were restored.

For patients who are impaired but not incompetent, the mental health evaluators should be asked to provide suggestions concerning the structure of the trial that would help the defendant compensate for areas of reduced functioning. For example, the evaluators might suggest that trial sessions be shortened or that there be frequent recesses.

Perhaps the most difficult reform would be to define with more precision what incompetency means. (This issue is discussed in more detail at the end of the chapter.) It may be impossible to define incompetency with absolute precision, but the efforts to more fully define what it means in the trial context should be expanded. In part, the structure of incompetency should include a recognition of the special skills that a defendant will need for the trial and specific charges he or she will face. A defendant facing a complicated felony charge will need talents considerably different than those of the defendant charged with simple assault. The process of better defining competency requires not just identification of the skills that are needed, but also definition of the *level* of impairment of those skills that is acceptable.

CAPACITY TO MAKE A WILL

A will is a legal means of indicating how property should be distributed after death. Interestingly, between the end of the twelfth century and middle of the sixteenth century, the will was regarded as contrary to public policy, and property was distributed to the family according to strict rules of descent. The concept of mental competency to make a will, or testamentary capacity, became important with the amendments to the Statute of Wills in 1572, shortly after the recognition of right to enforce wills.[55] Challenges to the validity of wills occur from time to time today on the basis that the person making the will (testator) lacked testamentary capacity. With the aging population, the number of challenges based on incompetency may well increase.

The conceptual basis for requiring testamentary capacity is that a legal will is what a deceased wished or "willed" to be done with property after death. If mental incapacity destroys a person's ability to possess a will, or to express wishes, then the reason for recognizing wills as a means of distributing property is also destroyed. In addition to this conceptual basis for the rules regarding testamentary capacity, they are also meant to protect other interests. First, it protects the family of an incompetent person from having property irrationally or accidentally passed to those outside the family. In addition, it protects the public from bizarre distributions of property that are of limited social value and serve no real purpose. Finally, it protects incompetents from their own irrational behavior.

If it is determined that testamentary capacity did not exist at the time a will was made, then the will is generally void and given no effect. (In a few instances involving "insane delusions," only part of the will may be invalid.) If the person had a previous valid will which the "incompetent" will sought to revoke, then the earlier will may be used to distribute property. If there was no earlier will, the person is considered as having died intestate, and the property is distributed according to statutory guidelines of intestate succession.

Standards of Competency

There are two general forms of incompetency to make a will. The first is the inability to know enough or to form the intention to dispose of property. It is generally agreed that to form testamentary capacity, people must be able to (1) understand the nature and extent of their property, (2) realize the persons who are the natural objects of their bounty (relatives and friends), (3) understand the distribution of the property contained in the will, (4) understand the nature of a will and be able to form an intent to make a disposition of property that will be carried out after death and (5) generally know how these elements relate to each other and form an orderly scheme for the disposition of property.[56] Neither eccentricities, mistaken beliefs, old age, nor unreasonable provisions in the will establish incompetence.[57]

Most of these elements are cognitive and relate only to the ability to know or understand limited amounts of information. It is generally said that less capacity is needed to make a will than to make a contract or transact business. A will is a single-party instrument and the possibility of fraud in the formation of a will is therefore theoretically less than with two-party transactions such as contracts.

The second type of incompetency is the existence of an insane delusion. (This is, apparently, as opposed to a "sane" delusion or an "insane" reality, neither of which is specifically mentioned in the law.) Today, this is seldom the basis for a challenge. Some people who are capable of understanding the distribution of property in wills they are making and are in that sense competent may nonetheless have minds "so warped and deranged that they are unable to form a rational testamentary plan." An insane delusion is broadly defined as "a belief in things which do not exist and which a rational mind would not believe to exist."[58] This test is extremely vague, but it is generally stated that the issue is not whether a reasonable person would adhere to the belief but whether it is so extravagant or unbelievable as to indicate lack of reality. False beliefs or prejudices regarding the person's family or friends are generally not considered insane delusions no matter how unfounded or if based on the flimsiest type of evidence.[59]

If there is any evidence whatsoever to confirm the delusion, it is no longer considered irrational. For example, the belief that the Vikings buried a stone during a visit to Minnesota would not be an insane delusion, but a belief that they returned nightly to polish the stone could be. To invalidate part or all of the will the insane delusion must have directly effected part of the will.[60] For example, the belief that the Vikings were polishing a rock in his back yard each night would not necessarily invalidate a will, unless, say, that belief led the testator to establish a fund to provide snacks for them.

The critical time regarding incompetency is the point at which the will is signed. The will of a person who later became completely incompetent cannot be invalidated on that basis. On the other hand, the fact that someone became competent after signing a will would not necessarily validate a will signed while the person was incompetent, unless it were ratified during a period of competence.

Evidence of Capacity and Mental Health Experts

The issue of incompetency arises when the will is probated. The issue is the mental state of the testator at the time the will was signed, which may have been years before. Generally the issue is raised only if someone disappointed by the terms of the will challenges it. Once it is demonstrated that the will was properly executed, signed, and witnessed, then those attacking the will will have the burden of proving incompetency.

A wide range of evidence is admissible to demonstrate the lack of testamentary capacity. Circumstantial evidence as well as direct evidence is appropriate. For example, the language or provisions of the will itself may be evidence of an insane delusion. The testator's physical condition, behavior, irrational conduct, physical weakness, or disease are admissible, but not conclusive. Inferences may also be drawn from hallucinations, weaknesses of memory, or being under the influence of drugs or liquor. Again, these are not conclusive. Expert witnesses may be called to give opinions about the mental state of the testator.[61]

Mental health experts called as witnesses in will contests face a number of difficult problems. Assume, for example, that a mental health expert is asked to express an opinion in the following case: A person who left a significant estate was extremely forgetful, at times quite confused with what appears to have been at least a moderate senile dementia complicated by varying states of paranoia directed at his neighbors and some relatives. Is it likely that a patient in this condition could understand what his property was, know the natural objects of his bounty, and form a definite plan for the disposition of property? Did the paranoia so interfere with his rational thought at the time the will was made as to make the disposition unreasonable? The mental health expert may never have examined or even met the testator. Even in the unlikely event that the expert knew the decedent, an examination was probably not conducted at the time the will was signed. Therefore the expert must engage in a speculation. In addition, it is the mental state at a particular moment that is relevant. Even if it can be determined that a testator suffered from a certain condition, experts may not know how severe it was at any given moment. For example, someone suffering schizophrenia may have delusions come and go. It would often be impossible to know the state of mind of the person at the time of the signing of the will.

An ethical question facing experts asked to testify is whether it is professionally appropriate to render an opinion concerning the mental state of someone who the expert never met and who is now dead. One physician noted that "no jurist or psychiatrist has indicated a precise point where sanity ceases and insanity begins. Perhaps it would be easier to decide the exact instance when dusk surrenders to darkness."[62] Others have noted that "the question of past mental state is, in the strictest sense, unanswerable."[63]

If the deceased was a patient other ethical issues arise. There is now the issue of the confidentiality of a now dead patient. Many privileges do not apply in will contests or after the death of the patient. Therefore, such communications may not be legally protected by a privilege and the mental health professional may be called to testify. The professional must consider the degree to which he or she will cooperate with such inquiry. One way of avoiding some of these ethical issues is for a mental health expert to be involved with the person at the time of the signing of the will with the express understanding that he or she will be permitted to testify concerning the person's mental condition. A strong argument can be made, in such circumstances, for the examiner to be a professional who has not treated the patient.

Capacity to Make a Will in Practice

There is surprisingly little research available concerning the actual operation of the process of determining incompetency to make a will. For some years, close observers have suggested that courts are subverting the intended purpose of testamentary capacity and instead are using it as a convenient way to impose the court's ideas of fairness or reasonableness in the case of individual wills.[64] The lack of testamentary capacity may be a legal excuse for overturning wills that courts do not like. One critical commentator suggests that in a contest no one is really interested in the mental state of the testator. "Questioning the testator's sanity serves to set aside a will which injures the community's sense of fair play in the inheritance game. In such a contest, the issue is not the testator's mental capacity, but who will inherit the property."[65] The absence of any clear definition of testamentary capacity and particularly of the level of disability that causes incompetency is likely to lead to misuse of the legal rules. If we want heirs to be able to challenge "unfair" or even "unreasonable" wills, then society should provide a direct legal mechanism for doing so, but using the incompetency rules to achieve this purpose is inappropriate.

Reforms

Several reforms in the way wills are signed and in the legal structure would avoid unnecessary and costly will contests and the uncertainty that accompanies them. To help avoid the posthumous guessing about the mental state of the testator, experts could examine the testator when the will is signed. (This should be accompanied by a report from the mental health experts.) This would be done with the understanding that the experts might be called as witnesses should there be a will contest involving testamentary capacity. While some evidentiary problems may be raised about admitting the reports, this process could nonetheless be valuable in helping to prove the validity of a will. In addition, if the experts doubt the competency of the person, it would be possible to re-sign or reaffirm the will if and when competency can be enhanced. If someone other than a mental health professional who is treating the person is used as an expert there is less chance that the highly personal or confidential information will be released during a will contest. It is not necessary that the mental health experts be aware of the person's prior mental health history. The experts who conduct such a survey should, of course, be familiar with the legal tests for competency to make a will.

Another proposal for avoiding unnecessary claims of incompetency is the use of a videotaped interview with the maker of the will at the time the will is signed. It may be conducted by mental health experts or by others but in either case it should deal with the mental state of the person and the possibility of insane delusions. This could be very profitably used in conjunction with the mental competency assessment described above.

There are, of course, dangers associated with these two techniques. Notably, they may well provide evidence to demonstrate the person was not competent at the time a will was made. In fact presenting a videotape of a person who is even mildly confused or forgetful to a judge or jury may seem much worse than it actually is and be misleading evidence.

When the competency of someone is in doubt at the time a will is signed it would be useful to have an immediate judicial determination of competency. That way the person could be interviewed and examined, and if incompetency was found there would be the possibility of executing a will at a later time. The evaluation of competency should be conducted by a court-appointed interdisciplinary team similar to the one we proposed earlier for conducting competency to stand trial assessments. The difficulty with making such a process available is that it might not allow those who oppose the will to be able to participate in the competency proceeding; they might not know what was in the will or even have notice of the hearing. On the other hand, competency should not be judged by whether a testator has made a potential heir unhappy and it would be possible to conduct these testamentary capacity hearings without their being based on an adversarial process. A potential, if unlikely, problem is that these competency hearings would be so popular that they would become a part of the execution of every will and would thereby flood the courts. A team would report their findings to a court which would make the final judgment.

A more precise definition of testamentary capacity, including "insane delusion" is desirable. As we noted earlier, the absence of a more precise definition of incompetency probably results in abuse of the concept, unequal application of the law, and uncertainty about how property will be distributed. Efforts should be made to more precisely define the level of knowledge or understanding that is necessary for testamentary capacity. As with other incompetency definitions this is a most difficult task.

Death, the Ultimate Incompetency: Testamentary Wills as Paradigm

Death may be viewed as the ultimate incompetency: the deceased cannot tell us from the grave how their properties should be distributed. The way we have dealt with the problem of this kind of incompetency is to let people tell us in a dependable way while alive what to do with their property after death. This approach might serve as a paradigm for other forms of incompetency, such as the ability to give or refuse consent to treatment or to make other personal care decisions. We believe that such living wills, psychiatric wills, treatment wills, and similar devices should be encouraged as a way of allowing individual decision making even in the face of incompetency.

Objections have been raised to such devices on the basis that they are unrealistic because the person making them is not actually facing the treatment situation.[66] These objections are not completely persuasive. Similar arguments could be made about testamentary wills; that is, they are always executed by people who are not now dead nor have ever been dead and therefore cannot fully know what distribution they would like made of their property when they are dead. Beyond that, it is possible that the testator had a change of mind about the distribution of property after signing the will. We permit that change of mind to be given effect if the testator cared enough to change the will.

Other problems with psychiatric or treatment wills are that the competency of the person at the time of signing the will could be called into question, provisions in it may be unclear or uncertain, and it would be possible for fraudulent wills to be presented. These are all legitimate concerns of varying risks and similar objections could be made against testamentary wills. The point of all wills is not that they present an optimal form of decision making; they do not. It would be optimal to have the person fully competent to make decisions at the time the decisions have to be made. When that is impossible, however, the question is whether the device of a will is the best way of coming as close as possible to what a person would make if competent. As is the case with posthumous distribution of property, on balance, wills are probably the best method of protecting legitimate autonomy in bad situations.

GUARDIANSHIP

The decision to declare people incompetent to make decisions for themselves concerning financial and personal matters is correctly classified as being among the most weighty and complex that the law makes. Guardianship has the potential both for protecting and caring for those who cannot care for themselves, and for great abuse.[67] Both the value and the risk of guardianship is that authority for making all decisions is transferred from an incompetent ward to a guardian.[68] The guardian takes control of property and manages it, and in addition, makes personal-care decisions, such as whether or not the ward will be placed in an institution, where the ward will live, and whether or not to consent to treatment for physical and mental conditions. The ward may also lose a few rights which the guardian may not exercise. For example, the right to vote may be removed with a determination of complete incompetency.

The guardianship system exists primarily to protect the incompetent from personal and financial harm, but it also protects society and the family of the incompetent. The history of legal protection for the property of the mentally disabled is much longer than protection of the incompetent person. By the time of Cicero, in ancient Rome, for example, there were elaborate provisions for the protection of the property of the incompetent. In Medieval England the lord of the manor had responsibility for both the property and person of the insane. Later this authority became a duty of the crown. In colonial

America, several colonies had statutes designed to protect the property of the incompetent even before those colonies became concerned with the personal welfare of the mentally disabled. All states now provide for some form of guardianship.[69]

Until recently, guardianship was commonly a part of civil commitment. The conservator managed the property of the patient, and the guardian made personal-care decisions. These functions were merged and as a practical matter the hospital often made decisions about the kinds of treatment the ward would receive. Recently the concept of limited or partial guardianship has been recognized where a guardian is appointed to make some, but not all, decisions for a partially mentally disabled person.

Standards for Determining Incompetency

The statutory criteria defining incompetency have traditionally been very vague. They might simply describe an incompetent as someone who is "incapable of caring for himself" or is "unable to manage his own affairs." Other states have adopted more "modern" definitions of incompetency that are only a bit more definite. States adopting the Uniform Probate Code, for example, may define the incompetent as someone who lacks "sufficient understanding or capacity to make, communicate or implement responsible decisions concerning his personal property."[70] Another type of statute adopts a functional or therapeutic approach that defines as incompetent someone who is likely to suffer substantial harm because of an inability to provide for personal needs for food, clothing, shelter, health care or safety, but these statutes may also define incompetency as the inability to manage property or financial affairs.[71]

Mental illness, "mental deficiency," or mental retardation may be the basis for incompetency. Many states also include chronic intoxication, drug addiction, old age, or serious physical infirmity. In the past being a spendthrift was also a basis for incompetency. An example of such a provision is the Wisconsin statute that includes as incompetent (as a spendthrift) someone who because of "the use of intoxicants or drugs or of gambling, idleness, or debauchery or other wasteful course of conduct is unable to attend to business or thereby is likely to affect the health, life or property of himself or others so as to endanger the support of himself and his dependents or expose the public to such support."[72]

Hearings and Process

Guardianships are established following a judicial hearing, which may include a jury, depending on the jurisdiction. Testimony may be taken from those who know the person and generally there is expert testimony concerning the mental state of the person. Most often these experts are appointed and called by the court and are sometimes referred to as impartial experts. States have recently begun to tighten the hearing procedures. Many now provide for an attorney, the person's presence at the hearing, and the right to call and examine witnesses. In some states the person can be found incompetent only if incompetency is demonstrated through clear and convincing evidence. These reforms may be more apparent than real.[73]

Incompetency permits the state to severely limit personal liberty and property rights. Therefore at least some constitutional due process provisions apply to guardianship proceedings.[74] Compared with civil commitment and criminal incarceration, relatively little attention has been given to due process issues in these cases. These questions will undoubtedly be raised more frequently in the future.[75]

Special problems may arise if a person is incarcerated for an evaluation while awaiting a competency hearing. Unless an immediate emergency exists, there is little reason for this deprivation of freedom since the necessary tests and evaluations can be conducted on an outpatient basis.

Following a hearing, a court may decide that the person is competent, in which case the person maintains control of personal and properties decisions. However, in most jurisdictions another petition claiming incompetency can be filed shortly thereafter. If the person is found incompetent following a hearing, a guardian is appointed by the court. This may be a family member, friend, or other person interested in the welfare of the incompetent. In some cases it is difficult to find someone willing to act as guardian. Many states now provide for public guardians as part of a social services system.

Incompetency Without a Hearing

A person may be completely incapable of making decisions, but never have gone through a formal determination of incompetency. The law recognizes this and provides, for example, that contracts made by someone unable to understand the nature and consequences of entering into them may be voidable or disclaimed by the incompetent person. Marriages entered into when one party does not have the capacity to understand the nature of a marriage may be subject to annulment. These kinds of incompetency, which do not depend on a prior court determination, provide protection for an incompetent person. They permit the unraveling of certain transactions when it appears they have harmed an incompetent person or advantage has been taken of the incompetent person.[76] The problem of determining incompetency when there has been no formal judicial proceedings has particularly been a problem in obtaining consent for treatment and is discussed in chapters 18 and 19.

Duty of Guardians

Guardians are obligated to act as fiduciaries, making decisions that are in the best interest of their wards. Generally, guardians must periodically account to the court concerning their handling of the property of their wards. Less frequently they are called to review for the court their actions to protect the physical and mental state of incompetents.

At the end of this chapter we discuss the difficulty in deciding what basis to use for making personal decisions for a ward. Similar problems can arise in determining how to handle the ward's assets. For example, suppose a ward has a habit of giving 10 percent of current income to charities. Should the guardian continue to make such awards? If so, to what charities? In some instances the guardian has a potential conflict of interest with the ward. Where the guardian is a beneficiary in a ward's will, for example, there may be some disincentive to spend large amounts of money to provide the very best care for the ward.

Restoration of Competence and Limited Guardianship

When incompetency no longer exists, the court will declare the person's competency restored. Depending upon the state, the restoration may occur after hearing or upon the certification of mental health experts.

A promising development has been the increasing availability of limited or partial guardianships, which recognize that a person may have inadequacies only in certain areas.[77] To maximize the autonomy of that person, decision-making authority should be removed only in specific areas of incompetence, with the ward retaining authority in all other areas. For example, a person might be incompetent to handle a complicated portfolio of stocks and commodities futures, but be able to make personal care decisions and to decide how to spend the money.

Unfortunately, limited guardianships have not been widely used.[78] This may reflect in part the fact that this is a new concept not fully understood by judges and attorneys and in part the fact that there are some practical problems with it. It may be difficult for mental experts to determine precisely which areas are so seriously affected as to make someone incompetent. Thus, creating accurate, specific reports for limited guardianships may be difficult for mental health experts. In addition, for some patients the areas of incompetence may change from day to day and week to week. The precision required to properly maintain a limited guardianship may make it difficult to keep up with shifting specific areas of incompetence.

Despite its shortcomings and problems, the concept of limited guardianship suggests an important way of reducing the invasions of liberty posed by complete guardianships, and it should be used more frequently.

Public Guardians

Most states now have established a public guardian which is a public agency with the duty to exercise the powers of a guardian. Ordinarily public guardians act for those for whom a private guardian cannot be found. Most of the wards of public guardians are poor.[79]

The major complaint about public guardians is that they are highly bureaucratized with very heavy caseloads that fail to provide any personal relationship.[80] A study of public guardians suggests the validity of this complaint. Caseloads varied from 30 to 341 wards per staff member with an average of 100 wards.[81] Because of these and other problems the President's Commission on Mental Health suggested several alternatives to public guardians, including the use of private nonprofit groups and public trusts to carry on the work.[82] One useful function of public guardians might be to encourage the development of such private, charitable organizations that will assume the role of guardianship including the demonstration of a real personal interest in their wards. However, it seems likely that with an aging population, and somewhat less cohesive family structures, the use of public guardians will probably continue to increase.

Special Decisions Concerning Incompetents: Sterilization and Lifesaving Treatment

Some very important decisions require special consideration when a guardian is consenting to them on behalf of a ward. Examples of these decisions are consent to permanent sterilization and consent to the withdrawal of lifesaving treatment. Courts have generally been reluctant to permit guardians broad authority to consent to sterilization. Usually a separate court hearing on the issue is required.[83] It must be demonstrated that there is a profound incompetency which is permanent, that the incompetency would prevent the ward from ever understanding the consequences of sexual intercourse or prevent her from being able to care for a child, and that there is no less restrictive alternative way of dealing with these problems.[84] These proceedings are generally for sterilization for incompetent women.

In very limited circumstances courts have been willing to permit the withdrawal of lifesaving treatment from incompetent patients where there is no hope that they will ever regain consciousness or where the treatment would be so painful and confusing with such limited benefit that it is sensible to refuse the treatment. The process of developing the standards and procedures for these decisions continues.[85]

Guardianship in Operation

After surveying the literature on the operation of guardianship, one group of commentators reported, "the professional literature relating to guardianship contains very little that is supportive of general guardianship practice or that argues forcefully for guardianship."[86] Indeed the commentary on the guardianship system has sometimes been as scathing as in any area of the law. "The law in most of the United States applies conservatorship: for inappropriate reasons . . . ; according to invalid standards; under the dubious pretense of medical expertise; and without seeing to the representation of the proposed ward."[87]

"Recognize guardianship for what it really is: the most intrusive, non-interest serving, impersonal device known and available to us and as such, one which minimizes personal autonomy and respect for the individual, has a high potential for doing harm and raises at best a questionable benefit/burden ratio."[88]

"When examined in the larger context of social programming through which we purport to help the less advantaged, involuntary guardianship emerges as an official initiation rite for the entry of the poor and the inept into the managed society."[89]

There are a limited number of strong studies on the operation of the incompetency system, but the evidence that exists suggests that too often the system is haphazard, uncertain, and not necessarily for the benefit of the ward. For example, despite the incompetent's right to attend the competency hearing and to be represented by attorneys, studies in Los Angeles and New York found that wards were seldom present and seldom adequately represented by attorneys. In Los Angeles, for example, in 84 percent of the cases the only people present at the hearing were the judge, the petitioner (the person trying to have the potential ward declared incompetent), and the petitioner's attorney. In California, case records showed that the person was physically unable to attend a hearing in circumstances in which that was clearly untrue.[90] "Despite the widespread trend for reform of state guardianship statutes, many still lack those elements traditionally associated with due process in other settings. The alleged incompetent does not always receive notice of the hearing. . . . Though lawyers may represent the patient, they are frequently not required to do so; if the patient cannot afford a lawyer, often none is available."[91]

One study of guardianship found that the proceedings tend to be nonadversarial, exceedingly brief, and subject to a large number of due process deficiencies.[92] Other important findings concerning the competency process are that applications for guardianship are invariably granted, restoration to competency is so rare as to be virtually nonexistent, despite laws providing for them, partial or limited guardianships are rarely established, and the review of guardianships is perfunctory if it is done at all.[93]

The absence of any clear standards of guardianship make it almost inevitable that inconsistent and inappropriate bases will be used for decision making. The process has been criticized for allowing guardianship to be used to prevent socially disapproved behaviors in the elderly or as a way of dealing with patients who refuse to do what professionals advise.[94]

Preliminary studies suggest that the operation of guardianships may not be in the best interest of the wards. In one study in Cleveland comparing a high level of social intervention (guardianship-like) with a control group, the experimental (high-intervention) group had a higher rate of institutionalization and death than did the controls.[95] Another review of elderly incompetents in New York concluded that the incompetent was generally in a worse position after being adjudicated incompetent than before.[96] In addition, the ward may be subject to physical or mental abuse at the hands of the guardian or the institution.[97] The ideal of a guardian who cares very deeply about the ward and sees to personal as well as financial needs is too often a myth. A significant number of private individuals, in one study, were discovered who held guardianships for many wards—an attorney had 50 wards at one time and a minister had 95.[98]

There is also increasing evidence that the guardianship system is overloaded and unable to keep up with the level of use of the system. Part of this reflects the growing number of aged in our society. It also undoubtedly reflects the increased emphasis on informed consent where a guardianship is sought to consent to medical treatment. There have also been changes in the process of civil commitment. There is evidence that some patients who cannot be civilly committed under current standards are instead found incompetent and then committed by guardians to institutions. Guardianship is one of the few areas in which a *parens patriae* justification exists for the involuntary institutionalization of patients.[99]

Reforms

These data sugest that the guardianship system is in need of continued reform, and that the reforms undertaken in the last decade or
two have not produced all of the desired changes. The purposes of
the reforms are to narrow the interference with fundamental decision
making rights by eliminating abuse and narrowing the use of guardianship, and to protect from harm those people who are truly incompetent. Changes in the procedures for determining incompetency
should be combined with enhanced periodic reviews of the necessity
for continued guardianship. Because guardianship is such a powerful
instrument, we believe that full due process rights should be provided. Unless there is vigorous and competent legal representation
by attorneys it is unlikely that any of these reforms will be very meaningful. There has been a debate about the appropriate role of attorneys in guardianship and civil commitment hearings. This is really a
debate about the legal representation deserved by those who do not
have their own attorney. There is no doubt that a client could demand
vigorous representation by a privately retained attorney; if one attorney refused to provide that assistance another could be retained.
However, those who must depend on appointed counsel may not have
the luxury of demanding vigorous representation. This distinction
between representation of retained and appointed counsel should be
unacceptable to the legal profession (imagine a similar claim made
regarding criminal representation).[100]

Other procedural reforms would help ensure that guardianships
are not extended unnecessarily and that guardians meet their obligations to protect the welfare of wards. Effective periodic reviews of
the need for continued guardianship should be undertaken. One way
to accomplish this would be to provide for limited terms of incompetency, much as many states now do with civil commitment. Under
this system a new hearing on incompetence would have to be held
periodically, perhaps every six or twelve months. Guardians should
be required to report periodically to courts not just about the financial affairs of the ward but also about the physical and mental welfare
of the ward. These reports should include evidence that the guardian
has physically seen the ward at least once a month and consulted with
the care facility at least that often.

Interdisciplinary evaluation teams, much like those described in the section on incompetency to stand trial, should be used.[101] These teams would include attorneys as well as a variety of mental health professionals. This would help ensure that the legal standards for incompetency are part of the review.

Several reforms could also reduce the invasion of autonomy when someone is partially disabled. Limited guardianships, as we have noted, are seldom used. States should require their use, and require that courts specifically justify any failure to use a limited guardianship. Particularly when personal decision making authority is removed, the basis for that form of incompetency should be clearly set out in writing. Other, voluntary legal mechanisms may reduce the need for incompetency proceedings. (These documents must be executed while the person is competent.) For example, greater use should be made of durable powers of attorney in lieu of formal incompetency hearings. A durable power of attorney appoints someone to make decisions should a person ever become unable to do so.[102] The use of specialized trusts, as well as documents such as living wills and treatment wills, should be used and recognized as a way of permitting extension of an incompetent person's decision-making authority.[103]

Perhaps the most important reform involves the standards used to define incompetency, which should be refined and more clearly stated. The philosophical basis for removing decision-making authority has not been adequately considered in most states. Current definitions lack a clear focus because no clear formulation exists about what it means to be incompetent. We noted earlier how powerful the declaration of incompetency is. Current definitions of incompetency are much too slender a reed to support this powerful concept. The breadth and vagueness of current definitions invite overuse, abuse, and inconsistent application of the law.

DEFINING INCOMPETENCY

We have repeatedly noted instances in which the definition of incompetency needs to be clarified. The search for a single precise definition of incompetency is undoubtedly the search for the Holy Grail.[104] Incompetency is used to refer to several different legal concepts which cannot be defined as precisely the same thing. In addition, Roesch and Golding suggest that competency is a construct that is evolving and changing and is not completely reducible to a set of rules.[105] Incompetency is situationally based; its existence depends on the task.

Even if we can never define competency in absolute terms as a single concept, we should endeavor to be as clear and precise as possible. There are two aspects to defining incompetency: first, we must describe the talents or abilities that are essential; second, we must establish the quality or level of achievement one needs. If, for example, we were to say someone must be able to read to perform a certain task, do we mean reading at the third-grade, seventh-grade, or college level?

Standards for Determining Incompetency

Decision-making capacity includes the ability to receive information and to understand that a decision must be made, the willingness to make the decision, the ability for some mental processing and manipulation that permits a decision to be made, and the ability to communicate the decision (or to carry it out oneself). The mental processing ability that is necessary to make one minimally capable of making a decision is difficult to establish.

In chapter 19 we suggest three mental functions establish the minimum mental processing for competency.

1. Memory must be adequate to permit a person to hold information in mind long enough to make a decision.

2. A competent person must be able to assess or recognize facts. In some instances, the ability to obtain factual data independently is a related necessary skill.

3. To be competent someone must have functional logic, *the ability* for some level of logical thinking. This allows the consideration and weighing of alternatives and options. It is not necessary that every decision be logical. It is, however, essential that the ability to engage in the logical thinking be present and available.

This formulation specifically avoids the consideration of values, beliefs, preferences, emotions, and feelings in deciding whether someone is or is not competent. These are the aspects of personality which autonomy rights are meant to protect.

Levels of Competency

The second inquiry is the level of impairment in any of the functions described above that will destroy competency. The nature and level of functioning in each of the areas should be determined in the context of the kinds of decisions that must be made and the consequences arising from an incorrect decision. The more harmful and permanent an injury that may result from a decision, the higher should be the level of functioning required of someone to be competent.[106]

SUMMARY

Incompetency is a very strong legal concept in a free society. Through it society removes the ability to make important decisions. In guardianship, for example, the ability to make personal care decisions and to control financial assets may be completely removed from a person. In this sense incompetency is even a stronger invasion of personal decision making than is involuntary civil commitment or punishment. This legal power, as well as the potential for abuse and the very vague standards that have been a part of incompetency determinations in the past, may make incompetency a major mental health civil rights issue of the future. The conflicting goals in incompetency are to protect autonomy and individual decision-making capacity as much as possible while protecting mentally disabled people from exploitation and unnecessary harm. Although incompetency plays a minor role in many legal areas, in three areas incompetency is of great importance: ability to stand trial, capacity to make a will, and guardianship.

Criminal defendants are generally considered incompetent to stand trial if they are unable to understand the charges against them, adequately to participate in their own defense, or understand the legal process. Defendants found incompetent to stand trial may be held for a reasonable time to determine if competency can be restored. If competency is restored, then a defendant may be tried. The issue of the competency to stand trial may be raised by the defense, the prosecution, or the judge. If there is cause to believe that a defendant may be incompetent then the person is sent for assessment (usually to a mental hospital). Following that there is a hearing to determine competency. Judges usually decide the competency issue, although they almost always follow the conclusions of mental health experts.

Professionals often confuse incompetency with the insanity defense, civil commitment, or psychosis. Several studies have examined the actual operation of incompetency to stand trial. A surprisingly small percentage of defendants sent for evaluation are in fact found incompetent to stand trial. There is great confusion among mental health experts concerning what is required to meet the legal test for incompetency. Courts depend heavily on the testimony of mental health experts, whose testimony is generally couched in conclusory terms, therefore mental health experts' confusion about incompetency to stand trial is likely to result in incorrect legal decisions.

We propose a number of reforms to improve the operation of incompetency to stand trial. These include the use of an interdisciplinary team, including a lawyer, to conduct the incompetency evaluation, the establishment of more definite standards for incompetency, and confidentiality for information revealed during assessment procedures. We also suggest that an enhanced hearing be held to determine that it is likely that the defendant has committed the crime. If the likelihood of guilt cannot be established, the defendant cannot be held by the state to reestablish competency.

A valid will requires that the person making it have testamentary capacity. The doctrine is meant to protect testators, their families, and society from irrational distributions of property that do not reflect the true wishes of the testator. Competency to make a will requires that people know what their property is, understand the natural objects of their bounty (family and friends), and be able to form an orderly plan for the distribution of property. An "insane delusion" that directly affects the provisions of the will may be the basis for invalidating part of the will.

Mental health experts may be asked to testify about the mental health of someone they may never have met and about the mental state of the person at the time the will was signed. There is some concern that it is not ethical for mental health experts to make these kinds of guesses about mental conditions.

Among the most important areas of incompetency is guardianship. People who are unable to make decisions for themselves may have a guardian appointed. The purpose is to protect these incompetent people from harm. The criteria for the appointment of guardians are ordinarily broadly stated as a person's "being unable to manage his affairs" or "unable to care for his property or himself." More modern standards are hardly more specific, sometimes referring to "impairment by reason of mental illness to the extent that he lacks efficient understanding or capacity to make or communicate responsible decisions."

Following the filing of a petition requesting that a guardian be appointed, the person is ordinarily examined by mental health professionals and a hearing is held to determine competency. If the person is incompetent, a guardian is appointed who assumes decision-making responsibility for the ward. There are provisions for another hearing to restore competency if the ward becomes able to again assume responsibility.

The concept of limited guardianship has been developed where a guardian is appointed to make only those kinds of decisions the ward is incapable of making; other decisions stay with the ward. Unfortunately, limited guardianships are apparently only infrequently used. In some cases, it is impossible to find a next of kin or a friend of the incompetent who is willing to assume the role of guardian. In such instances a public guardian, who may be employed by social service agencies, may assume the role.

Studies of the actual operation of guardianships suggest that they often do not operate in the interest of the people declared incompetent. Applications for guardianship are almost always granted, restoration to competency is very unusual, limited guardianships are rarely established, incompetency proceedings are subject to a large number of due process deficiencies, and a few private individuals hold guardianships for many wards. There may be a relationship between guardianship and the use of civil commitment for mental illness; the restrictions on the use of civil commitment may increase the use of guardianship or other forms of incompetency.

The current operation of guardianship should be modified. The process of determining incompetency should be tightened considerably, interdisciplinary evaluations should be used, periodic reviews of the condition of those found to be incompetent should be undertaken, the use of limited guardianship should be required, and the standards for determining incompetency should be much more clearly defined and limited.

Throughout the chapter the need for better definitions of incompetency is noted. The failure to provide clear and consistent definitions of incompetency has led to a system that encourages inconsistent and unfair exercise of an exceedingly strong interference with individual liberties. We believe that the efforts to define incompetency and to improve the operation of the legal system's determinations of incompetency will be a mental health imperative in the future. We provide a formulation to more precisely define incompetency in chapter 19.

NOTES

1. In some instances, incompetency may result from something other than mental capabilities—for example, from someone's inability to communicate or from a physical disability.

2. More than 30 legal areas have been identified involving incompetency, each requiring legal tests. Mezer & Rheingold, Medical Capacity and Incompetency: A Psycho-Legal Problem, 118 *Am. J. Psychiatry* 827 (1962).

3. See Poythress & Stock, Competency to Stand Trial: A Historical Review and Some New Data, 8 *J. Psychiatry & L.* 131 (1980); Silten & Tullis, Mental Competency in Criminal Proceedings, 28 *Hastings L. J.* 1053 (1977).

4. Dusky v. United States, 362 U.S. 402 (1960). For a general review of competency to stand trial see American Bar Association, *Criminal Justice Mental Health Standards* (approved 1984); George, The American Bar Association's Mental Health Standards: An Overview, 53 *Geo. Wash. L. Rev.* 338 (1985).

5. R. Roesch & S. Golding, *Competency to Stand Trial* 19 (1980). This work is an excellent review of theory and practice in competency to stand trial processes.

6. Ford v. Wainwright, 106 S. Ct. 2595 (1986). Nearly all states with death penalties recognize the right not to be executed while incompetent. Hazard & Louisell, Death, the State and the Insane: Stay of Execution, 9 *UCLA L. Rev.* 381 (1962); Kenner, Competency on Death Row, 8 *Int'l J. L. & Psychiatry* 253 (1986); Note, The Eighth Amendment and the Execution of the Presently Incompetent, 32 *Stan. L. Rev.* 765 (1980); Ward, Competency for Execution: Problems in Law and Psychiatry, 14 *Fla. St. U. L. Rev.* 35 (1986); Note, Insanity of the Condemned, 88 *Yale L. J.* 533 (1979).

7. In fact, the rejection of amnesia as the basis for incompetency to stand trial appears to be the position of the majority of courts. E.g., Hansford v. United States, 365 F.2d 920 (D.C. Cir. 1966); United States v. Sermon, 228 F. Supp. 972 (W.D. Mo. 1964); Cummins v. Price, 421 Pa. 396, 218 A.2d 758, *cert. denied*, 385 U.S. 869 (1966). To the extent that these cases are based on the proposition that amnesia does not automatically require a

determination of incompetency, they are probably correct. However, they seem to go too far toward suggesting that amnesia probably cannot be the basis for incompetency. It is possible that more recent decisions are moving toward a more realistic consideration of amnesia. See Wilson v. United States, 391 F.2d 460 (D.C. Cir. 1968) (discussed in note 8, *infra*); Commonwealth v. Lombardi, 378 Mass. 612, 393 N.E.2d 346 (1979).

8. In Wilson v. United States, 391 F.2d 460 (D.C. Cir. 1968), the court suggested that six factors should be considered in determining whether or not amnesia makes a defendant incompetent to stand trial: (1) the effects of the amnesia on the defendant's ability to assist his attorney, (2) the ability to testify in his own behalf, (3) the ability to reconstruct evidence even with the amnesia, (4) the degree to which the government assisted the defendant in that reconstruction, (5) the strength of the prosecution's case, and (6) "any other facts" relevant to determining whether a fair trial could be conducted even with the amnesia. *Id.* at 463–64. See Roesch & Golding, Amnesia and Competency to Stand Trial: A Review of Legal and Clinical Issues, 4 *Behav. Sci. & L.* 87 (1986).

9. Schoeller v. Dunbar, 423 F.2d 1183 (9th Cir. 1970) (Hufstedler, dissenting); Note, Competency to Plead Guilty: A New Standard, 1974 *Duke L. J.* 149.

10. Allard v. Helgemoe, 572 F.2d 1 (1st Cir.), *cert. denied*, 439 U.S. 858 (1978).

11. R. Roesch & S. Golding, *Competency to Stand Trial* 18–19, 71 (1980). See Pfeiffer, Eisenstein & Dabbs, Mental Competency Evaluations for Federal Courts, 144 *J. Nervous & Mental Disease* 320 (1967).

12. Roesch & Golding, *supra*, note 11, at 13, 50. These findings are consistent with Rosenberg & McGarry, Competency for Trial: The Making of an Expert, 128 *Am. J. Psychiatry* 82 (1972).

13. C. Kanno & P. Scheidemandel, *The Mentally Ill Offender: A Survey of Treatment Programs* 20 (1969); A. R. Matthews, *Mental Disability and the Criminal Law: A Field Study* (1970). See Steadman & Hartstone, Defendants Incompetent to Stand Trial, in *Mentally Disordered Offenders: Perspectives from Law and Social Sciences* 39 (J. Monahan & H. Steadman eds. 1983).

14. Geller & Lister, The Process of Criminal Commitment for Pretrial Psychiatric Examination: An Evaluation, 135 *Am. J. Psychiatry* 53 (1978); Golding, Roesch & Schrieber, Assessment and Conceptualization of Competency to Stand Trial, 8 *L. & Hum. Behav.* 321 (1984); Stone, Comment [on Geller & Lister article *supra*], 135 *Am. J. Psychiatry* 61 (1978).

15. Drope v. Missouri, 420 U.S. 162 (1975); Pate v. Robinson, 383 U.S. 375 (1966). See Bennett, A Guided Tour Through Selected ABA Standards Relating to Incompetency to Stand Trial, 53 *Geo. Wash. L. Rev.* 375 (1985).

16. See Roesch & Golding, *supra*, note 11, at 69–106; Bennett, Competency to Stand Trial: A Call for Reform, 59 *J. Crim. L. Criminology & Police Sci.* 569 (1968); McGarry, Competency for Trial and Due Process Via the State Hospital, 122 *Am. J. Psychiatry* 623 (1965).

17. Compare, Brown v. State, 245 So.2d 68 (Fla. 1971) [subsequent history omitted], with State v. Aumann, 265 N.W.2d 316 (Iowa 1978).

18. See A. L. McGarry, W. Curran, et al., *Competency to Stand Trial and Mental Illness* (1973); A. Stone, *Mental Health and Law: A System in Transition* 206–15 (1975); D. Wexler, *Criminal Commitments and Dangerous Mental Patients: Legal Issues of Confinement, Treatment and Release* (1976).

19. Roesch & Golding, *supra*, note 11, at 38–67. See Laben, Kashgarian, Nessa & Spencer, Reform From the Inside: Mental Health Center Evaluations of Competency to Stand Trial, 5 *J. Community Psychology* 52 (1977); Schreiber, Assessing Competency to Stand Trial: A Case Study of Technology Diffusion in Four States, 6 *Bull. Am. Acad. Sci. & L.* 439 (1978).

20. Lipsitt, Lelos & McGarry, Competency for Trial: A Screening Instrument, 128 *Am. J. Psychiatry* 105 (1971).

21. A. L. McGarry et al., *supra*, note 18.

22. See note 19, *supra*.

23. Maxson & Neuringer, Evaluating Legal Competency, 117 *J. Genetic Psychology* 267 (1970).

24. Bukatman, Foy & DeGrazia, What Is Competency to Stand Trial?, 127 *Am. J. Psychiatry* 1225 (1971).

25. The Laboratory of Community Psychiatry at Harvard, which produced the CST and CAI as part of a five-year project, also developed the Courtroom Apperception Test. The full discussion of the project is interesting and worth review. McGarry et al., *supra*, note 18. Regarding these evaluations generally see T. Grisso, *Evaluating Competencies: Forensic Assessments and Instruments* (1986).

26. Roesch, Jackson, Sollner, Eaves, Glackman & Webster, Fitness to Stand Trial Interview Test: How Four Professions Rate Videotaped Fitness Interviews, 7 *Int'l J. L. & Psychiatry* 115 (1984).

27. Golding, Roesch & Schrieber, Assessment and Conceptualization of Competency to Stand Trial, 8 *L. & Hum. Behav.* 321 (1984).

28. Shatin, Brief Form of the Competency Screening Test for Mental Competency to Stand Trial, 35 *J. Clinical Psychology* 464 (1979).

29. Burling & Saylor, Empirically Based Assessment of Competency to Stand Trial: Instrument Development and Preliminary Findings, 8 *Behav. Sci. & L.* 219 (1984).

30. McGarry, The Fate of Psychotic Offenders Returned for Trial, 127 *Am. J. Psychiatry* 1181 (1971). See Geller & Lister, The Process of Criminal Commitment for Pretrial Psychiatric Examination: An Evaluation, 135 *Am. J. Psychiatry* 53 (1978); Group for the Advancement of Psychiatry, *Misuse of Psychiatry in the Courts: Competency to Stand Trial* (1974); Steadman & Braff, Effects of Incompetency Determination on Subsequent Criminal Processing: Implications for Due Process, 23 *Catholic U. L. Rev.* 754 (1974).

31. Hess & Thomas, Incompetency to Stand Trial: Procedures, Results and Problems, 119 *Am. J. Psychiatry* 713 (1963). See B. Ennis, *Prisoners of Psychiatry: Mental Patients, Psychiatrists and the Law* (1972); T. Szasz, *Law, Liberty, and Psychiatry: An Inquiry into the Social Uses of Mental Health Prac-*

tices (1963); Foote, A Comment on Pretrial Committee of Criminal Defendants, 108 *U. Pa. L. Rev.* 832 (1960).

32. Jackson v. Indiana, 406 U.S. 715 (1972).

33. *Id.* at 738. Jackson had the mental capacity of a preschool child.

34. R. Roesch & S. Golding, *Competency to Stand Trial* 121–27 (table 5.2) (1980).

35. *Id.* at 117–19 (summarizes a dozen proposals for treatment limitations and disposition of charges).

36. In many instances, of course, the person who is incompetent to stand trial will also be incompetent to make personal-care decisions. In those cases, their consent to treatment must be obtained from a guardian. Whether a guardian should consent to treatment, to return an incompetent person to competency so he can stand trial may be a difficult question. Suppose the person is charged with a capital crime. It is not clear that it is in the incompetent's best interest to stand trial on the charge.

37. T. Gutheil & P. Appelbaum, *Clinical Handbook of Psychiatry and the Law* 265–66 (1982) note and reject this argument. See Smith, Psychiatric Approaches to the Mentally Ill Federal Offender, 30 *Fed. Probation* 23 (1966).

38. Winick, Psychotropic Medication and Competency to Stand Trial, 1977 *Am. B. Found. Research J.* 769. Winick found that while most courts have permitted defendants taking psychotropic medicine to stand trial, a significant minority do not permit it. Winick argues that the refusal to permit a trial while a defendant is taking medicine is a violation of the Constitution.

39. See Group for the Advancement of Psychiatry, *Misuses of Psychiatry in the Courts: Competency to Stand Trial* (1974); Haddox, Gross & Pollack, Mental Competency to Stand Trial While Under the Influence of Drugs, 7 *Loyola L.A. L. Rev.* 425 (1974); Winick, note 38 *supra.*

40. Comment, Antipsychotic Drugs and Fitness to Stand Trial: The Right of the Unfit Accused to Refuse Treatment, 52 *U. Chi. L. Rev.* 773 (1985).

41. An excellent review of the operation of competency to stand trial in one state, and of the literature, is contained in R. Roesch & S. Golding, *supra,* note 34.

42. The impact of competency to stand trial is not insignificant. It is estimated that there are 25,000 defendants evaluated annually for competency and more than $185 million spent on these evaluations (not including costs attributable to attorneys and court time). Winick, Restructuring Competency to Stand Trial, 32 *UCLA L. Rev.* 921, 922–38 (1985).

43. See Golding, Roesch & Schreiber, Assessment and Conceptualization of Competency to Stand Trial, 8 *L. & Hum. Behav.* 321 (1984); Stone, Comment, 135 *Am. J. Psychiatry* 61 (1978). See the citations in notes 30 to 35 *supra.*

44. Geller & Lister, The Process of Criminal Commitment for Pretrial Psychiatric Examination: An Evaluation, 135 *Am. J. Psychiatry* 53 (1978).

45. Department of Health Education and Welfare, *Legal Status of Inpa-*

tient Admissions to State and County Mental Hospitals (Statistical Note 105) 74–76 (1974); Joost & McGarry, Massachusetts Mental Health Code: Promise and Performance, 60 *A.B.A.J.* 95 (1974).

46. Roesch & Golding, *supra,* note 34, at 47–50.

47. Laczko, James & Alltop, A Study of 435 Court-Referred Cases, 15 *J. Forensic Sci.* 311 (1970); Steadman & Braff, Crimes of Violence and Incompetency Diversion, 66 *J. Crim. L. & Criminology* 73 (1975).

48. See note 11 *supra.*

49. Rosenberg & McGarry, Competency for Trial: The Making of an Expert, 128 *Am. J. Psychiatry* 82 (1972).

50. Roesch & Golding, *supra,* note 34, at 191–96.

51. *Id.*; McGarry, Competency for Trial and Due Process Via the State Hospital, 122 *Am. J. Psychiatry* 623 (1965); Pfeiffer, Eisenstein & Dabbs, Mental Competency Evaluation for Federal Courts, 144 *J. Nervous & Mental Disease* 320 (1967).

52. A number of the proposals for reform described here are consistent with suggestions made elsewhere. Many of these proposals are reviewed in R. Roesch & S. Golding, *supra,* note 34, at 201–20; American Bar Association, *Criminal Justice Mental Health Standards* (1984); Winick, Restructuring Competency to Stand Trial, 32 *UCLA L. Rev.* 921 (1985).

53. Roesch & Golding, *supra,* note 34, at 204. See Wulach, The Incompetency Plea: Abuses and Reforms, 8 *J. Psychiatry & L.* 317 (1980).

54. For a description of a variety of proposals for provisional trials, and objections to them, see Roesch & Golding, *supra,* note 34, at 209–16.

55. See Keeton & Gower, Freedom of Testation in English Law, 20 *Iowa L. Rev.* 326 (1935).

56. Epstein, Testamentary Capacity, Reasonableness and Family Maintenance: A Proposal for Meaningful Reform, 35 *Temple L. Q.* 231, 236–38 (1962); Houts, Alzheimer's Disease and Testamentary Capacity, 26 *Trauma* 1 (1985); Note, Testamentary Capacity: Is the Alcoholic Incapacitated?, 46 *Mont. L. Rev.* 437 (1985).

57. Epstein, *supra,* note 56, at 238.

58. S. Asch, *Mental Disability in Civil Practice* (1973); T. Atkinson, *Wills* 234 (2d ed. 1953). See Comment, Psychology and Law: An Examination of the Concept of Insane Delusion, 1960 *Wis. L. Rev.* 54.

59. Steinkuehler v. Wempner, 169 Ind. 154, 81 N.E. 482 (1907); Newman v. Dixon Bank and Trust, 205 Ky. 31, 265 S.W. 456 (1924); *In re* Hemingway's Estate, 195 Pa. 291, 45 A. 726 (1900).

60. E.g., *In re* Hemingway's Estate, *supra,* note 59; Appeal of Kimberly, 68 Conn. 428, 36 A. 847 (1896).

61. Regarding the use of various types of evidence, and concern about what courts really do with the evidence, see Green, Proof of Mental Incompetency and the Unexpressed Major Premise, 53 *Yale L. J.* 271 (1944).

62. Usdin, The Physician and Testamentary Capacity, 114 *Am. J. Psychiatry* 249, 254 (1957). See Bauer, Mental Illness and Will Contests, 13 *Colo. Law.* 985 (1984).

63. Pfeiffer, Eisenstein & Dabbs, Mental Competency Evaluation for the Federal Courts, 144 *J. Nervous & Mental Disease* 320, 321 (1967). See Spaulding, Testamentary Competency: Reconciling Doctrine with the Role of the Expert Witness, 9 *L. & Hum. Behav.* 113 (1985).

64. Epstein, *supra,* note 56; Green, Proof of Mental Incompetency and the Unexpressed Major Premise, 53 *Yale L. J.* 271 (1944).

65. T. Szasz, *Law, Liberty and Psychiatry: An Inquiry into the Social Uses of Mental Health Practices* 75 (1963).

66. Vatz, The "Psychiatric Will" Debate: Illogic and Hidden Agendas, 11 *J. Psychiatry & L.* 361 (1983).

67. Alexander, Premature Probate: A Different Perspective on Guardianship for the Elderly, 31 *Stan. L. Rev.* 1003 (1979); Jost, The Illinois Guardianship of Adults Legislation of 1978 and 1979: Protecting the Disabled From Their Zealous Protectors, 56 *Chi.-Kent L. Rev.* 1087 (1980).

68. This assumes a complete guardianship. Some jurisdictions provide for limited guardianships in which only some decision making authority is removed. Regarding the decision-making process for wards see S. Jordan, *Decision Making for Incompetent Persons: The Law and Morality of Who Decides* (1985).

69. For a short history of incompetency and guardianship see S. Brakel & R. Rock, *The Mentally Disabled and the Law* 250–51 (2d ed. 1971), and the excellent third edition cited, *infra,* note 70.

70. A broad review of statutory provisions concerning incompetency may be found in American Bar Association Commission on the Mentally Disabled, *Guardianship and Conservatorship* (1979); S. Brakel, J. Parry & B. Weiner, *The Mentally Disabled and the Law* (3d ed. 1986).

71. Nolan, Functional Evaluation of the Elderly in Guardianship Proceedings, 12 *L. Med. & Health Care* 210 (1984).

72. Wis. Stat. Ann. §§880.01(9), 880.03 (West Sup. 1984). This type of provision illustrates the need to narrow the basis for guardianships. Regan, Process & Context: Hidden Factors in Health Care Decisions for the Elderly, 13 *L. Med. & Health Care* 151 (1985) (noting ease of obtaining guardianships for the elderly).

73. A description of the hearing process is contained in S. Herr, S. Arons, & R. Wallace, *Legal Rights and Mental Health Care* 128–134 (1983).

74. Atkinson, Towards a Due Process Prospective in Conservatorship Proceedings for the Aged, 18 *J. Fam. L.* 819 (1980).

75. Morris, The Use of Guardianships to Achieve—Or Avoid—the Least Restrictive Alternative, 3 *Int'l J. L. & Psychiatry* 97 (1980).

76. See Brakel, Parry & Weiner, *supra,* note 70.

77. Frolik, Plenary Guardianship: An Analysis, A Critique, and a Proposal for Reform, 23 *Ariz. L. Rev.* 599 (1981); Comment, Guardianship of Incapacitated Adults, 1982 *Utah L. Rev.* 427.

78. American Bar Association, Commission on the Mentally Disabled, *Exercising Judgment for the Disabled: Report on an Inquiry into Limited Guardianship* (1979).

COMPETENCY 585

79. W. Schmidt, K. Miller, W. Bell & B. E. New, *Public Guardianship and the Elderly*, 167–77 (1981) (an excellent review of public guardianship); Schmidt, The Evolution of a Public Guardianship Program, 12 *J. Psychiatry & L.* 349 (1984).

80. A. Stone, *Mental Health and the Law: A System in Transition* 168–70 (1975); Mitchell, Involuntary Guardianship for Incompetents, 12 *Clearinghouse Rev.* 451 (1978).

81. Schmidt, et al., *supra*, note 79, at 169.

82. President's Commission on Mental Health, Task Force on Legal and Ethical Issues, *Report* (Vol. 4) 1395–97 (1978).

83. See Ross, Sterilization of the Developmentally Disabled: Shedding Some Myth-Conceptions, 9 *Fla. St. U. L. Rev.* 599 (1981); Note, Procreation: A Choice for the Mentally Retarded, 23 *Washburn L. J.* 359 (1984). The sterilization of incompetents in earlier years was particularly abusive. See Lombardo, Three Generations, No Imbeciles: New Light on *Buck v. Bell*, 60 *N.Y.U. L. Rev.* 30 (1985) (an excellent description of the misconduct that led to the involuntary sterilization of many considered to be incompetent to have children).

84. Sherlock & Sherlock, Sterilizing the Retarded: Constitutional, Statutory and Policy Alternatives, 60 *N.C. L. Rev.* 943 (1982); Note, *Ruby v. Massey*: Sterilization of the Mentally Retarded, 9 *Cap. U. L. Rev.* 191 (1979); Note, Sterilization Petitions: Developing Judicial Guidelines, 44 *Mont. L. Rev.* 127 (1983). The issues of sterilization are not fully settled. It may be unconstitutional for a state to prohibit all sterilization of incompetents. Mildred G. v. Valerie N., 40 Cal.3d 143, 707 P.2d 760, 219 Cal. Rptr. 387 (1985). But there are strict limits on the ability of guardians to consent to sterilization without court approval, Anonymous v. Anonymous, 469 So.2d 588 (Ala. 1985).

85. E.g., Superintendent of Belchertown v. Saikewicz, 373 Mass. 728, 370 N.E.2d 417 (1977); *In re* Quinlan, 70 N.J. 10, 355 A.2d 647, *cert. denied*, 429 U.S. 922 (1976); In the Matter of Storar, 52 N.Y.2d 363, 438 N.Y.S.2d 266, 420 N.E.2d 64, *cert. denied*, 454 U.S. 858 (1981).

86. Schmidt et al., *supra*, note 79, at 10.

87. Alexander, Who Benefits from Conservatorship?, 30 *Trial* 32 (May 1977).

88. Cohen, Protective Services and Public Guardianship: A Dissenting View, paper presented to Annual Meeting of the Gerontology Society, Nov. 20, 1978, quoted in W. Schmidt et al., *supra*, note 79, at 11. These difficulties may impose special obligations on mental health professionals to protect patient rights. Pleak & Appelbaum, The Clinician's Role in Protecting Patients' Rights in Guardianship Proceedings, 36 *Hosp. & Community Psychiatry* 77 (1985).

89. Mitchell, Involuntary Guardianship for Incompetents: A Strategy for Legal Service Advocates, 12 *Clearinghouse Rev.* 451, 466 (1978).

90. Schmidt et al., *supra*, note 79, at 14–15.

91. T. Gutheil & P. Appelbaum, *Clinical Handbook of Psychiatry and the Law* 227 (1982).

92. Schmidt et al., *supra*, note 79, at 172.

93. *Id.* at 172–73.

94. Mitchell, Involuntary Guardianship for Incompetents: A Strategy for Legal Services Advocates, 12 *Clearinghouse Rev.* 451 (1978); Nolan, Functional Evaluation of the Elderly in Guardianship Proceedings, 12 *L. Med. & Health Care* 210 (1984); Note, The Disguised Oppression of Involuntary Guardianship: Have the Elderly Freedom to Spend?, 73 *Yale L. J.* 676 (1964).

95. M. Blenkner, M. Bloom, M. Nielson & R. Weber, *Protective Services for Older People: Findings from the Benjamin Rose Institute Study* (1974); Berger & Piliavin, The Effect of Casework: A Research Note, 21 *Soc. Work* 205 (1976).

96. G. Alexander & T. Lewin, *The Aged and the Need for Surrogate Management* (1972).

97. Law & Kosberg, Abuse of the Elderly by Informed Care Providers: Practice and Research Issues, paper presented Annual Meeting of the Gerontological Society, Nov. 20, 1978, reported in Schmidt et al., *supra*, note 39, at 12. See Note, R. for the Elderly: Legal Rights (and Wrongs) Within the Health Care System, 20 *Harv. Civ. Rts.-Civ. Liberties L. Rev.* 425 (1985).

98. Schmidt et al., *supra*, note 79, at 173.

99. Gutheil & Appelbaum, *supra*, note 91, at 227–28; M. Kapp & A. Bigot, *Geriatrics and the Law: Patient Rights and Professional Responsibilities* (1985) (chapter 8 deals extensively with guardianship and other protective services); Cohen, Autonomy and Paternalism: Two Goals in Conflict, 13 *L. Med. & Health Care* 145 (1985) (arguing for limited paternalism and a service system that promotes autonomy).

100. The role of the attorney in the civil commitment process is discussed in chapter 17. Similar considerations apply to representation of clients in incompetency proceedings.

101. See Hafemeister & Sales, Interdisciplinary Evaluations for Guardianships and Conservatorships, 8 *L. & Hum. Behav.* 355 (1984).

102. Dickman, Court Enforcement of Durable Power of Attorney, 17 *U. San Fran. L. Rev.* 611 (1983).

103. Callahan, The Use of a Convertible Trust in Planning for Disability, 53 *N.Y. St. B. J.* 422 (1981).

104. Meisel, Lidz & Roth, Tests of Competency to Consent to Treatment, 134 *Am. J. Psychiatry* 279, 283 (1977).

105. Roesch & Golding, *supra*, note 41, at 11–13.

106. For an interesting review of applying different levels of competency to determinations of competency, see Drane, The Many Faces of Competency, 15 *Hastings Center Rep.* 17 (April 1985).

CHAPTER 17
INVOLUNTARY CIVIL COMMITMENT AND PREDICTIONS OF DANGEROUSNESS

Involuntary civil commitment is the process of hospitalizing mentally ill people who are dangerous (in some states, "gravely disabled"). The primary purpose of commitment is to prevent the mentally ill from harming themselves and to protect society from being harmed by them.

Civil commitment may be seen as one form of therapeutic intervention for dealing with certain antisocial or harmful behaviors. In that sense it is an alternative to punishment. There are similarities between imprisonment and civil commitment. Both result in an involuntary loss of freedom, and both carry a significant stigma. Because commitment is such a significant interference with liberty, it has become surrounded with procedural protections to prevent misuse.

The theory of commitment is, however, quite different than the criminal process in that it seeks to prevent injury through intervention and is not meant to be punitive in nature. The focus, therefore, is not what the patient has done in the past, but rather what he may do in the future.[1]

A distinction must be drawn between civil commitment and legal incompetency.[2] When someone is incompetent, a guardian is authorized to make decisions. In civil commitment, one may be hospitalized because of dangerousness even though completely competent to make decisions, and even over the rational objections of the patient.

In this chapter we briefly review the history of noncriminal commitment, and consider the commitment process, the bases for modern civil commitment, major ethical and legal issues in commitment, and proposed reforms. We then review the problems associated with the prediction of dangerousness.

HISTORY OF CIVIL COMMITMENT

There has been a great variety in treatment of the noncriminal deviant. In ancient times, some groups treated the insane with veneration, viewing them as persons who had been touched by God; other societies persecuted people with the same ailment, thinking they were possessed by devils.[3] By the middle ages there was in Europe a nearly uniform intolerance of deviants. The mentally ill or retarded were driven out of settlements. They were sometimes imprisoned, at other times transported to deserted colonies. At first, Colonial America treated the deviant in much the same way. Before long, however, an effort was made to treat these persons in a more humanitarian manner. Records dating back to 1689 indicate that some town governments paid their sheriffs to keep "mad men" in jail. In the early 1700s larger settlements built houses of correction to hold the "crazy," "vagrant poor," and retarded as well as criminals and delinquents. By 1773 the first hospital for the mentally deranged had been built in Williamsburg, Virginia.

Mental conditions were poorly defined and those we now consider mentally ill were treated the same as criminals and other deviants until the mid-1700s. Toward the end of the eighteenth century, chiefly as a result of the efforts of the French physician Pinel, noncriminal deviant behavior began to be regarded as an illness. The acceptance of the "medical model" of deviance led to a relative improvement in the lot of those held in mental hospitals. Fresh air, exercise, and proper diet and living quarters were provided some patients.

By the mid-nineteenth century many states allowed involuntary commitment under statutes that were extremely vague. Often they allowed husbands to commit their children or wives merely by obtaining the acquiescence of one physician who would sign commitment papers. Slowly reform movements began which sought to require greater specificity in commitment procedures.

In this century there have been numerous efforts to improve the lot of the involuntarily committed and to reduce their number. Serious debate concerning the rights of the mentally ill and the place of involuntary civil confinement in a free society has drawn renewed attention to the process of involuntary commitment. The debate ranges from whether it should be easier or more difficult to commit someone than it now is, to the procedures of commitment hearings, to the question of whether involuntary commitment should ever be permitted.[4]

The number of involuntarily committed patients in mental hospitals has, in recent years, been decreasing.[5] It has been estimated that about 30 to 40 percent of the patients in state and local public hospitals are involuntarily committed. It is, however, impossible to tell in how many of the "voluntary" admissions the patient was coerced to enter the hospital voluntarily under the threat of involuntary commitment.[6]

The reasons for the decrease in the number of involuntarily committed patients include the increased judicial supervision of the commitment process and the general trend toward deinstitutionalization of mental patients.

COMMITMENT PROCESSES

Every state has a civil commitment law, but these vary in the criteria and procedures used. State commitment laws have been modified frequently during the last two decades, with the tendency to narrow the grounds for commitment and to make the commitment process more detailed and complex. The commitment laws described in this chapter are based on the typical state law.[7]

Federal constitutional law is playing an increasingly important role in commitment law. The due process clause of the Fourteenth Amendment, the constitutional right of privacy, the prohibition on cruel and unusual punishment, and the First Amendment may limit the state's use of commitment. The Constitution requires reasonably fair commitment procedures and limits the criteria that a state may use to commit people.

The Process

Typically the civil commitment process is started through an emergency commitment when a mental health professional, peace officer, or hospital official fears that someone is dangerous and mentally ill. The professional arranges to have the person restrained at or taken to a mental health facility for examination. If it appears that the individual probably meets the standards for emergency detention, he is kept at the facility on an emergency basis. The detention generally continues for only two or three days, until a more careful and thorough review process can be undertaken.

The purpose of the emergency process is to provide for immediate action when someone is so dangerous that it is impractical to provide for judicial review of commitment. Theoretically, the loss of freedom will be for such a short time that no great harm will be done. At the same time, emergency does cause the loss of liberty for a period, and may carry a significant stigma.[8] Statutory changes and some court decisions have tried to ensure that emergency commitment is not abused. However, it appears that emergency commitment is the predominant route to commitment even when no real emergency exists.[9]

The commitment process may also be started by petitioning a court for a commitment warrant. After reviewing evidence supporting commitment, the court may have the person apprehended and held at the mental health facility. This "judicial" route to commitment should provide some greater protection against abuse because there is a limited hearing before the person is taken to the hospital.

After the patient is taken to, or held at, the mental health facility, he or she is examined by a mental health professional to determine that commitment is proper.[10] If the professional determines that the commitment is not proper, the patient is released. If it is proper, within a relatively short time (ranging from 7 hours to 20 days, depending on the state) a preliminary hearing before a judge is held. The purpose of this hearing is to provide a judicial determination that the patient is being properly held.[11] A full judicial hearing on the issue of commitment must be held, usually within 2 weeks, although states vary, allowing from 2 to 30 days to elapse.[12]

Hearings may be informal, and are generally held without a jury. Mental health professionals testify, and the patient has the opportunity to question them about their conclusions. Family members or others may present evidence, and the patient may call witnesses. Following the hearing the patient is committed or released. In some cases the commitment proceeding will be dismissed on condition that the patient voluntarily enter the hospital.[13]

In recent years the groups of medical and mental health professionals participating in the commitment process have increased considerably. For many years, in most states, only psychiatrists and other physicians were authorized to make commitment examinations. The use of physicians who were not psychiatrists created problems because the lack of behavioral science training often meant that they were not qualified to make psychiatric judgments.[14] It is now increasingly common for other professionals, including psychologists, social workers, and psychiatric nurses, to be part of the commitment process.

Release

In most states patients must be released from the mental health facility if they no longer meet the criteria for commitment. Ordinarily no judicial hearing is necessary to release a patient, and the patient may voluntarily stay at the hospital. In addition, of course, patients may be released following any hearing at which it is determined that the patient does not meet the criteria for commitment.

Procedural Rights

Many of the elements of due process commonly found in criminal cases are provided either by state statute or as a matter of constitutional right.[15] There is now broad agreement that a patient has the right to notice of the commitment hearing, to have an attorney present, to an impartial hearing officer, and to present evidence at the hearing. Some states grant the right to a jury trial. However, there is no right to bail, to a jury trial or to protection from self-incrimination.[16] In some instances the very nature of commitment patients makes these rights impossible to implement. For example, bail makes no sense for a person who is immediately suicidal.[17]

Another question that may arise in commitment hearings is the right to be free of psychotropic medication during the hearing. The drugs may, of course, prevent the patient from preparing for the hearing and from presenting the best defense possible. On the other hand, for many patients the drugs will greatly assist in making the best presentation to the court. Patients and their attorneys should therefore probably play a role in determining whether they will take medication that may affect their court appearances.[18] In any case, the court should be informed of the medication the patient has received prior to the hearing.

The degree to which the Constitution mandates the rights of patients has not yet been fully decided by the Supreme Court. The Court has, however, noted the great importance of commitment decisions and has suggested that special due process rights apply at commitment hearings. However, the Court has clearly refused to apply all criminal process rights to commitment hearings.[19] For example, the Court has held that a state is not constitutionally required to prove the need for commitment beyond a reasonable doubt, but is constitutionally required to prove the need for commitment by more than a preponderance of the evidence. Thus the state must prove the commitment case by "clear and convincing evidence," a standard between the usual civil and criminal standards.[20] The Court appears to see the Constitution providing significant due process protection to the commitment patient, but not as much due process protection as it provides criminals.[21]

Most states now establish a specified maximum period of commitment (without an additional hearing), or require periodic review of patients to determine if they should be released. In the not too distant past, indeterminant commitments were common and some patients were essentially committed for life without serious review. It is now unusual for commitment to extend for more than a year without review.

Criteria for Commitment

The requirements for commitment in most states are mental illness, and dangerousness to self or to others. (Some states consider one to be dangerous if "gravely disabled" or unable to provide for the necessities of life.) It is common for states to provide additional criteria for commitment, e.g. that treatment is available, or that the commitment is the least restrictive alternative available to the state to deal with the person. To be committed, a person must meet all of the criteria specified by the statute.

Most civil commitment statutes are fairly broad or leave the major terms poorly defined. "Mental illness" is often undefined or very broadly defined to include almost any mental condition—even those that are not serious. "Dangerous" is also often vague. It may refer to threats to persons, to property, to someone else's mental health, or to the tranquility of others; it may refer to relatively a minor threat or to a serious threat; it may involve threats to self or to others; it may be an immediate threat or a long-term threat. The tendency, by judicial decision or by statute, has been to define danger as a fairly serious, physical, imminent, threat to self or others.

The refusal of states to statutorily define dangerousness has left the issue to be decided by courts. State courts, however, have also been reluctant to provide clear and precise definitions of dangerousness, and behavioral experts examining patients are granted great latitude to, in effect, adopt their own definition of dangerousness.[22] As a consequence, this critical concept in commitment is likely to be applied very unequally among patients, and dangerousness may take on such an expanded meaning that it may become almost worthless.[23] A major deficiency in commitment laws today is that they do not clearly define the most critical word: dangerousness.

Although civil commitment is generally based on dangerousness, it could be based on any number of other concepts. Until recently it was common for states to provide commitment for someone mentally ill and in need of hospitalization, or mentally ill and not seeking needed treatment. Proposals are currently being debated which would broaden or change commitment to include a sophisticated form of the "in need of treatment" standard. One proposal, for example, is to permit commitment if the person will suffer severe distress associated "with significant impairment of judgment, reason, or behavior" causing a "substantial deterioriation" of ability to function on his own.[24] These proposals are based on the inability of the person to make decisions for themselves, and therefore resemble a form of incompetency rather than civil commitment.

It is clear that there are limits on the criteria that a state can use for civil commitment. It could not, for example, constitutionally commit someone for being a Republican or for believing in the theory of evolution or that the earth is flat. May a state, however, constitutionally commit someone who is mentally ill, but who is not immediately dangerous? The state might claim a strong interest not only in preventing physical harm to its citizens, but also in treating mental illness.[25]

The Supreme Court has not clearly defined the circumstances under which a state can commit a person. In *O'Connor v. Donaldson* the Court held that a state "cannot constitutionally confine, *without more,* a nondangerous individual who is capable of surviving safely in freedom by himself or with the help of willing and responsible family members or friends"[26] (emphasis added). In that case the Court was not called upon to decide whether it would be constitutional for the state to commit nondangerous people who could care for themselves. The case has been read by some as prohibiting the commitment of nondangerous people, and it is true that there is language in the decision that indicates that the Court might one day reach such a conclusion; it did not do so in the *O'Connor* case, however.

CIVIL COMMITMENT IN REALITY

The commitment process discussed above is essentially as described in statutes and judicial decisions. A number of studies, spanning more than a decade,[27] and our observations, suggest that in operation the system is often quite different. The process varies considerably from one locale to another, of course, but the following is probably a fair general description of the commitment process in many parts of the country.

A patient is usually brought to a mental hospital by a peace officer or upon the complaint of a member of his family. The patient may be given no psychiatric examination until after his arrival at the hospital. During the days between his arrival at the institution and the formal hearing, the patient is likely to be given treatment, generally in the form of medication. A few days before the hearing he will receive notice that it is forthcoming. Sometimes this notice is merely taped to the front of his chart.

The patient is likely to be seen by one or more court-appointed professionals before the hearing. An attorney may be appointed by the court; very few patients are represented by attorneys they have retained themselves. The attorney is likely to meet at least briefly with the patient before the hearing.

The hearing may involve little more than the professionals' report that the patient is mentally ill and dangerous, with few questions from the patients' attorneys. The judge will rely heavily, almost exclusively, upon the experts' testimony and will not release the patient if they agree that commitment is proper.

This process is slowly changing. A mental health bar with an interest and expertise in commitment and related issues is probably having an influence on their conduct. At the same time a number of behavioral scientists with expertise in the legal system are improving the quality of the evidence available to courts. It appears, however, that there is room for further improvement if the commitment statutes are to work as they are designed.

VOLUNTARY COMMITMENT

The above process, of course, does not prevent people from voluntarily entering a mental hospital regardless of whether they meet the criteria for commitment. In fact the commitment statutes in a number of states indicate a preference for voluntary admissions to hospitals.

Adults

Many technically voluntary admissions are related to civil commitment in that consent to hospitalization is gained on the threat that otherwise commitment proceedings will be initiated. This coerced admission is perhaps the civil commitment equivalent of plea bargaining. It has the advantage of avoiding court hearings and the stigma of involuntary commitment. On the other hand, it also operates without the protections of formal commitment, including the oversight of the judicial system. The appropriateness of this process may be of particular concern because the pressure is applied to people when their mental conditions make them most subject to coercion by mental health officials. In any case, it is likely that the effect of the civil commitment system extends well beyond those actually committed.[28]

Children

Traditionally parents have been responsible for making health care decisions for their children.[29] There are, however, limits on this right. We now recognize that child rearing rights of parents must be limited by some long-term interests of the child. Thus parents ordinarily cannot refuse lifesaving treatment or consent to permanent sterilization for a child.[30]

In *Parham v. J.R.* the Supreme Court considered whether minors should be permitted to refuse hospitalization on the basis of their own right of privacy, or whether parents should have the authority to overrule these objections on the basis of the parent's right of child rearing.[31] The Court rejected the argument that a full adversary hearing is necessary every time a child is admitted to a mental hospital. At the same time the Court noted that there are risks to important rights of minors in allowing parents to institutionalize their children for mental health care without some review. Therefore the Court held that some inquiry should be made by a "neutral factfinder" to determine whether or not institutionalization is appropriate and in the best interests of the child. The child's need for continuing commitment must also be reviewed periodically by an independent neutral factfinder.[32] It is interesting to note that while the Court felt some review of admissions decisions was necessary, it was willing to leave that review to mental health professionals rather than to judges. It also left the standards for making the decision very broad.

It appears that most older minors make decisions like adults, and it would be appropriate to recognize their interests in avoiding unwanted commitment.[33] The criticism of the Court's decision in *Parham* has been directed at its failure to adequately understand the competency and interests of adolescents.

Other Forms of Commitment

There are forms of incarceration that are in some ways similar to commitment. These systems have received less notice than civil commitment, and are generally less important. The commitment of those abusing or addicted to alcohol or drugs is perhaps most closely related to civil commitment of the mentally ill. It is based on a form of *parens patriae* and, perhaps, incompetency concepts.[34]

Criminal defendants found not guilty by reason of insanity may be committed. The state must in some manner show, or be able to reasonably imply, that the defendant meets the criteria for commitment. It cannot automatically commit someone for a significant period of time on the basis of the insanity verdict alone.[35] The state may be able to use an insanity verdict as a presumption that the defendant is mentally ill and dangerous.[36] The state may continue the commitment only so long as the defendant/patient meets the appropriate criteria, but the commitment may last longer than the maximum prison term for the crime with which the defendant was charged,[37] and the defendant may have to prove the *absence* of dangerousness to secure release.[38]

Criminal defendants who are incompetent to stand trial may be incarcerated for treatment of the mental condition. The purpose of this incarceration is different from commitment. It is directed at restoring sufficient competency to defendants to permit them to stand trial. This incarceration may occur whether or not the defendant is dangerous. If there is no reasonable possibility that the defendant will become competent, the state cannot continue to hold the person incompetent to stand trial without proceeding through the commitment process.[39] The state may impose treatment aimed at restoring competency even over the objection of the patient. In this way the incompetency to stand trial commitment may be more powerful than ordinary civil commitment. Both provide for incarceration without conviction of a crime, but it is probably easier to impose treatment through the incompetency process.[40]

Sexual psychopath laws, described in chapter 14, also have elements of commitment, although they are based on past sexual criminal conduct and are therefore more clearly punitive than is civil commitment. Incompetency in some cases has aspects of civil commitment, as was discussed in the previous chapter.

The institutionalization of the mentally retarded is permitted through processes common to civil commitment. In reality, however, these are competency decisions because they are based on the mental inability of the retarded person to make personal decisions.[41]

PROFESSIONAL ROLES

Mental health professionals and lawyers play several roles in the civil commitment process. Sometimes these roles are unusual or even inconsistent with the parts they customarily play in the legal system.

Mental Health Professionals

Mental health professionals play two major roles in commitment, expert witness and decision maker. As expert witnesses in commitment hearings, they are asked to assess whether or not patients are mentally ill and whether they are dangerous.[42] In almost all commitment cases in which mental health professionals testify, they are appointed by the court rather than any interested party. This, of course, differs from the usual civil or criminal case.

Perhaps in part because of their impartiality, mental health professionals appear to have a much greater impact in commitment hearings than in almost any other area of the law. Their opinion that a patient meets the criteria for commitment almost always results in the commitment of the patient, and it is extremely unusual for a judge to decide a commitment case against the advice offered by the mental health experts.[43] An additional reason for the deference to the experts is that the issues in commitment hearings (mental illness and dangerousness), rightly or wrongly, appear to judges to be those mental health experts are uniquely qualified to decide. Still another reason is that courts are at a loss about how to make such judgments, and fear that predicting incorrectly can cause real trouble. Relying completely on mental health experts may be a handy way for judges of letting someone else make the tough decisions.

Another unusual aspect of the testimony presented by mental health professionals in civil commitment hearings is that cross-examination is often superficial or nonexistent.[44] Its absence can probably be attributed to the lack of preparation of many attorneys in commitment proceedings, to the modification of the adversary process in the hearings, and to the fact that the experts have not been called by a party in interest.

In commitment cases mental health experts are decision makers, an unusual role for them in the legal process. They determine when most patients who are committed will be released. In this sense they determine whether the power of the state should continue to be used to restrain the patient, which is somewhat different than the usual decision to discharge a patient from a hospital. The decision to discharge a voluntary patient is medical, while the decision to release an involuntary patient is partly a legal question. Thus, the decision to release requires knowledge of the legal test to be used to determine whether the patient may be retained as a patient, as well as a medical judgment concerning the patient's condition. In this role mental health experts should not act as advocates for the patient, nor even necessarily in the best interest of the patient; they should decide whether the patient fits the legal criteria for commitment.

Attorneys

The role of attorneys in the commitment process is often unclear. Attorneys are usually obligated to zealously represent their clients. When incarceration is possible, that generally means seeking freedom for the client. Attorneys do not decide whether a case should be won or lost for the client based on the client's best interest. It would be an unusual, and unethical, attorney who did not mount a defense to a criminal case on the theory that a prison term would "be a good thing" for the client, or good for society.

The appropriate role of attorneys representing clients is not as clear in commitment hearings, however. This question is not a small one, because as a matter of statutory right—and perhaps constitutional right—almost all commitment patients have the right to counsel.[45] There are at least two schools of thought about the appropriate role of the attorney representing a patient in a commitment hearing: (1) paternalistic: the attorney should seek to do what she thinks is best for the patient, even if that is involuntary commitment; (2) adversarial: the obligation of the attorney is to act, as usual, as an advocate seeking to preserve the client's freedom by all legal and ethical means available.[46] In the past most attorneys who participated in the commitment system seem to adopt the first approach.[47]

Part of the confusion concerning the role of attorneys comes from a lack of clarity about whether commitment hearings are adversarial. If they are, then it is surely the obligation of the attorney to act as advocate for the patient. If they are inquisitorial (a system of justice not commonly found in this country), then the obligation of advocacy is not as strong.

Although the ideal of an informal process, without advocates, has some theoretical attraction, the attraction is less strong in practice. If a patient retains a private attorney the patient can expect, and demand, forceful advocacy from the attorney. It is contrary to our usual notions of fairness to permit effective advocacy only for those rich enough, or savvy or competent enough, to retain private counsel. The ethical obligation of an attorney cannot rest on being court appointed or privately retained. Beyond that, commitment hearings involve citizens who are often least able to be advocates on their own behalf and who often have only a vague notion of what the hearings will be like. The hearings often involve complex expert opinions in an area notoriously inexact. Under such circumstances it is particularly important that there be aggressive challenges to the testimony and that an advocate protect the interests of those who are often not in good positions to protect their own interests.

On the other hand, it is essential that both sides of the issue in controversy be represented. In some instances in which the attorney for the patient is actively opposing commitment there is no attorney forcefully representing the procommitment position. This half-an-adversarial approach may result in only part of the relevant information being presented to the court, and lead to bad decisions.[48]

Another source of confusion regarding the role of the attorney is that the patient/client may be unable or unwilling to issue instructions. Many do not express strong opinions about what they want the attorney to do. One approach is to assume, if there is any question of competency, that the goal should be to work to avoid commitment because if the patient wishes to voluntarily stay at the hospital, the patient may choose to do so. If the patient is incompetent to decide whether or not to stay, there are legal proceedings which should be undertaken to declare the patient legally incompetent. Absent such a proceeding, the argument goes, the patient should be presumed competent and therefore have the opportunity to leave the hospital. The other approach is that if there is a question of competency it is the attorney's role to help determine what is best for the client and work for that, whether the client wants it or not. This latter position is again somewhat inconsistent with the role of the attorney in other settings, and it is probably inappropriate to expect attorneys alone to decide whether or not a client is competent.[49]

ISSUES AND REFORMS

Involuntary civil commitment is a powerful device in a free country. It permits a major invasion of individual freedom based on a prediction of what someone will do in the future. It is not surprising, therefore, that great controversy surrounds commitment and that there are many proposals to reform it.

Should Mental Illness Be the Basis for Commitment?

The existence of mental illness is the basis for commitment. Only dangerous people who are mentally ill are committed; dangerous people who are not mentally ill are not. This has been criticized on several grounds: mental illness does not exist; even if mental illness does exist it cannot be determined with sufficient accuracy to be the basis for legal decision making; and it is improper to draw distinctions between groups of dangerous people based on mental illness.

A few people take the view that mental illness is not really an illness, but just behavior patterns that society finds unacceptable. Under this distinctly minority view commitment is seen as a method of social control "punishing" behavior that is not illegal, but which we find annoying.[50] If one accepts this view of mental illness, it is difficult to justify any commitment based on mental illness. Instead people should be responded to on the basis of what they do.

Others take the view that in practice the diagnosis of mental illness is uncertain and often inaccurate,[51] or that much of what is labeled mental illness is really just undesirable or bothersome conduct.[52] The issue of whether the definition of mental illness is sufficiently precise and certain to be used in critical legal decisions cannot be said to have been resolved. Nevertheless, there does not appear to be any effort to abandon the concept in commitment laws.

Perhaps the most serious attack is whether it is rational to commit dangerous people only if they are mentally ill, rather than *all* dangerous people regardless of mental status.[53] Three rationales might be suggested for committing the dangerous mentally ill: (1) through the insanity defense we provide that the insane cannot be held responsible for their actions and on the same basis we can commit them to protect them and us; (2) mental illness and dangerousness are so closely connected that it is rational to depend on mental illness for commitment; (3) the mentally ill cannot rationally choose what to do and they therefore should be treated differently.

Upon close examination, none of these rationales is persuasive. Commitment of the mentally ill extends well beyond those who could successfully use the insanity defense. Therefore commitment in lieu of criminal responsibility cannot be a legitimate basis for dividing the mentally ill from the "mentally well." Limiting commitment to those who because of mental illness could not tell right from wrong or conform their conduct to the requirements of the law might provide a rational basis for committing the mentally ill, but commitment is not so limited.

Mental illness and dangerousness are certainly not synonymous. In fact there does not appear to be any major difference between the level of dangerousness of the mentally ill and the mentally well.[54]

The claim that the mentally ill cannot, like others, decide whether or not to engage in dangerous behavior is really a claim that they are incompetent to make decisions for themselves. If that is the case, they are incompetent and should be treated as such whether or not they are dangerous. Even if there is incompetency or impaired judgment because of mental illness, such people may not be any more dangerous than fully competent people.

The question of mental illness and dangerousness might be turned around: why commit only the dangerous mentally ill? Why not commit all the mentally ill (or at least those who could benefit from hospitalization)? At one time it was in fact common to commit, under a *parens patriae* theory, anyone who was in need of treatment. This is much less common today. It is not certain that nondangerous commitment is constitutionally valid.[55] Theoretically there is a much stronger state interest in committing the dangerous than the nondangerous (whether mentally ill or not). By committing the dangerous the state is protecting the lives of citizens and avoiding unnecessary physical injuries. Such an interest does not exist for those who pose no danger.

Are the Criteria for Commitment Too Broad?
Are They Too Narrow?

There is considerable disagreement about the proper criteria for commitment. Major issues in the debate recently have included the proper definition of dangerousness, the propriety of committing patients for their own good or because they are in need of treatment, and requiring that the "least restrictive alternative" be considered in commitment decisions. We have noted that the tendency has been to narrow the grounds for commitment. Commonly, although not universally, dangerousness and mental illness are now required, although there are different definitions of dangerousness.[56]

The criteria for commitment that one supports depends in large part on one's philosophy of individual freedom and the proper role of government. Someone who believes that liberty is extremely important is likely to disagree with the incarceration of the mentally ill to prevent minor damage or because someone is seriously mentally ill. Those who believe that nobody can really be free while afflicted by a mental illness may approve the commitment of those refusing to seek available treatment.

Disagreements about the criteria also reflect different views about several practical aspects of commitment. For example, perceptions about the consequences of commitment to the patient, and the ability to accurately determine who meets the criteria, affect opinions on those criteria. The more negative the net consequences of commitment are perceived to be, the more one is likely to oppose broad criteria that will expand the number of people committed. The less confident someone is of the ability to correctly determine who meets the criteria for commitment, the less likely one is to favor an expansion of the criteria, because the expansion may result in the wrongful commitment of a greater number of people.[57]

Our view is that the criteria for commitment should be narrowly stated and applied. Serious physical dangerousness to self or others should define dangerousness. This is not to ignore other kinds of harm, such as injury to property or emotional injury. However, commitment is a very significant invasion of liberty and it is proper for society to exercise this kind of power only for the most compelling reasons, when the harm threatened is fairly catastrophic. Our view is fortified by a low level of confidence in the accuracy of predictions (overpredictions) of dangerousness. The tendency of definitions of dangerousness to "expand" also argues for narrow commitment criteria. "Harm to property" may become writing bad checks,[58] and "emotional harm" may become injury to family members in seeing a loved one act crazy or go without treatment for an emotional condition.[59] Broad criteria for commitment invite an extremely broad application of commitment to the unusual, the bothersome, and the difficult.

There has been some move toward permitting commitment for those "gravely disabled" or "in need of treatment." The American Psychiatric Association has proposed such an approach which has been adopted by a few states.[60] We would reject these *parens patriae* commitments. Treatment without consent should be undertaken with adults only for the most extraordinary reasons. Treatment should be forced on a nondangerous person only if he is incompetent, and civil commitment should not be used in place of the formal incompetency process. Many nondangerous, mentally ill people are competent to make decisions, and they should be permitted to decide whether they want treatment, including hospitalization. In addition, commitment should be permitted only if it is the least restrictive method available to the state to deal with the dangerousness.[61] If, say, outpatient therapy is likely to succeed, then the state should be required to pursue that approach.

Is the Process of Commitment Adequate?

The proper process to follow in commitment is a debate which tends to divide along lines related to views about commitment, with those opposing commitment favoring rigorous procedures, and those supporting very broad commitment laws favoring more limited ones. The debate over procedures is often really a debate over the substantive issue of commitment criteria.

One important element of the debate over process is the degree to which commitment decisions should be left to mental health professionals and the degree to which decisions should be made by judges. We have seen that mental health professionals now effectively make most commitment decisions. This rather extraordinary reliance on

experts is legitimate if they understand the legal criteria for commitment and are particularly adept at predicting dangerousness and assessing mental illness. There is reason to believe that predictions of
dangerousness are not particularly reliable. When mental health
professionals make decisions that directly affect legal rights, it is essential that they fully understand, and be willing to implement, the
law. There is reason to believe that there is often confusion about
legal criteria in commitment.

Can the Commitment Process Work in the Real World?

As we noted earlier, the actual operation of commitment often varies
considerably from the way the law is written. The law in practice
seldom matches perfectly the law in theory, so the question should
probably be: How closely can the operation of the commitment law
match the commitment law in theory? A key to this question may
rest with the attorneys representing patients. Ordinarily an attorney
for a client will ensure that the client's procedural rights are protected; no other participant is likely to protect these rights if the
attorney does not. If attorneys for patients do not act as fairly aggressive advocates for patients, it is unlikely that the procedures used
in the commitment process will match the statutory requirements.

Even if the procedural rights are ensured, several factors may con-
found the intended operation of the law. Predictions of dangerousness are, as we shall see, difficult, uncertain, and speculative—the
kinds of decisions which are subject to caprice and abuse. This may
lead to guessing about whether a person is dangerous, or a decision
based on factors other than dangerousness. A mental health expert
who believes a patient should be hospitalized may be tempted to
testify to dangerousness because that is the "button" that will get the
patient committed. And it would be difficult to prove the testimony
wrong. The strong reliance on the conclusion of experts often without significant cross-examination may also encourage weakly supported conclusions. Judges often know so little about mental health
principles and are reluctant to actually make the decisions concerning
dangerousness that they effectively turn over the decisions to the
mental health experts. Given the nature of the decisions in the commitment area and the absence of reliable predictions of dangerous-

ness, it is likely that commitment practice will not match theory. This may lead to one of several conclusions: that the system should be tightened to eliminate variance between theory and practice, that the basis for commitment should be narrowed to take account of the variance in the system, that the variance is something that will just have to be tolerated, or that the variance is an argument for abolishing the commitment system.[62]

Should Civil Commitment Be Abolished?

Several arguments are made for abolishing involuntary commitment or at least greatly limiting it: commitment does not work in practice and is often used to remove people who are bothersome; it is morally wrong for society to incarcerate someone on the basis of what he or she might do in the future rather than on the basis of past misconduct; most dangerous patients could be treated in a less restrictive setting; and the existence of mental illness is not a reasonable basis of classification on which to base loss of freedom. As we shall see shortly, another argument for eliminating commitment is that dangerousness cannot be predicted with sufficient accuracy to justify making decisions.

The arguments in favor of civil commitment are: the system is effective in preventing needless injury and death to, and by, the mentally ill; it is a caring act of kindness to prevent these people from harming themselves or others; and it is a legitimate function of society to prevent serious harm. Proponents may also argue that even if there are mistakes and some mentally ill are committed who are not dangerous, great harm is not necessarily done to the person who probably needed treatment and as a result of commitment received some therapy. The alternative to commitment, they argue, is imprisonment for misconduct or additional deinstitutionalization, resulting in terrible conditions for the mentally ill, who are often on the streets without protection or necessities of life.[63]

The issues in the debate concerning civil commitment and treatment are important, but at times the debate has been unnecessarily harsh. Perhaps this is because of the failure to recognize that the disagreements reflect good faith differences in values concerning the nature of freedom, autonomy, paternalism, and mental illness. It also results from failing to properly identify fundamental issues, e.g., recognizing nondangerous commitment as a question of competency.

Much of the debate concerning abolition may really be about narrowing the basis for commitment. Most would agree that it makes sense to restrain someone who is about to jump off a bridge because voices are telling him to do so. Making threatened or attempted suicide a crime is one way to restrain the person through prison; civil commitment is another way. Commitment includes the flexibility to permit release when treatment is no longer needed rather than when a sentence is served. The bridge example does not, however, express the circumstances in which most commitments occur. When the threat is less certain or the harm less grave, the consensus disappears. Even when the statutes have been written to require the threat of serious physical harm, it appears that the laws are applied much more broadly. Commitment is too often a handy instrument to deal with less serious problems.

Whatever the disagreements about values and other issues in the commitment debate, under most laws the issue of the prediction of dangerousness is critical. Civil commitment ultimately must depend on the ability accurately to predict who is dangerous. Otherwise, it is little more than a lottery.

PREDICTING DANGEROUSNESS

The prediction of dangerousness has become an increasingly important legal issue. Behavioral scientists are now called upon to predict dangerousness not only for commitment, but also in proceedings to decide whether a criminal defendant should be executed or not,[64] to determine whether an offender should be released on parole or probation,[65] to decide whether an involuntary patient should be required to accept treatment because of dangerousness,[66] and for a variety of other purposes.[67] Paradoxically, as the law has increased its reliance on the ability of professionals to predict dangerousness, the evidence that they are unable to do so with accuracy has increased.

It is now widely accepted that long-term predictions of dangerousness are not very accurate.[68] Major professional organizations have recognized the inaccuracy. For example, the American Psychological Association through a report[69] and the American Psychiatric Association through briefs filed with the Supreme Court[70] have called such predictions unreliable. Both legal and social science scholars have concluded that predictions of dangerousness are unreliable and ordinarily not an adequate basis on which to make many legal decisions.[71] There is some hope expressed that predictions of violent behavior may reach 50 percent "among some groups of clinical interest,"[72] although even this is optimistic.

It is virtually impossible to do controlled studies to determine the accuracy of predictions of dangerousness. One obviously cannot identify a group of people predicted to be dangerous and then randomly release half of them and commit half of them. However, several "natural studies" have been conducted. Ordinarily these occur when patients are released or placed in less restrictive incarceration over the objection of professionals who have predicted the patients to be dangerous. The study consists of reviewing the dangerousness of the released-but-predicted-dangerous patients by determining the number who commit dangerous acts. For example, such studies were possible when a court decision resulted in the transfer from criminal or civil hospitals of about a thousand people classified as extremely dangerous.[73] Studies of these patients did not find that they were particularly dangerous, even though they had all been predicted to be so.[74]

As is true with most natural experiments, these studies have methodological problems, particularly in gathering sufficient information about the patients to determine whether or not such persons actually committed violent or dangerous acts. However taken together the studies do provide significant information about predictions of dangerousness in practice.

Reviewing these and other studies, Monahan concluded that "the 'best' clinical research currently in existence indicates that psychiatrists and psychologists are accurate in no more than one out of three predictions of violent behavior." This one-in-three accuracy rate was found over a period of years among institutionalized patients diagnosed as mentally ill.[75]

The prediction of dangerousness is difficult because it really involves more than an assessment of the mental condition or prediliction of the patient. Whether someone will be violent or not may be seen as depending upon at least three factors: mental emotional condition, the circumstances of environment in which one is placed, and the dynamics of the interaction between the emotional condition and the environment. Someone may be dangerous in one set of circumstances, but not dangerous under others. Therefore the prediction of dangerousness requires not only a correct assessment of the emotional condition of someone, but also a prediction of the circumstances or environment that the person will experience, and an understanding of the interaction of that mental condition and that environment. An analogy is predicting whether someone will have a diabetic coma. This requires not only a knowledge of whether or not the person has diabetes, but also a prediction of whether the patient will take the correct amount of insulin, what he will eat, and the interaction between the food and the amount of insulin taken. Accurately assessing emotional conditions is often more difficult than diagnosing physical conditions, but accurately predicting environmental factors is beyond the bounds of science.

It is possible that short-term predictions of dangerousness may be more accurate than long-term ones. Short-term predictions with careful efforts to find all violent acts may provide accurate rates above those long-term rates described above.[76] It remains to be seen whether these rates will be duplicated, but it is reasonable to expect that the accuracy of short-term predictions is higher.[77] Predictions of outpatient dangerousness may also be more accurate than those concerning long-term institutional patients. There is also some hope that improved testing and the use of actuarial methods may improve predictions.[78]

The difficulty in predicting dangerousness, of course, results in some underpredictions (incorrect predictions that someone is not dangerous), but it results in very substantial overprediction (incorrect prediction that someone is dangerous). Two major factors for the overprediction can be identified here: the low base rate of actual dangerousness and the comparative consequences to the predictor of incorrect false positives and false negatives.

The number of people who will be violent over a given period is very small. Therefore even small rates of incorrect predictions of dangerousness will result in a relatively large number of people predicted to be dangerous.[79]

The consequences of an incorrect prediction encourage overprediction. A false prediction of dangerousness will result in the hospitalization of the patient (who the professional probably sees as needing help anyway) with few negative consequences to the professional. A false prediction of non-dangerousness has the real possibility of bad publicity, blame for releasing a dangerous person, and a potential lawsuit.

Policy Implications

What are the policy implications of data concerning the predictions of dangerousness? We should not depend on these predictions when we require a high degree of dependability for the evidence on which decisions are made. Particularly when we cannot tolerate a high false positive rate, such as in the criminal law where we require a high level of confidence to convict someone, these predictions should not be depended upon. For example, the mental health professions have suggested that the use of such predictions in capital sentencing is not appropriate because society is anxious to avoid wrongfully sentencing anyone to death.[80] Opinions from experts concerning dangerousness deserve very close examination and testing, generally including cross-examination. Experts who testify that they are certain about long-term dangerousness are making a ridiculous claim. Unfortunately in our opinion, the Supreme Court has approved such testimony.[81]

Given the inaccuracies of predictions of dangerousness, it may be questioned whether mental health experts ought to present opinions on the topic at all. A decision to not give such opinions might be based on the feeling that the testimony is so speculative not to be scientific, or that mental health experts are being exploited to make decisions on unstated criteria (e.g., race, sex, age) which courts are unwilling to make.[82] There are no ethical requirements that specifically prohibit testimony regarding dangerousness, so each professional is left to decide whether or not to present such opinions to courts.[83]

Should predictions of dangerousness be used as the basis for involuntary civil commitment? The predictions of dangerousness are so inaccurate, the invasion of liberty so substantial, and the opportunity for misusing the prediction of dangerousness so great, that we believe the use of predictions of dangerousness in commitment should be limited. There should be a strong presumption that one is not dangerous. The reasons for predicting someone to be dangerous should be clearly stated and narrow. Although they should provide factual information about patients, experts should not be permitted to testify to the conclusion that someone is or is not dangerous. There is no reason to believe that experts are any better at predicting dangerousness than anyone else, and therefore no reason to permit the prediction as testimony.[84]

SUMMARY

Civil commitment is the process of involuntarily hospitalizing mentally ill people who are thought to be dangerous. Commitment is ordinarily based on the existence of mental illness and predictions of future dangerousness, although some states include other commitment criteria, such as a requirement that hospitalization be the least restrictive alternative. Debate continues over the proper criteria to use in commitment. Some would replace or supplement dangerousness by permitting commitment when it is in the best interest of the patient.

Commitment is most often initiated through emergency processes that permit mental health professionals or others to hold patients or to take them to a mental health facility. Commitment may also be initiated by applying to a court for authority to have someone committed to a mental hospital. Whether initiated through an emergency or a judicial process, the initial commitment must be reviewed by a court with a full hearing prior to any long-term commitment. At this hearing involuntary patients have many, but not all, of the procedural rights afforded to criminal defendants. There has been a tendency to increase the formality of the process or to "legalize" commitment.

The actual operation of the commitment system is not consistent with the system described in the law books. Commitment hearings are often little more than a report by mental health experts of their findings and opinions, often unchallenged by patients' attorneys. Dangerousness is often not defined in the statutes. The absence of such definitions, and of challenges to expert conclusions, invites an extremely broad interpretation of dangerousness, and in some instance may mean only that the patient could profit from hospitalization.

Patients are released from involuntary commitment when they are determined by mental health professionals to no longer meet one or more of the criteria for commitment. Ordinarily this decision to release a patient does not have to be approved by a court. Professionals often play roles that are unfamiliar in the legal system, as when mental health professionals decide when patients no longer meet legal criteria for commitment. The proper role for attorneys representing patients in commitment proceedings is not settled. Ordinarily the role of an attorney is to provide zealous representation. There is debate over whether the attorney should seek to do what the attorney believes is best for the client (including permitting commitment), or whether the attorney should always seek freedom for the client.

Many important issues about civil commitment have been raised, including whether mental illness is a proper basis for commitment (why commit only those dangerous people who are mentally ill?), whether the criteria for commitment are too broad, whether *parens patriae* commitment should be permitted, whether the commitment process is adequate, whether commitment can ever work properly in the real world, and whether civil commitment should be abolished or substantially limited. Commitment based on predictions of future dangerousness is a powerful interference with individual liberty. In light of this and of the overprediction of dangerousness we have argued that for competent adults commitment should be limited to extraordinary circumstances involving threats of immediate serious physical harm. Proposals to permit commitment when someone is "in need of treatment" or "gravely disabled" are basically claims of incompetency and would be better handled as such.

Predictions of dangerousness are at the heart of the civil commitment process and several other important legal decisions. There is strong evidence that long-term predictions of future dangerousness are not very accurate. Short-term predictions may be more accurate, but even these probably involve substantial overprediction. The legal system should be cautious of predictions of dangerousness and should carefully examine experts on their bases for such predictions. Particularly when we are unwilling to tolerate a high false positive rate (e.g., in capital sentencing) predictions of dangerousness should not be the basis of decision making.

NOTES

1. The term "patient" refers to one who is subject to a civil commitment process, or the "respondant" in such a process. Some may object that it is

inappropriate to label as a "patient" one held involuntarily by the state, and that calling detainees "patients" suggests an inappropriate role for them. The term is commonly used, and appropriate or not, these people are generally treated as patients by the institutions in which they are held.

2. Some states permit the commitment of one who is "gravely disabled" or "unable to provide for his basic needs." These are probably forms of incompetency, although they may be handled as civil commitment cases. In this sense there is some overlap between civil commitment and incompetency.

3. Regarding the history of involuntary commitment see generally S. Brakel, J. Parry & B. Weiner, *The Mentally Disabled and the Law* (3d ed. 1986); N. Kittrie, *The Right to be Different* (1971); Taylor, A Critical Look into the Involuntary Civil Commitment Procedure, 10 *Washburn L. J.* 237 (1971).

4. E.g., A. Stone, *Mental Health and Law: A System in Transition* (1975); Morse, A Preference for Liberty: The Case Against Involuntary Civil Commitment for the Mentally Disordered, 70 *Calif. L. Rev.* 54 (1982); Roth, A Commitment Law for Patients, Doctors, and Lawyers, 136 *Am. J. Psychiatry* 1121 (1979); Szasz, Involuntary Psychiatry, 45 *U. Cin. L. Rev.* 347 (1976).

5. In 1981 there were about 138,000 persons each day subject to commitment in state and county mental hospitals. This was down from 276,000 persons per day in 1972, and from 560,000 persons per day in 1955. Stromberg & Stone, A Model State Law on Civil Commitment of the Mentally Ill, 20 *Harv. J. Legis.* 275, 277 (1983).

6. Gilboy & Schmidt, "Voluntary" Hospitalization of the Mentally Ill, 66 *Nw. U. L. Rev.* 429 (1971); Olin & Olin, Informed Consent in Voluntary Mental Hospital Admissions, 132 *Am. J. Psychiatry* 938 (1975).

7. For a review of the major provisions of all state commitment statutes see 7 *Mental & Physical Disability L. Rep.* 358, 358–69 (1983).

8. The problems of protecting individual interests while providing for a mechanism to deal with immediate dangerousness are considered in Affleck, Wintrob & Peszke, Psychiatrists' Evaluations of Emergency Involuntary Hospitalization, 21 *Comprehensive Psychiatry* 13 (1980); Peszke, Affleck & Wintrob, Perceived Statutory Applicability Versus Clinical Desirability of Emergency Involuntary Hospitalization, 137 *Am. J. Psychiatry* 476 (1980); Note, "We're Only Trying to Help": The Burden and Standard of Proof in Short-Term Civil Commitment, 31 *Stan. L. Rev.* 425 (1979).

9. For a careful study of the operation of the commitment process see National Center for State Courts, *Provisional Substantive and Procedural Guidelines for Involuntary Civil Commitment* (1982). Some recent changes in commitment laws may actually encourage emergency commitments. Mestrovic, Admission Patterns at South Carolina's State Psychiatric Hospitals Following Legislative Reform, 10 *J. Psychiatry & L.* 457 (1982).

10. Commitment is supposed to be to a mental health facility or hospital. However, in some areas patients may be held at least temporarily in jails because of space or transportation problems.

11. In some states, hearings are held only if the patient requests them.

A few states eliminate the preliminary hearing and require an early full hearing on the issue of commitment.

12. A few states permit quasi-judicial officers (hearing officers) to determine civil commitment cases. Miller, The Involvement of Judicial Officers Other Than Judges in Decision Making in Involuntary Civil Commitment, 10 *J. Psychiatry & L.* 491 (1982). Most states permit mental health professionals rather than judges determine when patients should be released.

13. In a few states, the failure of the patient to accept voluntary commitment is a condition which must exist before commitment is permitted. The rationale for this is that if voluntary admission is achieved there is no need for the state to exercise its power to force admission. On the other hand, such provisions may increase coercive voluntary commitments.

14. It appears that there are substantial differences between the commitment examinations conducted by psychiatrists and by other physicians. One study found nonpsychiatric physicians were much less likely to obtain adequate evidence of mental illness and of dangerousness. Miller & Fiddleman, The Adequacy of Commitment Evaluations Performed by Psychiatric and Non-Psychiatric Physicians, 10 *J. Psychiatry & L.* 45 (1982).

15. Lessard v. Schmidt, 349 F. Supp. 1078 (E.D. Wis. 1972), *vacated on other grounds,* 414 U.S. 473 (1973) considers many of the procedural issues in involuntary civil commitment. Concerning the effect of this case see Zander, Civil Commitment in Wisconsin: The Impact of *Lessard v. Schmidt,* 1976 *Wis. L. Rev.* 503. See generally Stefan, Right to Counsel in Civil Commitment Proceedings, 9 *Mental & Physical Disability L. Rep.* 230 (1985); Slovenko, Criminal Justice Procedures in Civil Commitment, 24 *Wayne L. Rev.* 1 (1977).

16. Aronson, Should the Privilege Against Self-Incrimination Apply to Compelled Psychiatric Examinations?, 26 *Stan. L. Rev.* 55 (1973); Wesson, The Privilege Against Self-Incrimination in Civil Commitment Proceedings, 1980 *Wis. L. Rev.* 697; Note, Civil Commitment of the Mentally Ill, 87 *Harv. L. Rev.* 1190 (1974). The Supreme Court is unlikely to apply self-incrimination rights to civil commitment hearings. Allen v. Illinois, 106 S.Ct. 2988 (1986) (regarding sexual psychopath commitments); French v. Blackburn, 428 F. Supp. 1351 (M.D. N.C. 1977), *summarily aff'd,* 443 U.S. 901 (1979).

17. The increasing use of preventive detention may have the effect of removing the opportunity for bail from those who are charged with a crime and predicted to be dangerous. See chapter 12.

18. The refusal of treatment should probably be permitted unless the patient is dangerous within the institution without the medicine and cannot be restrained in any less restrictive way, or unless the patient is determined to be incompetent. See discussions in chapters 3, 16, and 19.

19. Addington v. Texas, 441 U.S. 418 (1979).

20. *Id.* There is some doubt, however, about what must be demonstrated by clear and convincing evidence. Whether, for example, each criterion for dangerousness must be demonstrated by that level of proof. See Note, De-

velopments in the Law—Civil Commitment of the Mentally Ill, 87 *Harv. L. Rev.* 1190, 1253 (1974).

21. A state is free to adopt a standard of proof higher than clear and convincing evidence if it wishes to do so, but it cannot constitutionally adopt a lower standard of proof. The Court seemed to be concerned about adopting a higher standard because "there is a serious question as to whether a state could ever prove beyond a reasonable doubt that an individual is both mentally ill and likely to be dangerous." Given the problems identified later in determining that a person is mentally ill and in predicting dangerousness, it may be that the "clear and convincing" standard should be difficult to meet in many cases.

22. A very good review of the inadequacies of current definitions of dangerousness is Brooks, Defining the Dangerousness of the Mentally Ill: Involuntary Civil Commitment, in *Mentally Ill Offenders* 280 (M. Craft & A. Craft eds. 1984). Brooks proposes using several factors in deciding whether a person is dangerous: nature, magnitude, imminence, frequency, and likelihood of harm; circumstances and conditions "that affect the likelihood of harm occurring"; and the "substantive due process interest balancing between the alleged harm on one hand and the nature of society's intervention on the other." *Id.* at 295–305.

23. In reviewing the actual operation of commitment Wexler noted that, "the literal meaning of dangerousness is admittedly ignored in favor of the best interest of the patient, i.e., whether he will benefit from treatment." Wexler & Scoville, The Administration of Psychiatric Justice: Theory and Practice in Arizona, 13 *Ariz. L. Rev.* 1, 100 (1971). A more recent study surprisingly suggests that psychiatrists who are given the statutory definition of dangerousness were less consistent in their predictions of dangerousness than were those who did not use it. The authors speculated that the inability to incorporate new information into existing belief systems could explain the apparent paradox. Beigel, Berren & Harding, The Paradoxical Impact of a Commitment Statute on Prediction of Dangerousness, 141 *Am. J. Psychiatry* 373 (1984).

24. The concept of dangerousness to self, it is proposed, should be replaced with a definition permitting commitment if the person "(1) is likely in the near future to inflict substantial physical injury upon himself, or (2) is substantially unable to provide for some of his basic needs such as food, clothing, shelter, health, or safety, or (3) will if not treated suffer or continue to suffer severe and abnormal mental, emotional, or physical distress, and this distress is associated with substantial impairment of judgment, reason or behavior causing a substantial deterioration of his previous ability to function on his own." Stromberg & Stone, A Model State Law on Civil Commitment of the Mentally Ill, 20 *Harv. J. Leg.* 275, 302–3 (1983). Stone and Roth are among the most articulate proponents of *parens patriae* commitment criteria. (See note 60, *infra.*)

25. See Vernon, Due Process and Substantive Accountability: Thoughts Toward a Model of Decisionmaking, 38 *La. L. Rev.* 919 (1978).

26. O'Connor v. Donaldson, 422 U.S. 563 (1975).

27. Among the studies and discussions of the commitment process in operation are the following, Hiday, Reformed Commitment Procedures: An Empirical Study in the Courtroom, 11 *L. & Soc'y Rev.* 654 (1977); Miller & Fiddleman, Involuntary Civil Commitment in North Carolina: The Result of the 1979 Statutory Changes, 60 *N.C. L. Rev.* 985 (1982); Stier & Stoebe, Involuntary Hospitalization of the Mentally Ill in Iowa: The Failure of the 1975 Legislation, 64 *Iowa L. Rev.* 1284 (1979); Warren, Involuntary Commitment for Mental Disorder: The Application of California's Lanterman-Petris-Short Act, 11 *L. & Soc'y Rev.* 629 (1977); Wexler & Scoville, The Administration of Psychiatric Justice: Theory and Practice in Arizona, 13 *Ariz. L. Rev.* 1 (1970). For another perspective see S. Pfohl, *Predicting Dangerousness* (1978).

28. Questions may also be raised about the competency of some voluntary patients. It appears that many patients may not understand the consequences of admission or consent to treatment. See C. Lidz, A. Meisel, E. Zerubavel, M. Carter, R. Sestak & L. Roth, *Informed Consent: A Study of Decisionmaking in Psychiatry* 24–30, 73–139 (1984); Appelbaum & Bateman, Competency to Consent to Voluntary Psychiatric Hospitalization: A Theoretical Approach, 7 *Bull. Am. Acad. Psychiatry & L.* 390 (1979). See Miller, Maher & Fiddleman, The Use of Plea Bargaining in Civil Commitment, 7 *Int'l J. L. & Psychiatry* 395 (1984).

29. E.g., Parham v. J. R., 442 U.S. 584 (1979); Bonner v. Moran, 126 F.2d 121 (D.C. Cir. 1941); Ewald, Medical Decision-making for Children: An Analysis of Competing Interests, 25 *St. Louis U. L. J.* 689 (1982).

30. E.g., Jehovah's Witnesses v. Kings County Hosp., 278 F. Supp. 488 (W.D. Wash. 1967), *aff'd per curiam*, 390 U.S. 598 (1968); Smith, Life and Death Decisions in the Nursery: Standards and Procedures for Withholding Lifesaving Treatment from Infants, 27 *N.Y. L. Sch. L. Rev.* 1125 (1982); Note, Judicial Limitations on Parental Autonomy in the Medical Treatment of Minors, 59 *Neb. L. Rev.* 1093 (1980).

31. See Bennett, Allocation of Child Medical Care Decision-Making Authority: A Suggested Interest Analysis, 62 *Va. L. Rev.* 285 (1976); Note, Parents, Children and the Institutionalization Process—A Constitutional Analysis, 83 *Dick. L. Rev.* 261 (1979); Note, "Voluntary" Admission of Children to Mental Hospitals: A Conflict of Interest Between Parent and Child, 36 *Md. L. Rev.* 153 (1976).

32. Parham v. J. R., 442 U.S. 584 (1979).

33. E.g., Melton, Toward "Personhood" for Adolescents: Autonomy and Privacy as Values in Public Policy, 38 *Am. Psychologist* 99 (1983); Schoenberger, "Voluntary" Commitment of Mentally Ill or Retarded Children: Child Abuse by the Supreme Court, 7 *U. Dayton L. Rev.* 1 (1981); Zenoff & Zienta, If Civil Commitment is the Answer for Children, What are the Questions?, 51 *Geo. Wash. L. Rev.* 171 (1983); Note, A Chance to be Heard: An Application of *Bellotti v. Baird* to the Civil Commitment of Minors, 32 *Hastings L. J.* 1285 (1981) (suggesting that adolescents should have the right

to make civil commitment decisions similar to those they enjoy in the area of abortion).

34. See D. Wexler, *Mental Health Law* 41–51 (1981). A review of statutes permitting involuntary commitment for drug or alcohol abuse is S. Brakel, J. Parry & B. Weiner, *The Mentally Disabled and the Law* 144–45 (3d ed. 1986).

35. See Baxstrom v. Harold, 383 U.S. 107 (1966).

36. Jones v. United States, 463 U.S. 354 (1983). The D.C. statute essentially established a presumption of dangerousness from insanity acquittal. However, as *Jones* indicated, the acquittal could be for a minor property offense (e.g., shoplifting) and therefore not really demonstrate dangerousness. Nevertheless, the Court upheld the statute.

37. *Id.*; Comment, *Jones v. United States*: Automatic Commitment of Individuals Found Not Guilty by Reason of Insanity, 68 *Minn. L. Rev.* 822 (1984).

38. The D.C. code involved in the *Jones* case required that successful insanity defendants prove their lack of dangerousness before they could be released from custody. Jones v. United States, *supra*, note 36.

39. Jackson v. Indiana, 406 U.S. 715 (1972).

40. It is possible that the availability of forced treatment through incompetency procedures is subject to abuse. Someone could be charged with a minor criminal offense, and even over the defendant's objections a hearing held to determine competency to stand trial. Upon a finding of incompetency to stand trial the defendant would be incarcerated and perhaps subject to involuntary treatment.

41. Dybwad & Herr, Unnecessary Coercion: An End to Involuntary Civil Commitment of Retarded Persons, 31 *Stan. L. Rev.* 753 (1979).

42. Mental health experts may also be asked, for example, whether there are less restrictive alternatives available or whether treatment is available for the patient.

43. See studies cited in note 27 *supra*.

44. See the description of commitment practices in the articles cited in note 27 *supra*.

45. Sarzen v. Gaughan, 489 F.2d 1076 (1st Cir. 1973); Stamus v. Leonhardt, 414 F. Supp. 439 (S. D. Iowa 1976); Lessard v. Schmidt, 349 F. Supp. 1078 (E. D. Wis. 1972), *vacated on other grounds,* 414 U.S. 473 (1974); Note, Constitutional Right of Counsel: Role of the Attorney in Civil Commitment Proceedings 61 *Marq. L. Rev.* 187 (1977); Note, Constitutional Right to Court Appointed Counsel for the Involuntarily Committed Mentally Ill: Beyond the Civil-Criminal Distinction, 5 *Seton Hall L. Rev.* 64 (1973).

46. Blinick, Mental Disability, Legal Ethics, and Professional Responsibility, 33 *Albany L. Rev.* 92 (1968); Hiday, The Role of Counsel in Civil Commitment: Changes, Effects, Determinants, 5 *J. Psychiatry & L.* 551 (1977); Miller & Fiddleman, The Adversary System in Civil Commitment

of the Mentally Ill: Does it Exist, and Does it Work?, 9 *J. Psychiatry & L.* 403 (1981).

47. A study of the attitudes and actions of judges and attorneys participating in commitment hearings found that both groups thought that attorneys shoud operate in a "paternalistic" model rather than vigorously press for release of the client. The representation of patients was not vigorous; in only 4.7 percent of the cases studied did the outside attorney challenge a written medical report. Hiday, The Attorney's Role in Involuntary Civil Commitment, 60 *N.C. L. Rev.* 1027 (1982).

48. Miller & Fiddleman, *supra,* note 46 at 409–11.

49. See Andalman & Chambers, Effective Counsel for Persons Facing Civil Commitment: A Survey, a Polemic and a Proposal, 45 *Miss. L. J.* 43 (1974); Cohen, The Function of the Attorney and the Commitment of the Mentally Ill, 44 *Tex. L. Rev.* 424 (1966); Litwack, The Role of Counsel in Civil Commitment Proceedings: Emerging Problems, 62 *Calif. L. Rev.* 816 (1974).

50. T. Szasz, *The Myth of Mental Illness* (1961); Szasz, Involuntary Psychiatry, 45 *U. Cin. L. Rev.* 347 (1976).

51. An interesting study of mental illness and hospitalization is reported in Rosenhan, On Being Sane in Insane Places, 179 *Science* 250 (1973), in which researchers entered a hospital claiming systems of delusions, but claiming no symptoms thereafter. The psychiatrists did not discover most of these non-mentally-ill subjects.

Reviews of psychiatric diagnoses include Helzer, Clayton, Pambakian, Reich, Woodruff & Revely, Reliability of Psychiatric Diagnosis: The Test-Retest Reliability of Diagnostic Classification, 34 *Archives Gen. Psychiatry* 136 (1977); Beck, Ward, Mendelson, Mock & Erbough, Reliability of Psychiatric Diagnosis: A Study of Consistency of Clinical Judgments and Ratings, 119 *Am. J. Psychiatry* 351 (1962); Spitzer & Fleis, A Re-Analysis of the Reliability of Psychiatric Diagnosis, 125 *Brit. J. Psychiatry* 341 (1974). These studies involved diagnosis under earlier classification systems (DSM-II). The more recent DSM-III system is somewhat more precise, and should give greater precision in diagnosis. But see J. Ziskin, 1 *Coping With Psychiatric and Psychological Testimony* 138–44 (3d ed. 1981); Morse, A Preference for Liberty: The Case Against Involuntary Commitment of the Mentally Disordered, 70 *Calif. L. Rev.* 54, 70–73 (1982).

52. T. Sarbin & J. Mancuso, *Schizophrenia: Medical Diagnosis or Moral Verdict* (1980); Ennis & Litwack, Psychiatry and the Presumption of Expertise: Flipping Coins in the Courtroom, 62 *Calif. L. Rev.* 693 (1974); Morse, Crazy Behavior, Morals and Science: An Analysis of Mental Health Law, 51 *S. Cal. L. Rev.* 527 (1978).

53. In reality the reliance on a connection between mental illness and dangerousness is so direct that commitment patients must be dangerous *because* of the mental illness. See generally Chodoff, Involuntary Hospitalization of the Mentally Ill as a Moral Issue, 141 *Am. J. Psychiatry* 384 (1984).

54. There is no solid foundation for the widely held assumption that the

mentally ill are particularly dangerous. Morse, A Preference for Liberty: The Case Against Involuntary Commitment of the Mentally Disordered, 70 *Calif. L. Rev.* 54 (1982); Rabkin, Criminal Behavior of Discharged Mental Patients: A Clinical Appraisal of the Research, 86 *Psychological Bull.* 1 (1979); Steadman, Vanderwyst & Ribner, Comparing Arrest Rates of Mental Patients and Criminal Offenders, 135 *Am. J. Psychiatry* 1218 (1978). Nor does it appear that hospital deinstitutionalization was a significant factor in the increase in prison populations. Steadman, Monahan, Duffee, Hartstone & Robbins, The Impact of State Mental Hospital Deinstitutionalization on United States Prison Populations, 1968–1978, 75 *J. Crim. L. & Criminology* 474 (1984).

55. In O'Connor v. Donaldson, 422 U.S. 563 (1975) the Supreme Court held that a state could not constitutionally commit a nondangerous patient without providing treatment. It did not decide whether the state could commit nondangerous people if treatment were provided. There are suggestions, however, that nondangerous commitments would be unconstitutional. see Doremus v. Farrell, 407 F. Supp. 509 (D. Neb. 1975); Doe v. Madonna, 295 N.W.2d 356 (Minn. 1980).

56. E.g., Connecticut v. Lafferty, 192 Conn. 571, 472 A.2d 1275 (1984) (compulsive gambling). See Brooks, Defining the Dangerousness of the Mentally Ill: Involuntary Civil Commitment, in *Mentally Abnormal Offenders* 280 (M. Craft & A. Craft eds. 1984).

57. Paradoxically, a reduction in the certainty of correctly applying commitment criteria properly might argue for expansion of the criteria to ensure that the really dangerous patients are committed. In reality none of this may have a great impact on the number of people committed. Appelbaum, Standards for Civil Commitment: A Critical Review of Empirical Research, 7 *Int'l J. L. & Psychiatry* 133 (1984) (a review of the studies of the effects of the changes in the criteria for commitment demonstrates that most are flawed and the better studies reach conflicting conclusions on the question).

58. Overholser v. Russell, 283 F.2d 195 (D.C. Cir. 1960).

59. See Overholster v. Lynch, 288 F.2d 388 (D.C. Cir. 1961) (bad checks), *rev'd*, 369 U.S. 705 (1962); Connecticut v. Lafferty, 192 Conn. 571, 472 A.2d 1275 (1984) (compulsive gambling).

60. The APA statute permits commitment for dangerousness or if the patient if not treated will suffer distress associated with significant impairment of judgment, reason, or behavior causing a "substantial deterioration of his previous ability to function on his own," and he also lacks "*capacity to make an informed decision* concerning treatment." Stromberg & Stone, A Model State Law on Civil Commitment of the Mentally Ill, 20 *Harv. J. on Legis.* 275 (1983) (emphasis added). A very few states have adopted legislation similar to this. Alaska, North Carolina, Texas and Washington permit this form of commitment. Brakel et al., *supra*, note 34 at 114–21. The requirement that the person lack "capacity" essentially makes this a form of incompetency. For another view on the proposal see Schmidt, Critique of the American Psychiatric Association's Guidelines for State Legislation on Civil Commitment of the Mentally Ill, 11 *New Eng. J. Crim. & Civ. Con-*

finement 11 (1984). See Appelbaum, Is the Need for Treatment Constitutionally Acceptable as a Basis for Civil Commitment?, 12 *L. Med. & Health Care* 144 (1984) (reviewing adopted and model statutes which permit commitment on "need for care" bases, and suggesting such statutes may be constitutional).

61. Chambers, Alternatives to Civil Commitment of the Mentally Ill: Practical Guides and Constitutional Imperatives, 70 *Mich. L. Rev.* 70 (1972); Hiday & Goodman, The Least Restrictive Alternative to Involuntary Hospitalization: Outpatient Commitment, Its Use and Effectiveness, 10 *J. Psychiatry & L.* 81 (1982); Keilitz, Conn & Giampetro, Least Restrictive Treatment of Involuntary Patients: Translating Concepts into Practice, 29 *St. L. U. L. J.* 691 (1985); Keilitz & Hall, State Statutes Governing Involuntary Outpatient Civil Commitment, 9 *Mental & Physical Disability L. Rep.* 378 (1985). Concerning the importance of dealing directly with the issue of competence to make decisions, Brown, Psychiatric Refusal, Patient Competence, and Informed Consent, 8 *Int'l J. L. & Psychiatry* 83 (1986); Hermann, Barriers to Providing Effective Treatment: A Critique of Revisions in Procedural, Substantive, and Dispositional Criteria in Involuntary Civil Commitments, 39 *Vand. L. Rev.* 83 (1986).

62. Duizend & Zimmerman, The Involuntary Civil Commitment Process in Chicago: Practices and Procedures, 33 *De Paul L. Rev.* 225 (1984) (noting both strengths and weaknesses in the operation of the commitment system in Chicago). But see Myers, Involuntary Civil Commitment of the Mentally Ill: A System in Need of Change, 29 *Vill. L. Rev.* 367 (1984) (the commitment system does not adequately take account of the broad array of community-based services).

63. The arguments for abolishing or limiting commitment are extremely well presented in Morse, A Preference for Liberty: The Case Against Involuntary Commitment of the Mentally Disordered, 70 *Calif. L. Rev.* 54 (1982). Arguments in favor of commitment are noted in Chodoff, The Case for Involuntary Hospitalization of the Mentally Ill, 133 *Am. J. Psychiatry* 496 (1976). See also, Appelbaum & Gutheil, The Boston Hospital Case: "Involuntary Mind Control"—The Constitution and the "Right to Rot," 137 *Am. J. Psychiatry* 720 (1980); Rachlin, Pam & Milton, Civil Liberties Versus Involuntary Hospitalization, 132 *Am. J. Psychiatry* 132 (1975); Reich & Siegel, The Emergence of the Bowrey as a Psychiatric Dumping Ground, 50 *Psychiatric Q.* 191 (1978).

64. Barefoot v. Estelle, 463 U.S. 880 (1983); Estelle v. Smith, 451 U.S. 454 (1981).

65. Tarasoff v. Regents Univ. Calif., 17 Cal.3d 425, 551 P.2d 334, 131 Cal. Rptr. 14 (1976).

66. Dangerousness without treatment is widely accepted as a basis for overcoming an involuntary patient's refusal of treatment. E.g., Rogers v. Okin, 478 F. Supp. 1342 (D. Mass. 1979), *aff'd in part and rev'd in part,* 634 F.2d 650 (1st Cir. 1980), *vacated and remanded sub nom.* Mills v. Rogers, 457 U.S. 291 (1982), *on remand,* 390 Mass. 489, 458 N.E.2d 308 (1983);

738 F.2d 1 (1984); 638 F. Supp. 934 (1986); Rennie v. Klein, 462 F. Supp. 1131 (D. N.J. 1978), *supplemented* 476 F. Supp. 1294 (D. N.J. 1979), *modified and remanded* 653 F.2d 836 (3d Cir. 1981), *vacated and remanded,* 458 U.S. 1119 (1982), *on remand* 720 F.2d 266 (3rd Cir. 1983); Rivers v. Katz, 67 N.Y.2d 485, 495 N.E.2d 337, 504 N.Y.S.2d 74 (1986).

67. Shah, Dangerousness: A Paradigm for Exploring Some Issues in Law and Psychology, 33 *Am. Psychologist* 224 (1978).

68. "A recently published volume contains chapters on aggression and violence including 691 references to the literature. Not a single reference imputes any possibility of prediction of violence to any test or combination of tests." Kozol, Dangerousness in Society and Law, 13 *Toledo L. Rev.* 241, 254 (1982), citing R. Green & E. O'Neal, *Perspectives on Aggression* (1976).

69. American Psychological Association, Report of the Task Force on the Role of Psychology in the Criminal Justice System, 33 *Am. Psychologist* 1099, 1110 (1978).

70. Brief of the American Psychiatric Association at 11–18, Barefoot v. Estelle, 463 U.S. 880 (1983); Brief of the American Psychiatric Association at 11–17, Estelle v. Smith, 451 U.S. 454 (1981). See also American Psychiatric Association, *Clinical Aspects of the Violent Individual* (1974).

71. Among the large number of books and articles that raise doubts about the accuracy of predictions of dangerousness are the following. J. Monahan, *Predicting Violent Behavior: An Assessment of Clinical Techniquess* (1981); A. Stone, *Mental Health and Law: A System in Transition* (1975); Albers, Pasewark & Meyer, Involuntary Hospitalization and Psychiatric Testimony: The Fallibility of the Doctrine of Immaculate Perception, 6 *Capital U. L. Rev.* 11 (1976); Cocozza & Steadman, The Failure of Psychiatric Predictions of Dangerousness: Clear and Convincing Evidence, 29 *Rutgers L. Rev.* 1048 (1976); Ennis & Litwack, Psychiatry and the Presumption of Expertise: Flipping Coins in the Courtroom, 62 *Calif. L. Rev.* 693 (1974); Kahle & Sales, Due Process and the Attitudes of Professionals Toward Involuntary Civil Commitment in *New Directions in Psycholegal Research* (Lipsitt & Sales eds. 1980); Steadman, Some Evidence on the Inadequacy of the Concept and Determination of Dangerousness in Law and Psychiatry, 1 J. Psychiatry & L. 409 (1973).

72. Monahan, The Prediction of Violent Behavior: Toward a Second Generation of Theory and Policy, 141 *Am. J. Psychiatry* 10, 11 (1984); Slobogin, Dangerousness and Expertise, 133 *U. Pa. L. Rev.* 97 (1984).

73. Baxtrom v. Herold, 383 U.S. 107 (1966).

74. Cocozza & Steadman, Some Refinements in the Measurement and Prediction of Dangerous Behavior, 131 *Am. J. Psychiatry* 1012 (1974); Steadman & Halton, The Baxtrom Patients: Backgrounds and Outcome, 3 *Seminars in Psychiatry* 376 (1971); Steadman & Keveles, The Community Adjustment and Criminal Activity of the Baxstrom Patients: 1960–1966, 129 *Am. J. Psychiatry* 304 (1972). See T. Thornberry & J. Jacoby, *The Criminally Insane: A Community Follow-up of Mentally Ill Offenders* (1979); Cocozza, Melick & Steadman, Trends in Violent Crimes Among Ex-Mental Patients,

16 *Criminology* 317 (1978); Kozol, Boucher & Garofalo, The Diagnosis and Treatment of Dangerousness, 18 *Crime & Delinq.* 371 (1972).

75. J. Monahan, *Predicting Violent Behavior* 77 (1981).

76. The prediction of dangerousness in some circumstances may be better than 1 in 3. Monahan, *supra,* note 72; Hall, Catlin & Boissevain, Short-Term Violence Prediction: A Prospective Study, paper presented to the American Psychological Association, Toronto, Canada, Aug. 24, 1984 (short-term predictions may be quite accurate).

77. J. Monahan, *supra,* note 75 at 90–91.

78. See material cited in note 76 *supra.* See generally Aldrich, The Clouded Crystal Ball: A 35-Year Follow Up of Psychiatrists' Predictions, 143 *Am. J. Psychiatry* 45 (1986); Lion, Clinical Assessment of Violent Patients, in *Clinical Treatment of the Violent Person* (L. Roth ed. 1985); Madden, Psychotherapeutic Approaches in the Treatment of Violent Persons, in *Clinical Treatment of the Violent Person* (L. Roth ed. 1985).

79. Assume 1 person in 1000 will kill someone, and we can predict with 95 percent effectiveness those who will kill from those who will not. If 100,000 people are tested, 95 of the 100 who will actually kill would be correctly determined. But of the 99,900 who would not kill, 4995 would be predicted to be killers. In reality, the overprediction in commitment is worse because the rate of accurate prediction is much below 95 percent. What the rate of real violence is in the population tested in the commitment process might be difficult to determine.

80. See notes 69–70 *supra.* Some states use the prediction of long-term dangerousness as the basis for imposing the death penalty. Texas has received attention for its use of dangerousness in death decisions. E.g., Dix, The Death Penalty, Dangerousness, Psychiatric Testimony, and Professional Ethics, 5 *Am. J. Crim. L.* 151 (1977).

81. Barefoot v. Estelle, 463 U.S. 880 (1983).

82. The factors most closely related to violent behavior are previous violent acts, race, sex, age, socioeconomic status and alcohol or drug abuse. J. Monahan, *supra,* note 75 at 121–27.

83. Some have proposed that there should be ethical prohibitions on mental health experts' presenting opinions concerning dangerousness, at least in capital cases. Ewing, Ethical Ban on Psychiatric and Psychological Predictions on Dangerousness in Capital Sentencing Proceedings, 8 *Am. J. L. & Med.* 407 (1983).

84. The Supreme Court has not refused the use of expert opinion concerning dangerousness as a matter of constitutional law; therefore a state may constitutionally permit such testimony if it chooses to do so. It need not, however. The Court permitted predictions of dangerousness noting that such predictions are not always wrong, and saying that there is no reason to exclude psychiatrists from making such predictions just because they are no more accurate than anyone in making the predictions. Barefoot v. Estelle, 463 U.S. 880 (1983). This decision is puzzling. Presumably expert testimony should be permitted only if it helps the court reach a correct decision, not

because it is no worse than could be provided by nonexperts. The fact that a prediction is not always wrong is hardly a reason for admitting it into evidence and depending on it to make decisions. (Indeed, if it were always wrong, it should be admitted so that just the opposite could be done.) The real issue is whether a one-in-three accuracy rate is sufficiently accurate to make critically important decisions. See Justice Blackmun's dissenting opinion in *Barefoot*.

CHAPTER 18

THE RIGHT TO TREATMENT AND THE RIGHT TO REFUSE TREATMENT

The rights to treatment and to refuse it are two aspects of the same right: the ability to make basic decisions about one's own mental health. The law recognizes that we have a strong individual interest in controlling what is done to our bodies. This interest has constitutional protection and is central to privacy recognized by the Supreme Court.[1] It is also the primary reason for requiring that informed consent be obtained before significant treatment such as surgery.

If the individual right to make decisions concerning treatment is important in physical therapy, it may be even more important where the treatment involves changing mental activity. This treatment may have physical consequences (e.g., side effects from certain psychotropic drugs or from electroconvulsive therapy), mental consequences (changing the thought patterns or ability to have certain thoughts), and social consequences (e.g., loss of job or friends because of the stigma associated with some forms of treatment). Thus a patient might refuse treatment to avoid personality changes, physical side effects or social stigma. On the other hand, the failure to offer effective treatment may unnecessarily prolong the pain and debilitating effects of mental illness, and result in extended involuntary hospitalization. To make proper decisions, the patient must be offered treatments which may be effective, be given adequate information, and be able to decide whether or not to accept them.

The rights described here are most commonly considered in connection with involuntary mental patients, but issues may also arise regarding other institutionalized persons such as prisoners. The incompetent also raise difficult treatment issues because they are not permitted by the law to make some decisions for themselves.[2] Even voluntary mental patients may raise some right to treatment issues.

Most of the attention to these legal issues is of relatively recent origin. The increased interest in the rights of mental patients generally, the development and widespread use of psychotropic drugs, greater understanding of the consequences and side effects of certain kinds of therapy, and public awareness of the conditions in some major mental health institutions all contributed to the development of this interest. Because they have only recently won extensive recognition, the extent and nature of these rights are poorly defined.[3]

The debate is likely to continue to be important and intense. The existence of clearly effective therapies may make the right to receive treatment more important for some people, while it may cause other people to refuse treatment to prevent a form of governmental "mind control."[4]

WHAT IS TREATMENT?

A central question is, what is treatment? A variety of general types of treatment have been identified. These include milieu therapy in which the patient benefits from participating or being in the general "milieu" of a mental institution; traditional "talk" psychotherapy including group therapy; behavior modification techniques including token economies and aversive therapy; and intrusive therapies such as psychotropic drugs, electroconvulsive therapy, and psychosurgery.

These forms of treatment vary from the relatively noninvasive (traditional talk therapy) to the very intrusive (psychosurgery), from the standard (group therapy) to the experimental (new psychotropic drugs), from the relatively safe (milieu therapy) to the relatively dangerous (some forms of psychotropic medication), from the relatively reversible (behavior modification) to the relatively irreversible (psychosurgery), and from the relatively effective, which produces some clear result (some forms of psychotropic medication) to the relatively ineffective, which does not produce any particularly noticeable result (milieu therapy). The interest in refusing treatment is likely to be greater, of course, when the treatment is dangerous, intrusive, and ineffective than when it is safe, nonintrusive, and effective.

There is no uniform legal definition of treatment. Most commonly, treatment refers to a form of intervention aimed at eliminating or improving some form of disease or disorder. Whether this definition includes a process that reduces the symptoms of a disease is open to debate. We may, for example, say there is no treatment available for someone with cancer even though the person is receiving medication to reduce pain. However we might say someone with a headache was treated with aspirin. In the discussions of treatment relative to mental illness courts have not commonly drawn a distinction between treating a disease and treating its symptoms.

The difficulty in defining mental health treatment is increased by the absence of a clear understanding of what is effective and can therefore legitimately be considered treatment. Aspirin is not, for example, to be considered a treatment for severe depression because it is not effective in reducing the depression or eliminating the cause of it. The real efficacy of many forms of treatment for many kinds of patients and many kinds of mental illness are not fully and convincingly established, making it difficult to determine whether these therapies are in fact treatment. For example, some states in defending their absence of full treatment programs for state patients, have claimed that they are providing "milieu therapy."[5] They are, in effect, claiming that just being part of the environment of a mental health hospital could be considered treatment for some patients. Although the legitimacy of this claim may be doubted, without proof of the efficacy or inefficacy of such treatments, it may be difficult to determine whether the state is in fact providing treatment.

A further problem in defining treatment is to determine when treatment stops and punishment begins. Certain forms of aversive therapy, for example, are extremely frightening and painful. Prison systems may be precluded from using some forms of it just for this reason.[6] The state, furthermore, may be prohibited from punishing certain conduct or conditions but might be permitted to treat it— drug addiction for example.[7] The distinction between punishment and treatment may become more significant. The Supreme Court has indicated that incarceration for treatment (even in a maximum security institution) need not include all of the constitutional protections associated with punishment.[8] Therefore, states may increasingly try to define some incarceration as treatment rather than punishment.

Among the criteria which might be considered in determining whether an activity is treatment or punishment are the effects of the activity (whether it in fact improves the "patient"), whether the person or persons providing the "treatment" intend for it to be punishment, whether it is directly related to the patient's misconduct, whether it is stigmatizing, how intrusive it is, how it is perceived by the patient, and whether the patient agrees to it.[9]

THE RIGHT TO REFUSE TREATMENT

When the right to refuse treatment is mentioned, the public may have the image of the patient in Ken Kesey's *One Flew Over the Cuckoo's Nest*, who was forced to accept treatment and became a listless and zombie-like creature. Or, the image may be of the use of psychotherapy (particularly medication and electroconvulsive therapy) to exercise mind control for political or social reasons, as is apparently not uncommon in the Soviet Union. These popular images hint only vaguely at the real issues in the right to refuse treatment. They involve a conflict between some of the most important interests of the individual and those of the state.[10]

Informed Consent

The "right to *refuse* treatment" in one sense is a misnomer and confusing. The appropriate concern is consenting to the treatment. The concept at the heart of treatment issues is informed consent, which requires that diagnosis and treatment procedures be performed on competent adults only with their permission. Beyond that, the patient must be given sufficient information to make a reasoned and "informed" decision about which treatment will be undertaken.[11] The primary reason for informed consent is to protect individual autonomy. So important is this concept that in certain particularly invasive treatments, such as surgery, informed consent is now almost uniformly formalized and given in writing. The failure of health officials to obtain informed consent prior to treatment may result in civil (malpractice) liability.

Ideally psychotherapy is provided to a patient after the patient has understood the nature of, alternatives to, and risks associated with the proposed treatment and the consequences of refusing the treatment. In the absence of some form of consent, treatment ordinarily should not be given. Thus, the emphasis should be on the affirmative act of consenting to treatment, not on the patient's refusal of it, or on the assumption that treatment may continue unless the patient objects to it.

In reality, informed consent is probably not commonly sought from psychiatric patients, particularly involuntary patients. In most institutions, unless patients object to treatment, they will probably receive it. The legitimacy of such a procedure is doubtful. Patients do not give up their rights to make important decisions by virtue of their hospitalization. Any claim that patients have impliedly consented to whatever treatment is necessary when they entered the hospital is of doubtful validity when applied to voluntary patients[12] and would be ridiculous when applied to involuntary ones. If patients are incompetent to give consent, that should be specifically determined. Absent such a determination of incompetence, the doctrine of informed consent should apply to involuntary patients.[13] The doctrine of informed consent, however, assumes a *legally competent* adult. Not all mental patients are competent and the question of the legal competence of mental patients may be raised and be a major factor in the right to treatment.[14]

Legal Incompetence: Adults and Minors

Determining competency to make decisions is considered extensively in chapters 16 and 19. Competency issues involve three questions: (1) What standards should be used in defining competence? At what level do fears and eccentricities make someone incompetent to make personal decisions?[15] (2) Who should decide when incompetency exists?[16] (3) What process should be used to determine that someone is incompetent?[17]

The refusal itself cannot be a legitimate basis for determining competency, which relates to the ability to make a decision, not to the decision itself. Nor does a determination of incompetency automatically authorize an institution or physician to proceed with treatment. Incompetency means only that someone must make treatment decisions for the patient. The "substitute" decision maker may refuse treatment on behalf of the patient. The necessity of shifting decision-making authority to guardians can be reduced by using "living" or "therapeutic" wills,[18] implementing durable powers of attorney, delaying treatment decisions until competency is restored and using special informed consent procedures.

Minors are generally legally incompetent to make treatment decisions, and their parents or guardians are authorized to make treatment decisions for them. The age of majority, however, is considerably above the age at which most minors are capable of making treatment decisions.[19] A very strong argument can therefore be made for permitting those over 14 to participate fully in treatment decisions. The law appears to be moving in that direction.[20]

The Supreme Court has held that parents may play a major role in determining that a child should be admitted to a mental hospital.[21] Whether an analogous principle would permit parents, with the approval of a mental health professional, to consent to all forms of mental health treatment for adolescents is not clear.

Reasons for Imposing Treatment Without Patient Consent

If the patient is likely immediately to be dangerous to himself or others without treatment, forced treatment can perhaps most easily be justified. As with involuntary civil commitment such treatment should be narrowly defined to avoid abuse, and be imposed as a last resort. Otherwise, the concept could become so broadly defined as to virtually destroy the right to refuse treatment.[22]

Other reasons to require a patient to accept treatment have been suggested, including a *parens patriae* doctrine of providing care because the patient is in need of it or could benefit from it, the state's interest in reducing its institutional costs by having mental patients treated and released from mental institutions as soon as possible, the claim that involuntary civil commitment can be justified only if the state not only offers but also requires treatment of those involuntarily committed,[23] the state's interest in reducing the social costs (broken homes, suffering and loss of productivity) of mental illness by having patients released from institutions as soon as possible, and the desire to establish a "therapeutic environment" where treatment is commonly and routinely provided within the mental institution.[24] Few of the stated reasons, however—except the need to prevent imminent dangerous behavior—are particularly compelling in light of the strong interest in autonomy.

The *parens patriae* rationale cannot provide a very extensive basis for forced treatment of competent adults. It could destroy the concept of individual autonomy by justifying broad intrusions whenever the state claims that it is doing something for someone's own good. The *parens* argument is actually a special incompetency claim: the state should force treatment because the patient does not *really* understand what is best or cannot make good decisions for himself because of the mental illness. If applied only to those who refuse treatment this may become a "Catch 22" argument—the patient is not competent to refuse treatment because competent people would not refuse available treatment. At some point a person is mentally incapable of rejecting or accepting treatment. Until that point is reached, however, there is no clear reason the state's ability to intrude in the decisions of *competent* mental patients is any greater than it is to intrude into the life and treatment decisions of others. One purpose of the right of autonomy, of course, is to prevent the state from doing things to us "for our own good."[25]

The state's interest in reducing the costs of mental illness undoubtedly exists, but financial interests generally are not as strong as the interest in individual liberty and autonomy.[26] Any state interest in maintaining a "therapeutic environment" within an institution may not require that every patient accept the treatment suggested for him, nor is it likely that the state's interest in maintaining such an environment in the institution is strong enough to overcome autonomy rights.

It certainly is not essential that the state force treatment on patients in order to justify involuntary civil commitment.[27] If the interest of the state in civil commitment is in preventing dangerousness, then removal of the patient to a mental institution may itself serve to prevent the dangerous behavior. If the patient in the institution is still physically dangerous to himself or to others, and if no less intrusive means are available to avoid the dangerousness, then the state has a legitimate interest in forcing treatment to prevent the dangerous activity. It may be that the right to treatment requires that the state offer treatment to involuntary patients, but this is not to say that the patient must accept it to justify the civil commitment. The right to treatment is better seen as the right to have treatment made available.

Interests of the Individual

The interests of the individual in the legal right to refuse treatment have been identified as the interest in individual liberty and personal autonomy. Patients will refuse treatment when, from their perspectives, the risks outweigh the benefits. It is the patient's perception that is important here. The risk of loss (say of memory or sexual function) will obviously be more important to some patients than others. A patient might also refuse treatment because of fear that the treatment will be too effective—that it will produce changes in thought, beliefs or personality which the patient (as opposed to society) does not find desirable or attractive. Religious objections may play a role in the refusal of treatment, as may interests in the right to form and express thought. Thus, the refusal of treatment may involve the most important and fundamental of all rights and the state's interest in preventing serious injury or death is one of the very few compelling reasons to impose treatment on a legally competent patient.

It is reasonable to ask whether there is, in a mentally impaired person, a reduction of individual interests or strengthening of state interests which permits the imposition of involuntary treatment which would not otherwise be justified. The justification for treating the impaired but competent patient differently might rest on three propositions: (1) The autonomy interest depends on the ability to make rational decisions, when there is interference with the rational decision process, the individual interest in autonomy is reduced; (2) as decision-making capabilities are reduced, the state's interest in protecting incompetent citizens is strengthened, even if the impairment does not make the person completely incompetent; (3) the increased state interest in protecting the impaired can be "added" to other state interests to produce a total of state interests which in sum are compelling. Each of these grounds has an element of reason, but none is fully persuasive upon careful examination.

While it is true that the exercise of autonomy rights does require some level of mental competency, autonomy is not a concept which protects only fully rational decision making. To the contrary, it is intended to permit people to make decisions which others may find irrational. It thereby allows significant individual differences to be expressed in decision making.

The state does have an important interest in protecting the incompetent which translates to some interest in protecting the impaired. The appropriate expression of that interest is to help promote the opportunity for meaningful decision making, not to remove authority from the impaired patient. For example, the state might reasonably ensure that the impaired receive full information about proposed treatment, or that they are not induced by fraud to accept or refuse it. The state does not therefore necessarily have a stronger interest in imposing treatment on the impaired but competent than it does in doing so for other patients, but it does have a strong interest in ensuring that the consent procedures permit the impaired patient to make as informed a decision as possible.

The validity must be questioned of any claim that a state interest in protecting the impaired can be added to other state interests to produce a compelling state interest. Compelling state interests are qualitatively different than others. Two *strong* state interests do not equal one *compelling* state interest. Thus, state interests in protecting the impaired cannot be added to other state interests to establish a compelling state interest. As a practical matter, the compelling state interest doctrine, although generally accepted, limits fundamental rights by permitting some state infringement of those rights. As such, it should be strictly limited. If the state were permitted to add non-compelling interests together to claim a new compelling level of interest, it would seriously weaken constitutional protections of fundamental rights.

Philosophical Assumptions

Obviously a strong philosophy of individual decision making and self-determination of best interest underlies much of our discussion of the right to refuse treatment. It is consistent with most of the fundamental concepts of a free country. That philosophy, however, is not the only philosophical basis for making treatment decisions.

Starting from a different philosophy, the right to refuse treatment could look quite different. For example, a broad "utilitarian" approach might be used—that is, one would receive the treatment which would promote the greatest good for the greatest number. Thus, a patient might be required to accept treatment if it would be less expensive for others or bring great comfort to the patient's family. Or, the obligation of the patient might be seen as to the state, in which case the patient would have to accept treatment that would be in the best interest of the state. Under such a "collective" system, the treatment provided would be that which was least costly to the state and would return the patient to productivity. Still another philosophical approach would be to require the treatment which was in the patient's best interest in the view of another party (such as the physician, the state, or a court). Such a "paternal" approach recognizes the importance of the individual, but suggests that they are generally not capable of making some complex or difficult decisions for themselves, hence the need for the substitute decision maker. There are of course various degrees of paternalism, all of which are characterized by finding incompetency to make decisions at a fairly low level of dysfunction.

Of the philosophical approaches discussed, only those of free choice and limited paternalism have received any serious support in the United States. Medical paternalism, for competent patients, was declining in popularity in recent years as being inconsistent with fundamental concepts of personal autonomy, although there are now signs it may be making a comeback. Free choice and paternalism will undoubtedly continue to be central in the debate over the right to refuse treatment.[28] As the government assumes a larger responsibility for health costs, the debate may even expand to include a broad utilitarian or collective perspective. Should paternalism, utilitarianism, or collectivism become a dominant philosophy, the nature of the right to treatment debate would, of course, be dramatically altered.

Although perhaps not a philosophy of treatment, another approach is based on distribution of scarce mental health resources. Far fewer mental health services are available than there is need for them. The argument is that the treatment, and the effort to impose it on those who do not want it (even if they need it), would be more effectively spent on those who both need and want treatment.[29] This approach does not fully take account of the possible increased costs of not providing treatment (extended inpatient stays), or the possibility that those who do not want the services need them most. Nevertheless, as a practical matter this resources argument is a strong one that deserves serious consideration.

Sources of a Right to Refuse Treatment

Several constitutional sources of the right to refuse treatment have been suggested, including the Fourteenth Amendment's guarantees of basic liberty, the right of privacy, the freedoms of religion and speech guaranteed by the First Amendment, and the Eighth Amendment's prohibition on cruel and unusual punishment (particularly with prisoners). In addition, there may be state constitutional provisions which limit the ability to a state to impose treatment.[30]

Statutes and state common law are other sources of a right to refuse treatment. Mental patients may, for example, by state statute have the right to refuse some or all forms of treatment. Regulations promulgated by the state or the hospital may also guarantee some right to refuse treatment.[31] The ethical codes of therapists may also impose some limits on the imposition of psychotherapy over the objections of the patient.

Judicial Recognition of the Right to Refuse Treatment

Courts have only begun to consider the right of mental patients to refuse treatment. So far, this right remains rather poorly defined. The Supreme Court in *Mills v. Rogers* declined to clarify this right of refusal and decided the case on a procedural ground. The case, which had originally been known as *Rogers v. Okin,* had caused a considerable stir as it went through the federal courts.[32] The lower courts had determined that mental patients have a constitutional right to decide for themselves whether or not to submit to drug therapy and that this right is not automatically lost by involuntary civil commitment, but that there were some circumstances (such as emergencies) in which the state could impose treatment over the objection of a mental patient.

In *Rennie v. Klein* a constitutional right to refuse treatment was also recognized. In *Rennie,* the district court provided for a review of all medication refusals by an independent psychiatrist retained by the state.[33] Thus, under this approach the reviewer is not a judge but a psychiatrist. A more recent, important right to refuse treatment case is *Rivers v. Katz* in which the New York court unanimously found a state constitutional right to refuse treatment which the state can invade only if the patient is dangerous or incompetent.[34] The court also held that for forced treatment purposes, competency must be determined in a judicial hearing. This is an important case because of the clarity of the decision and the unanimity of the New York court. Although a number of courts have been asked to decide matters related to the right to refuse treatment, the final resolution of this matter will undoubtedly have to await a decision of the Supreme Court on the substantive issues which it declined to decide in *Rogers* and *Rennie.* The Court has shown an inclination to depend on mental health professionals to make treatment decisions, but it is not certain that this inclination would extend to the forced treatment of mental patients.[35]

Courts have also been faced with claims by prisoners that they have been wrongfully subjected to certain forms of psychotherapy, such as aversive psychotherapy or psychosurgery, token economies or even psychological counseling without having given adequate informed consent.[36] In *Knecht v. Gillman,* for example, inmates claimed that those with behavior problems were given aversive therapy, which consisted of the injection of apomorphine. This caused vomiting which lasted from 15 minutes to an hour. A federal court held that this treatment could be considered cruel and unusual punishment administered without informed, voluntary consent.[37]

While physical danger to self or others is, of course, the clearest reason to impose treatment,[38] less serious threats to self—for example the fear that a delay in treatment will reduce the chance of recovery from mental illness—represent much less compelling reasons to do so. We are generally ready, as a society, to prevent immediate death; we are much less willing to prevent people from doing foolish things which will be harmful and might well result in serious or imminent harm. While we would not be willing to let a heart patient jump to his death from a bridge, we would let the same heart patient smoke three packs of cigarettes a day.

Least Restrictive Alternative Treatment

Generally when the state invades a fundamental personal right in pursuit of a compelling state interest, that invasion should be as limited as reasonably possible, the "least restrictive alternative."[39] When treatment is administered to avoid dangerousness, there should be available no less invasive means of preventing the danger. Psychosurgery would not be least restrictive if a short period of seclusion would prevent the dangerousness. Criteria which relate to the least restrictive treatment include the possibility of irreversible changes in mind or body, the duration of the treatment, the degree to which the treatment is restraining, the physical invasiveness of the treatment, the probability and seriousness of adverse side effects, and the degree of pain or discomfort involved in the treatment.[40] This doctrine has less relevance when a guardian consents to treatment on behalf of an incompetent because the guardian should consent to the treatment which is in the best interest of the patient even if that is not the least restrictive form of treatment. Even here, however, consent to irreversible or risky treatment should be undertaken only with caution.

In some instances it is difficult to determine which is the least restrictive alternative. For example, there is disagreement over which of the following is least restrictive: two weeks of physical restraint in near isolation, treatment for the same period with antidepressant drugs, or one ECT treatment.[41] The answer to that question is likely to depend on the patient. Someone with deeply held (perhaps religious) views against all medicine may find the physical restraint less confining,[42] while someone with a fear of physical restraint, who has had a bad reaction to drugs, may find the ECT treatment least restrictive. Thus informed consent may play an important role in determining which involuntary treatment is imposed. When a dangerous patient is competent and treatment is going to be imposed involuntarily, it would be proper to offer the patient a choice among the alternative forms of treatment.

Process for Imposing Treatment

The process for determining whether treatment will be ordered over the patient's objection must take into account the variety of circumstances in which a patient may be dangerous. There is a significant difference between the patient who is brandishing a knife and the patient who is likely to become dangerous in a few days. The process for determining that treatment will be imposed involuntarily must balance the need for decisive action with the strong personal-liberty interests of the patient that are at stake.[43]

The process of civil commitment might be a useful model for making involuntary treatment decisions. The difference between emergency and nonemergencies is recognized in commitment hearings. Mental health professionals, under such a system, would be authorized to impose limited temporary treatment when necessary to prevent immediately dangerous behavior, with a review of the involuntary treatment decisions within a short time (e.g., 72 hours). This emergency treatment should avoid the most intrusive forms of treatment, such as psychosurgery. Any long-term use of involuntary treatment would be permitted only after a full hearing analogous to the civil commitment hearing. Mental health experts would present evidence regarding the dangerousness of the patient within the institution, and the least restrictive form of treatment. The hearing officer should of course be a neutral party, perhaps a judge. Although some courts are reluctant to require them before treatment is given,[44] such due-process hearings seem essential. It is important that patients have a full opportunity to prove that their fundamental liberties need not be invaded, and it is important to ensure that legal principles are followed in making involuntary treatment decisions. (Providing treatment for incompetent patients involves different procedural questions which are considered in the next chapter.)

As we continue to define the right of mental patients to refuse treatment, we will face three types of issues: (1) What standards should be used for imposing treatment on an unwilling patient; that is, can treatment be imposed involuntarily except when the patient is incompetent or immediately physically dangerous to himself or others? (2) Who decides when involuntary treatment can be imposed? Should it be a judge? the treating physician? an independent mental health expert? a jury? (3) What procedure should be used to make this decision? Should it be a full evidentiary hearing with counsel and sworn testimony? Should it be an informal "hearing" at which the decision maker consults informally with the psychiatrist, reviews the "chart" and talks to the patient?

The informed consent doctrine and the limits on nonconsensual treatment outlined above will mean that some competent patients who are not seriously dangerous within the institution will decline treatment even when mental health professionals believe it to be desirable. The decision may appear to many to be foolish. For *competent* patients this is no more a basis for governmental intervention than it is for heart patients who decline to take the heart medicine their cardiologists prescribe. The right to choose the unusual or, from the point of view of others, the incorrect course of action is an important part of freedom.

The emphasis on the competence of a patient to make a decision is important. Much of the debate about the right of the state to impose treatment is implicitly a claim that the patient is not competent to make decisions. It would be better to deal explicitly with the issue of competence than to suggest a poorly defined and unclear right of the state to impose treatment for the patient's own good.

RIGHT TO TREATMENT

While some patients refuse treatment, more commonly patients wish to have it. One basis for the right to treatment is that if the state is involuntarily holding someone, it has an obligation to make available treatment which will permit the patient to regain liberty. The questions are: When does the state have a legal obligation to provide treatment and what form of treatment is legally sufficient?[45]

As with the right to refuse treatment, the right to treatment involves issues related to prisoners, voluntary mental patients, children and others, but it is most commonly thought of in connection with involuntary (civil commitment) mental patients. Prisoners have an interest in treatment if it will reduce the chance of recidivism or increase the chance of early release from prison. Their claim is legally less significant because they are incarcerated for misconduct, and for reasons having nothing to do with rehabilitation (e.g., retribution). Involuntary mental patients and prisoners also share with all other people a general interest in having treatment available which will improve their mental condition. This broad interest does not command significant legal protection.

Despite the long history of mental institutions and the abuses to those held under involuntary civil commitment,[46] it was not until 1960 that the existence of a right to treatment became recognized. Dr. Morton Birnbaum, a psychiatrist as well as a lawyer, wrote in the *American Bar Association Journal* that as part of due process of law, "Courts must be prepared to hold that if an inmate is being kept in a mental institution against his will, he must be given proper medical treatment or else the inmate can obtain his release at will in spite of the severity or the existence of his illness."[47]

There are, of course, some circumstances in which no effective treatment is known. While the state interest in holding untreatable people in order to prevent violence may justify incarceration, the state cannot legitimately involuntarily incarcerate people for the purpose of providing treatment and then fail to provide it.[48]

Legal Sources of the Right to Treatment

Legal bases for the right to treatment have been found in statutes and in the Constitution. Some federal and many state civil commitment statutes specify at least limited rights to treatment.[49] For example, in the relatively early case of *Rouse v. Cameron* the federal courts noted that the Federal Hospitalization of the Mentally Ill Act of 1964 provided that "a person hospitalized in a public hospital for mental illness shall, during his hospitalization, be entitled to medical and psychiatric care and treatment."[50] Often those rights are diluted because the statute states only that a patient is entitled to treatment "to the extent that facilities, equipment, and personnel are available." In few states do the statutes assert a clearer right to treatment.

Because statutory rights to treatment are not universal and can easily be changed by the legislatures, the constitutional right to treatment has received increasing attention. This right to treatment could be based on the Fourteenth Amendment due process clause or the related right to privacy, the Eighth Amendment cruel and unusual punishment provisions, or conceivably upon a right to mentation springing from the First Amendment.

The Supreme Court suggested in *Youngberg v. Romeo* that there is at least some limited constitutional right to treatment.[51] The Pennsylvania courts had found that Romeo was severely retarded and unable to care for himself and committed him to the Pennhurst State School and Hospital. The Supreme Court determined that the Fourteenth Amendment's due process clause requires that the state provide reasonably safe conditions of confinement and freedom from unreasonable bodily restraints. The Court also said the state has a limited obligation to provide training or "habilitation." The Court held that the state is constitutionally obligated to provide "minimally adequate or reasonable training to ensure safety and freedom from undue restraint." In other words, the state must provide reasonable habilitation to the extent that it will help avoid unnecessary restraint and to ensure the patient's safety. For a mental patient this could require that the state offer treatment which could return the person to the community.[52]

The Court also held "persons who have been involuntarily committed are entitled to more considerate treatment and conditions of confinement than criminals whose conditions of confinement are designed to punish." The Court noted that deference should be given to the judgment of qualified mental health professionals in determining what training or treatment was reasonable and in choosing among several professionally acceptable forms of treatment. The Court essentially required that Romeo be given reasonable treatment in light of his interests in liberty, all of the circumstances surrounding his case, and the range of professionally acceptable forms of training (or treatment) available. It did not require the best, but only "adequate" or reasonable treatment.

In *Romeo* the Supreme Court dealt with a mentally retarded person's right to habilitation or training. Involuntarily mental patients would appear to have very closely analogous rights to limited treatment for emotional conditions, including the right to safe conditions, freedom from unnecessary restraint, and reasonable treatment which would permit them to enjoy freedom from bodily restraint.[53]

In *O'Connor v. Donaldson* the Supreme Court determined that a finding of "mental illness" alone cannot justify a state's locking up a person against his will and keeping him indefinitely in simple custodial confinement.[54] The Court specifically did not decide whether a dangerous person had a constitutional right to treatment, nor did it determine whether a nondangerous person could ever be involuntarily committed. The case did at least help establish, however, the constitutional right to treatment for involuntary patients who are not dangerous and who are capable of living safely outside of an institution.

The Supreme Court has not defined the specific nature of the right to safety, freedom from undue restraint, and limited treatment. One of the most comprehensive efforts to specifically define the elements of the right to treatment is *Wyatt v. Stickney*.[55] Wyatt was confined to the Bryce Hospital, Alabama's primary mental institution. The hospital had approximately 5000 patients, the majority of whom were involuntarily committed. For these patients the hospital at one point had only one Ph.D. clinical psychologist, three medical doctors (none a board certified psychiatrist), and two MSW social workers among the employees whose duties involved direct patient care in hospital therapeutic programs. Patients were assigned compulsory, nontherapeutic work, were often poorly clothed and fed, and had little privacy. The institution was seriously overcrowded, lacked a number of basic sanitation facilities, and had a number of fire and other emergency hazards.

After the state failed to dramatically improve conditions at the hospital, the federal district court listed with great specificity steps that the hospital was required to take to provide for the basic safety and treatment of the patients.[56] For example, it provided for specific minimum space per patient, sanitary facilities, educational opportunities, nutrition, and minimum staff/patient ratios. It adopted specific standards to protect patients' right to privacy, to be free from unnecessary restraint and medication, to send and receive sealed mail, to be compensated for labor, and to provide informed consent to treatment or experimentation. It required that individual treatment plans be developed and that written restraint and medication orders be filed and periodically reviewed. The court also appointed a committee within the institution to review all rehabilitation programs and to assist patients whose legal rights might be infringed.

What Does the Right to Treatment Mean?

Much of what has been considered "right to treatment" in fact seems to be more in the nature of the right to comfort or at least the right to safety. The Supreme Court emphasized the right to safety and freedom from restraint in the *Romeo* case; many of the standards in *Wyatt v. Stickney* really related more to safety and comfort than to mental health treatment.

Even when the courts actually deal with treatment issues, there is a serious question of whether courts are recognizing the right to *effective* treatment.[57] The courts have shown great reluctance to become involved in determining whether treatment is effective, or in second-guessing the treatment decisions of mental health professionals. In *Romeo,* for example, the Supreme Court noted that great deference would be given to the treatment decisions of professionals if those decisions were in the realm of professionally accepted treatment.[58]

One reason the courts have been reluctant to clearly define a right of effective treatment is the lack of clear understanding of which treatments are in fact effective. Without such understanding, the right to treatment is too often nearly an empty gesture.[59] If all forms of psychotherapy are approximately equally effective, then any form of treatment (even milieu therapy) should be acceptable to the court.[60] The right to treatment, however, ultimately depends on there being available some form of treatment that is likely to improve the condition of the patient and maximize his liberty and safety. The development of clearly effective "standard" forms of treatment will be essential to the full recognition of the right to treatment and to making that right meaningful.

Charging Patients

In many instances, states have not provided treatment to patients because of the absence of public funds for mental health facilities. This has led some to suggest that states assess the cost of treatment to patients who are able to pay. There are statutes in most states which provide for some form of financial responsibility for voluntary or involuntary patients in state mental institutions or their families.[61] Although a number of constitutional attacks have been mounted against these statutes (based in part on equal protection, due process, and taking of property without just compensation) these attacks have generally failed and the Supreme Court has refused to declare them unconstitutional.[62] States often ignore, or do not try to fully enforce, these pay-for-care statutes. As it relates to involuntary patients, these private pay statutes are criticized on the basis that civil commitment is often for the benefit of society and it is inappropriate to charge the patient for involuntary confinement.[63]

Enforcing the Right to Treatment

In upholding statutory or constitutional rights to treatment, courts have faced the difficult question of how to enforce patients' rights. Commonly, the implementation of a right of treatment involves major changes in a state's mental institutions. This, of course, often requires the expenditure of substantial funds. Because federal courts have generally been reluctant to directly order states to make massive expenditures of state funds, finding a method of enforcing constitutional rights to treatment has been somewhat frustrating. One method is to threaten to release involuntarily committed patients through a writ of habeas corpus. The courts are then giving the state the choice of implementing a right of treatment or facing the possibility of not being able to involuntarily commit anyone. The difficulty with this approach is that courts are understandably reluctant to actually release potentially dangerous mental patients wholesale.

An alternative is to order the states to provide adequate treatment. This, of course, was done by Judge Johnson in *Wyatt v. Stickney*. If, however, state officials refuse to abide by the order, the federal courts face a very difficult decision of enforcing the order. Federal courts would be understandably reluctant to hold a state legislature in contempt for failure to provide adequate resources to ensure treatment. In the *Wyatt* case, Judge Johnson suggested that if the legislature failed to provide adequate funds to meet the constitutional right of treatment, "It will be necessary for the court to take affirmative steps, including appointing a master, to ensure that proper funding is realized and that adequate treatment is available for the mentally ill of Alabama." The appeals court found this threat to be a problem and somewhat inappropriate.[64]

Another alternative is for money damages to be given to individuals whose rights are violated by the state. States are generally protected from ordinary civil damages through the doctrine of sovereign immunity and the Eleventh Amendment. Officials of the state and mental health professionals may be sued individually for damages. States (or their officials) may be liable for damages under federal civil rights statutes.[65] In the two cases involving the right to treatment described earlier that went to the Supreme Court, *Romeo* and *O'Connor,* civil rights damages were sought from the state officials and mental health institution personnel. The Supreme Court has established a defense against such cases when filed against state officials or employees if the employee did not violate "clearly established" rights.[66] Essentially, if the employees were acting in good faith they are not liable for civil rights damages. In addition, of course, state employees cannot be held individually liable for the failure of the state to provide adequate resources to provide for adequate treatment. Nevertheless, the use of federal civil rights statutes is a potentially effective way of enforcing constitutional rights involving the right to and the right to be free from treatment.

The Supreme Court may be making it more difficult procedurally for federal courts to decide right to treatment cases.[67] If the Court significantly reduces the role of federal courts in right to treatment cases, the right to treatment may be of little practical significance in most states.

The search for effective ways of enforcing the right to treatment must continue. The use of civil liability for patients whose right to treatment has been violated was a promising enforcement mechanism, the states' claim of sovereign immunity protection from many forms of liability, and state officials' claims of broad "good faith" and "limited resources," are making civil damages enforcement of treatment rights somewhat ineffective. Perhaps the threat of a variety of sanctions—habeas corpus, civil liability, direct supervision of institutions, loss of federal funds—will be effective in enforcing the right to treatment. In overcrowded state prisons, federal courts have placed specific limits on the number of prisoners that can be housed in an institution. This leaves it to state officials to decide which persons to hold in light of the resources available. Similar numerical limits could be imposed on state mental hospital populations pending provision of adequate facilities and staff.

Others' Rights to Treatment

We have concentrated on the right of involuntary mental patients to treatment. Others have some rights, however. Prisoners may also have limited statutory rights to mental health treatment. The Supreme Court has held that the Eighth Amendment requires that the state provide elementary physical care for prisoners, and that a state violates a prisoner's Eighth Amendment rights when it is deliberately indifferent to the prisoner's needs.[68] This case involved physical injury. However, under the right circumstances the Eighth Amendment right to treatment might be expanded to include minimal mental health care. At least one court has suggested that there would be a right to mental health care treatment if there were evidence of a serious disease which could be cured or substantially alleviated with reasonable cost and time and that the potential for harm to the prisoner by delay of care would be substantial.[69] The court indicated that it could not second guess reasonable treatment decisions made by mental health professionals concerning prisoners. It is likely that the right of prisoners to mental health care will only gradually be recognized.[70]

SUMMARY

The right of autonomy is at the core of the right to refuse and the right to treatment. A competent adult generally has the right to make personal medical decisions. That right is limited if the person presents a threat of substantial harm to himself or others. The right to make major mental health treatment decisions is as important as, if not more important than, the right to make physical treatment decisions, as mental health treatment may change the personality and very essence of a person.

The right to refuse treatment is best considered part of the doctrine of informed consent. The "right to *refuse* treatment" may suggest that treatment is provided unless the patient objects to it and does not suggest the more important affirmative duty to provide the patient with sufficient information from which to decide whether or not to accept it. Informed consent requires that competent adults be informed of the nature of proposed treatment as well as its risk, and of any alternatives.

The nature of the right to refuse treatment has not been fully defined. The very strong interest in autonomy suggests that mental health treatment should be provided without consent only in two circumstances: (1) if the patient is incompetent and therefore unable to make treatment decisions or (2) if there is a compelling state interest (such as the prevention of immediate physical harm) which cannot be satisfied in a less invasive way. In either case, the state should ensure that the invasion of personal liberty is as limited and as temporary as possible. For example, treatments which are irreversible or highly invasive should be avoided if possible. Particularly when a proposed treatment is very intrusive, experimental, dangerous, or irreversible, extreme caution should be exercised in ordering treatment without consent of the patient.

Incompetency to make personal decisions is an extremely complicated matter and discussed more extensively in the next chapter. The fact that someone has unusual views, fears, or feelings is not in itself enough to make one incompetent. Some patients with impaired judgment may be able to understand the nature and consequence of the refusal of treatment if special efforts are made to provide full information about the alternatives and risks available. Other patients who are incompetent from time to time will have lucid periods. The "living will" concept, discussed in chapter 3, also might help implement the concept of informed consent.

Who should decide whether a patient is competent to make decisions or is dangerous to himself or others and what treatment is appropriate in either circumstance? The Supreme Court in *Parham* and *Romeo* demonstrated a desire to avoid second guessing psychiatrists concerning treatment decisions.[71] Nevertheless, we feel that, except in emergencies, it is appropriate for a court to determine whether the legal standards for imposing treatment without consent have been met and whether the treatment proposed is in fact the least restrictive form available. To make these kinds of decisions, some process is required to receive and consider information about proposed treatments. This implies the necessity of at least an informal hearing at which the patient has the opportunity to present information in an effective form.

The above suggests a "legalization" of the treatment process, and it may be that. It also runs the risk of increasing the number of patients who refuse treatment and who may "rot with their rights on."[72] The involuntary civil commitment process, however, is already of necessity "legalized." The involuntary incarceration and involuntary treatment involve interference with fundamental forms of liberty. It is essential that legal procedures ensure that the system is not abused. Some competent patients make decisions inconsistent with what a mental health professional recommends, but that is no reason to impose treatment any more than the refusal of a competent adult to take medicine to control high blood pressure justifies compulsory treatment.

Among the most difficult treatment refusal issues is the right of adolescents to refuse treatment requested by their parents. At least in circumstances in which the treatment is highly invasive, irreversible or experimental, adolescents probably should have the right to reject certain forms of treatment.

The right to make treatment decisions assumes that treatment will be available. The right to treatment for those involuntarily committed seems fundamental. The state's interest in avoiding spending money for such treatment hardly seems sufficient to overcome the individual's interests in liberty. It is, after all, the actions of the state which have caused the deprivation of liberty for the involuntary patient. A strong argument can therefore be made that patients should be given not just minimally adequate treatment, but real treatment choices as a *quid pro quo* for involuntary commitment. It has been only very recently that even minimal rights to treatment have been recognized by the courts. The courts have thus far not been willing to extend the right to treatment very far. One problem is that it is often difficult to determine what treatments are effective. As mental health care becomes a more precise science, we might anticipate that courts will increasingly demand that states provide effective psychotherapy for involuntarily committed patients. At the very least, however, states have the obligation to provide safe confinement with as little physical restraint and loss of liberty as is reasonable.

The enforcement of the right to treatment has been difficult for courts. The use of money damages provides a strong economic incentive for states to correct unconstitutional conditions and may be the most effective method of enforcing treatment rights. In some prison cases, the courts have limited the number of prisoners that an institution can accept. Similar sorts of limitations on the number of patients who may be admitted to a mental health facility may also be effective in implementing treatment rights.

NOTES

1. The right of individuals to make fundamental personal decisions has been recognized by the Supreme Court as a constitutional right. E.g., Akron v. Akron Center for Reproductive Health, 462 U.S. 416 (1983); Roe v. Wade, 410 U.S. 113 (1975); Griswold v. Connecticut, 381 U.S. 479 (1965). Some people may refuse treatment as a religious belief. Thus, refusal may be related to First Amendment rights. See generally O'Connor v. Donaldson, 422 U.S. 563 (1975).

2. "Incompetent" and "ward" are used interchangeably to include those who are legally unable to make treatment decisions for themselves.

The text and notes in chapters 3, 16 and 19 also deal with other right to refuse treatment issues.

3. There is currently a considerable degree of misunderstanding about conflicting legal principles and treatment practices. Gutheil & Mills, Legal Conceptualizations, Legal Fictions, and the Manipulation of Reality: Conflict Between Models of Decision-Making in Psychiatry and Law, 10 *Bull. Am. Acad. Psychiatry & L.* 17 (1982).

4. At least one prisoner has objected to psychotherapy counseling on the basis that it infringed upon his right of mentation and privacy. The court was not impressed with his claim. United States v. Stine, 675 F.2d 69 (3d Cir.), *cert. denied*, 458 U.S. 1110 (1982). See generally S. Herr, S. Aarons & R. Wallace, *Legal Rights and Mental Health Care* (1983); Bonnie, The Psychiatric Patient's Right to Refuse Medication: A Survey of the Legal Issues, in *Refusing Treatment in Mental Health Institutions—Values in Conflict* (A. E. Doudera & J. Swazey eds. 1982); Sidley, The Rights of Involuntary Patients in Mental Institutions to Refuse Drug Treatment, 12 *J. Psychiatry & L.* 231 (1984).

5. See e.g., O'Connor v. Donaldson, 422 U.S. 563 (1975); Covington v. Harris, 419 F.2d 617 (D.C. Cir. 1969); Hendrix v. Faulkner, 525 F. Supp. 435 (N.D. Ind. 1981), *aff'd in part and vacated in part, sub nom.* Wellman v. Faulkner, 715 F.2d 269 (7th Cir. 1983), *cert. denied*, 468 U.S. 1217 (1984). In at least one instance a patient complained of a denial of treatment because he was *not* given milieu therapy. Jackson v. Amaral, No. 80-219-Z, slip op. (D. Mass. 1982).

6. Knecht v. Gillman, 488 F.2d 1136 (8th Cir. 1973).

7. Robinson v. California, 370 U.S. 660 (1962).

8. Allen v. Illinois, 106 S. Ct. 2988 (1986).

9. See Symonds, Mental Patients' Rights to Refuse Drugs: Involuntary

Medication as Cruel and Unusual Punishment, 7 *Hastings Const. L. Q.* 701 (1980).

10. It is interesting to consider the consequences of recognizing a right to refuse treatment. Bloom, Faulkner, Holm & Rawlinson, An Empirical View of Patients Exercising Their Right to Refuse Treatment, 7 *Int'l J. L. & Psychiatry* 315 (1984). Reviewing several studies of patients who refuse treatment, as well as their own data from an Oregon hospital, the authors conclude that, a request to override the right to refuse treatment was surprisingly common, the patients involved were seriously disturbed, there was a high degree of consensus among psychiatrists about the appropriateness of overriding refusals (a patient's right to refuse treatment, in this study, was overridden 95 percent of the time), excessive treatment was not used, and there were considerable costs in the refusal of treatment.

Other empirical studies of the refusal of treatment include Appelbaum & Gutheil, The Boston Hospital Case: "Involuntary Mind Control," the Constitution and the Right to Rot, 137 *Am. J. Psychiatry* 720 (1980); Hassenfeld & Grumet, A Study of the Right to Refuse Treatment, 12 *Bull. Am. Acad. Psychiatry & L.* 65 (1984); Rodenhauser, Treatment Refusal in a Forensic Hospital: Ill-Use of the Lasting Right, 12 *Bull. Am. Acad. Psychiatry & L.* 59 (1984). Concerning the difficult issues regarding consent to treatment see the very thorough study C. Lidz, A. Meisel, E. Zerubavel, M. Carter, R. Sestak & L. Roth, *Informed Consent: A Study of Decision Making in Psychiatry* (1984).

11. See Canterbury v. Spence, 464 F.2d 772 (D.C. Cir.), *cert. denied,* 409 U.S. 1064 (1972).

12. Even the fact that voluntary patients could "walk away from treatment," does not provide an "implied consent" to all treatment. See Lojuk v. Quandt, 706 F.2d 1456 (7th Cir. 1983), but see Doe v. Public Health Trust, 696 F.2d 901 (11th Cir. 1983).

13. Brown, Psychiatric Refusal, Patient Competence, and Informed Consent, 8 *Int'l J. L. & Psychiatry* 83 (1986) (noting the importance of studying consent, competence and refusal together); Macklin, Some Problems in Gaining Informed Consent from Psychiatric Patients, 31 *Emory L. J.* 345 (1982); Note, The Doctrine of Informed Consent Applied to Psychotherapy, 72 *Georgetown L. J.* 1637 (1984).

14. The competency of patients is not something that has been defined with precision. Even among voluntary patients there is a significant problem of understanding. One study found that half of the patients who had *voluntarily* admitted themselves to a mental hospital claimed that they did not have mental problems or need hospitalization. Only 14 percent of the voluntary patients were aware of the consequences of hospitalization, adverse effects, and the like. Appelbaum, Mirkin & Bateman, Empirical Assessment of Competency to Consent to Psychiatric Hospitalization, 138 *Am. J. Psychiatry* 1170 (1981).

15. Lidz & Roth, Tests for Competence to Consent to Treatment, 134 *Am. J. Psychiatry* 279 (1977); Michels, Competency to Refuse Treatment, in

Refusing Treatment in Mental Health Institutions—Values in Conflict 116 (A. E. Doudera & J. Swazey eds., 1982); Roth, A Commitment Law for Patients, Doctors and Lawyers, 136 *Am. J. Psychiatry* 1121 (1979). See Roth, The Right to Refuse Psychiatric Treatment: Law and Medicine at the Interface, 35 *Emory L. J.* 139 (1986).

16. There has been some suggestion that the determination of incompetency is best made by courts. See the controversial decision, *In re* Guardianship of Roe III, 383 Mass. 415, 421 N.E.2d 40 (1981). For a review of the state criteria for imposing treatment, see S. Brakel, J. Parry & B. Weiner, *The Mentally Disabled and the Law* (3d ed. 1986).

17. Although some courts are suggesting that these "competency to refuse treatment" decisions can be made informally by the hospital (e.g., United States v. Leatherman, 580 F. Supp. 977 [D.D.C. 1983], *remanded,* 729 F.2d 683 [D.C. Cir. 1984]), we will argue in the next chapter that these decisions are so important that there should be some minimal hearing before a disinterested party.

18. Somewhat analogous is a proposal to establish irrevocable treatment contracts, or "Ulysses" contracts. While competent, one would sign a contract consenting to treatment for mental illness, and instructing the physicians to disregard any subsequent refusal of treatment. Dresser, Ulysses and the Psychiatrists: A Legal and Policy Analysis of the Voluntary Commitment Contract, 16 *Harv. Civ. Rts.—Civ. Liberties L. Rev.* 777 (1982).

19. G. Melton, G. Koocher & M. Saks eds., Children's Competence to Consent (1983); Melton, Children's Participation in Treatment Planning: Psychological and Legal Issues, 12 *Prof. Psychology: Research & Prac.* 246 (1981).

20. E.g., Planned Parenthood v. Ashcroft, 462 U.S. 476 (1983); Bellotti v. Baird, 443 U.S. 622 (1979); Carey v. Population Services, 431 U.S. 678 (1977).

21. Parham v. J.R., 442 U.S. 584 (1979).

22. An example of criteria (which permit only limited imposition of treatment) adopted by some state courts is People v. Medina, 705 P.2d 961 (Colo. 1985). Treatment may be administered without consent only if (1) there is an immediate and substantial threat to the life or safety of the patient or others, or (2) at an adversary hearing there is clear and convincing evidence that (a) the patient is incompetent, (b) treatment is needed to prevent long-term harm, (c) less intrusive treatment is not available, and (d) the need for treatment is sufficient to override any interest in refusing it.

23. See Appelbaum & Gutheil, The Right to Refuse Treatment: The Real Issue is Quality of Care, 9 *Bull. Am. Acad. Psychiatry & L.* 199 (1981); Appelbaum, Mirkin & Bateman, *supra,* note 14.

24. Brooks, The Constitutional Right to Refuse Antipsychotic Medications, 8 *Bull. Am. Acad. Psychiatry & L.* 179, 201–12 (1980); Callahan & Longmire, Psychiatric Patients' Right to Refuse Psychotropic Medication: A National Survey, 7 *Mental & Physical Disability L. Rep.* 494 (1983) (noting considerable differences among states concerning the right to refuse treat-

ment); Keuma, Current Status of Institutionalized Mental Health Patients' Right to Refuse Psychotropic Drugs, 6 *J. Legal Med.* 107 (1985); Parry, Legal Parameters of Informed Consent Applied to Electroconvulsive Therapy, 9 *Mental & Physical Disability L. Rep.* 162 (1985) (concluding that the law regarding ECT is clear, in that a state cannot completely prohibit a competent person from consenting to ECT, and that in the absence of an emergency or incompetency adjudication patients have a right to accept or decline it).

25. See generally S. Herr, S. Aarons & R. Wallace, *Legal Rights and Mental Health Care* (1983); Coleman & Solomon, Parens Patriae "Treatment": Legal Punishment in Disguise, 3 *Hastings Const. L. Q.* 344 (1976).

26. The refusal of treatment undoubtedly is costly. See note 10, *supra.*

27. But see Stensvad v. Reivitz, 601 F. Supp. 128 (W.D. Wis. 1985). This case permitted imposition of treatment based on the civil commitment statute's purpose of providing treatment, and on the opinion that those committed are incompetent to make treatment decisions. Neither of these approaches has been generally adopted by other courts.

28. E.g., Brooks, The Constitutional Right to Refuse Antipsychotic Medications, 8 *Bull. Am. Acad. Psychiatry & L.* 179 (1980); Rachlin, One Right Too Many, 3 *Bull. Am. Acad. Psychiatry and L.* 99 (1975); Rhoden, The Right to Refuse Psychotropic Drugs, 15 *Harv. Civ. Rts.—Civ. Liberties L. Rev.* 363 (1980). The autonomy/paternalism debate is found in other areas of law-health conflicts. See Baron, Medical Paternalism and the Rule of Law, 4 *Am. J. L. & Med.* 337 (1979); Relman, The *Saikewicz* Decision: Judges as Physicians, 298 *New Eng. J. Med.* 508 (1978).

29. See generally Morse, A Preference for Liberty: The Case Against Involuntary Commitment of the Mentally Disordered, 70 *Calif. L. Rev.* 54 (1982). The process of deinstitutionalization has left the mentally ill on the streets without services. In many instances it is the failure to offer adequate social services to those who want them that is the problem. See P. Brown, *The Transfer of Care: Psychiatric Institutionalization and Its Aftermath* (1985).

30. Brakel et al., *supra,* note 16 at 342–47. See generally Gelman, Mental Hospital Drugs, Professionalism, and the Constitution, 72 *Georgetown L. J.* 1725 (1984) (concluding that the involuntary use of drugs is at least as invasive of fundamental rights as was the use of physical restraints).

31. An excellent review of all state statutes permitting patients to refuse treatment is contained in Brakel et al., *supra,* note 16; Note, Medicating Committed Psychiatric Patients Over Their Objections: Balancing Patients' Interests and Quality of Mental Health Care, 14 *Rutgers L. J.* 685 (1983). See Goedecke v. Dep't of Institutions, 198 Colo. 407, 603 P.2d 123 (1979); Bonnie, The Psychiatric Patient's Right to Refuse Medication: A Survey of the Legal Issues, in *Refusing Treatment in Mental Health Institutions—Values in Conflict* (A. E. Doudera & J. Swazey eds. 1982); Note, Right to Refuse Antipsychotic Medication: A Proposal for Legislative Consideration, 17 *Ind. L. Rev.* 1035 (1984).

Regardless of the source of treatment, it may be meaningless without an effective way of enforcing the right. See Furrow, Public Psychiatry and the Right to Refuse Treatment: Toward an Effective Damage Remedy, 19 *Harv. Civ. Rts.—Civ. Liberties L. Rev.* 21 (1984).

32. Rogers v. Okin, 478 F. Supp. 1342 (D. Mass. 1979), *aff'd in part, rev'd in part,* 634 F.2d 650 (1st Cir. 1980), *vacated, sub nom.* Mills v. Rogers, 457 U.S. 291 (1982), *later proceeding,* 390 Mass. 489, 458 N.E.2d 308 (1983), *remanded,* Rogers v. Okin, 738 F.2d 1 (1st Cir. 1984), 638 F. Supp. 934 (D. Mass. 1986).

33. Rennie v. Klein, 462 F. Supp. 1131 (D. N.J. 1978), *later proceeding,* 476 F. Supp. 1294 (D. N.J. 1979), *modified* 653 F.2d 836 (3d Cir. 1981), *vacated* 458 U.S. 1119 (1982); *on remand,* 720 F.2d 266 (3d Cir. 1983). The *Rogers* and *Rennie* cases are the most notable federal refusal of treatment cases. Another, more recent federal case is Bee v. Greaves, 744 F.2d 1387 (10th Cir. 1984), *cert. denied,* 105 S. Ct. 1187 (1985) (pre-trial detainee had the right to refuse treatment absent an emergency).

34. Rivers v. Katz, 67 N.Y.2d 485, 495 N.E.2d 337, 504 N.Y.S.2d 74 (1986).

35. See Youngberg v. Romeo, 457 U.S. 307 (1982); Parham v. J.R., 442 U.S. 584 (1979); O'Connor v. Donaldson, 422 U.S. 563 (1975).

36. United States v. Stine, 675 F.2d 69 (3d Cir.), *cert. denied,* 458 U.S. 1110 (1982).

37. Knecht v. Gillman, 488 F.2d 1136 (8th Cir. 1973). Also see Mackey v. Procunier, 477 F.2d 877 (9th Cir. 1973); Pena v. New York State Division for Youth, 419 F.Supp. 203 (S.D. N.Y. 1976); Nelson v. Heyne, 355 F.Supp. 451 (1972) *aff'd* 491 F.2d 352 (7th Cir.), *cert. denied,* 417 U.S. 976 (1974). In the *Kaimowitz* case, the court suggested that the environment of a prison might be inherently coercive and prevent a prisoner from giving full and free informed consent to psychosurgery in the prison setting. Kaimowitz v. Michigan Department of Mental Health, Civil Action No. 73-19434-AW (Cir. Ct. Wayne County, Mich. July 10, 1973, *reprinted in* A. Brooks, *Law, Psychiatry and the Mental Health System* 902 (1974).

38. E.g., Rennie v. Klein, *supra,* note 34; *In re* K.K.B., 609 P.2d 747 (Okla. 1980); Opinion of the Justices, 123 N.H. 554, 465 A.2d 484 (1983).

39. Zlotnick, First Do No Harm: Least Restrictive Alternative Analysis and the Right of Mental Patients to Refuse Treatment, 83 *W. Va. L. Rev.* 376 (1981).

40. See generally Keilitz, Conn & Giampetro, Least Restrictive Treatment of Involuntary Patients: Translating Concepts into Practice, 29 *St. Louis U. L. J.* 691 (1985); Ransohoff et al., Measuring the Restrictiveness of Psychiatric Care, 33 *Hosp. & Community Psychiatry* 361 (1982).

41. See Gutheil, Restraint Versus Treatment: Seclusion as Discussed in the Boston State Hospital Case, 137 *Am. J. Psychiatry* 718 (1980).

42. See Osgood v. District of Columbia, 567 F. Supp. 1026 (D. D.C. 1983).

43. See notes 15–17, *supra.*

44. E.g., Project Release v. Prevost, 722 F.2d 960 (2d Cir. 1983); but

see Davis v. Hubbard, 506 F. Supp. 915 (N.D. Ohio 1980); Goedecke v. State Dep't of Institutions, 198 Colo. 407, 603 P.2d 123 (1979); Rivers v. Katz, *supra*, note 34.

45. See generally Rubin, Generalizing the Trial Model of Procedural Due Process: A New Basis for the Right to Treatment, 17 *Harv. Civ. Rts.—Civ. Liberties L. Rev.* 61 (1982); Spece, Preserving the Right to Treatment: A Critical Assessment and Constructive Development of Constitutional Right to Treatment Theories, 20 *Ariz. L. Rev.* 1 (1978).

46. See generally Lessard v. Schmidt, 349 F. Supp. 1078 (E.D. Wis. 1972), *vacated* 414 U.S. 473 (1974) (this case has had an interesting history of reviews by the federal courts, *on remand*, 379 F. Supp. 1376 [E.D. Wis. 1974], *vacated*, 421 U.S. 957 [1975], *on remand*, 413 F. Supp. 1318 [E.D. Wis. 1976]).

47. Birnbaum, The Right to Treatment, 46 *A.B.A. J.* 499 (1960).

48. O'Connor v. Donaldson, 422 U.S. 563 (1975).

49. See generally Slovenko, Past and Present of the Right to Treatment: A Slogan Gone Astray, 9 *J. Psychiatry & L.* 263 (1981).

50. Rouse v. Cameron, 373 F.2d 451 (D.C. Cir. 1966).

51. Youngberg v. Romeo, 457 U.S. 307 (1982).

52. The full meaning of the case, and the consequences for treatment and the right to refuse it are the subject of debate. See Comment, The Right to Treatment in the Least Restrictive Alternative: The Confusion Remains After *Youngberg v. Romeo*, 19 *New Eng. J. L.* 175 (1983). The *Youngberg* case was expanded somewhat by Thomas S. v. Morrow, 781 F.2d 367 (4th Cir. 1986), *cert. denied, sub nom.* Kirk v. Thomas S., 106 S.Ct. 1992 (1986). In *Thomas S.*, the Fourth Circuit ordered the state to transfer a former patient to a suitable community placement, and to provide counseling, educational and training services.

53. Note, The Constitutional Right to Treatment in Light of *Youngberg v. Romeo*, 72 *Georgetown L. J.* 1785 (1984).

54. O'Connor v. Donaldson, 422 U.S. 563, 575 (1975).

55. Wyatt v. Stickney, 325 F. Supp. 781 (M.D. Ala. 1971), *later decision*, 334 F. Supp. 1341 (M.D. Ala. 1971), *later decision*, 344 F. Supp. 373 (M.D. Ala. 1972), *later proceeding* 344 F. Supp. 387 (M.D. Ala. 1972), *aff'd in part rev'd in part, sub nom.* Wyatt v. Aderholt, 503 F.2d 1305 (5th Cir. 1974).

56. Wyatt v. Stickney, 344 F. Supp. 373 (M.D. Ala. 1972) (subsequent case history described, *supra*, note 55).

57. Schwitzgebel, The Right to Effective Mental Treatment, 62 *Calif. L. Rev.* 936 (1974).

58. See Meyer & Soskin, Romeo, Romeo, Where Art Thou Romeo: Before the Court at the Mercy of Institutional Professionals, 10 *J. Psychiatry & L.* 205 (1982).

59. Brown & Bremer, Inadequate Means to a Noble End: The Right to Treatment Paradox, 6 *J. Psychiatry & L.* 45 (1978).

60. See McGuire & Frisman, Reimbursement Policy and Cost-Effective Mental Health Care, 38 *Am. Psychologist* 935 (1983); Shapiro & Shapiro,

Meta-Analysis of Psychotherapy Outcome Studies: A Replication and Re-finement, 92 *Psychological Bull.* 581 (1982); Smith, Meta-Analysis of Psy-chotherapy Outcome Studies, 32 *Am. Psychologist* 751 (1977). These and other outcomes issues are reviewed in chapter 4.

61. The state statutory provisions providing for private responsibility for the costs of care in state mental institutions are considered in Kapp, Residents of State Mental Institutions and Their Money (Or The State Giveth and the State Taketh Away), 6 *J. Psychiatry & L.* 287, 305 (1978).

62. Department of Mental Hygiene v. Kirchner, 380 U.S. 194 (1965) (decided on procedural grounds).

63. See Kapp, *supra,* note 61.

64. Wyatt v. Aderholt, 503 F.2d 1305 (5th Cir. 1974).

65. See 42 U.S.C. §§1983, 1984 (1982).

66. Harlow v. Fitzgerald, 457 U.S. 800 (1982). However, in right to treatment cases, even if the absence of funds is a defense in suits for money damages, it is not a defense to prevent an injunction from being issued or-dering the state to provide adequate services in the future. Thomas S. v. Morrow, 781 F.2d 367 (4th Cir. 1986), *cert. denied, sub nom.* Kirk v. Thomas S., 106 S.Ct. 1992 (1986).

67. Pennhurst v. Halderman, 465 U.S. 89 (1984), *later proceeding* 610 F. Supp. 1221 (E.D. Pa. 1985). See Parry, *Youngberg* and *Pennhurst* Revisited, 10 *Mental & Physical Disability L. Rep.* 154 (1986).

68. Estelle v. Gamble, 429 U.S. 97 (1976).

69. Bowring v. Godwin, 551 F.2d 44 (4th Cir. 1977), but see Illinois v. Marshall, 114 Ill. App.3d 217, 448 N.E.2d 969 (4th Dist. 1983).

70. Brenner & Galanti, Prisoners' Rights to Psychiatric Care, 21 *Idaho L. Rev.* 1 (1985); Neisser, Is There a Doctor in the Joint? The Search for Constitutional Standards for Prison Health Care, 63 *Va. L. Rev.* 921 (1977).

71. Brant, *Pennhurst, Romeo,* and *Rogers*: The Burger Court and Mental Health Law, 4 *J. Legal Med.* 323 (1983).

72. Appelbaum & Gutheil, "Rotting With Their Rights On": Consti-tutional Theory and Clinical Reality in Drug Refusal by Psychiatric Patients, 7 *Bull. Am. Acad. Psychiatry & L.* 306 (1979); Treffert, Dying With Their Rights On, 130 *Am. J. Psychiatry* 1041 (1973).

PART IV

CONCLUSION

CHAPTER 19
DECISION MAKING AND RESPONSIBILITY

There are several recurrent themes in law and the behavioral sciences. One is the importance of ethics in guiding professionals in meeting obligations to clients and patients, to other professionals, and to society. A second theme is the law's influence on mental health practice—e.g., through licensing, testimonial privileges, malpractice, and reimbursement. Another theme has been the significant impact that mental health professionals can have on the law directly (by participating in the legal system as witnesses and consultants) and indirectly (through the study of the legal system, virtually every subject in this book has been the subject of empirical research by behavioral scientists).

Of all of the themes in the law of mental health and human behavior, no theme is so pervasive, central, and complex as the question of when people should be able to make decisions for themselves and be held responsible for their decisions.[1] This question raises the issues of autonomy, decision-making ability, and responsibility. These issues are understandably controversial: They involve fundamental questions of freedom, the proper authority of the state, and the nature of human beings.

We suggest here a method of analysis concerning competency to make decisions consistent with a strong sense of individual liberty and freedom while providing for those who are unable to make decisions for themselves. We also review who should decide when someone is incompetent and how decisions should be made for those who are incompetent. We then discuss how decision-making ability is related to the issue of responsibility. In closing we briefly discuss the kinds of research that are needed in law and the behavioral sciences.

THE IMPORTANCE OF
DECISION-MAKING AUTHORITY

Declaring people incompetent is an extremely powerful concept. It permits the government to remove from people important rights including determining where they will live, what treatment they will accept, whether to vote and how to use their property. Many of the difficult issues discussed in this book are essentially a question of whether we should remove those rights. Incompetency is the central issue in guardianship, the right to refuse treatment, nondangerous civil commitment, criminal responsibility, and consent.

Despite the importance of defining standards for determining decision-making capacity, current legal definitions often remain extremely broad and vague. The failure to clearly define standards for determining incompetency invites abuse. Removal of decision-making authority is, of course, intended to protect incompetent people, but this power is subject to misuse and abuse. Justice Brandeis wrote in a different context, "experience should teach us to be the most on our guard to protect liberty when the government's purposes are beneficent."[2] In commenting on this opinion, judge, later Chief Justice, Warren Burger rejected the notion that individuals possess "rights only as to sensible beliefs, valid thoughts, reasonable emotions, or well-founded sensations. I suggest he [Brandeis] intended to include a great many foolish, unreasonable and even absurd ideas which do not conform, such as refusing medical treatment even at great risk."[3]

Because removal of the decision-making authority is so powerful and current standards are so vague, incompetency may be the next great mental health civil rights issue.

STANDARDS FOR DETERMINING
DECISION-MAKING CAPABILITY

The challenge is to design standards for determining incompetency that rest on the minimum mental facilities necessary to make decisions, but that avoid defining competency in terms of beliefs, feelings, attitudes, preferences, and emotions. Too often legal definitions of incompetency have relied on "rational" or "reasonable" decision making, and these definitions in effect do depend upon values, beliefs, and preferences. Improving the definition of competency requires a willingness to give up the vagueness of current definitions. These definitions may be valued by some because of their vagueness which allows decisions to be made on the basis on unstated principles or prejudices.

In the past, too little effort has been devoted to describing the skills or abilities necessary for people to be competent to make decisions for themselves. Successful efforts to fully define competency are likely to require substantial and sustained research efforts. The effort to find a single, perfectly precise definition of incompetency is perhaps the search for the Holy Grail.[4] However, efforts should be made to make it as definite as possible.

A variety of approaches to incompetency have been suggested. Appelbaum and Roth, for example, identified four standards for judging competency: evidencing a choice, factual understanding of issues, rational manipulation of information, and appreciation of the nature of the situation.[5] The President's Commission for the Study of Ethical Problems in Medical and Biomedical and Behavioral Research suggested that decision-making capacity requires the possession of values and goals, the ability to understand and to communicate information, and the ability to reason and deliberate.[6] Others suggest that reality testing or ability to retain information are the standards of incompetency;[7] or that people are competent if they have an awareness of their situation, a factual understanding of the issues with which they must deal and the ability to manipulate information rationally.[8] Another approach identifies the mental abilities that go into producing competency as including memory, intellectual functioning, orientation, and judgment; impairment in rationality, mood, hallucinations, and delusions might interfere with this proper functioning.[9] This small sample of the variety of definitions of decision-making capacity demonstrates the diversity of views concerning competency.

We believe that for people to be competent to make decisions they must:

1. Be able to receive and appreciate information necessary for making a decision, and about the issues that must be decided.

2. Be willing to make a decision.
3. Be able in some way to communicate (or implement) the decision.
4. Be able to manipulate the information in some way to produce the decision.[10]

The first three criteria are virtually self-evident. They require that the person know a decision must be made, and be able to tell others what that decision is or carry it out. The communication may be elementary or nonverbal, but it must be able to convey ideas and information.

The level of mental processing required for someone to be competent, the fourth criterion, is much more difficult to define. Many discussions of the criteria for competency suggest that "rational thought" or "reason" are the essence of competency. However, such definitions are likely to be misunderstood. It is common to speak of some beliefs, values, or preferences as being "irrational." For example, it is sometimes described as irrational or crazy to believe that blood transfusions are sinful or to favor (or oppose) abortion. In a free society, we should be unwilling to take decision-making authority from a person because the majority disagrees with those beliefs or because we see them as "irrational." Appropriate definitions of decision-making competence should therefore avoid judging feelings, values, or beliefs.

The mental processing might be thought of as the interaction of a set of values, beliefs, emotions, preferences, and feelings with several elements:

1. *Memory* sufficient to hold relevant information in mind long enough to make a decision. (In some instances the ability to obtain factual data independently is a necessary related skill.)
2. The ability to assess or recognize *facts* (facts being narrowly defined here not to include opinions).
3. The ability for *functional logic*.

A person with these abilities, if provided sufficient information, generally can assess the consequences of behavior as well as the relative risks and benefits of alternatives. The presence of these elements does not guarantee "rational" decisions (in the way that term is often used), with which most other people would agree. It means only that the person is capable of recognizing (and accepting or rejecting) normal or rational (or generally accepted) solutions to problems.

Decision-making competency should be defined on the basis of mental *abilities,* and should avoid judgments regarding values, emotions, feelings, beliefs, and preferences; freedom regarding these factors is at the heart of liberty and autonomy. The fact that unorthodox views cause someone to make decisions that would be rejected by the vast majority of the population cannot be the basis for determining incompetency. Therefore, we eliminate from the definition of incompetency any such evaluations. Decision-making capacity, then, may be defined as including the following:

1. The ability to receive and appreciate information necessary for making a decision.
2. The willingness to make a decision.
3. The ability in some way to communicate the decision (or otherwise implement it).
4. The ability to manipulate the information in some way to produce the decision. This requires:
   a. Memory sufficient to hold relevant information in mind long enough to make a decision.
   b. The ability to assess or recognize facts (not opinions), and in some instances the ability to obtain factual data independently.
   c. The ability for functional logic.

A person cannot make a decision without being able to hold information in mind long enough to do so. The kind and strength of memory required will vary. For example, the strength of memory required to participate actively in managing a complex investment portfolio is considerably greater than is necessary to remember relatives long enough to complete a will. In many instances, the level of memory required may be relatively low. This would be true where the relevant information can be provided in a short time and a decision is made immediately thereafter.

The ability to recognize facts or reality is difficult to define, in part because it is difficult to distinguish fact from opinions or beliefs. For our discussion, "facts" may be divided into three types.

1. Those facts completely indisputable and established beyond all question. An example is the existence of gravity. The failure to accept these facts may be the basis for determining someone's incompetence if material to the decision making in question.
2. Those facts generally accepted as true, but not *absolutes*. For example, it is generally recognized that it is healthy to eat a balanced diet. Someone may reject the benefits of one food group and still be considered competent, provided he is able to recognize that he is rejecting a fact generally accepted by most people.
3. Matters about which reasonable people may disagree. These are not facts at all, although they are sometimes incorrectly labeled as such. They often contain an element of opinion, belief, or prediction about the future. Examples of these "facts" are that IBM is currently a good investment or that saccharin causes cancer. The rejection of such "facts," of course, does not mean that someone is incompetent.

Not included as "facts" in this discussion are theories (even if very widely held, e.g., evolution), matters of opinion, or predictions about the future. It is possible for someone to have delusions and yet be able to adequately distinguish reality. For example, someone who hears voices may also know that others do not hear them and they do not represent ordinary audible sound transmission. In some cases, beliefs or values may be the basis for overcoming the existence of facts, and in these instances the belief does not necessarily establish incompetency. Thus, while the failure to recognize the existence of gravity is to reject a fact, the belief that God may suspend such physical laws is not.

It is critical that opinions and beliefs not play a role in determining facts. For example, whether someone would be "better off" with or without treatment is not a fact, but depends on what "better off" means. A generally accepted fact, however, might be a statement of the percentage of people who experience a particular outcome following treatment.

In some instances the ability to obtain factual information may also be relevant. For example, the ability to manage a complex financial estate may be related to the ability to obtain expert advice. The competency to stand trial depends on the ability to assist an attorney concerning the trial process and this may require, in some cases, some ability to remember or seek facts. In these instances it is appropriate that the ability to obtain basic facts be considered as part of competency.

The ability to engage in functional logic permits someone to apply values, beliefs and preferences, and facts, to solve a problem and to come to a decision. Functional logic refers to the ability to engage in basic reasoning processes. It is the *ability* to conduct logical reasoning that is critical, not whether the decision that is made is apparently "logical." Beliefs, feelings, or emotions that are unstated may cause someone to make a decision that is not totally logical in light of his or her expressed values or emotions. For example, selecting among treatment alternatives involves a complicated balancing of one kind of risk against others. Such a process often requires the application of values or emotions that are not or cannot be fully stated. If a person is capable of logical reasoning he or she has available the opportunity to know what is apparently logical. However, the person should also have the freedom to reject apparently logical decisions on the basis of intuitive or unstated feelings, beliefs, values, or emotions. Without the *ability* to engage in functional logic, however, a person cannot even have available for decision making an understanding of what apparently a logical conclusion is nor understand consequences of alternatives.

This formulation of decision-making capacity focuses upon the ability to exercise certain mental skills. It specifically avoids judging beliefs, values, preferences, feelings, and emotions. As such, it implements to the extent possible concepts of autonomy by avoiding a judgment of those parts of personality or mental processing that deal not with skills but with the way one views or reacts to the world. It is probably a somewhat narrower view of incompetency than is generally applied now. The very vague definitions of competency currently in use, however, make it difficult to know precisely how broad existing definitions are.

LEVEL OF COMPETENCY REQUIRED

The second part of decision-making capacity is the level of impairment in any of the necessary functions (memory, ability to determine facts, and ability for logical reasoning) that will destroy competency. No single level of functioning can be described for all kinds of competency. Rather, the nature and level of functioning in each of the areas described must be determined in the context of the kinds of decisions that must be made and the consequences arising from an incorrect decision.[11]

When the outcome of a decision is likely to be profound, with high probability of permanent, great harm, then enhanced or high levels of functioning in the three areas (memory, fact assessment, and functional logic) should be required. When the risk of harm is lower, or the harm likely to be less profound or not permanent, then a much lower level of functioning in the three areas is required. When there is little risk of significant, if any, harm, then only a minimal level of functioning in these areas should be required. For example, the refusal of lifesaving treatment, perhaps a blood transfusion, by an adult requires greater competence than the decision not to take an aspirin to relieve a headache.

INCOMPETENCY AND OTHER
STATE INTERVENTION

This formulation of standards and levels of functioning defines decision-making incompetency only. It suggests when the state can legitimately interfere with decision making of people solely on the basis of their incapacities. It does not, however, define the entire range of appropriate government interference with autonomy. Criminal incarceration and civil commitment are other examples. Someone who is delusional and likely to harm a family member or someone who is seriously depressed and likely to commit suicide can appropriately be civilly committed. Such people, however, should not be considered incompetent. Thus, the state has several alternatives for dealing with conduct that is related to mental illness and is dangerous or harmful, it need not depend on incompetency to serve these purposes. Criminal punishment and civil commitment serve particular social purposes and are limited in scope and surrounded with protections against abuse. The state should not seek to use incompetency to accomplish the specific goals of civil or criminal commitment (or vice versa) by removing decision-making authority from someone.

Furthermore, if the state wishes to interfere with specific decisions to protect people from bad decisions, it should do so directly, and not on the basis of incompetency. For example, if we want to prevent people from becoming destitute, we should directly limit the types of gifts they can make. We should not try to determine (essentially on the basis of the gift itself) that someone who gives most of his money to an offbeat church, or to a friend, is incompetent. If we start making determinations of competency on such bases, we will in effect be making legal decisions on the legitimacy of others' religious beliefs, values, and preferences.

Finally, the state has the authority to offer assistance to someone whether competent or not. Many people of marginal competency (e.g., some deinstitutionalized mental patients) could benefit from the availability of services which they would voluntarily choose to accept. Nor is incompetency the only way of protecting the civil (e.g., financial) interests of the mentally disabled. Laws preventing fraud and misrepresentation, and consumer protection, tenant rights, and civil rights laws can all be used to protect them. It is not necessary, or appropriate, to declare them incompetent in order to make available to them the necessities of life or to protect them from harm.

DETERMINING INCOMPETENCY

Whatever standards are used to determine incompetency, a second issue is, who has the authority to determine when incompetency exists. In chapter 16 we saw circumstances in which courts determine the question of competency. In other instances someone other than a court must make this judgment. For example, informed consent given by an incompetent person may not be effective and a contract made by an incompetent person may not be enforceable. Therefore, those treating or contracting with someone who may be incompetent must make a determination of competency. Ultimately, however, the decision will be made by a court even in these circumstances (e.g., if the enforcement of the contract becomes a legal issue), usually on the advice of mental health experts.

One area in which the debate concerning determination of incompetency has not been fully settled is whether mental health experts may determine the incompetency of an involuntary civil commitment patient and, having made a determination of incompetency, proceed to provide involuntary treatment. Some cases have argued that such an informal, nonjudicial process is appropriate because the level of competency changes rapidly, requiring a judicial determination would take too much time, and treating professionals should have the best interest of the patient in mind.[12] It might also be argued that because courts overwhelmingly rely on the conclusions of mental health experts, professionals are, in effect, the decision makers in incompetency cases anyway.[13] On the other hand, there is strong reason to believe that mental health experts often misunderstand or misapply the legal standards for establishing incompetency.[14]

To protect legal rights, the following should be required before any determination of significant legal rights is delegated or left in the hands of nonjudicial decision makers:

1. The legal standards for making the determination should be clear and unambiguous and be understandable by the decision maker.
2. The decision maker must be neutral and able to apply the standards fairly.
3. The person whose rights will be affected must be given notice that the decision will be made and have the opportunity to present information to the decision maker. In many cases, this will require access to pertinent information and an adviser, perhaps even an attorney.
4. The decision maker should state (preferably in writing) the reasons for the decision in a way that indicates that legal standards were understood and applied reasonably.
5. There should be some opportunity for judicial review of unreasonable decisions.

Involuntary treatment decisions made in hospitals are likely to be inadequate under these criteria. If incompetency determinations are to be made in a nonjudicial form, we recommend that they be made by an interdisciplinary team including mental health professionals and at least one attorney.[15] The person under review should be given the chance to present information and have an adviser. If incompetency is determined, a brief written report should be required and there should be relatively easy access to the evaluation team to have competency reestablished.[16]

DECISION MAKING FOR INCOMPETENTS

Substitute Decision Makers

In most instances when people cannot make decisions for themselves, substitute decision makers (guardians) make decisions for them. In a few instances, there is no way of substituting for the incompetent (incompetency to stand trial) or the law presumes a specific decision (distribution of property if a will is invalid).

Refusal of Treatment

The refusal of treatment by mental patients is the source of considerable controversy about the nature and consequences of a determination that a patient is not competent to refuse treatment. Incompetency is not relevant only to patients who refuse treatment. Patients may be incompetent whether they reject or accept treatment. Either patients are competent to make certain kinds of decisions or they are not. The refusal itself cannot be a legitimate ground for determining the question of competency.[17] Ideally, a decision concerning competency should be made before consent is sought, and incompetency should not in itself authorize the institution to proceed with treatment. There is some suggestion, however, that treatment can properly proceed for incompetents without obtaining the informed consent of a guardian or next of kin.[18] Such an approach is inconsistent with the role guardians should play in protecting the best interests of incompetents. It is a shortcut that should not be acceptable to the legal system.

The Basis for Substitute Decisions

Another critical issue is deciding what approach a guardian should use, or be required by the law to use, in making decisions. The guardian is commonly said to be obligated to act in the best interests of the ward. This is not a very helpful principle, because the question remains, what is the best interest of the ward? From whose point of view should the patient's best interests be viewed? There are at least three approaches to making decisions for an incompetent:

1. Decisions may be made on the basis of what the incompetent probably would have wanted ("substituted judgment").
2. Decisions may be based on what most people in the incompetent's position would want or, in the case of treatment decisions, what the mental health professional recommends. Presumably, these are generally the same thing ("best interest" standard).[19]
3. Decisions may be based on what the guardian would have wanted under the circumstances.

Suppose a psychotic patient, now incompetent, had previously expressed opposition to the use of psychotropic medications but spoke very favorably of ECT. In fact, on several occasions, he had expressed a desire to have ECT if there were any chance that it could help his condition. There is some realistic chance that ECT could help the patient, but the treating psychiatrist suggests the use of psychotropic medication, and there is every reason to believe that the majority of people with the patient's condition would accept medication. The guardian says that if she were to face a similar situation herself, she would refuse both ECT and psychotropic medication. She says she realizes that the rejection of all treatment might result in a longer period of incompetency and longer hospitalization. Which treatment option should the guardian be obligated to select—the patient's, the doctor's, or her own?

Because the major purpose of the consent process is to protect autonomy and to permit important personal decisions to be based on the patient's value system, beliefs, feelings, and emotions, the "best interest" of the patient must be viewed from the eyes of the patient. That is, someone's best interest can be legitimately judged only on the basis of what he sees as his own best interests. To promote this policy, the guardian should try to make treatment decisions that are consistent with what the patient would have decided.

This "substituted judgment" approach has attracted considerable attention, but not unanimous support. Two objections are that the patient's wishes in the matter, described while the patient was competent, are not dependable because the patient was not actually facing the situation at the time, and that it is often difficult to determine with certainty what the patient would have decided. The fact that patients do not really face the consequences of opinions expressed about decisions they would like made if they should become incompetent may make them less careful and thoughtful in the decision process. Therefore, the person's announced preference may be different than if the person actually immediately faced the decision. Furthermore, people's views may change and therefore the incompetent person's decision preference may have changed over time but not have been communicated to anyone. These criticisms accurately suggest that the substituted judgment doctrine cannot operate perfectly in the real world, but they are not necessarily persuasive reasons to abandon the doctrine. These objections could be raised to all wills. For example, enforcement of testamentary wills is a form of substituted judgment. There is a chance that those executing testamentary wills cannot really be making legitimate choices about the distribution of property after their deaths. After all, when they execute the will they have never been dead, and they may change their minds about the property before their deaths.[20] Despite these potential problems, the law recognizes these wills because by doing so society is more likely to give effect to the individual's wishes than it is without the will. Substituted judgment is never an optimal way of making decisions, but it is often the "least bad" method available.

A much more serious problem is that in many instances, it is difficult for a guardian to determine what an incompetent would have decided. Suppose the now incompetent made conflicting statements over time or (as is more likely the case) made no indication at all. It is often necessary, therefore, for the guardian to engage in informed speculation. In some instances it is impossible to even reasonably speculate about what the patient would have decided. Such is the case, for example, when someone has never been competent. The guardian must then make decisions on the basis of what other similarly situated patients would do and on reviews about what is "best" for most people. Even these "objective" decisions should be made in light of the special circumstances and needs of the ward. For example, painful treatment might be refused, even though it is life-prolonging, for a mentally retarded ward who would be extremely confused and upset by the treatment or who is particularly sensitive to pain.[21]

The substituted judgment approach requires that guardians take seriously their obligations to act for their wards and take the time to study carefully the decisions that must be made. Given the perfunctory attention given wards by many guardians we might expect that this would not be universally accomplished.[22] Guardians have fiduciary responsibilities to act with care to protect their wards. The failure to be careful in the management of the assets may make the guardian subject to liability. Neglect of the responsibility for nonfinancial decisions is also a breach of fiduciary responsibility and grossly inadequate guardians should be held legally responsible for nonfinancial as well as financial accountability.

Several policies will help limit the uncertainty of substituted judgment decision making or reduce the need for it. The execution of living wills or treatment wills should be encouraged. The formal nature of these documents should help to ensure that people consider what they are signing, rather than making offhand comments. In addition, they give a relatively clear set of instructions concerning decisions that should be made.[23] Such are some of the purposes of the formal execution requirements for testamentary wills. Other mechanisms such as the durable power of attorney and some trusts serve similar purposes by permitting people while competent to place decision-making capacity in people (much like guardians) who will have decision-making authority for them should they become incompetent.[24]

In addition, decisions should not be made for incompetents if they can be voided. For example, where there is hope that competency will be restored, one good way to promote autonomy is by delaying decisions when doing so will not result in any substantial risks or losses. For example, decisions on elective surgery or on the sale of a piece of property (assuming the decision need not be made immediately) can be temporarily put off if a return to competency is expected. Even when someone does not currently have decision-making capacity, the person's wishes during the time of incompetency should be given weight unless to do so would result in unnecessary and significant risks or harm. For example, an incompetent patient's desire to refuse a pain medication should generally be respected even though the person is incompetent and does not have full legal decision-making authority. These techniques will help narrow as much as possible the decisions that must be made for an incompetent.

Perhaps the most important means of avoiding making unnecessary decisions for others is to strictly limit the determinations of incompetency. The standards for determining incompetency suggested earlier in this chapter would help to accomplish this. In addition, limited guardianships (discussed in chapter 16) should be required and used as extensively as possible to reduce the areas in which decision-making authority is lost.[25]

RESPONSIBILITY

Competency and criminal responsibility are related concepts. The decision-making competency described in this chapter is also useful in defining criminal responsibility. If some people are so incompetent that society is unwilling to let them make decisions for themselves, then at that stage of disability they may not be responsible for their decisions. Put simply, if people are incompetent because they cannot make responsible decisions, they cannot be responsible for their decisions. The factors described earlier to determine when someone is incompetent to make decisions can also be used to determine when the person is responsible for decisions. In the area of contract law, competency to contract is the basis for responsibility.[26] However, it is the area of criminal law in which the concept of responsibility is most central. If memory, fact determinating ability, and functional logic are grossly impaired, then it makes little sense to impose criminal guilt. We believe that the insanity defense should be replaced with the defense of criminal incompetency. (This incompetency, of course, must be distinguished from incompetency to stand trial.) Those who are incompetent to make very basic decisions should not be criminally responsible.

The concept of criminal incompetency is consistent with the various philosophical bases for imposing criminal responsibility and the reasons for punishment. Professor Moore has eloquently argued, for example, that a form of incompetency (the absence of practical reasoning) is the proper basis for not imposing "just deserts" punishment on some people.[27] The basis of criminal responsibility, as we noted in chapter 11, is often identified as free will or choice, sometimes identified as varying levels of "strong" or "weak" free will or autonomy. Thus, the core of responsibility has been decision-making ability. For those seeing a form of free choice as being the critical feature of responsibility, incompetency removes the ability to make free or reasoned choices, and therefore removes the "just deserts" basis for punishment. Therefore, the elements that serve to make someone incompetent should also serve to remove responsibility for decisions that the person does make.

Strong behaviorists or determinists reject free choice as the basis for imposing punishment, and instead look to the potential for deterrence, rehabilitation, or removal from society. Instead of moral blameworthiness as the basis for criminal punishment, the ability of the law to change the environment in which decisions are made and to change behavior (decisions) is the central point.[28] For those with a strong determinist philosophy, incompetency is likely to destroy much of the ability of the law to affect behavior. Furthermore, the law is not likely to be a deterrent for those who are so incompetent as to be legally incapable of making decisions.[29] Generally, there is no reason to convict incompetent people of crimes for restraint or rehabilitation purposes; guardianship provisions of the civil law provide the proper legal response because guardianship can be more precisely tailored to the special conditions and needs of the incompetents.

Replacing the insanity defense with a defense of incompetency might be criticized on several grounds. Some would argue that it is too narrow to define the absence of criminal responsibility. (Incompetency would not, of course, be the only exception to criminal liability. Justification—such as self-defense—or the absence of a specific state of mind—such as premeditation—would also be available as defenses.) An example of the narrowness argument would be the person who has bizarre beliefs. Some may see such a belief as a reason for removing criminal responsibility through an insanity defense. However, in most states the current insanity defense would ordinarily not be available based solely on such beliefs.

The "irresistible impulse" type of insanity defense would not always be available if the insanity defense were replaced with a criminal incompetency defense, although this part of the insanity defense is being narrowed or limited in many jurisdictions anyway. Another problem is that criminal incompetency cannot be used with mathematical precision. Especially difficult is defining the level of functioning necessary to establish a capacity for criminal incompetency. This difficulty is, however, an improvement over the problems with current definitions of insanity because the incompetency concept is conceptually sounder and expresses criminal responsibility issues in terms that are somewhat more definite and testable.

A doctrine of not guilty by reason of incompetency, if closely related to guardianship-type incompetency, might reduce the current problems of disposition following a determination of not guilty by reason of insanity. Not guilty by reason of incompetency should be the basis for removing decision-making authority from the defendant, unless it is demonstrated that competency was restored between the time the crime was committed and the time of trial. In cases where the state has proved that the defendant committed the act which would be a crime but for the incompetency, it would be appropriate for the state to play a role in determining (with the guardian) where the incompetent defendant will be living, to ensure that the defendant is not a threat to society. Such a role is somewhat analogous to state civil commitment. However, because the incompetent person is already without the right to make important personal decisions, the state's participation in the decision of where such a defendant will live may be somewhat less intrusive than is ordinary civil commitment. It is apparent that significant protection would be necessary to ensure that the incompetency process was not used to permit unfair state interference with decision making for incompetents. Several of the principles suggested in chapter 16 for dealing with incompetency to stand trial might be adapted to reduce the risk of abuse of not guilty by reason of incompetency.[30]

AUTONOMY

Throughout this volume the importance of individual autonomy has been emphasized. Autonomy is important to those who accept free will or other free choice views of human behavior. It is the expression of choices that gives any meaning to the free will.

Autonomy, as we have used the concept, also has an important place as a basis for legal principles for those who accept a strong behavioral/determinist point of view. Autonomy is the ability to express a personal preference concerning what will happen to oneself. The strong behavioral/determinist position is that preferences, beliefs, and values are not internally generated as part of a free will, but are rather the result of a complex combination of hereditary and environmental factors. Under this philosophy, the expression of autonomous decisions is not a free choice of options, but rather determined by these factors. It is therefore sometimes assumed that freedom and autonomy are meaningless concepts in a strong behavioral/determinist philosophy.[31] If people are not really making free choices, why give legal protection to autonomy? Whatever the cause of someone's wanting to choose one course of action or another, the failure to implement that choice is likely to cause frustration and anger.

If a person makes a decision to do X, it does not matter whether that decision results from some form of free will or from hereditary and environmental factors. A legal requirement that the person do Y instead of X will result in unhappiness and discomfort. This sense of harm will to some extent be shared by others who will be concerned that their "choices" (real or apparent) will be frustrated by government action. Therefore, autonomy is a real interest to be protected no matter what one's philosophical views are concerning human behavior.

A FINAL WORD ABOUT RESEARCH IN LAW AND THE BEHAVIORAL SCIENCES

If this volume demonstrates anything, it is that there are extraordinarily difficult and important unresolved problems and issues involving law and the behavioral sciences. Three broad types of research—analytical, empirical, and philosophical—are available to grapple with those problems. Analytical studies have been the traditional form of research in law and are also of importance in the behavioral sciences. This research analyzes existing law and often proposes reform based on existing social policy. It is through this research that reforms can be formulated and proposed. Empirical research has gathered considerable momentum in recent years and is a mainstay of behavioral science, if not legal, scholarship. Much of it has centered on examining how legal and social services systems work, with some efforts directing toward experimental studies designed to test assumptions about the legal system or proposed reforms. Philosophical studies involving law and the behavioral sciences have received too little attention, but are an essential part of progress in law and the behavioral sciences. One call for more philosophical studies reminds us that the philosophies of behavioral sciences and of law "are simply the disciplines themselves, carried on at somewhat higher levels of abstraction than those employed by typical practitioners in each."[32] Ultimately, philosophical positions define what the law will be and the direction it will take. Keynes suggested that "practical men, who believe themselves quite exempt from intellectual influences, are usually the slaves of some defunct economist"[33] So too, the practitioners of law and the behavioral sciences are often the slave of some defunct philosopher and too seldom recognize the importance of philosophical considerations.

Our disciplines will undoubtedly be strengthened by the growth of a reliance on all three of these research tools. These tools are considerably enhanced by the interdisciplinary efforts that have characterized some of the research in law and the behavioral sciences. The size and importance of the questions with which these disciplines must deal require legal research and reasoning, good empirical research, sound statistical analysis, and solid philosophical footings, and the creative interaction of all of the disciplines. Studies in law and the behavioral sciences are relatively new, and those who have worked in the area thus far are perhaps more accurately characterized as pioneers than as laborers in cleared fields.

SUMMARY

Much of this book has been concerned with issues relating to when individuals have, or should have, legal capacity to make decisions for themselves, and should be legally responsible for their decisions/actions. We have proposed criteria that should be central in defining decision-making capacity.

1. The ability to receive and appreciate information necessary for making a decision.
2. The willingness to make a decision.
3. The ability in some way to communicate the decision (or otherwise implement it).
4. The ability to manipulate the information in some way to produce the decision. This requires:

a. Memory sufficient to hold relevant information in mind long enough to make a decision.
b. The ability to assess or recognize facts (not opinions), and in some instance the ability to obtain factual data independently.
c. The ability for functional logic.

Under this formulation, values, beliefs, preferences, and emotions are not considered in determining whether a person is competent. This formulation is intended to fully protect autonomous decision making. The level of functioning in each of the three areas which is necessary for decision-making capacity depends on the nature and consequences of the decisions. If consequences are life threatening or very harmful and irreversible, then a relatively high level of functioning in the three areas is required.

We suggest that criminal responsibility can generally follow the same functions described for decision-making authority. We would substitute a concept of criminal incompetency for the traditional insanity defense. Ordinarily only a very low level of functioning would be required to oppose criminal responsibility.

The law and the behavioral sciences have three tools with which to grapple with difficult issues: analytical, empirical, and philosophical studies. All three of these areas have important contributions to make to the understanding of the law, mental health and human behavior. These tools are enhanced by interdisciplinary studies which are important in the study of law and the behavorial sciences.

NOTES

1. The issues of decision-making capacity, autonomy and responsibility have been considered in one way or another in almost every chapter in the book. For example, an informed consent to treatment and to the release of information, a major effort to protect autonomy and decision-making interests, is important in issues of malpractice, confidentiality, the intrusive therapies, mental health care, testing, research, competency, and the right to refuse treatment. The concept of responsibility is important in dealing with the insanity defense, punishment, juvenile justice, the psychopath, the truth finding process, sexual variations, and competency.

2. Olmstead v. United States, 277 U.S. 438, 479 (1928) (Brandeis, dissenting, in a different context).

3. Application of President and Directors of Georgetown College, 331 F.2d 1010 (D.C. Cir.), *cert. denied,* 377 U.S. 978 (1964) (Burger, dissenting).

4. Roth, Meisel & Lidz, Tests of Competency to Consent to Treatment, 134 *Am. J. Psychiatry* 279, 283 (1977).

5. Appelbaum & Roth, Competency to Consent to Research, 39 *Archives Gen. Psychiatry* 951 (1982).

6. President's Commission of the Study of Ethical Problems in Medical and Biomedical and Behavioral Research, *Making Health Care Decisions* (1982).

7. Olin & Olin, Informed Consent in Voluntary Mental Hospital Admission, 132 *Am. J. Psychiatry* 938 (1975). See generally B. Gert & C. Culver, *Philosophy in Medicine* (1982).

8. T. Gutheil & P. Appelbaum, *Clinical Handbook of Psychiatry and the Law* 217–18 (1982).

9. *Id.* See also Roth, Meisel & Lidz, *supra,* note 4.

10. The incompetency may occur because of physical disability (e.g., total inability to communicate), mental disability (e.g., mental retardation) or emotional illness (e.g., a psychosis).

11. A very good statement about the need for more than one level of competency is Drane, The Many Faces of Competency, 15 *Hastings Center Rep.* 17 (Apr. 1985). Regrding the process of evaluation see T. Grisso, *Evaluating Competencies: Forensic Assessments and Instruments* (1986).

12. E.g., Doe v. Gallinot, 657 F.2d 1017 (9th Cir. 1981); Rennie v. Klein, 653 F.2d 836 (3rd Cir. 1981) (en banc), *vacated,* 458 U.S. 1119 (1982), *on remand,* 720 F.2d 266 (3d Cir. 1983). But see Rogers v. Okin 634 F.2d 650 (1st Cir. 1980), *remanded, sub nom.* Mills v. Rogers, 457 U.S. 291 (1982) (subsequent history, *infra,* note 14); Rivers v. Katz, 67 N.Y.2d 485, 495 N.E.2d 337, 504 N.Y.S.2d 74 (1986).

Similar issues arise in the refusal of lifesaving treatment by incompetent patients. See generally e.g., *In re* Quinlan, 70 N.J. 10, 355 A.2d 647, *cert. denied,* 429 U.S. 922 (1976); Matter of Storar [Eichner v. Dillon], 52 N.Y.2d 363, 420 N.E.2d 64, 438 N.Y.S.2d 266, *cert. denied,* 454 U.S. 858 (1981).

13. Studies described in chapters 16 and 17 indicate that mental health experts' recommendations are almost invariably followed by courts when making decisions concerning involuntary civil commitment, competency to stand trial and guardianship. It might be argued that because courts routinely adopt the recommendation of mental health experts in making these decisions, little would be lost by giving mental health experts direct authority for making the decision.

14. See generally Rogers v. Okin, 634 F.2d 650 (1st Cir. 1980), *remanded, sub nom.* Mills v. Rogers, 457 U.S. 291 (1982), *later proceeding,* Rogers v. Department of Mental Health, 390 Mass. 489, 458 N.E.2d 308, *on remand,* Rogers v. Okin, 738 F.2d 1 (1st Cir. 1984), 638 F. Supp. 934 (D. Mass. 1986).

There is reason to believe that mental health professionals who testify as expert witnesses may misunderstand the legal issues to which they are testifying. See R. Roesch & S. Golding, *Competency to Stand Trial* 69–91, 140–200 (1980).

15. The value of an interdisciplinary team is that the mental health expert can review the mental health questions while the attorney provides guidance about the legal standards on which decision should be based. In addition, the combination of the different approaches of law and the behavioral sciences might produce a healthy new perspective on these decisions. See Levine, Scientific Method and the Adversary Model, 29 *Am. Psychologist* 661 (1974); Smith, Life and Death Decisions in the Nursery: Standards and Procedures for Withholding Lifesaving Treatment From Infants, 27 *N.Y. L. Sch. L. Rev.* 1125, 1181–82 (1982).

16. The issues involved in moving legal decisions to mental health professionals are examined in Berger, The Psychiatric Expert as Due Process Decision-Maker, 33 *Buffalo L. Rev.* 681 (1984).

17. Incompetency has to do with the *ability* to make a decision, not the decision itself. However, those who do what professionals advise are less likely to find themselves the subject of incompetency proceedings. Nolan, Functional Evaluation of the Elderly in Guardianship Proceedings, 12 *L. Med. & Health Care* 210 (1984). It appears, therefore, that the decision itself, rather than the ability to make it, is often an initial basis for determining competency. The *ability* to refuse (or consent to) treatment rather than the decision is, of course, the appropriate question in competence. See Brown, Psychiatric Refusal, Patient Competence, and Informed Consent, 8 *Int'l J. L. & Psychiatry* 83 (1986).

18. See notes 12 and 14, *supra*; Note, The Doctrine of Informed Consent Applied to Psychotherapy, 72 *Georgetown L. J.* 1637 (1984).

19. S. Jordan, *Decision Making for Incompetent Persons: The Law and Morality of Who Should Decide* (1985).

We follow the traditional labeling of these standards as "best interest" and "substituted judgment." These labels are, however, somewhat inappropriate and misleading. Substituted judgment is not substituting someone else's judgment for the incompetent, rather it is trying to determine and implement the incompetent person's own judgment. At the same time, the best interest judgment does substitute someone else's decision (of an objective or "average person" standard) for the incompetent person's judgment. Because determining what is in the incompetent person's best interest is the difficult question being considered, labeling one of the options as the "best interest" is particularly confusing.

20. See Buchanan, The Limits of Proxy Decision-Making for Incompetents, 29 *UCLA L. Rev.* 386 (1981); Gutheil & Appelbaum, The Substituted Judgment Approach: Its Difficulties and Paradoxes in Mental Health Settings, 13 *L. Med. & Health Care* 61 (1985); Gutheil & Appelbaum, Substituted Judgment and the Physician's Ethical Dilemma: With Special Reference to the Problem of the Psychiatric Patient, 41 *J. Clinical Psychiatry* 303 (1980); Isenberg & Gutheil, Family Process and Legal Guardianship for the

Psychiatric Patient: A Clinical Study, 9 *Bull. Am. Acad. Psychiatry & Law* 40 (1981).

21. In Superintendent of Belchertown v. Saikewicz, 373 Mass. 728, 370 N.E.2d 417 (1977), for example, the court approved withholding painful chemotherapy from an incompetent patient with terminal cancer. The court noted that the treatment would have been painful and that unlike fully competent patients, the incompetent could not understand the reason for the pain and therefore the treatment was likely to be even more confusing and hurtful to the incompetent patient than it would be to the competent patient.

It is possible that incompetent mental patients may be similarly more confused or hurt by certain procedures than would competent patients. Jacobs & Kotin, Fantasies of Psychiatric Research, 128 *Am. J. Psychiatry* 9 (1972); Siris, Docherty & McGlashan, Intrapsychic Structural Effects of Psychiatric Research, 136 *Am. J. Psychiatry* 12 (1979) (dealing with confusion of psychiatric treatment and research, including EEGs and spinal taps). Regarding the competency of mental patients generally see C. Lidz, M. Meisel, E. Zerubavel, M. Carter, R. Sestak, & L. Roth, *Informed Consent: A Study of Decisionmaking in Psychiatry* (1984).

22. In chapter 16, we note that some people or institutions may serve as guardian for more than 100 wards. Public guardians often are responsible for a large number of incompetent people with low incomes. See W. Schmidt, K. Miller, W. Bell & B. E. New, *Public Guardianship and the Elderly* (1981).

23. Compare Reinert, A Living Will for a Commitment Hearing, 31 *Hosp. & Community Psychiatry* 857 (1980) and Szasz, The Psychiatric Will: A New Mechanism for Protecting Persons Against "Psychosis" and Psychiatry, 37 *Am. Psychologist* 767 (1982); with Chodoff & Peele, The Psychiatric Will of Dr. Szasz, 13 *Hastings Center Rep.* 11 (1983).

24. A durable power of attorney gives legal decision-making authority to a specific, named individual. It is "durable" in that if it is executed while someone is competent, it continues in effect even if the person becomes incompetent. (Most states provide that the durable power of attorney ends if there is a formal court proceeding to declare someone incompetent. Thus, the durable power continues to be effective between the time someone in fact becomes incompetent, and the time someone raises the incompetency in court through a guardianship proceeding.) This is a change in common-law power of attorney, which ended if incompetency occurred. Most states require that a durable power of attorney specifically note that the power of attorney is durable, or should survive incompetency. Dickman, Court Enforcement of a Durable Power of Attorney, 17 *U. San Fran. L. Rev.* 611 (1983); Note, Appointing an Agent to Make Medical Treatment Choices, 84 *Colum. L. Rev.* 985 (1984). But see Buchanan, The Limits of Proxy Decisionmaking for Incompetents, 29 *UCLA L. Rev.* 386 (1981).

Several legal trust arrangements may provide for the management of property. The convertible and protective trusts are suggested as appropriate. Callahan, The Use of a Convertible Trust in Planning for Disability, 53 *N.Y. St. B. J.* 422 (1981). Such instruments, however, do not provide for personal care decisions, but only financial decisions. See L. M. Russell, *Alternatives: A Family Guide to Legal and Financial Planning for the Disabled* (1983).

25. A limited guardianship provides for declaring someone to be incompetent only in certain areas. In a limited partnership, only some decision-making authority is removed from the person. Unfortunately, they are infrequently used by courts. Schmidt et al., *supra,* note 22 at 172.

26. A contract made by someone who is incompetent is not legally enforceable, whether or not the person has formally been declared incompetent in a court proceeding. Comment, The Mentally Ill and the Law of Contracts, 29 *Temple L. Rev.* 380 (1956).

A much different approach is taken in tort liability, where incompetency or mental disability is ordinarily no defense to tort liability. Curran, Tort Liability of the Mentally Ill and Mentally Deficient, 21 *Ohio St. L. J.* 52 (1960); Note, Insanity as a Defense, 54 *Marq. L. Rev.* 245 (1971).

27. M. Moore, *Law and Psychiatry: Rethinking the Relationship* 233–46 (1984). Moore distinguishes between "strong" free will or autonomy (which means freedom from causation of one's actions) and "weak" free will or autonomy (which refers to the existence of sufficient causal power over their bodies to achieve some of their wants). *Id.* at 109, 361–62. Moore also proposes that the insanity defense be stated, "Is the accused so irrational as to be nonresponsible?" Moral responsibility is based on the ability to do practical reasoning. *Id.* at 243–45. A summary of the arguments are presented in Moore, The Relevance of Philosophy to Law and Psychiatry 6 *J. L. & Psychiatry* 177 (1983).

28. See B. F. Skinner, *Beyond Freedom and Dignity* (1971).

29. The availability of an incompetency defense could, however, reduce the general level of deterrence of the insanity defense by leading some who could be deterred to believe that they could use (or misuse) the defense to escape punishment.

30. These procedures include requiring a finding of not guilty unless the state proves that the defendant committed the crime (with not guilty by reason of incompetency being reserved for those who would otherwise be found guilty), the period of incompetency (without periodic rehearings) being limited to the average sentence for those found guilty, and interdisciplinary team evaluations.

31. See generally B. F. Skinner, *Beyond Freedom and Dignity* (1971).

32. Moore, *Law and Psychiatry,* supra, note 27, at 423.

33. J. M. Keynes, *The General Theory of Employment, Interest and Money* (1936).

INDEX OF REFERENCES

The Index of References is a listing of the references appearing in the book. The format is the same used in the notes, as described in the Note on Notes (pages xiii–xiv). Entries are alphabetical rather than grouped by author.

Following the citation, the chapter (in roman numerals) and note in which the work is cited are given. Thus, II–n.73 refers to note 73 in Chapter 2.

Abarbanel, Shared Parenting After Separation: A Study of Joint Custody, 49 *Am. J. Orthopsychiatry* 320 (1979), XIII–n.47.

Abbott, Professional Ethics, 88 *Am. J. Soc.* 855 (1983), I–n.19.

C. Abel, *Punishment and Restitution: A Restitutionary Approach to Crime and the Criminal* (1984), XII–n.85.

Abel, Becker & Cunningham-Rather, Complications, Consent, and Cognitions in Sex Between Children and Adults, 7 *Int'l J. L. & Psychiatry* 89 (1984), XIV–n.13.

Abel, Blanchard & Becker, An Integrated Treatment Program for Rapists, in *Clinical Aspects of the Rapist* (R. Rada ed. 1977), XIV–n.15.

Abille v. United States, 482 F. Supp. 703 (N.D. Cal. 1980), I–n.79.

Abramowitz, Psychological Outcomes of Sex Reassignment Surgery, 54 *J. Consulting & Clinical Psychology* 183 (1986), XIV–n.39.

Abrams, What's New in Convulsive Therapy, in *New Dimensions in Psychiatry* 85 (S. Arieti and G. Chrzanowski eds. 1975), III–n.27.

Action for Mental Health, IV–n.67.

Adams, Medical Research and Personal Privacy, 30 *Vill. L. Rev.* 1077 (1985), VI–n.37.

Addington v. Texas, 441 U.S. 418 (1979), XVII–n.19, XVII–n.20.

Adelman & Howard, Expert Testimony or Malingering: The Admissibility of Clinical Procedures For the Detection of Deception, 2 *Behav. Sci. & L.* 5 (1984), VIII–n.21, VIII–n.22, VIII–n.69.

Aden v. Younger, 57 Cal. App. 3d 662, 129 Cal. Rptr. 535 (4th Dist. 1976), III–n.86.

Adney, Winning Through Effective Client Appearance, 15 *Trial Lawyers Q.* 51 (1983), VII–n.16.

T. Adorno, E. Frenkel-Brunswick, D. Levinson & R. Sanford, *The Authoritarian Personality* (1950), VII–n.36.

Affleck, Wintrob & Peszke, Psychiatrists' Evaluations of Emergency Involuntary Hospitalization, 21 *Comprehensive Psychiatry* 13 (1980), XVII–n.8.

Ake v. Oklahoma, 470 U.S. 68 (1985), XII–n.104.

Akron v. Akron Center for Reproductive Health, 462 U.S. 416 (1983), I–n.60, VI–n.68, XIV–n.23, XVIII–n.1.

Albemarle Paper Co. v. Moody, 422 U.S. 405 (1975), V–n.21.

Albers, Pasewark & Meyer, Involuntary Hospitalization and Psychiatric Testimony: The Fallibility of the Doctrine of Immaculate Perception, 6 *Capital U. L. Rev.* 11 (1976), XVII–n.71.

Albert, Fox & Kahn, Faking Psychosis on the Rorschach: Can Expert Judges Detect Malingering?, 44 *J. Personality Assessment* 115 (1980), VIII–n.27.

Aldrich, The Clouded Crystal Ball: A 35-Year Follow Up of Psychiatrists'

Aldrich (*Continued*)
Predictions, 143 *Am. J. Psychiatry* 45
(1986), XVII–n.78.

Alexander, Premature Probate: A Different Perspective on Guardianship for
the Elderly, 31 *Stan. L. Rev.* 1003
(1979), XVI–n.67.

Alexander, Who Benefits from Conservatorship?, 30 *Trial* 32 (May 1977),
XVI–n.87.

F. Alexander & H. Staub, *The Criminal,
the Judge, and the Public: A Psychological Analysis* (rev. ed. 1956), XV–n.19.

G. Alexander & T. Lewin, *The Aged and
the Need for Surrogate Management*
(1972), XVI–n.96.

Allard v. Helgemoe, 572 F.2d 1 (1st
Cir.), *cert. denied,* 439 U.S. 858
(1978), XVI–n.10.

F. Allen, *The Decline of the Rehabilitative
Ideal: Penal Policy and Social Purpose*
(1981), XI–n.86.

R. Allen, E. Ferster & J. Rubin eds.,
Readings in Law and Psychiatry
(1975), II–n.29.

Allen v. Illinois, 106 S. Ct. 2988
(1986), XII–n.54, XIV–n.46, XIV–
n.48, XVII–n.16, XVIII–n.8.

Allred v. State, 554 P.2d 411 (Alaska
1976), II–n.34, II–n.35.

Alpher & Blanton, The Accuracy of Lie
Detection: Why Lie Tests Based on
the Polygraph Should Not Be Admitted Into Evidence Today, 9 *L. & Psychology Rev.* 67 (1985), VIII–n.98,
VIII–n.111, VIII–n.115, VIII–n.164.

American Association for Counseling
and Development, *Ethical Standards*
(1981) I–n.5.

American Bar Association, *Annotated
Code of Professional Responsibility*
(1981), I–n.4, I–n.18.

American Bar Association Commission
on the Mentally Disabled, *Exercising
Judgment for the Disabled: Report on
an Inquiry into Limited Guardianship*
(1979), XVI–n.78.

American Bar Association Commission
on the Mentally Disabled, *Guardian-

ship and Conservatorship* (1979), XVI–
n.70.

American Bar Association, *Criminal Justice Mental Health Standards* (1984),
XVI–n.4, XVI–n.52.

American Bar Association Criminal Justice Section, *Guidelines for Fair Treatment of Victims and Witnesses in the
Criminal Justice System* (1983), XII–
n.13.

American Bar Association, *The Model
Rules of Professional Conduct,* I–n.4.

American Bar Association, *Standards for
Criminal Justice* (2d ed. 1980), XII–
n.38.

American Bar Association's *The Insanity
Defense,* 51 U.S.L.W. 2476–77
(1983), XI–n.76.

American Friends Service Committee,
Struggle for Justice 146 (1971), XII–
n.6, XII–n.26.

American Law Institute, *Model Penal
Code, Proposed Official Draft* 401
(1962), XI–n.28.

American Law Institute, *Model Penal
Code* (Tent. Draft No. 4, 1956), XV–
n.2, XV–n.64.

American Medical Association, *The Insanity Defense in Criminal Trials and
Limitation of Psychiatric Testimony* (approved Dec. 6, 1983), XI–n.60.

American Medical Association, *Physical
Abuse of Children—Suggested Legislation* (1965), II–n.55.

American Medical Association, *Revised
Principles of Medical Ethics* (1980), I–
n.15, I–n.16, I–n.17.

American Nurses' Association, *Code for
Nurses with Interpretive Statements*
(1968), I–n.6.

American Personnel and Guidance Association, *Ethical Standards* (1981), II–
n.7, II–n.8.

American Psychiatric Association, Amicus Brief in Barefoot v. Estelle, 463
U.S. 880 (1983), XII–n.106, XII–
n.108, XVII–n.70.

American Psychiatric Association, Amicus Brief in Estelle v. Smith, 451 U.S.

Barefoot v. Estelle, 463 U.S. 880 (1983), XII–n.107, XVII–n.64, XVII–n.81, XVII–n.84.

Barish, A Response to "Training for Responsible Professional Behavior in Psychology and Social Work," 11 *Clinical Soc. Work J.* 184 (1983), I–n.23.

Barland & Raskin, Validity and Reliability of Polygraph Examinations of Criminal Suspects (Report No. 76–1, Dept. Justice, 1976), VIII–n.118, VIII–n.133, VIII–n.138.

H. Barnes, *The Story of Punishment* (2d ed. 1972), XII–n.1, XII–n.30, XII–n.36, XII–n.88, XII–n.93.

Barnett & Field, Character of the Defendant and Length of Sentence in Rape and Burglary Crimes, 104 *J. Soc. Psychology* 271 (1978), VII–n.15.

Baron, Medical Paternalism and the Rule of Law, 4 *Am. J. L. & Med.* 337 (1979), XVIII–n.28.

Barrett, Johnson & Meyer, Expert Witness, Consultant, Advocate: One Role is Enough, 6 *Bull. Am. Acad. Forensic Psychology* 5 (1985), X–n.1.

R. Barnett & J. Hansel eds., *Assessing the Criminal* (1977), XII–n.17.

Bartels, Capital Punishment: The Unexamined Issue of Special Deterrence, 68 *Iowa L. Rev.* 601 (1983), XII–n.115.

Bartholomew, The Ethics of Non-Therapeutic Clinical Research on Children, in *Research Involving Children,* Appendix 3, VI–n.74.

C. Bartol, *Psychology and American Law* (1983), VIII–n.45, VIII–n.84, VIII–n.88, VIII–n.130, X–n.9.

C. Bartol & A. Bartol, *Criminal Behavior* (1986), XI–n.82, XI–n.86.

Bassford, The Moral Role Differentiation of Experimental Psychologists, 15 *Soc. Sci. & Med.* 27 (1981), VI–n.49.

Bassiouni, Baffes & Evrard, An Appraisal of Human Experimentation in International Law and Practice: The Need for International Regulation of Human Experimentation, 72 *J. Crim. L. & Criminology* 1597 (1981), VI–n.8.

Batavia, Preferred Provider Organizations: Antitrust Aspects and Implications for the Hospital Industry, 10 *Am. J. L. & Med.* 169 (1984), IV–n.76.

Bates v. State Bar of Arizona, 433 U.S. 350 (1977), I–n.2.

Batson v. Kentucky, 106 S.Ct. 1712 (1986), VII–n.131, VII–n.133.

Bauer, Mental Illness and Will Contests, 13 *Colo. Law.* 985 (1984), XVI–n.62.

Baumrind, Nature and Definition of Informed Consent in Research Involving Deception, in *The Belmont Report,* Appendix, 23, VI–n.48.

Baumrind, Research Using Intentional Deception: Ethical Issues Revisited, 40 *Am. Psychologist* 165 (1985), VI–n.20, VI–n.61.

R. Bausell, *Experimental Methods* (1986), VI–n.48, VII–n.58, VII–n.59, VII–n.115.

Baxstrom v. Herold, 383 U.S. 107 (1966), XVII–n.35, XVII–n.73.

Bazelon, Psychiatrists and the Adversary Process, 230 *Sci. Am.* 18 (June 1974), X–n.12.

J. Beatty, *Biological Basis of Behavior* (1987), III–n.34, XV–n.20.

T. Beauchamp, R. Faden, R. J. Wallace & L. Walters eds., *Ethical Issues in Social Science Research* (1982), VI–n.12, VI–n.27.

Beck v. Alabama, 447 U.S. 625 (1980), XII–n.103.

Beck v. Beck, 86 N.J. 480, 432 A.2d 63 (1981), XIII–n.47.

Beck, When the Patient Threatens Violence: An Empirical Study of Clinical Practice After *Tarasoff,* 10 *Bull. Am. Acad. Psychiatry & L.* 189 (1982), II–n.93.

Beck, Ward, Mendelson, Mock & Erbough, Reliability of Psychiatric Diagnosis: A Study of Consistency of Clinical Judgments and Ratings, 119

Bershoff, Hospital Privileges and the Antitrust Laws, 38 *Am. Psychologist* 1238 (1983), IV–n.45, IV–n.46.

Bersoff, Regarding Psychologists Testimony: Legal Regulation of Psychological Assessment in the Public Schools, 39 *Md. L. Rev.* 27 (1979), V–n.35.

Bersoff, Testing and the Law, 36 *Am. Psychologist* 1047 (1981), V–n.35.

Besharov, Child Abuse and Neglect: Liability for Failing to Report, 22 *Trial* 67 (1986), II–n.67.

Besharov, Child Protection: Past Progress, Present Problems and Future Directions, 17 *Fam. L. Q.* 151 (1983), I–n.102, II–n.56.

Besharov, "Doing Something" About Child Abuse: The Need to Narrow the Grounds for State Intervention, 8 *Harv. J. L. & Pub. Policy* 539 (1985), II–n.69.

Besharov, State Intervention to Protect Children: New York's Definition of "Child Abuse" and "Child Neglect," 26 *N.Y.L. Sch. L. Rev.* 723 (1981), XIII–n.66.

Biglan, VanHasselt & Simon, Visual Impairment, in *Handbook of Development and Physical Disabilities* (V. VanHasselt, P. Strain & M. Hersen eds. 1986), IX–n.17, IX–n.18.

Binder v. Ruvell, Civil Docket 52C2535, Circuit Court of Cook County, Illinois, June 24, 1952, Judge Harry M. Fisher presiding, reported in Note, Confidential Communications to a Psychotherapist: A New Testimonial Privilege, 47 *Nw.U. L. Rev.* 384 (1952), II–n.34.

Bingham v. Lifespring, No. 82–5128 (E.D. Pa. July 31, 1984) reported in 28 ATLA L. Rep. 139 (1985), I–n.112.

Binner, DRGs and the Administration of Mental Health Services, 41 *Am. Psychologist* 64 (1986), IV–n.58.

Binner, Halpin & Potter, Patients, Programs and Results in a Comprehensive Mental Health Center, 41 *J.*

Consulting & Clinical Psychology 148 (1973), IV–n.89.

Birnbaum, The Right to Treatment, 46 *A.B.A. J.* 499 (1960), XVIII–n.47.

Blachly, Attitudes, Data, and Technological Promise of ECT, 14 *Psychiatric Opinion* 9 (1977), III–n.9, III–n.15, III–n.30, III–n.38, III–n.45.

Blackburn, Cortical and Autonomic Arousal in Primary and Secondary Psychopaths, 16 *Psychophysiology* 143 (1979), XV–n.18.

Blackburn, An Empirical Classification of the Psychopathic Personality, 127 *Brit. J. Psychiatry* 456 (1975), XV–n.15.

Blackburn & Lee-Evans, Reactions of Primary and Secondary Psychopaths to Anger-Evoking Situations, 24 *Brit. J. Clinical Psychology* 93 (1985), XV–n.50.

4 *Blackstone's Commentaries* 21 (4 Lewis ed. 1898), XI–n.4, XI–n.17.

Blaney, Contemporary Theories of Depression: Critique and Comparison, 86 *J. Abnormal Psychology* 203 (1977), III–n.51, III–n.52.

Blau, An Evaluative Study of the Role of the Grandparent in the Best Interests of the Child, 12 *Am. J. Fam. Therapy* 46 (1984), XIII–n.49, XIII–n.59.

T. Blau, *The Psychologist as Expert Witness* (1984), X–n.10.

M. Blenkner, M. Bloom, M. Nielson & R. Weber, *Protective Services for Older People: Findings from the Benjamin Rose Institute Study* (1974), XVI–n.95.

Blinick, Mental Disability, Legal Ethics, and Professional Responsibility, 33 *Albany L. Rev.* 92 (1968), XVII–n.46.

S. Block & P. Chadoff eds., *Psychiatric Ethics* (1981), I–n.7.

Blonstin & Marclay, HMOs and Other Employee Health Plans: Coverage and Employee Premiums, 6 *Monthly Labor Rev.* 28 (1983), IV–n.52.

Bloom, Faulkner, Holm & Rawlinson, An Empirical View of Patients Exercising Their Right to Refuse Treatment, 7 *Int'l J. L. & Psychiatry* 315 (1984), XVIII–n.10.

Blue Shield of Virginia v. McCready, 457 U.S. 465 (1982), IV–n.76.

Blythe, A Critique of Outcome Evaluation in Child Abuse Treatment, 62 *Child Welfare* 325 (1983), XIII–n.82, XIII–n.85.

Boehm, Mr. Prejudice, Miss Sympathy and the Authoritarian Personality: An Application of Psychological Measuring Techniques to the Problem of Jury Bias, 1968 *Wis. L. Rev.* 734, VII–n.37.

Bonner v. Moran, 126 F.2d 121 (D.C. Cir. 1941), XVII–n.29.

Bonnie, The Moral Basis of the Insanity Defense, 69 *A.B.A. J.* 194 (1983), XI–n.75.

Bonnie, The Psychiatric Patient's Right to Refuse Medication: A Survey of the Legal Issues, in *Refusing Treatment in Mental Health Institutions—Values in Conflict* (A. E. Doudera & J. Swazey eds. 1982), XVIII–n.4, XVIII–n.31.

Boor, Effects of Victim Competence and Defendant Opportunism on Decisions of Simulated Jurors, 100 *J. Soc. Psychology* 315 (1975), VII–n.10.

Bordas, Tort Liability of Institutional Review Boards, 87 *W. Va. L. Rev.* 137 (1984), VI–n.32.

Bordens & Horowitz, Joinder of Criminal Offenses: A Review of the Legal and Psychological Literature, 9 *L. & Hum. Behav.* 339 (1985), VII–n.85.

R. Boruch & J. Cecil eds., *Solutions to Ethical and Legal Problems in Social Research* (1983), VI–n.28, VI–n.37.

Borus, Issues Critical to the Survival of Community Mental Health, 135 *Am. J. Psychiatry* 1029 (1978), IV–n.70.

Bouhoutsos, Holroyd, Lerman, Forer & Greenberg, Sexual Intimacy Between Psychotherapists and Patients, 14 *Prof. Psychology: Research & Prac.* 185 (1983), I–n.61.

Bourne & Newberger. "Family Autonomy" or "Coercive Intervention?" Ambiguity and Conflict in the Pro-

posed Standards in Child Abuse and Neglect, 57 *B.U. L. Rev.* 670 (1977), II–n.65.

Bowers V. Hardwick, 106 S. Ct. 2841 (1986), XII–n.12, XII–n.71, XIV–n.27, XIV–n.28, XIV–n.29, XIV–n.31.

Bowers & Pierce, The Illusion of Deterrence in Isaac Ehrlich's Research on Capital Punishment, 85 *Yale L. J.* 187 (1975), XII–n.113.

Bowers & Pierce, Racial Discrimination and Criminal Homicide Under Post-Furman Capital Statutes, in *The Death Penalty in America* (3d. ed. H. Bedau 1982), XII–n.117.

Bowring v. Godwin, 551 F.2d 44 (4th Cir. 1977), XVIII–n.69.

Brady & Krizay, Utilization and Coverage of Mental Health Services in Health Maintenance Organizations, 142 Am. J. Psychiatry 744 (1985), IV–n.78.

Bradley Center, Inc. v. Wessner, 250 Ga. 199, 296 S.E.2d 693 (1982), I–n.91, I–n.97.

Bradley & Janisse, Accuracy Demonstrations, Threat and the Detection of Deception, 18 *Psychophysiology* 307 (1981), VIII–n.97, VIII–n.141.

Brainerd, Kigma & Howe, On the Development of Forgetting, 56 *Child Dev.* 1103 (1985), VII–n.76, IX–n.38.

S. Brakel, J. Parry & B. Weiner, *The Mentally Disabled and the Law* (3d ed. 1986), II–n.29, III–n.106, XIV–n.41, XVI–n.70, XVI–n.76, XVII–n.3, XVII–n.34, XVII–n.60, XVIII–n.16, XVIII–n.30, XVIII–n.31.

S. Brakel & R. Rock, *The Mentally Disabled and the Law* 250–51 (2d ed. 1971), XVI–n.69.

Brant, *Pennhurst, Romeo,* and *Rogers*: The Burger Court and Mental Health Law, 4 *J. Legal Med.* 323 (1983), XVIII–n.71.

Bremer v. State, 18 Md. App. 291, 307 A.2d 503 (1973), *cert. denied,* 415 U.S. 930 (1974), II–n.74.

Brenner & Galanti, Prisoners' Rights to Psychiatric Care, 21 *Idaho L. Rev.* 1 (1985), XVIII–n.70.

L. Breslow ed., *Annual Review of Public Health* (1986), III–n.85.

Bridgeman & Marlowe, Jury Decision-Making: An Empirical Study Based on Actual Felony Trials, 64 *J. Applied Psychology* 91 (1979), VII–n.86, VII–n.103, VII–n.104.

Brigham & Barkowitz, Do They All Look Alike? Experience, Attitudes, and the Ability to Recognize Faces, 8 *J. Applied Soc. Psychology* 306 (1978), IX–n.28.

Brigham & Bothwell, The Ability of Prospective Jurors to Estimate the Accuracy of Eyewitness Identifications, 7 *L. & Hum. Behav.* 19 (1983), IX–n.94.

Brigham & Wolfskiel, Opinions of Attorneys and Law Enforcement Personnel on the Accuracy of Eyewitness Identification, 7 *L. & Hum. Behav.* 337 (1983), IX–n.2.

Brodsky, The Mental Health Professional on the Witness Stand: A Survival Guide, in *Psychology in the Legal Process* 269 (B. Sales ed. 1977), X–n.11.

Brongersma, Aggression Against Pedophiles, 7 *Int'l J. L. & Psychiatry* 79 (1984), XIV–n.6, XIV–n.13.

Brooks, The Constitutional Right to Refuse Anti-Psychotic Medications, 8 *Bull. Am. Acad. Psychiatry & L.* 179 (1980), III–n.71, III–n.73, XVIII–n.24, XVIII–n.28.

Brooks, Defining the Dangerousness of the Mentally Ill: Involuntary Civil Commitment, in *Mentally Abnormal Offenders* 280 (M. Craft & A. Craft eds. 1984), XVII–n.22, XVII–n.56.

A. Brooks, Law, *Psychiatry and the Mental Health System* (1974), Pre–n.5, III–n.110, XII–n.78, XVIII–n.37.

Brooks, Polygraph Testing: Thoughts of a Skeptical Legislator, 40 *Am. Psychologist* 348 (1985), VIII–n.146, VIII–n.150.

Brown, Employment Tests: Issues Without Clear Answers, 30 *Personnel Administrator* 43 (1985), V–n.17.

Brown, Psychiatric Refusal, Patient Competence, and Informed Consent, 8 *Int'l J. L. & Psychiatry* 83 (1986), XVII–n.61, XVIII–n.13, XIX–n.17.

P. Brown, *The Transfer of Care: Psychiatric Institutionalization and Its Aftermath* (1985), XVIII–n.29.

Brown & Bremer, Inadequate Means to a Noble End: The Right to Treatment Paradox, 6 *J. Psychiatry & L.* 45 (1978), XVIII–n.59.

Brown, Deffenbacher & Sturgill, Memory for Faces and the Circumstances of the Encounter, 62 *J. Applied Psychology* 311 (1977), IX–n.1, IX–n.17, IX–n.43, IX–n.50, IX–n.54.

D. Brown & E. Fromm, *Hypnotherapy and Hypnoanalysis* (1986), VIII–n.47, VIII–n.50.

Brown & Truitt, Civil Liability in Child Abuse Cases, 54 *Chi.-Kent L. Rev.* 753 (1978), I–n.104, II–n.68.

Brown & Uhl, Mandatory Continuing Education: Sense or Nonsense?, 213 *J.A.M.A.* 1660 (1970), IV–n.27.

Brown v. Board of Education, 347 U.S. 483 (1954), V–n.26.

Brown v. State, 245 So.2d 68 (Fla. 1971), XVI–n.17.

Browne & Finkelhor, Impact of Child Sexual Abuse: A Review of the Research, 99 *Psychological Bull.* 66 (1986), XIII–n.78.

Brownell & Stunkard, The Double-Blind in Danger: Untoward Consequences of Informed Consent, 139 *Am. J. Psychiatry* 1497 (1982), VI–n.47.

Brummer & Looney, Grandparent Rights in Custody, Adoption, and Visitation Cases, 39 *Ark. L. Rev.* 259 (1985), XIII–n.59.

Bruner, The Course of Cognitive Growth, 19 *Am. Psychologist* 1 (1964), IX–n.33.

Bruner, Olver & Greenfield eds., *Studies in Cognitive Growth* (1966), IX–n.33.

formance, 3 *Behaviorometric* 74 (1973), IX–n.39.

Cheifetz & Salloway, Patterns of Mental Health Services Provided by HMOs, 39 *Am. Psychologist* 495 (1984), IV–n.78.

In re Cheryl H., 153 Cal. App. 3d 1098, 200 Cal. Rptr. 789 (2d Dist. 1984), XIII–n.68.

Child Support Enforcement Amendments (Pub. L. No. 98–378), XIII–n.52.

Chodoff, The Case for Involuntary Hospitalization of the Mentally Ill, 133 *Am. J. Psychiatry* 496 (1976), XVII–n.63.

Chodoff, Involuntary Hospitalization of the Mentally Ill as a Moral Issue, 141 *Am. J. Psychiatry* 384 (1984), XVII–n.53.

Chodoff & Peele, The Psychiatric Will of Dr. Szasz, 13 *Hastings Center Rep.* 11 (1983), XIX–n.23.

Chodoff & Peele, The Psychiatric Will of Dr. Szasz, 13 *Hastings Center Rep.* 11 (April 1983), III–n.103.

Choninard, Jones & Annable, Neuroleptic-Induced Supersensitive Psychosis, 135 *Am. J. Psychiatry* 1409 (1978), III–n.82.

Christian v. Randall, 33 Colo. App. 129, 516 P.2d 132 (1973), XIII–n.40.

Christiansen, Sweeny & Ochalek, Influencing Eyewitness Descriptions, 7 *L. & Hum. Behav.* 59 (1983), IX–n.48, IX–n.53.

F. D. Chu & S. Trotter, *The Madness Establishment* (1974), IV–n.64.

Ciccone & Clements, The Ethical Practice of Forensic Psychiatry: A View from the Trenches, 12 *Bull. Am. Acad. Psychiatry & L.* 263 (1984), I–n.24.

Ciccone & Clements, Forensic Psychiatry and Applied Clinical Ethics, Theory and Practice, 141 *Am. J. Psychiatry* 395 (1984), I–n.25.

Civil Rights Act of 1964, 42 U.S.C. §2000 (1982), V–n.32.

Clark, Clinical Limits of Expert Testimony on Diminished Capacity, 5 *Int'l J. L. & Psychiatry* 155 (1982), XI–n.36.

S. Clark, *The Moral Status of Animals* (1977), VI–n.104.

H. Cleckley, *The Mask of Sanity* (4th ed., 1964), XV–n.7.

Clingempeel & Reppucci, Joint Custody After Divorce: Major Issues and Goals for Reform, 91 *Psychological Bull.* 102 (1982), XIII–n.27, XIII–n.28, XIII–n.32, XIII–n.48.

Clovis, The Boards—What Price Glory, 128 *Am. J. Psychiatry* 784 (1971), IV–n.33.

Cocozza, Melick & Steadman, Trends in Violent Crimes Among Ex-Mental Patients, 16 *Criminology* 317 (1978), XVII–n.74.

Cocozza & Steadman, The Failure of Psychiatric Predictions of Dangerousness: Clear and Convincing Evidence, 29 *Rutgers L. Rev.* 1048 (1976), XVII–n.71.

Cocozza & Steadman, Some Refinements in the Measurement and Prediction of Dangerous Behavior, 131 *Am. J. Psychiatry* 1012 (1974), XVII–n.74.

R. Cohen & W. Mariano, *Legal Guidebook in Mental Health* (1982), I–n.74.

Cohen, Autonomy and Paternalism: Two Goals in Conflict, 13 *L. Med. & Health Care* 145 (1985), XVI–n.99.

Cohen, Effect of Media: Survey of 5 Cases: Jurors Not Swayed, *Los Angeles Times,* Apr. 11, 1976, VII–n.62.

Cohen, The Function of the Attorney and the Commitment of the Mentally Ill, 44 *Tex. L. Rev.* 424 (1966), XVII–n.49.

Cohen, Protective Services and Public Guardianship: A Dissenting View, paper presented to the Annual Meeting of the Gerontology Society, Nov. 20, 1978, quoted in W. Schmidt, K. Miller, W. Bell & B. E. New, *Public Guardianship and the Elderly* 11 (1981), XVI–n.88.

Cohen, Selective Incapacitation: An Assessment, 1984 *U. Ill. L. F.* 253, XII–n.11, XII–n.24.

Cohen & Harnick, The Susceptibility of Child Witnesses to Suggestion, 4 *L. & Hum. Behav.* 201 (1980), IX–n.21.

Cohen & Hunter, Mental Health Insurance: A Comparison of a Fee-for-Service Indemnity Plan and a Comprehensive Mental Health Center, 42 *Am. J. Orthopsychiatry* 146 (1972), IV–n.93.

Cohen & Peterson, Bias in the Courtroom: Race and Sex Effects of Attorneys on Juror Verdicts, 9 *Soc. Behav. & Personality* 81 (1981), VII–n.51, VII–n.52.

Cohen & Squire, Retrograde Amnesia and Remote Memory Impairment, 19 *Neuropsychologia* 337 (1981), III–n.24.

Coe & Sarbin, An Experimental Demonstration of Hypnosis as Role Enactment, 71 *J. Abnormal Psychology* 404 (1966), VIII–n.52.

Coker v. Georgia, 433 U.S. 584 (1977), XII–n.55, XII–n.101, XIV–n.14.

Coleman, Creating Therapist-Offender Exception to Mandatory Child Abuse Reporting Statutes—When Psychiatrist Knows Best, 54 *Cin. L. Rev.* 1113 (1986), II–n.70, XIII–n.69.

Coleman & Solomon, Parens Patriae "Treatment": Legal Punishment in Disguise, 3 *Hastings Const. L. Q.* 344 (1976), XVIII–n.25.

R. Colligan, D. Osborne, W. Swenson & K. Offord, *The MMPI: A Contemporary Normative Study* (1983), VIII–n.13.

Colussi, The Unconstitutionality of Death Qualifying a Jury Prior to the Determination of Guilt: The Fair Cross-Section Requirement in Capital Cases, 15 *Creighton L. Rev.* 595 (1981–82), VII–n.46, VII–n.50.

Comment [Annual Review], Homosexual Parent and Custody, 8 *J. Juv. L.* 291 (1984), XIII–n.40.

Comment, Antipsychotic Drugs and Fitness to Stand Trial: The Right of the Unfit Accused to Refuse Treatment, 52 *U. Chi. L. Rev.* 773 (1985), XVI–n.40.

Comment, Antipsychotic Drugs: Regulating Their Use in the Private Practice of Medicine, 15 *Golden Gate U. L. Rev.* 331 (1985), III–n.71.

Comment, Assessing Children's Best Interests When a Parent is Gay or Lesbian: Toward a Rational Custody Standard, 32 *UCLA L. Rev.* 852 (1984), XIII–n.40.

Comment, Child Custody: Best Interests of the Child versus Constitutional Rights of Parents, 81 *Dick. L. Rev.* 733 (1977), XIII–n.31.

Comment, Do the Eyes Have It? Psychological Testimony Regarding Eyewitness Accuracy, 38 *Baylor L. Rev.* 169 (1986), IX–n.90.

Comment, Guardianship of Incapacitated Adults, 1982 *Utah L. Rev.* 427, XVI–n.77.

Comment, Guilty But Mentally Ill: Historical and Constitutional Analysis, 53 *J. Urban L.* 471 (1976), XI–n.65.

Comment, Hypnosis in Our Legal System: The Status of its Acceptance in the Trial Setting, 16 *Akron L. Rev.* 517 (1982–83), VIII–n.58, VIII–n.61, VIII–n.62.

Comment, Hypnosis—Should the Courts Snap Out of It?—A Closer Look at the Critical Issues, 44 *Ohio St. L. J.* 1053 (1983), VIII–n.64.

Comment, Injuries Precipitated By Psychotherapy: Liability Without Fault as a Basis for Recovery, 20 *S.D. L. Rev.* 401 (1975), I–n.30, I–n.115.

Comment, *Jones v. United States*: Automatic Commitment of Individuals Found Not Guilty by Reason of Insanity, 68 *Minn. L. Rev.* 822 (1984), XVII–n.37.

Comment, Laetrile: Statutory and Constitutional Limitations on the Regulation of Ineffective Drugs, 127 *U. Pa. L. Rev.* 233 (1978), III–n.85.

Currie, Legislative Initiatives in Hospital Practice, paper presented American Psychological Association (1983), IV–n.44.

D.C. Code Ann. §22–3503 (1981), XIV–n.44.

D.M. v. Hoeston, No. 47744 (Mo. Ct. App. Dec. 20, 1983), reported in 8 *Mental & Physical Disability L. Reporter* 121 (1984), II–n.69.

D'Ver, The End of the Pound Dog, 10 *Lab Animal* 23 (1981), VI–n.102.

Danish, Considering Professional Licensing from a Social and Historical Context, 9 *Counseling Psychologist* 35 (1980), IV–n.5.

Darling v. Charleston Community Memorial Hospital, 33 Ill. 2d 326, 211 N.E.2d 253 (1965), *cert. denied,* 383 U.S. 946 (1966), I–n.110.

Darrow quoted in *Capital Punishment: Hearings Before Subcommittee No. 3 of The Committee on the Judiciary, House of Representatives,* 92d Cong., 2d Sess. 19 (1972), XII–n.119.

Davidson, How Trustworthy is the Witness?, 2 *J. Forensic Med.* 14 (1955), XV–n.70.

Davison, Not Can, But Ought: The Treatment of Homosexuality, 46 *J. Consulting & Clinical Psychology* 170 (1978), XIV–n.40.

Davidson, Validity of the Guilty Knowledge Technique: The Effects of Motivation, 52 *J. Applied Psychology* 62 (1968), VIII–n.122.

K. Davis, *National Health Insurance* (1975), IV–n.107.

S. Davis, *Rights of Juveniles* (2d ed. 1983), XIII–n.13.

Davis, Kunreuther & Connick, Expanding the Victim's Role in the Criminal Court Dispositional Process: The Results of an Experiment, 75 *J. Crim. L. & Criminology* 491 (1984), XII–n.15, XII–n.87.

Davis v. Alaska, 415 U.S. 308 (1974), II–n.52.

Davis v. Hubbard, 506 F. Supp. 915 (N.D. Ohio 1980), XVIII–n.44.

Davis v. United States, 160 U.S. 469 (1895), XI–n.31.

Dawidoff, The Malpractice of Psychiatrists, 1966 *Duke L. J.* 696, I–n.35.

Dawson, Physiological Detection of Deception, 17 *Psychophysiology* 8 (1980), VIII–n.108, VIII–n.115, VIII–n.131, VIII–n.132, VIII–n.134.

Deardorff, Cross & Hupprich, Malpractice Liability in Psychotherapy: Client and Practitioner Perspectives, 15 *Prof. Psychology: Research & Prac.* 590 (1984), I–n.27.

Decker & Kohfeld, A Deterrence Study of the Death Penalty in Illinois, 1933–1980, 12 *J. Crim. Just.* 367 (1984), XII–n.114.

Deffenbacher, Eyewitness Accuracy and Confidence: Can We Infer a Relationship?, 4 *L. & Hum. Behav.* 243 (1980), IX–n.9, IX–n.10, IX–n.82.

Deffenbacker, Bothwell & Brigham, Predicting Eyewitness Identification from Confidence: The Optimality Hypothesis, paper presented to the American Psychological Association (1986), IX–n.10, IX–n.87.

Deffenbacher & Loftus, Do Jurors Share a Common Understanding of Eyewitness Behavior?, 6 *L. & Hum. Behav.* 15 (1982), IX–n.94.

Dekruai & Sales, Privileged Communications of Psychologists, 13 *Prof. Psychology: Research & Prac.* (1982), II–n.27.

DeLeon & VandenBos, Psychotherapy Reimbursement in Federal Programs: Political Factors in *Psychotherapy: Practice, Research, Policy* (G. VandenBos ed. 1980), IV–n.57, IV–n.105, IV–n.108.

Demsky, The Use of Depo-Provera in the Treatment of Sex Offenders: The Legal Issues, 5 *J. Legal Med.* 295 (1984), XIV–n.16.

Denicola & Sandler, Training Abusive Parents in Child Management and Self-Control Skills, 11 *Behav. Therapy*

Furrow (*Continued*)
tive Damage Remedy, 19 *Harv. Civ. Rts.—Civ. Liberties L. Rev.* 21 (1984), XVIII–n.31.

J. Gackenbach, *Sleeping and Dreams: A Sourcebook* (1985), IX–n.36.

G. Galaway & J. Hudson eds., *Offender Restitution in Theory and Action* (1978), XII–n.16.

Gallucci, Prediction of Dissimulation on the MMPI in a Clinical Field Setting, 52 *J. Consulting & Clinical Psychology* 917 (1984), VIII–n.8.

Ganzer & Sarason, Variables Associated with Recidivism Among Juvenile Delinquents, 40 *J. Consulting & Clinical Psychology* 1 (1973), XV–n.1.

Gardner v. Florida, 430 U.S. 349 (1977), XII–n.103.

Garnett, Children as Witnesses: Competency and Rules Favoring Their Testimony, 12 *Colo. Law.* 1982 (1983), XIII–n.93.

Garrison, Why Terminate Parental Rights?, 35 *Stan. L. Rev.* 423 (1983), XIII–n.30.

Garvey, Freedom and Choice in Constitutional Law, 94 *Harv. L. Rev.* 1756 (1981), III–n.94.

Gasser & Taylor, Role Adjustment of Single Parent Fathers With Dependent Children, 25 *Fam. Coordinator* 397 (1976), XIII–n.36.

In re Gault, 387 U.S. 1 (1967), XIII–n.12.

Gay Alliance of Students v. Matthews, 544 F.2d 162 (4th Cir. 1976), XIV–n.36.

Gay Student Services v. Texas A & M University, 737 F.2d 1317 (5th Cir. 1984), *appeal dismissed,* 105 S. Ct. 1860 (1985), XIV–n.36.

Gay Students Organization v. Bonner, 367 F. Supp. 1088 (D.N.H.), *modified,* 509 F.2d 652 (1st Cir. 1974), XIV–n.36.

P. Gebhard, J. Gagnon, W. Pomeroy & C. Christenson, *Sex Offenders: An Analysis of Types* (1965), XIV–n.17.

Geddes & Newberg, Cuff Pressure Oscillations in the Measurement of Relative Blood Pressure, 14 *Psychophysiology* 198 (1977), VIII–n.91.

Geiselman, Fisher, MacKinnon & Holland, Eyewitness Memory Enhancement in the Police Interview, 70 *J. Applied Psychology* 401 (1985), IX–n.70.

Geiser & Rheingold, Psychology and the Legal Process: Testimonial Privileged Communications, 19 *Am. Psychologist* 83 (1964), IV–n.8.

Gelenberg, Prescribing Antidepressants, 9 *Drug Therapy* 95 (1979), III–n.78.

Geller, Alternatives to Deception: Why, What and How?, in *The Ethics of Social Research: Surveys and Experiments* 40 (J. Sieber ed. 1982), VI–n.63.

Geller & Lister, The Process of Criminal Commitment for Pretrial Psychiatric Examination: An Evaluation, 135 *Am. J. Psychiatry* 53 (1978), XVI–n.14, XVI–n.30, XVI–n.44.

Gelman, Mental Hospital Drugs, Professionalism, and the Constitution, 72 *Georgetown L. J.* 1725 (1984), III–n.114, XVIII–n.30.

Gendreau & Suboski, Classical Discrimination Eyelid Condition in Primary Psychopaths, 77 *J. Abnormal & Soc. Psychology* 242 (1971), XV–n.40.

Genesis 18:20–19:26, XIV–n.3.

George, The American Bar Association's Mental Health Standards: An Overview, 53 *Geo. Wash. L. Rev.* 338 (1985), XVI–n.4.

Gerbasi, Zuckerman & Reis, Justice Needs a New Blindfold: A Review of Mock Jury Research, 85 *Psychological Bull.* 323 (1977), VII–n.14, VII–n.41, VII–n.42, VII–n.63, VII–n.116.

Gerow, Attitudes Towards the Use of the Polygraph, 6 *Polygraph* 266 (1977), VIII–n.98.

B. Gert & C. Culver, *Philosophy in Medicine* (1982), XIX–n.7.

Gutheil & Mills (*Continued*)
Psychiatry & L. 17 (1982), XVIII–
n.3.

Guttmacher & Weihofen, Privileged
Communications Between Psychiatrist
and Patient, 28 *Ind. L. J.* 32 (1952),
II–n.27.

H. L. A. Hart, *Law, Liberty and Morality*
(1963), XIV–n.50.

H. L. v. Matheson, 450 U.S. 398, 411
(1981), II–n.64.

Haas & Fennimore, Ethical and Legal
Works in Professional Psychology: Selected Works, 14 *Prof. Psychology: Research & Prac.* 540 (1983), I–n.8.

Haberstroh v. Montanye, 493 F.2d 483
(7th Cir. 1974), IX–n.77.

Haddox, Gross & Pollack, Mental Competency to Stand Trial While Under
the Influence of Drugs, 7 *Loyola L.A.
L. Rev.* 425 (1974), XVI–n.39.

Hafemeister & Sales, Interdisciplinary
Evaluations for Guardianships and
Conservatorships, 8 *L. & Hum. Behav.*
355 (1984), XVI–n.101.

Hafemeister, Sales & Suggs, Behavioral
Expertise in Jury Selection, in *Law
and Mental Health: International Perspectives,* vol. 1 (D. Weisstub ed.
1985), VII–n.120, VII–n.123, VII–
n.124, VII–n.138.

Hagan, Victims Before the Law: A
Study of Victim Involvement in the
Criminal Justice Process, 73 *J. Crim.
L. & Criminology* 317 (1982), XII–
n.87.

Hale, The Illusion of Effective Regulation, 35 *Clinical Psychologist* 10
(1981), IV–n.6.

Hall, Psychiatry and Criminal Responsibility, 65 *Yale L.J.* 761, 765 (1955–
56), XI–n.8.

Hall, Catlin & Boissevain, Short-Term
Violence Prediction: A Prospective
Study, paper presented at the American Psychological Association, Toronto, Canada, Aug. 24, 1984, XVII–
n.76.

Hall, Loftus & Tousignant, Postevent
Information and Changes in Recollec-
tion for a Natural Event, in *Eyewitness
Testimony: Psychological Perspectives* (G.
Wells & E. Loftus eds. 1984), IX–
n.47.

Hall v. State, 255 Ga. 267, 336 S.E.2d
812 (1985), I–n.109, II–n.13.

Hall & Hare-Mustin, Sanctions and the
Diversity of Ethical Complaints
Against Psychologists, 38 *Am. Psychol-
ogist* 714 (1983), I–n.20.

Halleck, "The Psychiatrist and the Legal
Process," 2 *Psychology Today* 25
(1969), XI–n.44, XI–n.46.

Halleck, Responsibility in Psychiatry
and Law, in *Law and Mental Health:
International Perspectives,* vol. 1 (D.
Weisstub ed. 1986), X–n.3, X–n.15.

Halpern, The Fiction of Legal Insanity
and the Misuse of Psychiatry, 2 *J. Legal Med.* 18 (1980), XI–n.2.

Hammer v. Rosen, 7 N.Y.2d 376, 165
N.E.2d 750, 198 N.Y.S.2d 54
(1960), I–n.66.

Hammersley & Read, The Effect of Participation in a Conversation on Recognition and Identification of
Speakers' Voices, 9 *L. & Hum. Behav.*
71 (1985), IX–n.63, IX–n.64.

Haney, Psychology and Legal Change:
On the Limits of Factual Jurisprudence, 4 *L. & Hum. Behav.* 147
(1980), Pre–n.2.

V. Hans & N. Vidmar, *Judging the Jury*
(1986), VII–n.4, VII–n.138.

Hans & Slater, "Plain Crazy": Lay Definitions of Legal Insanity, 7 *Int'l J. L.
& Psychiatry* 105 (1984), XI–n.54.

Hans, Jury Selection in Two Countries:
A Psychological Perspective, 12 *Cur-
rent Psychological Rev.* 283 (1982),
VII–n.28, VII–n.117, VII–n.124,
VII–n.165.

Hansford v. United States, 365 F.2d.
920 (D.C. Cir. 1966), XVI–n.7.

Harcourt, Brace & World v. Graphic
Controls Corp., 329 F.Supp. 517
(S.D. N.Y. 1971), V–n.12.

Loftus, Altman & Geballe, Effects of Questioning Upon a Witness' Later Recollections, 3 *J. Police Sci. & Ad.* 162 (1975), IX–n.44.

Loftus & Monahan, Trial By Data, 35 *Am. Psychologist* 270 (1980), IX–n.91.

W. Loh, *Social Research in the Judicial Process* (1985), VII–n.1, VII–n.64, VII–n.82, VII–n.110, IX–n.1.

Lojuk v. Quandt, 706 F. 2d 1456 (7th Cir. 1983), XVIII–n.12.

Lombardo, Three Generations, No Imbeciles: New Light on *Buck v. Bell*, 60 *N.Y.U. L. Rev.* 30 (1985), XVI–n.83.

London & Flerman, Boundaries Between Research and Therapy, Especially in Mental Health, in *The Belmont Report*, Appendix 15, VI–n.25.

Longo, Administering a Comprehensive Sexual Aggressive Treatment Program in a Maximum Security Setting, in *The Sexual Aggressor: Current Perspectives on Treatment* (J. Greer & I. Stuart eds. 1983), XIV–n.15.

Lora v. Board of Education, 74 F.R.D. 565 (E.D.N.Y. 1977), II–n.83.

Lorenz, Criminal Confessions Under Narcosis, 31 *Wis. Med. J.* 245 (1932), VIII–n.74.

Louisell & Hazard, Insanity as a Defense, The Bifurcated Trial, 49 *Calif. L. Rev.* 805 (1961), XI–n.63.

Lsagna, Special Subjects in Human Experimentation, in *Experiments With Human Subjects* 262 (C. Freund ed. 1970), VI–n.91.

Lutzker & Rice, Project 12-Ways: Measuring Outcome of a Large In-Home Service for Treatment and Prevention of Child Abuse and Neglect, 8 *Child Abuse & Neglect* 519 (1984), XIII–n.78.

Lykken, The Detection of Deception, 86 *Psychological Bull.* 47 (1979), VIII–n.109, VIII–n.110, VIII–n.112, VIII–n.121, VIII–n.122, VIII–n.128, VIII–n.135, VIII–n.142, VIII–n.162.

Lykken, Psychology and the Lie Detector Industry, 29 *Am. Psychologist* 725

(1974), VIII–n.92, VIII–n.121, VIII–n.122, VIII–n.143, VIII–n.148, VIII–n.162.

Lykken, The Psychopath and the Lie Detector, 15 *Psychophysiology* 137 (1978), VIII–n.135.

Lykken, A Study of Anxiety in the Sociopathic Personality, 55 *J. Abnormal & Soc. Psychology* 6 (1957), XV–n.11, XV–n.13, XV–n.14, XV–n.36.

D. Lykken, *A Tremor in the Blood* (1981), VIII–n.93, VIII–n.109, VIII–n.110, VIII–n.121, VIII–n.122, VIII–n.148, VIII–n.162.

Lyles v. United States, 254 F.2d 725 (D.C. Cir. 1957), XI–n.50.

Lyman & Roberts, Mental Health Testimony in Child Custody Litigation, 9 *L. & Psychology Rev.* 15 (1985), XIII–n.94.

Lynch & Graves, Participants' Perceptions of Ethical Issues in Research with Humans, 52 *Psychological Rep.* 231 (1983), VI–n.53.

Maben v. Rankin, 55 Cal.2d 139, 10 Cal. Rptr. 353, 358 P.2d 681 (1961), I–n.69.

J. Macauley & L. Berkowitz eds., *Altruism and Helping Behavior* (1970), VII–n.43.

Macciocchi & Meyer, unpublished paper, University of Louisville (1981), VIII–n.113.

Mackey v. Procunier, 477 F.2d 877 (9th Cir. 1973), XII–n.73, XVIII–n.37.

Macklin, Some Problems in Gaining Informed Consent from Psychiatric Patients, 31 *Emory L. J.* 345 (1982), III–n.94, XVIII–n.13.

Madden, Psychotherapeutic Approaches in the Treatment of Violent Persons, in *Clinical Treatment of the Violent Person* (L. Roth ed. 1985), XVII–n.78.

Maddux & Rogers, Effects of Source Expertness: Physical Attractiveness and Supporting Arguments on Persuasion: A Case of Brains Over Beauty, 39 *J. Personality & Soc. Psychology* 235 (1980), VII–n.60.

S. Mednick & K. Christiansen, *Biological Basis of Criminal Behavior* (1977), XV–n.27.

P. Meehl, *Clinical v. Statistical Predictions: A Theoretical Analysis and Review of the Evidence* (1954), VIII–n.15.

Meeker, Dombrink & Geis, State Law and Local Ordinances in California Barring Discrimination on the Basis of Sexual Orientation, 10 *U. Dayton L. Rev.* 745 (1984), XIV–n.35.

Mehrabian, Nonverbal Betrayal of Feelings, 5 *J. Experimental Research in Personality* 64 (1971), VIII–n.42.

D. Meichenbaum, *Cognitive Behavior Modification* (1977), XV–n.63.

Meier v. Ross General Hospital, 69 Cal.2d 420, 445 P.2d 519 71, Cal. Rptr. 903 (1968), I–n.79.

R. Meiners, *Victim Compensation* (1978), XII–n.16.

Meisel, The "Exceptions" to the Informed Consent Doctrine: Striking a Balance Between Competing Values in Medical Decisionmaking, 1979 *Wis. L. Rev.* 413, I–n.47.

Meisel, The Expansion of Liability for Medical Accidents: From Negligence to Strict Liability By Way of Informed Consent, 56 *Neb. L. Rev.* 51 (1977), III–n.102.

Meisel & Kabnick, Informed Consent to Medical Treatment: An Analysis of Recent Legislation, 41 *U. Pitt. L. Rev.* 407 (1980), I–n.45.

Meisel, Lidz & Roth, Tests of Competency to Consent to Treatment, 134 *Am. J. Psychiatry* 279 (1977), XVI–n.104.

Melton, Children's Competency to Testify, 5 *L. & Hum. Behav.* 73 (1981), IX–n.21.

Melton, Children's Participation in Treatment Planning: Psychological and Legal Issues, 12 *Prof. Psychology: Research & Prac.* 246 (1981), III–n.105, XVIII–n.19.

Melton, Minors and Privacy: Are Legal and Psychological Concepts Compatible?, 62 *Neb. L. Rev.* 455 (1983), II–n.16, II–n.64.

Melton, Toward "Personhood" for Adolescents: Autonomy and Privacy as Values in Public Policy, 38 *Am. Psychologist* 99 (1983), II–n.16, XVII–n.33.

G. Melton, G. Koocher & M. Saks eds., *Children's Competence to Consent* (1983), XVIII–n.19.

Memory Drug Piracetam Now Being Researched in U.S., 2 *Brain/Mind Bull.* 3 (1977), III–n.23.

Memphis Telephone Co. v. Cumberland Telephone and Telegraph Co., 231 F. 835 (6th Cir. 1916), VIII–n.1.

Menges, Openness and Honesty v. Coercion and Deception in Psychological Research, 28 *Am. Psychologist* 1030 (1973), VI–n.51.

K. Menninger, *The Crime of Punishment* (1968), XII–n.2, XII–n.90.

7 *Mental & Physical Disability L. Rep.* 358 (1983), XVII–n.7.

Mentally Infirm, see National Commission for the Protection of Human Subjects of Biomedical and Behavioral Research, *Research Involving Those Institutionalized as Mentally Infirm* (1978).

C. Mercier, *Criminal Responsibility* (1926), XI–n.11.

Merriken v. Cressman, 364 F. Supp. 913 (E.D. Pa. 1973), II–n.82.

Merrill, Compensation for Prescription Drug Injuries, 59 *Va. L. Rev.* 1 (1973), I–n.52.

Merton, Confidentiality and the "Dangerous" Patient: Implications of *Tarasoff* for Psychiatrists and Lawyers, 31 *Emory L. J.* 263 (1982), I–n.95.

Messenger & McQuire, The Child's Conception of Confidentiality in the Therapeutic Relationship, 18 *Psychotherapy: Theory, Research & Prac.* 123 (1981), II–n.16.

Mestrovic, Admission Patterns at South Carolina's State Psychiatric Hospitals Following Legislative Reform, 10 *J.*

Mulder, Who is Right About Animal Rights?, 29 *Lab. Animal Sci.* 435 (1981), VI–n.104.

Mullen & Reihehr, The Mentally Ill Offender: A Comparison of Prison Inmates, Forensic Psychiatric Patients and General Psychiatric Patients, 9 *J. Psychology & L.* 203 (1981), XI–n.84.

Mullen v. United States, 263 F.2d 275 (D.C. Cir. 1958), II–n.36.

Munetz, Loren & Roth, Informing Patients About Tardive Dyskinesia, 42 *Archives Gen. Psychiatry* 866 (1985), III–n.102.

J. Murphy, *Retribution, Justice and Therapy* (1979), XII–n.6, XII–n.7.

Murray, Genetic Testing at Work: How Should it be Used, 30 *Personnel Administrator* 91 (1985), V–n.17.

J. Murray, *Status Offenders: A Sourcebook* (1983), XIII–n.25.

Musetto, The Role of the Mental Health Professional in Contested Custody: Evaluator of Competency or Facilitator of Change, 4 *J. Divorce* 69 (1981), XIII–n.96.

Mutual Life Insurance Co. v. Terry, 82 U.S. 580 (1873), XI–n.35.

Myers, Involuntary Civil Commitment of the Mentally Ill: A System in Need of Change, 29 *Vill. L. Rev.* 367 (1984), XVII–n.62.

Myers et al., Six-Month Prevalence of Psychiatric Disorders in Three Communities, 41 *Archives Gen. Psychiatry* 959 (1984), IV–n.48.

Nagle, The Polygraph in Employment: Applications and Legal Considerations, 14 *Polygraph* 1 (1985), VIII–n.149.

Nakell, The Cost of the Death Penalty, in *The Death Penalty in America* 241 (3d ed. H. Bedau ed. 1982), XII–n.116.

National Association of Social Workers, *Code of Ethics* (1979), I–n.10, I–n.14, I–n.61, II–n.6, II–n.8.

National Association of Social Workers, *Legal Regulation of Social Work Practice* (1973), IV–n.40.

National Center for State Courts, *Provisional Substantive and Procedural Guidelines for Involuntary Civil Commitment* (1982), XVII–n.9.

National Commission for the Protection of Human Subjects of Biomedical and Behavioral Research, *Report* (1976), III–n.60, III–n.91.

National Commission for the Protection of Human Subjects of Biomedical and Behavioral Research, *The Belmont Report: Ethical Principles and Guidelines for the Protection of Human Subjects of Research* (1978), VI–n.10, VI–n.25, VI–n.30, VI–n.48, VI–n.81.

National Commission for the Protection of Human Subjects of Biomedical and Behavioral Research, *Institutional Review Boards* (1978), VI–n.14, VI–n.17, VI–n.19.

National Commission for the Protection of Human Subjects of Biomedical and Behavioral Research, *Research Involving Children* (1977), VI–n.70, VI–n.74, VI–n.75.

National Commission for the Protection of Human Subjects of Biomedical and Behavioral Research, *Research Involving Prisoners* (1976), VI–n.88.

The National Commission for the Protection of Human Subjects of Biomedical and Behavioral Research, *Research Involving Those Institutionalized as Mentally Infirm* (1978), VI–n.79, VI–n.82.

The National Commission on the Insanity Defense, *Myths and Realities: A Report* (1983), XI–n.76.

National Gay Task Force v. Board of Education, 470 U.S. 903 (1985), XIV–n.24, XIV–n.33.

National Institute of Mental Health, *Electro-Convulsive Therapy: Consensus Development Conference* (1985), III–n.9, III–n.10, III–n.24, III–n.39, III–n.53, III–n.90.

National Research Council, *Punishment and Deterrence* (1978), XII–n.22, XII–n.24.

Neil v. Biggers, 409 U.S. 188 (1972), IX–n.76.

Neiland, Malpractice Liability of Psychiatric Professionals, 1 *Am. J. Forensic Psychiatry* 22 (1979), I–n.33.

Neisser, Is There a Doctor in the Joint? The Search for Constitutional Standards for Prison Health Care, 63 *Va. L. Rev.* 921 (1977), XVIII–n.70.

B. Nelson, *Making Child Abuse an Issue* (1984), XIII–n.65.

Nelson v. Heyne, 355 F.Supp. 451 (1972), *aff'd*, 491 F.2d 352 (7th Cir.), *cert. denied*, 417 U.S. 976 (1974), XVIII–n.37.

Nevares-Muniz, The Eighth Amendment Revisited: A Model of Weighted Punishments, 75 *J. Crim. L. & Criminology* 272 (1984), XII–n.55.

Newberger, The Helping Hand Strikes Again: Unintended Consequences of Child Abuse Reporting, 12 *J. Clinical Child Psychology* 307 (1983), II–n.54, XIII–n.69.

G. Newman, *Just and Painful* (1983), XII–n.18, XII–n.89.

Newman v. Dixon Bank and Trust, 205 Ky. 31, 265 S.W. 456 (1924), XVI–n.59.

Newman & Kosson, Passive Avoidance Learning in Psychopathic and Nonpsychopathic Offenders, 95 *J. Abnormal Psychology* 252 (1986), XV–n.35.

Newmark, The MMPI, in *Major Psychological Assessment Instruments* (C. Newmark ed. 1985), VIII–n.11.

C. Newmark ed., *Major Psychological Assessment Instruments* (1985), V–n.2.

Newsom, Favell & Rincover, Side Effects of Punishment, in *The Effects of Punishment on Human Behavior* 285 (S. Axelrod & J. Apsche eds. 1983), XII–n.81.

Newsome v. Commonwealth, 366 S.W.2d 174 (Ky. 1962), *cert. denied*, 375 U.S. 887 (1963), XI–n.32.

A. Nicholi ed., *The Harvard Guide to Modern Psychiatry* (1978), III–n.70.

W. Nichols, *Marriage and Family Counseling: A Legislative Handbook* (1974), IV–n.41.

M. Nietzel, *Psychological Consultation in the Courtroom* (1979), VII–n.33.

M. Nietzel & R. Dillehay, *Psychological Evaluations in the Courtroom* (1986), VII–n.55, VII–n.71, VII–n.99, X–n.11.

Nietzel & Dillehay, Psychologists and Voir Dire: A Strategy and Its Applications, paper presented at American Psychological Association (1979), VII–n.5, VII–n.99, VII–n.117, VII–n.137.

Nogrady, McConkay & Perry, Enhancing Visual Memory: Trying Hypnosis, Trying Imagination, and Trying Again, 94 *J. Abnormal Psychology* 195 (1985), IX–n.65.

Nolan, Functional Evaluation of the Elderly in Guardianship Proceedings, 12 *L. Med. & Health Care* 210 (1984), XVI–n.71, XVI–n.94, XIX–n.17.

Noll, The Psychotherapist and Informed Consent, 133 *Am. J. Psychiatry* 1451 (1976), I–n.53.

Norborg, A Warning Regarding the Simplified Approach to the Evaluation of Test Fairness in Employee Selection Procedures, 37 *Personnel Psychology* 483 (1984), V–n.21.

Northern California Psychiatric Society v. Berkeley, No. 566 778-3 (Cal. Super. Ct. Sep. 14, 1983), *aff'd*, 178 Cal. App. 3d 90, 233 Cal. Rptr. 609 (1st Dist. 1986), III–n.2.

Norwood v. Tucker, 287 F.2d 798 (8th Cir. 1961), V–n.27.

Note, Admissibility of Present Recollection Restored by Hypnosis, 15 *Wake Forest L. Rev.* 357 (1979), VIII–n.71.

Note, Admission of Expert Testimony on Eyewitness Identification, 73 *Calif. L. Rev.* 1402 (1985), IX–n.78.

Note, Antipsychotic Drugs: Regulating Their Use in the Private Practice of

Note, *Ruby v. Massey*: Sterilization of the Mentally Retarded, 9 *Cap. U. L. Rev.* 191 (1979), XVI–n.84.

Note, R, for the Elderly: Legal Rights (and Wrongs) Within the Health Care System, 20 *Harv. Civ. Rts.-Civil Liberties L. Rev.* 425 (1985), XVI–n.97.

Note, The Scope of a Psychiatrist's Duty to Third Persons: The Protective Privilege Ends Where the Public Peril Begins, 59 *Notre Dame L. Rev.* 770 (1984), I–n.98.

Note, Standard of Care in Administering Non-Traditional Psychotherapy, 7 *U. Cal. Davis L. Rev.* 56 (1974), I–n.112.

Note, Sterilization Petitions: Developing Judicial Guidelines, 44 *Mont. L. Rev.* 127 (1983), XVI–n.84.

Note, Stipulation Cannot Make Polygraph Results Admissible, 47 *Mo. L. Rev.* 586 (1982), VIII–n.155.

Note, Survey on the Constitutional Right to Privacy in the Context of Homosexual Activity, 40 *U. Miami L. Rev.* 521 (1986), XIV–n.26.

Note, Testamentary Capacity: Is the Alcoholic Incapacitated?, 46 *Mont. L. Rev.* 437 (1985), XVI–n.56.

Note, Testimonial Privileges and the Student-Counselor Relationship in Secondary-Schools, 56 *Iowa L. Rev.* 323 (1971), II–n.23.

Note, The Testimony of Child Victims in Sex Abuse Prosecutions: Two Legislative Innovations, 98 *Harv. L. Rev.* 806 (1985), XIII–n.93.

Note, Tort Liability of the Psychotherapist, 8 *U. San Fran. L. Rev.* 405 (1973), I–n.69.

Note, Tort Remedies for Incestuous Abuse, 12 *Golden Gate U. L. Rev.* 609 (1983), XIII–n.63.

Note, Toward Legal Rights for Laboratory Animals?, 10 *J. Legis.* 198 (1983), VI–n.100.

Note, Underprivileged Communications: Extention of the Psychotherapist-Patient Privilege to Patients of Psychiatric Social Workers, 61 *Cal. L. Rev.* 1050 (1973), II–n.23.

Note, The Use of Hypnosis to Refresh Memory: Invaluable Tool or Dangerous Device?, 60 *Wash. U. L. Q.* 1059 (1982), VIII–n.71.

Note, Vanishing Exception to the Psychotherapist-Patient Privilege: The Child Abuse Reporting Act, 16 *Pac. L. J.* 335 (1984), II–n.69.

Note, Visitation Rights of a Grandparent Over the Objection of a Parent: The Best Interest of the Child, 15 *J. Fam. L.* 51 (1979), XIII–n.61.

Note, "Voluntary" Admission of Children to Mental Hospitals: A Conflict of Interest Between Parent and Child, 36 *Md. L. Rev.* 153 (1976), XVII–n.31.

Note, "We're Only Trying to Help": The Burden and Standard of Proof in Short-Term Civil Commitment, 31 *Stan. L. Rev.* 425 (1979), XVII–n.8.

Note, Where the Public Peril Begins: A Survey of Psychotherapists to Determine the Effects of Tarasoff, 31 *Stan. L. Rev.* 165 (1978), II–n.93.

Nuremberg Military Tribunal, The Nuremberg Code, 2 The Medical Cases 181-82 (G.P.O. 1947), VI–n.8, VI–n.9, VI–n.99.

N.Y. Education Law §340 (McKinney 1984 Supp.), V–n.7, V–n.36.

O'Brien & Robuck, Experimentally Produced Self-Repugnant Behavior as a Function of Hypnosis and Waking Suggestion: A Pilot Study, 18 *Am. J. Clinical Hypnosis* 272 (1976), VIII–n.51.

A. J. O'Callaghan & D. Carroll eds., *Psychosurgery: A Scientific Analysis* (1983), III–n.59.

O'Connor v. Donaldson, 422 U.S. 563 (1975), I–n.70, I–n.71, XVII–n.26, XVII–n.55, XVIII–n.1, XVIII–n.5, XVIII–n.35, XVIII–n.48, XVIII–n.54.

Plotkin, Limiting the Therapeutic Orgy: Mental Patients' Right to Refuse Treatment, 72 *Nw. U.L. Rev.* 461 (1977), III–n.67, III–n.68.

Plutchick & Stewart, Jury Selection: Folklore or Science, 1 *Crim. L. Bull.* 3 (1965), VII–n.157, VII–n.158.

Podlesny & Raskin, Effectiveness of Techniques and Physiological Measures in the Detection of Deception, 15 *Psychophysiology* 344 (1978), VIII–n.91, VIII–n.100, VIII–119, VIII–n.129, VIII–n.143.

Pogrebin, Regoli & Perry, Not Guilty by Reason of Insanity: A Research Note, 8 *Int'l J. L. & Psychiatry* 237 (1986), XI–n.51, XI–n.83.

Pollack, Psychiatric Consultation for the Court, 1 *Bull. Am. Acad. Psychiatry & L.* 267 (1973), X–n.3.

Pollack, Gross & Weinberger, Dimensions of Malingering, in *New Directions for Mental Health Services: The Mental Health Professional and the Legal System* (B. Gross & L. Weinberger eds. 1982), VIII–n.2.

Pope, Keith-Spiegel & Tabachnik, Sexual Attraction to Clients, 41 *Am. Psychologist* 147 (1986), I–n.61.

Pound, Introduction to F. Sayre, *Cases on Criminal Law* (1927), Pre-n.4.

Powell v. Texas, 392 U.S. 514, 546 (1968), XI–n.24, XII–n.53, XV–n.69.

Poythress & Stock, Competency to Stand Trial: A Historical Review and Some New Data, 8 *J. Psychiatry & L.* 131 (1980), XVI–n.3.

President's Commission for the Study of Ethical Problems in Medicine and Biomedical and Behavioral Research, *Compensating for Research Injuries: A Report on the Ethical and Legal Implications of Programs to Redress Injuries Caused by Biomedical and Behavioral Research* (1982), VI–n.97.

President's Commission of Mental Health, *Report of the President's Commission on Mental Health* (1980) IV–n.48.

President's Commission on Mental Health, *Report of the Task Force on Legal and Ethical Issues,* (1978), XVI–n.82.

President's Commission of the Study of Ethical Problems in Medical and Biomedical and Behavioral Research, *Making Health Care Decisions* (1982), XIX–n.6.

President's Task Force on Victims of Crime, *Final Report* (1982), XII–n.13, XII–n.86.

Prince v. Massachusetts, 321 U.S. 158, 166 (1944), II–n.64.

Project Release v. Prevost, 722 F.2d 960 (2d Cir. 1983), XVIII–n.44.

Prygoski, Of Predispositions and Dispositions: An Attitudinal Study of Decision-making in Child Abuse and Neglect Cases, 21 *Houston L. Rev.* 883 (1984), XIII–n.71.

Pub. L. No. 79–487 (1946), IV–n.66.

Pub. L. No. 88–164 (1963), IV–n.68.

Pub. L. No. 96–398 (1980), IV–n.72.

Pub. L. No. 97–291 (1982), XII–n.14, XII–n.85.

Pub. L. No. 98–378 (1984), XIII–n.52.

Pub. L. No. 98–473, 98 Stat. 1837 (1984), XI–n.78, XII–n.14, XII–n.27.

Pub. L. No. 99–319 (1986), IV–n.73.

Purwin, D'Agostino & Brown, Loaded for Acquittal? Psychiatry in the Jury Selection Process, 7 *U. W. L.A. L. Rev.* 199 (1975), VII–n.155.

Pyszczynski & Wrightman, The Effects of Opening Statements on Mock Juror's Verdicts in a Simulated Criminal Trial, 11 *J. Applied Soc. Psychology* 301 (1981), VII–n.74, VII–n.77, VII–n.78.

Quay, Psychopathic Personality as Pathological Stimulation Seeking, 122 *Am. J. Psychiatry* 180 (1965), XV–n.52.

Quen, Anglo-American Criminal Insanity, An Historical Perspective, 2 *Bull. Am. Acad. Psychiatry & L.* 115 (1974), XI–n.12.

In re Quinlan, 70 N.J. 10, 355 A.2d 647, *cert. denied,* 429 U.S. 922 (1976), XVI–n.85, XIX–n.12.

Quinn & Hutchinson, Status Offenders Should Be Removed from the Juvenile Court, 7 *Pepperdine L. Rev.* 923 (1980), XIII–n.22.

Quinsey, Warneford, Pruesse & Link, Released Oak Ridge Patients: A Follow-Up Study of Review Board Discharges, 15 *Brit. J. Criminology* 264 (1975), XV–n.1.

Rabkin, Criminal Behavior of Discharged Mental Patients: A Clinical Appraisal of the Research, 86 *Psychological Bull.* 1 (1979), XVII–n.54.

Rachlin, One Right Too Many, 3 *Bull. Am. Acad. Psychiatry and L.* 99 (1975), XVIII–n.28.

Rachlin, Pam & Milton, Civil Liberties Versus Involuntary Hospitalization, 132 *Am. J. Psychiatry* 132 (1975), XVII–n.63.

R. Rada, *Clinical Aspects of the Rapist* (1977), XIV–n.15.

Rahaim and Brodsky, Empirical Evidence Versus Common Sense: Juror and Lawyer Knowledge of Eyewitness Accuracy, 7 *L. & Psychology Rev.* 1 (1982), IX–n.94.

Ransohoff et al., Measuring the Restrictiveness of Psychiatric Care, 33 *Hosp. & Community Psychiatry* 361 (1982), XVIII–n.40.

Rappeport, Psychiatrist-Patient Privilege, 23 *Md. L. Rev.* 39 (1963), II–n.27.

Raskin, The Polygraph in 1986: Scientific, Professional and Legal Issues Surrounding Application and Acceptance of Polygraph Evidence, 1986 *Utah L. Rev.* 29, VIII–n.155.

Raskin, Scientific Assessment of the Accuracy of Deception: A Reply to Lykken, 15 *Psychophysiology* 143 (1978), VIII–n.134.

Raskin & Hare, Psychopathy and Detection of Deception in a Prison Popula-

tion, 15 *Psychophysiology* 126 (1978), VIII–n.102.

Raskin & Podlesny, Truth and Deception: A Reply to Lykken, 86 *Psychological Bull.* 54 (1979), VIII–n.129.

F. Reamer & M. Abramson, *The Teaching of Social Work Ethics* (1982), I–n.24.

W. Redd, A. Porterfield & B. Anderson, *Behavior Modification* (1979), XIV–n.40.

Redlich, Ravitz & Dession, Narcoanalysis and Truth, 107 *Am. J. Psychiatry* 586 (1951), VIII–n.75.

Redmont, Persuasion, Rules of Evidence and the Process of Law, 4 *Loy. L.A. L. Rev.* 253 (1970), VII–n.97.

T. Regan, *All That Dwell Therein* (1982), VI–n.101.

Regan, Process & Context: Hidden Factors in Health Care Decisions for the Elderly, 13 *L. Med. & Health Care* 151 (1985), XVI–n.72.

Regeir, The Nature and Scope of Mental Health Problems, in *Primary Care: Variability and Methodology in Mental Health Services in General Health Care,* vol. 1 (1979), IV–n.95.

Rehabilitation Act of 1973, 29 U.S.C. §701 (1982), V–n.32.

Reich & Siegel, The Emergence of the Bowrey as a Psychiatric Dumping Ground, 50 *Psychiatric Q.* 191 (1978), XVII–n.63.

Reid & Bottinger, Genetic Aspects of Antisocial Disorders, 1 *Hillside J. Clinical Psychiatry* 87 (1979), XV–n.20.

J. Reid & F. Inbau, *Truth and Deception: The Polygraph Technique* (1966), VIII–n.86, VIII–n.87, VIII–n.100, VIII–n.114.

W. Reid, D. Dorr, J. Walker & J. Bonner eds., *Unmasking the Psychopath* (1986), VIII–n.101, XV–n.8, XV–n.19.

R. Reiff, *The Invisible Victim* (1979), XII–n.86.

Judgments, 6 *J. Applied Soc. Psychology* 64 (1976), VII–n.13.

Rumsey & Rumsey, A Case of Rape: Sentencing Judgments in Males and Females, 41 *Psychological Rep.* 459 (1977), VII–n.25.

Rush v. Akron General Hospital, 171 N.E.2d 378 (Ohio App. 1957), I–n.106.

L. M. Russell, *Alternatives: A Family Guide to Legal and Financial Planning for the Disabled* (1983), XIX–n.24.

Rutledge, State Regulation of Marriage Counseling, 22 *Fam. Coordinator* 81 (1973), IV–n.11.

Ryback v. Cobb County Dept. of Family and Children Services, 163 Ga. App. 165, 293 S.E.2d 563 (1982), XIII–n.50.

Sabin, Individual Risk v. Societal Benefit, in *Experiments With Human Subjects* 127 (C. Freund ed. 1970), VI–n.92.

Sackett & Decker, Detection of Deception in the Employment Context, 32 *Pers. Psychology* 487 (1979), VIII–n.124.

R. Sadoff, *Forensic Psychiatry: A Practical Guide* (1975), X–n.11.

Sadoff, Practical Ethical Problems of the Forensic Psychiatrist in Dealing with Attorneys, 72 *Bull. Am. Acad. Psychiatry & L.* 243 (1984), I–n.25.

M. Saks, *Jury Verdicts* (1977), VII–n.121.

Saks, Judicial Notebook, 15 *APA Monitor* 19 (1984), VIII–n.140.

Saks, Social Science and Jury Selection: A Consumer Advocate Position, paper presented at American Psychological Association (1981), VII–n.153, VII–n.156, VII–n.159.

M. Saks & R. Hastie, *Social Psychology in Court* (1978), VII–n.121, VII–n.165.

Salazar v. State, 559 P.2d 66 (Alaska 1976), II–n.53.

B. Sales, *Laws Affecting Mental Health: Arizona* (1985), Pre–n.1.

B. Sales ed., *The Professional Psychologist's Handbook* (1983), IV–n.33.

B. Sales ed., *Psychology in the Legal Process* 269 (1977), X–n.11.

B. Sales, *The Trial Process* (1981), VII–n.4, VII–n.81, VII–n.150.

Salmon & Meyer, Neuropsychology and Its Implications for Personal Injury Law, in *Psychology in Product Liability and Personal Injury Law* (M. Kurke & R. Meyer eds. 1986), VII–n.93.

Saltzman, Protection for the Child or Parent? The Conflict Between the Federal Drug and Alcohol Abuse Confidentiality Requirements and the State Child Abuse and Neglect Reporting Laws, 1985 *S. Ill. U. L.J.* 181, II–n.14, II–n.69.

Salzman, The Use of ECT in the Treatment of Schizophrenia, 137 *Am. J. Psychiatry* 1032 (1980), III–n.40, III–n.49.

H. Sandhu & C. Heasley, *Improving Juvenile Justice* 37 (1981), XIII–n.7.

Sanford, The Criteria of a Good Profession, 6 *Am. Psychologist* 668 (1951), IV–n.7.

Sank & Shapiro, Case Examples of the Broadening Role of Psychology in Health Maintenance Organizations, 10 *Prof. Psychology: Research & Prac.* 402 (1979), IV–n.79.

Santosky v. Kramer, 455 U.S. 745 (1982), XIII–n.29, XIII–n.72.

Santrock & Warshak, Father Custody and Social Development in Boys and Girls, 35 *J. Soc. Issues* 112 (1979), XIII–n.36.

T. Sarbin & J. Mancuso, *Schizophrenia: Medical Diagnosis or Moral Verdict* (1980), XVII–n.52.

Sarzen v. Gaughan, 489 F.2d 1076 (1st Cir. 1973), XVII–n.45.

Sattler, The Psychologist in Court: Personal Reflections of One Expert Witness in the Case of *Larry P. v. Wilson Riles*, 11 *Sch. Psychology Rev.* 306 (1982), V–n.33.

Saunders, Vidmar & Hewitt, Eyewitness Testimony and the Discrediting

Saunders, Vidmar & Hewitt (*Cont.*) Effect, in *Evaluating Witness Evidence: Recent Psychological Research and New Perspectives,* (S. Lloyd-Bostock & B. Clifford eds. 1983), IX–n.6.

Saxe, Dougherty & Cross, The Validity of Polygraph Testing: Scientific Analysis and Public Controversy, 40 *Am. Psychologist* 355 (1985), VIII–n.94, VIII–n.123, VIII–n.147.

Sayre, Mens Rea, 45 *Harv. L. Rev.* 974 (1932), XI–n.3.

Schachter, Amnesia and Crime: How Much Do We Really Know, 41 *Am. Psychologist* 286 (1986), VIII–n.45.

Schachter & Lantane, Crime, Cognition, and the Automatic Nervous System, in *Nebraska Symposium on Motivation* 221 (M. Jones ed. 1964), XV–n.39.

Schall v. Martin, 467 U.S. 253 (1984), XII–n.67, XIII–n.11.

Scheiner, Musetto & Cordier, Custody and Visitation Counseling: A Report of an Innovative Program, 31 *Fam. Relations* 99 (1982), XIII–n.41.

Schlesinger, Distinctions Between Psychopathic, Sociopathic, and Anti-Social Personality Disorders, 47 *Psychological Rep.* 15 (1980), XV–n.3.

Schlesinger, Mumford & Glass, Mental Health Services and Medical Utilization, in *Psychotherapy: Practice, Research, Policy* (G. VandenBos ed. 1980), IV–n.94, IV–n.97.

Schmauk, Punishment Arousal, and Avoidance Learning in Sociopaths, 76 *J. Abnormal & Soc. Psychology* 325 (1970), XV–n.14, XV–n.35, XV–n.37.

Schmid, Appelbaum, Roth & Lidz, Confidentiality in Psychiatry: A Study of the Patient's View, 34 *Hosp. & Community Psychiatry* 353 (1983), II–n.92.

Schmidt, Critique of the American Psychiatric Association's Guidelines for State Legislation on Civil Commitment of the Mentally Ill, 11 *New Eng.*

J. Crim. & Civ. Confinement 11 (1984), XVII–n.60.

Schmidt, The Evolution of a Public Guardianship Program, 12 *J. Psychiatry & L.* 349 (1984), XVI–n.79.

Schmidt, Health Maintenance Organizations and the McCarran-Ferguson Act, 7 *Am. J. L. & Med.* 437 (1984), IV–n.76.

W. Schmidt, K. Miller, W. Bell & B. E. New, *Public Guardianship and the Elderly* (1981), XVI–n.79, XVI–n.81, XVI–n.86, XVI–n.88, XVI–n.90, XVI–n.92, XVI–n.93, XVI–n.98, XIX–n.22, XIX–n.25.

Schneider & Kintz, The Effect of Lying Upon Foot and Leg Movement, 10 *Bull. Psychonomic Soc.* 451 (1977), VIII–n.42.

Schoeller v. Dunbar, 423 F.2d 1183 (9th Cir. 1970), XVI—n.9.

Schoenberger, "Voluntary" Commitment of Mentally Ill or Retarded Children: Child Abuse by the Supreme Court, 7 *U. Dayton L. Rev.* 1 (1981), XVII–n.33.

Schopp, Punishment as Treatment and the Obligations of Treatment Providers, 7 *Int'l J. L. & Psychiatry* 197 (1984), XII–n.72.

Schornhorst, The Waiver of Juvenile Court Jurisdiction: *Kent* Revisited, 43 *Ind. L. J.* 583 (1968), XIII–n.19.

Schreiber, Assessing Competency to Stand Trial: A Case Study of Technology Diffusion in Four States, 6 *Bull. Am. Acad. Sci. & L.* 439 (1978), XVI–n.19.

Schuchman, Confidentiality: Practice Issues in New Legislation, 50 *Am. J. Orthopsychiatry* 641 (1980), II–n.3.

H. Schuchman, L. Foster & S. Nye, *Confidentiality of Health Records* (1982), II–n.15.

Schulman, Shauer, Coleman, Enrich & Christie, Recipe for a Jury, 6 *Psychology Today* 37 (1973), VII–n.138.

Schulsinger, Psychopathy: Heredity and Environment, 2 *Life History Research*

D. Shapiro, *Psychological Evaluation and Expert Testimony* (1984), X–n.2, X–n.3, X–n.10.

Shapiro, The Right of Privacy and Heroin Use for Painkilling Purposes by the Terminally Ill Cancer Patient, 21 *Ariz. L. Rev.* 41 (1979), III–n.85.

Shapiro & Shapiro, Meta-Analysis of Psychotherapy Outcome Studies: A Replication and Refinement, 92 *Psychological Bull.* 581 (1982), IV–n.84, IV–n.87, XVIII–n.60.

Shapley, Jury Selection: Social Scientists Gamble in an Already Loaded Game, 185 *Science* 1033 (1974), VII–n.152.

Shastrom, Group Therapy: Let the Buyer Beware, in *Clinical Psychology Today* 149 (B. Henker, ed. 1967), I–n.111.

Shatin, Brief Form of the Competency Screening Test for Mental Competency to Stand Trial, 35 *J. Clinical Psychology* 464 (1979), XVI–n.28.

Shaw & McMartin, Effect of Who Suffers in an Automobile Accident on Judgmental Strictness, 1 *Proc. 81st Ann. Convention of Am. Psychological A.* 239 (1973), VII–n.12.

Sheehan & Tilden, The Consistency of Occurrences of Memory Distortion Following Hypnotic Induction, 34 *Int'l J. Clinical & Experimental Hypnosis* 122 (1986), VIII–n.54.

M. Shepard, *The Love Treatment: Sexual Intimacy Between Patients and Psychotherapists* (1971), I–n.64.

Sherlock & Sherlock, Sterilizing the Retarded: Constitutional, Statutory and Policy Alternatives, 60 *N.C. L. Rev.* 943 (1982), XVI–n.84.

Sherman, Guilty but Mentally Ill: A Retreat From the Insanity Defense, 7 *Am. J. L. & Med.* 257 (1981), XI–n.64.

Shichor, Historical and Current Trends in American Juvenile Justice, 34 *Juv. & Fam. Ct. J.* 61 (1983), XII–n.60, XIII–n.2.

Shinn, Father Absence and Children's Cognitive Development, 85 *Psychological Bull.* 295 (1978), XIII–n.36.

Shlensky, Psychiatric Expert Testimony and Consultation, 24 *Med. Trial Tech. Q.* 38 (1977), X–n.3.

Shuman, The Origins of the Physician-Patient Privilege and Professional Secret, 39 *Sw. L.J.* 661 (1985), II–n.3.

D. Shuman, *Psychiatric and Psychological Evidence* (1986), X–n.10.

Shuman & Weiner, The Privilege Study: An Empirical Examination of the Psychotherapist-Patient Privilege, 60 *N.C. L. Rev.* 893 (1982), II–n.26, II–n.90.

F. Shumer, *Abnormal Psychology* (1983), III–n.77, III–n.79.

Shuttlesworth v. Birmingham Board of Education, 162 F.Supp. 372 (N.D. Ala.), *aff'd*, 358 U.S. 101 (1958), V–n.27.

Sidley, The Rights of Involuntary Patients in Mental Institutions to Refuse Drug Treatment, 12 *J. Psychiatry & L.* 231 (1984), XVIII–n.4.

J. Sieber ed., *The Ethics of Social Science Research: Surveys and Experiments* (1982), VI–n.63.

Sieber, Evaluating the Potential for Harm or Wrong (parts I, II & III), *IRB: A Review of Human Subjects Research* Nov. 1982, Jan.–Feb. 1983, June 1983, at 1 (each issue), VI–n.60.

Siegal, Privacy, Ethics and Confidentiality, 10 *Prof. Psychology: Research & Prac.* 249 (1979), II–n.1.

Sierles, Correlates of Malingering, 2 *Behav. Sci. & L.* 113 (1984), VIII–n.6.

Silber, Ethical Relativity and Professional Psychology, 29 *Clinical Psychologist* 3 (1976), X–n.3.

Silten & Tullis, Mental Competency in Criminal Proceedings, 28 *Hastings L. J.* 1053 (1977), XVI–n.3.

Silverberg & Jonas, *Plalmore v. Sidoti,* Equal Protection and Child Custody Determinations, 18 *Fam. L. Q.* 335 (1984), XIII–n.39.

Walker, Thibant & Andreoli, Order of Presentation at Trial, 82 *Yale L. J.* 216 (1972), VII–n.79.

P. Wall, *Eyewitness Identification in Criminal Cases* (1975), IX–n.5, IX–n.7, IX–n.27, IX–n.41, IX–n.43.

Wallace, Occupational Licensing and Certification: Remedies for Denial, 14 *Wm. & Mary L. Rev.* 46 (1972), IV–n.4, IV–n.23.

Wallerstein, Child of Divorce: An Overview, 4 *Behav. Sci. & L.* 105 (1986), XIII–n.27.

G. Walters & J. Grusec, *Punishment* (1977), XII–n.83.

Ward, Competency for Execution: Problems in Law and Psychiatry, 14 *Fla. St. U. L. Rev.* 35 (1986), XVI–n.6.

Warren, Involuntary Commitment for Mental Disorder: The Application of California's Lanterman-Petris-Short Act, 11 *L. & Soc'y Rev.* 629 (1977), XVII–n.27.

Washington v. Davis, 426 U.S. 229 (1976), V–n.23.

Washington v. Texas, 388 U.S. 14 (1967), VIII–n.165.

Watkins & Watkins, Malpractice in Clinical Social Work, 1 *Behav. Sci. & L.* 55 (1983), I–n.27.

Wayne, An Examination of Selected Statutory Licensing Requirements for Psychologists in the United States, 60 *Personnel & Guidance J.* 420 (1982), IV–n.14, IV–n.17.

Wecht, Medical, Legal and Moral Considerations in Human Experimentation Involving Minors and Incompetent Adults, 4 *J. Legal Med.* 27 (1976), VI–n.3.

Weems v. U.S., 217 U.S. 349 (1910), XII–n.47.

Weinberg & Vatz, The Mental Illness Dispute: The Critical Faith Assumptions, 9 *J. Psychology & L.* 305 (1981), XI–n.40.

Weiner, *American Medical News,* Aug. 6, 1982 at 3, XI–n.68.

Weiner & Power, The Use of ECT Within the Veterans Administration Hospital System, 21 *Comprehensive Psychiatry* 22 (1980), III–n.36, III–n.42, III–n.44.

Weiner & Shuman, Privilege—A Comparative Study, 12 *J. Psychiatry & L.* 373 (1984), II–n.90.

Weiner, Volow, Gianturco & Cavenar, Seizures Terminable and Interminable with ECT, 137 *Am. J. Psychiatry* 1416 (1980), III–n.26.

Weiner, Whanger, Erivin & Wilson, Prolonged Confusional State and EEG Seizure Activity Following Concurrent ECT and Lithium Use, 137 *Am. J. Psychiatry* 1452 (1980), III–n.26.

Weinstein, How Should Forensic Psychiatry Police Itself? Guidelines and Grievances: The AAPL Committee on Ethics, 12 *Bull. Am. Acad. Psychiatry & L.* 289 (1984), I–n.25.

Weinstein, On the Teaching of Legal Ethics, 72 *Colum. L. Rev.* 452 (1972), I–n.24.

D. Weisstub ed., *Law and Mental Health: International Perspectives* (1985), VII–n.120, VII–n.123, VII–n.124, VII–n.138, VIII–n.8, VIII–n.31, X–n.3, X–n.11, X–n.15.

Weiten, The Attraction-Leniency Effect in Jury Research: An Examination of External Validity, 10 *J. Applied Soc. Psychology* 340 (1980), VII–n.17, VII–n.117.

Welfel & Lipsitz, Ethical Orientation of Counselors: Its Relationship to Moral Reasoning and Level of Training, 23 *Counselor Educ. & Supervision* 35 (1983), I–n.24.

Wellner & Zimet, The National Register of Health Service Providers in Psychology, in *The Professional Psychologist's Handbook* 185 (B. Sales ed. 1983), IV–n.33.

Wells, Expert Psychological Testimony: Empirical and Conceptual Analyses of Effects, 10 *L. & Hum. Behav.* 83 (1986), X–n.9.

Wells, Lawyer Credibility, 7 *Trial* 69 (1985), VII–n.53.

INDEX

DATE DUE			

E. LOUISE PATTEN LIBRARY
Piedmont College
Demorest, GA. 30535